Public Management Reform

Public Management Reform

A Comparative Analysis

SECOND EDITION

Christopher Pollitt

and

Geert Bouckaert

OXFORD

UNIVERSITY PRESS

Great Clarendon Street, Oxford OX2 6DP

Oxford University Press is a department of the University of Oxford.
It furthers the University's objective of excellence in research, scholarship,
and education by publishing worldwide in

Oxford New York

Auckland Bangkok Buenos Aires Cape Town Chennai
Dar es Salaam Delhi Hong Kong Istanbul Karachi Kolkata
Kuala Lumpur Madrid Melbourne Mexico City Mumbai Nairobi
São Paulo Shanghai Taipei Tokyo Toronto

Oxford is a registered trade mark of Oxford University Press
in the UK and in certain other countries

Published in the United States
by Oxford University Press Inc., New York

British Library Cataloguing in Publication Data
Data available

Library of Congress Cataloging in Publication Data
Pollitt, Christopher.
Public management reform: a comparative analysis/Christopher
Pollitt and Geert Bouckaert.
p. cm.
Includes bibliographical references and index.
1. Public administration. 2. Comparative government.
3. Organizational change. I. Bouckaert, Geert. II.Title.
JF1351.P665 2000 351—dc21 99-37269
ISBN 0–19–926848–7
ISBN 0-19-926849-5 (pbk)

1 3 5 7 9 10 8 6 4 2

Typeset in StoneSerif
by Kolam Information Services Pvt. Ltd, Pondicherry, India
Printed in Great Britain
on acid-free paper by
Antony Rowe Ltd, Chippenham, Wiltshire

For our parents,
Freda, John, Leen and Michel

■ ACKNOWLEDGEMENTS

Unsurprisingly, for a book of this scope, our debts are too numerous and go too far back in time for us to adequately acknowledge them all in a small space here. Thus we are, uncomfortably, obliged to be somewhat selective in our expressions of gratitude.

A first acknowledgement must go to our sheltering institutions, Erasmus University Rotterdam and Katholieke Universiteit Leuven. Over the years they have supported our research efforts and, more specifically, enabled us to spend time together to work on this second edition.

A second acknowledgement is due to our network of colleagues and friends who share an interest in comparative public administration. Our citations make clear how extensively we have drawn on the work of others, but, in addition to the normal processes of benefiting from each other's publications, we have received a generous portion of informal assistance and comments from a number of individuals during the preparation of this text. We particularly wish to acknowledge Jonathan Breul, Maurice Demers, Jan-Eric Furubo, John Halligan, Sigurdur Helgasson, Jan-Coen Hellendoorn, Annie Hondeghem, Patricia Ingraham, Helmut Klages, Walter Kickert, Roger Levy, Elke Löffler, Rudolf Maes, John Mayne, Nicole de Montricher, Guy B. Peters, Jon Pierre, Rune Premfors, Luc Rouban, Donald Savoie, David Shand, Hilkka Summa, Colin Talbot, Sandra van Thiel, and Petri Uusikylä.

Third, we have received some special help with this expanded second edition. Elio Borgonovi and Eduardo Ongaro at Universita Bocconni in Milan, who produced an excellent Italian translation of the first edition, generously allowed us to draw on their material on recent Italian reforms. Nick Thijs has laboured mightily to update much of the empirical data in chapter 5 and Appendix B. Christel Vandeurzen and Anneke Heylen have patiently and accurately absorbed our many changes to the typescript.

Finally, we would like to acknowledge those organizations that have contributed—indirectly but significantly—to this book by being willing to fund serious empirical research into public management reform. In the age of the 'sound bite' and the 'packaged' management consultancy solution, it takes some institutional courage to invest in the kind of time-consuming research which almost always reveals variety and complexity. As this book makes clear, however, if politicians' hopes, public money, and civil servants' time are not to be wasted, such research is desperately needed. We therefore gratefully acknowledge the support we have at various times received from Brunel University, the Canadian Centre for Management Development, the Finnish Ministry of Finance, the Public Management Institute and the Research Council of the Katholieke Universiteit Leuven, and the UK Economic and Social Research Council.

Christopher Pollitt
Geert Bouckaert

■ CONTENTS

LIST OF FIGURES   x

LIST OF TABLES   xi

ABBREVIATIONS   xii

Introduction   **1**

1   **The nature of public management reform**   6

2   **Problems and responses: a model of public management reform**   24

3   **Many houses: types of politico-administrative regime**   39

4   **Trajectories of modernization and reform**   65

5   **Results: through a glass darkly**   103

6   **Politics and management**   143

7   **Trade-offs, balances, limits, dilemmas, contradictions, and paradoxes**   159

8   **Reflections: management and governance**   182

APPENDIX A: THE SOCIO-ECONOMIC CONTEXT   203

APPENDIX B: COUNTRY FILES   210

  AUSTRALIA   210

  BELGIUM   216

  CANADA   224

  EUROPEAN COMMISSION   232

  FINLAND   239

  FRANCE   247

  GERMANY   256

  ITALY   264

  NETHERLANDS   270

  NEW ZEALAND   277

  SWEDEN   285

  UNITED KINGDOM   292

  UNITED STATES OF AMERICA   300

BIBLIOGRAPHY   309

WEBSITES: OVERVIEW   327

INDEX   333

■ LIST OF FIGURES

1.1 Four levels of public management reform: a first approximation   17

2.1 A model of public management reform   25

4.1 The concept of a trajectory   66

5.1 The input/output model   106
5.2 Trust in government, USA (1958–2000)   133

8.1 Three interactive systems   183
8.2 Distancing and blaming   185
8.3 Tightening traditional controls   186
8.4 Modernize the administrative system   187
8.5 Marketize the administrative system   188
8.6 Minimize the administrative system   189

A.1 Population aged 65 and over as a percentage of the population aged 15–64   207
A.2 Percentage of people aged 80 and over in the whole population   208

LIST OF TABLES

3.1	Types of politico-administrative regime: five key features of public administration systems	42
3.2	Percentage shares of public employment by levels of government	44
3.3	State structure and the nature of executive government	47
3.4	Indicators on cultures in different countries	56
4.1	Aspects of trajectories: context (what) and process (how)	67
4.2	Budget trajectories	70
4.3	Accounting trajectories	71
4.4	Audit trajectories	73
4.5	Strategic choices in decentralization	87
5.1	Changes in government outlays, 1985–2000	109
5.2	Government consumption as a percentage of GDP	110
5.3	General government net lending, 1980–2002	111
5.4	Central government debt as a percentage of GDP	112
5.5	Changes in government employment and compensation of government employees, 1985–99	113
5.6	Policy shifts: the case of the Netherlands	114
5.7	Productivity in the Swedish public sector by policy area, 1960–90	116
5.8	Productivity trends of Swedish central government, excluding defence, and rate of change in public consumption, 1960–90	117
5.9	EFQM scores for benchmarked UK agencies	119
5.10	Service quality indicators—UK National Health Service	121
5.11	Service quality ratings for public and private providers, Canada, 1998–2000	122
5.12	A summary assessment of the US National Performance Review	124
5.13	Trust in institutions, 1981–2000	132
5.14	Trust in national governments, 2002	133
A.1	Selected key economic variables (2001)	204
A.2	Social expenditure (% of GDP) 1980–98	205
A.3	Composition of households by type of household in 1995 (%)	209
A.4	Foreign and foreign-born population as a percentage of total population	209
B.1	Public employment at the different levels of Belgian government	218
B.2	Stages of German administrative reform	259
B.3	Swedish economic growth, 1970–93 (%)	285

■ ABBREVIATIONS

APS	Australian Public Service
BPR	Business Process Re-engineering
CAF	Common Assessment Framework (EU quality system, based on EFQM)
CCT	compulsory competitive tendering
DG	Directorate General (the main organizational division within the EU Commission and in a number of other continental European administrations)
The Three 'Es'	Economy, Efficiency and Effectiveness
EFQM	European Foundation for Quality Management
EMS	Expenditure Management System (Canada)
EU	European Union
GAO	General Accounting Office (USA)
GDP	gross domestic product
GPRA	Government Performance and Results Act (USA)
HRM	human resource management
ICT	information and communication technology
IMF	International Monetary Fund
JUG	joined-up government
KRA	Key Results Area (New Zealand)
MAP 2000	Modernizing Administrative and Personnel Policy 2000 (EU Commission)
MbO	Management by Objectives
MP	Member of Parliament (UK)
MTM	market-type mechanism
NAO	National Audit Office (UK)
NHS	National Health Service (UK)
NPM	New Public Management
NPR	National Performance Review (USA)
NWS	Neo-Weberian State
OECD	Organization for Economic Co-operation and Development
PAR	Programme Analysis and Review (UK)
PEMS	Policy and Expenditure Management System (Canada)
PI	performance indicator
PMA	Partisan Mutual Adjustment
PPBS	Planning, Programming and Budgeting System (USA)
PPP	Public–Private Partnership
PUMA	Public Management Service of the OECD
PS 2000	Public Service 2000 (Canada)
quango	quasi non-governmental organization

RIA	Regulatory Impact Analysis
RCB	Rationalisation des Choix Budgetaires (France)
SAI	Supreme Audit Institution (national audit office—their association is called the International Organization of Supreme Audit Institutions, or INTOSAI)
SEM 2000	Sound and Efficient Management 2000 (EU Commission)
SES	Senior Executive Service
SIGMA	Support for Improvement in Governance and Management in Central and Eastern European Countries (a joint initiative of the OECD and the EU)
SOA	Special Operating Agency (Canada)
SRA	Strategic Results Area (New Zealand)
TQM	Total Quality Management
ZBB	Zero-based Budgeting (USA)
ZBO	Zelfstandige Bestuursorganen ('autonomous public bodies'—Netherlands)

Introduction

The first edition of this book was—we acknowledged in its introduction—ambitious. The positive reception of that original has encouraged us to be bolder yet. We have extended the geographical coverage from ten countries to twelve, much expanded our treatment of the European Commission, further developed both our theoretical framework and our interpretation of trends, updated the empirical data, and revised the text throughout. The original aims of the work still stand and its broad structure is retained, but much else has changed. This is halfway to being a new book.

It may be worth recapping our original aims before going on to identify the innovations in this second edition. The background to the book was an awareness of the 'pandemic of public management reforms which have swept across much of the OECD world' (1st edn., p. 1). That pandemic continues to rage—few governments, it seems, can now afford to be without some programme of public sector modernization. Furthermore, it is clear that, while each country or jurisdiction exhibits its own unique features, there are also many reform concepts, techniques, and practices that are items of international trade. This trade is not new (Japan copied certain western administrative arrangements during the nineteenth century; Brazil adopted elements of US 'scientific management' during the 1930s) but it appears to have increased in volume. More recently we have seen (to take just two of many possible examples) citizens' charters appear in the UK (1991), France (1992), Belgium (1992), Portugal (1993), and Italy (1993), and programmatic commitments to the creation of central government executive agencies in (*inter alia*) the UK (from 1988), the Netherlands (from 1994), Jamaica (from 1999), Tanzania (from 1996), and Japan (from 2000). This importing and exporting of public management ideas and practices has also been greatly facilitated by international and supranational bodies such as the Public Management Service of the OECD (PUMA), the World Bank, and the European Commission.

Against this background—and listening to the endless litany of improvement claims made by governments of all political hues—we saw the need for a book that would take a cool, analytic look at this mass of reforms, and which would do so through a comparative perspective. We quote the six claims we made (our 'added value') when we wrote the first edition in 1999. In particular, we aimed to strengthen the then-existing literature in a number of ways:

• By strengthening the field of comparative texts. There are rather few systematic comparisons of more than two countries. Those which exist tend to be edited collections rather than single, integrated works (though the edited *genre* includes some well-planned and highly informative works, especially Flynn and Strehl 1996; Kickert 1997; Lane 1997). We have attempted to compare ten countries, and to say something about the

European Commission (EU). Our selected countries are Australia, Canada, Finland, France, Germany, the Netherlands, New Zealand, Sweden, the UK, and the USA.

- More particularly, by giving full attention to countries such as Germany and France, which have not participated so enthusiastically in the vogue for the 'New Public Management' (NPM) which has swept the anglophone world.

- By integrating the study of management change with an analysis of political systems and contexts. We share the view that management changes in the public sector cannot be satisfactorily understood as some set of free-floating, generic phenomena. Instead they require to be interpreted as one element in a broader shift in the pattern of political problems and responses. In short, public management is always a part of the broader agenda of public governance.

- By developing explicit models and taxonomies of management reform and thus (we hope) enhancing a literature that is frequently untheoretical and primarily descriptive.

- By assessing the available evidence as to the *results* of the reforms in each country. What do we reliably know about the consequences of the huge administrative upheavals of the last two decades?

- By reflecting more generally upon what can reasonably be *expected* of management reform—its potential but also its inbuilt limitations as a means for improving democratic governance.

We preferred to do all this not through the conventional route of setting a number of chapters countrywise side by side, but rather by exploring a set of key issues and themes crossnationally and internationally. The strong sales and wide usage of the first edition have encouraged us to believe that we then correctly identified an unsatisfied need. Translations have been made into three other European languages, and Chinese, and a summary has been translated into Japanese. However, the world moves on and, what is more, readers of the first edition have been fertile in suggestions for improvements. So, in this second edition, we have

- added two 'new' countries to the comparison—Italy and Belgium. Italy is important because, as a number of commentators have pointed out, our original set of ten countries was 'Mediterranean-lite', which was a serious limitation given the distinctive structural and cultural characteristics of Mediterranean administrations. Belgium is of special interest as a small, federal country with an unusually complex federal structure, and a relatively recently expressed determination to reform, following a long period of relative administrative stagnation. In adding these two countries we have stuck to our original guideline that we would not write about countries where we had not been recent visitors, or where, for language reasons, we had little access to the relevant documentation. For these same reasons we regretfully resisted some other suggestions we received, including Switzerland, Japan, and Brazil.

- expanded our treatment of the European Commission, which was somewhat vestigially treated in the first edition. It now has its own section in Appendix B, and we offer a commentary on the recent reforms led by Vice-President Kinnock.

• updated empirical data throughout. Feedback from students and academic colleagues indicated that the first edition was useful to many simply as a handy, clearly organized, record of reforms. Given the continuing flood of such changes we have weeded and replanted the various tables and appendices, adding in a good deal of material about developments that took place between 1999 and 2003.

• elaborated our theoretical perspective. We now take account of theoretical developments that were only just beginning when we wrote the first edition, and of innovations and adjustments in our own thinking, encouraged partly by debates about what we said in the first edition. In so doing, we have made a more explicit attempt to incorporate the influences of administrative law, administrative cultures, and the rapid development of information and communication technologies (ICTs). We have also developed a clearer view of the limitations of discussing reform exclusively in terms of 'more or less NPM'. To put it briefly, we suggest that it is not simply a case of some countries being reluctant or opposed to the NPM: it is more the case that there are alternative and positive concepts of modernization, one of which we describe as the 'Neo-Weberian State' (NWS).

• added a (we hope judicious) selection of the considerable academic literature which has appeared since we first went to press.

All in all, we trust these improvements make the second edition of significantly greater value to its various users—academic colleagues, students, and practising public servants. It remains only to give a brief indication of how we have organized our material.

Chapter 1 sets out our basic understanding of the nature of public management reform. It asks what kinds of activities are involved, who is affected, what the main concepts in play appear to be, and where the boundaries can be drawn between management reforms and other kinds of changes. In setting out our position on these matters we refer to some of the more problematic aspects of the subject, noting the existence of significant debates as to the scope and nature of public management.

Chapter 2 then presents a model of management reform. It begins by identifying the stimuli that appear to have provoked the wave of management changes referred to above. What are the problems that have prompted politicians and civil servants to reach for the instruments of administrative modernization and change? How have these perceived problems interacted with the main flows of ideas, the play of political interest and power, and movements of popular opinion to generate specific agendas for reform? What constraints and distortions may have influenced the extent to which these agendas have been implemented? Our basic argument is that the construction of a broad model or map is both useful and possible, even though countries may well have combined the various elements in very different ways. More specific theories are needed to 'fill in' the map—to explain particular topographical features in particular countries and periods.

While Chapter 2 establishes a common conceptual vocabulary for the discussion of management reform, Chapter 3 is more concerned with *differences* between our twelve countries, and also with the unique character of the EU Commission. It develops a taxonomy of regime types and locates each state within this scheme. In some cases the very possibility of management change may be less than in others—at least in the short term—because of constitutional, political, or institutional features specific to the country or sector concerned. Many of the basic issues for public administration turn out to be *relational*. For example, in the 1980s a British prime minister abolished the local authority responsible for governing the capital city, whereas in Finland or Sweden, constitutionally and politically, a prime minister simply could not make a change of that kind. Or again, relations between the political elite and the civil service elite—which are crucial for management reform—vary significantly between countries. In France the two elites are thoroughly interpenetrating (e.g. 'mandarins' frequently become ministers) while in Canada or the UK the two groups are largely separate.

Chapter 4 uses the concept of a 'trajectory' to describe the varying combinations of ideas, actions, and inactions that particular states have adopted. Each country begins its trajectory in a different place and therefore travels across a somewhat different terrain, even if two or more countries are ultimately aiming at roughly similar objectives. For each trajectory, however, it is possible to apply some general tests; for example, how coherent is the trajectory? Are reforms in the areas of, say, finance, personnel, and organizational structure mutually consistent and reinforcing? Are some areas or sectors left outside the reform process altogether? Are there strong guiding ideas and rhetoric or is there a more fragmented, ad hoc approach? It is here that we first introduce the notion of Continental European alternatives to the largely Anglo-Saxon NPM. We call the main alternative the Neo-Weberian State, and it comes in two main varieties.

Having described the main trajectories in Chapter 4, Chapter 5 moves on to look for evidence of the results of reform. First, it is necessary to give some consideration to what we are going to count as a 'result' and how different kinds of impact may be conceptualized. When this ground has been cleared, we move to ask what we know about what has been achieved, and how secure our knowledge is. Here we draw on various types of data. The Organization for Economic Cooperation and Development (OECD) and other international bodies provide some macrocomparative data, such as trends in public expenditure and changes in the size of the civil service in different countries. By itself, however, this kind of data poses almost as many questions as it answers, and so it is necessary to go deeper, to examine particular countries, to take into account specific evaluations, and to interpret changing rhetoric. In some ways there is a notable absence of 'hard', 'scientific' data (Pollitt 1995). In other ways one *can* begin to construct a picture, though only by carefully weighing and combining different types of evidence generated by different investigators pursuing different purposes. This is what Chapter 5 seeks to accomplish.

Chapters 4 and 5 particularly (though also other parts of the book) are supported by two appendices. Appendix A draws a general picture of some of the socio-economic pressures that have been acting on our twelve countries. Appendix B offers tabulated factual and chronological material on each country, and on the European Commission. Readers are invited to refer to this *corpus* of material as they go through the book. We have done our best to make it accurate and have thoroughly updated it for this second edition, but we recognize that any such selection is bound to leave out some items that others will consider to be of importance (as well as unwittingly including errors or challengeable interpretations).

In the later chapters the 'mood' of the book shifts. Instead of modelling, identifying, and categorizing public management reforms, we move to a more reflective (and reflexive) interpretation of the record of the past two decades. Chapter 6 considers the implications of management reform for politicians and political roles. Some versions of the NPM, for instance, appear to envisage the politicians of the future principally as strategy-makers and definers of guiding values, who will leave operational matters to cadres of performance-oriented professional managers. But are most politicians—or political systems—attuned to such a role? In an era in which the scope for launching grand new programmes appears to have diminished, and during a time when many indicators seem to show a decline in the public's confidence in governments—and when media pressures are more intense than ever—what advantages and disadvantages do politicians see in involving themselves in management reform?

If Chapter 6 partly takes the perspective of the politician, looking at public administrative organizations from 'above' or 'outside', Chapter 7 examines some of the same issue from 'inside' or 'below'. It raises the issue of the limits of administration (Hood 1976; Pressman and Wildavsky 1973)—what can we reasonably expect from management improvements: 'citizen empowerment' (as some would have it) or merely shorter queues? There may be logical, categorical, and/or economic reasons why management improvements are often bound to have the character of a trade-off or a marginal rebalancing of awkward alternatives rather than a 'great leap forward'. Furthermore, our state of knowledge about effective institutional design is probably less scientific and more proverb-like than we usually care to admit (Goodin 1996; Hood and Jackson 1991; Simon 1946). There is at least some evidence to suggest that certain types of reform contain the seeds of their own decay. Consider the setting-up of decentralized, single-purpose delivery agencies—a popular reform in a number of countries, including Canada, the Netherlands, New Zealand, and the UK. These new organizations were created in the name of debureaucratization, increased productivity, and greater user-responsiveness. However, after a few years, concern grew about the 'flip side' of these virtues, namely, loss of coordination, overconcentration on output targets rather than overall effectiveness, and reduced accountability to ministers and/or Parliaments (see, e.g. Bouckaert et al. 2000; Office of Public Services Reform 2002; Pollitt 2003b). Is it possible that some public management initiatives end up, in practice, in circling round administrative dilemmas rather than solving administrative problems?

In Chapter 8 we briefly return to the 'big questions' about the role of public management within the evolving framework of democratic governance. What types of strategy can be discerned, and what are the strengths and weaknesses of each? Has the international experience of the last twenty years generated reliable knowledge from which one can draw 'lessons for the future'? This is a suitably speculative note on which to conclude.

Last, but by no means least, we offer the two substantial appendices (A and B). Readers using the first edition indicate that these factual summaries of developments in each country have been extremely useful. They bring together, in a 'potted' format, a vast amount of data. They protect the reader from the danger of an 'all-ideas-and-no-facts' book. When we wrote the first edition we argued between ourselves about the value of such a substantial 'tail' to the book. Subsequently, students have convinced us that the effort of collection is worthwile.

To support this book, there is a website containing teaching and learning exercises, information updates, and other relevant materials. Go to http://www.oup.com/uk/booksites/content/0199268495/.

1 The nature of public management reform

The noble art of losing face
Will one day save the human race.

(A real public manager—Hans Blix, Executive Chairman, UN Monitoring, Verification,
and Inspection Commission, quoted in Younge 2003, p. 3)

1.1 Why public management reform?

Public management reform is usually thought of as a means to an end, not an end in itself. To be more precise we should perhaps say that it is potentially a means to *multiple* ends. These include making *savings* (economies) in public expenditure, improving the *quality* of public services, making the operations of government more *efficient*, and increasing the chances that the policies which are chosen and implemented will be *effective*. On the way to achieving these important objectives, public management reform may also serve a number of *intermediate* ends, including those of strengthening the control of politicians over the bureaucracy, freeing public officials from bureaucratic constraints that inhibit their opportunities to manage, and enhancing the government's *accountability* to the legislature and the citizenry for its policies and programmes. Last, but not least, one should mention the *symbolic and legitimacy benefits* of management reform. For politicians these benefits consist partly of being seen to be doing something. Announcing reforms, criticizing bureaucracy, praising new management techniques, promising improved services for the future, restructuring ministries and agencies—all these activities help to attract favourable attention to the politicians who espouse them. A cynic might observe that, in these days when the power of individual governments to act independently is increasingly called into question by a complex interplay of local, national, and international constraints, the one thing that ministers usually *can* do—with the appearance of dynamism but at little immediate cost—is to announce changes in their own machinery of governance. There are also legitimacy benefits for those senior officials who, almost invariably, play important parts in shaping and implementing such initiatives. They may gain in reputation—indeed, make a career out of—'modernizing' and 'streamlining' activities.

If management reform really does produce cheaper, more efficient government, with higher-quality services and more effective programmes, and if it will simultaneously enhance political control, free managers to manage, make government more transparent, and boost the images of those ministers and mandarins most involved, then it is little wonder that it has been widely trumpeted. Unfortunately, however, matters are not so simple. There is a good deal of evidence to show that management reforms can go wrong. They may fail to produce the claimed benefits. They may even generate perverse effects that render the relevant administrative processes worse than they were previously.

Furthermore, even if a particular reform clearly 'succeeds' in respect of one or two of the objectives mentioned above (savings, say, and an improvement in quality), it is unlikely that it will succeed in all. Indeed, we shall argue later that certain trade-offs and dilemmas are exceedingly common in administrative change, so that the achievement of one or two particular ends might well be 'paid for' by a lowered performance in other respects: 'rule over specialised decision-makers in a bureaucracy is maintained by selective crackdowns on one goal at a time, steering the equilibrium—without ever acknowledging that tightening up on one criterion implies slackening off on another' (Dunsire 1993, p. 29). For example, if we subject public servants to more effective political supervision and control, can we simultaneously gift them greater freedom and flexibility to manage? The optimists will say yes, by laying down a clearer, simpler framework of rules within which managers can 'get creative'. The sceptic will say no, pointing to survey evidence that the managers themselves think that political 'interference' has *increased* and arguing that it is unrealistic to expect politicians to 'leave well alone' in politically sensitive operations such as social security, health care, education, or the prison service.

In any case, public management reform is only one way to achieve most of the desirable ends identified in the first paragraph. To be adequate, any description of its nature will need to take into account that governmental performance can be improved by a variety of routes and that management reform is frequently undertaken in conjunction with other types of policy initiative. Comparing administrative developments in a number of countries, one academic observed recently: 'Administrative reform... is a subset of *all* policy performance, not a separable set of technical efforts' (Ingraham 1997, p. 326).

Other routes to improved government performance include *political reforms* (such as changes in electoral systems or legislative procedures) and substantive *changes in key policies* (such as new macroeconomic management policies, labour market reforms, or fundamental changes in social policy). The New Zealanders, for example, combined management reforms with fundamental changes in both macroeconomic policies and, later, the electoral system. As you read through the book it is important to bear in mind that, although our focus is on *management* reforms, in practice these are frequently accompanied by policy and/or political changes.

To make matters more complicated, there is, as many commentators have noticed, a delay that affects a good deal of public management reform. The full benefits of major changes in the processes and structures of public agencies normally cannot be harvested until three, four, five, or even more years after a reform programme has been launched. To begin with, new legislation might well be needed. Then it will be necessary to analyse the status quo, and subsequently to design, formulate, and refine new operating procedures, train staff to work with them, define new roles and the appropriate reward and appraisal systems, set new measurement systems in place, inform service users and other stakeholders, and work hard to reduce the anxiety all these novelties have probably caused, both among users and staff. But this is not the kind of timescale that most senior politicians are comfortable with. Their focus is more intensely short-term: on the next election, the next government reshuffle, or even today's television news. The searchlight of political attention moves about from one issue to another much more quickly than complex organizational change can be accomplished. This has always been the case (Pollitt 1984, pp. 148–9) but the discrepancy between the politician's need for 'something to show now' and the organization reformer's need for time, commitment, and continuity has probably grown as a result of the general intensification and acceleration of the political process in many western democracies.

1.2 What is public management reform?

But what *is* public management reform? As with all definitional questions, this can be answered in a number of different ways. As a first approximation we could say that *public management reform consists of deliberate changes to the structures and processes of public sector organizations with the objective of getting them (in some sense) to run better.* Structural change may include merging or splitting public sector organizations (creating a smaller number of big departments to improve coordination or a larger number of small departments to sharpen focus and encourage specialization). Process change may include the redesign of the systems by which applications for licences or grants or passports are handled, the setting of quality standards for health care or educational services to citizens, or the introduction of new budgeting procedures that encourage public servants to be more cost-conscious and/or to monitor more closely the results their expenditures generate. Management reform frequently also embraces changes to the systems by which public servants themselves are recruited, trained, appraised, promoted, disciplined, and declared redundant—these would be another kind of process change.

This way of describing public management reform is helpful, if not very sophisticated. Chapters 3, 4, and 5 will discuss the specifics of structures and processes in a range of countries and in the European Commission. However, this is not the only way of approaching the question of definition. The relevant literature offers a number of more analytical or synoptic definitions, and it is worth exploring some of these, if only to get a feel of the breadth of current thinking on this issue. There are at least two components to our definitional enquiry, namely 'public management' and 'reform'. We will deal first with public management:

1. 'Public management is a merger of the normative orientation of traditional public administration and the instrumental orientation of general management.' (Perry and Kraemer 1983, p. x)
2. 'The field of public management is better defined analytically than institutionally. No clear institutional distinction can be drawn . . . The critical area of public management is the management of organizational interdependence, for example, in the delivery of

services or in the management of the budgetary process. Public management is concerned with the effective functioning of whole systems of organizations . . . What distinguishes public management is the explicit acknowledgement of the responsibility for dealing with structural problems at the level of the system as a whole.' (Metcalfe and Richards 1987, pp. 73–5)

3. 'We conceive public administration as the key output linkage of the state towards civil society. However, the interface between public administration and civil society is a two-way street, including public policy implementation as well as policy demands from private actors towards policy-makers.' (Pierre 1995, p. ix)

4. 'We talk about the *managerial* state because we want to locate managerialism as a cultural formation and a distinctive set of ideologies and practices which form one of the underpinnings of an emergent political settlement.' (Clarke and Newman 1997, p. ix)

5. 'Public administration may be interpreted as a social system existing and functioning in accordance with its own order but, on the other hand, it also depends on environmental conditions in a complex and changing society.' Also: 'In the light of the modern society's functional differentiation, state and market are notable for their own characteristic strategies to control the supply of goods. The type, scope, and distribution of private goods are decided on by harmonising the individual preferences within the market mechanism; decisions on the production of public goods, on the other hand, result from a collective, i.e. politico-administrative, development of objectives.' (König 1996, pp. 4, 59)

The above quotations reflect a range of views not only on the extent of the field of public management, but on its nature and on the most appropriate strategy for conceiving and defining that nature. All five are broad, but in different ways. The first, from a pair of American scholars, relates the nature of public management to certain specific developments in the organization of the field as an academic subject. During the 1970s and 1980s the teaching of public management in the USA (and to some extent in the UK—Pollitt 1996a) tended to migrate from university departments of political science to business schools or other business-related units where 'management' was regarded as a generic subject (how to manage anything). Generic management studies tend to be fairly functional/instrumental in orientation: management is about getting things done as quickly, cheaply, and effectively as possible—and usually about getting things done through other people ('staff', 'the work force', 'personnel', 'human resources'). The study of public administration, by contrast, although sharing a concern with effectiveness, was typically also focused on 'public sector values' such as democracy, accountability, equity, and probity. Hence the proposed purpose for the field of public management studies as being 'to develop an understanding of how public, primarily governmental, organizations may accomplish the missions charged to them' (Perry and Kraemer 1983, p. xi). Note that the field of public management is seen here as being relatively new. There does not seem to be much use of the term before the 1970s, and 'public administration' is still preferred as the title for the leading academic journals in the UK and the USA. Interestingly, both journals accommodated the new trend by acquiring fresh section headings:

'Public Management Forum' for the American *Public Administration Review* and 'Public Management' as a part of the British *Public Administration*. Significantly, in France, Germany, and the Nordic countries, scholars continue to translate the title of their field of study as 'public administration' or 'administrative science' more frequently than as 'public management' (e.g. Ahonen and Salminen 1997; Derlien 1998; König 1996; Premfors 1998; Trosa 1995).

To return to the Perry and Kraemer account, here public management consists, in effect, of a benign merger between generic (overwhelmingly commercial, private sector) management and the more traditional concerns of public administration. The concern for democratic values is fully retained but the enterprise is given a sharper cutting edge in terms of risk-taking, flexibility, performance measurement, and goal achievement. Thus construed, public management sounds unobjectionable, indeed 'bland' (Gunn 1987, p. 35). Much depends, however, on just how compatible the different components that have been integrated to produce this middle-of-the-road vehicle actually are. Hood (1991), for one, has questioned whether the values of the NPM are easily combined with those of traditional public administration. He argues that *in practice* NPM has meant great stress being placed on 'sigma-type values' (efficiency, matching resources to clear goals) but points out that, even if it were to be proved beyond reasonable doubt that such values had been realized in practice, 'it remains to be fully investigated whether such successes are bought at the expense of honesty and fair dealing [theta values] and/or of security and resilience [lambda values]' (Hood 1991, p. 16; see also Pollitt 2003*a*, chapter 6).

The definition offered by Metcalfe and Richards is very different from that of Perry and Kraemer. It deals not so much in values as in processes. It is, in effect, an argument that there are certain processes which are unique to the public sector, and that these constitute the core of public management. The processes in question are those of managing whole sets of organizations, rather than a single organization, and of attempting to adjust the structure of the entire system of public governance. In a later paper Metcalfe expanded on this theme, writing: 'The innovative task of public management as a macro process is to develop new and quite distinctive *macro-organizational* capacities to deal with structural change at the interorganizational level' (Metcalfe 1993, p. 183).

By contrast, the task of public management at lower levels is seen as 'imitative'—that of adapting business or other management ideas to improve the micro-organizational abilities of governments. This is in many ways an ingenious line of argument. It draws attention to the limits of generic management ideas and the existence of unique, 'higher-order' functions which, if they are to be tackled at all, must be tackled by the public sector. These functions have also attracted the neologism 'governance', a term that has become very fashionable since the late 1990s. Among the confusing variety of meanings ascribed to it, one of the more considered definitions was by Keohane and Nye (2000, p. 37; see also Pierre and Peters 2000):

By governance we mean the processes and institutions, both formal and informal, that guide and restrain the collective activities of a group. Government is the subset that acts with authority and creates formal obligations. Governance need not necessarily be conducted exclusively by governments. Private firms, associations of firms, nongovernmental organizations (NGOs), and associations of NGOs all engage in it; sometimes without government authority.

There is a connection between this approach and Metcalfe's for both envisage that government may well be involved in steering nongovernmental organizations and firms, or in cooperating with them, in the pursuit of collective purposes.

Similarly, one may note Goodin's definition: 'Governance . . . is nothing less than the steering of society by officials in control of what are organizationally the "commanding heights" of society.' 'Steering' or 'guidance' is the preferred term across much of Continental Europe (see, e.g. Kaufmann et al. 1986; König 1996). In these systems approaches, the boundaries between individual institutions become less significant than the question of how the whole ensemble dances (or fails to dance) together. It is a perspective within which the conventional boundaries between politics and administration are perhaps less significant, and which enables large social questions to be approached more directly than from within the narrower perspective of traditional public administration. The main boundaries are not so much institutional as between larger systems that operate according to different principles of guidance, such as the market economy, civil society, and—of immense importance within the Continental European approach but much less so within the Anglo-American world—the state.

Unfortunately, the Metcalfe and Richards definition of public management also has some significant drawbacks. In this book we are committed to try to integrate theory and empirical evidence. Empirically, a huge amount of the change that has taken place under the banner of 'public management reform' has been, in Metcalfe's terms, micro-organizational. Most public managers do not spend their time designing 'macro-organizational capacities to deal with structural change at the interorganizational level'—the latter is a task that usually falls to a relatively small number of elite *hauts fonctionnaires*. Therefore, wholeheartedly to adopt the Metcalfe and Richards approach would be to exclude a large slice of our intended subject matter—and to use the term 'public management' in a much more restrictive and specialized sense than do most public servants and politicians. This is not to deny the claim that there are certain high-level, structural adjustment functions that fall mainly to governments and have no close parallel in the world of commerce. It is simply to say that much of the discourse of public management reform treats less elevated problems, and that we wish to include this more mundane territory within our scope too. Indeed, we would go further and suggest that the nature of the high-level, 'macro' functions have an influence on microlevel operations (it would be strange if they did not) and therefore the latter also often have a degree of distinctiveness in the public sector.

There are also issues of interpretation around Metcalfe and Richards' use of the terms *structural*, *system*, and *responsibility*. What does it mean to take responsibility for structural problems across a system? Systems are often collections of organizations with differing bases of power and legitimacy (e.g. EU institutions). Is it possible for any person, group, or even institution to 'take responsibility' for such an entity? If it is not, how is democratic accountability for steering the system supposed to be articulated? Furthermore, how are we to distinguish between 'structural' problems and other kinds of problem?

The third definition clearly denotes a field of much greater scope than high-level 'macro-organizational capacities'. Pierre employs a conventional political science division of society into two spheres—the state and civil society. Public administration (not 'management', note) is then the buckle that joins these two. It is an 'output linkage' (i.e. it serves to transmit information and resources from the state to civil society), but it is also an 'input linkage' (because it delivers demands from actors in civil society back to the state). Again, this is a definition that makes a useful point, reminding the reader that public administration is a 'two-way street', and that, far from being just a technical exercise in achieving the best value for money, it is an instrument of state power. Indeed, Pierre goes on to identify the type of relationship that obtains between political career patterns and administrative careers as one of the key variables in determining the character of public administration (Pierre 1995, p. 208, see also Hood 2002).

Note that Pierre does not use the term 'management' at all, though it is clear that many of the developments he is describing and analysing are what other writers have referred to as 'managerialism' (Pollitt 1993) or the 'NPM' (Hood 1991 and many subsequent publications). 'Management' can be seen as a new way of conducting the business of the state, occupying much of the same territory as traditional 'administration' but differing in style and emphasis (Dunleavy and Hood 1994). This progressive replacement of 'administration' by 'management' was noted and described as early as 1972 by the English civil servant Desmond Keeling. He characterized the differences between the two as follows:

- *Administration*: 'the review, in an area of public life, of law, its enforcement and revision; and decision-making on cases in that area submitted to the public service.'
- *Management*: 'the search for the best use of resources in pursuit of objectives subject to change' (Keeling 1972).

Of course, not all activity by public servants—not the whole of the 'output linkage'—becomes wholly 'managerialized'. Nor are Keeling's two types absolutely pure—administrators need to keep an eye on efficiency and policy objectives, just as managers cannot ignore the law in their pursuit of optimal resource use. But Keeling captured a real and enduring difference of emphasis, and one that we will need to revisit later in the book, particularly when we examine the *Rechtsstaat* regime in Germany and the French, Belgian, and Italian systems of administrative law and control.

The fourth definition is different again. In one sense it is closer to the first than the second or third in that it stresses ideas and values rather than institutions or activities. Yet Clarke and Newman go much further than Perry and Kraemer by introducing the notion of managerialism as an *ideology* and by relating the rise of management ideas to a distinct *political settlement* (in their case, the political realignments around the reconstruction of the British welfare state). To regard the concepts and values that have guided public management reform in many countries as an ideology is not new. One of us has made a detailed case for the usefulness of this perspective elsewhere (Pollitt 1993). In this context an ideology may be defined as follows:

The essential characteristics of an ideology are, first, that it consists of values and beliefs or ideas about states of the world and what it should be. Second, these cognitive and affective elements form a framework. In other words, ideology is not simply a summation of a set of attitudes, but consists of some kind of relatively systematic structuring (though the structuring may be psychological rather than logical). Third, ideologies concern social groups and social arrangements—in other words, politics in its widest sense of being concerned with the distribution and ordering of resources. Fourth, an ideology is developed and maintained by social groups, and thus is a socially derived link between the individual and the group . . . Fifth, ideology provides a justification for behaviour. (Hartley 1983, pp. 26–7)

The fact that Clarke and Newman make a close link between ideologies, practices, and a particular political 'settlement' has a significant implication for their analysis. The implication is that the exact configuration of the ideology—the weightings and emphases as between its particular themes and values—will vary somewhat from one country (and even from one organization) to another. This is because the 'penetration' of the ideology will be influenced by whatever are the prevailing local political forces—the kind of political 'starting point' from which the spread of new ideas and practices begins. In fact this is precisely what we shall be arguing at greater length later in the book.

The fifth and final definition comes from a distinguished German scholar. We should note that he envisages 'public administration' as a system that works according to a distinctive set of principles ('its own order'), yet is influenced by developments in the society in which it is embedded. Its distinctiveness is the result of a more general process of 'functional differentiation' which is universally characteristic of modern societies. The particular quality that defines this state system is that its outputs (decisions, services, goods) are produced according to priorities set by the politico-administrative system rather than by the impersonal forces of the economic market, or by the relational affinities and obligations of civil society. Furthermore, these priorities can ultimately be backed up by the state's monopoly of the legitimate use of force and coercion. This approach therefore stresses the *distinctiveness* of public administration and the uniqueness of the state as a separate sphere of institutional activity, albeit one that is influenced by developments in civil society and economic markets.

We can now look back over the five definitions and draw out some general points. Our aim in doing this is not to arrive at a single, stipulative definition of what public management *really* is. That kind of semantic imperialism is very much out of fashion after the 'linguistic' or 'argumentative' 'turn' in so many social science disciplines (Fischer and Forester 1993). However, what a comparison of definitions can achieve is a better appreciation of the varying meanings and the multiple dimensions of the concept in question. In short, one can grasp *how* the terms 'public management' and 'public administration' are currently used, and what basic assumptions lie behind particular usages.

First, it is clear that the term 'public management' may be used in at least three main senses. It may denote the *activity* of public servants and politicians. Or it may be used to refer to the *structures and processes* of executive government (e.g. to the use of a technique such as Total Quality Management (TQM) or results-oriented budgeting). Or, finally, it may mean the *systematic study* of either activities or structures and processes. The older term 'public administration' was also used in each of these three ways (Pollitt 1996*b*). In this book we will be concentrating on the first two meanings of 'public management' and making only tangential references to its status as a field of systematic academic and professional study.

Second, it is equally clear that public *management* is often seen as a new kind of activity, and is contrasted with the older form, public *administration*. It is regarded as a symptom of modernization—a dynamic force for change. Thus it can act as a legitimizing label for those politicians and public officials who wish to identify themselves with the 'forces of progress'. Here is the then American Vice-President, Al Gore:

President Clinton and I are just as proud of making government work better as we are of making it smaller. It isn't good enough yet, or small enough yet, but we sure have things headed in the right direction. (Gore 1996, p. 4)

Our stance towards these aspects of public management could be described as 'sceptically open-minded'. In other words, we doubt whether most of the ideas behind, for example, the NPM are quite as new as some of their more enthusiastic proponents claim (see also Hood 1998; Hood and Jackson 1991). Furthermore, we regard the matter of 'making government work better' (or even smaller) as quite a complicated one, requiring some discussion of whose values and perspectives are being adopted and what kind of evidence is on offer. While we are perfectly well convinced that real benefits have been secured in certain specific circumstances, we doubt whether this can validly be enlarged into more sweeping claims of 'better government' on a large and unqualified scale. This is hardly the first time that the strength of the case for the benefits of managerialism has been questioned (Foster and Plowden 1996; Hood 1991; König 1996; Pollitt 1995; Wright 1997).

Third, the relationship between *public* management and *generic* management is a contested one. Almost all writers about public management reform (including ourselves) acknowledge that, in many countries, the last twenty years have witnessed extensive borrowing by public sectors of management ideas and techniques which originated in the commercial sector. However, how far this has been 'a good thing' and how far it should go are much debated. Some think it should go further, others, that it has already gone too far (of course, both views could be valid if commercial techniques 'fit' some parts of the public sector but not others). The positions taken by commentators range from the proposition that public administration is a unique and separate field and that it should not be sullied by 'the methods of commerce' to the diametric opposite, that is, that business methods and a business culture are the solution to a wide range of pathologies which are said to be endemic in traditional public administration (Gunn 1987). The Metcalfe and Richards definition fell somewhere between these two extremes, suggesting that at a microlevel public administration might have much to imitate from the world of business, but that at the macrolevel it was *sui generis*. Our own position is also 'in between', but not in the same sense. We argue that the applicability and appropriateness of business-derived approaches vary not only with the *level* (macro/micro) but also with the technical and political characteristics of the activity in question (Bouckaert 2002*b*; Clarke and Newman 1997, pp. 99–101; Lane 1997, p. 307; Pollitt 2003; Stewart 1992). There is also, of course, a skill factor: even if political and technical characteristics are favourable to the introduction of a technique of business origin, the implementor may lack the necessary skills and 'make a mess of it'.

Fourth, all five of the definitions remind us, in different ways, that management is not some neutral, technical process, but rather an activity which is intimately and indissolubly enmeshed with politics, law, and the wider civil society (Bouckaert 2002*a*). It is suffused with value-laden choices and influenced by broader ideologies.

A fifth point follows from the fourth. The different definitions carry rather strong implications for the *scope* of public management, and therefore, by extension, of government action. The Perry and Kraemer definition is quite narrow, at least in the sense that it seems to imply a merger of public sector norms and private sector instruments within the conventional setting of individual public sector organizations. Metcalfe and Richards then broaden that to consideration of a *set* of organizations. Pierre takes the broadening still further by stressing the link between the public sector as a whole and civil society. Clarke and Newman also broaden the scope of the definition, but along another dimension—instead of embracing more institutions or sectors, they see managerialism as a cultural formation and an ideology—a whole new way of thinking about the world. König takes a very broad systems approach, stressing not the existence of individual institutions, or even sets of institutions, but rather strategic differences between contrasting logics for the supply of goods in society. When governments adopt programmes of public management reform, much may thus depend on how broadly or narrowly they conceptualize their task. Indeed, there may be a difficult balance to be struck—finding a way of conceptualizing and operationalizing 'public management' or 'public administration' that is inclusive enough to avoid narrow technicism, yet not so broad as to fall beyond the bounds of feasibility for a government operating within the usual constraints of time, resources, and legitimacy.

Having dealt with 'public management' we can now turn to the other term in our title—'reform'. In English we are conscious that 'reform' is only one among the congeries of alternative and competitor terms (including, significantly, several from the business world, e.g. 'transformation' and 'reinvention', as well as others with a longer public sector history, e.g. 'modernization' and 'improvement'). Like all these other words, 'reform' is a 'loaded' term, in the sense that it strongly implies not just change but *beneficial* change—a deliberate move from a less desirable (past) state to a more desirable (future) state. We accept this as an appropriate characterization of the intentions of many of those who pushed for management improvements, while always holding open the possibility that the actual effects of change could be experienced as less rather than more desirable by any or all of the main 'players'. Thus our use of the term should not be interpreted as a sign that we are believers in inevitable improvement, progress, or 'evolutionism'.

In addition, we are aware that 'reform' is a term with deep roots in the politics of improvement. English schoolboys have for many decades been required to study the 'great reform acts' of the nineteenth century (acts that successively extended the parliamentary franchise). However, nowadays 'reform' does not carry the sense of rapid, across-the-board change, which is conveyed by the American 'transformation' or, possibly to a slightly lesser extent, by 'reinvention'. Nor does it seem to convey quite the dynamism that continental European states have invested in the term 'modernization' (König 1996, pp. 75–6). In short, it has become a more sober, yet still explicitly political term. It refers not to total innovation, but to the reshaping of something that is already there (*re*form). We find this particularly appropriate because it seems to us that the outcomes of many management reforms have very much depended upon the nature of the administrative–political systems in which they have taken place. It is also useful to bear in mind that reforms may be classified as more or less fundamental in character: 'At the most basic level we find adaptation and fine-tuning of accepted practices. The second order extends to the adoption of techniques. The third is concerned with sets of ideas which comprise the overall goals, the framework guiding action' (Halligan 1997, p. 19).

Some contemporary sociologists see continuous 'reform' as a central feature of modern life, contrasting with the premodern emphasis on holding fast to (largely un-examined) traditions: 'The reflexivity of modern social life consists in the fact that social practices are constantly re-examined and reformed in the light of incoming information about those very practices, thus constitutively altering their character' (Giddens 1990, p. 38).

Thus one might say that the structures and processes of public administration are constantly being revised in the light of fresh information about how things are going. Yet, put as baldly as this, the proposition sounds too straightforwardly empirical and far too crudely functional. We share the view expressed by many commentators to the effect that the 'incoming information' is not necessarily straightforward at all, and neither is the way in which it is interpreted and acted upon:

Policy reforms are...symbolically mediated change processes which can be understood only if we uncover the action-motivating reasons that guide efforts to alleviate practical problems...Claims about policy reforms are products of frames of reference; that is, they are systematically related assumptions that provide standards for appraising knowledge claims. (Dunn 1993, pp. 259, 270)

Thus it would be inadequate to conceive of reforms as simply a string of connected actions. If they are to be understood then they must also be considered as processes of debate to which different participants may bring, first, different objectives (including the achievement of symbolic purposes) and, second, different frameworks and standards for identifying and accepting relevant 'evidence'.

To conclude, if we return to our original, working definition of public management reform, we can see that—with some important qualifications and elaborations—it will still serve our present purposes. We proposed that public management reform had to do with *deliberate changes to the structures and processes of public sector organizations with the objective of getting them (in some sense) to perform better.* To this we now need to add that:

- Such deliberate changes are informed by specific sets of ideas, some of which have the characteristics of ideologies, and which merit study in their own right.

- Such ideas may be more or less well specified, more or less adequate for their purposes. Success at getting things to run better should be tested rather than assumed.

- Changes are likely to be influenced by the actors at both ends of the 'output linkages' between the state, the market and civil society, that is, by politicians and civil servants at one end and by private actors (citizens)—also those with an economic interest such as management consultants and big corporations—at the other. (It is remarkable how the powerful corporate players that in practice dominate so many Washington lobbies have disappeared almost entirely from the account of government–citizen relations conveyed by the American best-seller on public management reform, *Reinventing Government* (Osborne and Gaebler 1992).)

- Thus the management reforms in any particular country will almost certainly be shaped by the local preoccupations and priorities of the politicians and private actors most concerned. These local frames of reference are likely to vary a good deal. The successful application of a single template for reform right across the globe (or even across the liberal democracies of Western Europe, North America, and Australasia) is therefore inherently improbable.

• Reforms occur at different levels and may be of broader or lesser scope. A useful distinction is made by Lynn and colleagues (2001, pp. 35–7). They distinguish between four levels. At the 'top' is the global and national cultural environment. This tends to form a set of pervasive influences rather than being an explicit target for reform (although occasionally reformers will make large claims about how they are going to 'transform the culture'). Then comes the level of institutional framework, where there are issues of (re)design and choice. Next there is a managerial level, where key actors develop strategies and shape relationships. Finally, there is the technical or primary work level, where the efficiency and cost of specific functions are a central focus. In the original version—not in our simplified adaptation—there is also a fifth level of 'political assessment'. This scheme is summarized in Figure 1.1. As the arrows indicate, all four levels interact—the figure is not meant to imply a top-down hierarchy. Our book will be mainly concerned with the middle two levels—institutional design and the managerial level—

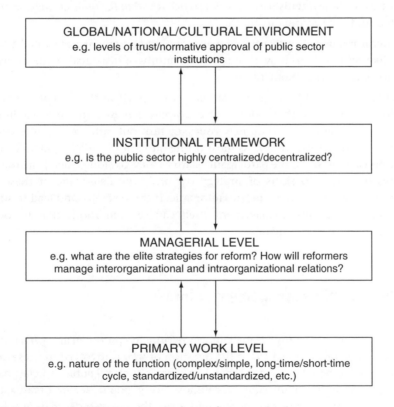

Figure 1.1 Four levels of public management reform: a first approximation.

Source: Adapted from Lynn et al. 2001, p. 37.

but will also regularly refer to both the top level of global and national cultural contexts and the basic level of primary work processes.

• 'To run better' may mean different things to different individuals and groups, and improving performance on one dimension or against one objective may lead (intentionally or unintentionally) to a lower performance in other dimensions.

• As well as seeking evidence about substantive performance improvement, we need to pay attention to the legitimation aspects of management reforms. Simply announcing, discussing, and beginning to implement reforms may bring benefits to some politicians and public servants, even if the later, more 'substantive' effects are elusive or counterproductive.

• The very language of change—'reform', 'transformation', 're-engineering', 'modernization'—is suffused with assumptions about the speed, nature, and value of what is being described or represented. In analysing management texts there is a need to carefully identify who is speaking and who is the intended audience, and to remember that frames of reference shift over time, and that the meanings of words are slippery and variable (see, e.g. Sahlin-Andersson 2001). This is obviously true when moving from one language to another. For example, Finnish has no exact equivalent for the English 'public management', and even the French *gestion publique* carries somewhat different connotations. However, these linguistic slippages also occur *within the same language* as words are transferred from one context to another.

• Furthermore, once the rhetoric of managerial improvement has gained hold it can become, like other reform movements, a 'community of discourse', with its own logic, vocabulary, and internal momentum.

• Finally, although this is implicit rather than explicit in the quotations we chose, it should be remarked that reform is a *learning process*. Attempts to implement reforms very frequently throw up new issues, or turn out rather differently from what had been expected at the outset. As most of the quotations indicate, management is a dynamic process, in which the participants learn as they go along. Such learning can and sometimes does lead to shifts of strategy (we will chronicle some of these in later chapters). But learning is by no means automatic. It can be faulty and lead to superficial or mistaken conclusions. Management itself can set conditions that encourage or discourage analysis and evaluation.

1.3 Who is public management reform?

To complement the preceding ideas about *why* reforms are proposed and *what* is meant by public management we now turn to the question of *who* is involved in these activities. To begin, it should be acknowledged that, in a sense, almost *all* public officials have been 'involved', because in many countries almost every public sector organization has been influenced, to some extent, by the reforms of the last two decades. Similarly, one might argue that almost every citizen has been involved too—affected especially by changes in public service delivery. These have included, for example, the publication of citizen's charters in Belgium, France, Italy, Portugal, and the UK and the privatization of major public utilities such as airlines, telecommunications companies, water companies, or the postal service in a considerable number of countries, including Australia, France, the Netherlands, New Zealand, and the UK.

However, while it is important to bear in mind that the ripples from management changes can thus spread out to touch almost the entire population, our main focus is on the key animators—those groups or individuals which supplied the power, the ideas, or the skills that drove or enabled the process of reform.

In all the twelve countries we examine in this book (and in the European Commission) significant public management reform required the acquiescence, and more usually the active support, of leading politicians, particularly presidents, prime ministers, and ministers of finance. The record shows that, since the early or mid-1980s, restructurings have been popular with significant elites in most of these countries. In the mid-1990s the European Commission launched a programme entitled 'Sound and Efficient Management 2000' (SEM 2000), and then, following the collapse of the Santerre Commission in 1999, formulated a yet more ambitious programme of administrative reform (European Commission 2000). However, the record also shows that some countries have proceeded with management change much more slowly, or on a much narrower front, than others. In Chapter 2 we will offer a preliminary model of the reform process that will identify the sources of such diversity between states.

Alongside executive politicians, senior civil servants have in almost every case themselves been crucial actors in the reform programmes. Indeed, in some countries they have been the prime moving force. This may seem strange—there is a stereotype that depicts senior civil servants ('mandarins') as instinctively conservative and opposed to change. However, the record shows that this is not the case. In countries as diverse as New Zealand, Finland, and France, 'mandarins' have been active in generating reform ideas and pushing for their implementation. Meanwhile, in the academic world, new theories have been developed to explain this phenomenon. For example, Dunleavy (1991) has elaborated a model of 'bureau-shaping', in which senior officials actually gain from reorganizing their subordinates, both by distancing themselves from certain kinds of operational problems (through decentralization) and by casting themselves more and more in a high-status and intellectually more interesting role of institutional design and regulation. Of course, junior- and middle-level officials may not feel so positive about reform: for them it may mean heightened job insecurity, the need to learn new skills, more intense workload pressures, and so on. As Wright (1997, p. 10) expressed it: '[C]urrent evidence suggests that top bureaucrats are not at all allergic to reform programmes, which, on the whole, impact most acutely on the lower ranks and which often open up more exciting opportunities of policy-oriented managerialism.'

Beyond the politicians and their senior official advisers, certain groups of 'outsiders' have played prominent parts in the reform process—at least in some countries. Three such groups deserve specific mention: management consultants, independent 'think tanks', and academics (some individuals are active in more than one of these categories). In the USA, Australasia, and the UK management consultants have been used on a vast scale (Saint-Martin 2000). In the UK, for example, the civil service reforms of the 1960s were carried out largely as an internal matter, whereas almost every reform in the 1980s and 1990s included participation by one or more of the big management consultancies, such as PricewaterhouseCoopers, Andersen, Ernst and Young, Deloitte and Touche, KPMG (and their merged and renamed successor organizations). In the USA Presidents Reagan, Bush, and Clinton, whatever their other differences, all made continuous use of advice from the business world (so much so, indeed, that in 1997 we find the US Vice-President proudly issuing a booklet entitled *Businesslike Government: Lessons Learned from America's Best Companies* (Gore 1997)). In both countries the influence of generic models of management, derived from private sector theory and practice, has been enormous (Pollitt 1993).

In some countries political 'think tanks' have been influential. Thatcher's interest in the ideas generated by right-wing think tanks such as the Adam Smith Institute, the Centre for Policy Studies, and the Institute for Economic Affairs has been well documented (Denham and Garnett 1998; Stone 1996). These ideas frequently included specific proposals for the reform of institutions such as the National Health Service (NHS) or the state schooling system. Similarly, in the USA bodies like the American Enterprise Institute, the Heritage Foundation, and the Hoover Institution found many sympathetic ears among the conservative administrations of Reagan and Bush (Weiss 1992). In Germany the Bertelsmann Foundation sees itself as a workshop of reform, dedicated to removing the social, political, and bureaucratic inflexibilities which may obstruct democratic development.

Finally, the academic world has not been without its influence. Quite commonly individual professors have made contributions to the work of the think tanks discussed above. Others have been hired as consultants, either by individual governments, or the European Commission, or by the PUMA (Halligan 1996a). During the 1990s PUMA was one of the nodal points in an international network, bringing together civil servants, management consultants, and academics (and occasionally politicians themselves) who were interested in public management. It helped to shape what has now become an international 'community of discourse' about public management reform (Premfors 1998 offers a sharp critique of the PUMA 'line'). The World Bank, the International Monetary Fund (IMF), and the Commonwealth Institute have also been international disseminators of management reform ideas. Less influential, but not without significance, have been the more academically oriented networks of the International Institute for Administrative Sciences (IIAS) and its European Group for Public Administration (EGPA). Within particular countries specific university centres have been important— such as the Speyer Postgraduate School of Administrative Sciences in Germany (Schröter and Wollmann 1997, p. 197). Finally, some professors have attempted to exert their influence by staying in their offices and writing books and tracts. As the authors of this book are only too painfully aware, the academic literature on public management reform has become enormous. The number of public management journals has increased. The list of references at the end of this book is long enough, yet represents only a selection of what is currently available.

1.4 **Our approach**

The present text is a work of synthesis. It represents a bringing-together of many previous, comparative studies with which, jointly and severally, the two of us have been engaged (e.g. Bouckaert 1996a, 2002a; Bouckaert and Verhoest 1999; Bouckaert et al. 2002; Halachmi and Bouckaert 1995; OECD 1997a; Pollitt 1993, 2002; Pollitt and Bouckaert 1995; Pollitt et al. 1997, 1999, 2001; Pollitt and Talbot 2004). This corpus of previous work was itself in need of systematization and revision, and, during that process, we have been able both to refine our underlying models of change and collect additional empirical data, especially in respect of countries that we had not included in our previous research.

In this labour of synthesis we have worked in stages. First, a broad model of public management reform was constructed, mainly on an inductive basis, in the light of a review of previous research by ourselves and many others (see Chapter 2). This model is intended to provide a framework within which the main forces for and against management change can be identified and placed in relation to one another. It is also a comparative model in the sense that it permitted country-by-country differences in the pattern of these forces to be mapped and subsequently incorporated into interpretations and explanations. It was therefore the vehicle for what comparative methodologists would term a 'small-N analysis'—a systematic comparison of a limited number of cases (King et al. 1994). This approach permits the testing of theories and the construction of generalized statements, but as *analytic* rather than statistical generalizations (Yin 1994, p. 10).

Incidentally, our decision to move fairly swiftly to the presentation of a model of management reform has meant that we have not had space for a conventional 'literature review' chapter. Instead we have reviewed the most relevant literature as and when we have needed to, in terms of the logic of the book's own sequence rather than as a separate exercise.

Our second step, working initially with countries we knew well, was to test the model to see if it made reasonable sense, both as a way of structuring descriptions of developments in the countries concerned and, beyond that, as a vehicle for explanation. Several refinements to the model were made during this stage.

In the third stage the revised model was used to guide a process of collecting further comparative data from additional countries. Comparativists will not be surprised to learn that this was, in part, a frustrating process because, despite the heroic efforts of organizations such as the OECD, there are still many issues for which relevant data are either non-existent, of doubtful reliability, or of doubtful comparability. We would agree with the American expert, Allen Schick, who wrote:

The nature of management reform is such that an assessment cannot be grounded solely on hard evidence of what succeeded or failed. One's own judgement must be brought to bear, as well as that of others—participants and observers—who have seen the reforms in operation and have thought much about how the system is operating. (Schick 1996, p. 9)

Finally, following the thinking in the above quotation, we attempted to validate the descriptive generalizations, interpretations, and explanations that application of the model to the experiences of twelve countries had yielded by placing them before selected academic and practitioner experts in the countries concerned. The question for these experts was basically: 'Is our interpretation/explanation of what has happened in your country accurate, and does it make sense?' We remain profoundly grateful for the generous (and entirely unremunerated!) assistance we were given at this final stage.

1.5 Concluding remarks

There is a growing fashion for the authors of academic texts to 'confess' their own perspectives and likely biases. On the whole, we agree that this is a useful convention, although perhaps prone to 'Californian' excesses of lengthy introspection. We will therefore keep this last section brief. In any case, we suspect that the discerning reader will already have deduced some of the main features of our *point de vue*.

We are an Englishman and a Flemishman, formally educated with degrees in modern history, philosophy, engineering, and government. We share several values and beliefs: for example, that the public sector *is* distinctive; that public sector (collective) approaches to many social problems are desirable/necessary/ultimately unavoidable; that the dull stuff of administrative implementation is actually crucial to the final effects of reforms; that the eventual impacts on citizens are usually the most powerful (though often fiendishly difficult to execute) test of the 'success' or 'failure' of a management 'improvement'. Further, we recognize that language is both rich and treacherous, and that the rhetorical dimension of public management reforms is substantial, in most countries. That is *not* to say that such reforms are mainly 'blather' but, on the contrary, that some understanding of rhetoric is crucial to the identification of the character and dynamism of reforms. Anyone who tries to read Osborne and Gaebler's *Reinventing Government*, or indeed the European Commission's 2001 white paper of reform, under the illusion that they are neutral, scientific texts will find themselves in considerable difficulty. Reform language is very frequently deployed with an overtly persuasive purpose, and much may hang upon implied or claimed associations between, on the one hand, the (often boring) details of managerial change and, on the other, values that at least some sections of the potential audience hold dear ('autonomy', 'fairness', 'efficiency', 'responsiveness', 'integrity', etc.).

We do not think that we are the slaves of any single theory or approach. On the other hand, it would be absurd to claim that we are somehow 'totally objective' or 'theory-free'. Our general stance is probably what some social scientists have come to call 'critical modernist'. In other words, we still hold to the importance of the empirical testing of theories and hypotheses, although accepting that this is only one kind of test, and that arguments concerning whether the appropriate conditions for falsification have been met will never cease. In brief, we are more sympathetic to the perspective of radical modernity than to a wholesale postmodernity (finding, e.g. Giddens 1990 more illuminating than Boje et al. 1996 or Burrell 1997). Reality is socially constructed, but not all constructions have equal claim to our credulity and certainly some constructions prove more durable than others. Careful interpretations of texts and analysis of the evolution of reform language can be highly illuminating (e.g. Smullen 2003), but we want more than that. However quaint this may seem to radical deconstructionists, we remain interested in what *happens*, as well as what is written and said. We want to know how far practices correspond to promises. One important test is correspondence with such empirical evidence as may be available. Another is the extent to which the theory or hypothesis concerned resonates with the articulated experiences of those who have been directly affected by the phenomenon under discussion. A third is the extent to which a theory or model is internally clear and consistent, in a logical sense. The simultaneous application of all three of these tests may not steer us towards some ultimate and immaculate 'truth', but it should at least help us discriminate between more—and less—adequate descriptions and explanations.

Although fairly catholic in our approach to theory, it will become obvious that, in the sense of a general emphasis rather than adherence to a very specific set of propositions, we find that *institutionalist* explanations carry considerable power. This is *not* to deny the importance of politics or global economic forces or, sometimes, local technical factors (Figure 1.1—see also Chapter 2, and Pollitt 2003*a*). Neither is it to confess an unwavering addiction to some particular school of 'new institutionalism' (Lowndes 1996). Rather it is simply to recognize that—at least in the field of public management reform—the broader forces of economics and politics are almost always mediated through networks of *institutions*. The specific characteristics of these networks, and of the individual institutions that compose them, frequently have a profound shaping effect upon what actually happens during the course of reform, and therefore upon the final results and outcomes of the change process. Of course the networks themselves can and do change, though often not nearly as swiftly as reform rhetoric would lead one to believe. Sometimes, quite distant historical compromises are found still inscribed upon the face of our constitutional and institutional order. In this limited sense we are probably closer to a mildly constructivist historical institutionalism than to either rational choice or the more strongly constructivist sociological institutionalism (Premfors 1998). We acknowledge the frequent constraining importance of path dependency (Pierson 2000), but also repeatedly stress the role of agency and choice.

So it is at a middle level of analysis that most of this book is pitched—between, on the one hand, big political ideas and global economic pressures and, on the other, the 'microflow' of interactions between specific individuals, units, and departments which makes up so much of the everyday life of public servants. This is a level of generality that reveals both interesting patterns and striking variations. In Chapters 2 and 3 we deal with, first, the convergences and then the divergences.

2 Problems and responses: a model of public management reform

> Reform means change in a direction advocated by some groups or individuals. It does not necessarily mean improvement.
>
> (Rubin 1992, p. 20)

2.1 Why has there been so much reform?

Over the last two decades there appears to have been a huge amount of public management reform. It is difficult to be certain—there are no readily available, common and commensurable units in which we can count and compare what has been happening. Yet the present authors share, with many other commentators (e.g. Christensen and Lægreid 2001; Kettl 2000), an impression of a wave of reforms across many countries. Of course, there was also reform in earlier periods (see, e.g. Bouckaert 1994; König 1996, pp. 44–5; Pollitt 1984; Savoie 1994). However, the changes since 1980 have—in many countries—been distinguished by an international character and a degree of political salience that mark them out from the more parochial or technical changes of the preceding quarter century. In some countries there have been deliberate attempts to remodel the state. In many countries reform has been accompanied by large claims from politicians to the effect that wholesale change, with sharp improvements in performance, was both desirable and achievable. To put it more colloquially, there has been more 'hype' about administrative change, in more countries, more or less simultaneously, than ever before.

If this impression is even approximately correct, then one question must be 'why?' What are the forces driving the reformers? Is this just a policy fashion, or are there deeper influences at work? Why is it that, on the one hand, many countries have participated in the stampede to remodel their public sectors while, on the other, some have been much more cautious? How can we explain both the similarities and the differences between what has happened in this country as compared with that? The development of answers to these questions will occupy a good part of the remainder of this book. A useful first step, however, is to develop a general model of management reform, and that is the task we address in this chapter.

2.2 A model of public management reform

The model we will propose is intended as a first approximation. Its purpose is to provide a framework for subsequent discussion by depicting the broad forces that have been at work in both driving and restraining change. A model such as this is a conceptual map, a diagram of forces, and a heuristic device. From it and within it we will develop more detailed sets of typologies and more specific theories that will classify and explain specific patterns and trends, both within individual countries and across groups of countries. Thus, later in the book, sections of the model presented below will be elaborated and modified, as evidence is introduced and our arguments are developed. The model is therefore a way of learning—as anyone attempting to draw even a simple diagram of the influences on reform will quickly discover for themselves.

Figure 2.1 shows our general model. It represents a synthesis of what we have learned about the process of reform in many countries. It is as simple as we could make it without doing injustice to the real complexity of the processes we are endeavouring to identify and assess. Even so, it is complex enough to require some explication.

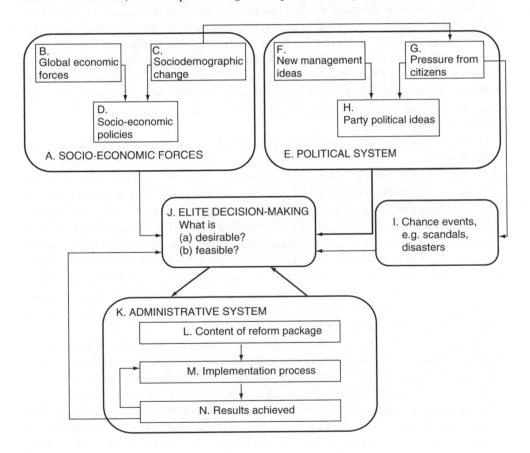

Figure 2.1 A model of public management reform.

2.3 The forces at work

Let us first consider the broad architecture of the model, since this embodies a number of our key assumptions and concepts. At the centre of the figure lies the process of elite decision-making. That is no accident, since one of our theories is that most of the changes we are concerned with have been predominantly 'top-down', in the sense of having been conceived and executed by executive politicians and/or senior civil servants. They are thus elite, essentially voluntaristic activities. Of course (as the diagram explicitly acknowledges), these elites may be heavily influenced by ideas and pressures from elsewhere and, furthermore, their plans may be blown off course. Nevertheless, public management reform—certainly in central governments—is a process that tends to begin in the upper rather than the lower reaches of governance, and that allows for a measure of choice as to the specific instruments and techniques that are chosen. Notice that, within box J, we distinguish between elite perceptions of what reforms are *desirable* and elite perceptions of what reforms are *feasible* (the elites are the same in both cases). This distinction reflects the commonplace of political life that, as Mick Jagger once sang, 'You can't always get what you want' (even if you are a president or prime minister). There are obstacles—economic, ergonomic, and legal—and there are conservative forces that resist change. Reformers are frequently in the position of desiring something more than what they actually propose, but 'censoring' their own aspirations in the interests of framing a lesser package that stands a better chance of being accepted. Notice, also, that perceptions of what is desirable are not merely identifications of what is technically optimal. They are very much *cultural* as well as technical, as, equally, are perceptions of what is feasible.

There are two other general points to be made about the centrality of elite decision-making in the model. First, it is the exception rather than the rule for reform schemes to be comprehensive, even in intent. Reformers try to improve an institution or a programme, or sometimes a whole sector (health, education), but they seldom attempt to remodel the entire sweep of public sector institutions in one go. Goodin (1996, p. 28) expresses this point well: 'Typically there is no single design or designer. There are just lots of localized attempts at partial design cutting across one another, and any sensible scheme for institutional design has to take account of that fact.' Even the reforms in New Zealand, which were unusual for the extent to which they formed a coherent whole and were (initially at least) driven by one small group, evolved over time and were significantly affected by a host of practical considerations which blunted the purity of the theories that lay behind them (Boston et al. 1996, pp. 81–6).

The second general point is that it is easy to exaggerate the *degree of intentionality* in many reforms. The final results of reform efforts (box N) in the diagram may bear only a loose relationship to the intentions embodied in the elite's original manifesto for change (box L). Again, Goodin (1996, p. 28) makes the point: 'Institutions are often the product of intentional activities gone wrong—unintended by-products, the products of various intentional actions cutting across one another, misdirected intentions or just plain mistakes.' Thus, although we locate elite decision-making at the centre of the process of reform, and although we would maintain that intentional acts of institutional redesign have been crucial to the story we have to tell, this should not be read as an elevation of organizational elites into Godlike designers who are routinely able to realize bold and broad schemes of improvement. On the contrary, we envisage their schemes as frequently vulnerable to cognitive limitations, cross-cutting actions, polit-ico-administrative roadblocks, and unforeseen developments of a wide variety of kinds (see March and Olsen 1995, Chapter 6 for an extended account of the pitfalls, both cognitive and motivational, and Hammond 1996 for a brilliantly argued demonstration of why having more of one kind of desired result often inevitably means having more of another kind of problem as well). The most prominent of these complicating factors are discussed further later in this chapter, and subsequently.

Surrounding the elite decision-making at the heart of Figure 2.1 there are three large groups of elements. In the top left there is a group of economic and sociodemographic factors (box A, including B, C, D). In the top right there is a group of political and intellectual factors (E, including F, G, H). In the bottom half of the figure there is a group of administrative factors (box K, including L, M, N). It is from the interplay between these principal elements that management changes emerge. A German scholar expressed the matter thus: 'Extensive welfare state tasks, reduced financial latitude, economic structural crises, and the internationalization of public matters have put state administrations under reform pressure' (König 1996, p. 31).

We will now proceed to examine each of these influences in more detail, beginning with the socio-economic factors (box A). Box A itself represents the general set of these factors, which is both broad and diverse. Some such factors can be thought of as *structural*, in the sense that they are deep-rooted and long-lasting. The population struc-ture would be one example. Others may be more ephemeral, such as short-term eco-nomic cycles of upturn and downturn. Certain of these are likely to have a definite and discernible impact on state administrations, and it is these that are identified in boxes B, C, and D.

Box B represents the influence of global economic forces. Some commentators ascribe a large and dominating influence to these (for thoughtful critiques of such arguments, see Held 1998; Scholte 2000). It is often said that the globalization of capital markets and the growth of multinational corporations and international trade have weakened the control national governments are able to exert over 'their' economic policies. It is therefore no longer possible for a government to sustain for very long a level of public spending that global money markets deem imprudent (hence König's reference to 'reduced financial latitude'). The intensification of international competition has also obliged governments to give greater attention than ever before to the competitiveness of 'their' firms. Firms are unlikely to compete effectively if they are weighed down by either high taxes (to finance high public spending) or by tedious and heavy bureaucracy. What is more, national and local governments are more restricted than they used to be in their ability to address costly and painful social problems such as unemployment:

As a consequence of increased capital mobility and tax competition, the power of all national governments to tax capital assets and capital incomes has been reduced. By the same token, national monetary policy can no longer reduce interest rates below the international level in order to stimulate productive investment, and higher rates of tax mean that running fiscal deficits to expand aggregate demand has become more expensive. National governments have thus largely

lost their ability to avert rising unemployment through the strategies of macroeconomic management that were still effective in the 1960s and 1970s. Hence, the more social policy systems were
implicitly premised on continuing full employment, the more they have come under stress.
(OECD 1997c, p. 211)

Thus we have one set of reasons for widespread public sector reforms—to restrain public
spending, lighten the bureaucratic burden and reshape social policies that can no longer
be afforded (see also Appendix A).

These are powerful arguments. They are widely rehearsed and believed. However, it is
important not to exaggerate their explanatory power. Whilst it seems entirely probable
that global economic forces have been a vital background factor in prompting consideration of administrative reform, they do not determine the precise form or timing or
degree of that reform. Some of the detail necessary to support this contention will be
presented later, but it can immediately be pointed out that the pattern of management
change has differed considerably from country to country, suggesting that the effects of
global markets are not uniform. Furthermore, the timing of particular reforms in particular countries frequently does not correlate at all to economic crises. Finally, it should be
noted that economic pressures do not themselves translate directly into some particular
type of management reform. Reformers need ideas—models or patterns or plans or
visions of how the public sector could be better organized. Markets may provide the
pressure but they do not supply the ideas.

In practice, a further problem with those commentators who present 'globalization' as
a dominant and determining influence on institutional changes is that the concept itself
is frequently deployed in a vague or even contradictory manner. For a satisfactory
analysis one would need, at a minimum, to distinguish the different mechanisms and
modalities involved in the increasing interconnectedness of world financial markets,
extensions to free trade, technological standardization and internationalization
(e.g. the global spread of certain brands of computer software or hardware), and what
one might term cultural globalization (McDonald's, certain films, fashions, sporting
events, etc.). Too often these rather different processes are all lumped together in a single,
utopian or dystopian fashion.

In short, *economic* forms of globalization do seem to have been a major influence on
institutional change, but one which has acted through a number of other intervening
variables. These other variables have been crucial in determining the precise shape and
timing of the reforms in particular countries.

Sociodemographic change (box C) is a second background pressure of considerable
importance. By this we refer to the pressures arising from changes in the pattern of life for
millions of citizens in each of our countries. They are too numerous to list in their
entirety here, but include, most notably, increased life expectancy, changes in the patterns of family life (especially a higher incidence of single-parent and single-person
households), and a considerable rise in the average level of unemployment as compared
with the boom years of 1950–73. Some data on these trends are given in Appendix A. The
basic effect of many of these social changes has been to increase the demand falling upon
state-provided or state-financed services—particularly health care, social care, and social
security. For example, in the early 1990s estimates of the average amount of health care
resources consumed by the average British or American person over the age of 75 ranged

between six and ten times the amount consumed by a middle-aged person. Thus to have an increasing proportion of elderly people in a population implies a considerable growth in welfare expenditure. In most modern states social security (pensions, unemployment benefits, and other benefits in cash and kind) is the largest single item in the state budget, and health care is frequently the second largest. Broad changes in the levels of demand for these services therefore translate into significant public expenditure increases—just as global economic pressures are pushing in the other direction. In some countries commentators have painted frightening scenarios of state finances collapsing under unsupportable welfare burdens, with millions of citizens being deprived of their expected rights and benefits (for a flavour of the American debates, see Marmor et al. 1990).

How does all this affect public management reform? Again, as with the globalization of capital and trade flows, the impacts are indirect. An increase in the number of pensioners or the unemployed does not by itself produce a particular type of organizational change. But what it does do is provide powerful incentives for politicians and civil servants to look for ways of easing the strain on the system. These may include lowering the rates of increase in benefits (e.g. by de-indexing them from wages and salaries), narrowing the categories of eligibility (so as to concentrate on the 'most needy'), or increasing charges and co-payments by the beneficiaries. But they have also tended to include changes that have more obvious impacts on the ways in which such services are organized and managed. For example, streamlining may be implemented with a view to reducing administrative overheads; commercial and voluntary sector participation in the process of provision may be encouraged; and/or there may be wholesale restructurings of the relevant departments and agencies in an attempt to build in stronger incentives to economy and efficiency (see, e.g. for the US, Petersen 2000; for Sweden, Micheletti 2000).

These background pressures therefore reflect themselves in foreground socio-economic policies (box D) which may oscillate quite rapidly over time. For example, in pursuit of social security savings, some European governments have raised the minimum age for entitlement to a state pension. Or, in the economic field in the mid and late 1990s, EU member states struggled to meet the Maastricht 'convergence criteria', which would qualify them to join the European single currency. This put downward pressure on public spending and public debt, and may well have somewhat increased the numbers of unemployed, at least in the short term. It was therefore a policy with considerable and diverse effects on the administrative apparatuses of those states concerned. It was of particular interest as a *supranational* initiative.

We can now move to the second cluster of influential factors—those concerned with the political system. To begin with we need to take into account the general, structural features of this system, which are represented in Figure 2.1 by box E. These features may make management reform more or less straightforward. For example, in Germany a strict constitutional law makes it difficult, if not impossible, for major restructurings to take place at the federal level, whereas in the UK the process of changing the machinery of government has long been remarkably easy, usually involving only secondary legislation that can easily be passed through the legislature by the executive (Pollitt 1984). Note here the important role the law can play in facilitating, shaping, or sometimes restraining public management reform. Moving to another aspect of the political system, it may be observed that in countries such as Finland or Belgium, which are characterized by consensual political systems and coalition governments, the process of management reform is likely to be less harsh and combative than in countries such as Australia, New Zealand or the UK, where the political systems are more adversarial. A final example would be the high degree of protection that the constitutions of Germany and the Nordic countries afford to regional/local/municipal government. This usually means that central governments in these countries find it relatively difficult to extend the reforming process to the local level—unless and until there is a reasonable coalition of political support for reform at that level itself. Contrast this with Thatcher's ability, in the UK during the 1980s, to actually *abolish* the Greater London Council and the six metropolitan county authorities when she found herself in disagreement with their politics and policies (Stoker 1988, pp. 142–4). These contrasting features of different political systems are to some extent *structural*—as in the electoral system and the corresponding pattern of political parties, and to some extent *cultural*—as with the heavy emphasis on relatively 'polite' collective discussion and agreement, which characterizes systems such as those of the Netherlands and Sweden.

In contrast with the constraints and restraints that often flow from the deep structures of political systems, there are also, within those same systems, dynamic elements. One such that is of particular importance for our theme is the influx of new management ideas into the public sector (box F). Over the last two decades this has generated a rich flux of ideas about how to manage almost anything, from a corner shop to 'Great Britain, plc'. These ideas have echoed around business schools, corporate boardrooms, government seminars, and even airport bookstands (see Pollitt 2003a, Chapter 7). There has been considerable intercountry borrowing, facilitated by international bodies such as PUMA of the OECD and the World Bank. Savoie (1994) details several important instances of mutual borrowing between the conservative regimes of Thatcher in the UK (1979–90), Reagan in the USA (1980–8), and Mulroney in Canada (1984–93). There can be no doubt that the selling of management ideas was one of the growth industries of the 1980s and 1990s (Saint-Martin 2000). Equally there can be little doubt that the writings of the gurus and the presentations of the management consultants have influenced political and civil service leaders in a number of the countries examined in this book. Perhaps the most celebrated case was the intellectual line of descent that ran from generic management writers such as Peter Drucker and Tom Peters through the authors of the American best-seller *Reinventing Government* (Osborne and Gaebler 1992) to the major US federal government report *Commonsense Government: Works Better, and Costs Less* (Gore 1995).

Of course, management ideas, however fashionable, very seldom get translated in a pure form directly into specific reforms. Rather they flow into a larger pool of ideas, drawn from a variety of sources, which are made use of by political and administrative elites (box J). Nevertheless, generic management ideas have been prominent on the face of public sector reforms, perhaps especially in Australasia, North America, and the UK. In these countries (and, to a lesser extent, in others) generic approaches and techniques such as Management by Objectives (MbO), TQM, benchmarking, outsourcing, and Business Process Re-engineering (BPR) have been widely adopted within the public sector (Bouckaert 2003a; Lane 2000; Pollitt and Bouckaert 1995; Thompson 2000). Alongside these management ideas, and often interwoven with them, organizational design principles based on microeconomic theories have also been extensively used. In New Zealand, for example, public choice theory, agency theory, and transaction cost economics were all influential (Boston et al. 1996, chapter 2).

In the quotation we used near the beginning of this section, König referred to the 'internationalization of public matters'. Certainly this has become increasingly true of management ideas, both those generated by gurus and business schools and those that derive from microeconomic theory. Departments and units charged with administrative reform have their own international networks, both bilateral and multilateral. The PUMA of the OECD was an influential nodal point in these networks from the late 1980s onwards (see, e.g. OECD 1993*b*, 1995, 1997*a*; Halligan 1996*a*; Premfors 1998). Furthermore (although we cannot deal with it within the covers of this book), there is a complex story to tell concerning the dissemination of 'western' ideas of public management reform to many countries in the developing world—not always with particularly impressive results (see, e.g. Manning 2001; Pollitt and Talbot 2004).

Box G in Figure 2.1 represents pressure from citizens. It should immediately be acknowledged that management reform is not usually at the top of the citizenry's list of priorities. Neither is it a topic upon which most men and women in the street have very specific suggestions to offer. However, although lay citizens are unlikely to be brimming with concrete proposals for better management, they can and, on occasion, do exert pressure for change. If, for example, citizens become used to very rapid and customer-friendly transactions in banks, building societies, and shops, they may become progressively more and more discontented with post offices or benefits payment agencies that are slow, inflexible, and inhospitable. Such discontent with low standards of service in state institutions may then be expressed to political representatives, or the media, who communicate them onwards to the elites (box J). More dramatically, if it is widely believed that civil servants are corrupt, or that a particular service is being delivered in a seriously inequitable way, then public opinion may mobilize to create pressure for reform. Thus, while the views of citizens seldom seem to be the driving or shaping force for particular reforms, there can be circumstances in which they constitute an important background influence. For example, the fatal explosion of a firework store in the Dutch city of Enschede in 2001 crystallized a major debate in that country concerning alleged laxity and 'cosiness' in regimes of public regulation.

Box H identifies party political ideas as a further influence on public management change. Political parties acquire ideas about how they would like to govern, and these include issues of structure, style, and process. For example, a party may decide that it wishes to 'reduce bureaucracy' or to 'decentralize and put power closer to the people'. Or it may adopt more specific proposals such as creating a special ministry or agency for the environment, the regions, the family, inland security, or any other topic which happens to be prominent or fashionable. Party political ideas may be more or less ideologically charged. One doctrine that was influential in a number of countries during the 1980s and 1990s was that of privatization. When construed as a consistent preference for private over public provision, this doctrine had a very obvious and immediate impact on the public sector—it reduced its size. Australia, New Zealand, and the UK all pursued vigorous privatization programmes of this type, and the doctrine was also applied, albeit in a less unremitting way, in Canada, France, the Netherlands, and the USA. More recently a number of political leaders have proclaimed the need for more 'joined-up' government, with greater integration between hitherto separate policies or services (see, e.g. OECD 2001; Pollitt 2003*b*).

Party political ideas (box H) are sometimes internally generated and derived from a specifically political agenda that party activists are developing. On other occasions the ideas may come from outside, from popular movements among the electorate (box G), or from the worlds of business or academia (box F). It is clear, for example, that in relation to public management issues, the ideas of the 1980s Conservative governments in the UK, and the 1984–90 Labour governments in New Zealand were extensively influenced by the theories of public choice-school of economists (Boston et al. 1996; Pollitt 1993). Equally, the Republican administration of President Reagan was heavily populated with business advisers, while its Democratic successors during the mid-1990s also made deliberate use of what it called 'lessons learned from America's best companies' (Gore 1997).

It should be noted, *en passant*, that all these flows of ideas can be greatly strengthened by amplification in the mass media. Political systems have become more and more closely attuned to, and bound in with, the mass media, and if a reform idea can achieve exposure on national TV or in the main newspapers, it will be virtually guaranteed at least some serious political attention. While the detailed technicalities of reform (e.g. accruals accounting versus cash-based accounting) are unlikely to catch the attention of TV pundits or mass-circulation daily newspapers, more general ideas (that the railways are a mess and need reorganizing, or that too many people are defrauding the welfare system) do receive wide media exposure, and help to increase pressure for management reform. We have not devoted a specific box to the media in Figure 2.1, but one can perhaps think of the TV and the press as a general influence that can (sometimes quite suddenly) 'heat up' a particular part of the diagram, amplifying the volume and force of communications and discussions of particular issues. Summing up the play of ideas, one scholar wrote:

Public sector reform is in fashion and no self-respecting government can afford to ignore it. How a fashion is established is one of the most intriguing questions of public policy. Part of the answer lies in *policy diffusion* brought about by the activities of international officials (whose zeal for administrative reform mysteriously stops short at the door of their own organisations), by meetings of public administrators, academics and the so-called policy entrepreneurs. (Wright 1997, p. 8)

There is one influence that operates outside the main groupings of socio-economic forces, political system factors, and elements of the administrative system. Box I represents the effect of chance events such as scandals, natural or man-made disasters, accidents and unpredictable tragedies such as shootings or epidemics. Whilst these can clearly partake of socio-economic or political factors (trains can collide because of lack of public investment in maintenance or signalling equipment; a crazed gunman may bear a grudge against the government), their most obvious features are their newsworthiness and their unpredictability. The effect of such events on reform programmes may not be obvious, but occasionally it is significant. For example, the Cave Creek disaster in New Zealand (when an observation platform collapsed in a public reservation) sharply focused media attention on the issue of public accountability in a newly decentralized system (Gregory 1998). The explosion at Enschede, mentioned earlier, had a similar effect in the

Netherlands. Or again, failures in the UK NHS breast cancer screening programmes were interpreted by the new Labour government of 1997 as evidence that the market-type mechanisms (MTMs) the previous (Conservative) government had introduced were inappropriate and required reform (Laurance 1997). In the USA the disaster that destroyed the space shuttle *Challenger* led to a major overhaul of the National Aeronautics and Space Administration (NASA), one of the largest federal agencies. At a more personal level, senior ministers are prone to a variety of 'accidents' and occasionally individuals with strong reforming ideas may arrive or depart for reasons quite unconnected with their management priorities.

Taking a broad view, therefore, the upsurge of reforms in the last twenty years or so can be attributed to an intensification of a number of factors, but perhaps particularly to global economic forces, socio-economic change, and the supply of new management ideas (boxes B, C, and F). However, these pressures do not enjoy free play over a smooth surface. On the contrary, they soon wash up against countervailing forces—not only the recalcitrance of those groups with a vested interest in the status quo, but also less animated sources of resistance. Existing ways of doing things may be entrenched in laws or regulations or cultural norms, which take time or political majorities (or both) to change. At the extreme, a particular kind of management change requires an adjustment to a country's constitution or—in the case of EU institutions—to the founding treaties. Furthermore, even if the majority agreed that the existing administrative structures or procedures are inadequate, it may be hard to agree on what to do instead (especially if, as is often the case, reform in one direction raises risks in another). Or it may simply be that to manage in a new and desired way may require a considerable investment in new information technology, new accounting systems, and/or new training programmes for the staff concerned before it can be put into practice. All these factors represent the *costs of change*. Often reformers underestimate the extent of these until they get close to them (as they approach or get into implementation—box M).

Many of the costs of change can be thought of as being associated with the dismantling of existing political and administrative systems in order to 'make room' for the new. In every country, much history and many political bargains—and therefore some wisdom— is built into existing systems. Such systems are archaeological maps of past struggles and settlements. Economists and political scientists increasingly employ theories of 'path dependency' to show how certain laws, rules, and institutions can create heavy disincentives for change because so much is already invested in the existing ways of doing things (Pierson 2000). Consider the business of the UK driving on the left, while most of Europe drives on the right. At first sight it seems a pointless and occasionally irritating or even dangerous anomaly—why not just pass a law that requires all countries to drive on the same side of the road? But then think of all the previous investments in the UK in favour of driving on the left—car plants, which make right-hand drive cars, road markings, road signs, driving tests, and many other things that would have to be (expensively) changed. Then there would have to be a huge campaign to retrain every driver, and complex and possibly disruptive arrangements for the day when the changes would actually be made. All in all, the disincentives against change are considerable, even without allowing for the fuss about 'surrendering to the Brussels bureaucracy', which the nationalist media would presumably make.

Similarly, with management reform, staff have to relinquish old ways and learn new. Well-oiled networks of information and influence are disturbed, and new, less certain ones put in their place. Politicians who were used to one configuration of authority within those state agencies that most interested them now have to get used to a new pattern, and possibly one that will be more difficult for them to influence or communicate through. And so on. We have already discussed the restraining effects of political structures (box E) and we will now move on to look at the corresponding structures of *administrative* systems. The two act jointly to temper the ardour of the reformers with the sober difficulties of shifting the status quo. Thus we depict them as enclosing and surrounding the more specific and dynamic pressures of the moment.

Administrative systems (box K) are often difficult to change in more-than-incremental ways. For example, the UK civil service is built around a core of generalists whereas many Continental civil services, including the French and German, consist mainly of staff trained in law. A cultural and disciplinary difference of this type cannot be eliminated overnight—it influences the way in which officials conceptualize and approach a wide variety of issues. Structural differences can also be significant: in Sweden and Finland central government for long consisted of a group of modest-sized ministries surrounded by a circle of relatively independent administrative agencies, which had responsibility for most operational issues. This was a more decentralized system than that which obtained (until recently, at least) in France or the UK. Many of the issues for which local or municipal authorities in the UK would deal directly with a central ministry would be taken care of by agencies in Finland or Sweden. For the Nordic countries to change required new legislation and a reconsideration of the highly political issue of relations between central government and municipalities. It could be done (and to some extent has been), but not quickly or lightly. A third example would be personnel regulations. These are clearly necessary to ensure that public servants behave with propriety and consistency. Yet they tend to develop a momentum of their own. Over the years huge manuals are built up, with each unusual occurrence leading to more paragraphs or pages being added to the *magnum opus*. It can be very difficult fundamentally to reduce or revise this tangle of interlocking rules and regulations. When in 1993 the US Vice-President launched the National Performance Review (NPR), the federal personnel manual was ceremonially burned on the lawn of the White House. The reality was less impressive than this publicity stunt—a huge civil service could not really throw away all its internal rules, and most agencies seem to have continued to apply most of the rules as before. As one American colleague put it to us, 'the copy that was burned cannot have been the only one'. Personnel regulations have become notable constraints on reform in a number of countries—perhaps especially Belgium, France, and Italy—and also for the European Commission.

At a more pedestrian level, administrative systems can still be hard to budge. Consider a straightforward benefits-claiming system. Claimants come to a social security office and fill in a form. The form is then checked by counter staff who, if the claim is in order, make the appropriate payment. Let us suppose that a decision is made to reform this system by introducing computerized technology. In theory the new procedures will be quicker and less staff-intensive. Large efficiency gains are predicted. In practice even this simple-sounding reform can involve extensive complications. Hundreds, if not thousands of staff will need training to use the new computer technology. The educational qualifications needed for counter staff may need to be increased. Public service unions are likely to be concerned about any such changes, and are even more likely to resist attempts to reap efficiency gains that take the form of staff reductions. The purchase of the necessary computer software may be less than straightforward (Bellamy and Taylor 1998, pp. 41–51; Hudson 1999; Margetts 1998). Questions about linking the data held on the new system to other computerized government data banks and about the security of personal details held on file may also arise, and these are likely to have legal implications. And so on. To manage the change well will take considerable forethought, planning, and time. To announce the reform is the easy part, to carry it through requires patience and resolve. During the 1980s and 1990s the UK Department of Social Security struggled hard to implement a huge computerization project called the 'Operational Strategy', but in the end the results fell well short of what had been forecast (National Audit Office 1999, p. 25).

Despite these potentially formidable obstacles to radical or rapid change, reform programmes *are* launched, and frequently make an impact. In Figure 2.1, boxes L, M, and N represent this more dynamic aspect of the administrative system. These activities—announcing reform packages, implementing changes, and achieving results—are the main focus of the remainder of our book, and their treatment here will be correspondingly brief.

The *content* of reform packages (box L) is the product of the interaction between the desirable and the feasible, mentioned above. When announced, such packages frequently display a considerable rhetorical dimension, playing harmonies on the styles and ideas of the moment. They attempt to establish, or reinforce, discourses that support the particular institutional changes under consideration. Here is an example from the USA:

If somebody had said in 1993 that within 10 years the federal government would be smaller, customer-driven, worker-friendly, and run like America's best companies, they would have drawn...jeers.

But that was the challenge that President Clinton handed down four years ago when he asked me to reinvent the federal government—to put the wheels back on. We agreed right then that we needed to bring a revolution to the federal government: we call it reinventing government. (Gore 1997, p. 1)

Or this, from the Minister of Finance in a new, right-wing Danish government in the Autumn of 2002:

The public sector must learn to think, act and be managed on the same terms as the private sector. The old bureaucrats must be smoked out! (Pederson 2002, p. 2)

Reform announcements are therefore as much texts to be interpreted as they are blueprints for administrative action. Some reform announcements come to rather little, so it is always advisable to check how far the initial promises have been realized in the medium term. In this they are no different from most other political manifestos. March and Olsen (1995, p. 195) put it like this:

[M]ost democracies undertake comprehensive reforms of administration from time to time. They create special commissions or parliamentary initiatives to overhaul the administrative machinery of government. Those efforts regularly have their beginnings hailed, their aspirations praised, and their recommendations ignored.

In our view this is somewhat of an overstatement—*comprehensive* reforms are actually fairly rare, and it is quite common for at least some recommendations from some of the reviews to be implemented. Nevertheless, March and Olsen suggest an important idea, namely that *announcing* reforms and *making recommendations* may become activities in their own right, without any necessary follow-through. Politicians, consultants, and academics can make quite a decent living out of producing statements and reports, even if little else happens in the longer run. Many countries can show at least some examples of political rhetoric outrunning measured achievement.

The process of *implementation* (box M) is a particularly important stage of the reform process. The 'science' of administration is hardly exact. Much is learned during the attempt to put reform ideas into practice, and some of that learning frequently translates into departures from the original design. During the 1970s an Anglo-American academic literature focusing on this stage appeared, and much of it was fairly pessimistic about the chances of reform packages actually unfolding according to plan. One particularly influential work was subtitled 'How great expectations in Washington are dashed in Oakland' (Pressman and Wildavsky 1973). It explained how top-down reforms were implemented through long chains of decisions and many levels of administration, and the chances of success were no better than the strength of the weakest link. Although subsequent scholarship has suggested that this mainly linear model of the implementation process is too simple, the basic point about the complexity of the process running from ideas to actual accomplishments stands firm (Hill and Hupe 2002).

Indeed, the complexity of implementation processes may well be on the increase. More and more programmes are delivered through networks of organizations rather than by a single implementor (Kickert et al. 1997; Osborne 2000; Rosenau 2000). These networks may include different levels of government, independent public corporations, public/private hybrid bodies, commercial firms, and voluntary, nonprofit associations. Increasingly, implementation networks need to be international—most obviously for policies in fields such as telecommunications, transport, environment, or communicable diseases. The implications of all this for management reform are complex. If such reforms are to be effective, it seems they will often have to take the whole of a network as their 'unit of analysis', rather than just a single organization. However, both the available theories and the available authority could easily be inadequate for such a task. Ideas about how to design or redesign networks of different types of organization are in short supply (Pollitt 2003a, Chapter 3). And the authority to carry through integrated reform of a whole network may not exist—each member of the network being its own master in the matter of management change.

Another problem that can arise during implementation is that individual reforms, though they may make good sense in themselves, may contradict or detract from other reforms that are being carried through at the same time. For example, the Assistant Auditor General of Canada, commenting on the slow progress made by various public service quality improvement initiatives during the early 1990s, observed:

Our review of relevant documents and our discussions with service managers indicated that they had many reasons for not having made more progress toward the government's repeated commitments. The reasons included the public service strike of 1991, government reorganisation in 1992, the change of government in 1993 and the subsequent Program Review and associated cutbacks, as well as re-engineering exercises carried out by individual departments. (Auditor General of Canada 1997, para 14.65)

Implementation is also a crucial stage in the sense that it can directly feed back to the elite decision-makers' ideas about what to do next—whether to continue along a given path or change tack. For example, in New Zealand a particularly elaborate and sophisticated performance management system was put in place from the mid-1980s onwards. By the mid-1990s, as this system matured, it was recognized that there were dangers in too tight a focus on measurable outputs. The ultimate objectives of programmes (to educate children, lower unemployment, etc.) could be displaced by an intense concentration on how well lessons were delivered, how many unemployment training courses had been held, and a host of other measures of process and output. With this concern in mind the New Zealand Senior Public Managers' Conference for 1997 had the title and theme 'Raising our game: from outputs to outcomes'.

Finally we come to the end of this long and complicated road—the achievements that eventually accrue from the process of reform (box N). These might, or might not, bear a close resemblance to the original aspirations of the politico-administrative elite. Whether they do or not, like the implementation phase, these 'results' are likely to feed back into earlier stages of the process—particularly to elite perceptions of what types of change are desirable and feasible (box J). In practice—as we shall see in Chapter 5—the 'final results' of reform are frequently difficult to identify with any confidence. Rhetoric and reality can be very hard to disentangle. Indeed, ultimately 'the final reality' *cannot* be wholly separated out, because it is so thoroughly impregnated with the competing discourses through which it is constituted. Furthermore, although new administrative structures and processes may unmistakably exist, it is often a problem to know just how far they can be attributed to some preceding reform (Pollitt 1995; Pollitt and Bouckaert 2003). In interviews practitioners very often trace specific impacts back to a variety of influences, of which a particular reform is only one.

2.4 Concluding remarks

We have now presented our model of public management reform. It depicts the process as multifaceted and liable to modification at a number of different stages. It embodies interactions between background socio-economic influences, political pressures, and features of the administrative system itself. It identifies both pressures *for* change and sources of resistance *against* change. It reserves a role for the unintentional and the accidental. It already hints at, and allows for, considerable variation between countries, not least because they enter into the process of change from different starting points, in the sense that each country has its own distinctive political and administrative system (boxes E and K). It incorporates several important feedback loops, as reformers learn from the process of implementation (and with the internationalization of the 'market' in management ideas governments frequently look for lessons from the experiences of other countries, not just their own).

Nevertheless, there is still a lot to be 'filled in'. In particular, to breathe life into the model we need more detailed accounts of what goes on inside some of the key boxes— particularly typologies of different types of political (box E) and administrative (box K) regime. Once we have those in place it should be possible to further develop the dynamic features of the model, by relating specific regime types to specific trends in reforms. At that point the schematic and heuristic model (see Figure 2.1) can begin to accommodate specific explanatory theories. For the moment it is simply a starting point—a logical model, not a unified theory. It could accommodate within its 'boxes' quite a wide variety of more specific theories—more, in fact, than we will have room to introduce within this book. We will, however, make a start. The socio-economic forces of box A, though important, will be treated primarily as background factors, and are analysed comparatively in Appendix A, and for individual states in the country files of Appendix B. In Chapter 3 we therefore focus on boxes E and K—the political system and the administrative system. Here, we will argue, one is able to see quite a strong set of explanatory connections between the types of system and the particular patterns of management reform.

3 Many houses: types of politico-administrative regime

Every house has many builders, and is never finished.

(Paavo Haavikko, in Lomas 1991, preliminary page)

3.1 The starting point for management reforms

The model of public management reform developed in Chapter 2 laid considerable stress on the characteristics of the existing political and administrative systems as shaping influences over processes of management change (boxes E and K in Figure 2.1). These systems provide, as it were, the existing terrain—the topography over which reformers must travel. To continue the analogy, it is obvious that different countries display different topographical features, and therefore different challenges to those who wish to carry through reform. In this chapter we will offer relevant classifications for such differences, and will then use these to examine and locate the twelve countries that fall within our scope. We will also attempt to use the strategy on the other entity in our study—the European Commission—although its application in that unique case is less straightforward (Section 3.8).

Some accounts of public management reform say little or nothing of contextual differences of the kind to which the discussion of this chapter is devoted. They concentrate entirely on the characteristics of the reform instruments themselves—TQM, results-oriented budgeting, performance contracts, or whatever. In our view such accounts are seriously incomplete. Their attention is, in effect, confined to the intervention alone, with minimal analysis of variations in the contexts in which the intervention takes place. Yet there is ample evidence from the study of public administration that 'implementation habitats' can make a huge difference to the effects yielded by a particular piece of management change (Manning and Parison 2003; Pollitt 2003a; Pollitt et al. 1998; Pressman and Wildavsky 1973; Schröter and Wollmann 1997). We are convinced that a conceptually identical, or at least very similar, reform develops differently in one national (or sectoral or local) context as compared with another. There is very frequently a distinct element of *path dependency*, as explained in Chapter 2.

However, it would be misleading to think of politico-administrative systems as some kind of unchanging bedrock to which every reform must adapt itself or fail. In our model (Figure 2.1), *every* element is subject to change, though at different speeds. Thus even the fundamentals of political systems (e.g. constitutions) and administrative systems (e.g. the educational and cultural characteristics of the higher civil service) may change over time. The phrase from Paavo Haavikko's poem, which introduced this chapter, well sums up the situation. However, these kinds of systemic features usually tend to change only gradually—or infrequently—and may therefore be regarded as much more stable/less dynamic features of the reformer's environment than, say, the play of economic forces or the changing fashions in management ideas (Lijphart 1999, p. 254).

Towards the end of the chapter (Section 3.9) we comment on another type of regime—the *ancien régime*, or 'traditional bureaucracy', which recent reforms are often said to be departures, or escapes, from. We raise some questions about the accuracy of this picture of the past, and about the value shifts that are both explicit and implicit in the contemporary debate over 'bureaucracy'.

3.2 Politico-administrative systems: the key features

From the very beginning, comparative approaches to the study of politics and public administration have been intimately concerned with the question of what features to select as the most sensible and illuminating basis for comparing one state, or subnational jurisdiction, with another. In the fourth century BC Aristotle was already suggesting what the most important dimensions might be:

Of good constitutions there are three: Monarchy, Aristocracy, and Polity. Of bad there are also three: Tyranny, Oligarchy, Extreme Democracy. (Aristotle 1963, p. 12)

Whilst it is not feasible for us to replay all the twists and turns in the story of comparative methodology during the intervening 2,300 years, we will at least attempt to explain and justify our own selection.

It makes sense to concentrate on features that, prima facie, seem likely to affect the process of management reform. Fortunately, in the relevant academic literature, there is no shortage of suggestions as to what these might be. We have borrowed heavily from this corpus of comparative work. Typically, the key features identified by leading authors include *structural*, *cultural*, and *functional* elements (see Lalenis et al. 2002 for a useful overview). Those we have chosen are as follows:

1. The state structure (including the constitution)—this is clearly a structural feature.

2. The nature of executive government at the central level—this is a mixture of structural and functional elements. This includes the nature of the political system—in particular whether it operates according to majoritarian or consensus-oriented principles (Lijphart 1984, 1999).

3. The way relationships work between political executives (ministers) and top civil servants ('mandarins')—a functional element, but heavily conditioned by cultural values and assumptions. One way to think of this is to regard it as a bargain between the two elites (Hood 2002). For example, top civil servants may be treated as an entirely

independent group ('magistrates', 'trustees', or 'technocrats'), or they may be regarded as 'battle troops for political masters to command and redeploy' (Hood 2002, p. 319). As trustees, top officials receive a generous share of discretionary authority and a high social status. As agents of the politicians they may receive operational autonomy and the pleasures of being trusted confidants, closely protected by the politicians, at least as long as the latter are in power. The German (Hegelian) idea of a civil service probably comes closer to the former (trustee) model, while the top American officials are more of the 'battle troops'. The career paths of the two elites may be largely separate, as in the UK, or extensively intertwined, as in France, where, for example, the recent Prime Ministers Jospin and Juppé and the recent Presidents Mitterand and Chirac had all attended the famous training school for top civil servants, the *Ecole Nationale d'Administration* (ENA).

4. The dominant administrative culture. We here take administrative culture to refer to the expectations the staff of an organization have about what is 'normal' and 'acceptable' in that organization. It therefore provides the context for ethical relations within the public sector. Such beliefs and attitudes manifest themselves in numerous different ways, including the symbols and rituals of the organization, and its stories, jokes, and myths (Geertz 1973; Handy 1993; Hofstede 2001). Cultures will vary from country to country and, indeed, from one organization to another (Lalenis et al. 2002, pp. 18–41).

5. The degree of diversity among the main channels through which the ideas come that fuel public management reform—this reflects both cultural and functional elements.

These five key features are depicted in tabular form in Table 3.1. In the following sections we discuss each feature in turn.

3.3 The basic structure of the state

Here there are two basic dimensions. The first refers to the degree of *vertical* dispersion of authority—that is, how far authority is shared between different levels of government. Some states are highly centralized, with all significant decisions concentrated at the top level; some much more decentralized. The second dimension concerns the degree of *horizontal* coordination at central government level—that is, how far central executives are able to 'get their acts together' by ensuring that all ministries pull together in the same direction. This dimension ranges from the pole of 'highly coordinated' to 'highly fragmented'.

In terms of the first dimension, the vertical dispersion of authority tends to be greatest within federal constitutions and least within the constitutions of unitary and centralized states. In a unitary state there is no *constitutionally entrenched* division of state power. Central government retains ultimate sovereignty, even if particular authority is delegated to subnational tiers of government. In a federal state the constitution itself prescribes some division of sovereignty between different bodies—for example, in the USA between

Table 3.1 Types of politico-administrative regime: five key features of public administration systems

	State structure	Executive government	Minister/ Mandarin relations	Administrative culture	Diversity of policy advice
Australia	Federal Coordinated	Majoritarian	Separate Mildly politicized	Public interest	Mainly civil service until 1980s
Belgium	Federal	Consensual	Politicized	*Rechtsstaat*	Mainly consultants and universities
Canada	Federal	Majoritarian	Separate	Public interest	Mainly civil service
Finland	Unitary Decentralized Fairly fragmented	Consensual	Separate Fairly politicized	Tending to *Rechtsstaat*	Mainly civil service
France	Unitary Formerly centralized Coordinated	Intermediate	Integrated Fairly politicized	Predominantly *Rechtsstaat*	Mainly civil service
Germany	Federal Coordinated	Intermediate	Separate Fairly politicized	*Rechtsstaat*	Mainly civil service (plus a few academics)
Italy	Unitary Increasingly decentralized	Coalition	Politicized	*Rechtsstaat*	A broad mixture
Netherlands	Unitary Fairly fragmented	Consensual	Separate Fairly politicized	Originally very legalistic, but has changed to pluralistic/ consensual	A broad mixture: civil servants, academics, other experts
New Zealand	Unitary Centralized Mildly fragmented	Majoritarian (until 1996)	Separate Not politicized	Public interest	Mainly civil service
Sweden	Unitary Decentralized	Intermediate	Separate Increasingly politicized	Originally legalistic, but has changed to corporatist	A broad mixture: corporatist processes bring in academic experts and trade unions
UK	Unitary Centralized Coordinated	Majoritarian	Separate Not politicized	Public interest	Mainly civil service until 1980s Recently think tanks, consultants, political advisers
USA	Federal Fragmented	Intermediate	Separate Very politicized	Public interest	Very diverse: political appointees, corporations, think tanks, consultants

the federal government and the state governments or, in Germany, between the federal government and the *Länder*. Of the countries included in this study Australia, Belgium, Canada, Germany, and the USA are federal states.

However, we wish to distinguish further within the category of 'unitary' states. Some of these may be highly centralized (e.g. France, at least until the 1980s decentralization reforms; New Zealand; the UK), whilst others are extensively decentralized (e.g. the Nordic states, where many powers have been delegated from ministries to agencies, and where local governments (counties, municipalities, etc.) have statutorily well-protected independence from central government). In such circumstances the degree of de facto decentralization in a unified state can equal or even exceed the decentralization of a federal state. In Sweden, for example, the reforms of the 1980s and 1990s further decentralized an already decentralized state, expanding the 'local state' at the expense of an increasingly anorexic group of central ministries (Micheletti 2000; Molander et al. 2002).

What are the consequences of these distinctions for public management reform? All other things being equal, reforms in highly decentralized states (whether they be unitary or federal) are likely to be less broad in scope and less uniform in practice than in centralized states. In decentralized states different entities are likely to want and to be able to go in different directions, or at least not all in the same direction at the same time. The federal governments in Washington, DC or Brussels or Canberra simply *cannot* order the subnational governments to reform themselves in particular ways. In Germany the *Länder* have tended to grow in strength (even aspiring to separate representation at European Community level), and different *Länder* have adopted varying stances towards administrative reform (Schröter and Wollmann 1997). Indeed, it is often argued that federal states have the advantage that they form 'natural laboratories', where one approach can be tried in one state or at one level, while another is tried elsewhere. Even if external pressures are similar, states within a federation may adopt quite widely varying trajectories for management reform (see Halligan and Power 1992 for Australia; see Vancoppenolle and Legrain 2003 for Belgium). By contrast, one may once more refer to the actions of Thatcher's administration in the unitary UK when, in 1986, irritated with certain local authorities for a mixture of doctrinal and administrative reasons, central government simply abolished the Greater London Council and the six largest metropolitan county councils (Cochrane 1993, pp. 28–47).

Another possible contrast between a highly centralized state and a highly decentralized state concerns the *focus* of management reforms. Central governments in centralized states tend to be more heavily involved in the business of service delivery (education, health care, etc.) than do the central governments of decentralized states (where these functions tend to be taken care of by lower tiers of government). It has been suggested that this may lead reformers in such centralized states towards a narrower focus on service-specific outputs and results (as in New Zealand during the late 1980s and early 1990s) rather than towards a more strategic concern with policy impacts and overall outcomes (as in Australia during the same period—see Holmes and Shand 1995). Behind this concern one may often detect budgetary preoccupations—if central government is responsible for running major welfare state services, such as social security, health care, or education, these are likely to dominate its overall spending profile. When pressures to restrain public spending mount, it is to these services that ministries of finance are obliged to turn their attention.

Among our unitary states, Finland and Sweden have been rather decentralized throughout the period under consideration. New Zealand and the UK have remained highly centralized throughout the same period. These latter two are also the countries that have carried through the most vigorous, broad-scope management reforms among the twelve states under consideration (which therefore fits with our analysis). France is an interesting case because, having been famously and highly centralized until the early 1980s, it then embarked upon a series of structural decentralizations, the full effects of which have been profound (and which are still working themselves out). The impacts of these changes appear to have included a modest decline in central government's share of both total public expenditure and total taxation (Steunenberg and Mol 1997, pp. 238–9, see also Table 3.2).

Table 3.2 Percentage shares of public employment by levels of government

Country	Central government				Other levels of government		
	1985	1990	1994	2000		1994	2000
Australia	—	15.0	14.6	12.1^d	State	73.3	77.1^d
					Local	12.1	10.8^d
Belgium	—	53.7^a	39.9^b	34.3	Regional	14.1^b	14.8
					Local	46.0^b	50.8
Canada	16.8	17.9	17.1	13.2	Provincial	44.1	51.9
					Local	38.9	35.0
Finland	33.3	24.3	25.2	23.4^e	Municipalities	74.8	76.6^e
France	56.3	55.0	48.7	51.6^c	Subnational	30.7	25.3^c
Germany	22.1	21.6	11.9	11.5	*Länder*	51.0	52.2
					Municipalities	37.1	36.3
Italy	62.9	63	63	57.9^c	Regional	23.0	26.8^c
					Municipalities	14.0	15.3^c
Netherlands	68.4	70.1	—	74.2^e	Regional	—	4.7^e
					Municipalities	—	21.1^e
New Zealand	—	90.1	89.7	90.9	Local	10.3	9.1
Sweden	27.2	26.7	17.3	—	Regional	24.6	—
					Municipalities	58.1	—
UK	48.0	47.7	47.7	47.6^c	Local	52.3	52.4^c
USA	17.9	16.7	15.2	13.5	State	22.6	23.1
					Local	61.1	63.4

Note: Figures 2001, Public Management Service for ^{a}1989; ^{b}1995; ^{c}1997; ^{d}1998; ^{e}1999.
Source: OECD (Summary of the PSPE data analysis and future direction for HRM data collection).

Thus, various indicators of decentralization can be constructed. Central government shares in total public spending and in total taxation are two possibilities. A third is to examine the percentages of public servants who work for central governments, as compared with the proportion working for subcentral governments—states, regions, counties, municipalities, and so on. Mapping our twelve countries like this (Table 3.2) reveals some large differences.

Clearly some countries are much more 'centre-heavy' than others. New Zealand shows 90 per cent of its public servants as working for the centre. Italy, France, and the UK are also quite high scorers on this indicator, with 72 per cent, 52 per cent, and 48 per cent respectively. Germany, however, employs fewer than 12 per cent of its public servants at the centre, and the Nordic countries are quite low too (Finland = 23 per cent and Sweden = 17 per cent—figures refer to slightly varying years, see Table 3.2 for details).

We now turn to the second dimension of structure—the degree of horizontal coordination within central government. How far are one or two central ministries able to ensure that all the others take the same approach to matters of particular interest? This is a difficult variable to estimate, because it tends to be more a matter of convention and less clearly written down in constitutional or statutory provision than are questions of the distribution of powers between different levels of government. One is obliged to rely more on the impressions of knowledgeable observers and participants. Allowing for this, there appears to be some significant differences between countries.

In some countries there is a tradition that one or sometimes two ministries 'call the shots' as far as administrative reform is concerned. Other ministries have to fall in line. In New Zealand, for example, the Ministry of Finance and the State Services Commission were able to drive through the huge changes of the ten-year period after 1984 (Boston et al. 1996). In the UK the Treasury is usually able to get its way, especially when it is in agreement with the Cabinet Office. Other countries, however, are more fragmented in this regard. In the Netherlands no ministry enjoys the degree of pre-eminence held by the New Zealand Ministry of Finance or the UK Treasury. In Finland the Ministry of Finance is certainly powerful, but in matters of administrative change shares responsibility with the Ministry of the Interior. In the USA the picture is complicated by the unusual strength of the legislature. The strong direct links between, on the one hand, the Senate and the House of Representatives and, on the other, the individual departments and agencies, and Congress's ability to 'micromanage' federal organizations, sometimes cut across the intentions of the president and the executive leadership (see Appendix B: USA, country file; Peters 1995). In France, although the *grands corps* form a strong 'glue' at the top of the system, the state as a whole is a 'fragmented machine' and 'ministerial structures are always in turmoil' (Rouban 1995, pp. 42, 45). Germany is more fragmented still: 'Instead of having one single powerful actor or agency, possibly at the national level, that would take the lead, and have the say in public sector reform issues, the German politico-administrative system has a multitude of such arenas and actors' (Schröter and Wollmann 1997, p. 187).

3.4 The nature of executive government

Whatever the *scope* of central government might be, what goes on within that scope will be shaped by the working habits and conventions of that particular executive. Comparativist scholars have developed a useful typology of these conventions, the basic features of which are as follows:

- *Single-party or minimal-winning or bare-majority*: where one party holds more than 50 per cent of the seats in the legislature;

- *Minimal-winning coalitions*: where two or more parties hold more than 50 per cent of the legislative seats;

- *Minority cabinets*: where the party or parties composing the executive hold less than 50 per cent of the legislative seats; and

- *Oversized executives or grand coalitions*: where additional parties are included in the executive beyond the number required for a minimal-winning coalition (Lijphart 1984; see also a slightly changed but fundamentally equivalent classification in the later Lijphart 1999, pp. 90–1).

The importance of these types is that each tends to generate a different set of governing conventions. Of course, following elections the executive of a given country *can* change from one of these types to another, but in practice such shifts are comparatively rare. In most countries the electoral system produces fairly stable results and thus executives tend to build up entrenched habits of government. In general terms these habits tend to become more consultative and consensus-oriented/less adversarial the further one moves down the above list (i.e. single-party majorities tend to go along with majoritarian styles of governance while minority cabinets and grand coalitions tend to behave in a more consensual fashion). The implication of this for public management reform is that the sweeping changes—which are highly likely to be those that will disturb the widest range of interests—are less and less feasible the further one moves away from the first category of executive government, that is, single-party or minimal-winning or bare-majority governments. We do not wish to suggest that the pattern of reform can simply be 'read off' from the type of executive—but it is a significant background influence, which shapes the boundaries of what is politically feasible (in terms of Figure 2.1, this is the political system (box E) influencing elite perceptions of what is feasible (box J)).

The 'track records' of our twelve countries would appear to lend general support to this line of reasoning. If we examine the clearly majoritarian governments (Australia, Canada, New Zealand until 1996, and the UK) and compare them with the clearly consensual regimes (Finland, Italy, and the Netherlands), there can be little doubt that the scope and intensity of management reforms were greater in the former group than in the latter. If we look at the period 1945–96 the contrast is stark. One-party cabinets were in power in Australia for 69.2 per cent of the time, Canada for 100.0 per cent, New Zealand for 99.2 per cent, the UK for 93.3 per cent, but in Finland, Italy, and the Netherlands for 10.9 per cent, 10.3 per cent, and 0.0 per cent of the time respectively (Lijphart 1999, pp. 110–11). However, there is also an intermediate category where the application of this 'rule of thumb' does not work out so clearly.

The first two features—the state structure and the nature of executive government—combine to exercise a very significant influence on the speed and scope of public management reform. In Table 3.3 we show the two factors together, and the groupings it reveals seem to fit rather well with much of the recent history of management reforms that we will be unfolding in Chapter 4 and in Appendix B. *Very crudely* (and we will want to refine this proposition as we go along) *the speed and severity of management reform have declined as one moves from left to right, and the scope of reform (the amount of the public sector any one reform programme affects) has declined as one moves from top to bottom.*

This kind of analysis rests on a whole set of definitions and approximations, and it is important to examine these carefully. However, its value in relation to public management reform can be straightforwardly stated. It leads to two important propositions. First, deep and rapid structural reforms to the administrative apparatus tend to be less difficult in majoritarian regimes than in consensual ones. The general reason for this is that such changes usually create 'winners' and 'losers', and the more consensual the regime, the more likely it is that the losing interests will be directly represented in the executive, and will seek to prevent, delay, or dilute the envisaged changes. Thus consensual regimes are less inclined to, and, in terms of political feasibility, less capable of, dramatic, radical reforms than are strongly majoritarian executives. The latter can force through their own schemes even against opposition from a range of other interests. In case this sounds like a 'plug' for majoritarian regimes, let it also be said that these same qualities mean that majoritarian governments may be more prone to disruptive policy reversals. In the UK, for example, the alternation between Labour and Conservative executives between 1945 and 1989 led to the nationalization, denationalization, renationalization, and, under Thatcher, reprivatization of the steel industry.

The second proposition is that more centralized countries find it less difficult to carry out sweeping, synoptic reforms than more decentralized ones. This is one reason why, for example, we will find that management reforms in New Zealand and the UK have been

Table 3.3 State structure and the nature of executive government

| | NATURE OF EXECUTIVE GOVERNMENT | | |
	Majoritarian←——Intermediate——→Consensual		
Centralized (unitary)	New Zealand UK	France	Italy Netherlands
Intermediate	Sweden		Finland
Decentralized (federal)	Australia Canada USA	Belgium Germany	

Source: Adapted from Lijphart, 1984, p. 219 and 1999, pp. 110–11, 248.

deeper and wider than in Canada and the USA (both federal, decentralized states), despite the fact that all four of these countries are usually majoritarian rather than consensual democracies.

The form of the political executive can thus affect change at several stages in the process of reform. First, it influences the degree of leverage that can be created to launch a programme of reform. Second, it may affect the stability of reforms, once carried through (consensually based innovations are hypothesized to have a higher life expectancy than single party–based innovations, which may be overturned when a rival party gets back into power). Third, there may also be an impact on the sense of 'ownership' of reform measures. In so far as these are seen to have emerged from a broadly based consensus of political opinion, they may assume a legitimacy among the public servants who have to carry them out. If, however, specific reforms are perceived as the doctrinaire instruments of a single party or group, then public servants may resist taking any 'ownership', regarding them with resentment, as alien impositions which may be delayed or diluted as much as possible. This kind of resistance may be even more likely where senior civil servants are independent, high-status 'trustees' rather than politically patronized 'agents' (Hood 2002). In terms of Figure 2.1, the nature of executive government (box E) may thus affect not only perceptions of desirability and feasibility (box J) but also the content of reform packages (box L), the implementation process (box M), and the extent of reform eventually achieved (box N).

We have looked at the clearest-cut cases—the extremes of majoritarianism and consensualism. Now let us examine some more 'mixed' examples. France is in an intermediate position—it has a multiparty system, but possesses a very strong executive figure in the shape of the president. When the president is of a party that is also a major party in the government, France has quite a majoritarian 'tinge'. During these periods (e.g. 1982–4, 1988–92, and 2002–) extensive public management reforms have been carried out (see Appendix B: France, country file). However, at other times, the president has had to work with a prime minister who is not of the same party (*cohabitation*) and during these interludes policy-making is likely to be more cautious. Overall, France may be said to have an intermediate regime, and to be a 'middling' player in terms of the extent and intensiveness of its management reforms. Thus the hypothesized connection still stands.

Italy is a second 'mixed' case. During the 1990s it experienced deep political crisis, and moved from a proportional/coalition system towards a more majoritarian system, and from a highly centralized system towards a system with strong regions, provinces, and municipalities. The executive continues to be a coalition, but usually now with a dominant party. These shifts have been accompanied by a wave of administrative reforms. From the perspective of our model, it would be convenient to claim that the upsurge in administrative reform was linked to the move towards a more majoritarian system. In truth, however, what we have witnessed during the past ten years has been a confusion of initiatives, heading in several different directions. The smoke has not yet cleared from the various political and administrative battles, and Italy is hard to classify with much confidence. If there is ever a third edition of this book, we may then be in a position to make a more settled judgement.

A third case would be Finland, again an intermediate case, but further towards the consensual end of the spectrum than France or Italy. Here the state structure is unitary and oversized coalitions are common. The political culture is one of consensual caution and mutual accommodation. Interparty disputes certainly occur, but their tone is seldom as fierce as is common in France or the UK. In the Finnish case we find a history of substantial but nondoctrinaire reforms, which have been implemented calmly and continuously over a period of more than ten years and which have traversed the periods of office of three coalition governments of widely varying mixtures of parties (see Appendix B; Pollitt et al. 1997).

Before concluding this section it is worth examining two further cases, Germany and the USA. In the German case the *structure* of the state is federal and extensively decentralized (the 'subsidiarity principle'), while the form of executive government has usually, but not always, been that of a minimal-winning coalition (for 71% of the time between 1945 and 1996—Lijphart 1999, p. 110). The effects of the state structure have been profound:

Lacking a single, possibly centrally located powerful protagonist and trend-setter in public sector reform matters and, instead, disposing of a multitude of such arenas and actors each interacting in its own right, it almost follows from the 'logic' of the German federal system that public sector reform activities are bound to proceed in a disjointed and incrementalist rather than a comprehensive and 'wholesale' manner. (Schröter and Wollmann 1997, p. 188)

The effect of the nature of executive government has been less clear. In theory the minimal-winning coalition provides a strong chancellor with good possibilities for carrying through reforms. In the specific case of public administration, however, this possibility tends to be outweighed by the structural factors referred to above. Most public servants are not employed by, and most public programmes are not administered at, the federal level. Also, the federal government's freedom of manoeuvre is restricted by the Federal Civil Service Framework Law. Considerable change has taken place at the level of the *Länder* and of cities such as Berlin, Dortmund, Duisberg, Hanover, Heidelberg, Cologne, Munich, Nuremberg, Offenbach, and Saarbrucken. However, 'Compared to these developments the federal government has not yet put forward any strategic approach towards modernizing its administrative apparatus in a managerial fashion' (Schröter and Wollmann 1997, p. 198).

Finally, the USA is a fascinating example of an executive with mixed characteristics. On the one hand, in relation to the nature of executive government it is quite strongly majoritarian (one-party cabinets for 89% of the period 1945–96). This would lead one to hypothesize the possibility of vigorous, broad-scope management reforms—at least during those periods when the president is of the same party as holds the majority in Congress (at other times there may be an American parallel with the French *cohabitation*, although one in which the legislature is relatively much more powerful than it is in France). However, state structure pushes in quite a different direction. The USA is a decentralized, federal state, with a somewhat rigid constitution. One further element needs to be taken into account. The US legislature (House of Representatives plus Senate) is unusually strong relative to the executive, and, furthermore, the executive does not wield the same control over same-party members in the legislature as is enjoyed by, say, the British Cabinet. These factors further qualify the picture of majoritarian strength, and change the hypothesis in the direction of a more cautious assessment of the executive's reform capacity. When one comes to examine the track record of reform, it is a mixture. From time to time presidents have loudly proclaimed their intentions fundamentally to reform the management of federal departments and agencies, but actual achievements have lagged far behind (General Accounting Office 2001; Ingraham 1997; Mihm 2001; Pollitt 1993; Radin 1998, 2000; Schick 2001). This 'more-mouth-than-muscle' picture closely corresponds with the two dimensions depicted in Table 3.3.

Of course, although state structure and the nature of executive government do seem to be important determinants of change, they usually act in combination with other factors. They permit, but do not, of themselves, 'drive'. That requires the intervention of some dynamic agency, such as a flow of new ideas allied to determined leadership. Rhodes (1997, p. 44) expresses this clearly as he reviews the UK experience:

[W]hy was the pace of change in Britain greater than elsewhere in Western Europe? Three factors were of overriding importance. First, Margaret Thatcher pushed through reform of the civil service. The phrase *political will* is commonly used to explain the government's determination. *Strong, directive and above all persistent, executive leadership* is longer but more accurate.

Second, there are few constitutional constraints on that leadership, especially when the government has a majority in Parliament . . . Central administrative reform in Britain does not require a statute, only the exercise of Crown Prerogative, or executive powers.

Finally, the government evolved a clear ideological strategy to justify and sell its various reform packages. It attacked big government and waste, used markets to create more individual choice and campaigned for the consumer.

3.5 Minister/mandarin relations

In all countries, major public management reforms usually involve both executive politicians and senior public servants (as described in Chapter 2). Together they usually constitute the main part of the elite which makes the crucial decisions about reform (box J in Figure 2.1).

However, the relationships between these two elite groups vary considerably from one country to another, and over time. This is the question of what kind of 'bargain' or deal exists between top politicians and top civil servants? What do they expect from each other? For example, are political careers separate from, or integrated with, the careers of 'mandarins'? (Pierre 1995). Are senior civil service positions themselves politicized, in the sense that most of their occupants are known to have (and have been chosen partly because they have) specific party political sympathies? Mandarins can still be politicized in this sense even if their careers are separate from those of politicians. Or again, how secure are senior civil service jobs? Do mandarins enjoy strong tenure, remaining in post as different governments come and go? Or are their fortunes tied to party political patronage, so that they face some form of exile—of 'being put out to grass' if the party in power changes? Or are they employed on performance-related contracts, so that they can survive changes of government, but not a repeated failure to reach their performance targets? (Hood 2002).

Unfortunately, scholars have as yet failed to agree on a single, robust way of classifying these important differences. The literature does discuss these issues, but we have been unable to find any suitable scale or classification that could be simply displayed in the way that, say, centralization/decentralization and majoritarianism/consensualism are handled by Lijphart and other comparativist political scientists. Hood has made a promising start by distinguishing between eight types of public service 'bargain', but he acknowledges that even these categories 'are neither mutually exclusive nor jointly exhaustive' (Hood 2002, p. 322). We are therefore left with a slightly messy situation, in which we are reasonably convinced that the type of bargain *is* likely to affect the direction and speed of public management reform, but where we have to describe that connection in a fairly ad hoc, descriptive way.

The effects of different 'bargains' on management reforms may be quite subtle. They concern, in particular, 'ownership' of reforms at different levels within the administrative system. Thus, where ministerial and mandarin careers are integrated, one might imagine that the ownership of reforms at the highest levels would be more easily achieved than in systems where the two career paths are entirely distinct. So in a system such as that of the *grands corps* in France, where many ministers would share closely intertwined careers with the senior civil servants, the shaping of reform packages can rely upon shared perspectives and a common professional socialization to an extent that would not usually be the case in, say, Canada or the UK. However, in a French-type system of integrated careers the problem of ownership may reappear lower down the hierarchy, where rank-and-file public officials feel little kinship or identification with the politicized high-flyers of the *grands corps*. In terms of Figure 2.1, the French problem may be with the implementation process (box M) more than with the original shaping of the 'package' (box L)—as does indeed seem to have been the case.

Another of the variables mentioned above—that of the politicization of top posts—adds its influence in roughly the same direction. It creates a bigger gap between the mandarins and the rank and file than would otherwise exist, and may lower the legitimacy of the former in the eyes of the latter. However, in its extreme form—where the occupancy of top civil service positions changes on a large scale following the election of a new political executive—the effect may be one of creating instability in the reform process. This would particularly dog administrative reform because reshaping organizations and standard operating procedures tends to take several years to carry through. We can illustrate this with several examples. Germany (Götz 1997) and Finland (Tiihonen 1996) offer cases of moderate politicization where the party political affiliations of senior officials are important but where a change of government does not result in the wholesale 'slaughter' and replacement of the mandarinate. In the Finnish case the governments are usually coalitions and the style is consensual, and these factors have enabled considerable continuity and stability to be achieved in public management reform (Pollitt et al. 1997). In the German case the effects were masked by the long tenure of the Kohl-led Conservative–Liberal coalition, and, in any case, when German governments change, there are opportunities for mandarins who are unsympathetic towards the new regime to take study leave or be moved to a variety of less politically sensitive roles (Götz 1997). The American example is more extreme. The 'spoils system' results in an incoming president rapidly replacing a large number of senior officials in

Washington, DC producing an odd situation, which one American academic has memorably described as a 'government of strangers' (Heclo 1977). The number of political appointees grew from 451 in 1960 to 2,393 in 1992 (Kettl et al. 1996, p. 82). Change on this scale certainly disturbs continuity. As we will see later, the reform programme of the NPR, which had been given great prominence by Democratic President Clinton and Vice-President Gore during the mid and late 1990s, almost instantly disappeared when Republican George W. Bush came to power in 2000. One group of American scholars describe the general problem as follows:

It is one thing to rely on political appointees to set basic agency policy. It is quite another to appoint so many political appointees that they extend deeply into an agency's middle management. These extra layers increase the distance from the government's top to its bottom and can frustrate the ability of top leaders to give voice to their policies. The layers complicate the flow of information in both directions. They hinder the always difficult job of translating broad goals into specific goals and manageable objectives. They create an artificially low ceiling on the career paths for the bureaucracy's long-term officials and, therefore, impose additional frustrations on the federal government's career work force. (Kettl et al. 1996, p. 83)

This state of affairs may be contrasted with what passes for normalcy in Canada, New Zealand, or the UK. In these countries few overtly party political appointments are made to the upper reaches of the public service, and 'mandarins' can normally expect to serve out all or most of their working lives within the upper reaches of the state machine. This brings, in equal measure, the benefits of continuity and accumulated knowledge and the drawbacks of conservatism ('seen it all before') and limited breadth of experience. In these countries the career patterns of ministers and mandarins are largely separate.

3.6 The philosophy and culture of governance

Having considered the 'normal habits' of government (consensualism, majoritarianism, and their variants) and the relations between ministers and mandarins, we can now begin to examine the 'normal beliefs' of administration. Can distinctive administrative cultures be identified, each with its own characteristic pattern of values and assumptions and, if so, how do these affect the process of administrative reform?

A number of writers have argued for the existence of two particularly strong models: 'Most public administrative systems seem to be guided either by the *Rechtsstaat* model or by the Anglo-Saxon notion of the "public interest"; very few systems fall between these two models, which appear to be inherently inconsistent and irreconcilable' (Pierre 1995, p. 8).

From the *Rechtsstaat* perspective, the state is a central integrating force within society, and its focal concerns are with the preparation, promulgation, and enforcement of laws. It follows from this that most senior civil servants will be trained in law and, indeed, that a large and separate body of specifically *administrative* law will have been created. In such a culture the instinctive bureaucratic stance will be one of rule-following and precedent, and the actions of both individual public servant and individual citizen will be set in this context of correctness and legal control. The oversight of such a system will require a hierarchy of administrative courts, such as the *Conseil d'Etat* in France and Belgium or the *Bundesverwaltungsgericht* in Germany. The typical values of this approach will include respect for the authority of the law as a socially necessary and integrating force, attention to precedent, and a concern with equity, at least in the sense of equality before the law. All in all,

it has become sufficiently clear now that, in countries like France and Germany, the issue of New Public Management in the civil service meets with cultural premises that differ from those in Anglo-Saxon countries. (König 1997, p. 222)

By contrast, the 'public interest' model accords the state a less extensive or dominant role within society (indeed, use of the phrase 'the state' is rare within originally 'Anglo-Saxon' states such as Australia, New Zealand, and the UK). 'Government' (rather than 'the state') is regarded as something of a necessary evil, whose powers are to be no more than are absolutely necessary, and whose ministers and officials must constantly be held to public account by elected parliaments and through other means. Of course, the law is an essential component of governance, but its particular perspectives and procedures are not as dominant as within the *Rechtsstaat* model. All citizens are under the law, but law is usually in the background rather than the foreground, and many senior civil servants have no special training in its mysteries (as in the UK case, where the majority of senior officials are 'generalists'). Civil servants are regarded as simply citizens who work for government organizations, not some kind of special caste or cadre with a higher mission to represent 'the state'. The process of government is seen as one of seeking to obtain the public's consent (or, at least, acquiescence) for measures devised in the public (general, national) interest. It is recognized that different social interests groups compete with one another, sometimes in fiercely adversarial ways. In this context, the government's job is to play the part of a fair and trusted referee, and not to get drawn in on one side or another. Fairness and independence of the play of sectional interests are therefore key values, with pragmatism and flexibility as qualities that may be prized above technical expertise (or even above strict legality).

What are the implications of each of these approaches for public management reform? In general terms we might expect that *Rechtsstaat* systems would be 'stickier' and slower to reform than public interest regimes. This is because management change would always require changes in the law and, culturally, because senior civil servants who are highly trained in administrative law may find it more difficult than generalists to shift to a 'managerial' or 'performance-oriented' perspective. There is at least some circumstantial evidence to support this interpretation. For example, French and German civil servants often find it surprising that the UK executive agency programme could have, within a decade, transferred more than two-thirds of nonindustrial civil servants out of ministerial departments and into a new form of organization without a single new statute being required (see Appendix B: UK, country file). By contrast, the small amount of restructuring that has taken place in the federal German government has sometimes been explained as partly a result of the constraining nature of the basic framework laws in that country (Schröter and Wollmann 1997).

However, one may question whether the bipolar categorization of administrative cultures as either 'public interest' or *Rechtsstaat* is really adequate. In a number of the countries under consideration there has been a considerable shift away from a highly legalistic state form, but towards something other than a straightforward public interest model. The Netherlands, Finland, and Sweden all fall into this third category. The Netherlands went through a period of 'dejuridification' after the Second World War, and its administrative culture now appears as a complex mixture, with a rather open attitude that brings a range of experts and representative groups into the policy-making process. There are also remnants of the old 'pillarization' mindset, in so far as it can still be considered important to ensure that the administrative decision-making process balances representation from each of the major social groups. It is an essentially consensual approach, very different from the more closed and juridical purity of a full *Rechtsstaat* philosophy. In both Finland and Sweden a training in law has in the past been normal for higher public officials, but, as with the Netherlands, this juristic dominance has been considerably diluted over the past forty or fifty years. In both countries civil servants now come from a wide variety of disciplinary backgrounds, and the culture of upper civil service could be said to have as much to do with satisfying the demands of meso-corporatist intermediation practices as with a strict application of law. In both countries, also, there is a sense of the weight, centrality, and continuity of the state—senior public servants are not quite the anxious, harassed breed one finds often in Washington, DC or sometimes in Whitehall.

There is therefore much more to administrative culture than just a bipolar scale running from *Rechtsstaat* to public interest—as an explosion of writing about organizational cultures over the past two decades testifies (see, e.g. Hood 1998). To summarize all that literature is well beyond us, but it may be worth selecting one particular approach, so as to illustrate the additional insights that a cultural perspective can afford. Hofstede's *Culture's Consequences* (2001) examines variations in values and organizational norms across fifty countries. It is based on a quarter century of research and a wide range of studies and surveys. It is relatively unusual in that it actually attempts to quantify certain dimensions of culture. It produces measures for what Hofstede argues are five critical cultural elements:

• Power distance: the difference between the extent to which a boss can determine the behaviour of a subordinate and the extent to which the subordinate can determine the behaviour of the boss. This is closely connected with the norms that exist in a given culture about equality and inequality. A high power distance implies a high tolerance for the existence and manifestation of inequality. For example, Hofstede tells a story of seeing a Dutch prime minister holidaying at an ordinary Portuguese campsite, and suggests that while this was not unusual in the Dutch culture (power distance index 38), it would be much less likely to be the choice of a French prime minister (power distance index 65).

• Uncertainty avoidance: the extent to which the members of a culture feel threatened by uncertain or unknown situations. Here one might compare, say, Belgium (index 94) with Sweden (index 29).

• Individualism versus collectivism: 'Individualism stands for a society in which the ties between individuals are loose: everyone is expected to look after him/herself and his/her immediate family only. Collectivism stands for a society in which people from birth onwards are integrated into strong, cohesive in-groups, which throughout people's lifetime continue to protect them in exchange for unquestioning loyalty' (Hofstede 2001, p. 225). The USA, a famously individualistic society, scores 91 on the individualism/collectivism index, while Finland scores only 63.

• Masculinity versus femininity: 'Masculinity stands for a society in which gender roles are clearly distinct: men are supposed to be tough, assertive, and focused on material success; women are supposed to be more modest, tender, and concerned with the quality of life. Femininity stands for a society in which social gender roles overlap: both men and women are supposed to be modest, tender, and concerned with the quality of life' (Hofstede 2001, p. 297). On this dimension the scores of Germany (66) and Italy (70) can be contrasted with the lower masculinity/higher femininity scores of Sweden (5) and the Netherlands (14).

• Long-term versus short-term orientation: 'Long-term orientation stands for the fostering of virtues oriented towards future rewards, in particular, perseverance and thrift. Its opposite pole, short-term orientation, stands for the fostering of virtues related to the past and present, in particular, respect for tradition, preservation of "face" and fulfilling social obligations' (Hofstede 2001, p. 359). Here the variation between 'our' countries does not appear to be so great, but there is nevertheless a significant difference between, on the one hand, Canada (23) and the USA (29) and, on the other hand, the more past-and-present (short-term) orientation of Finland (41) and the Netherlands (44).

Table 3.4 sets out Hofstede's findings for the twelve countries covered in our book. What, the reader may well ask, does all this have to do with public management reform? Quite a lot, we would suggest. Although Hofstede's measures are usually taken from general surveys, and are not focused specifically on civil servants or politicians, they presumably reflect the broad cultural climates in which management reforms will have to be announced, interpreted, promoted, and resisted in each particular country. They help us understand why what appears to be exactly the same reform may be very differently received in different cultures. We would expect, for example, equal opportunities regulations to have an easier passage in Sweden than Italy. We would expect quality improvement techniques that rely upon egalitarian discussion circles as their main mechanism to work less well in France than the Netherlands—at least if staff of different ranks were involved in the same discussion group. We would expect people in high uncertainty avoidance cultures to be more alienated from, and suspicious of, their governments, and therefore, on average, less 'believing' in their responses to reform (Hofstede 2001, p. 171). We would also expect staff in high uncertainty avoidance cultures to be more concerned with rule-following and more reluctant to risk changing jobs—both factors of some importance for those reformers who want to deregulate bureaucracies and encourage more rapid job change in the public service. As we will see in Chapters 4 and 5, the introduction of flexible employment contracts in civil service jobs does

Table 3.4 Indicators on cultures in different countries

Country	Power distance		Uncertainty avoidance		Individualism/Collectivism		Masculinity/Femininity		Long/Short-term orientation	
	Index	Rank	Index	Rank	Index	Rank	Index	Rank	Index	Rank
Australia	36	41	51	37	90	2	61	16	31	22–24
Belgium	65	20	94	5–6	75	8	54	22	38	18
Canada	39	39	48	41–42	80	4–5	52	24	23	30
Finland	33	46	59	31–32	63	17	26	47	41	14
France	68	15–16	86	10–15	71	10–11	43	35–36	39	17
Germany	35	42–44	65	29	67	15	66	9–10	31	22–24
Italy	50	34	75	23	76	7	70	4–5	34	19
Netherlands	38	40	53	35	80	4–5	14	51	44	11–12
New Zealand	22	50	49	39–40	79	6	58	17	30	25–26
Sweden	31	47–48	29	49–50	71	10–11	5	53	33	20
UK	35	42–44	35	47–48	89	3	66	9–10	25	28–29
USA	40	38	46	43	91	1	62	15	29	27

Note: Rank 1 = highest rank.
Source: Hofstede, 2001, p. 500.

indeed appear to have gone much further in New Zealand and the UK (uncertainty avoidance scores of 49 and 35) than in Belgium or France (UAI scores 94 and 86).

At the very least, this kind of analysis may challenge, or at least refine, the kind of crude parading of national stereotypes to which discussions of different countries' bureaucracies and political systems so often seem to descend. At best it may offer an insight into the specific ways in which particular reforms are extensively 'translated' as they move from one country to another (Czarniawska and Sevón 1996).

3.7 Sources of policy advice

The final significant aspect of the administrative system that we wish to suggest is the diversity of the key sources of advice to ministers on reform issues. (We are here referring exclusively to advice on management reform issues. Advice on other types of policy innovation, such as defence policy or economic policy, may be taken from different networks.) In principle, political executives could take management advice from a wide range of sources—from their own political parties, mandarins, management consultants, academic specialists, business corporations, or political or policy think tanks. The basic proposition here is that the wider the range of customary sources of advice, the more likely it is that new ideas—especially those from outside the public sector—will reach ministers' ears in persuasive and influential forms. Thus, for example, new management ideas (box F in Figure 2.1) will have an earlier and better chance of getting a sympathetic hearing from executive politicians.

Beyond this, the source of a particular reform idea may influence its perceived legitimacy and 'ownership' (a point already made in the section on minister/mandarin relations). Rank-and-file civil servants may be more suspicious of innovations that are believed to come from one particular political party or from 'whizz-kids' in a fashionable think tank. Achieving 'ownership' of reform right down the hierarchy may be less difficult if it is perceived as having a significant 'home-grown' element, that is, if the innovation is seen to be based on accumulated experience within the civil service itself, rather than being a forced 'import' from Rank Xerox or Motorola. Of course, these reactions will themselves be influenced by the administrative culture. Ideas from big business may be accorded greater face legitimacy in a pro-business, antigovernment culture such as prevails in the USA, than in a strong, proud, state-centred culture such as has existed for some time in France.

Contrasts are not hard to find. Consider the differences between France and the UK during the 1980s. In France reform policies emerged from within the 'usual networks' of members of the *grands corps*—mandarins and politicians with shared ENA backgrounds and intertwined careers. In the UK Thatcher was well known for her suspicions of the civil service and went out to right-wing think tanks for many of her reform ideas. Or again, we may note a similar contrast between Germany and the USA. In Germany most reform projects have been hatched within the public service itself, sometimes helped by advice from specialist academics at the Speyer Institute of Administrative Sciences (Schröter and Wollmann 1997). In the USA President Reagan called in teams of businessmen to propose changes in the federal administration, most infamously the Grace Commission and its 2,000 businessmen (Pollitt 1993, pp. 91–5). In 1984 Grace delivered 2,478 recommendations for improving efficiency and cutting 'waste', but the implementation of many of these ideas seems to have been lost track of within a fragmented, sceptical, and probably resentful federal bureaucracy. In Canada, too, Prime Minister Mulroney exhibited considerable suspicions of the career bureaucrats and made a virtue of seeking business advice (Savoie 1994).

Finland, the Netherlands, and Sweden are each different again. The Finnish public management reforms of the decade from 1987 owed most to the thinking of senior public servants. External participation from business people or consultants was the exception rather than the rule (though one or two of the civil servants themselves had some business experience). By contrast, Dutch reforms emerged from a procession of committees and enquiries that featured not only civil servants but also academics, auditors, and individuals from the business world—there was a fairly open market place of advice and ideas. Sweden probably fell some way between Finland and the Netherlands—there was some 'external' debate and participation, but senior public servants kept a firm grip on the helm, and were never in the position of US or British or Canadian civil servants in being obliged to implement a reform agenda that had been substantially set by business advisers to the government, external think tanks, or management consultants.

3.8 The European Commission: a special case

The European Commission is obviously a special case because it is not a sovereign nation state. Furthermore, as a supranational authority, much of its business is conducted *with* nation states, and thus cannot be considered in the same breath as relations between a national government and its own subnational tiers of government. We agree with the many commentators who have warned against simple comparisons between EU institutions and national governments. However, despite these *sui generis* aspects, much of the analysis that we have applied above to the twelve countries in our set can also be applied to the Commission. We would argue that the third, fourth, and fifth features of our general analysis (see Sections 3.5, 3.6, and 3.7) can be related to the Commission without too much difficulty, and that the main differences arise with the first and second—state structure and the style of executive government. So we will tackle these two more problematic features first.

In terms of the vertical dispersion of authority we cannot neatly label the Commission as either federal or unitary. Certainly it is not federal in the sense of having inferior tiers of authority below it, sharing powers in a way that is defined by a single constitution. Yet there are some resemblances: the Commission very much operates within the framework of treaties (Rome, Maastricht, Nice) and these define the relationships that are supposed to obtain between the Commission, other EU institutions, and member states themselves. In this sense one might speak of the Commission working within a quasi-federal, treaty-framed environment, although one in which the other 'levels' are not at all 'inferior'. One obvious difference, for example, has been that, whereas the national level in most federal states retains responsibility for foreign and defence policies, within the EU, member states have fiercely guarded their independence in these respects, and moves towards developing common approaches in these areas, though significant, remain limited and fragile.

The definition of 'unified' does not seem to fit very well either, because, although the Commission is itself a unified body, so much of its work depends on arriving at cooperative agreements with member states, each of which is an independent sovereign power in its own right. In this sense, therefore, only the most extreme Europhobes would liken the Commission to a powerful unitary state on the model of France or the UK.

Moving onto the question of horizontal coordination, we may immediately observe that the Commission has strong vertical divisions and is often difficult to coordinate (Middlemass 1995; Page 1997). Each Directorate General (DG) is to a significant extent a law unto itself. The most powerful horizontal controls have traditionally emanated from the personnel DG (although current reforms are lessening these—see Appendix B). In short, however, the Commission is vertically a quite fragmented body.

Given these structural characteristics, what might one deduce about management reform? Perhaps simply that broad-scope, radical reform of the kind carried through in unified, centralized states such as New Zealand and the UK would be difficult. The historical record would seem to bear this out. There has been a tortuous history of partial, incremental reforms (and failed reforms—Spierenberg 1979). Until the mid-1990s there was no general restructuring or reorientation towards modern styles of management— indeed, 'management' itself was not seen as particularly important by most senior Eurocrats (Stevens and Stevens 2001, p. 148). The Commission was, for the most part, an old-fashioned bureaucracy.

The second 'key feature' in our analysis is the nature of executive government—the habits or style of governance. In the Commission's case this is much more consensual than majoritarian, although political parties play only a very subdued role. The Commission itself (i.e. the body of commissioners) is an expressly collegial body, where it is vital for proposers of reform to gain common assent (sometimes through complicated trade-offs between apparently unrelated issues) or at least to secure reluctant acquiescence. It is composed of people with executive political experience (typically ex-ministers from the member states) but they must deal with what is, in effect, a rival, and in some ways more powerful political executive in the shape of the Council of Ministers. The Commission is also accountable to the European Parliament. The latter was not a particularly strong political force, but since the late 1990s it has acquired new powers and has begun to flex its muscles.

Moving onto what in Table 3.1 is termed 'minister/mandarin relations' we may say that the Commission is unique, and uniquely complex. To begin with, it has what in terms of most nation states would be regarded as an 'extra' political layer. The 'mandarins' are the directors-general, the permanent heads of the Commission's services. Above them floats the first political layer—the commissioners, who, although appointed, are generally politicians by background (see previous paragraph). However, beyond the commissioners lies another powerful body of executive politicians, the Council of Ministers from the member states. Just to make matters more complicated still, each commissioner has a *cabinet* of personally appointed officials, who offer policy advice and (not infrequently) clash with the directors-general. Finally, we may note that, while *cabinet* positions are temporary (they do not last beyond the tenure of the individual commissioner), both they and the career directors-general, and the two grades immediately below them ('A2s' and 'A3s'), are politically influenced appointments (Page 1997). The upshot of all this is a very complex set of relations between senior career officials and 'their' commissioners. Their careers are not usually intertwined after the French fashion, but the mandarin ranks are certainly politicized, and there is a large group of politicized temporary officials in the shape of the *cabinets*. Yet for most of the permanent officials the 'bargain' seems to be more of 'trustees' or 'technocrats' than 'battle troops' for a particular political regime (the terms are taken from Hood 2002 and referred to in Sections 3.2 and 3.5). They enjoy extremely strong tenure and, at the time of writing, are only just beginning to be subject to any organized form of individual appraisal (Levy 2003). Many of them serve most of their careers in Brussels, where they enjoy high salaries and a variety of privileges.

As for the administrative culture of the Commission, it would probably be fair to say that it still bears strong traces of the predominant French influence during its formative years. Many French practices and titles continue, including the existence of strong separate hierarchies (in the DGs) and the predominantly regulatory and legalistic cast of mind. Although there is considerable internal variation (as one might expect in an organization whose staffing policies deliberately mixed officials from such a diverse range of national backgrounds), the predominant impression is of a hierarchy that would score quite highly on both Hofstede's power distance index and index of uncertainty avoidance (see Section 3.6). 'Playing it safe', not challenging one's superiors, addressing problems by making and then following very detailed procedural rules—these are familiar cultural 'norms' within the Commission to this day. The Commission is thus more *Rechtsstaat* than public interest, and can seem a strange place for new arrivals from countries such as Sweden or the UK, which have somewhat different traditions.

With respect to policy advice, that which reaches commissioners may be said to be fairly diverse. In addition to advice from the DGs, commissioners take the views of their own *cabinets*, and, not unusually, may tap sources within the administration of their own member states. They are also bombarded with evidence and demands from the multiplicity of pressure groups that have set up in Brussels. Whilst this is an exceedingly complex system it is not a closed one; indeed the channels are almost certainly more diverse than in some member states (such as Finland, Germany, or even France).

In sum, therefore, one could say that, within the Commission, the feasibility threshold over which management reforms must pass is particularly high. The Commission is a collegial, consensual body and its operative DGs are vertically and strongly divided from each other. No single source of power and authority is therefore strong enough to drive through across-the-board changes against significant resistance. The pressure of public opinion is weak and indirect: this is because of the intervening 'layer' of member states, because of the relative feebleness of the European Parliament (whose own legitimacy, as indicated by electoral turn-outs, is not high), and because the Commission anyway does not itself provide the kinds of public services that would bring it into direct contact with the public. Other 'difficult-to-change' factors should also be mentioned. The Commission mandarins have separate and secure careers—they do not need constantly to 'show results' in order to keep their jobs (Page 1997, p. 87). The top three grades in the hierarchy are fairly politicized, but in a way that tends to focus the occupants on sexy political topics and on what can be achieved within the four-year term of a Commission rather than on longer-term structural change. The administrative culture carries significant elements of *Rechtsstaat*, and the resort to legal rules and standard procedures is, if anything, intensified by the difficulties of running such a multilingual, multicultural organization. All these features combine to make the life of the would-be management reformer difficult.

Despite all this, broader political pressures and external currents of management ideas have at least placed large-scale administrative modernization on the Commission's agenda. When a new Commission took office in 1995, it launched SEM 2000. This was quickly followed by 'Modernizing Administrative and Personnel Policy 2000' (MAP 2000), which focused on internal reforms to the Commission's own machinery. However, this (Santerre) Commission collapsed in disgrace and an unprecedented mass resignation in 1999. The circumstances of the fall of Santerre and his fellow commissioners guaranteed that reform would be high on the agenda of the new leadership (the Prodi Commission), and, under the leadership of Vice-President Kinnock, significant reforms in audit, financial management, and human resource management (HRM) were proclaimed (European Commission 2000). At the time of writing these are still in progress. It appears that real changes are being made, but that progress is quite slow, and that the main emphasis of the reforms has become—in path-dependent fashion—centralizing and regulatory (Levy 2003; Stevens and Stevens 2001—see Appendix B for further details).

3.9 Traditional bureaucracy: the *ancien régime*?

A good deal of the rhetoric associated with public management reform vividly contrasts the new (= good) with the old (= bad). The name given to the old—that against which the modern, reformed public sector organization stands out as superior—is usually something like 'traditional bureaucracy' (e.g. Hughes 1998, chapter 2). Before concluding this review of regime types it is therefore necessary to explore this *ancien régime*—to understand what was supposed to be wrong with it and to clarify its relationships with the various dimensions of the politico-administrative world, which have been discussed in Sections 3.2 to 3.8.

Osborne and Gaebler (1992, pp. 11–12) are fairly typical of at least the Anglo-American-Australasian critique of traditional bureaucracy:

Our thesis is simple. The kind of governments that developed during the industrial era, with their sluggish, centralised bureaucracies, their preoccupation with rules and regulations, and their hierarchical chains of command, no longer work very well. They accomplished great things in their time, but somewhere along the line they got away from us. They became bloated, wasteful, ineffective. And when the world began to change, they failed to change with it. Hierarchical, centralised bureaucracies designed in the 1930s or 1940s simply do not function well in the rapidly changing, information-rich, knowledge-intensive society and economy of the 1990s.

This traditional model is commonly linked with the ideal-type rational/legal bureaucracy proposed and analysed in the writings of Max Weber (1947). This type of organization was characterized by:

- fixed spheres of competence;
- a defined hierarchy of offices;
- a clear distinction between the public and private roles (and property) of the officials;
- specialization and expertise as the basis for action;
- full-time, career appointments for officials; and
- management by the application of a developing set of rules, knowledge of which was the special technical competence of the officials concerned.

This then is the type of regime that is said to be in need of replacement by more flexible, fast-moving, performance-oriented forms of modern organization. Of the various types of administrative culture that have been discussed earlier in this chapter, it is fairly clear which one is closest to the traditional model—it is the *Rechtsstaat*. The culture is one of high power distance and high uncertainty avoidance—indeed, the reduction of uncertainty and the increase in predictability are claimed to be among its chief virtues. The critique favoured by Osborne and Gaebler, Hughes, and many others, therefore leads towards the conclusion that countries like Germany are 'behind' and need to take up 'reinvention' or the 'NPM' more vigorously—to follow the 'leaders' such as New Zealand, the UK, or the US NPR.

Unfortunately, however, what one might term the 'NPM story' is misleadingly neat and oversimple. There are many detailed criticisms which could be made of it (see Pollitt 2003*a*, chapter 2), but here we will confine ourselves to just three general points. First, as is dazzlingly clear from the earlier sections of this chapter, for many years there has not been just one type of administrative regime in existence, but several. So to reduce the past to a single system is to do a considerable injustice to the variety of history. Second (by way of extension to the first), even if some parts of some public sectors 'fitted' the image of the traditional bureaucracy, others definitely did not. For example, in the UK (as in most other western European states) the most expensive and labour-intensive sectors of state administration—health care and education—were never legalistic bureaucracies. On the contrary, they were heavily professionalized organizations in which individual professions were able to exercise a great deal of discretion, sometimes in a collegial rather than a hierarchical manner. Clarke and Newman (1997) call this 'bureau-professionalism', to distinguish it from pure bureaucracy. Third, the accounts of traditional bureaucracy given by the NPM 'school' tend to be rather one-sided. They emphasize the negatives such as 'rigidity' and 'centralization' but ignore or underplay the positives, such as continuity, honesty, and a high commitment to equity in dealing with the citizen-public. In his seminal article on the NPM, Hood terms these 'theta-type core values', and comments that, even if NPM reforms do increase frugality and efficiency, these gains could be 'bought at the expense of guarantees of honesty and fair dealing and of security and resilience' (Hood 1991, p. 16—see also, for a sophisticated defence of bureaucratic characteristics, Du Gay 2000).

Our conclusion is *not* that the negative features of the 'traditional model' are fantasies, with no basis in reality. Every reader can probably vouchsafe some personal experience testifying to the capacity of public (and private) bureaucracies to work in infuriatingly slow and inefficient ways. However, it is a long—and unjustified—leap from there to the idea that the governments of the industrialized world previously operated their public sectors as Weberian-style traditional bureaucracies, and are now able to move, without significant loss, to a new, modern type of organization which avoids all the problems of the past. As this book will continue to demonstrate, public sectors have not all come from the same place and are not all headed in the same direction. Modernization often involves losses as well as gains (Chapter 7 is particularly concerned with this theme). Each country is different (though there are some groups and patterns) and within each public domain, individual sectors have distinctive organizational cultures of their own. The idea of a single, and now totally obsolete, *ancien régime* is as implausible as the suggestion that there is now a global recipe which will reliably deliver 'reinvented' governments.

3.10 Concluding remarks

The main points of this chapter can be straightforwardly summarized. Features of the existing politico-administrative regime are likely to exert a significant influence over both the choice of reforms to be adopted and the feasibility of implementing certain types of reform. State structures, the nature of central executive government, relationships between ministers and mandarins, the prevailing administrative culture, and the diversity of channels of advice all have effects on which ideas get taken up and how vigorously and widely these are subsequently implemented. Thus, certain regimes look as though they are much more open to the 'performance-driven', market-favouring ideas of the NPM than others: particularly the 'Anglo-Saxon' countries, Australia, Canada, New Zealand, the UK, and the USA. Other countries—especially the Continental European states of Belgium, France, Finland, Germany, and Italy—are structurally and culturally less hospitable to such ideas, but may be expected to respond to pressures by developing a different reform mix of their own. However, whatever type of reform may be desired, not every country has an equal capacity to *implement* new arrangements in a coherent, broad-scope way (Manning and Parison 2003). For structural reasons, executive power is less centralized and focused in, say, Belgium, or even the USA, than in New Zealand or the UK.

Continental Europe is significantly different. It is dominated by Germany and France, each with its own strong administrative tradition. Of the two, France finds it less difficult to make broad changes, to the extent that it remains fairly centralized and is governed by a president with strong powers. In federal Germany some of the constraints on change are entrenched in constitutional law, so one might expect change to be difficult at the federal level, though possibly more in evidence at the lower levels of *Länder* and municipalities. Belgium is federal, and therefore structurally closer to Germany, but carries an inheritance of administrative arrangements that is predominantly in the French style. Unsurprisingly, with this background, change has hitherto been slow.

Italy is in transition, and consequently rather hard to 'read'. Finally, there are the three north-western European states—Finland, the Netherlands, and Sweden. These differ among themselves in a variety of ways, but share a general disposition towards consensual, often meso-corporatist styles of governance. This tends to blunt the sharper corners of the NPM, leading to less outright criticism of the state bureaucracy, a cautious rather than a wildly enthusiastic approach to MTMs and to privatization, and a less rapid (some would say less ruthless) style of implementation than prevailed in New Zealand and the UK.

The above remarks are a brief foretaste of what is to come. In Chapter 4, and in Appendix B, there will be more detailed accounts of the reform trajectories in each of the twelve countries, and of the EU Commission. These will therefore provide a test for the predictive powers of the politico-administrative variables here identified and discussed.

4 Trajectories of modernization and reform

Why are Anglo-American countries the centre of the reform universe? How do the reforms fare when they are taken from that context and placed into different political and administrative environments?

(Peters 1996a, p. 115)

4.1 From regimes to trajectories

In the previous chapters we examined the relatively enduring—yet slowly changing—politico-administrative regimes of twelve countries, plus the European Commission. Now we shift focus to more rapid and short-term forms of change: the reforms themselves. Is it true that the Anglo-American countries are the centre of the reform universe, or is that a perspective largely confined to Anglo-Americans? How far can it be said that everyone has been following the same route, albeit from different starting points in terms of their politico-administrative regimes? Are there clear patterns, or is the story really one of ad hockery dressed up as strategy?

These are questions we will address in this chapter, and continue to pursue throughout the remainder of the book. There are, as always, too many 'facts' for anyone to master them all, so any explanation is bound to be selective (and therefore interpretive). Our first step was to use the model of change advanced in Chapter 2 to organize the elements of what seemed to be the 'basics' of each country's experience into some sensible categories. The results of that exercise may be seen in tabular form in Appendix B, where there is a summary for each country, and chronological tables. Appendix B should be used as an adjunct to the whole book, and especially to this chapter. In this chapter itself we adopt a broad comparative perspective, looking for patterns of similarity and difference. We do this by employing the concept of *trajectories* to help us sort out the data.

4.2 Trajectories and scenarios: a conceptual preliminary

A trajectory, as defined here, is more than a trend. A trend is simply some pattern in the data (e.g. if the rainfall goes up every year for ten years, that is a trend). A trajectory, by contrast, is an *intentional* pattern—a route that someone is trying to take. It leads from a

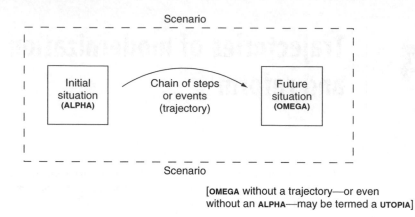

Figure 4.1 The concept of a trajectory.

starting point (an alpha) to some desired place or state of affairs in the future (an omega). Thus a *scenario* consists of three basic elements, an initial state, a trajectory, and a future state (see Figure 4.1).

Scenarios may exist at various levels of specificity. They may amount to little more than a set of vague ideas and orientations. Or they may be developed into a strategic plan, with specified actions, timescales, and objectives. Scenarios are not always complete, in the sense that one or more of the three basic elements may be missing. For example, if there is only an omega—a vision of the desired future—but no clear specification of alpha or of trajectory, then we speak of a *utopia*. Alternatively, there may exist a critique of the status quo (alpha) and a desire to move in a certain direction (trajectory) but no well-developed picture of the final state that is aimed for. This could be thought of as a kind of drifting with the tide, and there is certainly evidence of a good deal of that in the world of management reform ('everyone seems to be doing this so we had better try it too').

To anticipate, we are of the view that fully worked-out scenarios, with each of the three main elements clearly analysed and described, are definitely the exception rather than the rule in public management reform. The real world is usually more untidy, with poorly specified visions of the future, inadequate analyses of the status quo, and partial and sometimes conflicting or oscillating trajectories for different aspects of the administrative apparatus.

4.3 **The main components of reform**

Table 4.1 sets out some of the main components of reform trajectories, and these headings will be used as a template for the following sections and subsections.

We have selected four main components for the substance (or 'what') of reform, plus three for the process (or 'how'). The divisions are fairly conventional: finance, personnel, organization, and performance measurement constituting the 'what' and top-down/

Table 4.1 Aspects of trajectories: context (what) and process (how)

Starting position: alpha	*What trajectory: scope and components*	End position: omega
	– Finance: budget, accounts, audits	
	– Personnel: recruitment, posting, remuneration, security of employment, etc.	
	– Organization: specialization, coordination, scale, (de)centralization	
	– Performance Measurement Systems: content, organization, use	
	How trajectory: process of implementation	
	– Top-down / bottom-up	
	– Legal dimensions	
	– Task allocation: (new) organizations	

bottom-up, legal dimensions and organizational processes constituting the 'how'. These topics are reviewed in the following subsections, before a final overview is given in Section 4.9.

4.4 Trajectories in financial management reform

Budget reforms have been widespread, and have been driven by two particular external pressures. The first has been to restrain the growth of public expenditure, for macroeconomic reasons. Clearly, this need goes up and down with the economic cycle and the strength or weakness of the particular economy. The Norwegians, for example, with a small population and a huge revenue from offshore oil and gas, have experienced less budgetary pressure than any of the twelve countries covered by this book. The second pressure has been for performance improvement within the public sector—for types of budgeting and financial management that will stimulate greater efficiency or effectiveness, or higher quality, or some mixture of the three.

Taken together, these pressures have led to what in effect has been an expansion in the scope or purpose of budgeting. Instead of a situation where budgets were mainly a process by which annual financial allocations were incrementally adjusted, legalized, and made accountable to legislatures, budgeting has become more intimately linked with other processes—planning, operational management, and performance measurement. Greater integration of these different systems has been a common objective (Bouckaert 2000*b*, 2002*c*; Bouckaert and Van Reeth 1998; Le Loup 1988; OECD 2002*b*; Pollitt 2001). Caiden (1988) describes this broadening and complexifying of the budget agenda as the emergence of 'super budgeting'. The OECD says: 'Since the early 1990s almost all OECD member countries have been working to improve the quality of their public expenditure by implementing a focus on results to their management and budgeting systems' (OECD 2002*b*, p. 2). In parallel, financial management, which often used to be the preserve of financial management specialists, has now become an element in the training and professional socialization of many, if not most, middle managers and professionals (see Zifcak 1994 on initiatives in Australia and the UK). If one examines, for example, the Local Management of Schools Initiative in the UK in the late 1980s and early 1990s, one can see how delegation of budgets from local governments to individual schools turned most head teachers into financial managers, whether they liked it or not (Pollitt et al. 1998, chapter 6).

The reforms that have served the *savings* objective have not always fitted well with the reforms that would be required to encourage performance improvement. For example, the first reaction of some governments to expenditure pressures was to 'cheese-slice', that is, to strengthen the hand of central finance ministries to cut back programmes from the top-down. In a study of budgetary behaviour in Australia, Canada, Germany, Japan, Mexico, and the UK, the US General Accounting Office (GAO) concluded: '[A]ll six governments departed from previous budgeting approaches and imposed "top-down" overall limits on government spending . . . Despite . . . variation, each represented a multi-year approach that sought to reduce overall real spending' (General Accounting Office 1994, p. 6).

The depth and incidence of the cuts depended on the political opportunities (some targets are politically 'harder' than others—e.g. it may be easier to cut new weapons systems than to cut pensions) and on the severity of the macroeconomic position (e.g. New Zealand in 1984 and Finland in 1992 were in more severe circumstances than in 1998). In general, however, this kind of approach sits uneasily with performance improvement. This is because opportunistic cheese-slicing generates a highly unpredictable and negative environment for operational managers, in which they may suddenly find they have lost part of their budget for no good performance-related reason. Managers come to see themselves as the victims of particularistic interventions from seemingly all-powerful central finance departments.

A second route to savings was perhaps more compatible with performance improvement (though no programme manager enjoys budget reductions, however they are executed). It was to adopt or increase the use of frame- or block-budgeting, as was done by a number of countries, including Finland, Sweden, the USA, Belgium, and more recently Italy, as part of its *decentramento* (decentralization) reforms. Here the central ministry sets and polices broad ceilings (frames), but within those delegates responsibility for allocation to particular services, programmes, or projects to local politicians and/or managers. In Finland, for example, the introduction of frame-budgeting in 1994 meant a change from a system where central agencies had been heavily involved in regulating and controlling individual local services to a new relationship in which central government fixed a formula-determined total for each municipality and left local politicians to decide how to distribute that total between the various activities (see Appendix B: Finland, country file). This approach does permit the local determination of priorities. However, as many commentators have pointed out, it also neatly delegates the unpopular business of making painful choices between competing priorities—in Italy, for example, the process of decentralization has been accompanied by vocal concerns from the provinces and regions that they are being delegated new tasks from the centre without adequate resources to carry them out. Frame-budgeting also required some redesign of budgetary procedures, in that there needed to be clear and separate phases to the budgetary discussion—first, the determination of aggregate financial frames (and therefore a debate about what the most appropriate formulae should be) and second, a detailed local discussion of what allocations there should be to specific programmes (and how the performance of those programmes should be measured).

Turning to those aspects of financial management reform that are more related to *performance* rather than savings, one finds a number of partial trajectories. A first step is sometimes simply to publish some performance information alongside the annual budget documents (though it may be difficult or impossible to relate specific 'performances' to specific financial allocations). A second step is to begin to change the format and contents of the budget itself, typically by moving away from line item-budgeting towards some more performance-sensitive type of categorization, or by trying to link up budgeting with new processes of strategic planning. A third and more ambitious step is to change the procedure of budgeting itself, for example, by altering the incentives to key budget actors or by fundamentally changing the structure or timing of the budget discussion, or even by attempting to alter the role of the legislature in the budget process (Pollitt 2001).

Before moving to greater detail it should be emphasized that caution is required in the interpretation of the evidence of budgetary reform. Budgeting is an intensely political process, and actual behaviours can be very difficult to change—even when formal procedures are modified. Furthermore, headline statements such as 'Country X adopted performance budgeting from 1995' seldom tell the whole story. Even when budgetary reform is implemented successfully, it may take years for all the various organizations concerned to become comfortable with, and fully practise, the new procedures. A recent OECD overview showed that, even after a decade or more of performance-oriented budget reforms, there was still considerable confusion between outputs and outcomes, and that only about half the countries showed performance information for most government programmes. Despite undoubted shifts in many countries towards more attention being given to performance information, 40 per cent of senior budget officials surveyed from twenty-eight countries thought that this data did not usually influence budget allocations (OECD 2002*b*, pp. 12–21). Finally, the process of budget reform is continuous, so it is inevitable that by the time this book is in print, further initiatives, not recorded here, will have been launched.

Bearing these caveats in mind, one can discern a broad pattern in budget reform. Major changes to enhance the performance focus of budgeting have been implemented in Australia, Finland, New Zealand, Sweden, and the UK. For example, from the late 1970s, 'results-oriented budgeting' has formed a central plank of the management reform process in both Finland and Sweden (Pollitt and Summa 1997). All these countries therefore fall in the 'third-step' category (see Table 4.2). We have also included Canada in this category because, although the links between performance information and budgetary allocations are still rather general, the timing and periodicity of the budget have been altered, and efforts have been made to discover formats that will encourage members of the legislature to make more informed use of performance data.

Canada provides a good illustration of the aforesaid difficulty of 'reading' budget reforms. In the early 1980s the federal government introduced a range of budget-

Table 4.2 Budget trajectories

Budget status	Routes
Input-oriented line item budget	1: Germany/Belgium
A: include some performance information	2: France/EU/Italy
A + B: change format and content and add other documents	3: USA
A + B + C: adapt procedures and timing	4: Netherlands/Canada/Sweden/Finland
A + B + C + D: adapt method of charging (accrual basis)	5: UK/Australia/New Zealand

modernizing measures—a Policy and Expenditure Management System (PEMS), a Multi-Year Operational Plan (MYOP), and an Operational Framework Plan (OFP). On paper this system sounded highly rational. In practice, however, under the Mulroney administration from 1983, the PEMS system singularly failed to persuade or enable ministers to achieve their expenditure targets. It was partially replaced in 1989 and then in 1995 completely superseded by a new Expenditure Management System (EMS). Though EMS managed to deliver the first balanced budget for more than a decade, the relationship between budget allocations and performance was still debatable. Indeed, this is far from being just a technical issue. During almost half a century many countries have experienced considerable and persistent difficulties in trying to establish close links between the performance of programmes and their budget allocations (General Accounting Office 1997; Pollitt 2001). There is no particular reason to believe that the latest generation of budget reforms will enjoy more than marginally greater success than previous efforts.

Other countries have not gone quite so far as those in the bottom row of Table 4.2. The Dutch and US governments have taken steps to change the format of budget documents, and to display much more performance information (either in the basic budget document or alongside it) than would have been usual twenty, or even ten, years ago. In 2001 the French government made a major shift to programme-budgeting, which one book described as 'une véritable réforme de l'Etat'. However, this still left the French some way short of the intensity of performance linkage which had been achieved in New Zealand nearly a decade earlier (Trosa 2002—the quotation comes from the back cover). The German federal government and the EU Commission have also made changes: type A in the German case, type A + B in the case of the post-1999 European Commission (see, e.g. European Commission 2001*b* on Activity-Based Budgeting).

If we move from budgetary reform to the modernization of accounting systems, we find a roughly similar pattern of country trajectories (Table 4.3). Again, Australia, New Zealand, the UK, and, in this case, Sweden are among the countries that appear to have made the most far-reaching changes, with Finland, the USA, and the Netherlands having moved, but not quite so far, and the least change being visible in Belgium, Germany, Italy, and the EU Commission. This is the pattern that seems to appear if one defines three broad positions, beginning with a traditional, cash-based accounting system, then a shift to double-entry bookkeeping, possibly with elements of cost analysis, modified

Table 4.3 Accounting trajectories

Accounting status	Routes
A: cash-based system	1: Germany/EU
B: double-entry bookkeeping	2: USA/Netherlands/Finland/Canada/ France/Italy/Belgium
C: accruals-accounting with extended cost calculation supported by performance measurement system	3: Sweden/Australia/New Zealand/UK

cash, or modified accrual, and, finally, the development of full accrual accounts with a focus on providing performance-related information.

This is not a place for a full exposition of the different bases for keeping public accounts. There is space only to point to the very basics of our threefold classification. In pure cash accounting, a public sector entity is given a budget, calculated in cash terms, and proceeds to spend the money, keeping records of each cash disbursement so as to ensure neither an overspend (which may actually be illegal) nor an underspend (which is likely to act as an invitation to the political level to arrive at the conclusion that not so much money is needed, and that the budget can therefore be cut in the following year). In the EU Commission, for example, an elaborate cash system used to operate until recently, in which each piece of expenditure had to be approved by three separate officials: first—legal, second—in accordance with the programme, third—affordable (there is sufficient cash to pay it). This is a system that had been traditional in much of the francophone world for some time. A problem with it is that, by itself, it gives few incentives for efficiency, or even economy. The name of the game easily becomes that of simply spending the money allocated, within the financial year. Large expenditures are rushed through in the last few weeks. EU officials, for example, seem to worry about 'absorption' (i.e. their ability to spend all the money allocated) at least as much as they do about efficiency and effectiveness of expenditure. Even after the reforms of 2001–2, the EU budgetary system contains few incentives to 'save'. The money in the budget is there, it cannot be saved or switched for use elsewhere, and therefore it has to be spent.

The shift to double-entry bookkeeping marks a significant change from this position. It brings public accounts closer to the private sector model. Every transaction is entered on the accounts twice—once as a credit and once as a debit. If wages are paid, for example, the sum involved can be shown as a *credit* to the organization's central cash account and, simultaneously, a *debit* to the wages account. This approach is founded on the perspective that the organization is a separate business, in which its total assets must, by definition, remain equal to its capital plus its liabilities. It can be used to raise consciousness of a wider range of management issues than is usually provoked by cash-based accounting. In particular, if double-entry bookkeeping includes capital assets (land, buildings), it can stimulate managers to make more efficient use of these resources, rather than treating them as a 'free good', as often occurs in cash-based systems. On the other hand, much depends on the *level* at which the books are balanced, and on the extent to which links to performance are made explicit. If double-entry systems are confined to a high level, and accounting itself is performed as a very centralized function, far from 'street-level' management, then the impact on most managers may be limited.

Our third stage, accruals-accounting, brings the public sector onto as near as possible a comparative basis to the private sector (lowering 'grid' in anthropological terms—Hood 1998). It means that government organizations report commitments when they are incurred (rather than when the cash is actually disbursed), allow for the valuation and depreciation of all capital assets, and present annual 'balance sheet-type' financial statements (Likierman 1998*a*, 1998*b*). When coupled with a system of decentralized financial management, it can form the basis for a close link between resource allocation and performance management at the level of individual agencies and programmes. At the time of writing, full accruals accounts for public sector entities were being produced by Australia, New Zealand, Sweden, and the UK. 'The majority of OECD member countries are budgeting and accounting on a cash basis' (OECD 2002*b*, p. 19).

The significance of these shifts in accounting practices for management is considerable. So long as a cash-based system prevails, without double-entry bookkeeping or accruals-accounting, it is hard to make either global or specific links between expenditure and cost, and between cost and performance. Managers are not faced with the full costs of their use of assets, and performance measurement, if it exists, tends to be a separate system from financial management. On the other hand, the application of accruals systems is not equally straightforward for all different types of service and circumstance, and reform can create perverse incentives as well as advantages (Gillibrand and Hilton 1998; Pollitt 2001; Straw 1998).

When reform takes place it has frequently been a step-by-step process, moving from pilot projects to larger scale roll-outs, or from one part of the public sector to others (which means that distortions can arise during the sometimes long transitional periods, when one part of the public sector is operating according to one set of accounting principles and another is following a different set). For example, in the UK, accruals-accounting was introduced in the NHS before it was adopted for central government, and in the Netherlands double-entry bookkeeping has been required for some agencies but not for their parent ministries. In Italy, at the time of writing, a version of accruals-accounting is being used in the health service and some other parts of the public sector, but not in central government. Furthermore, our three broad 'stages' of accountancy are inevitably a somewhat overneat classification of detailed practice. In the real world, governments blur these categories considerably by adding performance elements to basically cash-based systems or by introducing partial accruals-accounting with lots of exceptions and special features (see HM Treasury 1998, pp. 132–54). In the late 1990s, for example, the Finnish Ministry of Finance had a project aiming at introducing a full accruals system by the beginning of 1998. However, what was implemented was both later and less than the original proposals.

Completing the financial circle, we now turn briefly to reforms in public sector *auditing*. Again, we distinguish three stages (and again, these should be regarded as no more than rough approximations to the complexities of detailed practice within each country and sector). The first stage is traditionally that of financial and compliance-auditing. Here the basic concern of the auditor is with legality and procedural correctness. Has the money been spent on duly approved objects, through the correct procedures? Is there evidence of unauthorized expenditure or corruption? The second stage is to add investigations of some performance issues. For example, auditors may be empowered to search for waste—items that have been purchased at unnecessary expense, or items that have been perfectly legally purchased but which are not being used very much (the school purchases a computer but no teacher can use it, so it sits in the storeroom). Another extension of traditional audit is a deeper questioning of data quality ('valid-ation'). The figures presented to parliament or audit office may add up, but how reliable are they? Have all transactions been recorded, and recorded accurately? This is, in effect, an audit of the performance of the organization's internal auditing system. The third stage is the development of full-blown performance-auditing as a distinct activity, usually with a separate unit or section of the National Audit Office (NAO) to develop perform-ance-auditing expertise. The development of performance-auditing over the last fifteen years has been considerable, but it has been taken much further in some countries than others (Pollitt et al. 1999). Performance-auditors claim to focus directly on the 'three Es', economy, efficiency, and effectiveness (see Figure 5.1). These three stages are the basis for Table 4.4.

Performance-auditing is fully established, with its own procedures and staff, in Australia, Canada, Finland, the Netherlands, New Zealand, Sweden, the UK, and the USA. In some countries Supreme Audit Institutions (SAI) (the imposing title that NAOs give themselves) have gone further and set up groups that concentrate specifically on evaluation (New Zealand, USA—though in the mid-1990s the USA dissolved the evalu-ation and methodology section which had existed within the GAO since the 1970s). In other countries the SAIs have taken an active interest in evaluation, and have examined the scope for borrowing techniques and concepts from evaluation, but have not created separate units to carry out evaluations per se (e.g. Sweden, UK). Elsewhere, however, the place of performance audit is not so developed or clear cut. In France there is no doubt that the magistrates of the *Cour des Comptes* can and often do analyse performance aspects, but the performance audit function has not been separated from more traditional, compliance-oriented forms of audit, and the general culture is still highly legalistic. In Germany the main emphasis of the *Bundesrechnungshof* has been on compli-ance and financial auditing, though some performance elements are also covered. Performance-auditing has also been slow to get off the ground in Italy. In Belgium the Court of Audit established a section on performance audits. The same might be said of the European Court of Auditors, which has a definite capacity for performance

Table 4.4 Audit trajectories

Audit status	Routes
A: traditional financial and compliance audit	1: Germany
B: traditional audit enriched with some elements of performance and evaluation	2: France/EU/Italy/Belgium
C: institutionalized financial, compliance, and performance-auditing	3: Netherlands/Sweden/Finland/Canada/UK/USA/Australia/New Zealand

audit but which, in practice, seems to find most of its staff resources drawn into the identification of fraud and the provision, since 1994, of an annual statement of assurance (DAS) to the European Parliament (National Audit Office 1996; Pollitt et al. 1999).

Thus far the discussion of audit has been exclusively in terms of external audit by independent audit offices. In practice the work of external audit organizations is made either much easier or much more time-consuming and difficult according to the state of sophistication of *internal* audit within public sector organizations. Thus, if the internal audit of a department concentrates solely upon compliance work, it becomes that much more difficult for the external audit body to conduct performance audit (partly because necessary types of data will not exist). In short, reform of auditing usually entails more than just remandating, retraining, and reskilling the NAOs. It also requires matching changes in internal audit services. We are not aware of substantial comparative research in this area, but our own impressions (no more) are that the same rough pattern as emerges for SAIs in Table 4.4 also fits the development of internal audit. Further changes are happening all the time. The crisis that led to the fall of the Santerre Commission in 1999 helped to ensure that the introduction of an internal audit service would be a high priority for the next leaders of the Commission (European Commission 2000). Similarly, in Belgium, the Copernicus reform announced in 2000 that henceforth each federal ministry would have an internal audit service.

4.5 Trajectories in personnel management/HRM

4.5.1 The volume and direction of reform

As Chapter 3 made clear, different countries entered the 1980s with contrasting legal and cultural assumptions about the nature of public service (even the words are treacherous here—'public service' already suggests an Anglo-American-Australasian perspective, by contrast to Continental countries in the *Rechtsstaat* tradition, which might rather regard civil servants as 'officers of the state', or some such term). Yet, despite differences of 'starting line', most countries suffered similar pressures and were obliged to find some response. Certainly there has been no shortage of activity (the following list is selective, not comprehensive):

- Australia: 1983 Amendment of the Public Service Act; 1987, 1993, 1995 Guidelines on Official Conduct of Commonwealth Public Servants; 1990 Guidelines on Appraisal of Performance of Senior Executive Service (SES); 1999 Public Service Act.

- Belgium: 1994 new civil service statute; 1997 introduction of a personnel appraisal system; 2000 Copernicus reform plan, including many aspects of personnel management.

- Canada: 1989 new Personnel Management Manual; Public Service 2000 initiative; Public Service white paper; 1992 Public Service Reform Act.

- Finland: 1994 State Civil Servants Act.

- France: 1989 Prime Ministerial circular on public service renewal included some personnel reforms. In the mid-1990s proposed personnel reforms helped provoke extensive public sector strikes.

- Germany: 1989 law amending working provisions for civil servants; 1994 Public Service Reform Act; 1996 amendments to the law relating to federal civil servants.

- Italy: reforms of public employment law in 1993 and 1997.

- Netherlands: 1993 delegation of detailed negotiations on labour conditions from Ministry of Home Affairs to eight sectors (state, judiciary, municipalities, etc.).

- New Zealand: 1988 State Sector Act; 1991 Employment Contracts Act.

- Sweden: 1990 modification of Public Employment Act.

- UK: 1992 Civil Service (Management Functions) Act; 1993 Civil Service Management Code; white papers—*The Civil Service: Continuity and Change* (1994) and *The Civil Service: Taking Forward Continuity and Change* (1995).

- USA: 1978 Civil Service Reform Act (including creation of an SES); 1994 Federal Personnel Manual abandoned (with ceremonial burning of a copy on the White House lawn, as part of the National Performance Review (NPR)); 1994 Federal Workforce Restructuring Act.

Most of these measures were characterized by the same broad orientation (Balk 1996; Farnham et al. 1996; Hondeghem and Nelen 2002; Horton et al. 2002). Politicians wanted civil services that were more flexible and responsive, more focused on getting results, more skilful and, if possible, less numerous (and therefore less expensive in total). Meanwhile, civil servants, while not averse to some of these demands, also sought to retain existing privileges and protections. They obviously did not want drastic downsizing with compulsory redundancies; neither did they want salary freezes or other arrangements that would further erode their material rewards in comparison with the private sector. In some places (France, the EU Commission) they had strongly entrenched unions and fought long and hard to stave off erosions of their basic conditions of service (Howard 1998). Elsewhere constitutional protections were so formidable that it was almost impossible for governments to effect radical change (as for German federal civil servants). In other cases resistance was either less well organized or less effective, and fundamental changes were driven through. For example, security of tenure was significantly reduced in Australia, New Zealand, and the UK. Substantial downsizing was carried through in Australia, Finland, New Zealand, the UK, and the USA (though one has to be careful in interpreting the statistics because in some cases most of the staff were transferred to other parts of the public sector). One common feature was that personnel changes seldom came first on the reform agenda. It was much more common for them to follow—sometimes at a considerable distance—innovations in financial management, organizational structures, and management techniques. In this respect Australia was not unusual (at least not for the Anglo-Saxon countries):

Financial management dominated the reform programme of the 1980s. In the latter half of the decade, the limitations of this emphasis were increasingly acknowledged and pressures to broaden the directions being taken to reduce the subservience of management processes to financial questions. Other forms of management were increasingly being advocated, human resource management assuming a prominence from the end of the 1980s. (Halligan 1996*b*, pp. 102–3)

It is perhaps easiest to describe the trajectories of change in respect to a 'base case'. This base case is very general, and applies to both the *Rechtsstaat* and the public interest countries (Section 3.6). In it a typical civil servant is assumed to be:

- A tenured, career appointment—not dependent on the whims of transient politicians or on one's civil service superior (although dismissible, with difficulty, in cases of extreme dereliction of duty or of criminal actions).
- Promoted principally in relation to qualifications and seniority.
- Part of a unified civil service, within a distinct and particular national framework of terms and conditions (including national pay scales).

These are all features that made being a civil servant different (and increasingly different during the 1970s and 1980s) from most private sector jobs. They are also features that, at least in the NPM countries, came to be seen as inhibiting the greater responsiveness and efficiency which it had become fashionable for politicians and public alike to demand. In Australia the Public Service Commissioner, explaining the main thrust of the 1999 Public Service Act, said:

As public servants we need to walk the same fields and gaze the same blue skies that inspire innovation in the private sector. Central to that is the need to bring our employment arrangements more into line with the wider Australian community. Does anyone really believe that, protected by a monopoly status and inadequate scrutiny, we can defend an approach to management that we now know is at least twice as expensive as best practice? (Shergold 1997, p. 33)

Note the elements in this quotation—the setting up of the private sector as the standard to be attained, the emphasis on cost-saving, and the suggestion that the public service is over-protected and 'feather-bedded'. One should beware of accepting all this at face value. For example, it is easy to exaggerate the prevalence and influence of the three distinctive features mentioned (e.g. many categories of civil servants in the UK never had particularly strong tenure, low pay was common, and there had long been many non-career and part-time appointments, especially in the clerical grades). Nevertheless, the popular stereotype of a tea-drinking, probably not very efficient, yet secure and well-pensioned civil servant was never far from media-reporting and political characterization, especially by neoconservatives. Even in France, a country with a proud tradition of a powerful and talented civil service, there was a period when 'from a model of social success, the civil servant became an awful figure, the pure representation of waste and incompetence' (Rouban 1997, p. 150). In the Netherlands, generally a more consensual and incremental politico-administrative system than Australia or New Zealand, the early 1990s saw steps being taken to 'normalize' the status of government employees, and in

1992 it was agreed that the general pension fund for public employees would be privatized. Even in Belgium and Italy steps were taken to lessen the differences between public sector and private sector employment (although the senior Italian civil servants—*la dirigenza*—remained a special case) (Brans and Hondeghem 1999; Hondeghem 2000; Hondeghem and Vandermeulen 2000; OECD 2003). In the European Commission the reforms at the beginning of the twenty-first century saw the introduction of regular individual appraisals and large-scale management training.

The three indicated characteristics therefore became easy foci for reform. In each case the tendency in the NPM countries was to reduce the distinctiveness of a civil service job—to make it more like jobs elsewhere (in the terms used by Dunleavy and Hood 1994 and Hood 1998, this was a deliberate lowering of 'group'). We will now look at each of the three features in turn.

4.5.2 A tenured career

The directions of change here were to make careers less secure, and to encourage greater inflows and outflows of staff so that a smaller and smaller proportion of civil servants were 'lifers' and a larger and larger proportion had experience of other ways of doing things. A typical development in NPM countries was the appointment of top officials (especially agency chief executives, but also, in some cases, the heads of ministries) on two-, three-, or five-year performance-related contracts. The most extreme case is again New Zealand. There all members of the SES (see Section 4.5.3) have to reapply for their own jobs after five years, except for the heads of ministries (called chief executives), who enjoy a provision that permits their contracts to be extended (Boston et al. 1996, pp. 117–20). UK ministers expressed themselves thus:

[T]here is a belief in some quarters that civil servants have a job for life. That is not the case. In the case of senior staff, more than 50 per cent of the individuals who have left the existing Senior Open Structure in the last seven years did so before the normal retirement age. 30 per cent of the departures were brought about by management through voluntary or compulsory early retirement. (Prime Minister et al. 1994, p. 43—the government in question was at that time just about to embark upon a programme of radical downsizing of a number of central ministries, which included reductions of, typically, 25 per cent of senior staff—see, e.g. HM Treasury 1994.)

Elsewhere, however, there has been much less change. In Belgium, Canada, Finland, France, Germany, and Sweden most top civil servants are career 'mandarins' with long experience and well-established personal networks (see, e.g. Bourgault and Carroll 1997). France is perhaps rather different from the other countries in this group, to the extent that the members of the *grands corps* frequently move in and out of jobs in the business world, and therefore could not be accused of being monkishly bureaucratic. Indeed, one problem is that, with falling civil service prestige, increasing numbers of these mandarins have been leaving for the better-paid positions in the private sector (Rouban 1997, p. 147). In the European Commission the permanent A grades continue to enjoy great security of tenure, although their performance may now come under somewhat more systematic formal appraisal than in the past. The USA is different again: here members of the SES have tended to be narrowly specialist and, in any case, are obliged to work within a system where so many of their colleagues are short-term political appointees (Kettl et al. 1996, p. 56; on the 'spoils system' see Appendix B: USA, country file).

4.5.3 **Promotion by seniority and qualifications**

Here the shift was to link promotion more to results and responsiveness, often by embodying the required results in an annual agreement or quasi-contract, containing specified individual targets and priorities. Usually the change was only partial—seniority and qualifications were still elements in the overall calculation—but the intention of making civil servants more sharply focused on specific and usually short-term objectives was quite clear. This new emphasis was frequently reinforced by linking pay as well as promotion to 'track record' in achieving results (see Section 4.5.4).

A further important development in a number of countries was the creation of some form of SES (Australia, Canada, New Zealand, and the USA—see Ban and Ingraham 1984; Boston et al. 1996, pp. 117–20; Halligan 1996*b*, pp. 86–7). In the UK the Conservative government favoured a 'senior management group' employed on the basis of written contracts (Prime Minister et al. 1994). This kind of grouping was supposed to bring a variety of benefits ('supposed' because in every case there were significant difficulties in achieving the originally proclaimed goals). Basically an SES was intended (with slightly different emphases in each country) to create a more mobile, flexible, responsive, and managerially competent group at the top of the public service. An SES would be more mobile because provisions would allow the easier recruitment of competent executives from outside the normal career ladder of the civil service, and because the terms and conditions would explicitly include horizontal movement within the politico-administrative machine ('horses for courses'). It would be more responsive partly because the right (wo)man could be moved into the right place at the right time, but also because promotion was intended to be for the 'can do' individuals with track records of achievement, rather than by seniority and precedence. As the UK Conservative government put it:

Entry to the Senior Civil Service from within a department or agency would be marked for the individual concerned by leaving negotiated group pay arrangements and moving to individually determined pay, and by acceptance of a written contract of service. (Prime Minister et al. 1994, p. 37)

This type of system was usually backed up by some form of performance-related pay (in both Australia and the USA this was also intended to be a way of circumventing general civil service pay restrictions so as to be able to retain 'high-flyers'). Experiments with performance pay have been implemented in most of our twelve countries, and elsewhere, but often with mixed or downright disappointing results (Gaertner and Gaertner 1985; OECD 1993*b*; Perry and Pearce 1985). Again, the pattern is of the widest use in the NPM countries (and, on this score, the USA) with more cautious and limited projects in the Nordic countries and France (Vallemont 1998). It is perhaps typical of the more sceptical approach of the Continental European countries that, in Finland and Sweden, while performance-related pay is legally possible, many public departments and agencies decline to avail themselves of it, arguing that it would be

divisive and unhelpful. Additionally, managerial competence can be increased by bringing in outsiders with managerial backgrounds as well as by the provision of intensive
high-level management training programmes. The advantages of this trajectory are thus
obvious, but it has potential disadvantages too. Concerns about the dangers of increasing
the number of 'yes-men' (and 'yes-women') and endangering the promotability and
security of those who give 'frank and fearless' advice have been expressed in several of
the NPM countries.

4.5.4 **Part of a unified national service**

In this case the thrust in quite a few countries was towards decentralization of personnel
authority, initially for the day-to-day management of individuals, but increasingly also in
terms of a widening range of terms and conditions, so that, ultimately, line managers
could hire and fire on terms they set according to local conditions, and the concept of a
unified public service was for all practical purposes abandoned. This direction of change
had many ramifications. Pay, hours of work, required qualifications, disciplinary and
dismissal procedures—all these and more might cease to be matters of national negotiation by management and union leaders and be decentralized by organization, region, or
occupational group. The new philosophy was succinctly enunciated in a UK white paper
in 1994:

No two civil service organisations are identical, any more than two organisations elsewhere in
the public or private sectors. It is right that pay and grading systems, like other management
arrangements, should be attuned to individual circumstances and relevant labour markets. (Prime
Minister et al. 1994, p. 26)

In Australia, as in the UK, the outline shell of a unified public service was retained but,
with the 1997 Public Service Act,

[i]t is departmental secretaries and agency heads who will determine the remuneration, conditions
and terms of employment. No longer will the legislation distinguish between public servants on
the basis of whether they are permanent or fixed-term. It is secretaries who will decide how they
will employ public servants and on what conditions of engagement. It is they who will assign
duties and delegate responsibility. (Shergold 1997, p. 34)

In New Zealand the government moved away altogether from the concept of a
single, unified service. The 1988 State Services Act established departments, under
their chief executives, as the employers of their own staff. The Annual General
Adjustment (of pay) and public service-wide negotiation of nonpay conditions of service
were abolished (Boston et al. 1996, chapter 10). The public sector came under
the provisions of the Labour Relations Act, which had previously been meant for the
private sector.

This kind of 'normalizing' trajectory, where the civil service is 'deprivileged'
and increasingly treated on the same fragmented and locally varying terms as private
sector employment, has certainly not been followed by all countries. France, Germany,
and the European Commission are notable and weighty exceptions (if 'exception' is
the word). In Italy the terms of civil service employment have been brought somewhat

closer to those prevailing in the private sector, but there are still significant differences, especially for more senior grades. The MAP 2000 initiative by the European Commission was proclaimed a major decentralization in personnel management, and this tendency was taken further by the Kinnock reforms (see Appendix B: European Commission, country file). Nevertheless, by comparison with what had already been implemented by the NPM countries, it was quite timid and conventional (European Commission 1997*b*, 2000). Within such 'central European' jurisdictions (Belgium, Germany, France, the EU Commission) the state servant remains a very distinct category—legally, culturally, and politically. As we saw to be the case with financial management reforms, the more northern European states have followed a path somewhere between the NPM enthusiasts and the more conservative *Rechtsstaat* regimes. Finland and Sweden have made provisions for performance-related pay, and for more decentralized and results-oriented styles of personnel management—for example, in 1992 each Swedish agency became responsible for the training and development of its own staff. Yet these countries have not more than marginally dismantled the essential unity of the civil service. The same could be said of the Canadian federal civil service (Bourgault and Carroll 1997). In the Netherlands career management of top civil servants was actually *centralized* during the mid-1990s (Mazel 1998).

The USA is once more a unique case. In theory a scrupulously fair and impersonal merit system provides a national framework for recruitment and job classification:

However, the federal government's uniform merit system today is neither uniform, merit-based, nor a system. It now covers barely more than half—56%—of the federal government's workers. Only 15% of the federal government's new career employees enter through the system's standard testing-and-placement process. (Kettl et al. 1996, p. 1)

Despite much debate during the 1980s and 1990s, no comprehensive reform was agreed or implemented (so in this respect the USA was unlike Australia and New Zealand). The problem, in the complex and fragmented US political system, is that:

Civil service reform is on everyone's list of jobs that must be done—but it is high on virtually no one's list. It has too little sex appeal to excite political interest; and though everyone agrees on the need for change, the consequences of *not* reforming the civil service never seem great enough to force it onto the policy agenda. (Kettl et al. 1996, p. 2)

In short, the USA, while far from the European *Rechtsstaat* model in political temperament and rhetoric, was nevertheless home to an often rigid and unreformed (or perhaps one should say partially and incoherently reformed) bureaucracy.

In general, therefore, while trends to 'de-privilegization' are clearly visible in a number of countries, there are also cases where the 'bargain' between politicians and mandarins mentioned in Chapter 3 remains one in which senior civil servants are treated as an independent group of technocrats or magistrates (Hood 2002). There is more than one omega, and more than one trajectory, but the overall direction of travel is that of reducing the distinctiveness of the rules governing many public service jobs.

4.6 Organizational trajectories

The restructuring of organizations is a ubiquitous feature of public sector management reforms (OECD 1994, 1995; see Appendix B for details on the twelve countries). Of the many different possible ways of classifying these restructurings we have chosen a fourfold scheme which is fairly 'mainstream' in terms of classical organization theory, namely:

- specialization (should institutions be single-purpose or multi-purpose?)
- coordination (by what means should coordination across different functions, levels, and sectors be achieved?)
- centralization/decentralization (what functions should be centralized/decentralized, and to what degree?)
- scale (what is the optimal size for organizations?)

We will deal with each of these dimensions in turn, but first a brief overview may be useful. As a broad generalization it can be said that the main thrust of the Australian/New Zealand/UK reforms has been towards more specialized organizations; towards coordination by means of market mechanisms and contractual and quasi-contractual relationships instead of through hierarchies of authority; towards decentralization of authority from the centre towards the periphery (in both hierarchical and geographical terms) and towards decreasing the size of public organizations by breaking up and downsizing large bureaucratic organizations (Boston et al. 1996; O'Toole and Jordan 1995; Peters and Savoie 1998; Pollitt and Talbot 2004). Trends towards specialization and fragmentation have also been discernible in Canada, France, and the Netherlands (though to a lesser degree than in the NPM countries), but are much less marked in Belgium, Finland, Germany, Sweden, and the European Commission, each of which has retained its central ministerial or directorate structure with only limited fragmentation, downsizing, or 'hiving off'. The USA already possessed a fairly fragmented and specialized administrative system (see Appendix B: USA, country file) and has been concerned in trying to develop overall systems that will permit greater coherence (e.g. common accounting procedures, common reporting procedures through the Government Performance and Results Act (GPRA)). As for decentralization, almost everyone seems to believe in it, though, as we shall see, it takes on a different personality in different contexts. The four dimensions will now be examined in sequence.

Specialization. Alternation between a preference for broad-scope, multi-purpose organizations and, by contrast, a predilection for tight-focus, specialized organizations has been one of the salient features of the history of administrative thought. The idea that specialization is the basis of good administration can trace its supporters back through Adam Smith and Jeremy Bentham. The opposite doctrine—that consolidation is good—has been advanced by, *inter alia*, Sir Edwin Chadwick and Karl Marx (Hood and Jackson 1991, pp. 114–16). The pendulum may swing within a single generation, witness the shift in UK central government from a preference for large, omnibus central ministries (favoured by both Labour and Conservatives in the late 1960s and early 1970s) to the 1990s model of downsized and relatively focused ministries surrounded by shoals of specialized executive agencies (O'Toole and Jordan 1995; Pollitt 1984). Since the advent of the New Labour government in 1997, preferences have swung back again. Blair's government has criticized the fragmentation caused by the intensive agencification of 1988–97, and has launched various initiatives to ensure 'joined-up government' and greater coordination between policy and implementation (Office of Public Services Reform 2002; Pollitt 2003*b*).

During the 1980s the international swing was towards more specialization, most clearly in those countries that were the most influenced by the application of microeconomic reasoning to questions of institutional design. This took place at all levels—micro, meso, and macro. Thus in New Zealand 'the preference for single-purpose organisations and the separation of potentially conflicting functions has led in some cases to a plethora of functionally distinct, but nonetheless quite interdependent, organisations' (Boston et al. 1996, p. 88). By the late 1990s there were signs that the pendulum had reached its furthest point and was beginning to return: there was much discussion in New Zealand government circles of the drawbacks of having such a large number of ministries to deal with such a small population.

New Zealand is probably the clearest but not the only case. In the UK the Next Steps Programme, launched in 1988, led within ten years to the creation of more than 140 specialized executive agencies (Chancellor of the Duchy of Lancaster 1997). In France more than 200 *centres de responsabilité* have been set up since 1989. In the Netherlands many Zelfstandige Bestuursorganen (ZBOs) were created during the 1980s, and since 1991 more than twenty specialized agencies have also appeared (Ministerie van Financiën 1998; Roberts 1997; Smullen 2004). The Canadians moved more cautiously, but there too some 'Special Operating Agencies' (SOAs) were carved out of the federal ministries (the first five appeared in 1989—see Appendix B: Canada, country file). In Italy legislative decree number 3000 of 1999 led to the setting up of a number of *agenzie*, some with their own legal personalities and some as units within ministries. Germany, however, is generally an exception to the trend. There the main 'receiving positions' for the flow of decentralized functions have not been specialist agencies (though some of those have been set up) but rather multifunctional local authorities (Wollmann 2001).

If one moves away from central government to examine other public functions the trend is equally, if not even more, clear. Most of our twelve governments hastened to give distinctive organizational forms to commercial or potentially commercial activities within their public sectors. At the extreme, of course, there has been large-scale privatization, especially in New Zealand and the UK and, to a lesser but still substantial extent, in France and the Netherlands. Most other countries had less to privatize in the first place, but selective privatization nevertheless occured in Finland, Germany, Sweden, and the USA (see Appendix B for details). Short of full-blooded privatization, a number of countries have preferred to invent other specialized corporate forms—such as the state enterprises and state-owned companies in Finland and Sweden, or the state-owned enterprises in New Zealand. Some of these have survived, while others have acted as brief staging posts on the route to full privatization.

In local governance, too, specialization has been in evidence. In the UK the setting-up of MTMs (quasi-markets) in health care, education, and social care entailed a good deal of de facto specialization into separate purchaser and provider units (Pollitt et al. 1998). The

Conservative governments of 1979–97 also supported the creation of several types of specialized educational institution (e.g. City Technology Colleges) and infrastructural renewal organizations (e.g. Urban Development Corporations) plus diverse other quasi-autonomous nongovernmental organizations (quangos). Taken together, these constituted a rather crowded new environment of specialized entities with which traditional local authorities had to try to deal (Painter et al. 1996). Furthermore, the process of compulsory competitive tendering (CCT) for local authority and health services meant that, even where an 'in-house' bid won the contract, it usually had to recreate itself as a distinct, specialized organization (e.g. for refuse collection or laundry or building maintenance—see Ascher 1987; HM Treasury 1991). Again we must remember that Germany is a significant exception to the trend towards fragmentation and specialization at local level.

In sum, one might say that the use of specialized administrative and managerial bodies appears to have grown in at least ten of our twelve countries. The creation of agencies has been particularly popular (Peters and Bouckaert 2003; Pollitt and Talbot 2004). This trend has given rise to criticism in some countries, focused on the sometimes uncertain legal and political status of these new creations. As a recent comparative article put it:

Indeed, the growth in, and use of, quasi-autonomous nongovernmental organisations (quangos) is evident at all levels of society from local quangos to regional and central government agencies and also at the European level where new bodies have been created which reflect similar problems of accountability and legitimacy, the European Monetary Institute, for example. (Greve et al. 1999)

Assessments of the problems associated with increased specialization and decentralization are not, however, the job of this chapter. This task will be taken up later, especially in Chapters 6 and 7.

Coordination. In a traditional hierarchy, coordination is ensured by the exercise of authority from the top. Coherent and consistent orders are passed down the line. Central staff units, supporting the top administrators, check lower-level proposals to ensure that they all fit the strategy, that precedents are observed, that division X does not set out along a line that contradicts what is being done at division Y. Regulations are issued from the centre, which all must observe. When new situations occur, new regulations are formulated to deal with them, and these are fitted into the existing body of law and procedure that guides every part of the organization. Such exercise of hierarchical authority is, however, not the only way of achieving coordination. It can also be achieved less formally, by voluntary cooperation within a network. This form of 'solidarity' tends to be more easily achieved where objectives are widely shared among all network members, communication is easy and full, and the scale of operations is modest (Pollitt 2003a, chapter 3). A third mode of coordination is the market mechanism. The miracle of the market is that a price mechanism enables the activities of many producers/sellers and consumers/buyers to be coordinated without any central authority ordering it. The 'hidden hand' of supply and demand does the work, and with the assistance of modern communications and information technologies that work can be accomplished with great speed.

Thus coordination may be achieved by hierarchy, network, or market (Kaufmann et al. 1986; Thompson et al. 1991). The main thrust of NPM reforms has been, de facto, that market forms of coordination should wherever possible be substituted for hierarchical coordination. Although it is conceded that under certain conditions—most influentially specified in theoretical terms by Williamson (1975)—hierarchies may be preferable to markets, the main weight of argument has been that there are many hitherto unseen opportunities to 'marketize' relationships within the public sector. Indeed, just as certain words such as 'decentralization' and 'empowerment' have become unassailably positive in their connotations, 'hierarchy' and 'hierarchical' have become invariably negative—at least within the NPM discourse. Even where an indisputably hierarchical relationship remains, there may be an attempt to package it into a quasi-contract, where the 'agent' ('subordinate' in old-fashioned hierarchical terms) agrees to supply the 'principal' (superior, boss) with a defined set of outputs within a fixed period and at a predetermined cost. In the countries that have been most enthusiastic about NPM, there has therefore been a wide-scale substitution of market and quasi-market coordination and contractualization for hierarchical coordination (Lane 2000 develops the theoretical underpinning for this tendency). In New Zealand, for example, the chief executives who run ministries agree an annual quasi-contract with their minister, promising to deliver specified outputs, which are then supposed to lead to the outcomes at which the minister and his or her government are aiming. In most countries contractualization has not infiltrated so high up the chain of minister/mandarin command. Slightly lower down, however, contractualization and marketization have spread widely in Australia, New Zealand, the USA, and the UK, and to a lesser extent in Canada and Sweden. It has gone hand in hand with many of the measures of specialization referred to in the previous subsection. Thus, for example, where a pre-1991 District Health Authority in the UK might have given an instruction to a local hospital, in the post-1991 'provider market' it contracted for defined services with a legally independent corporation—the NHS trust, which the previously 'directly managed' hospital had become. The two parts of the previously hierarchical NHS had specialized into a purchaser and a provider, joined by contract. The example of the Canadian SOAs provides a further illustration of the general logic:

The SOA is based on the same theoretical models as organisational forms being adopted by other governments and large corporations. The models are more contractual than hierarchical; provide greater autonomy to individual units of the whole; and rely more on market mechanisms than central decisions to allocate resources. (Auditor General of Canada 1994, p. 2)

This spread of contractual and quasi-contractual relationships has provoked a certain amount of academic concern, both by legal theorists worried about the inadequacies of the relevant areas of administrative law (Bouckaert 2002*a*; Harden 1992) and by public administrationists who have pointed to the difficulties of writing 'complete' contracts in conditions where the providers of services have much more information than the purchasers and/or users (Le Grand and Bartlett 1993).

Not all countries have been as enthusiastic about the potential of MTMs and contractualism as New Zealand, the UK, and the USA. Such devices have been used more sparingly in Germany, France, and even the Nordic countries (see, e.g. Wollmann 2001). Here limited local experiments have been more characteristic than sweeping marketizations of entire sectors.

The connection between specialization and coordination is important. All other things being equal, increasing specialization implies a need for *greater* efforts at coordination, at least if the level of overall coherence of policy and services is to be maintained. Otherwise the danger is that newly specialized agencies, many of which also enjoy decentralized authority, will go their own ways. No country has been content to rely entirely on MTMs to address this problem. Even those states that have favoured MTMs have added new hierarchical devices to try to ensure that coordination is preserved or enhanced.

At a local microlevel 'one-stop' or 'one-window' service delivery arrangements have proved popular. Quite a number of local authorities have tried them in the UK. In 1994 France adopted a programme of integrated Rural Service Outlets in country areas, which necessitated cooperation between different services (Ministère de la Fonction Publique 1994*b*). One-stop ideas have also been implemented in the Netherlands, Finland, and Sweden, where the arrangement of having one integrated outlet in remote and thinly populated areas has an obvious logic.

At higher levels a variety of new coordinating mechanisms have been created. In Germany there is some evidence of greater coordination between the *Länder*: 'What increased during the 1980s was, perhaps, less the scope for regional policy makers to develop and implement independent initiatives than their determination to make use of the hitherto neglected potential for subcentral policy making' (Benz and Götz 1996, p. 7). In France a simpler and more coordinated arrangement for the central states' regional and provincial services has been developed. The *sous-préfet* now has a major role in directing and coordinating deconcentrated service delivery (Comité pour la réorganisation et la déconcentration de l'administration 1995). In the UK, too, the 1980s saw central government implementing stronger regional coordination of the work of the various ministries. In Finland provincial units of central administration have been merged and reduced in number. In both the Netherlands and New Zealand the number of local government jurisdictions has been reduced—an interesting case of a different organizational logic being applied at local level from that being simultaneously implemented for the central state.

Within central governments themselves the signs of attempts at improved coordination are clear (although in some cases they have appeared as rather late responses to the fragmentation caused by earlier enthusiasms for specialization and decentralization). One popular initiative has been to develop some form of strategic planning. This has been tried (in different ways) by Australia, Canada, Finland, New Zealand, and the UK. The New Zealand system of Strategic Results Areas (SRAs) and Key Results Areas (KRAs) is probably the best known (Boston et al. 1996, pp. 282–3; Matheson et al. 1997). In Canada the 1994 Program Review exercise was intended to put an end to the fragmented and volatile policy-making which was seen as a characteristic of the preceding Mulroney administration (Aucoin and Savoie 1998). In Finland there has been a more recent attempt to develop a Strategy Portfolio and a strategic overview of government organization (*High Quality Services, Good Governance, and a Responsible Civic Society* 1998*a*, pp. 19–22; and the later consultancy report, Bouckaert et al. 2000). In the UK, following a period of distaste for central planning and coordination under Thatcher, the Blair Labour government has committed itself to better 'joined-up', horizontally coordinated policy-making. It has set up cross-departmental reviews in areas such as criminal justice, services for young children, and the countryside, and conducted a comprehensive review of all government spending (Chancellor of the Exchequer 1998, pp. 33–41; Pollitt 2003b). A brief assessment of strategic planning is made in Chapter 5.

Merging departments has for long been one way of improving coordination. Of course, this route rather contradicts the trend to specialization noted above, but it is a device that has been used by some countries. While New Zealand was allowing the number of its ministries to proliferate, its neighbour, Australia, was reducing its population of departments from twenty-eight to eighteen (1987—see Appendix B). In 1993 Canada followed suit, reducing the number of federal departments from thirty-two to twenty-four (see Appendix B). These initiatives were reminiscent of much earlier (1960s and early 1970s) attempts by UK governments to rationalize the pattern of ministries by creating large, 'strategic' departments (Pollitt 1984). In Italy in 2000 a population of more than twenty ministries was merged and slimmed to just a dozen.

Another feature in a number of central governments has been an attempt by politicians themselves to exert greater control over the bureaucracy. This phenomenon will be discussed in more detail in Chapter 6, but it should be noted here as, in effect, another species of coordination effort. It has been particularly noticeable in Australia, New Zealand, the UK, and the USA, but softer echoes have also been heard in Finland, the Netherlands, and Sweden. Australia offers perhaps the clearest case. As Halligan (1996b, p. 82) puts it: 'Reform programs [during the Labor governments of 1983–93] were driven by a foremost concern of Labor—political control—which had come to be regarded both as an end in itself and a means to implementing party policy. To achieve this required a redistribution of power between the bureaucracy and the politicians.' To attain this the capacity of the Prime Minister's Office and Cabinet was enhanced, the pattern of ministries was radically altered (1987), ministers made more active use than hitherto of their right to influence senior bureaucratic appointments, and much greater use was made of specially recruited ministerial advisers.

To conclude this review of coordination, it should be remarked that, even where traditional hierarchies remained in place, the instruments of hierarchical coordination tended to change. In particular there was a shift from control and coordination by rationing inputs and regulating procedures to a greater emphasis on coordination by targets and output standards. The majority of the twelve countries became active in developing indicator sets for the performance of almost every imaginable public service (for Australia see Department of Finance 1996; Department of Finance and Administration 1998a, 1998b; Development Team 1998; for Canada see Mayne 1996; Treasury Board of Canada 1996; for the Netherlands see Leeuw 1995; Mol 1995; for the UK see Boyne et al. 2003; Carter et al. 1992; Chancellor of the Duchy of Lancaster 1997; Likierman 1995; Pollitt 1986, 1990; for the USA see Radin 1998). Some, however, are still at a fairly undeveloped stage as far as performance measures and performance reporting are concerned. In Germany there has been much more reform at local and provincial (*Länder*) level than in the federal government. Large parts of the Belgian and Italian public sectors appear to have little in the way of output or outcome targets. Equally, the recent reform documents from the European Commission (2000, 2001a) stop well short of providing a set of quantitative criteria by which the success of individual reforms and programmes might later be judged.

Decentralization. Decentralization, ministers and mandarins have said, makes possible more responsive and speedy public services, better attuned to local and/or individual needs. It facilitates 'downsizing' by leading to the elimination of unnecessary layers of middle management. It even produces more contented and stimulated staff, whose jobs have been 'enriched' by taking on devolved responsibilities for financial and personnel management, and by escaping from the overburden of centralized regulation. Given all these benefits it is little wonder that almost everyone in every country (and in the European Commission) seems to be officially in favour of decentralization (Pollitt 2005). Like virtue, however, decentralization is differently construed by different parties, and is far easier to preach and praise than to practise. If we are to describe the actual trajectories in a way that carries some real meaning, we have to distinguish between different aspects of decentralization, different alphas, as well as between rhetoric and reality.

One way of deconstructing the concept of decentralization is to recognize that it is a process that contains at least three strategic choices. These are depicted in Table 4.5.

The first choice is therefore between *political* decentralization, where the decentralized authority is transferred to elected political representatives (e.g. when central government decentralizes a power to local government), and *administrative* decentralization, where authority is passed to an appointed body such as a UK Urban Development Corporation or a Swedish agency. The second choice is between transferring authority to another body that is selected by *competitive* means (e.g. through competitive tendering for a local authority refuse collection service) and transferring authority by *noncompetitive* means (e.g. where a District Health Authority transfers some of its authority to an NHS trust). A third choice is between *internal* decentralization (where the act of transfer takes place 'within the walls' of an existing organization) and *external* decentralization, where the authority is transferred to an independent external body (which might be an existing one or a new, specially created one). When authority to spend up to $X without seeking permission is delegated from the Principal Finance Officer to senior line managers, that is internal decentralization. When authority was transferred from a UK Local Education Authority to a grant-maintained school under Major's Conservative government, that was external delegation (Pollitt et al. 1998).

The balance between these different forms of decentralization has been rather different in different countries. Once more, different countries have *started* from very different positions. Thus, for example, in each of France, Sweden, Finland, and the UK central governments have praised the virtues of decentralization, but in the early 1980s France

Table 4.5 Strategic choices in decentralization

Either	Or
Political decentralization	Administrative decentralization
Competitive decentralization	Noncompetitive decentralization
Internal decentralization	External decentralization (devolution)

and the UK were relatively centralized countries while the two Nordic states were both already extensively decentralized (see Chapter 3 and Appendix B). Germany had been very decentralized since the Second World War, at least by Franco-British standards (Schröter and Wollmann 1997; Wollmann 2001). Taking this into account, we can say that administrative decentralization has been the preferred form in New Zealand and the UK, while political decentralization has been the dominant type in Belgium, Finland, Germany, France, and Sweden. Few new powers have been given to local governments in New Zealand and the UK. In each case decentralization has transferred authority to a range of specialized administrative bodies (such as grant-maintained schools and NHS trusts in the UK—see Pollitt et al. 1998). In France, by contrast, probably the most significant single reform of the last three decades was the decentralization to local and regional *elected* authorities carried out by the Mitterand presidency and the socialist government from 1982 (see Appendix B: France, country file Montricher 1996). In Germany local governments have probably gained most from the delegation of functions by higher levels in the three-tier system. In Finland and Sweden there has been both political and administrative decentralization, but the transfer of responsibilities to the municipalities and counties has been a central plank of their respective reform programmes. In Italy one of the consequences of the political crisis of the early 1990s was a marked swing towards decentralization (*decentramento*), both of a political and of an administrative kind. Meanwhile in Belgium the political tensions between the Flemish and Walloon communities have led to an increasing delegation of federal powers to the subfederal level. Thus, until recently, the UK was the 'odd one out' in the EU, because it had done so little to transfer responsibilities to elected subnational authorities. Under the Labour government since 1997, however, newly elected legislatures were set up for Scotland and Wales. Even so, the degree of control that the UK central government exerts over the elected local authorities must remain one of the highest in Europe.

Turning to the distinction between competitive and noncompetitive decentralization, we see a roughly similar pattern. The competitive approach was prominent in Australia, New Zealand, and the UK, but much less so in the central or northern European countries. The USA was fairly enthusiastic about contracting-out (but in a sense had less to commercialize, at least at the federal level) and Canada (again at the federal level) was generally more cautious. This, of course, follows from the pattern of enthusiasm and caution over the use of MTMs, as already discussed.

As for the internal/external distinction, it is safe to say that all countries practised both types to some extent, but that the NPM countries have probably undertaken more *external* decentralization, because they have been the ones who have been keenest to create new, autonomous, and specialized bodies, and then devolve powers to them. France has also been fertile in setting up new subnational authorities, in line with the government's wider strategy of political and administrative decentralization, and has also continued, over the years, to create many more or less autonomous *établissements publiques*. The picture in the Netherlands is complicated. The creation of ZBOs and departmental agencies can be taken as evidence of external decentralization by central departments. On the other hand, during the 1980s and 1990s, 'spending departments often held out resolutely (and with success) against the transfer of powers to provinces and municipalities' (Derksen and Korsten 1995, p. 83). At a detailed level one can trace how the concept of a decentralized executive agency, imported from the UK, was in Dutch central government successively 'translated' into something less radical and more narrowly focused on financial flexibility (Smullen 2004). Other countries (e.g. the Nordics) have also practised devolution, but have tended to rely more on existing local governments as the recipients of new responsibilities (Micheletti 2000). There has been some divergence between Finland and Sweden, however, with respect to central agencies. Whereas, during the mid-1990s, the Finns downsized the numbers and functions of their central agencies, the Swedish agencies remain extremely powerful and, in many cases, have received even greater devolved power from their ministries than hitherto (Molander et al. 2002; OECD 1998).

It would, however, be quite misleading to suggest that there was a global rush towards decentralization, with the only differences between countries being which types of decentralization they prefer and how far they have gone. Centralization is also part of the picture: as some authority has been decentralized, simultaneously there have been significant instances of a tightening of central control and oversight. One fairly prominent case has been the way in which pressures on public spending have strengthened the hands of treasuries and central finance ministries in a number of countries. For example, there is a general perception among officials that economic constraints have reinforced the dominance over other ministries of the Finnish Ministry of Finance and the New Zealand and UK Treasuries. Furthermore, centralization has not been exclusively a matter of finance. There are countless instances, especially perhaps in the NPM countries, of central authorities using performance indicator (PI) systems or standard-setting, to reassert control over lower tiers or local units. In the UK, central government forced national 'league tables' on every school and hospital, and from 1988 for the first time imposed a national educational curriculum on all state schools (Pollitt et al. 1998; Pollitt 2003*a*, Chapter 3). Under Blair's New Labour administration the intensity of central target-setting and monitoring has actually increased. In the EU there have been many examples where the 'harmonization' of some product or rule or procedure across Europe has resulted in a de facto centralization on the Commission in Brussels. Furthermore, the administrative reforms of the Prodi Commission have in some ways decentralized 'horizontal' functions to the DGs, only to rearticulate them in a particularly centralized and bureaucratic fashion within each individual DG. Thus the idea that everything is travelling in the direction of decentralization (still more 'freedom') is, to say the least, oversimple.

Scale. Obviously, scale is intimately connected with some of the other dimensions of organization discussed immediately above. In addition to the general pressure for 'downsizing', which arrives from the savings objective, the trends towards specialization and decentralization also indicate reductions in the average size of many public sector organizations. The ideal public sector agency, as envisaged by the enthusiasts and visionaries of the NPM and reinventing government movements, will be 'flat', flexible, specialized ('focused'), and decentralized, and therefore very probably quite *small*. These approaches to reform include a deep doctrinal suspicion of large central bureaucracies. Such organizations represent (as we will see in subsequent chapters) the 'old world' from which the reformers are determined to escape. The US Vice-President put it like this:

Big headquarters and big rule books never have kept the government from making big mistakes. In fact, they often kept front-line workers from doing things right. So we asked agencies to cut layers of supervisors, headquarters staff, and other management control jobs by 50%. (Gore 1996, p. 16)

However, the 'small-is-beautiful' vision is evidently not universally shared. For example, while central ministries have been considerably reduced in size in New Zealand and the UK (Boston et al. 1996; HM Treasury 1994), in Finland the reforms of the 1990s actually led to slight growth in their size, as they absorbed some of the functions previously performed by central agencies (Ministry of Finance 1997). In general the Continental European countries have been less enthusiastic about 'downsizing' as an overall goal. The EU Commission itself has grown considerably. Between 1977 and 1997 the number of Commission staff grew by 104 per cent, with an increase of 150 per cent in the policy-making A grades. However, it should be noted that the EU budget grew by 206 per cent in real terms over the same period, and, since it is widely acknowledged that the tasks of the Commission expanded rapidly during the 1980s, it can be argued that the extra staff were needed to cope with new responsibilities. Nevertheless, the organizational development of the Commission has certainly not followed the NPM trend: it has specialized only to a limited extent, has created only weak forms of horizontal coordination, did not begin to decentralize in any significant way until the very end of the 1990s, and has grown in size.

4.7 The measurement of performance

It is clear from the previous subsections that increased measurement of performance has been a central feature of public management reform in many countries. These accounts of financial and personnel management, and organizational restructuring, have already partly dealt with performance measurement, so this section can be correspondingly brief. There are, however, some generic measurement issues, which it makes sense to address under this separate heading.

Performance measurement certainly is not new (Bouckaert 1994). Indeed, it is as old as public administration itself. In the latter part of the nineteenth century there were already schemes in place in the UK and the USA for measuring the performance of teachers in state schools. Woodrow Wilson was writing about the need to design an administrative system that would perform well against efficiency criteria, and F. W. Taylor was advocating a generic approach towards measuring the efficiency of workers (Dunsire 1973). Acknowledging all this, however, does not prevent one from recognizing that interest in measuring public sector activities has blossomed over the last quarter century. It has developed along several dimensions:

Measurement is becoming more *extensive*. More levels . . . and more fields . . . are included. Performance measurement is becoming more *intensive* because more management functions are included (not just monitoring but also decision-making, controlling and even providing accountability). Finally, performance measurement becomes more *external*. Its use is not just internal, but also for the members of legislative bodies, and even for the public. (Bouckaert 1996*b*, p. 234)

It may be useful to look at each of these dimensions in turn. The growing *extent* of performance measurement was best exemplified in the NPM countries, although significant measurement initiatives were also to be found in Canada, France, the Netherlands, the Nordic states, and the USA. We therefore turn to the UK for an assessment of the full extent of the trajectory:

No public sector employee has escaped the ever-extending reach of performance evaluation schemes. The pressure to meet targets or performance standards, whether hospital waiting lists, school exam results, crime clear-up rates or university research ratings—has introduced profound changes in public organisations. As PIs have become increasingly linked to resource allocation and individual financial rewards, so organisational cultures and individual behaviours have been transformed. (Carter 1998, p. 177—if Carter had been writing as we are, early in 2003, after more than six years of New Labour, he would have had no reason to reduce the strength of his claim—on the contrary.)

Examples of the spread of performance measurement to new fields can be found in many countries. Often they have been tied in with developments in information technology (e.g. Bellamy and Taylor 1998, pp. 68–70). In the USA the 1993 GPRA effectively mandated PIs for every federal agency (Radin 1998). In Australia performance measures were widely introduced during the 1980s and the systems were tightened and toughened by the neoconservative Howard government after 1996 (Department of Finance and Administration 1998*a*, 1998*b*; McGuire 2004). In New Zealand the system of SRAs and KRAs (mentioned earlier) required wide-scope PI systems. In the Netherlands during the 1990s a strategy of progressively integrating performance measurement with the budget process has been pursued (Sorber 1996), and this took a further twist with the introduction of the VBTB budgeting system from 1999. In several countries initiatives to raise the quality of public services have led directly to a wider scope for performance measurement (e.g. the UK *Citizen's Charter* from 1991; the French Public Service Charter from 1993; the 1994 Declaration of Service Quality; and the 1995 Quality of Service Initiative in Canada).

One might suppose that the extension of PI systems would proceed in a rational fashion, with relatively straightforward, tangible services (e.g. refuse collection, the mail) being measured first and then more individually variable, less concrete services such as health care and education, and finally, perhaps, nontangible, nonroutine services with a high subjective content such as the provision of policy advice or the coordination of different agencies in the pursuit of some general policy goal (Bouckaert and Ulens 1998). In practice, however, any such logic is hard to find. In the UK, for example, one of the earliest national PI schemes (from 1983) was for the NHS (Carter et al. 1992; Pollit 1986). What is perhaps a clearer pattern is that the powerful have been better able to postpone or deflect the tide of measurement than other groups. Thus, within health services, the activities of nurses and receptionists have been measured far more intensively and openly than the quality of clinical decision-making by doctors. In the NPM countries, at least, the public can read plenty of reports containing measures of the performance of teachers, police, social workers, social security clerks, and specialist agencies, but few, if any, measuring the performance of Members of Parliament (MPs) or ministers (the USA may offer one of the rare exceptions to this generalization, at least in respect of the voting and attendance habits of members of Congress and Senate).

Extending PI systems is not only a matter of finding hitherto unmeasured sectors or organizations and subjecting them to 'the treatment'. It is also a question of broadening the scope of measurement in a more analytical sense—of beginning to measure efficiency and effectiveness, not just inputs, processes, and compliance. As noted elsewhere in this book, for example, many NAOs have extended their work beyond questions of regularity and legality, beyond even the hunting-down of waste, to embrace more sophisticated concepts of efficiency, effectiveness, and service quality. These are the focus of the field of performance audit, which has developed rapidly since the mid-1980s (Pollitt et al. 1999). This shift of measurement systems beyond the relatively mundane issues of input and process towards the more politically sensitive and methodologically challenging problems of assessing effectiveness has proved both difficult and controversial—in several countries and in many contexts (Bouckaert and Peters 2002; Bouckaert and van Dooren 2003). For example, consider the words of a New Zealand minister, reflecting upon the way in which, with one of the world's most sophisticated performance measurement systems, New Zealand public servants have nevertheless tended to overconcentrate on outputs (e.g. cases completed) at the expense of the final *outcomes* (e.g. satisfied clients) that their efforts are supposed to lead towards:

One [danger is that] risky, unattractive, but nevertheless important functions might start to fall between the cracks, or that absurd demarcation disputes might arise, of the kind that used to be endemic in the cloth-cap trade unions of old. If 'output fixation' distracts departments from outcomes, and 'contract fixation' encourages them to ignore everything that isn't actually specified, aren't these things very likely to happen? (East 1997)

These more ambitious uses of PIs—to assess impacts, guide programmes, or help decide the fate of policies—are perhaps less difficult for the public service cultures of the 'public interest' administrative systems to absorb than for the *Rechtsstaat* systems. The latter are more used to trying to guide administrative behaviour by the formulation of precise laws and regulations than by giving more discretion and then measuring results (Bouckaert 1996*b*, pp. 228–9).

The NPM countries have also been at the forefront of the more *intensive* use of PIs. Over the last twenty years one may discern a trajectory that runs from the use of PIs principally as supplementary or background information towards their use for a variety of management purposes—to inform specific decisions, to compare different organizations or functions (benchmarking), to determine budget allocations, and even as a major input to decisions concerning motivation, career development, and promotion of individuals (Bouckaert 2001). An example would be the research quality ratings given to UK university departments on the basis of their published output, research grants, and honours won, PhDs awarded, and other factors. This elaborate national exercise, which is conducted roughly every four years, now directly and formulaically produces each department's allocation of baseline research funding. Planning to achieve a 'high score' in this assessment has become a core component of the management of most university departments. In short, the use of PIs, having once been an 'extra' or novelty, has been progressively integrated with other aspects of management (Carter 1998). This can significantly sharpen the management of public services and the orientation of those services to their users. On the other hand, it can also lead to various pathologies where the activity of measurement itself distorts the administrative process in undesirable ways (Bouckaert 1995*b*; Bruijn 2002; Pollitt 2003*a*, chapter 2).

Finally, we turn to the *external* use of performance measurement—not exclusively for internal management purposes, but to inform legislatures, taxpayers, service users, and a variety of other stakeholders. For those who know where to look (and, more importantly, for those who are interested in looking) the official publications of the late 1990s contain far more performance information than was available in 1980. Publications such as the annual Next Steps agencies review or various NHS PI booklets (UK) or the GPRA reports (USA) or the Swedish Ministry of Finance reports on public sector productivity contain a great deal of potentially useful data (see Chancellor of the Duchy of Lancaster 1997; Swedish Ministry of Finance 1997). Gradually these data-sets are being refined so as to reduce the weaknesses and poor presentation of some of their early versions. In the case of the NHS, for example, the first national sets of PIs were unwieldy and unwelcoming, and overwhelmingly concerned process issues such as average lengths of hospital stay. Over the years, however, the presentation and explanation of this information has improved enormously, and, if there are still many possible improvements that can be discussed, at least some indicators or proxies for clinical outcomes are now included in the package (an example is shown in Chapter 5). In some cases performance information is given considerable publicity by the mass media (e.g. the 'league tables' of English state schools), although in others the 'take-up' of such data by politicians has been disappointing (Carter et al. 1992, p. 182). Some governments and parliaments have begun to take special steps to improve the relevance and accessibility of PI data for politicians (e.g. in the Canadian case, Duhamel 1996).

4.8 Modes of implementation

In this subsection we move from the 'what' of reform to the 'how'. This poses an immediate problem. It is usually harder for academics to obtain systematic information about how reforms are being put into practice than about what the reforms are. Governments are frequently keen to announce what they are going to do but are understandably less energetic in offering a blow-by-blow account of how things are going. Some aspects of implementation are particularly hard to research and write about: it is only rarely that we get scientific accounts of the strengths and weaknesses of individual leaders and managers, of the resentments and conflicts that reforms so easily stimulate, of the compromises and threats by which these are often settled, and so on (though journalistic treatments are more common). There is plenty of circumstantial evidence to indicate that such factors can be influential in determining the success or failure of some innovations, but these things can rarely be subject to rigorous testing.

What can be seen from the outside is the broad direction and energy of implementation that seems to be characteristic of a particular government during a particular period. Even this is partly impressionistic, but, pending more systematic comparative evidence, worth recording nonetheless. Here we will quickly review three aspects:

- The extent to which reform has been a *top-down/bottom-up* exercise.

- The extent to which *new organizations and structures* have been created specifically to advance reform (the alternative being the pursuit of reform through existing structures).

- The *intensity* of reform, that is, have governments barged ahead, trampling opposition underfoot, or have they tiptoed delicately, consulting and cooperating with the other stakeholders (such as public service unions) as they go?

The distinction between top-down and bottom-up reforms has itself to be used with some caution. These are not two separate categories but poles on a spectrum that passes through 'top-down-guided bottom-up'. So there are more intermediate cases than pure polar examples. Furthermore, since our focus is principally on central governments, it must be acknowledged that what constitutes the 'bottom' of central government may be far from immediately clear.

Bearing these caveats in mind, we can go straight to a major generalization about implementation: *all three aspects have in practice gone hand in hand*, that is, those countries that have employed more top-down strategies also tend to have created more new institutions *and* to have pushed on with reform at a more intense pace. Furthermore, *the Anglo-Saxon NPM countries again stand out as a separate group*—it is they, more than Germany and France, more than the consensual Dutch and the Nordics, more even than the voluble Americans or the somewhat quieter Canadians, who have driven reforms from the top, with relentless speed, throwing up all manner of new organizations—and new *types* of organization—as they have rushed onward. The range of implementation styles therefore matches very well the characteristics of politico-administrative regimes which were identified in Chapter 3.

There is space here only to offer brief illustrations of these generalizations, although evidence for them continues to accumulate throughout the remainder of the book. One way of doing this would be to compare the reform process in, say, Finland, Germany, the UK, and the USA (i.e. an active modernizer, a country that has been conservative with respect to management reform, an 'NPM enthusiast', and, in the case of the USA, a country where reform rhetoric has been loud, but reform achievements not necessarily commensurately impressive).

In Finland, considerable reforms have been implemented, and the number of civil servants has been markedly reduced, though in a low-key way and at a relatively leisurely pace. Furthermore, high levels of continuity have been maintained despite the existence of three different coalition governments over the relevant period. The reform programme that was launched in 1987/88 was still being 'rolled out' twelve years later (although by then there were naturally new items on the agenda as well). It was conceived and coordinated mainly by the Ministry of Finance and, in that sense, was fairly 'top-down'. It was of broad scope, affecting all or most of the central government, but could not directly apply to the municipalities, which enjoyed the constitutional autonomy that allowed them to decide on their own reforms. A good example of a central government reform would be results-oriented budgeting, one key element of the broader programme. It began with a small number of voluntary pilot projects from 1988, and then developed into a government decision to extend the system to all ministries and their agencies. The target was to have the system fully in place by the beginning of 1995—seven years after the launch. On the organizational dimension, new forms of state-owned company were a significant innovation, and the system of central agencies was extensively remodelled during the mid-1990s, but the ministries themselves remained largely undisturbed. Personnel reforms were placed on the statute book, but came into use only slowly and on a limited scale. The Finns paid close attention to reforms throughout the OECD world, and were active members of PUMA and other international bodies, but they imported reform ideas cautiously and selectively, adapting them to fit the Finnish politico-administrative system. Privatization and quasi-market mechanisms were elements of the NPM package that the Finns treated with considerable reserve. There was no 'rush to the market', and no large political constituency for the idea that the market was automatically superior to the 'nanny state' (Ministry of Finance 1997; Pollitt et al. 1997).

The federal German government was more conservative than its Finnish counterpart. There was no broad programme of management reform at the federal level (though there was considerable activity in a number of municipalities—see Appendix B). The main laws governing the civil service were not changed. No flocks of new organizations were created. There was no drastic downsizing. German activity at PUMA and in other inter-national *fora* was modest in terms of active participation in the global debate about management reform. Most of the leading German academics appeared to be lukewarm or actively hostile to NPM thinking (Derlien 1998; König 1996). When faced with the huge administrative challenge of reunification, the government decided not to innovate, but to transplant virtually the whole of the existing system in West Germany to the former East Germany—to create what was, in effect, a new Weberian state out of a defunct Communist one. Overall there was plenty of modernization in Germany, but it took place mainly at local and provincial levels, and it proceeded in an incremental fashion, with many local variations (König and Siedentopf 2001; Wollmann 2001).

The implementation process in the UK was more hectic, harsh, and sweeping than in either Finland or Germany (and it began in 1979, almost a decade earlier than in Finland). Wave after wave of broad-scope reform followed each other for more than two decades, often to the accompaniment of assertively doctrinaire statements by ministers. Most change was decidedly top-down. In central government Rayner Scrutinies (1979) were followed by the Financial Management Initiative (1982), the Next Steps Programme (1988), the *Citizen's Charter* (1991), the Private Finance Initiative, the downsizing of a number of ministries (1994–7), the introduction of accruals-accounting right across central government and various other new systems. Extensive personnel reforms led to wider application of individual contracts for senior public officials, extensive use of performance-related pay, and the decentralization of most personnel authorities to individual ministries and agencies. Central government also drove radical reforms in subnational and local government, often in a directive manner that would have been impossible in either Finland or Germany. MTMs were imposed on the NHS, education, and community care. Many new types of organization were created, including Urban Development Corporations, City Technology Colleges, grant-maintained schools, an Audit Commission, NHS trusts, various types of public housing agency, and so on (see Painter et al. 1996). Nor did the advent, after eighteen years in opposition, of a Labour government (1997) lead to any slackening of the pace of change. The catalogue of restructurings, realignments, and rebadgings continued (Office of Public Services Reform 2002; Pollitt 2003*b*; Prime Minister and the Minister for the Cabinet Office 1999).

The USA offers our last, and contrasting, illustration. Here there has been the surface appearance of top-down reform, with many presidentially sponsored commissions and councils during the 1980s, and then the NPR in the 1990s (see Appendix B: USA, country file). Behind this façade, however, it becomes apparent that the fragmented American politico-administrative system seldom allows reforms to be implemented via a concerted drive from the top (Peters 1995). The follow-through on a number of these reforms has been weak or uncertain (President Reagan's Grace Commission providing one example of this). The central executive does not have the untrammelled implementation ability of its counterparts in New Zealand or the UK. Some of the most interesting parts of the NPR have been the 'reinvention laboratories', and these show large variations from one agency to another (Ingraham 1997). New organizations have certainly been created, but not on the scale of the UK's Next Steps agencies. The pattern of departments has not changed that much, and certainly not in line with any centrally determined strategic plan. Personnel management, as was noted, has included a good deal of innovation, but there have been significant problems with the SES and performance-related pay, and more than half the federal workforce still falls within the somewhat rigid merit system (Kettl et al. 1996). Thus it could be said that reform *debate* has been quite intense—and sometimes highly doctrinaire—but reform implementation has been quite 'patchy', that is, energetic here but slow there.

4.9 Summary: multiple omegas, multiple trajectories, and unforeseen developments?

At the beginning of this chapter questions were posed as to whether all twelve states were following one, basically similar route (first mapped out by the Anglo-American countries) or whether, at the other extreme, there was no discernible pattern to the multiplicity of reforms—just a national and international game of reform ad hockery. On the basis of the evidence developed above—and set out at greater length in Appendix B—what can now be said in response to these propositions?

A first, perhaps rather obvious, observation is that the story as told here lies somewhere between the two extremes. There is more than one route but, on the other hand, the picture is not one of anarchy. Some trends and partial patterns seem to stand out rather clearly.

A second point is that trajectories would be much more likely to converge if every government in every country shared the same omega—the same vision of the desired future arrangements towards which the reforms were intended to propel that jurisdiction. However, it does not seem that there *is* such a universally shared vision. Although the question of visions of future states remains to be explored in greater depth in subsequent chapters (especially Chapters 5 and 8), it can already be suggested that there are different emphases as between our twelve countries. Some seem to have the relatively modest ambition of 'lightening' the existing bureaucracy, through deregulation and streamlining, and simultaneously saving money by tightening up on budgets and financial management. For most of the 1980s Germany fell into this category—at the federal level, though not locally—as did the European Commission at least until the SEM 2000 initiative in the mid-1990s. One might think of this as an essentially conservative strategy of *maintaining* as much as possible of the status quo by taking steps to make current structures and practices work better—tightening up rather than fundamentally restructuring. In the German case, however, it has to be remembered that this was (and remains) an unusually decentralized state, where the functions of the federal government are rather narrow in scope (Wollmann 2001).

A second group of states have been more adventurous. We term them the *modernizers*: they still believed in a large role for the state but acknowledged the need for fairly fundamental changes in the way the administrative system was organized. Such changes typically included budget reforms which move towards some form of results or performance-budgeting, some loosening of personnel rigidities (but not the abandonment of the concept of a distinctive career public service), extensive decentralization and devolution of authority from central ministries and agencies, and a strengthened commitment to improving the quality of public services to citizens. A greater emphasis on strategic planning is a further characteristic of such a trajectory. Within this group of modernizers there are different emphases as between managerial modernization (concentrating on management systems, tools, and techniques) and participatory modernization (giving greater salience to devolution of authority to subnational governments and to developing user-responsive, high-quality services and forms of public participation). Despite considerable differences between each other, Belgium, Finland, France, Italy, the Netherlands, and Sweden belong to this group. Within the group Finland, the Netherlands, and Sweden tend more towards participatory modernization, while Belgium, France, and Italy could be said to put more emphasis on managerial modernization. We might call the first group the 'northern Europeans' and the second the 'central Europeans'. Further, one might link these shades of difference with deeper cultural orientations—the northerners being more open and egalitarian, the central Europeans, more hierarchical and technocratic. Within both subgroups of modernizers, moves to privatize state-owned commercial organizations have been selective and gradual, with intermediate forms such as state-owned enterprises or companies being extensively resorted to before, or instead of, outright privatization. In a way Germany belongs to this group also—as is clear from the many subnational reforms that took place from the mid-1980s onwards. In Germany, however, there was also a striking increase in participation (again at the subnational levels), mainly through the introduction of locally binding referenda, from the early 1990s onwards (Wollmann 2001). However, our main focus here is on central governments and, at that level, a serious move towards modernization came very late (at the end of Chancellor Kohl's third term) and has still not gone far enough for us to evaluate it with any confidence.

A third group also want to make fundamental reforms, but hold a particular view of what the most successful kind of change is likely to be, namely the introduction of more competition and MTMs *within* the public sector. They are therefore *marketizers*. These countries favour quasi-markets, large-scale contracting-out and market-testing, contractual appointments and performance pay for civil servants, more people brought in from outside the traditional career pattern, and a general reduction of the distinctiveness of the public sector vis-à-vis the private. They are also the most enthusiastic about importing private sector techniques such as accruals-accounting, BPR, benchmarking, and franchising into the public sector. Australia, New Zealand, and the UK all fit this category, at least for considerable parts of the period under scrutiny. Occasionally the Netherlands, Finland, and Sweden (the 'northern Europeans') have ventured into this territory, but only selectively and cautiously, remaining more usually among the modernizers of the previous group.

Finally there is the omega of a *minimal state*, where everything that could possibly be privatized is privatized, leaving only a 'nightwatchman' administrative apparatus, performing core functions that the private sector is quite unable or unwilling to perform. Massive privatization and wholesale downsizing of public sector organizations would be key features of this approach. None of our twelve countries has consistently adopted this minimizing position, which exists in full-blown form only in the tracts of right-wing politicians and theorists. However, it has been at least flirted with under certain, usually right-wing, governments: during the late Thatcher period in the UK and under the 1990 National Party government in New Zealand and Howard's 1996 Liberal (neoconservative) government in Australia. Rhetorical empathy for such minimalism was also to be found on the lips of President Reagan, but there the gap between practice and vision was particularly wide. More generally, the USA remains difficult to classify: there have been strong elements of modernization, but also a considerable thrust towards marketization. Canada is also rather an 'awkward customer' from the point of view of this classification since, during the 1980s, it shared much of the marketizing rhetoric of Thatcher and Reagan, but did not in fact go far in implementing those ideas. Whilst the culture is not of a strong central state like France, or even the Netherlands or Italy, it has clung to the tradition of a fairly stable and neutral senior civil service, unlike the American 'spoils' system. One might say that it was in the Anglo-Saxon camp as far as its openness to marketizing ideas was concerned, but that its federal divisions and the continuing anchor of a nonpartisan central civil service have helped to moderate the scope and pace of change, and to preserve considerable elements of modernization.

Thus there *is*, in our view, a pattern. We might say that there are two obvious groupings, and then a few 'hybrid' or 'hard-to-classify' cases. The first and best-known grouping is that of the NPM marketizers—Australia, New Zealand, the UK, and, in words if not always in deeds, the USA. We will call this the *core NPM group*—they all see a large role for private sector forms and techniques in the process of restructuring the public sector. The second grouping is the Continental European modernizers—Belgium, Finland, France, the Netherlands, Italy, and Sweden (and Germany, if one goes below the federal level). They continue to place greater emphasis on the state as *the* irreplaceable integrative force in society, with a legal personality and operative value system that cannot be reduced to the private sector discourse of efficiency, competitiveness, and consumer satisfaction. They thus continue, in modern form, their nineteenth- and twentieth-century traditions of strong statehood and a high status for the top civil servants. Of course, the pace and precise mixture of change has differed between members of this modernizing group. Reform has come later to the 'central Europeans'—

Belgium, Germany, and Italy than to the 'northern Europeans'—Finland, the Netherlands, and Sweden. France has matched the pace of the northern group, but has been more resistant to marketizing ideas, and to much of the anglophone rhetoric around NPM. Further, the 'northerners' have given their modernization efforts a stronger citizen-oriented, participatory flavour than the central Europeans. Decision-making in Italy has inevitably been affected by the political turbulence it has experienced, in contrast, say, to the much more measured, consensual process of reform in Finland or the Netherlands. Nevertheless, when compared with the core NPM group, we can say that the Continental Europeans as a whole have shared a more optimistic attitude towards the future role of the state, a more constructive/less 'blaming' approach to the reform of the public services, and a less sweepingly enthusiastic attitude towards the potential contribution of the private sector within the public realm.

The NPM group are well known in the anglophone literature (Boston et al. 1996; Christensen and Lægreid 2001; Hood 1996; Kettl 2000; Lane 2000). The second group are much less so, and are sometimes portrayed simply as laggards or faint-hearts who have been slow to climb aboard the NPM train. Our interpretation, however, is much more positive. We believe that what we see in the Continental European states is a distinctive reform model, one which we have decided to call the *Neo-Weberian State* (NWS). We term it NWS because, in comparison with NPM marketization, it has the following emphases:

'WEBERIAN' ELEMENTS

- Reaffirmation of the role of the state as the main facilitator of solutions to the new problems of globalization, technological change, shifting demographics, and environmental threat
- Reaffirmation of the role of representative democracy (central, regional, and local) as the legitimating element within the state apparatus
- Reaffirmation of the role of administrative law—suitably modernized—in preserving the basic principles pertaining to the citizen–state relationship, including equality before the law, legal security, and the availability of specialized legal scrutiny of state actions
- Preservation of the idea of a public service with a distinctive status, culture, and terms and conditions

'NEO' ELEMENTS

- Shift from an internal orientation towards bureaucratic rules towards an external orientation towards meeting citizens' needs and wishes. The primary route to achieving this is not the employment of market mechanisms (although they may occasionally come in handy) but the creation of a professional culture of quality and service
- Supplementation (not replacement) of the role of representative democracy by a range of devices for consultation with, and the direct representation of, citizens'

views (this aspect being more visible in the northern European states and Germany at the local level than in Belgium, France, or Italy)

- In the management of resources within government, a modernization of the relevant laws to encourage a greater orientation on the achievement of results rather than merely the correct following of procedure. This is expressed partly in a shift in the balance from *ex ante* to *ex post* controls, but not a complete abandonment of the former

- A professionalization of the public service, so that the 'bureaucrat' becomes not simply an expert in the law relevant to his or her sphere of activity, but also a professional manager, oriented to meeting the needs of his or her citizen/users

We are aware that using the label Neo-Weberian State may surprise some Continental experts. Among German scholars, for example, the modernizers have sometimes characterized themselves as anti-Weberian or, at least, as moving away from the *Welt von Max Weber*. We would not disagree with their contention that many of their reforms could be seen as diluting or adding new features to the original Weberian ideal type. Nor would we deny that the conservatives who opposed these modernizers could be seen as wanting to hang on to the old systems and the old values—as defenders of the Weberian heritage. Yet, looked at from the outside, what is striking in comparison with the core NPM states is how far the underlying assumptions of a positive state, a distinctive public service, and a particular legal order survived as the foundations beneath the various packages of modernizing reforms. What was going on, it seems, was the modernization of the Weberian tradition, not its outright rejection: a process of addition, not demolition (even if some of the additions fitted on the foundations rather awkwardly). Consider the following summary of French reforms:

In France, the importance of administrative law, the successful experience of nationalized, monopoly, public service providers in the post war period, and the idea of a 'general interest', represented at local level by the prefect, explain many of the distinctive features of the hybrid modernization reforms. (Guyomarch 1999, p. 171)

Finally, the extreme marketizers and antistate minimizers who were quite common in the UK, New Zealand, and the USA never commanded the same degree of political voice in either the central European states or even the northern group. One might say that the omegas (Figure 4.1) were different. The prophets of the core NPM states envisaged an entrepreneurial, market-oriented society, with a light icing of government on top. The northern variant of the NWS foresaw a citizens' state, with extensive participation facilitated by a modernized system of public law that would guarantee rights and duties. Proponents of the central European variant of the NWS favoured a professional state—modern, efficient, and flexible, yet still uniquely identified with the 'higher purposes' of the general interest.

However, the precision of the NWS model—or the NPM for that matter—must not be exaggerated. As we said at the beginning of the chapter, omegas are frequently vague or incomplete or both. So the pattern is very rough and approximate, for both political and organizational reasons. Politically, governments change and may hold different visions of the future, so that, following elections, certain types of reform are de-emphasized and other types given greater salience. The arrival of Blair's Labour government in power in the UK in 1997 did not by any means completely alter the trajectory of UK reforms, but it did shift the emphasis. The automatic preference for private sector solutions was replaced with talk of partnerships. Some MTMs were partially dismantled (e.g. in the NHS), though others were retained. Greater emphasis was laid on horizontal coordination or 'joined-up' government. In general it might be said that the change of administration shifted the UK from the radical end of the 'marketizing' group towards the 'marketizing'/ 'modernizing' borderline. Similarly, in the US the arrival in power of the Clinton Democrats resulted in an end to the neglect and sometimes scorn that the federal civil service had suffered between 1980 and 1992. In rhetorical terms it shifted reform away from a mixture of minimalism (especially under Reagan) and marketization and towards modernization as the dominant motif. The election of President George W. Bush at first seemed likely to mark a swing back to marketizing and, indeed, plans for further large-scale contracting-out were announced. However, 9/11 introduced a new dimension, and the subsequent proposal for a new Department of Homeland Security at first sight strikes a somewhat inconsistent, centralizing, and interventionist note. The devil is in the detail, however, and the 2002 Homeland Security Act also contains provisions that, in true NPM style, weaken (federal) employee protection and strengthen management flexibility.

A second set of political reasons for 'untidiness' is to be found among the pressures represented by external socio-economic forces (Figure 2.1, box A) and by political demands (box E). These can blow chosen trajectories off course. Consider, for example, the balance between three basic types of reform objective. First there is the objective of reducing public expenditure, or, at least, restraining its rate of growth. Second, there is the laudable desire to design better-performing public services—higher quality, greater efficiency, and so on. Third, there is the aim of sharpening accountability and therefore, hopefully, enhancing the legitimacy of the administration in the eyes of the public. These three objectives—all of them widely held and proclaimed among our twelve countries—exist in some tension with each other. Trouble for governments may blow up on any of these three fronts at quite short notice. An economic downturn may heighten the need for economies and cuts. Revelations of low standards in, say, nursing homes or public transport may lead to strident and popular calls for something to be done. The discovery of cases of corruption or gross waste or concealment of important decisions may fuel calls for greater transparency and stricter accountability procedures (as happened with the European Commission crisis in 1999). When one or more such events occurs, political leaders and their senior officials have, temporarily at least, to alter the balance of their efforts. 'Firefighting' may lead to some neglect of longer-term tasks of forest management. Progress along a particular trajectory wobbles or halts. A small-scale example might be when the needs of the national economy seem to require a budget cut, and the impact on particular public service organizations is that they abandon their plans for service improvement, which can no longer be afforded. Alternatively, attempts to decentralize authority and increase managerial discretion and flexibility may be halted if a particular 'decentralized' manager is discovered to have acted corruptly, so that calls for tighter centralized control cannot be resisted.

Organizational factors also intrude to spoil the possibility of any truly neat pattern. Frequently there are implementation difficulties, and these can persuade governments to change instruments, or to 'soft pedal' on types of reform about which they were previously very enthusiastic. Major's Conservative government soon retreated from the rhetoric of vigorous competition with respect to the NHS provider market, and took steps to see that it was closely managed, in an effort to avoid volatility (Pollitt et al. 1998). Following criticism, the Dutch government of the mid-1990s became more cautious about creating highly autonomous ZBOs and tended to favour more controllable departmental agencies instead. In the 1990s Jospin's government in France retreated from some of its public service reform proposals when faced with large-scale strikes by resistant trade unions.

More fundamentally, different governments have different *capacities for reform*, according to regime type (as explained in Chapter 3). During the 1980s, for example, the gap between rhetoric and actual implementation was perhaps particularly wide in Canada and the USA. During the 1990s one may question the extent of actual reform achievements within the European Commission, despite the impressive-sounding rhetoric of SEM 2000 and MAP 2000 (Evaluation Partnership 1999; see also Appendix B: European Commision, country file).

Overall, therefore, our interpretation is that, whilst there has undoubtedly been great diversity and many trajectories turn out to be partial or interrupted, there is a rough but discernible longer-term pattern beneath the welter of detail. Whilst this pattern certainly does not mean that each individual reform instrument (performance budgets, contracting-out, etc.) can be ascribed exclusively to one single trajectory (still less to one group of countries and not to others), it *does* suggest that there are usually some continuing broad differences between different groups of countries. The trajectories and rhetoric of reform were significantly different as between, first, the Anglo-Australasian-American core NPM enthusiasts; second, the early and participatory modernizers in northern Europe (NWS, first variant); and, third, the somewhat later, more managerially oriented modernizers in central Europe and the EU Commission (NWS, second variant). It also seems likely that these differences are indeed related to the types of politico-administrative regimes which were analysed in Chapter 3. In terms of trajectories or strategies, not every country is playing the Anglo-Saxon game—not even all the Anglo-Saxon countries!

There is, of course, another, uncomfortably sharp question, which has been waiting in the wings throughout this chapter. It is: Do any or all of these trajectories actually *work*? That is, what have been the *results* of the many efforts at reform? Chapter 5 wrestles with this by-no-means straightforward issue.

5 Results: through a glass darkly

> One of the ideological outputs of organisations is *talk*. The political organisation sets great store by what it says, orally or in writing . . . Talk, decisions and products are mutually independent instruments used by the political organisation in winning legitimacy and support from the environment . . . hypocrisy is a fundamental type of behaviour in the political organisation: to talk in a way that satisfies one demand, to decide in a way that satisfies another, and to supply products in a way that satisfies a third.
>
> (Brunsson 1989, pp. 26–7)

5.1 Results: a slippery concept

The question of what has resulted from all the many reforms is obviously an absolutely fundamental one. Yet it is not at all simple. The label 'result' can be applied to many different aspects, and may incorporate a variety of concepts. As Brunsson says, talk and decisions, as well as actual actions, may be considered as important types of outputs. Furthermore, much depends on who is evaluating, for whom, and why. A full discussion of 'results' therefore embraces the wider questions of 'results for whom, defined by whom, against what criteria, and in pursuit of which objectives?'

There is a utopian quality to some of the political rhetoric around the reforms—particularly in the UK, Australasia, and North America. In Paradise citizens will enjoy services that are high-quality yet low-cost, easily accessed, and responsive. They will become more satisfied with their governments. Meanwhile civil servants will take on a new culture, infused with the values of economy, efficiency, effectiveness, and customer service. Citizens will be empowered, civil servants will be trusted by politicians and citizens alike, politicians themselves will provide 'leadership' and strategic guidance. If only all this could be bottled! Yet perhaps it can—a number of governments have been ambitious to export their reform products:

The Citizen's Charter is the most comprehensive programme ever to raise quality, increase choice, secure better value and extend accountability. We believe that it will set a pattern, not only for Britain, but for other countries in the world. (Prime Minister 1991, p. 4; more generally, see Pollitt 2002; see also Bouckaert 1995a, 1996b)

When expectations are pitched so high it becomes extremely hard for internal evaluations and reports to register anything less than good results. '*Tout est pour le mieux dans les meilleurs des mondes possibles*' (Voltaire, *Candide*). It was no surprise, two-and-a-half years after the launch of the UK *Citizen's Charter*, when the responsible minister reported that performance had been impressive—the political price of saying anything less would have been considerable. Some of the reasons why hubris and hyperbole are so common are explored in subsequent chapters, but here the main task is soberly to set out what we know (and do not know) of the results of reform.

To form a balanced picture is not easy. However, some materials are less gushing and more thoughtful than the 'headline' statements of ministers and other *parties pris*. There are reports from line departments, intended principally for internal consumption (Employment Service 1994; Ministry of Finance 1997). There are some attempts at academic assessments (e.g. Aucoin and Savoie 1998; Bouckaert 2000*a*; Boyne et al. 2003; Kettl 2000; Maas and van Nispen 1999; Peters 1998*a*; Pollitt 1995; Pollitt and Bouckaert 2003; Thompson 2000). There are reports by relatively independent public commissions or experts (e.g. Evaluation Partnership 1999; Schick 1996; Task Force on Management Improvement 1992). There are performance audits by national audit institutions (e.g. Auditor General of Canada 1993, 1997; National Audit Office 1995, 1999). Taking these together there are still many significant gaps, but there is enough to begin to sketch out a broad picture. The first message from this picture is that—unfortunately—there is often contradictory information and an ambiguous and changing reality.

Whilst this state of affairs may seem frustrating to the rationalist (or to the rationalist elements within each of us), it may also, as Brunsson's book suggests, carry some positive benefits. From a political viewpoint it may enable a discourse of high (but somewhat conflicting) ideals to be maintained even in conditions where the possibilities for concrete actions are quite limited:

We seldom reflect high values in action, and because of their unreal elevation and their internal inconsistencies our best values cannot be adequately reflected in action. The maintenance of high values involves sin, i.e. a discrepancy between values and actions. And if norms, which are not or cannot be adapted to action, are to be advocated, some hypocrisy is called for. Sin and hypocrisy are necessary to the creation and preservation of high morals. Those without sin or hypocrisy are those who pursue or advocate realisable goals, trading in their morality in exchange. (Brunsson 1989, pp. 233–4)

The remainder of the chapter is divided into seven sections. In Section 5.2 we distinguish between a number of different levels at which results can be defined and assessed. In the next five sections we look at some of the typical evidence that is available at each of these levels, and we also consider the (plentiful) problems of interpretation (5.3–5.7). Finally, in Section 5.8, we try to sum up what is known and what is not about the results of public management reform.

5.2 A brief taxonomy of results

It may be useful to distinguish between four levels of results, as follows:

First, *operational results*. This is perhaps the simplest and most concrete sense of 'result'. In principle, operational results are discrete and quantifiable. More outputs are obtained for the same inputs. Without additional expenditure a programme succeeds in reaching a higher percentage of its target population. The police crack down on car theft, and succeed in halving the number of vehicles that are broken into (and so on). Operational results may be found at the micro-, meso-, and macroscales. Examples might be a local office that provides the same service with fewer staff (micro) or a government that manages to reduce the overall rate of growth of public expenditure (macro).

Second, there could be improved *processes* of management or decision-making. Related matters (such as health care and housing) are better coordinated. 'One-stop shops'/ 'single-window arrangements' are examples of this—the particular decisions taken and the information given are not necessarily any different, but they are all conveniently available in one place. Processes are streamlined (e.g. planning applications are now processed in only 70 per cent of the average time that they used to take). In the language of economics, transaction costs are reduced. Much 're-engineering' is about this kind of improvement. The assumption is normally that process improvements of this type will lead directly to improvements in operational results—that is, to better or more outputs and outcomes. Of course, in practice it is necessary to check that this assumption actually holds—public sector re-engineering projects, for example, do not always produce identifiable effects on final outcomes, or even on outputs (Packwood et al., 1998).

Third, a 'result' may take the form of some broad change in the overall *capacity* of the political or administrative system. The pattern of institutions may be redesigned so as to be more flexible, with the intention that this will make the system more resilient in dealing with pressures which are expected to arise in the future. For example, it may be decided that all senior civil service appointments will be competitive and open to any applicant, rather than being confined to those already in the civil service and at the relevant level in the hierarchy.

Fourth, 'results' may be assessed relative to the degree to which the system has shifted towards some *desired or ideal state*. This is perhaps the most strategic sense of result. It is also the most obviously doctrinal or ideological. If the ideal is very small, 'light' state apparatus, with most activities undertaken within the private, market-oriented sector, then public management reforms may be judged in terms of how far they have moved the system in the direction of this vision.

It is immediately apparent that the first and second levels are more precise and concrete and—potentially at least—quantifiable than the third and fourth. The third and fourth are both 'systems-level' kinds of results, and both involve somewhat abstract and intangible changes, including value shifts and cultural transformations. In practice the borderline between these two is not always clear but, in principle, the third level is somewhat more specific and less explicitly normative than the fourth.

A moment's thought will also indicate that results—at any level—lead to further results. On level four the 'result' of a determined drive towards minimizing the state/ maximizing the market may, for example, be a backlash from voters who wish to safeguard the welfare state and who succeed in electing a different government which then slows or reverses the original strategic direction. On level one a 20 per cent improvement in the productivity of a particular tax collection agency may lead top management in the taxation service to launch an investigation as to why the other collection agencies are not making similar efficiency gains.

5.3 **Some key result concepts**

There is one last matter to be attended to before we come to the results themselves. We need to clarify our usage of familiar performance terms such as 'efficiency' and 'effectiveness'. Despite (or perhaps because of) the frequency of their usage, one should not assume that such terms always have the same meaning. On the contrary, we are aware of a wide range of meanings, both precise and vague, being attached to these central elements in 'performance vocabulary'. Therefore we want to set out *our* meanings— which we would suggest are fairly 'mainstream', not idiosyncratic or unusual.

Terms such as the famous 'three Es' (economy, efficiency, and effectiveness) are drawn from a generic input/process/output/outcome model that is very widely used in both the study and practice of public management (see Boyne et al. 2003 for an extended account). This model can be applied at various levels. For example, it can be deployed at a very high level of generality, taking the entire apparatus of public administration as the unit of analysis—the 'thing' that produces the output. More commonly, however, the input/output model is applied to programmes (e.g. health care, job creation, road construction) or to individual institutions or organizations (the Inland Revenue, the Driver and Vehicle Testing Agency). The model assumes that institutions and/or programmes are set up to address some specific socio-economic need(s). They establish *objectives* concerned with these needs, and acquire *inputs* (staff, buildings, resources) with which to conduct activities in pursuit of those objectives (see Figure 5.1 for

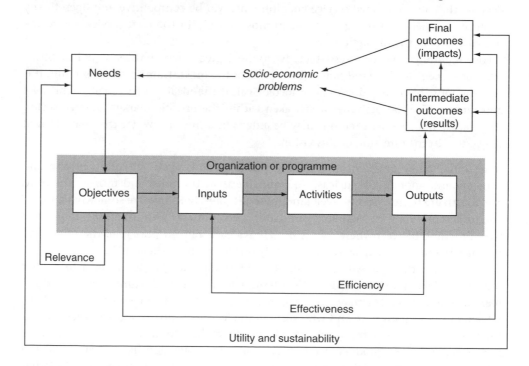

Figure 5.1 The input/output model.

a graphical representation of these relationships). *Processes* are then those activities that take place inside institutions, in order to generate outputs. These would thus include teaching in a school or recording and labelling within a warehouse. The *outputs* are the products of these processes—what the institution 'delivers' to the outside world (academic qualifications, school reports, or, in the warehouse case, issued stock). These then interact with the environment (especially with those individuals and groups at whom they are specifically aimed), leading to 'results' and, in the longer term, more fundamental 'impacts' (students getting jobs and achieving competence within them, or stock items being used by their purchasers). Both results and impacts may be termed *outcomes* (results are sometimes called 'intermediate outcomes' and impacts 'final outcomes'). Ultimately, the *value* of both the processes and the outputs rests on the outcomes. We will be using this vocabulary in the sections that immediately follow.

5.4 Operational results

5.4.1 Inputs and 'savings'

In the simplest case the operational result will be expressed quantitatively, and will be compared with some preset standard. In practice, however, the standard is often inferred rather than explicit (e.g. a licensing office may have cut costs by 5 per cent, but there may be no guidance on whether this is a great achievement, less than could reasonably be expected, or 'about right').

One of the commonest forms of operational 'result' can be seen in the traditional budget. The budget as made shows the resources appropriated for programme Z at $120 m. At the end of the year to which the budget refers the accounts are audited and show that in fact $119 m. was spent. This result indicates that input control is probably good—the amount spent is close to, but within, the amount budgeted (which was, in effect, the standard set).

At a higher level of aggregation one can ask about the total mass of public expenditure. Even if a government is successful at achieving its budget forecasts for some programmes, there may be others that get out of control so that the overall total is wide of what had been planned. So 'hitting the target' for public expenditure as a whole is also an important result.

As we have seen in earlier chapters, saving money has been a salient objective for many countries, and a major influence on public management reform. Governments have certainly striven to achieve overall savings 'targets', which may have been represented as a reduction in the rate of growth of public expenditure, a levelling-off of that expenditure as a proportion of gross domestic product (GDP), or even an absolute reduction of that share. The Canadian Program Review of 1994, changes to the UK Public Expenditure Survey, reforms to budgetary procedures in the Nordic countries, Belgium, Italy, and New Zealand—all these and many more were designed with savings in mind. One should also remember the EU's Maastricht 'convergence criteria', which included the standard that public sector deficits must be held below 3 per cent of GDP (and which were a major spur to reform in Italy and several other EU member states).

Yet, even with these apparently simple 'results' measures, ambiguity easily creeps in. As any experienced budget official knows, a 'saving' may mean any one or more of the following:

1. a reduction of the financial inputs compared with the previous year, using the current price basis in each year (i.e. not allowing for inflation);

2. a reduction of the financial inputs compared with the previous year, using the same price basis for both years (so that, e.g. if the nominal/current spend in the previous year was 100 and the nominal/current spend this year is 105, but general inflation has been 10 per cent, then this will be counted as a saving, despite the fact that the nominal spend is higher);

3. a reduction in the financial input for year X compared with the previous *forecast* input for year X (such reductions may still leave the inputs higher than they were in the previous year);

4. a reduction in inputs with no reduction of the services provided/activities conducted (i.e. an efficiency gain in terms of Figure 5.1);

5. a reduction in inputs that leads to a reduction in the services provided/activities conducted (which may even mean an efficiency *loss*, depending on what the relative proportions of the reductions in inputs and outputs turn out to be);

6. a reduction in unit costs (e.g. the cost per application processed). If activity volumes increase, then perfectly genuine savings in unit costs may nevertheless be accompanied by an increase in the budget (because the latter is determined by unit cost × quantity, so the increase in quantity may outweigh the reduction in unit costs);

7. the transfer of an activity from one part of the state to another (e.g. from central government to local government) so that one jurisdiction can show what appears to be a 'saving', though the system as a whole has made no saving;

8. the transfer of an activity out of the state sector altogether (privatization). In this case the government 'saves' money (at least in terms of gross public spending) and also wins a one-off receipt in the form of the sale price. The citizen may or may not benefit. Taxes may go down, or not; the citizen may now have to buy the same service from the private sector at the same or even a higher price; or may benefit from lower prices and higher efficiency—these outcomes all depend on situationally specific factors of markets, regulatory regimes, management skills, and other variables; and

9. a purely hypothetical future event (as in 'if we make these changes to our working patterns now, then in two years' time we should be able to reduce our overheads by 15 per cent').

Claims that savings have been made should therefore always be subject to further questioning and scrutiny, in order to determine precisely what is meant and what the implications may be for outputs and outcomes. With that caveat in mind we will now look at some of the broad evidence concerning 'savings'.

Table 5.1 shows changes in the ratio of government spending to GDP in the twelve countries from 1985 to 1990 to 2000. At first sight the GDP share appears to have fallen in nine countries, with three 'don't knows'. It is also noticeable that there appears to be a particularly rapid fall in New Zealand, which is a country known to have conducted an especially vigorous reform programme. Before jumping to the conclusion that this means public management reforms have been successful in producing savings, however, several qualifications must be made.

First, the pattern between countries does not always fit what one might expect from the record of management reform. For example, the Netherlands—a consensual regime—achieved a large reduction while the UK—a self-styled 'world leader' in reform—achieved something proportionately more modest. Meanwhile Finland, which implemented quite a substantial programme of reforms (Pollitt et al. 1997), hardly changed at all.

Second, the figures tell us little about what kind of 'savings' may have been involved here. In particular they give no clue as to whether reductions in the share of GDP taken by public spending have been achieved with no losses in efficiency, effectiveness, and quality, and small losses or severe deterioration in the overall standards and scope of public services (i.e. the difference between savings of types (4) and (5) in the above list). Neither do they tell us to what extent the 'results' have been gained by transferring large sets of activities to the private sector, nor what the consequences of this have been for the pockets of citizens—(issue (8) in the above list). In fact there are no good international, comparative data-sets to show what in these senses has been the 'price that has been paid' for 'savings'. Indeed, the methodological problems in constructing such a data-set are enormous.

Table 5.1 Changes in government outlays, 1985–2000 (% of nominal GDP)

Country	General government		
	1985	1990	2000
Australia	36.5	34.8	32.2
Belgium	—	53.3	46.8
Canada	46.0	46.7	41.9
Finland	43.8	45.4	43.7
France	52.2	49.8	47.5
Germany	47.0	45.1	44.5
Italy	—	53.1	44.1
Netherlands	57.1	54.1	41.7
New Zealand	—	57.5	36.4
Sweden	63.3	59.1	52.2
UK	44.0	39.9	37.7
USA	32.9	32.8	32.7

Source: OECD, Analytical database.

A third qualification is that much depends on the state of the economy at the time the measurement is taken. If the economy is depressed, various kinds of social protection expenditures rise and tax revenues fall. The public sector tends to remain large while the private sector contracts or ceases to grow so rapidly. For this reason the public spending : GDP ratio can change quite rapidly because of general economic conditions, without this implying anything about the underlying state of management reform. In the case of Table 5.1, for example, 1985 and 1990 were not terribly good years for most advanced economies, whereas 2000 was towards the end of a long boom, during which private sectors had been able to grow at a rapid pace. One way round this difficulty would be to exclude transfer payments (like social security and unemployment benefits) and concentrate only on government final consumption spending—a much smaller total. If we look at the United Nations figures for this we get the picture shown in Table 5.2.

Here the changes are less unidirectional and less striking than those of general outlays in Table 5.1. For three out of twelve countries consumption expenditure went *up*, despite favourable economic conditions during the 1990s and despite the fact that it was a decade of fairly constant management reform. And when we look at the averages for all developed countries (not just 'our' twelve), there is no change at all—it was 17.8 per cent in 1990 and still 17.8 per cent in 1997 (United Nations 2001, p. 152).

A fourth qualification—whether we are talking about 'government outlays (broader) or government final consumption (narrower)—is that *care must be taken not to attribute all savings to management reform, because the 'arrow of causation' may well be working in the opposite direction.* That is to say, it may be that hard-pressed governments have made relatively arbitrary cuts to public spending and it is these that have pushed public sector organizations into serious reform, not the other way round. In Sweden, the country that,

Table 5.2 Government consumption as a percentage of GDP (domestic prices), 1990–7

Country	1990	1997
Australia	17.2	16.8
Belgium	14.0	14.4
Canada	20.2	19.6
Finland	21.1	20.9
France	19.3	19.6
Germany	18.3	19.3
Italy	17.6	16.6
Netherlands	14.5	13.8
New Zealand	17.1	15.2
Sweden	27.4	25.8
UK	20.5	20.1
USA	17.7	15.3

Source: OECD, Analytical database.

among the twelve, has carried out the most comprehensive investigation of productivity changes within the public sector, it seems likely that cuts lead to reform or, at least, that reform is much more effective in raising productivity when it is carried out in a stringent fiscal climate. In a survey of productivity measures for the whole of the Swedish public sector from 1960 to the early 1990s, one expert concludes that 'public management reforms are necessary but not sufficient to make the public administration produce more value for money... it takes strict control of public budgets to realise the efficiency potential' (Murray 1998, p. 16). However, this example takes us beyond input savings into the realm of productivity, which will be described in detail later.

Tables 5.3 and 5.4 give us a further perspective on the question of 'savings'. Table 5.3 shows the net lending of the twelve governments in 1980, 1990, and 2002. Net lending is sometimes used as an indicator of public sector deficit (the larger the minus percentage, the larger the deficit).

The picture on net lending is mixed, though the overall trend appears to be virtuous. Seven out of nine countries recorded negative figures in 1980, whereas only five out of twelve were in deficit in 2002.

Again, though, we have to remind ourselves that 1980 was the beginning of a world recession and 2002 was the end of a boom. Some individual countries show large changes. New Zealand swung from −5.4 in 1990 to 0.1 in 2002. France travelled in the other direction, from 0.0 in 1980 through −1.6 in 1990 to −2.0 in 2002. An NPM enthusiast might remark that the three leading NPM countries—Australia, New Zealand,

Table 5.3 General government net lending, 1980–2002 (% of nominal GDP)

Country	1980	1990	2002
Australia	− 1.8	0.6	0.1
Belgium	− 15.7*	− 7.5[†]	0.0
Canada	− 3.1	− 4.5	1.0
Finland	2.8	5.4	3.2
France	0.0	− 1.6	− 2.0
Germany	− 2.9	− 2.1	− 2.8
Italy	—	—	− 1.4
Netherlands	− 4.2	− 5.1	0.1
New Zealand	—	− 5.4	0.1
Sweden	− 4.0	4.2	2.1
UK	− 3.4	− 1.2	− 0.8
USA	− 1.4	− 2.7	− 1.0

Notes: Net lending is often referred to as a measure of government deficits (−) or surplus.
* Figures for 1981.
[†] Figures for 1991.

Source: OECD, Analytical database.

Table 5.4 Central government debt as a percentage of GDP, 1990–2000

Country	1990	1995	2000
Australia	6.5	19.7	12.0
Belgium	109.5	117.2	102.1
Canada	43.7	54.9	43.2
Finland	10.3	63.3	48.0
France	28.6*	40.2	48.3
Germany	20.0	21.6	34.7
Italy	95.4	116.0	104.4
Netherlands	58.3	59.5	45.4
New Zealand	65.1*	49.9	34.3
Sweden	43.9	82.0	62.8
UK	25.8	51.4	44.9
USA	41.8	49.1	34.4

Note: * Figures for 1992.

Source: OECD, 2001, *Central Government Debt, Statistical Yearbook, 1980–2000*, p. 21.

and the UK—each shows an overall movement 'upwards', while the two of the 'least NPM-ish' states—Germany and France—show high and seemingly persistent negative scores. However, the qualifications expressed in respect of Table 5.2 also apply here.

Table 5.4 records the OECD's estimates of gross public debt as a percentage of nominal GDP in 1990, 1995, and 2000. What is surprising here is that the debt percentage has *increased* in seven out of twelve cases. This is hardly in line with the rhetoric of most governments during this period. We can see that the debt ratio climbed particularly fast in Finland and Sweden, and substantially in France, Germany, and the UK. There was a significant reduction in the USA, New Zealand, the Netherlands, and Belgium. There seems little correlation here with any of the four strategies (maintaining, modernizing, marketizing, minimizing) that were identified at the end of Chapter 4.

In sum, it is hazardous to draw any conclusions at all about public management reform solely from macroeconomic statistics of government spending and borrowing. The connections are too indirect and uncertain, and the spending figures are affected by too many other factors, which cannot be attributed to management reform. What is more, the figures themselves are riddled with inconsistencies and variations, which make them only very cautiously and approximately useful for intercountry comparisons (see United Nations 2001, Part 2 for a succinct account of some of these technical difficulties).

If we now turn from public money to public sector staff, we can perhaps get a little closer to the direct effects of management reform.

In Table 5.5 we can see which countries have made the biggest reductions in their public service staffs (columns 2–4) and their public service wage bills (columns 5–7),

Table 5.5 Changes in government employment and compensation of government employees, 1985–99

Country	General government employment (% of total employment)[*]			Compensation of general government employees (% of nominal GDP)[†]		
	1985	1990	1999	1985	1990	1999
Australia	17.6	16.2	—	12.7	11.6	8.2[b]
Belgium[‡]	—	18.4[a]	17.9[e]	—	10.8	11.3[c]
Canada	20.7	20.5	17.5	12.7	12.8	11.4[b]
Finland	19.2	20.9	24.3[c]	14.1	14.6	13.4
France	20.5	20.4	21.3[b]	14.6	13.2	11.0
Germany	15.5	15.1	12.3	10.6	9.7	7.9[d]
Italy	—	—	15.2	—	11.4	6.9
Netherlands	15.1	12.9	12.2	11.1	9.8	7.8
New Zealand	16.2	16.5	—	11.8	11.8	9.9
Sweden	33.3	32.0	—	18.9	18.8	16.1[b]
UK	21.7	19.5	12.6	12.1	11.6	7.8[b]
US	14.8	14.9	14.6	10.6	10.5	7.8[b]

Notes: [a] 1995; [b] 1997; [c] 1998; [d] 2000; [e] 2001.

Source: [*] OECD, 2001, *Public Management Service*.
[†] OECD, 2000, Summary of the PSPE data analysis and future direction for HRM data collection, OECD, PUMA/HRM, p. 3.
[‡] National Bank of Belgium

relative to total employment in their economies and the sizes of their GDPs respectively. Some countries (especially the UK) have made large reductions in staff as a percentage of total employment in their economies, whereas some others have actually experienced increases in this ratio (Finland). On this measure the performance of the UK is quite startling probably mainly because of the large-scale privatization of previously national-ized industries—not really a 'management reform' as such. The overall trend—for six countries out of the eight where there are trend data—is down.

Equally startling are the huge differences in the 1985 'starting points', ranging from Sweden, where a third of all employees were in the public sector, to the Netherlands and the USA, where the corresponding percentage was 14–15 per cent.

5.4.2 **Activities and outputs**

We have so far discussed operational results mainly in terms of 'savings', where savings is a concept (in all its many forms) closely linked to financial *inputs*. Yet, as noted earlier, much of the management reform of the past two decades has been intended to produce a more *output*- and *outcome*-oriented approach to public administration. Increasingly, therefore, operational results have been conceived in terms of outputs (or sometimes activities believed to lead directly to outputs) or outcomes, or some mixture of the two. Popular slogans such as 'doing more with less', 'not working harder but working smarter', and 'more bang per buck' all draw attention to the output side of the equation, linking it with efforts (inputs). This is perfectly sensible—to maintain level outputs may not sound very exciting, but if this has been accomplished against the background of steadily falling inputs, then it represents a significant productivity gain. Equally, for an agency to increase its activities under conditions of a static budget can be counted as a useful 'result'.

Information about changes in *activities* tends to be much more copious than information about productivity. Public sector organizations frequently keep detailed records of what they *do* even if they have much less information about what effects it has, or even how much each activity costs. There is a wealth of reports and studies showing how management reform has led to an intensification of activity (e.g. Carter et al. 1992; Chancellor of the Duchy of Lancaster 1997; Management Advisory Board 1994; Swedish Ministry of Finance 1997).

Activity has not only been intensified, it has also been transferred to a variety of alternative providers (i.e. the state still pays for a service but contracts out its provision to external organizations). We know that large-scale contracting-out and resort to public–private partnerships (PPPs) have taken place in a number of our twelve countries such as Australia, the Netherlands, New Zealand, the UK, and the USA (see Osborne 2000; Peterson 2000; Rosenau 2000). A summary of the trends in one country (the Netherlands) can be seen in Table 5.6.

Of course, some countries started from a position of heavier involvement in direct service provision than others, and therefore had more scope for contracting-out. Sweden and the UK, for example, were relatively heavy direct providers, Germany much less so (where voluntary, nonprofit, and charitable associations already played an important role in the provision of local services).

In sum, one might say that, while there has been a good deal of intensification of activities, delegation of activities to lower levels of government, and contracting-out of activities, the fact remains that activity data or output and activity data *alone* is of

Table 5.6 Policy shifts: the case of the Netherlands

Policy field in the Netherlands	Position of central government
Education	Careful withdrawal
Health	Partial expansion
Social security	Careful withdrawal
Social housing	Partial withdrawal
Environment	Clear expansion
Land use planning	Status quo but less detail
Emancipation/Minorities	Modest development

Source: Sociaal Cultureel Planbureau (SCP), 1991, The Netherlands.

limited value or meaning. Unless it is coupled with quality data and cost data, it floats in a vacuum (Boyne et al. 2003, pp. 17–18). To know that agency X now deals with 25 per cent more applicants, or that function Y is now performed by a company under contract, or that hospital Z will be built through a PPP is all very interesting, but to be meaningful for performance this information needs to be married to other data about costs and the quality of service.

Finally, there is the issue of validation. This concerns all performance and cost data. The question is, 'How do we know that the data we see is accurate?' This is a source of real concern, not least since there have been several cases where, upon inspection, perform-ance data has turned out to be seriously inaccurate. This may be inadvertent (no one actually intends the data to be wrong) or there can be deliberate cheating (e.g. Hencke 1998 reports how a jobcentre provided misleading figures for its success rate; Smithers 2002 provides evidence about the extent to which British schoolteachers currently cheat in order to obtain better success rates for their students in public examinations). In the Netherlands some schools sought to improve their performance and hence their related income. The same happened in German employment offices. The more intensive the measurement regime, and the closer performance scores are linked to resource alloca-tions and other rewards and punishments, the higher are the incentives to manipulate the data. A number of NAOs have expressed concern over the quality of performance data, and those in Finland, Sweden, and the UK have begun major attempts at validation (for a UK example, see the NAO report on the Meteorological Office—National Audit Office 1995). As the UK NAO put it in its 1997 annual report: 'The National Audit Office are at the forefront of developing the methodology by which performance measures can be validated and we would like to see greater public reporting and auditing of perform-ance data' (National Audit Office 1997, p. 1).

5.4.3 **Productivity ratios**

A productivity increase (or efficiency gain) is usually defined as an improvement in the ratio of outputs to inputs (see Figure 5.1). As such it may come about via a variety of quite different circumstances:

- where resources (inputs) decrease and outputs increase;
- where resources remain the same and outputs increase;
- where resources *increase* but outputs increase by an even larger amount;
- where outputs remain static but resources decrease; and
- where outputs *decrease* but inputs decrease by an even larger amount.

Clearly it is important to know which of these situations one is dealing with. For example, in the 1970s and 1980s both British Steel and British Coal considerably increased their average productivity. This sounds fine until one realizes that both corporations were contracting fast—closing down plants and throwing many people out of work. Productivity rose as fewer and fewer steel plants/coal mines—the most modern and productive ones—were left.

Comparative data on public service productivity (as distinct from the productivity of industries such as coal and steel) is rare. The most detailed figures come from single countries, especially Sweden and Finland (the USA also had a long-running statistical series, but it focused on labour productivity only). The Swedish data is shown in Table 5.7. The overall pattern appears to be a *decline* in productivity during the 1960s and 1970s, followed by a levelling-off in the 1980s, and an increase in the early 1990s. More detailed analysis indicates a strong correlation between bouts of spending cutbacks ('savings') and productivity increases (see Table 5.8).

A closer examination of specific, cases suggests that public management reforms *can* help to increase productivity, especially when carried out in conjunction with budget cuts or increases in demand for a service, which were not paralleled by any significant increase in resource inputs, but that management reforms in the absence of downward pressure on inputs are not necessarily terribly effective in improving productivity (Murray 1998; Swedish Ministry of Finance 1997).

Generally it might be said that there appears to be a great deal of productivity data around, but close inspection reveals much of it to be of questionable validity and/or

Table 5.7 Productivity in the Swedish public sector by policy area, 1960–90 (% of annual change)

	1960–5	1965–70	1970–5	1975–80	1980–5	1985–90
Central government						
General administration	−0.2	−3.6	−5.1	4.3	0.3	1.3
Justice/Police	−4.7	−2.5	−6.2	2.8	−1.4	−1.3
Defence			−0.1	−0.6	−0.6	−5.0
Education	−2.1	−10.5	−2.1	0.7	2.5	2.0
Social insurance	−1.0	−2.6	−4.8	−0.2	2.8	1.2
Social welfare	9.0	−6.4	−4.7	−1.7	6.1	−2.3
Community planning	5.0	−0.6	6.6	1.9		
Culture, recreation, theatres					−8.8	0.6
Economic services	−2.2	1.6	3.5	1.1	3.7	0.0
CENTRAL TOTAL	−1.3	−2.2	−2.1	1.1	0.8	−1.2
CENTRAL TOTAL EXCLUDING DEFENCE	−1.3	−2.2	−3.0	1.9	1.2	0.1
Local government						
Education	−4.1	−6.1	0.5	−3.7	−0.5	−1.5
Health care	−3.8	−3.4	−1.4	−2.2	−0.2	−1.4
Social welfare			−2.0	−1.0	0.5	0.1
Community planning			0.0	−9.7		
Culture, recreation	−4.9	3.0	1.1	−1.8	−1.2	−3.7
LOCAL TOTAL	−4.1	−4.9	−0.8	−2.6	−0.2	−1.1
PUBLIC SECTOR TOTAL	−3.7	−4.3	−1.1	−1.6	0.0	−1.1

Source: Swedish Ministry of Finance, 1997, pp. 25–6.

Table 5.8 Productivity trends of Swedish central government, excluding defence, and rate of change in public consumption, 1960–90 (% of annual change)

	1960–70	1970–80	1980–90
Productivity	− 1.8	− 0.6	0.6
Public consumption	3.7	1.8	0.6

Source: Swedish Ministry of Finance, 1997, p. 36.

reliability. An interesting example of this may be found in Boyne's review of contracting-out in US local government. Although it was widely believed that such contracting-out would produce higher levels of productivity—and despite the fact that a number of previous studies pointed to precisely such an outcome—Boyne found numerous methodological and other weaknesses in the supporting evidence. He concluded that 'public choice hypotheses on contracting are not directly supported or undermined by the empirical evidence' (Boyne 1998, p. 482).

Even the privatization of state-owned industries—the area in which, perhaps, one might expect productivity changes to be most transparent—has provoked a considerable debate. Changing to private ownership does not necessarily seem to have made much difference by itself. One well-known economist claims that 'empirical studies of the impact of privatization upon economic performance do not give much support to the proposition that privatized companies perform significantly better than nationalized utilities' (Jackson 2001, pp. 13–14). Large productivity gains have been more closely associated with intensification of competition, whether the corporation concerned had been privatized or was still in public ownership (see, e.g. Parker 1999). In fact economists themselves differ rather sharply on this point (see Parker 2000). Some studies find significant productivity gains *before* privatization, others afterwards. Even where productivity does improve there is no guarantee that the benefits of this will go mainly to consumers—other stakeholders, such as investors or top management may reap most of the rewards (Parker 2000, chapter 16). So the idea that there is some automatic upward shift in productivity, which comes from merely shifting into private ownership, looks very unconvincing.

5.4.4 Outcomes and impacts ('effects')

As was seen in the previous subsection, there are often difficulties in *attributing* productivity growth to a single, definite cause, or proportionately to a limited number of causes. These difficulties grow still larger when the focus shifts to outcomes. New Zealand is a case in point. Certain outcomes—both positive and negative—were observable in the period of the great management reforms of 1986–92 (see Appendix B: New Zealand, country file). Unemployment reached new heights and then, in the early 1990s, dropped. Inflation also rose and fell. Crime and youth suicides rose. And so on. Were these the results of *management* reforms, or policy changes, or changes in external circumstances (the continuing dynamic of the global economy), or some mixture of all three? As it happens, New Zealand was a country that built up an unusually sophisticated system of performance measures for its public services. Yet most of these measures were of outputs, not outcomes.

Attribution problems of this kind are present in almost every country. In Australia, for example, the 1992 evaluation of management reforms concluded that 'the new framework has strong support and is seen, overall, to have increased the cost effectiveness of the APS [Australian Public Service] including outcomes for clients' (Task Force on Management Improvement 1992, p. 52). However, closer inspection shows that the causal link suggested here was far from proven, and, in another part of the very same report, a rather different emphasis is given:

[S]ince the reforms took place at a time of rapid social and economic change, there is no definitive way of separating the impact on cost, agency performance and clients (among other things) of these broader changes and the government changes which accompanied them. (Task Force on Management Improvement 1992, p. 8)

This is quite typical: the same could be said of the Thatcher management reforms in the UK, the great French decentralization measures of the early 1980s, the multiple Swedish efforts to decentralize, and most other large-scale public sector restructurings. The conventional wisdom is: 'Experience has shown that developing performance measurement systems that are outcome oriented is critical for using performance measures to improve programmes' (Mayne 1996, p. 8). In practice, however, the availability of such outcome measures, confidently linked to programme interventions, is the exception rather than the rule. At the level of broad programmes of management reform we know of not a single study from our twelve countries that convincingly links the actions taken with a set of positive and safely attributable final outcomes. This kind of rationality may occasionally be possible for very specific programmes in particular, well-understood contexts (e.g. an evaluation of traffic management measures—see Bureau of Transport and Communications Economics 1995), but it is seldom, if ever, possible for broad strategies of reform such as those referred to above. Recent academic attempts to develop a 'theory of effective government' show what a wide range of information would be required—much wider than anything that is normally available, even in these electronically lubricated, data-rich times (Rainey and Steinbauer 1999, p. 3).

Nevertheless, the search for a rationally defensible notion of 'results' continues—indeed, appears to have intensified. One technique in which much effort has recently been invested in several countries is that of 'benchmarking' (Department of Finance 1996; National Performance Review 1997b; Next Steps Team 1998). There are several different species (internal benchmarking, functional benchmarking, competitive benchmarking, generic benchmarking, etc.). Most of these rest on the fundamentally simple idea of finding an organization that is good at some process or activity, comparing one's own performance at that same process or activity with the organization's, and then analysing in some detail how the superior performance is achieved, in order to be able to learn from it (Pollitt et al. 1994). However, the technique has been developed into a generic format which, it is claimed, can be used to compare virtually any organization, public or private sector, with any other. In Europe this has resulted in the

Business Excellence model of the European Foundation for Quality Management (EFQM) (1996). A simplified version of the model, known as the Common Assessment Framework (CAF), has been developed by the European Commission and the European Institute for Public Administration, and is being used by certain public sector bodies in a number of member states (see Innovative Public Services Group 2002 for some idea of the bewildering array of quality models and specific applications being deployed in EU public sectors).

An example of this is that some of the UK's Next Steps agencies participated in a pilot exercise in which, using the EFQM model, their performances were compared with each other and with high-performing private sector companies. The conclusion was that

[i]n comparison with the private sector, agencies scored well in the areas of customer satisfaction, business results, policy and strategy and the management of financial resources... The agencies tended to score rather less well than the private sector in the areas of leadership, human resources, processes and employment protection (Chancellor of the Duchy of Lancaster 1997, p. 10)

Table 5.9 shows some of the scores recorded in this pilot. With the EFQM model 50 per cent of the marks are awarded for 'results', weighted as 20 per cent customer satisfaction, 15 per cent business results, 9 per cent people satisfaction (staff), and 6 per cent impact on society. Perhaps the main point about a table such as this is that in one way it looks so final, but, in another, the process of arriving at the figures in each cell is fraught with contestable assumptions and compromises. In particular, it should be noted that less than 50 per cent of the overall score is attributable to outcomes as defined in Figure 5.1. More than 50 per cent is placed on 'enablers', such as leadership or people management. In Australia,

Table 5.9 EFQM scores for benchmarked UK agencies

Unweighted criterion	UK quality award standard	Private sector average	Agency average	Maximum agency score	Minimum agency score
Leadership	63	60	35	48	19
Policy and strategy	68	40	36	57	15
People management	66	50	36	50	18
Resources	68	60	41	52	17
Processes	75	50	35	53	14
Customer satisfaction	60	30	38	61	14
People satisfaction	66	40	22	45	7
Impact on society	55	30	17	30	0
Business results	86	50	46	63	23

Source: Next Steps Team, 1998; Cowper and Samuels, 1997.

international benchmarking is considered a priority by most countries. An international focus is necessary to capture public service activities where the only possible benchmark comes from similar public services in other countries. (Trosa 1997, p. 6)

Like so many other techniques adopted by public sectors during the course of reform, benchmarking had its origins in US private sector practice (Camp 1989). Its suitability for public sector applications is debated between optimists (Next Steps Team 1998) and those who wish instead to stress either its limitations (Talbot 1997) or the existence of preconditions that render its usefulness questionable in significant parts of the public sector (Pollitt et al. 1994).

Another form of benchmarking is the comparison of different units delivering the same or similar services within a single national organization. There has been a great deal of this in the UK. A small extract from one such exercise is shown in Table 5.10.

Tables including this and other data are published annually, and cover all NHS establishments in the country. Initially they contained very few direct measures of clinical outcomes but, over time, some clinical indicators have been added to the set. Table 5.10 is a tiny extract from a huge amount of data (there are many indicators for many hospitals). It shows examples of indicators under each of the three main headings—key targets, clinical focus, and patient focus—and it shows them (for comparative purposes) for two hospitals. Thus, for example, a key target for both hospitals was to eliminate all the very long waits for treatment—those over fifteen months or more. Good Hope Hospital failed to do this, with twenty patients waiting longer than the target. Wirral Hospital had no patients waiting this long. The clinical measure we have selected—the number of deaths within thirty days of surgery per 100,000 patients—shows that Good Hope was close to (slightly above) the national average of 2.922, whereas Wirral was significantly better than the national average, that is, fewer of its patients died within thirty days of surgery. Two indicators are shown from the patient focus—the first concerning waiting times for treatment and the second concerning the dignity and respect with which patients felt they were treated. Interestingly, Good Hope scores better than Wirral—and better than the national average—on six-month inpatient waits. How can this be, one may ask, if the same hospital was significantly worse than average on its key target of reducing long waits (fifteen months plus)? This can easily be so. It could indicate that *on average* people have shorter waits at Good Hope, but that a few people there have very long waits, whereas this very long wait category has been eliminated by Wirral. Table 5.10 may give a taste of the complexity of the notion of 'results', and of the huge amount of data collection and standardization that can be involved, even at the level of individual hospitals, let alone whole governments.

None of this is new—the existence of a national set of NHS PIs enjoyed its twentieth birthday in 2003. Similar league tables are published for schools, showing test scores, and for some other local authority services. This kind of public 'scoreboarding' has probably gone further in the UK than in any other country (possibly because of the unusual degree of control central government has over locally provided services), but evidence about whether and how the public actually use the data is still thin.

Another way of conceiving 'results' or impacts is to use citizens as final arbiters, and ask them to say how good or bad particular services are. The patient survey scores in

Table 5.10 Service quality indicators—UK National Health Service

KEY TARGETS

Hospital	Indicator	Current figure	Performance level
Good Hope Hospital (West Midlands)	15-month inpatient waits	20 patients waiting over 15 months	Significantly underachieved
Wirral Hospital (NW England)	15-month inpatient waits	0 patients waiting over 15 months	Achieved

CLINICAL FOCUS

Hospital	Indicator	Current national figure	Current hospital figure	Performance level
Good Hope Hospital	Deaths within 30 days of surgery	2,922[a]	3,322	Average
Wirral Hospital	Deaths within 30 days of surgery	2,922[a]	1,967	Significantly above average

PATIENT FOCUS

Hospital	Indicator	Current national figure (%)	Current hospital figure (%)	Performance level
Good Hope Hospital	6-month inpatient waits	76.7[b]	83.4[b]	Above average
Wirral Hospital	6-month inpatient waits	76.7[b]	81.6[b]	Average
Good Hope Hospital	Inpatient survey: respect and dignity	82.3[c]	78.2[c]	Below average
Wirral Hospital	Inpatient survey: respect and dignity	82.3[c]	85.8[c]	Above average

Notes: [a] Number of deaths within 30 days per 100,000 patients.
[b] These are the percentages of patients who were admitted to hospital after a wait of less than 6 months.
[c] These are scores derived from questionnaire surveys of inpatients asking various questions concerning the privacy, dignity, etc. of their treatment.

Source: Selected and adapted from the official Department of Health website, *http://www.doh.gov.uk/performanceratings/2002* on 20/12/02.

Table 5.10 were one example of this. Another is shown in Table 5.11. In 1998 a mail survey of 2,900 Canadian citizens was commissioned, seeking comparative judgements between selected public and private sector services. It produced the scores shown in Table 5.11 (although with a response rate of only 9.5% in 1998).

   Contrary to some popular beliefs, this piece of research shows that the public have quite selective views of the quality of services from public and private sectors—some public services (in bold) scoring high and others low, with the private sector services scattered through the top two-thirds of the same range, but not anywhere falling as low

Table 5.11 Service quality ratings for public (in bold) and private providers, Canada, 1998–2000

Service	Service quality (0–100)		Service	Service quality (0–100)	
	1998	2000		1998	2000
Fire departments	**78**	**77**	**Public libraries**	**75**	**75**
Supermarkets	74	73	Private mail carriers	68	69
Provincial electric utilities	63	64	**Provincial parks, campgrounds**	**64**	**64**
Police	**63**	**63**	Telephone companies	63	63
Private sector services in general	60	63	Department stores	—	62
Passport office	**60**	**61**	**Canada Post**	**55**	**60**
Insurance agencies	55	59	Taxis	57	58
Municipal government services	**53**	**57**	**Public transit**	**55**	**55**
CCRA	**50**	**54**	Cable-television companies	—	54
Banks	51	52	**Federal government services in general**	**47**	**51**
Provincial government services	**47**	**50**	**Public education system**	**47**	**49**
Hospitals	**46**	**49**	**Road maintenance**	**35**	**36**

Source: Erin Research Inc., 2000, *Citizens First*, Canadian Centre for Management Development p. 45.

as the very poor score accorded to road maintenance. In principle, such surveys could be undertaken before and after major reforms (this was not the design of the Canadian survey) and would provide one way of registering any shift in public satisfaction levels. In practice, such before-and-after studies are not terribly common, although there are a few (e.g. concerning passenger satisfaction with rail journeys before and after improvements, where changes have definitely translated into higher scores). We will return to this particular survey in Chapter 6, where we consider citizens' attitudes to public services in more depth.

5.5 Results as process improvements

5.5.1 Process measures: an overview

In the first chapter a working definition of management reform was adopted, which focused on changes in the structures and processes of public sector organizations made with the aim of getting them to perform better. This suggested that improving *processes* was frequently an important step towards achieving improved outputs and outcomes. It is also the case that process improvements may have a value of their own in a democratic state, where *how* things are done may be as important as what the operational results are (engaging values such as 'due process', fairness, transparency, and participation). For these reasons, therefore, changes in processes merit attention.

Changes in process may also signal a shift in administrative cultures—indeed they are often made with a definite consciousness of their symbolic impact. A status report on the US NPR lists ten pieces of evidence that government is starting to work better:

- over 90% of National Performance Review recommendations are underway;
- the President has signed 22 directives, as well as performance agreements with seven agency heads;
- over a hundred agencies are publishing customer service standards;
- nine agencies have started major streamlining initiatives;
- agencies are forming labour-management partnerships with their unions;
- agencies are slashing red tape;
- the government is buying fewer 'designer' products and doing more common-sense commercial buying;
- throughout the federal government 135 're-invention laboratories' are fostering innovation;
- the government is shifting billions of dollars in benefits to electronic payments; and
- the federal government is changing the way it interacts with state and local governments. (National Performance Review 1994, p. 5)

Clearly, the above items are *process* improvements, which are supposed to lead to improved final outcomes in due course.

Five years later another assessment of the NPR was made, this time by an independent academic. Thompson (2000) repays careful reading because his paper shows just how difficult it can be to evaluate a major public management reform, and how some evidence can point one way while other 'facts' point quite elsewhere. Table 5.12 gives Thompson's own assessment, drawing both on official surveys of the workforce and on his own investigations. You will see that the 'datum' column displays a mixture of evidence about attitudes, job numbers, financial estimates, and specific actions—some inputs, some information about activities, and some outputs, but no direct evidence about outcomes.

As the above example indicate, the main problem with process improvements is that the link with final outcomes is less than certain. If the administrative culture remains hostile to the spirit of the reform, then the new process may be observed in a minimalist and ritual way, but no real change may follow. For example, Rouban (1995, pp. 28–9) suggests that German and French civil servants may sometimes resist changes in the professional culture if they seem likely to threaten their social values and/or personal status.

Table 5.12 A summary assessment of the US National Performance Review

Objective	Specifics	Assessment
Downsizing	Reduce federal civilian employment by 272,900	By August 1998 this employment group had been reduced by 317,000 FTEs
Reduce administrative costs	Save $108 bn. over the 5 years to 1999	By September 1997 the NPR reported $82.2 bn. saved and another $30 bn. pending
Reform administrative systems	Reform the civil service, procurement and budgetary systems	The procurement system was significantly reformed, but not the budgetary or personnel reforms
Decentralize authority within agencies	Give front-line managers more authority on personnel, procurement, and budgets	A 1998 survey showed that 49% of supervisory/management employees felt they had been given more flexibility in the previous 2 years, but only 20% of this group said they had more flexibility in personnel matters
Empower front-line workers	Create partnerships/lessen adversarialism in labour relations	A 1997 survey showed 52% of management and labour representatives believed that labour relations had improved 'some' or 'much'
Cultural change	Change from 'complacency and entitlement toward initiative and empowerment'	A 1996 survey showed 20% agreement, but 47% disagreement with the statement 'The NPR has had a positive impact on bringing change to government'; two other (1998) surveys showed 37% and 35% agreement with the statement 'My organization has made the goals of the NPR a priority'
Improve quality of service	Tailor service to the needs and wants of the public	In a survey 21% agreed and 41% disagreed with the statement 'The NPR has had a positive impact on improving customer service to the public'
Improve efficiency of practices	Re-engineer basic work processes to achieve higher productivity at lower cost	61% responding to a survey agreed that, as a consequence of cuts, downsizing, or reinvention, the amount of work they had to do had increased; 49% also agreed that the productivity of their work unit had improved

Source: A simplified adaptation of Thompson, 2000, table 2. For full referencing of surveys, see original.

A further difficulty in interpreting lists of process changes—such as that quoted above from the 1994 NPR review of its own progress—is that they may be the products of an acute form of selection bias. That is, good examples are chosen from the best-performing parts of the public sector, and both side effects and the other parts of the public sector (which may even be getting *worse*) are ignored.

The next two subsections will be given over to an analysis of two of the most common and popular types of process improvement.

5.5.2 **Increasing client orientation**

The assumption here is that, by paying more attention to clients, public service organizations will learn to deliver better results, and that clients will notice the change and experience increased satisfaction.

The notion of putting clients, customers, users, patients, passengers (or whatever) first has been given tremendous rhetorical emphasis in many jurisdictions and in many countries. The NPR in the USA, the *Citizen's Charter* in the UK, the 1994 French programme *Année de l'accueil dans les services publiques*, the Belgian, Italian, Portuguese and Finnish service charters, and more—all claim to increase client orientation. Furthermore, modern quality improvement techniques such as TQM are founded on the centrality of customer requirements, and have been introduced in parts of the Australian, Belgian, Canadian, Dutch, Finnish, French, New Zealand, Swedish, UK, and US public sectors, as well as being promoted by some parts of the European Commission. In 1987 the OECD jumped on a rhetorical bandwagon that was then gathering speed and posed a shrewd question: 'If the public service already exists to serve the public, then why are so many OECD governments embarking on campaigns to make it happen?' (OECD 1987, p. 9).

However, achieving a client orientation is not straightforward. While the UK *Citizen's Charter*, which was strongly driven from the centre of government, made some impact, its Italian equivalent quickly faded out (Schiavo 2000). Or consider the case of the reforms to the APS. A 1992 survey of Australian citizens indicated that 73 per cent of those who had prior contact with a given agency thought its quality of service remained the same, and 26 per cent thought it changed (about three-quarters of whom thought it changed for the better). At the same time members of the Australian SES were asked whether *they* thought that the reforms led to an increased client focus, and 77 per cent thought it had. Only 51 per cent of lower-grade staff were of the same view. This—and other evidence within the same report—shows a complicated picture in which perceptions of client emphasis and of quality improvements depend to some extent on where the respondent sits. The senior staff appear to be more optimistic than junior staff, while only a minority of citizens notice much difference. Compare this with the situation shown in Table 5.12 where 41 per cent of respondents to a survey of US federal officials thought that the NPR did *not* improve customer service, whereas only 21 per cent thought it did.

Elsewhere we have suggested that the relevant variables are quite complex (Pollitt and Bouckaert 1995). Much depends on the expectations of the various parties concerned, and satisfaction levels may go up and down as much because *expectations* vary when the underlying 'producer quality' of the service changes. Indeed, one strategy for a cynical government that is determined to raise satisfaction scores might be to attempt to lower public expectations (which may almost have been the case with some governments in certain instances—e.g. for state pensions). Thus the measurement of perceived quality in public services is by no means just a technical issue. It has political and psychological elements, and these make 'satisfaction' a moving target, something that may jump to a new position as soon as or even before it is achieved.

5.5.3 Increasing performance orientation

A second common theme within the conception of results as improvements in process is that an increasing importance on processes that emphasize *performance* is a good thing. A performance orientation is frequently contrasted with a 'traditional' focus on inputs and procedural correctness (compliance). It is seen as a good in itself.

At different times and in different sectors every country in our set has praised the (supposedly) new stress on 'performance', which has sometimes been seen as virtually synonymous with 'getting results' (see Appendix B: country files). Similarly, the white paper on the reform of the European Commission contained a section headed 'Performance-oriented working methods' (European Commission 2000, Section III.3).

In addition to this general advocacy of a performance orientation, a number of countries have proposed a specific link between performance measurement and budgeting. It is widely assumed that the integration of budgeting processes with performance measurement will be 'a good thing'. The problem for this general approach is to explain why attempts to make this kind of integration have seemingly so often failed to take root in the past. It may be that economic logic and political logic do not lead to the same conclusions, and that, from a political perspective, application of strict economic rationality is not the final word (Pollitt 2001). Perhaps certain kinds of political deal can only be arrived at within contexts where objectives are left as somewhat ambiguous, and results information is inconclusive. In other words, it may be that better information about the results to be expected from particular allocations of resources does not actually help very much when politicians come to the point of having to make those allocation decisions. Mayne concluded a survey of attempts to use performance information in the budgetary process as follows:

In general performance measures are not being used to make decisions about the level of resources that a program or organisation will receive. This is true even for those who have defined a specific objective to do so... Resource allocation decisions continue to be driven, for the most part, by traditional budget practices... Performance information *supports* internal management decisions on setting priorities, adjusting operations and resource levels, etc. (Mayne 1996, pp. 13–14; see also OECD 2002*b*)

In the field of HRM the introduction of 'performance logic' is even more controversial. In some jurisdictions revisions to regulations have made it easier to dismiss or discipline individuals who persistently fall below the required performance. Presumably this has been beneficial in enabling public organizations to get rid of a few cases of really serious incompetence or laziness. Performance-related pay systems have been applied to a far larger number of staff, but have not always been a huge success (Gaertner and Gaertner 1985; OECD 1993*b*; Perry and Pearce 1985). The idea that current performance will become the only—or at least the dominant—criterion for tenure and advancement, carrying greater weight than seniority, loyalty, qualifications, and other factors, is far from universally popular. Support for this tendency seems to come more from politicians and senior civil servants (those who have already 'made it') than from lower ranks

(Bourgault et al. 1993). Part of the problem is that merit pay systems can be divisive—it is very common for civil servants to feel that such arrangements are unfair, too crude to register real differences in performance, or even open to a degree of manipulation. Another part is that the actual 'bonus' that is to be distributed frequently turns out to be either quite small per capita (and therefore likely to have little effect on motivation) or is larger but confined to a few outstanding individuals (in which case the majority feel disappointed that they have not received anything). A system that distributed sizeable bonuses to a substantial proportion of the total workforce would actually be rather expensive, if not downright unaffordable.

The development of strategic management can also be portrayed as a way of increasing the performance orientation of an organization. One or other variety of strategic approach has been much discussed and—to varying degrees—implemented in, *inter alia*, Australia, Canada, Finland, New Zealand, and the UK. The Kinnock/Prodi reforms to the European Commission have also laid considerable emphasis on articulating an 'annual policy strategy', which 'will be the Commission's main instrument for deciding on positive and—equally important—negative priorities' (European Commission 2000, Section III.1). One is tempted to add that, however important they may be in theory, negative priorities subsequently received remarkably little public discussion—political leaders seldom see much advantage in discussing what they have decided not to do.

The basic link in all this is that a strategic approach will permit the organization to focus more clearly and consistently on its high-priority goals, which will, in turn, lead to a more intensive pursuit of the results that are deemed to be of the greatest importance. New Zealand provides perhaps the best-known example. A system was developed that included an annual consideration of SRAs (broad, often cross-portfolio priorities set by the Cabinet) and their linkage to a more detailed set of KRAs (critical medium-term objectives, which are written into the contracts of the chief executives who head departments). The articulation of this system was not without its problems, but nevertheless led to

improved information flows, more substantial consultation with commercial interests and non-profit organisations, greater clarity about the Government's vision and priorities and a surprising synergy among agencies with a history of sometimes fractious relationships. (Matheson et al. 1997, p. 88; see also Boston et al. 1996, pp. 282–3, 359)

In Australia, also, reforms meant that 'ministers are now in a better position to set the strategic directions for their portfolios and to direct the efforts of their departments' (Management Advisory Board 1993*b*, pp. 9–10). In Finland, the Lipponen coalition government (1995–9) developed a Strategy Portfolio which contains the 'key results or strategic results areas of the government', and serves as one of the main platforms for overall steering and priority-making (*High Quality Services, Good Governance, and a Responsible Civic Society* 1998*a*, pp. 19–22). In the UK the incoming Labour government of 1997 laid great emphasis on carrying out a Comprehensive Spending Review, which formed the basis for a 'new, strategic approach to public spending' (Chancellor of the Exchequer 1998, Prime Minister's foreword). In the USA the GPRA was portrayed by some as an exercise in strategic planning, although by the end of the Clinton administration independent opinion was sceptical about the extent of change in government decision-making (General Accounting Office 2001; Radin 2000).

The fundamental difficulties in assessing most, if not all, of these strategic initiatives are those of determining how far (if at all) the quality of top-level decision-making is improved, and whether the new decision procedures ultimately lead to more efficiently produced outputs and/or substantively better outcomes. There is some testimony from insiders to indicate that the quality of decisions does benefit from more strategic approaches, but it is hard to be sure. Much is likely to depend on how receptive the broader civil service culture is to exercises of this kind. If the products of strategic exercises are placed in the public domain, then one benefit is that public accountability is improved to the extent that the relevant documents give reasonably clear and concrete descriptions of political priorities and intentions (e.g. Chancellor of the Exchequer 1998). It would be prudent, however, to remember Brunsson's point that political organizations frequently devote great energy to talk and decision procedures without these necessarily having much effect on external actions—or even being intended to have such an effect (Brunsson 1989).

5.6 Results as system improvement

5.6.1 The concept of systems improvement

In the previous section we briefly discussed strategic management initiatives as one type of process improvement. There is a sense in which the adoption of a more strategic approach shades upwards into the more general category of *systems improvements* (Bouckaert 2003*b*). The achievement of such improvements may be counted as a kind of 'result', in so far as a systems improvement leaves the entire governmental system more flexible, more quickly responding, with a higher capacity to learn and adapt, and so on. Thus (for example) the transformation of a rigid bureaucratic hierarchy into a flexible, 'flat', multidisciplinary organization could be said to have increased the capacity of that organization to cope with new developments in its environment. These could well include the kinds of global economic developments and new sociodemographic phenomena mentioned in Chapter 2 and documented in Appendix A.

A systems improvement is not a small thing, not a particular individual reform such as the introduction of PIs for the police force. Rather, it is something broad, which is intended to influence the whole structure or character of government. The Clinton/Gore NPR was claimed to be of this type, as was the Finnish government's 1998 resolution *High Quality Services, Good Governance, and a Responsible Civic Society* (1998*a*, 1998*b*). Such improvements are therefore virtually bound to have a number of different aspects and elements. For the sake of convenience they will here be divided into just two: structural improvements and cultural change.

5.6.2 **Structural change in systems**

Major reorganizations alter the architectures of politico-administrative systems, and thus the pattern of interactions within them and across their boundaries. In the UK, between 1988 and 1998, more than 70 per cent of the nonindustrial civil servants found themselves working for a new type of organization—the Next Steps executive agency. In New Zealand almost every public sector body underwent substantial restructuring in the decade following 1984. In Finland, during the early and mid 1990s, the whole range of central agencies was streamlined and remodelled, producing a much less heavy regulatory layer between the central ministries and the municipalities. In Italy the political crisis of the early 1990s led to a change in the electoral system, a fragmentation of the previous pattern of political parties, an extensive decentralization of state functions, and much else besides (see Appendix B: Italy, country file). These are just some of the many examples of efforts at widescale restructuring.

It is not unusual for politicians and senior civil servants to claim that such changes have significantly improved the system of government and, indeed, that is one of their central purposes. At the time of writing there is much international talk of 'capacity building'. To assess these claims is, however, difficult. To begin with, organization structures are intermediate variables, and there is no tried-and-tested, widely accepted model showing exactly what structural change will lead to what shift in outputs or final outcomes. On the contrary, it appears that the effects of particular structure or procedure are very frequently contingent upon contextual factors (Pollitt 2003a). Neither is there any easy way of measuring 'capacity', so claims here are hard to assess.

Furthermore, one may observe that the reformed structures themselves are frequently far from stable. Countries like New Zealand and the UK can be seen to have subjected some sectors to two or three waves of structural reform since 1980, and there is every sign that this process will continue. In France ministerial departments are frequently reshuffled, but few observers believe that this process fundamentally alters the nature of the system (Rouban 1997). A longer-term view reveals shifting fashions for different types of structure—big departments, small departments, regional-level organizations, local-level organizations, and so on (e.g. Pollitt 1984). All of which raises a doubt as to whether the process of securing systems improvements via structural change is a particularly stable or certain one. Detailed studies tend to reveal a complicated pattern of impacts, some of which could be counted as improvements (always depending on one's values) and some of which would probably be regarded by many observers as problematic (e.g. Boston et al. 1996; Halligan and Power 1992; Pollitt et al. 1998; Thompson 2000).

5.6.3 **Cultural change in systems**

The difficulties of evaluating cultural change are as great as, if not greater than, those of assessing widescope structural change. While there can be little doubt that organizational cultures can have a significant influence on organizational performance, the tasks of actually *measuring* that influence and knowing how to go about reshaping cultures in some desired direction are fraught with pitfalls and problems (Hofstede 2001 contains an extended discussion of such methodological problems).

In fact the empirical basis for conclusions about cultural change at the systems level is slender. The number of studies where researchers have been able to measure broad shifts in attitudes and beliefs over time (essential to a full identification of cultural shifts) is small indeed—even the Hofstede book is heavily reliant on one particular and unusual survey undertaken more than thirty years ago. Most of the limited number of works that do exist measure the results at a single point in time and then hypothesize what they imply for cultural change (Rouban 1995; Talbot 1994). Nevertheless, such fragments as we have help to cast some light on the claims that management reform has produced cultural change. A survey of 3,800 UK public service managers, conducted at the end of 1993, indicated that 'managers' willingness to accept and implement change was remarkably high; it was clear that managers' attitudes to change are broadly in line with the actual changes taking place'. Yet at the same time 'over 40% of managers feel inadequately supported for dealing with political influences' and 'almost a third of all respondents expect to leave the public sector within the next five years' (Talbot 1994, pp. 5–6). The message here—among managers, though not necessarily other categories of staff—seemed to be that a real change in attitudes was underway, but that some aspects of this change were negative. A survey of French civil servants, carried out in 1989, drew an interesting distinction between professional values and broader social values. It then concluded that:

[P]rofessional values depend closely on the nature of the job and the strategic position within ministerial circles. They can therefore evolve and can be improved with training. However, the transformation of these values cannot be so great as to modify the global conception that civil servants have of the relationship between public administration and political spheres, or the ranking of social values which determine their professional success. One cannot change civil servants' social values through administrative reform. Such a change requires extra-professional resources... (Rouban 1995, p. 51)

This line of interpretation may help to explain why, in a number of jurisdictions, it has seemed possible to change, for example, civil servants' attitudes towards the 'customer', but much less so other attitudes, such as a distrust of politicians or a scepticism towards the benefits of MTMs within the public service. Rouban went on to argue that the perceived legitimacy of administrative reforms varied up and down the hierarchy, usually being highest with senior civil servants, but only so long as they could continue to control the process of change itself. This finding of a variable adhesion to reforms, correlated with rank and position, has been replicated in other countries also. A large survey of staff carried out in conjunction with an Australian 1992 evaluation of the management reforms of the previous decade found evidence that public servants at different levels exhibited significantly different degrees of belief in the usefulness and impact of the reforms (Task Force on Management Improvement 1992). The rather high levels of scepticism shown by US federal staff towards the NPR and GPRA reforms of the 1990s have already been referred to (Table 5.12 and General Accounting Office 2001).

5.6.4 **Trust the system?**

One of the hoped-for outcomes of systems change is a reversal of falling levels of citizen trust in government. This is clearly stated in, for example, the US 1995 budget documents, where one of the headings, referring to the NPR, was 'Rebuilding public trust through results and service' (Executive Office of the President of the United States 1995, p. 158). To put it bluntly, do all the many reforms described elsewhere in this book persuade public to trust their governments more and to believe that public sector organizations are accessible, reliable, efficient, and sympathetic to their varied needs?

Once again, no clear and simple answer can be given. Some of the evidence on citizens' attitudes to management reforms is reviewed in the following chapter, but we can already say here that there is, as yet, no indication of a widespread national or international shift of public opinion in favour of governments that make public sector reform a central part of their programmes. As an example, we may examine the findings of a 'European Values Survey', in so far as these concern public confidence in institutions (see Listhaug and Wiberg 1995, pp. 304–5).

Table 5.13 shows shifts in public confidence towards specific institutions between 1981 and 2000—a period that saw extensive public management reforms in most of the European states covered in this book. If one were naive enough to think that confidence in the civil service was determined by the volume of reform, one might expect to see the highest score for the civil service entered against the UK, with rises everywhere, but dwindling towards low-reform countries such as Belgium or Germany. Unsurprisingly, the picture is nothing like this. Germany actually shows the largest *rise*, and the majority, including the UK, show a distinct *fall* in confidence in the civil service. It is also clear that different countries *start* from somewhat different positions: in 1981 the civil service commanded the confidence of 52 per cent of respondents in France but only 32 per cent in Germany.

Of course, much depends on exactly what questions are posed. Asking citizens about the civil service is not the same as asking them about their local fire service, or about whether they have noticed any improvement in the refuse collection service (again, we will have more to say about this in Chapter 6). If, instead of asking about the civil service, the question is changed to one about the degree of trust citizens have in national governments, we get the picture (for EU states) shown in Table 5.14.

Here again we see considerable variation, and of a type that cannot be satisfactorily explained by correlations with management reforms. Trust runs very low in the UK (33%) and Italy (also 33%)—both states where there has been endless and much-publicized reform during the 1990s. In Finland (54%) and the Netherlands (61%), however, a much gentler style and pace of reform is accompanied by much higher levels of trust. Even Belgium, where there was very little management reform at national level during the 1990s, scores well above Italy and the UK.

Roughly similar survey questions have been put to the American public. Figure 5.2 shows the findings since 1958—a history of considerable fluctuation, with no very strong pattern and certainly not one related to management reform.

Table 5.13 Trust in institutions, 1981–2000 (%)

	Belgium			Finland		France			Germany			Italy			Netherlands			Sweden			UK		
	1981	1990	2000	1981	2000	1981	1990	2000	1981	1990	2000	1981	1990	2000	1981	1990	2000	1981	1990	2000	1981	1990	2000
Church	62.9	49	42.9	49	58.1	53.2	50	45.7	43.0	40	39.5	57.0	63	67.1	38.8	32	29.6	39	38	45.4	46.0	43	34.4
Army	42.7	33	39.8	71	84.3	53.9	56	63.0	51.3	40	55.1	54.3	48	51.6	41.9	32	39.1	61	49	44.3	80.9	81	83.6
Education	79.1	80	77.9	83	88.8	56.6	66	68.4	43.3	54	72.6	53.9	49	53.2	73.0	65	73.1	62	70	67.8	59.3	47	66.3
Press/Media	35.5	20	38.3	34	36.3	33.5	38	35.6	30.3	34	36.0	31.6	39	35.3	28.2	36	55.4	27	33	45.8	28.3	14	15.8
Labour unions	33.1	51	37.8	56	53.5	40.3	32	34.7	38.8	36	37.8	28.8	34	28.7	39.6	53	58.6	49	40	42.5	25.5	26	28.1
Police	63.5	85	55.4	88	90.1	63.6	67	66.2	68.8	70	73.6	64.5	67	67.2	72.3	73	63.6	80	74	75.6	85.4	77	69.6
Parliament	38.2	53	39.1	65	43.7	54.8	48	40.6	51.4	51	35.7	30.0	32	34.1	44.5	54	55.3	47	47	51.1	31.4	46	35.5
Civil service	46.3	46	46.1	53	40.9	52.1	49	45.9	32.3	39	38.7	26.8	27	33.2	44.5	46	37.5	46	44	48.8	47.0	44	45.9
Social security	—	—	69.4	—	70.6	—	—	66.9	—	—	44.3	—	—	34.1	—	—	64.4	—	—	50.9	—	—	36.4
Health care	—	—	82.6	—	84.4	—	—	77.4	—	—	53.0	—	—	36.7	—	—	75.1	—	—	76.3	—	—	58.7
Legal system	57.8	67	36.4	84	65.8	56.4	58	45.8	42.4	65	61.5	66.5	32	31.5	65.1	63	48.2	73	56	61.0	65.8	54	49.1
Business enterprise	43.5	40	—	45	42.6	48.7	67	47.6	33.9	38	36.2	32.4	62	49.6	35.0	49	—	42	53	—	50.5	48	40.1

Source: Figures based on:
1. NIWI, 1981. *European Values Study*, Set P0830, Version 1.0, Steinmetz Archive Documentation.
2. Listhaug, Wiberg, 1995. pp. 298–322.
3. Halman, 2001. *The European Values Study: A Third Wave*, Source Book of the 1999–2000, European Values Study Surveys, Tilburg WORC, Tilburg University.

Table 5.14 Trust in national governments, 2002 (%)

	Belgium	EU (15)	Finland	France	Germany	Italy	Netherlands	Sweden	UK
Tend to trust	43	39	54	30	37	33	61	54	33
	(−8)	(−9)	(−6)	(−13)	(−10)	(−8)	(−9)	(−2)	(−10)
Tend not to trust	46	51	38	63	51	53	31	40	56
	(ⅰ4)	(+7)	(+4)	(+13)	(+8)	(+6)	(+9)	(+1)	(+7)
Don't know	11	10	7	8	12	14	8	6	10
	(+4)	(+1)	(+1)	(+1)	(+2)	(+2)	(+0)	(0)	(+1)

Note: (− or + *n*) signifies the difference with the percentage of 2001.

Source: European Commission, 2002, *Eurobarometer 57, First Results*.

Interpretation of broad survey data such as this is extremely difficult. As already indicated, macrolevel perceptions are not necessarily reflected at microlevels (e.g. it is very common for American citizens to have a low opinion of Congress but quite a high opinion of their local Congressmen). The more general the question (and the questions in Table 5.14 and Figure 5.2 are very general indeed), the harder it is to be confident in attributing the 'result' to any specific influence or influences. It is extremely rare to be able to attribute a shift in general views to a specific set of changes in the politico-administrative system (indeed, most citizens have very little knowledge of the existence of administrative reform programmes).

Ultimately, therefore, the main difficulties in assessing systems improvements are twofold. First, there is a need to separate the substance from the rhetoric, a distinction that is often far from straightforward. Many government documents and speeches, in several countries, have claimed a 'system transformation' of one kind or another, only for closer empirical study to show that there has actually been high continuity between the old and the new (e.g. Ingraham 1997 on the US NPR; Pollitt et al. 1998 on the British

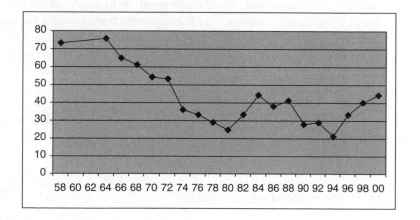

Figure 5.2 Trust in government, USA (1958–2000).

Source: National Election Studies (http://www.umich.edu/~nes/).

Conservative government's decentralization reforms of the late 1980s and early 1990s; more generally see Pollitt 2002). These commonplace divergences between words and deeds are discussed further in Chapters 7 and 8.

Second, there is an even more stubborn difficulty in assessing the claim that a system has acquired greater flexibility, capacity, and so on. How are these claims to be tested? Presumably the counterfactual is the way that the old (previous) system would have tackled the new circumstances and pressures. But that is a very difficult criterion to apply: who can say exactly how the old system would have performed? Nor does it help that the most prominent voices saying that the new system is better/worse are frequently insiders with strong and obvious interests in conveying a picture of either progress or decline.

All in all, the category of systems improvement, while appealing in theory, is very hard to pin down in empirical practice (Van de Walle and Bouckaert 2003b). The dangers of hindsight are considerable, and the risks of perceptions being distorted by a few salient incidents or episodes are high. There is also a temptation to see change in an overcoherent way, that is, to presume that all the changes one sees were intentional, rather than forced or accidental, and, further, to assume that they were related to each other within some overall 'systems approach' (this common bias is challenged at length in the intriguing book, *The Reforming Organization*, Brunsson and Olsen 1993). Such issues of coherence and intentionality are discussed further in the final chapter. It is also misleading to assume that there are singular entities called 'the public service culture', or 'public opinion about reform'. As indicated above, such research as has been carried out conveys a more fragmented and variegated picture. Organizational cultures seem to depend to some significant extent on role and rank, and they shift more quickly along some dimensions than others, with some basic elements of social values which may be beyond the power of reformers to change. As Hofstede (2001) indicates, the basic patterns of national cultures probably change only very slowly—over generations rather than between elections. Public opinion is also a complex issue, with no easy or straightforward link between the success of reforms and the perceived legitimacy of the politico-administrative system.

The most, perhaps, that one can say is that the politico-administrative system in some countries appears to have undergone deeper change than in others. As is clear from Chapters 3 and 4, high-change countries (in management terms) would include New Zealand and the UK, and low-change countries would include Belgium and Germany (although both underwent considerable change at subnational levels). The other countries considered in this book are stretched out somewhere in between. Whether the many innovations in the high-change countries are all to be considered as *improvements*, however, is another question altogether. Some commentators, for example, clearly believe that sticking with a strong existing system is better than playing around with flawed and ephemeral fashions in management reform (Derlien 1998).

5.7 Results as the realization of a vision

Sometimes management reforms are ad hoc and functional. Sometimes they are emergency measures, designed to stave off a crisis, real or anticipated. But there are also occasions when management reforms are carried through with the aim of realizing some larger vision of how things should be in some imagined future world. These imagined futures may be framed in very general terms, or in more specific ways, but they serve a useful function as rallying points and guidance for the faithful and as siren calls to the as-yet agnostic. In terms of the trajectories discussed in Chapter 4 they are highly normative omegas, which may or may not be accompanied by plans for how to get from here to there.

There was certainly something of this visionary element to Thatcher's reforms, encapsulated in the phrase from her 1979 election manifesto, 'Rolling back the state'. There was a similarly vivid (and almost certainly more coherent) vision informing the New Zealand reforms of 1984–94 (Boston et al. 1996, pp. 3–6). No one could accuse Vice-President Gore of being without a vision for the NPR—many publications elaborate on the theme of reinventing government so that it 'works better and costs less'.

In other countries the vision was perhaps less strongly enunciated, less combative towards the *status quo ante*, but there were nonetheless elements of idealism and futuristic imagery. The Finnish government recommitted itself to a combination of democracy and egalitarianism (*High Quality Services, Good Governance, and a Responsible Civic Society* 1998a). The new 1994 'purple coalition' in the Netherlands committed itself to the 'primacy of politics', and the reining-in of unaccountable quangos (Roberts 1997). In Germany one might say that there was at first a conscious rejection of 'fashions and fads' in favour of the virtues of the existing system (Derlien 1998), and then, at the end of the long chancellorship of Helmut Kohl, a brief flirtation with the vision of a 'lean state'. In Belgium, the new 'purple–green' coalition launched a modernization process called 'Copernicus', referring to a fundamental change based on a vision.

Of course, academics adore ideal models and utopian visions. They (we) take an intense interest at the merest whiff of a new 'paradigm', and tend to react by polishing, systematizing, and elaborating the fragmentary visions proclaimed by political leaders, so as to be able to analyse them—and subsequently often to damn or praise them. Politicians, on the other hand, usually have the street wisdom to cast their references to the desired future in rather more vague, malleable, and ambiguous terms. The purposes and skills of the two groups are different. Since we are academics rather than politicians it will come as no surprise when we say that the 'teasing-out' of visions can be a useful and illuminating exercise. This is not the place to do justice to all the various schemata that have been offered (though we have already introduced the NPM and the NWS), but it may be helpful to pause long enough to look at one example.

Peters (1996b) suggests that four main visions may be identified within the national and international rhetoric of public management reform:

- *The market model*, which holds out the prospect of extensive privatization and therefore of a much smaller public sector—and one that will itself be infused with MTMs. Citizens become consumers and taxpayers, and the machinery of government shrinks to a policy-making, lightly regulatory, and contract-letting core. This corresponds to the 'NPM group'—those countries that we identified as having a marketizing trajectory in the concluding section of Chapter 4.

• *The participatory state*, which lays great emphasis on the empowerment and partici-pation of citizens in the running of 'their' administration. Like the market model, it envisages radical decentralization and a sharp move away from bureaucratic hierarchies. Unlike the market model it is suspicious of the divisive and inegalitarian features of competitive markets and confident of citizens' ability and willingness to play a more creative part in their own governance. We would see this model as corresponding with the 'northern Europeans'—the NWS modernizers of Finland, Sweden, and the Netherlands.

• *Flexible government*, which is opposed to the rigidities and conservatism attributed to permanent organizational structures and individuals with permanent, highly secure careers. The remedy is a 'temporary state', with shifting squadrons of adaptable and readaptable organizations, each purpose-built to address the most salient issues in the current but rapidly changing environment. Advanced information technology is frequently seen as a major force in this new state of affairs, which can be represented as less 'doctrinaire' or 'ideological' than either the market model or the vision of participa-tory government (Bellamy and Taylor 1998; Hudson 1998). The temporary state is likely to be an extensively contract-based phenomenon. There is no one group of countries that we would suggest as exemplars of this particular vision. Rather it appears as a subsidiary element in many reform programmes, but probably more so in the NPM group of countries than the NWS group (and least so among the 'central Europeans'—Belgium, France, and Germany).

• *Deregulated government*, which is built on the assumption that the public service and its organizations are full of creative ideas, relevant experience, and well-motivated people—if only they can be released from the heavy constraints of bureaucratic regula-tions. This vision is perhaps the least widespread of the four, being mainly confined to those—such as public service unions and professional groups—who share its optimism about the character and motivation of civil servants. It is essentially a version of the modernized state, but rather different from the participatory state described above. Again, it is seldom the sole or dominant element in reform programmes, but can play an important subsidiary role, perhaps especially in the more heavily bureaucratized countries of Continental Europe.

As Peters makes clear, each of these visions has aspects of silence or even incoherence, lying quietly alongside its 'headline' messages. That none of the four has been imple-mented in a pure way will come as no surprise, given the constraints on radical change identified in Chapters 2 and 3. Nevertheless, in certain countries the 'flavour' of one dominant model can be tasted in the key speeches and documents of reform. Thus the New Zealand reforms clearly owed much to microeconomic thinking that favoured a market model (see Appendix B: New Zealand, country file). The Finnish reform docu-ments lean more towards the participatory model: '[E]arlier administrative reforms have been experienced to have increased the bureaucracy of administration. The government wants to ensure the democratic development of the policy of governance' (*High Quality Services, Good Governance, and a Responsible Civic Society* 1998a, p. 8). The recent Belgian Copernicus programme places great emphasis on modernizing personnel management and releasing civil servants from the shackles of outdated bureaucratic procedures (See Appendix B: Belgium, country file).

To conclude this section, it might be said that, while visions play an important role in shaping the rhetorical dimension of reform, it is hard to use them as a means of assessing the results of the reform process. For the zealots, the ever-closer approximation of reality to the vision is the abiding concern, but they are usually few in number. Even the most powerful spokespersons for a particular view are obliged to compromise and exercise patience. Thatcher left the level of UK public spending only marginally different from that which she had found in 1979. President Reagan bequeathed a huge public sector deficit and a federal civil service little altered in size by his eight years at the helm. The enthusiastic privatizers in the new Dutch government of 1982 and the new Swedish government of 1991 found that they could not transfer to private ownership anything like as much of their respective public sectors as they had at first envisaged. For the reasons developed in Chapter 3 (and to be elaborated in Chapter 7) purity of vision must almost always be tempered with an understanding of political, economic, and functional constraints and trade-offs. Therefore, even those who are advocates of a particular vision, and who wish to assess 'results' in terms of that vision, must make allowances for the strength of the forces of tradition, inertia, and recalcitrance—for path dependency. Talk, decisions, and actions frequently diverge. Our argument has been that the strength of these forces depends to a considerable extent on the nature of the politico-administrative regime in question, and the extent to which the new, proposed vision cuts across, or goes along with its grain.

5.8 Conclusion: what do we know and what can we say?

5.8.1 Different perspectives on results: what you look for is what you see

This has been a long chapter and the conclusions may be briefly stated. First (Sections 5.1 and 5.2) 'results' may be looked for in different ways, in different places, and on different levels. For some commentators the most significant evidence lies in the 'changed climate', the existence of new 'talk', and the promulgation of visions of privatization, marketization, participation, deregulation, and flexibility. In short, the crucial evidence is the growth of a new community of discourse, with its main production centres located in the 'Anglo-Saxon' countries and certain international organizations such as the OECD, the IMF, the Commonwealth Secretariat, and the World Bank. For others the focus is the record of decisions—the publication of white papers and national review documents, the enunciation of programmes such as citizen's charters or Public Service 2000 (PS 2000), and the passing of laws decreeing administrative reform. Others, however, look for 'hard' evidence in the form of actions and impacts. This is itself a large domain, within which one may look for macrolevel effects or local impacts, for concrete outputs or longer-term outcomes, and so on. One's judgement on the achievements of reform is likely to vary considerably according to which of these various types of evidence is given the greatest weight (Pollitt 2002).

Where one looks is, in turn, influenced by where one sits. The three most obvious sitting positions tend to generate rather different 'vibrations' about management reform. The state apparatus itself, and particularly the political heads of department, tend to report steady progress—everything is in hand and remaining issues are being addressed (e.g. Chancellor of the Duchy of Lancaster 1997; Commonwealth Secretariat 1993; Gore 1996). Management consultants tend to focus more on the future, on the potential of new techniques and systems to solve the perceived problems of today. They do issue warnings, but these are usually about the constraints that may inhibit progress rather than about the nature of that progress itself. This may be considered understandable for a group, the existence of which depends partly on their being able to sell innovatory concepts and techniques. Significantly, management consultants usually address themselves privately (as it were) to their clients, and only occasionally to the public domain, whereas the other two groups are accustomed to delivering their conclusions to a wider audience. Academics are undoubtedly the least optimistic of the three groups, worrying about what may be lost as well as what is gained, expressing caution about long-term effects, and generally hedging achievement claims with qualifications and critique (e.g. Boyne et al. 2003; Derlien 1998; Dunleavy and Hood 1994; Ingraham 1997; Pollitt and Bouckaert 2003; Radin 1998, 2000).

There are also differences *within* each group. The differences among members of the state elite itself are perhaps the most interesting, since this is the group that one might suppose would be most likely to speak with one voice. One obvious divide is between legislatures and executives. Another is between executives and independent audit offices (Pollitt et al. 1999 gives an extended treatment of audit offices' reactions to management reforms). A third is within the executive itself, between central finance departments (on the one hand) and operational departments (on the other). Two brief examples can illustrate these differences of perspective.

In 1996 the President of the Canadian Treasury Board made an annual report to the legislature, entitled *Getting Government Right: Improving Results Measurement and Accountability* (Treasury Board of Canada 1996). The minister claimed:

We have already achieved tangible results in this area. For example, modernizing the financial management system, better reporting to Parliament, improving how we use information technologies, and adopting alternative ways of delivering government services. (Foreword)

However, when the Auditor General's Office reviewed these documents, they made a number of strong criticisms, including:

[...] The President's report does not distinguish evaluation from other forms of review [...] The President's report presents an overly optimistic picture of progress for an activity which is undergoing major change and dealing with many important challenges [...] The Treasury Board should ensure that its report to Parliament credibly represents the performance of review and includes specific measures on evaluation. (Auditor General of Canada 1997, Sections 3.80, 3.83, 3.85, and 3.86)

At the same time a Parliamentary Working Group was considering the same documentation. In their own report they also expressed critical views:

One of the perceived shortcomings of these documents, as expressed by MPs, was the lack of objectivity in the reporting. Many respondents suggested that it was inappropriate for departments to be reporting on their own performance—the perceived result of which was 'feel good' documents that said little about the true performance of the department. (Duhamel 1996, p. 14)

To complete the circle, we might add that parliaments themselves—including the Canadian one—have been less than exemplary in making use of performance data, even when these have been supplied to them. There has perhaps been a tendency to succumb to the temptation of grabbing a few headlines by highlighting unusual or extreme statistics, but not to work through or try to understand the broad picture that is presented to them.

As for internal differences of perspective within executives, the European Commission offers many examples of tensions between different DGs, some of which involve management issues (e.g. Middlemas 1995, pp. 247–55). The SEM 2000 and MAP 2000 initiatives, for example, were seen as coming mainly from the 'horizontal' parts of the Commission—DGIX (personnel), DGXIX (budgets), DGXX (internal control), and the Secretariat General. As such, aspects of the reforms were regarded with suspicion and were slow-pedalled by certain 'operational' ('vertical') DGs, which regarded them as belonging to someone else's agenda, and potentially burdensome.

5.8.2 Data, criteria, attribution

The foregoing sections have been liberally peppered with references to the often incomplete, or downright inadequate, state of the available data. There is no need to repeat that at length here. What is very clear is that data availability varies sharply according to how one defines 'results'. The records of reform *talk* are voluminous, and the analyst's problems are mainly to do with information overload. The records of reform *decisions* are also very extensive—even a list of the titles of major reform legislation in the twelve countries runs to many pages. The situation with reform *actions and achievements* is more complex. The available information on inputs, savings, process improvements, and outputs is vast. There can be little doubt that, in many public sector organizations in many countries, the work process has intensified; more measured outputs are being generated per pound spent or per member of staff employed. Not all of this information may be entirely reliable, but it would take a giant dose of cynicism to arrive at the conclusion that nothing has changed and that the productivity of specific organizations has remained static.

Where the information begins to get thin is at the next two stages. First, what have been the costs of the many measured improvements in productivity, in terms of other activities foregone, stress and reduced loyalty or commitment among the public sector workforce, loss (or gain) of trust by the public, and so on? In most cases there are few answers: these hidden costs could be very high or very low, and there could also be hidden benefits, which the bald statistics of productivity fail to capture.

Second, more importantly, information about what may be regarded as the final stage—the ultimate outcomes of all the reform talk, decision-making, and action on society at large—is both sparse and ambiguous. This is partly because most governments do not seem to have looked very vigorously for this type of information, but partly also because such information is difficult and expensive to collect, and then hard to interpret.

There is therefore something of a paradox at the heart of the international movement in favour of performance-oriented management reform. The reformers insist that public sector organizations must reorient and reorganize themselves in order to focus more vigorously on their results. They must count costs, measure outputs, assess outcomes, and use all this information in a systematic process of feedback and continuous improvement. Yet this philosophy has clearly not been applied to many of the reforms themselves, which thus far have been evaluated relatively seldom, and usually in ways that have some serious methodological limitations (Pollitt 1995; Pollitt and Bouckaert 2003).

Finally, it may be observed that information itself means little until it is combined with some *criterion*. An increase of 5 per cent may be good if the criterion for success is an average increase elsewhere of 2 per cent, but poor if the average elsewhere is 8 per cent. Contracting out refuse collection may be deemed a success if the criterion to be applied is cost per bag collected but thought to be a problem if the criterion is promoting equal opportunity of employment. The main point here is that there is often room for debate about which criteria are the most appropriate and, in any case, there seem to be fashions for particular criteria or measures, which come and go. Indeed, there is quite a persuasive theory that suggests that this kind of change over time is necessary, to prevent particular PIs getting 'worn out' and becoming the target for excessive gaming and manipulation (Meyer and Gupta 1994). Even in the market sector, the dominant measures used to judge the performance of commercial firms have shifted several times:

[A] number of factors, especially the tendency of performance measures to run down or to lose the capacity to discriminate good from bad performance, trigger ongoing creation of new performance measures different from and therefore weakly correlated with existing measures. (Meyer and Gupta 1994, p. 309; see also Bruijn 2002)

Perhaps this is why a number of studies have found that it is difficult to construct good time series of indicators for public organizations, because they seem to change rather frequently (Pollitt et al. 1998; Talbot 1996).

5.8.3 **Who needs results?**

One mildly controversial conclusion can be drawn from the foregoing. It is that, if 'results' are defined in a narrow way as scientifically tested data describing the final outcomes of changes, then *the international management reform movement has not needed results to fuel its onward march*. This will come as no surprise to analysts who stress the symbolic and rhetorical dimensions of politics and institutional life (Brunsson 1989; Brunsson and Olsen 1993; Hood 1998; March and Olsen 1995; Meyer and Rowan 1991; Power 1997). Nevertheless, it does represent what might politely be termed a discontinuity within some of the paradigms used by the proponents of reform themselves—particularly the hard-edged, performance-driven visions of core NPM enthusiasts.

Equally, 'results' of another kind *are* needed to maintain the momentum of reform. A continuing high level of production of talk and decision-making is probably essential. Until now, the flow of white papers, charters, and 'new initiatives' has been unceasing since the early 1980s. Every country has to have a reform programme of some sort, or at least be seen to be discussing one. To the knowledge of the authors of this book, there are many international conferences on public management reform every year, and even more national ones (the brochures arrive without the need for any special research!). One may ask whether this procession of talk and decision is now a permanent feature of governance, or whether it is conceivable that the flood tide may begin to ebb. If management reform *did* fall from fashion, it would not imply that institutions would cease to change. It would simply mean that reforms were no longer so newsworthy—they would resume the status of technical adjustments, which is what they were mainly seen as during some periods in the past.

5.8.4 Regimes, trajectories, and results

Finally, we should ask what are the connections between the politico-administrative regimes described in Chapter 3, the reform trajectories chosen by different jurisdictions and commented upon in Chapter 4, and the picture of 'results' put together here in Chapter 5?

In an ideal world the regime types would influence the reform trajectories, and evidence would show that given trajectories led to specified but different mixtures of results. The connecting mechanisms or processes (what works and what does not) would also be clear, and the would-be reformer could thus inspect the local regime and then choose a reform trajectory that would generate the mix of benefits and costs which he or she most desired.

Unfortunately, neither we nor anyone else can 'fill in' all the spaces in this ideal model. Chapter 4 did show that some broad connections could be established between types of politico-administrative regime and the choice of reform trajectories. Even those links were subject to exceptions and deviations, temporary or otherwise. However, there is a considerable 'disconnect' between trajectories and results. The record does not permit confident and specific statements to be made concerning the different mixtures of results that will be harvested from each main trajectory. On the contrary, there are conflicting claims, with advocates advancing the respective merits of the 'New Zealand model' (Boston et al. 1996), the 'Canadian model' (Bourgon 1998), German 'disjointed incrementalism' (Derlien 1998), American 'reinvention' (National Performance Review 1997*a*, 1997*b*), and so on. These arguments are only occasionally backed up by results data, and, when they are, the attribution of effects is usually disputable.

On the other hand, it would be wholly mistaken to draw the conclusion that public management reform was a meaningless charade, played only by the cynical or the stupid. On the contrary, it is absolutely clear that many of the changes made have carried definite 'pay-offs' for particular groups and individuals, even if longer-term outcomes remain comparatively obscure (see, e.g. Boyne et al. 2003 for a summary of select UK reforms). It is also the case that some very broad consequences can be predicted on the basis of the different 'visions' or 'omegas' that reformers seem to have in mind. To explore these issues also requires a disaggregation of the 'players', and, in particular, a further examination of the role of management reform at the interface between politics and management. This will be undertaken in Chapter 6. It further requires the development of a closer analysis of some of the trade-offs and paradoxes that have come to light in Chapters 4 and 5. They will be the subject of Chapter 7. Finally, in Chapter 8, it will be possible to return to the overarching question of the likely connections between different reform strategies and their consequences for relations between politicians, public servants, and the rest of society.

6 | Politics and management

> [O]n the one hand we see policy-makers using administrative reform to displace accountability for public policy; on the other hand we see the very same policy-makers trying to increase their control over bureaucracy. Whilst this appears to be two inconsistent developments, they may in fact reflect a general desire among elected politicians to increase their influence over bureaucracy while at the same time avoiding responsibility for the bureaucracy's actions.
>
> (Pierre 1995, p. 3)

6.1 Forwards to the past?

At this point we shift gear. In Chapters 2, 3, 4, and 5 we have been engaged in building a model of management reform, classifying key contextual features that differentiate one country's regime from another, identifying alternative trajectories for change, and examining the evidence as to the results of this change. Each of these chapters has therefore been intended to help build up a general picture of what has been happening—in word and in deed—in the world of public management reform. In the remainder of the book, however, we stand back from this picture in order to reflect upon and interpret some of its broader features. We shift mood from construction towards deconstruction, from creating an accurate and convincing depiction towards exploring its contradictions and acknowledging its limitations. This exercise will carry us from the excitements of the ostensibly new ('transforming', 'joining-up', 'reinventing', 're-engineering', 'revitalizing', 'modernization') and take us back to some of the abiding, recurrent problems of governance in Liberal democratic regimes.

From the outset we have argued that public management cannot be adequately comprehended without reference to the crucial relationships that exist between administration and politics, and between administrators and politicians. In this we are at one with the many authors who have made an identical or similar point (e.g. Flynn and Strehl 1996; Götz 1997, p. 753; Hood 2002; Lynn et al. 2001; Peters 1996a, p. 20; Pierre 1995, pp. 205–7).

While there is wide agreement that this frontier is an important one, there appears to be sharply varying opinions as to what is taking place along the borderlines. Some have seen 'management' (in the sense of modernized public administration plus privatization) invading politics and taking over slices of political territory (e.g. Clarke and Newman

1997; Pollitt 1993, chapter 1; Stewart 1994). Others, in apparent contrast, suggest that management reform has been a vehicle by which executive politicians have gained a tighter grip on their officials (Halligan 1997; Pierre 1995). One recent comparativist goes so far as to assert that 'as far as most countries are concerned, the possible dominance of the civil service by political regimes seems to be of greater concern than the possible dominance of the political regime by the civil service' (Hojnacki 1996, p. 144). Less speculatively, a large poll of public service managers in the UK found that 'the largest single negative response in the whole survey was concerned with managers' ability to "resist political interference in operational management decisions"' (Talbot 1996, p. 38).

At this point it may be useful to examine more closely the concept of a 'frontier' between management and politics. It should immediately be emphasized that this frontier is related to, but by no means necessarily identical with, the boundary between civil servants and politicians. According to most contemporary definitions, 'politics' is not limited to certain persons (elected politicians) or to specialized arenas in which an action takes place (parliament, ministerial offices, 'smoke-filled rooms', etc.). More commonly politics is defined by the *processes* involved. In particular, political activity is that which involves the exercise of power, especially the mobilization of various kinds of resources in order to achieve a chosen set of ends in a situation where the interests of the various parties concerned potentially or actually conflict (Leftwich 1984). Thus, even public servants in Westminster-type systems, though they may remain 'neutral' and scrupulously avoid 'party politics', nevertheless frequently engage in 'political' processes, in the sense that they bargain and negotiate and deploy resources of money, information, and presentational skills in order to improve the chances of success for policies and programmes with which they are associated. For example, a senior civil servant charged with implementing his or her minister's policy of privatizing a public utility will negotiate with the various parties involved and attempt, on the minister's behalf, to make the policy work. Similarly, the chief executive of a hospital may negotiate with the local trade unions over redundancies or terms and conditions and the head of a government regional office will bargain with other powerful local figures (local government officers, local business leaders, and so on) to try to promote regional development. In these senses, then, many public servants are involved in 'politics', even if they stay clear of 'party politics'. To the popular definition of politics as the process that determines 'who gets what, when, and how' we would therefore add the thought that, albeit within legal frameworks and (possibly) under explicit guidance from elected politicians, the person making such determination will often be an appointed official.

From such a perspective some interesting interpretive possibilities open up. The apparently contrasting views referred to above (between those who believe that the domain of management is increasing and those who argue that political scrutiny is increasing) become more understandable and—to a degree, if not entirely—mutually reconcilable. For example, it could be simultaneously true that politicians are intervening more in public administration *and* that the sphere of public management has begun to encompass more and more issues that used to be mainly the preserve of politicians. Equally, the quotation from Jon Pierre that heads this chapter could be understood as identifying a strategy by executive politicians to shift issues into the management domain precisely so as to be able to 'disown' them when things go badly and then intervene and claim credit when things go well.

These are, then, crucial, boundary issues for public management, and they deserve more detailed consideration here. We will focus on three key questions:

1. Has public management reform shifted the borderline between politics and administration, and, if so, in what way?
2. What are the main implications of the new trajectories and models of public management for elected politicians (in both executive and legislative roles)?
3. What is the relationship between public management reform and public attitudes towards politicians and civil servants?

Our answers to all three of these questions—perhaps particularly to the third—are tentative. The available evidence is patchy. One of the features of the rhetoric surrounding a good deal of management reform (perhaps especially in the core NPM group of countries) has been that it has drawn attention *away* from these overtly political issues— the emphasis has tended to be placed on saving money or improving the public services received by citizens rather than on the effects of all this upon basic political and constitutional relationships. The implication has seemed to be that management can be a professional and technical exercise, relatively free of 'politics'. Typical of this dominant emphasis was Vice-President Gore's characterization of the US NPR exercise as one aiming at a government that 'works better and costs less'. Typical also was Thatcher's bold assertion that moving 70 per cent of the civil service out of conventional departments and into a new type of executive agency had no constitutional significance:

The government does not envisage that setting up executive agencies within departments will result in changes to existing constitutional relationships. (Prime Minister 1988, p. 9)

However, after two decades of intensive change across many countries, we are far from alone in suggesting that the 'three Es' and improved 'customer service' are only one dimension of the picture: the relations between politics and administration have changed too.

Having addressed the three questions listed above, the chapter concludes with some synthesizing comments on the extent to which 'politics' may represent a structural limit to the effectiveness and reach of management reform.

6.2 Has public management reform shifted the borderline between politics and administration?

There have, in any case, been significant changes in the nature of politics in many OECD countries, quite apart from the impacts of management reforms. Specifically, there has been an erosion of the perceived legitimacy of government and an increase in the volatility (decrease in the party loyalty) of most electorates. More sectors of politics— including management reform—have developed through international rather than purely national networks (Halligan 1996a; Held et al. 1998; Kettl 2000; Manning 2001). Finally, economic pressures have meant that in most OECD countries the era where ministers made their reputations by introducing big new programmes has long passed. We have moved into an era of largely 'technical politics' rather than the welfare state construction of 1945–75. Executive politicians are now usually engaged in streamlining, repackaging, marginally modifying, or actually downsizing ('decrementing') existing programmes, rather than any heroic new efforts. Public tend to be vigilant against reductions in popular and basic welfare state services (health care, education, pensions) yet more sceptical and more demanding (in terms of service standards) than in the past *and*, at the same time, more resistant to tax increases. Furthermore, in most countries the mass media have become more aggressive and sceptical, no longer accepting the 'official line' or deferring to the minister's authority or access to expertise. To put it bluntly, it is even more difficult being a minister than it used to be, partly because the kinds of things a minister gets to do today are inherently less popular than those that were being done during the boom years of the 1950s and 1960s, and partly because the public audience out there are more sceptical, less deferential, and less trusting. One should add that it is also more difficult being a 'mandarin'. Rouban (1997, p. 148) refers specifically to developments in France, but his words apply to most of our other countries as well:

The time is over when civil servants, representing an all-mighty State, could steer most actors of the social life and could impose their choice without too much difficulty. Moreover, the classic political game has been changed. Controversies are no longer built along the lines of ideological frontiers but involve technical arguments that often cross the political parties' boundaries.

Within this context, management reform ministers have been caught in the dilemma captured by the Pierre quotation at the beginning of this chapter: on the one hand they have sought greater control over the bureaucracy and its programmes but on the other they have seen advantages in decentralizing responsibility and trying to sit 'above' the dangerous cauldron of day-to-day operational failures and achievements. Generally speaking, it might be said that NPM style on the Anglo-Australasian model contains contradictory ideas (or, at least, ideas that exist in some tension with each other). NPM doctrine holds not only that decentralization is good, and letting/making managers manage is good, but also that political control and accountability need to be strengthened *and* that consumer power should be strengthened. This conundrum— which will be explored in more detail in Chapter 7—looks rather like an 'eternal triangle'. The grass in the other two corners is always greener. Nor have Continental European states—which, as we have seen, have not embraced NPM to anything like the same extent—been able to avoid problems. In France,

Many civil servants have perceived modernisation as a means to put them in charge of political choice that had not been decided upstream, as a tricky game whose winners are always the politicians who can get rid of embarrassing responsibilities in a time of budget cuts and, simultaneously, of high defensive corporatism. (Rouban 1997, p. 155)

Decentralizing devices such as frame-budgeting (Sweden, Finland) or delegation to provincial or regional tiers of government (Belgium, Canada, Italy, USA) have clearly been used partly in order to transfer the political pain of sharp prioritizations and downsizing from the national to subnational levels of government (from one set of elected politicians to another—although within each jurisdictional level there may also be some passing on of 'hot potatoes' to officials). However, at least in these cases the arguments have taken place *within* the political sphere, between different strata of elected representatives.

The precise ways in which these tensions play themselves out are therefore shaped by the type of regime in which they occur (see Chapter 3). In the 'Anglo-Saxon' regimes (Australasia, UK, USA) where politics and government in general tend to be held in lower esteem, it has been less difficult for politicians to retreat from responsibility for the management of public services (indeed, easier for them to pursue outright privatization). Look at Table 5.14, where the percentage tending to trust central government in Belgium (43), Germany (37), the Netherlands (61), Finland (54), and Sweden (54) all significantly exceed the UK (33). Thus many developments have seemed to signal a shift of the borderline in favour of management, so that its empire (both private and public) has grown while the empire of politics appears to have shrunk. This has been done in the name of efficiency and consumer responsiveness. Yet executive politicians have also been cunning. They have, in effect, reasserted the distinction between politics and administration (though now calling the latter 'management'), making managers responsible for achieving targets, but at the same time they have frequently retained powers of intervention so that, if things go badly wrong in the public eye, then the politicians can appear to ride to the rescue with inquiries, inspection teams, restructurings, and all the other paraphernalia of crisis management. This generalization would apply, for example, to UK executive agencies, grant-maintained schools, and NHS trust hospitals and to the Belgian Commission on the Dutroux (child abuse) scandal and the Dutch inquiry into the firework explosion at Enschede.

Beneath the surface, the process of letting—or making—public sector managers manage has not been so simple. There have been countervailing currents and considerable centralization, partly through the establishment of evermore sophisticated PI and target regimes, underpinned by rapidly advancing information technologies. In the UK a general shrinkage of the public sector has been accompanied by an extraordinary growth of central auditing, inspecting, and monitoring bodies (Hood et al. 1999; Power 1997). As we have seen, executive politicians have transferred their focus for control from inputs to outputs, via processes. This may account for the somewhat ambiguous responses from public service managers themselves—they have experienced greater freedom to deploy their inputs (e.g. switching money from staff to equipment, or vice versa) but at the same time they have felt themselves under closer scrutiny than ever before as far as their results are concerned. Even where an activity has been fully privatized—as with the UK public utilities such as gas, water, electricity, and telecommunications—politicians have gradually been obliged to give more attention to arrangements for the public regulation of the resultant private corporations (Foster 1992).

What is clear is that, in the UK, but also in other Westminster-influenced systems, the additional pressures that NPM reforms have put on traditional concepts of public accountability have not been met with any clear and coherent new doctrine to cope with the new circumstances. The problems are increasingly widely recognized, but most politicians have shrunk from the task of articulating a 'new model' (Barberis 1998; Behn 2001; Pollitt 2003*a*, chapter 4; Stone 1995).

In an interesting analysis of reforms in two strong NPM countries (Australia, New Zealand) and two modernizers from the 'northern European' group (Norway, Sweden), a pair of Norwegian scholars paid particular attention to the effects of the implementation of NPM practices on politicians. Their conclusions are worth citing:

The distance between political leaders, on the one hand, and the actors, institutions and levels to be controlled, on the other, is increasing, and autonomy from political leaders is more evident. The new administrative and institutional actors are less loyal than in the traditional system, more instrumental and individually oriented, and less preoccupied with collective interests, public accountability and ethos. (Christensen and Lægreid 2001, p. 304)

Note the emphasis here on a changing culture among the new administrative elites. Christensen and Lægreid go on to note the additional complexity these changes bring for accountability systems before finally delivering a sober verdict:

Our conclusion is that these changes may in fact undermine political control. Managerialism may allow executives to exercise greater control over state agencies, but it is greater control over less...The changes also create ambiguity concerning the role of managers, because they are caught in cross-pressure between politicians and customers. (Christensen and Lægreid 2001, p. 309)

In the more consensualist and decentralized regimes (the northern European group identified in Chapter 4) the 'antigovernment' theme has not been as strong as in the core NPM group. Instead the rhetoric has stressed modernization, with the political elites largely holding to their usual role of directing a substantial state apparatus, and the mandarins continuing to play a strategic role with relatively little challenge to their status and competence. Considerable decentralization has taken place (Sweden, Finland) but this has been more political decentralization (to subnational elected authorities) rather than managerial decentralization on the New Zealand/UK model. One should remember, however, that these countries were already administratively more decentralized than the UK, with both Sweden and Finland having strong traditions of national boards and agencies and Sweden, in particular, possessing only quite small central ministries (Molander et al. 2002). In general, change in the Nordic countries, although often flavoured with NPM ideas, was more incremental and cautious than in Australia or New Zealand (Christensen and Lægreid 2001). In the Netherlands the trajectory was slightly different, with a significant growth in appointed quangos (ZBOs) during the 1980s. However, this trend soon attracted political criticism (including some accusations that the ZBOs were being used to create well-paid jobs for sympathizers of the ruling Christian Democrat party), and in 1994 an incoming left–right 'purple coalition' made restoring 'the primacy of politics' one of its leading slogans (Roberts 1997). Departmental agencies with more sharply defined accountability became the preferred vehicle for decentralization of central government tasks, rather than ZBOs, and the NAO made a series of well-publicized reports aimed at improving the public accountability of autonomous bodies (e.g. Algemene Rekenkamer 1995, 2002).

In sum, neither in the Nordic states nor in the Netherlands has the borderline between management and politics moved much, one way or the other. On the other hand, these regimes have shared in the shift to systems of output rather than input controls, even if this move has not been as vigorously reinforced by personnel reforms (performance appraisals, annual results targets for individual public servants) as in the most pro-NPM countries.

In Germany and France the politics/administration frontier has not shifted very much either. Neither has significantly dismantled central civil service controls; neither has created flocks of powerful new quangos to take over functions formerly under direct political oversight (Germany already possessed a large and significant set of para-statal, corporatist organizations with responsibilities for carrying out public functions). France has implemented a significant privatization programme, but cautiously, and nowhere near as sweepingly as the UK or New Zealand. Germany was already extensively decentralized and France has carried through a major decentralization programme since 1982 but, as in the case of the Nordics, these have been primarily acts of political decentralization (to local and regional *elected* bodies), not pure managerial decentralization. Administrative decentralization has certainly taken place, but not on the same scale as in the UK or New Zealand (Guyomarch 1999; Trosa 1995). In short, political and civil service elites (which, significantly, in both countries are intermingled rather than separate—especially in France) have retained their grip. The politically led state, even if leaking legitimacy, is still seen as a major, socially integrating force to be reckoned with. There have been significant attempts to begin to shift large, rule-following bureaucracies towards a more performance-oriented approach, but this has been both patchy and a largely internal matter. It has not been accompanied (as in Australia/New Zealand/UK/ USA) by general rhetoric about how 'political influences' have to be removed/minimized and professional management/business-like approaches substituted. On the contrary, while the first edition of this book was being written a prominent German scholar expressed himself thus:

Not only would it be undesirable to once again in German history have senior civil servants conceal their functionally politicized role, it is also hardly imaginable how to turn them into a political managers. Possibly, the formal neutrality of civil servants in the UK and the absence of the safety valve of temporary retirement could be reasons for the easy adoption [in the UK] of a managerialist role understanding. (Derlien 1998, pp. 23–4)

Nor have the German or French public been copiously supplied with 'league tables' of 'results' as has been the fashion in the UK and, to a lesser extent, the USA and New Zealand. The Anglo-American-Canadian rhetoric of citizen 'empowerment' has been far more muted in *Rechtsstaat* regimes, where the dominant legal perspective and the distinctiveness of the state sphere make such concepts more difficult to conceive or fill with any sensible meaning. Citizen justice and citizen rights, *Conseil d'Etat* style is very different from consumer choice in the style of Major's *Citizen's Charter*.

Among the central European group of states, Belgium and Italy remain to be commented upon. Both have witnessed extensive political decentralization (see Appendix B: country files) but it is not clear that this has much altered the borderline between politics and administration or, at least, not in any lasting way. In Belgium the federal civil service has, if anything, probably lost some status, alongside politicians, amid the public anger at the Dutroux affair and other administrative and political scandals of the 1990s. In Italy confidence in the political system fell to very low levels in the late 1980s and early 1990s, and there were even two 'nonpolitical', technocratic governments in the mid-1990s. However, there too there is little evidence that the civil service has been the beneficiary of the loss of confidence in politicians. Rather it, too, has a low status in the eyes of the public. Table 5.13 showed 2000 levels of 33 per cent for Italian trust in the civil service, as against 46 per cent for Belgium, France, and the UK, 41 per cent in Finland, and 49 per cent in Sweden. Only Germany (39%) and the Netherlands (37%) joined Italy below the 40 per cent level. Although both countries have begun real reforms, it is hard to see that these have yet led to any restoration of the status and authority of national civil servants. Neither does the available evidence show any sustained reversal of the fall in the standing of politicians. Direct evidence of a shifting borderline between political and managerial power is not plentiful—either in Belgium or in Italy—but we can at least say that there is little to indicate a major accretion of authority to either ministers or mandarins (even though the Belgian 'purple–green' coalition made the 'primacy of politics' a key programme issue).

6.3 What are the main implications of the new trajectories and models of public management for elected politicians?

We will deal with the executive roles—that is, ministers—first. According to the NPM model, the new role held out for ministers is as strategists and opinion-leaders. They will clarify and communicate visions and values, choose appropriate strategies, and identify, allocate, and commit resources at the macrolevel. The managing/operations will then be done by professional managers, whose performance will subsequently be appraised against clear objectives and targets.

There seems little evidence that this is a credible vision of any likely reality. Most senior politicians, in most countries, have not been trained for such a role, and the pressures on them are not likely to encourage them to adopt it. They may learn the rhetoric—particularly if it enables them to shed responsibility for policy failures (the Prison Service and Child Support Agency cases in the UK)—but not much more. The story of the politically dismissed Director of the UK prison service vividly illustrates the dangers: a minister who, faced with an embarrassing series of incidents, tries to save his political reputation by blaming his official, even though the latter has achieved all the performance targets set out in his contract (Lewis 1987). There were similar events with the responsible CEOs for railways in the Netherlands and Belgium. Politically, the incentives are still short-term: to make popular announcements of new initiatives, to intervene dramatically when things appear to be going wrong, to follow popular opinion rather than try to educate it, to take up single issues (mirroring the media) rather than develop integrated strategies, and so on. And there is evidence that this is exactly what happens (Molander et al. 2002 for the steering of Swedish agencies; Radin 1998 for the GPRA in the USA; Talbot 1996 for the UK; Zifcak 1994, chapter 5, for Australia). 'While the intellectual exercise involved in defining goals and measures of success has its own rigor, it does not fit comfortably into the fragmented decision-making process in both the White House and the Congress' (Radin 1998, p. 313).

In consensualist political systems the attraction of the NPM vision of ministers as strategists seems even less than in the majoritarian systems of Australia, Canada, New Zealand, and the UK. In Belgium, the Nordic states, and the Netherlands ministers are not far-sighted strategists—their political success and survival depend upon their skills and creativity in putting together coalitions of support to steer through particular programmes. This is even more true for EU institutions. In these environments clear statements of strategies and priorities may actually prove counterproductive: the ability to be all things to all (wo)men is much more useful. Nothing in the NPM can change this political dynamic.

Again, as far as the substantive content of management reform is concerned, nothing has happened to alter the diagnosis made by many previous writers on public sector organizational reform, namely that such reforms have little interest for most ministers, as they are not 'vote-catchers' and because they yield results only over long periods of time, if at all. *Announcing* reforms may be mildly rewarding (e.g. Gore, Thatcher, Lange, Howard) but following them through and checking to see if they worked are not high-priority tasks for most politicians. As the OECD—a leading influence in NPM-type reforms for a decade or more—put it in 2002: 'There are political advantages in launching reform initiatives, and political disadvantages in carrying them through. Hence the prevalence of reform initiatives abandoned before the critical mass-point of cultural change' (OECD 2002*a*, p. 8). Of course, when organizational boundaries are changed, politicians take an interest, either to protect their 'patch' or to try to gain 'territory', but this is hardly the perspective of the strategic figure implied in much of the NPM litera-ture. At a supranational level one may cast one's mind back over the poor record of the Council of Ministers in respect of the attempts to reform EU institutions so as to make them more performance-oriented. The 'bottom line' has usually proven to be a national interest in holding on to a particular share of senior positions, or even a reluctance to aid the emergence of a more efficient and effective (and therefore potentially more powerful) Commission. During 2002 this could be seen once more, for example, in the UK position during the evolving debates within the EU Convention, where the UK government was initially very suspicious of proposals for a strengthened, elected President of the Commission, preferring instead a strengthening of the (nationally based) Council of Ministers.

The analysis in the previous paragraph is even more true for the second group of politicians—those in the legislatures. Their careers are hardly ever shaped by organiza-tional reforms, their constituents are seldom interested in them or knowledgeable about them, and there is little incentive to get involved in such matters, except in the most superficial ways, or as constituency advocates in particular cases when things go wrong ('crippled widow denied disability benefit' etc.). Legislatures have been very slow to make constructive use of the increase in performance information available to them (Carter et al. 1992, pp. 182–3). Most MPs simply do not have the time or inclination to get involved in the details of management. Describing the US Congress's reaction to the NPR, Kettl (1994, p. 49) vividly crystallized the problem:

Congress, by practice and the Constitution, attacks problems by passing laws. The NPR seeks to solve problems by improving performance. Congress as an institution works on the input side. The

NPR focuses on the output side. Congress has little incentive to worry about results and, in fact, has long indulged itself in a separation-of-powers fantasy that absolves it from any complicity in the executive branch's performance problems.

In the late 1990s this judgement was reinforced by Congress's treatment of the first set of reports that came out of the GPRA. The more quotable aspects of their contents were treated to a brief burst of publicity, but there was little sign of any appetite or plan on Congress's behalf to make more sober or systematic use of these much-heralded performance reports.

6.4 What is the relationship between public management reform and public attitudes towards politicians and civil servants?

On the face of it the question 'What do the citizens think about public management reform?' may seem both fundamental and straightforward. Surely, in a liberal democracy, this is the ultimate test of any government action or programme? Such assumptions are further supported by both political rhetoric around the issue of rebuilding citizens' trust in government and by academic discourse concerning the apparent loss of legitimacy by governments throughout the western (and Australasian) world. The academic fascination with this began a long time ago, and has embraced academics of very different theoretical persuasions (see, e.g. Habermas 1976; Nivette 1996; Nye et al. 1997). Some write of a loss of legitimacy, others of a decline in deference, others still of a loss of trust. There are interesting differences between these concepts (legitimacy/deference/trust), but from the point of view of management reform they all point towards a more critical and possibly recalcitrant audience for attempts to remodel at least those public sector organizations that deal directly with the citizenry.

Unfortunately, the question itself is packed with doubtful assumptions. For example, do most citizens know anything about the many reforms that have been proclaimed and implemented by OECD governments? They are seldom the stuff of TV news or newspaper headlines. Even if they may have encountered some references to reforms, are most citizens sufficiently interested to pay any attention? If we take one of the most extensively (and expensively) promoted reforms, the UK *Citizen's Charter*, one survey indicated that 71 per cent of citizens had heard of it (ICM 1993), but other research indicated that very few people possessed any accurate knowledge of what was in it (Beale and Pollitt 1994). This ignorance of actual mechanisms and substance survived despite a government campaign that had mailed a glossy leaflet to every household in the land. In Italy, to an even greater extent, the proud launch of a citizen's charter escaped the attention of most Italians (Schiavo 2000). In Belgium the citizen's charter was professionally published in the *State Monitor*, as royal and ministerial decrees, and therefore remained at the administrative level (Bouckaert et al. 2003). One imagines that more technical reforms—such as the 'reinvention labs' in the US NPR, or results-oriented budgeting in Finland and Sweden—would remain completely unknown to the vast majority of the populations of the countries in question.

Lack of knowledge may not be the most serious barrier. Equally distorting can be the possession of *false* information or serious conceptual misconceptions. Take, for example, the average American's view of the efficiency of federal programmes. Surveys show that most Americans believe that more than 50 per cent of the expenditure in social security programmes goes in overheads. The true figure is less than 2 per cent (Bok 1997, p. 56). Surveys in the UK in the 1960s were said simultaneously to reveal majorities against 'nationalization' but in favour of 'public ownership'.

However, let us set the (major) problems of citizen ignorance and indifference on one side for a moment, and concentrate on those issues where citizens do, it seems, hold definite opinions. After all, surveys in a number of countries have been carried out with questions such as 'How do you rate the overall performance of government?' or 'Do you have no confidence/some confidence/a great deal of confidence in politicians/civil servants/bank managers/doctors?', and there has been no difficulty in obtaining responses and adding them up to percentage 'answers'. It is on the basis of time series of surveys of this genre that political scientists have identified a problem of declining legitimacy and trust in many liberal democracies (for summaries, see Nye et al. 1997; Pew Research Centre 1998; see also Tables 5.13 and 5.14). These are certainly interesting data, but the problems of interpretation are considerable. For example, an important question is: What are respondents thinking of when they declare their opinions on the overall performance of government, or their level of trust? What they read in the newspaper last week? A recent TV appearance by the prime minister? The government's decision not to increase the state pension by the full rate of inflation? The poor service the respondent received in the post office that morning? Furthermore, there is the question of the rationale behind the opinion. *Why* does the respondent think that state pension decisions/macroeconomic policy/counter service at the post office is good or bad? What expectations did he or she bring to the question, and how were those expectations formed? Unfortunately, only a few surveys can offer any help with these sorts of questions—we may know *what* the average citizen thinks, but seldom *why* they think it (the 1993 ICM survey on the UK *Citizen's Charter* being a case in point).

Nevertheless, some provocative, if inconclusive, findings emerge from survey data. First, opinions as to overall governmental performance, or levels of trust, do not necessarily correlate closely with opinions on much more concrete and specific issues (e.g. How adequate is the postal service?). It seems quite possible for citizens to maintain a generalized cynicism or mistrust of 'government' whilst simultaneously being reasonably satisfied with many of the specific public services they actually make use of (Canadian Centre for Management Development 1998*a*, 1998*b*). The level of this generalized dissatisfaction with government is 'strongly connected to how people feel about the overall state of the nation' (Pew Research Centre 1998, p. 1).

It also seems that the belief that private sector services are generally much better regarded than public services is questionable. In Canada at least:

Many public sector services such as police, trash collection, weather services and fire services are rated more highly by the public than many private sector services such as banks, cable companies, and automobile dealers . . . In general they rate public and private sector services within much the same ranges. (Canadian Centre for Management Development 1998*b*, p. 5; see also Table 5.11, which shows considerable stability in these scores over a period of years)

In the UK too, the 1993 ICM survey found that the public's perceptions of improvements in services by no means put private sector services consistently above those provided by the public sector—for example, NHS doctors and state postal services were placed somewhat above building societies and far above banks (ICM 1993, p. 16).

Certainly, there is no firm ground for the assertion that the public would like the welfare state to be 'rolled back' and replaced by private modes of provision. For example, a 1993 attitudinal survey of New Zealanders showed

strong endorsement for the notion of a universalist rather than a residualist welfare state, including support for more taxes (although not necessarily a willingness to pay more tax personally), as well as an underlying conviction that politicians are out of touch and unworthy of the government's trust. (Vowles et al. 1995, p. 97)

Similarly, more recently, the 2002 Swedish election results could be interpreted as a vote for public services rather than tax reductions.

Even in the USA, supposedly the stronghold of antigovernment, pro-private sector sentiments, it has been shown that: 'Fully 72% of Americans believe that government should see to it that no one is without food, shelter or clothing . . . as many as felt that way in the 1960s' (Pew Research Centre 1998, p. 7). In the UK, before, during, and after the apex of Thatcherism, polls frequently showed a majority of voters favouring more public money being spent on public health care and educational services, and, in some cases, even a majority declaring itself willing to pay more taxes if they could be assured that the revenue thus raised would go to those causes.

Second, respondents are frequently able to distinguish between different groups of actors in the process of governance. Most commonly they extend a tolerable degree of trust towards civil servants, but a considerably lower (and falling) degree towards political leaders. For example,

Surveys suggest that the public's frustration is directed more at politicians who lead government than at civil servants who administer it. By a margin of 67% to 16% the public has more trust in federal workers than in their elected officials to do the right thing. In that vein 69% now say that they have a favorable opinion of government workers—an improvement from the 55% that held that view in a 1981 *Los Angeles Times* national opinion survey. (Pew Research Centre 1998, p. 2)

Thus, if President Reagan was right in saying that the federal government was part of the problem rather than part of the solution, it was the politicians rather than the bureaucrats he should have been aiming to reform! Furthermore—for the USA at least—it is not so much failures in the *efficiency* of elected politicians that provoke public distrust, as the perception that such leaders are failing to uphold high moral standards (Pew Research Centre 1998). This is extremely interesting material, as it carries the implication that public management reform is unlikely to contribute much to the enhancement of governmental legitimacy, for two solid reasons. First, the public *do* distinguish between political leaders and civil servants, and the bulk of their distrust is directed at the former. Second, the deepest roots of discontent with the political leadership do not grow out of perceptions of their incapacity to manage affairs but rather from their (perceived) untrustworthiness or low moral standards. Finally—just to complicate matters further—the public may well also draw distinctions between different *types* of politicians. They may trust local politicians more than national politicians. Or they may respond more favourably to a question about how far they trust 'parliament' than to one about how far they trust 'government'. All in all, it looks as though public may be quite discriminating and sophisticated in their judgements, and as though sweeping generalizations about a loss of public confidence in (by implication) *all* governments in *all* countries are inaccurate and misleading.

Third, citizen responses can be highly context-specific, and need to be interpreted in the light of that. For example,

[I]t appears that fire services are always rated highly by citizens while municipal planning services are rated much lower. This may reflect the nature of the services: one is an essential service; while the other is a regulatory function that may impact on some citizens negatively, in order to ensure fairness in protecting other citizens, such as in zoning regulations. *Thus a rating of 7.0 would be a poor score for a fire service, but an excellent score for a planning service.* (Canadian Centre for Management Development 1998*b*, p. 6)

Fourth, a decline in deference may mean that more citizens are willing—actively or passively—to resist and criticize public authorities, making life more difficult for the latter. What it does not necessarily mean, however, is that those citizens want to play a much bigger part in the process of reaching decisions or running public programmes. The evidence here is mixed: many members of the public may want 'more say' but that is a far cry from full-blooded and time-consuming participation. Offering more places on citizens' panels or in focus groups may well appeal to some, but it would be an unwarranted leap of logic to presume that lots more 'participation' was the principal answer to problems of recalcitrance and low trust (Pollitt 2003*a*, chapter 4).

Thus, ideally, analysis of citizen opinion needs to be topic-specific (some services are inherently more popular than others) and person-specific (politicians are distrusted more than civil servants). One also needs to know something about the citizens' own experiences. (Are responses coming from those who have little knowledge and no experience to be counted as equally valid as those from other citizens who are regular, indeed, 'expert' users of the particular service in question?) The question of 'trust in government' turns out to be as complex as government itself, and it is by no means clear what significance or meaning should be attached to large sample surveys which come up with the answer that 61 per cent of the population thinks this or that about some very generalized questions on trust or efficiency.

Indeed, the concept of legitimacy itself is far from simple (Held 1987). To say that one accepts the current government, or the current system of public administration, as legitimate is a statement that may conceal a range of states of knowledge and a variety of attitudes. As already noted, respondents to questionnaires (or, indeed, voters) may be very knowledgeable or profoundly ignorant about the topics that they are being asked to assess. Equally, with respect to attitudes, these may range from reluctant acquiescence ('I suppose there isn't any alternative') through lukewarm acceptance to enthusiastic approbation ('American democracy/the British NHS/the French system of *grands corps* is the best in the world').

In sum, we may conclude that the public's attitude to management reform in particular, and to public administration in general, is both complex and as yet only lightly researched. Most of the evidence we have found comes from the Anglo-Saxon countries, and it would be extremely useful to be able to compare that with equally sophisticated surveys carried out in the Nordic countries or in Germany or France. Most of the public probably know little about most specific reforms. Most of them are also capable of simultaneously maintaining a spectrum of attitudes towards the state apparatus, distinguishing between different groups of actors, different services, and questions of greater generality or specificity. Some of their attitudes may be deeply founded and hard to shift (e.g. the widespread apparent support, in many countries, for the continuance of the basic fabric of the welfare state), while other opinions may be quite volatile, easily altered by new information or experiences. Thus bold assertions that the public have lost confidence in public services, or that they 'want' less bureaucracy, or that they are demanding higher quality, frequently turn out to be fragile—and therefore inadequate as platforms upon which to erect specific programmes of reform.

6.5 Concluding remarks

The relationship between politics, public management, and public opinion is a contentious area, and one in which systematic data are at best patchy. Having made these caveats, we will attempt to draw out a few broad propositions from the evidence advanced above.

First, public management reforms *have* altered the relationships between elected and appointed officials, in a number of countries and in a number of ways. In this sense, at least, they are not 'neutral'. It seems likely that these changes have been greatest in the core NPM countries, somewhat less in the northern group of European countries, and smallest in the central European group. Second, there is an absence of convincing evidence concerning the willingness or ability of executive politicians to become the 'strategic managers' of their portfolios. The kindest thing that could be said about reform models that cast politicians in such roles would be that they are unproven and seem to fly in the face of known incentives to behave in a more traditional 'political' fashion. Third, managers do appear to have gained extra authority in a number of ways but at the same time political control has been vigorously reasserted in many of the twelve countries. There is no *necessary* contradiction between these two developments—the public sector is large and diverse enough for both to be happening at the same time. In specific cases, however, there may be a quite definite tension. Fourth, any suggestion that public management can be radically depoliticized (in the sense of 'political' outlined above) is either a misunderstanding or flies in the face of evidence from many countries. The allocation of, say, health care resources or decisions about educational standards or major public infrastructure projects are all inherently 'political' decisions, whether they are taken by powerful politicians or tough public managers (or, indeed, medical doctors or teachers). The public will often see the political authority as ultimately responsible—or, at least, sharing responsibility—however much ministers may protest that these are technical or professional decisions which have been taken by the appropriate officials. Fifth, there is a certain ambiguity in much of the rhetoric around strengthening accountability and increasing transparency, in so far as some executive politicians have used the new politics/administration split to redefine policy weaknesses as managerial failures. This enables political leaders to shuffle off direct responsibilities for things going wrong—or, at least, to try to. Furthermore, it appears that legislatures have been slow to take up and use the increased flow of performance data which greater transparency and the contemporary emphasis on outputs and outcomes afford. With Chapter 5 in mind, one might say that even when a 'real result' manages to climb over the conceptual, methodological, and political barriers, and escapes into the wider public world, it is often left wandering around looking for an audience. Sixth, few of the specific reforms appear to have been undertaken in direct response to 'public opinion'—although some such rationale has quite often been claimed. Privatization, the introduction of market mechanisms, downsizing, and the promotion of PI systems are the products of elite, not popular, agendas (even if public opinion has subsequently accepted some of these innovations and begun to make use of them). The sector of greatest tension would appear to be the welfare state, the basic elements of which remain enduringly popular in most countries but the expense of which inevitably draws it into the line of fire of the cost-cutters and downsizers (see Appendix A). Seventh, any simple picture of public opinion as being 'for' or 'against' 'big government' is misleading. Such evidence as is available shows that, however limited the public's knowledge may be of the specifics of reform, popular attitudes towards government are multifaceted and, in some respects, quite sophisticated.

One further conclusion that might be drawn is that there is a strong need for a more realistic model of the role politicians can and should play in the running of the state apparatus. Neither the representative democracy/public interest model of the Anglo-Saxon countries nor the Continental *Rechtsstaat* model seems sufficient to cope with the new forms and practices which have emerged. It is not so much that these traditional models are wrong, but that they are, by themselves, inadequate to present-day circumstances (for some fruitful ideas see, e.g. Bovens 1998; Klijn and Koppenjan 2000). More controversially, one might suggest that any rethinking of these matters ought to focus at least as much on the induction and training of politicians, and on the framework of incentives and penalties surrounding them, as on reforming the public service or yet again reshuffling its organizations. Why is it usually assumed that it is the civil servants who are in need of reform but not ministers or the other politicians who may hope to become ministers in due course? This is *not* to advocate some modern version of Platonic guardians and neither, certainly, is it a plea for MPs to be forced to take MBAs. However, it *is* to suggest that the preparation of politicians for high office has, in many countries, been a 'no-go' area for reformers for too long. If it is in fact the *politicians themselves* who are most widely and deeply distrusted, then perhaps there are sound democratic reasons for bringing their readiness for the tasks they are confronted with to the fore as an item on the agenda for public debate?

[T]he time has come for elected officials to recall the biblical injunction: 'heal thyself'. It is crucial that they look to their own institutions. Every government is being affected by the information revolution and the global economy. Yet, parliament and cabinet still function much as they did twenty years ago. (Bourgault and Savoie 1998, p. 16)

Trade-offs, balances, limits, dilemmas, contradictions, and paradoxes

[T]he major paradoxes, with their unpalatable medium-term and long-term implications, appear to be general and permanent in character and seem to be rooted in misunderstanding, in the policy contradictions which characterise the reforms and in the naivete of the reformers themselves.

(Wright 1997, p. 12)

7.1 Reform optimism/memory loss

A prominent, but frequently unremarked feature of the public sector reforms of the last twenty years has been a large optimism about the *potential of management itself* (Pollitt 1993, pp. 1–5). Few boundaries seem to be envisaged for the exercise of this set of dynamic and purportedly generic skills. At the beginning of the most intensive period of reform a British Cabinet minister expressed himself thus: 'Efficient management is the key to the [national] revival . . . and the management ethos must run right through our national life—private and public companies, civil service, nationalized industries, local government, the National Health Service' (Heseltine 1980). Such optimism stands in contrast to an older tradition of speaking and writing about the running of public sector organizations, one that sees these activities as subject to a number of widespread, 'built-in', and possibly inevitable limitations and trade-offs. In traditional, permanent bureaucracies, cautionary wisdom about such administrative constraints was built up, case by case and over time, and used by seasoned career officials to warn politicians of the likely limitations of their proposed innovations (which, in administrative form, were seldom as novel as the politicians may have supposed). Since the 1970s, however, in the most radically reforming countries this kind of cautious mandarin has gone out of cultural fashion in favour of the 'can-do' chief executive (see Pollitt 2003a, chapter 7 for an analysis of management gurus and the representation of managers as heroes and visionaries). Furthermore, in these same countries, a combination of downsizing, the spread of term contracts for senior officials, and higher rates of turnover of various categories of staff has operated to shorten institutional memories, so that fewer and fewer in the organization are likely to know of the precedents of ten or twenty years ago, or to wish to bring these inconveniences to the attention of their political masters. As one senior

Canadian public servant put it recently: 'some of the grey matter of the public service has disappeared' (seminar discussion, November 1998; see also Pollitt 2000).

The grip of the 'lessons of history' has been further weakened by the popularity of the notion that, catalysed by rapid economic and technological change, the business of management is constantly confronting *new* challenges, and therefore, by implication at least, rapidly leaving *old* concerns far behind. Best-selling texts with titles such as *Thriving on Chaos: A Handbook for a Management Revolution* (Peters 1987) or *Re-engineering the Corporation* (Hammer and Champy 1995) have encouraged the belief that the past is irrelevant. Consider the following advice from the founding fathers of re-engineering:

Re-engineering is about beginning again with a clean sheet of paper. It is about rejecting the conventional wisdom and received assumptions of the past. Re-engineering is about inventing new approaches to process structures that bear little or no resemblance to those of previous eras. (Hammer and Champy 1995, p. 49)

It might be objected that the cited sources are concerned with the private sector. In fact the management 'gurus' in question insist that their insights apply to *all* organizations (see, e.g. Hammer and Champy 1995, pp. 218–19) and their work has certainly been taken up and noticed by governments in a number of countries. Furthermore, there is a parallel stream of rhetoric specifically focused on government. Probably the most read and talked-about English language text on government reform of the last decade is replete with declarations such as the following:

[T]he bureaucratic model developed in very different conditions from those we experience today... Today all that has been swept away. We live in an era of breathtaking change... Today's environment demands institutions that are extremely flexible and adaptable... It demands institutions that *empower* citizens rather than simply *serving* them. (Osborne and Gaebler 1992, p. 15)

Without wishing to deny the evident truth of changing conditions for government, we do wish to register a profound scepticism concerning what one might term the 'history is dead, everything is new' school of management thought. On the contrary, as governments have geared up to tackle the problems of the late twentieth century, the record (as we read it) shows many examples of old constraints and trade-offs reappearing in new clothes. One might even observe that individuals who undergo extreme memory loss are usually referred to as suffering from dementia, and that at least some of the more frenetic reform pronouncements share that same, sad quality of a loss of touch with everyday, here-and-now reality (Pollitt 2000).

In this chapter, therefore, we wish to take seriously the concept of there being intrinsic constraints and limits to administrative reform. This is hardly revolutionary. It has been espoused, in different ways, by a number of the most distinguished academic writers on public administration and management. For example, Charles Perrow envisaged bureaucratic processes as being inherently beset with dilemmas, in which to organize in one way was inevitably to pay a serious price in another (Perrow 1972). Aaron Wildavsky and John Pressman argued that the implementation of public policies was a deeply chancy business in which the realization of the policy-makers' vision depended upon the weakest link in what was usually a very long chain of intervening decisions and interorganizational linkages (Pressman and Wildavsky 1973). Christopher Hood developed an extended typology of 'limits' to administration, in which administrative dilemmas and nonlinearities commonly conspired to distort the process of implementation in the direction of inefficiency, corruption, or even counterintentional effects (Hood 1976). Hood and Jackson have also drawn attention to the way in which administrative 'principles' often come in matching pairs, with advantages and disadvantages trading off as one moves from one polar principle to its opposite (Hood and Jackson 1991). More recently the same author has articulated an even more elaborate scheme of constraints, using grid/group cultural theory in an attempt to demonstrate that each administrative philosophy carries not only intrinsic limitations but, beyond that, the seeds of its own decay (Hood 1998). In a more 'applied', specific work, John Halligan, commenting on the deep and wide-ranging reforms carried through in Australia and New Zealand, observed that, even in these two cases: 'While management practice and discourse have been transformed, the perennial questions of public administration remain' (Halligan 1997, p. 43).

Whilst we do not follow any of these authors exactly, we do believe that their shared perception that the administration of public programmes commonly exhibits deep-seated and recurring types of dilemma and contradiction is accurate. The substitution in anglophone environments of the magical word 'management' for the unfashionable 'administration' does little to change the types of limits with which these analysts were concerned (though it may lead to an increase in the proportion of certain types of problem in relation to other types). Obtaining reliable information about tax evasion behaviours or coordinating a variety of agencies delivering services to the unemployed are activities that pose fundamentally similar organizational problems whether the public officials concerned deem themselves to be rule-following bureaucrats or performance-chasing managers. Neither do the wonders of information technology dissolve the need to balance, choose, and recognize limits. Vastly improved capacities for data processing and rapid communication certainly make possible styles of governance, coordination, and (not least) supervision that were difficult or unachievable previously (Bovens and Zouridis 2002). However, information and communication technologies (ICTs) cannot resolve logical contradictions, bruised motivations, ergonomic constraints, or problems of competing and divergent values (Hudson 1999). They may, however, help decision-makers to muster a clearer or more detailed picture of the options before them—whether this clarity is welcome or not.

In this chapter, as earlier in the book, a distinction is drawn between the more 'gung-ho' reform rhetoric in some countries and the more cautious discourses of others. We concentrate mainly on the claims of the more radical reformers (or, at least, the more ambitious rhetoricians). More specifically we mean the core NPM group—Australia, New Zealand, the UK, and the USA. Canada has sometimes also been a member of this 'community of discourse', and the 'northern Europeans'—Finland, Sweden, and the Netherlands—have occasionally borrowed from the rhetoric, though only selectively and cautiously from the practice. Germany has not been a member of the club (certainly not at the level of the federal government) and neither has Belgium although Flanders is more inclined to the northern European version of the NWS. France has kept its distance, while articulating a rather distinctive reform rhetoric of its own (Guyomarch 1999).

Italian reform rhetoric has swung about rather wildly, but although it has certainly contained elements of the NPM, the 'message' has not been either as consistent or as persistent as in the UK and New Zealand. The EU Commission only began to dabble, and then rather unconvincingly, in the NPM brand of reform rhetoric since the mid-1990s. Our critique therefore concentrates on the 'radical reformers' (and would-be radical reformers) with only occasional remarks about the others. A charitable preliminary interpretation might be that these NWS countries have been more sensitive to balances, limits, and the persistence of traditional problems from the outset. A less optimistic interpretation would be that they have yet to face up to some of the awkward choices involved in thoroughgoing modernization of their public sectors. Regrettably, we have neither the space nor the data to pursue these enquiries concerning 'the others' here.

7.2 **The vocabulary of balance and contradiction**

Thus far in this chapter we have referred to 'constraints', 'limits', 'trade-offs', and 'problems'. In an attempt to be slightly more precise we will henceforth distinguish between:

Trade-offs: where having more of one desideratum, or lessening one problem, inevitably diminishes some other wished-for quality or increases a different problem. This is therefore a situation where decision-makers are obliged to *balance* between different things that they want, but cannot feasibly have more of all at the same time—indeed, where to have more of one entails having less of another. An example that Hood (1976) gives is that of appointing long-serving local officials, which is likely to increase local knowledge and continuity but simultaneously to increase the number of instances where the local officials 'go native' or succumb to the temptations of corruption. On the other hand, one can send in mobile officials whose allegiances are to the centre and who know they will soon be posted elsewhere. Choosing this second route reduces corruption and the dangers of the official developing excessive sympathy for the perceived difficulties faced by the administered local population, but it also reduces the local knowledge available to the administering organization, and thereby increases the chances that the local population are managing to evade or pervert the intended system of controls.

Limits: we will use the dictionary definition of a limit as 'a point, degree or amount beyond which something does not or may not pass' (Harrap's *Chambers Encyclopedic English Dictionary* 1994, p. 741).

Dilemmas: situations in which the manager is faced with a choice of two or more unsatisfactory alternatives, that is, in which the available decisions about a given problem cannot be made in such a way as to *solve* the problem, but only to substitute one set of undesirable features for another. A dilemma is thus the limiting case of a trade-off, in that it is a trade-off in which the situation remains negative whichever option is chosen. Sometimes rooting out public service corruption and/or incompetence may take on the characteristics of a dilemma. To publicize the problem lowers the standing of that part of the public service, undermines public trust, and may even encourage increased citizen recalcitrance ('why should I pay my taxes if they are putting them in their own pockets?'). On the other hand, not to publicize the problem may allow it to continue and can prevent the formation of a sufficient coalition of support to ensure that real action is taken.

Another concept to which we will resort is the *paradox*. Paradoxes are *seeming* contradictions: statements that appear self-contradictory and false, and yet may contain a particular kind of truth. The dictionary example is often 'more haste, less speed'. Some commentators have found a whole string of paradoxes entwined in the rhetoric and practice of contemporary administrative reform (Wright 1997). Some of these are pitched at the level of whole countries or systems, others at the level of specific institutions or practices. Wright begins his account with a striking example of a macroparadox:

The first major policy paradox is that the most radical reform programmes appear to have been introduced in countries with the most efficient administrations, in other words, in those countries with the least need! (Wright 1997, pp. 9–10)

Earlier chapters in this book have contained some possible reasons for this curious state of affairs. Perhaps it has been the countries that are constitutionally and politically most *able* to make big changes to their administrative arrangements that have done so (Chapter 3). Yet these are also probably the countries *that had already made significant modernizations of their public sector organizations in the past* (for the same reason). Our own account will mainly address more specific propositions within the portfolio of current reform ideas. One might argue, for example, that the statements which have been made in a number of countries to the effect that public management reforms will make public servants more accountable to political leaders *and simultaneously more accountable to the citizens who use public services*, though appealing, are paradoxical. How can public officials serve two masters, masters who are quite unlikely to have identical needs or preferences? Further examples occur when policy-makers say that they intend to empower middle managers in the public service whilst at the same time radically downsizing the numbers of that group who will continue in public employment. *Perhaps* these apparent dissonances can be harmoniously reconciled, but it is not immediately obvious how.

It must be allowed that sometimes what sounds to be an incompatibility *is* an incompatibility, which cannot be reconciled. In such cases we may speak of straightforward *contradictions*. Guy B. Peters is one comparativist who has suggested that, while the contemporary nostrums of public management reform appear to contain a number of contradictions, some at least of these can be resolved into a question of finding an appropriate *balance* rather than a question of choosing between wholly incompatible alternatives (Peters 1998a). In effect he is saying that some contradictions are really trade-offs rather than absolute contradictions. Thus one may think of a contradiction as a case of a very steep-sided trade-off—that is, as a situation in which having more of one benefit immediately and sharply reduces another benefit. This is a notion we explore in more detail below.

7.3 Public management reform: some candidate contradictions

Many writers have noticed apparent contradictions or tensions within the body of contemporary management prescriptions, and each has offered a slightly different set (e.g. Hood 1991, 1998; Peters 1998a; Savoie 1994; Williams 2000; Wright 1997). We will draw on these to compile our own shortlist of 'candidate contradictions'—sets of prescriptions which at first sight appear incompatible, or at least unstable, and which therefore merit further discussion and investigation.

Our focus is on the substance rather than the process of management reform—on the types of reform to be put in place rather than on how the implementation of the change is managed. This is an important restriction, and we would be the first to acknowledge that there may be significant contradictions and paradoxes in process as well as substance (indeed, the arguments provided by some commentators concentrate as much, if not more, on implementation strategies as on actual types of reform, e.g. Peters 1998a). Obviously, implementation is important. A fundamentally sound reform can be 'messed up' through poor implementation and the worst effects of an unsound reform can be obscured, delayed, or otherwise diluted by shrewd management (Pollitt 2002). However, this is not principally a book on 'how to do it', and the 'comparative advantage' of an academic account probably lies with an analysis of the substantive content of reform rather than in attempting to second-guess the craft skills of the implementors.

Our selection includes some (seemingly) incompatible paired statements and some more complicated/less obvious combinations. Each will be explained in the sections that follow. We will begin with four 'candidate contradictions' at the level of the whole system of public administration in a country, and then move on to a further six that are pitched more at the level of specific operations, giving ten in all. The shortlist is set out below:

1. Increase political control of the bureaucracy/free managers to manage/empower service consumers.
2. Promote flexibility and innovation/increase citizen trust and therefore governmental legitimacy.
3. Give priority to making savings/improving the performance of the public sector.
4. 'Responsibilize' government/reduce the range of tasks that government is involved with.
5. Motivate staff and promote cultural change/weaken tenure and downsize.
6. Reduce burden of internal scrutiny and associated paperwork/sharpen managerial accountability.
7. Create more single-purpose agencies/improve horizontal coordination ('joined-up government'; 'horizontality').
8. Decentralize management authority/improve programme coordination.
9. Increase effectiveness/sharpen managerial accountability.
10. Improve quality/cut costs.

7.4 Increase political control of the bureaucracy/free managers to manage/empower service consumers

Each of these three admonitions features regularly in the rhetoric of public management reform. There is no doubt that reform leaders such as (among others) Thatcher, Reagan, and Mulroney wished to reassert (as they saw it) political control over the bureaucratic machine (Savoie 1994). So did, for example, the French political leadership (Rouban 1997) and at least some elements among Swedish politicians (Pierre 1995) and the Australian Labor governments of the 1980s (Halligan 1997). Equally, there is no doubt that increasing the freedom managers have to manage has been a recurrent theme in countless texts and speeches. For example, a key line in the report that led to the UK's creation of 130-plus executive agencies, employing more than two-thirds of the nonindustrial civil service, was: 'At present the freedom of an individual manager to manage effectively and responsibly in the civil service is extremely circumscribed' (Efficiency Unit 1988, p. 5).

Finally, the empowerment of customers is a theme that has been repeatedly on the lips of politicians bent on reform, especially in the Anglo-Saxon countries. One US NPR document puts it like this: 'Once President Clinton signed the Government Performance and Results Act in August 1993, strategic planning and listening to the "voice of the customer" was no longer just a good idea—it was the law' (National Performance Review 1997*b*, p. 6).

The problem with these superficially attractive formulations can be encompassed in the question 'How is it possible to give managers greater freedom and yet at the same time place them more under the control of ministers *and* oblige them to be more responsive to newly empowered consumers?' Is it conceivable that all three corners of this triangle can be strengthened simultaneously (minister power, manager power, consumer power), or is this simply a contradiction? As Hood (1998 p. 208) puts it: 'Since not everyone can be "empowered" at the same time, who exactly is to be empowered against whom, and how, is a key test of cultural bias in visions of modernization.'

If it is assumed that the appropriate concept of power and authority in this case is zero-sum (i.e. power is a fixed quantum, so that a gain here must be balanced by a loss somewhere else), then this particular NPM 'recipe' is a (double) contradiction. However, it is possible, on the basis of a different assumption, to interpret these guidelines in a more sympathetic, or paradoxical light. Such a defence might run along the following lines:

1. Managers can have greater freedom over the marshalling of their resources (combining inputs and processes in different and perhaps innovative ways) while at the same time ministers are offered a clearer picture of what is achieved—the outputs and outcomes of all the newly unencumbered management activity. So both politicians and managers can increase their control—though of somewhat different things. The clearest expression of this philosophy has been the New Zealand system in which ministers are deemed responsible for objectives and outcomes, and they then contract with the heads of departments (chief executives) for packages of measured outputs that are calculated to produce the desired outcomes (Boston et al. 1996; Halligan 1997).

2. Similarly, empowered consumers may have access to better information about the performance of a service, and may enjoy improved means of complaint/more efficient redress if things are not to their liking, and may participate in planning and prioritizing the service through a variety of mechanisms (these empowerments manifesting themselves in the shape of charters, better complaints systems, user panels, etc.—though whether the majority of citizens actually want to spend more time doing these things is an open question, as we saw in Chapter 6). At the same time managers can gain new freedoms to arrange their resources in ways that are calculated to maximize consumer satisfaction. There is no contradiction between these two separate but complementary spheres of autonomy.

3. Thus, all three groups—politicians, public service managers, and public service users—*can* gain greater control, each in their own corner. Power is not zero-sum but rather variable: everyone can be a winner.

Is this a convincing defence against the charge of contradiction? Perhaps, but only if certain fairly demanding conditions are met. Three deserve particular mention. First, politicians must refrain from interfering in the management sphere (the allocation, manipulation, and combination of different kinds of resource, the motivation of staff, the establishment and maintenance of suitable organizational structures, systems, and processes) and confine themselves to scrutinizing 'results' and taking action if the results are short of target. Second, the priorities and targets handed down by the political leaders must be both clear and reasonably congruent with the demands and expectations of consumers (otherwise managers will be asked to dance simultaneously to two discordant tunes). Third, where there are different organizations and levels involved in service delivery (as there very frequently will be), all must work within the same, shared set of objectives, targets, and—to some extent at least—procedures. Otherwise there is the likelihood that managers will receive conflicting messages from above and consumers will encounter different priorities, standards, and attitudes in different parts of the 'shop'. If one or more of these conditions is transgressed, the likelihood of the triangle being squared (so to speak) will be swiftly reduced.

The question of how often the above conditions actually *are* met (and how often they are not) is an empirical one, and the rate may vary with regime type, organizational culture, political ideology, and so on. What is clear is that there have been many occasions in many countries when the vision of mutual, three-cornered empowerment has been announced but not achieved. Some have been recounted earlier in this book. Particularly in welfare state services such as health care, education, personal social services, and social security the figure of the empowered service user has in practice been hard to find (e.g. Clarke and Newman 1997, chapter 6; Evers et al. 1997; Flösser and Otto 1998; Harrison and Pollitt 1994, pp. 125–34). 'Shop front' public service staff may have had customer service training and been enjoined to deal more flexibly with individual service users, but meanwhile managers seem often to have extended their domain without conceding any substantial space for 'consumer power'. In other cases managers have been pulled in different directions by irreconcilable demands from political bosses and service users (see Pollitt 2003a, chapter 4 for an extended analysis of these issues).

Nor is the evidence on the second side of the triangle especially encouraging. As we saw in Chapter 6, politicians have not been spectacularly willing to relinquish their former habits of detailed intervention. In some research, managers have recorded more political 'interference', not less (Halligan 2002; Talbot 1994). Nor have ministers necessarily been prepared to spell out their values in a sufficiently precise manner to give managers a clear set of priorities to work to (and therefore, by derivation, a clear set of targets to aim at).

As for the achievement of coordination between different levels and types of organization (the third condition), there can be no doubt that 'partnership' and 'networking' have become extremely fashionable in most of our twelve countries, and with the EU Commission (e.g. Chancellor of the Exchequer 1998; Osborne 2000; Pollitt 2003*a*, chapter 3; Rosenau 2000). Being in fashion and being well understood are, however, not at all the same thing. A rapidly burgeoning literature demonstrates that most governments are still on the steep part of the learning curve as far as these pluriform approaches to service delivery are concerned (e.g. Kickert et al. 1997; Lowndes and Skelcher 1998; Peters 1998*b*). The available 'technologies' for ensuring 'seamless' service are therefore still experimental and uncertain, so it would be reasonable to conclude that the third condition cannot be satisfied regularly and with certainty.

To sum up: first, the reformers' claims to empower consumers, free managers, and strengthen political control are not always and not necessarily contradictory. Unfortunately, however, the conditions for their simultaneous achievement are difficult to cultivate, so that, in practice, these three aims often do collide or, perhaps less dramatically, one or more of them is simply sidelined or forgotten. In a perfect world the three objectives might be compatible. In the real world public managers usually find themselves facing trade-offs or even downright contradictions.

7.5 Promote flexibility and innovation/promote citizen trust and increase legitimacy

The possible contradiction between these two appealing propositions is not necessarily obvious. The tension arises in those situations where continuity, trust, and predictability are likely to be the qualities most sought after by the majority of service users. In such circumstances the excitements of constant change and innovation become counterproductive. Confusion and mistrust may grow. Take, for example, the issue of local post offices, which have been a focus for debate in a number of our countries, including Finland and the UK. Many small (often rural) post offices are uneconomic to maintain. Therefore, efficiency-promoting innovations are proposed (remote electronic means of conducting the same transactions; the relocation of the postal services in local shops rather than separate premises). However, the public reacts against these 'improvements'. At least one section of the public values the cultural and social aspects of the local post office—they want stability and continuity. In Finland it seems that some persons trust a post office with their personal business but do not wish to reveal details of the same to their local shopkeeper (an interesting example of the public servant being perceived as more trustworthy than the business person).

Part of the problem with innovation is that it frequently requires users as well as service providers to learn new tricks. This tends to be far more difficult for some sections of society than for others, and innovations thus, unintentionally, acquire inegalitarian aspects. One could see this in the post office example mentioned above: citizens in rural areas lose their post offices and may have to learn to use remote systems, citizens in big cities get to keep them. An even clearer example occurred in the 1990s in a London borough that embarked upon a policy of installing automated electronic information kiosks for the public. The hope was that this innovation would extend service (through 24-hour availability) and enable the authority to economize on staff. Unfortunately, as subsequent research showed, matters were not so straightforward. Most of those who used the kiosks were male and under forty years of age—women and older residents used them much less. Furthermore, considerable difficulties were encountered in having all the (voluminous) information translated into all the ethnic languages represented in the area. Also, it emerged that some ethnic groups had a cultural norm that located trust in transactions only in face-to-face contacts with officials (needing to see a face). For all these reasons (and more) the actual effect of the automated kiosks tended to discriminate against the elderly, women, and certain ethnic groups.

A case which affects many millions of citizens in a number of countries is that of pensions. Governments have, in several instances, come to realize that their previous planning of pensions has been inadequate, and that they are unlikely to be able to afford all the demands that will fall on them in the future. Legislation is therefore introduced to change national pension systems—sometimes restricting eligibility, some-times changing terms, sometimes incentivizing citizens to take up occupational or personal pension schemes rather than rely on the state pension. Many innovations in pension provision are attempted—some with very good intentions, some to save money. The outcomes are mixed. One outcome has been that stability and predictability are lost in an area where they have been of essence over long time periods. Citizens have lost trust in the ability of the state to provide for their old age—there has been considerable anxiety, and some commercial pension companies have taken advantage of the confusion to advertise their wares (Marmor et al. 1990). In some cases commercial schemes have been perfectly satisfactory. In other cases there have been well-publicized examples of schemes being very poor value for money, or of companies failing, or of schemes being sold to citizens who did not really need them, thus adding to public disquiet.

Our overall analysis would be that *there is no fundamental or universal contradiction* between innovation on the one hand and stability and continuity on the other. Indeed, there are occasions when innovation is required in order to maintain continuity—such as when back-of-office automation allows the same service to be delivered to a larger number of users without unacceptable increases in cost. This having been said, however, there are also specific contexts in which public managers do face at least a trade-off between innovation and one or more of the values of stability, continuity, predictability, trust, and (as we saw in some of the above examples) egalitarianism. Such contexts confront public service managers with difficult problems of balancing divergent desiderata, and possibly disadvantaging certain sections of a community, even if an improved service is supplied to other sections of the community. Given the pervasive cost pressures and the prominence given to innovation within the reform ideology, it is likely that trade-off problems of this kind occur quite often. It is not our impression that the literature on management reform—either academic or professional—fully reflects this.

7.6 Make public expenditure savings/improve public sector performance

Tighter control of public expenditure has figured as one of the most frequent and most powerful motives for public management reform—in every country we have surveyed. If translated into reduced tax burdens, this may be popular (though in practice the overall tax burden on individuals may have increased, as it did, for example, under the UK Conservative administrations of 1979–97). However, if translated into cuts in popular welfare state services such as pensions, health care, or education, then 'savings' tend to be unpopular, as was noted in Chapter 6. Since these 'social protections' commonly take up the major share of the state budget, it is usually impossible to make large-scale savings without touching them (see Appendix A). Thus there appears, prima facie, to be a contradiction between the commitment to holding down public spending and the commitment to improving public services.

As a first step in exploring this tension, we may note that it reflects a background discontinuity in the stream of ideas that have been taken up and used by the reformers. As explained in Chapter 2, politicians and mandarins drew on various bodies of thought to guide their actions. One important source, especially in the Anglo-Saxon countries, was microeconomics. Indeed, one commentator goes so far as to label the entire wave of contemporary public management reform 'Ricardian' (Lane 1997). A quite different—but equally influential—source was the work of management and organization theorists, including 'gurus' such as Peter Drucker, Tom Peters, Robert Waterman, and Edward Deming. The two currents of thought have different emphases. Microeconomics is focused on the achievement of allocative and technical efficiency. Management thinking is also concerned with efficiency, but pursues a broader agenda including adaptation to new environments, cultural change, and the importance of measuring, meeting, and (some would say) manipulating customer expectations.

It is not that there is a direct contradiction between the two sets of ideas (though they do tend to use fundamentally different models of individuals) but rather that there is the difference of emphasis indicated above. One might say that microeconomic thinking would tend to prioritize efficiency and savings, while management thinking would focus more on improving performance in a broad sense, embracing higher-quality, more flexible, and 'customer-friendly' service. Management theorists also seem to embrace a slightly more optimistic, or at any rate varied, model of individual motivation, in that they allow for factors such as loyalty and cultural change, whereas microeconomists are stuck with their elegant but thin utility maximizers.

A second point is to note that it is possible to sidestep the apparent contradiction—at least on the level of rhetoric. In the field of social security in the UK, for example, much effort has been concentrated on improving the *process* of claiming—training counter staff to be more friendly, smartening up premises, speeding up processing activities, and so on. Not unreasonably, this is often referred to as 'quality improvement'. Meanwhile, however, the actual benefit levels have been tightly controlled, and, in the cases of a number of benefits, eligibility categories have been narrowed. Thus is the paradox resolved—expenditure (substance) is reined in but 'quality' (process) is improved.

A third step is to see that the apparent contradiction actually has a paradox folded within it. This 'nested' paradox is that the contradiction is more likely to hold in those jurisdictions *that are most efficient and effective in service delivery*. This is because the ability to make savings and at the same time improve service seems to be closely connected with the amount of spare capacity in the system (Murray 1998) and the most efficient jurisdictions are those that are carrying the least spare capacity. In jurisdictions that are already super-efficient there is no 'fat' left to cut, and enforced economies are bound to carve into the bone of real services.

A fourth step is to acknowledge that technological advance will sometimes be able to 'solve' the apparent contradiction. A technological leap forward may enable managers of a public service simultaneously to save money and to push up quality and productivity (see, e.g. some of the examples in National Audit Office 1999). There is an empirical question as to how often such technological breakthroughs occur, and there is a further empirical question about how well new technologies are implemented (Hudson 1999; Margetts 1998). Nevertheless, new ICTs will sometimes be able to resolve the contradiction, which is no doubt one reason why they are such a universal favourite as an ingredient of the rhetoric of public management reform.

We are left, then, with a context-dependent comment on the apparent contradiction between improved performance and expenditure savings. In contexts where a system is already fairly efficient, and where there is no technological breakthrough to hand, the contradiction may be real. In less efficient systems, the contradiction can be circumnavigated by drawing upon spare capacity. In systems where technological change is rapid, the contradiction may be solved by technological innovation, assuming it is competently implemented.

7.7 'Responsibilize' government/privatize

These two strands in the rhetoric of reform seem to sit uneasily together. How can governments become more responsible and responsive to public wishes if at the same time they are relinquishing control of huge public enterprises—that is, apparently reducing their ability to steer the economy and ensure the delivery of specific services and utilities? The UK Conservative governments of 1979–97 'returned' roughly half the public sector—and approximately 650,000 employees—to private ownership. The nationalized industries shrank from 9 per cent to less than 5 per cent of GDP. In New Zealand privatizations were, proportionately, even larger (Halligan 1997, p. 23). In other countries privatization has been a smaller component of reform, but significant sales of public assets have occurred in countries as diverse as Australia, Finland, France, and the Netherlands (see in Appendix B: country files).

There is also the argument that privatization makes the state appear more and more parasitic. It no longer has a hand in producing anything that can be sold at a profit. It becomes just a taxing and redistributing authority. At the same time it loses direct touch with the world of industrial or commercial service production, and has to seek information about that world from the outside, without the benefit of any direct experience itself (in the language of economics, there is increasing information asymmetry).

Of course, *if* privatization were what the public wanted, then it would be a straightforward matter to claim that 'responsive' and 'responsible' governments should vigorously pursue such a policy. In some cases privatization seems to have been popular (the UK case of British Telecom is the one usually quoted). In others, however, individual privatization measures have clearly run directly *against* public opinion—as with the privatization of water and of British Railways in the UK. Yet initial unpopularity need not be conclusive in itself. Governments can (and do) argue that responsible privatization, accompanied by the creation of a strong regulatory regime, can safeguard the public interest in the activities concerned, while simultaneously releasing the economic benefits that flow from the efficiency-inducing pressures of the commercial marketplace.

There is also a 'your-government-knows-better' argument to support privatization. In the UK, at least, ministers and mandarins knew how often nationalized industries had been informally 'interfered with' by ministers (e.g. to postpone needed price rises until after the next election). Privatization could be conceived of as a kind of political self-denying ordinance: 'We politicians know we are not to be trusted as managers of industrial corporations and large service operations and therefore the best thing is for us to shift them to a format where we *cannot* mess around with them.' This is 'responsible', in the same sense as an alcoholic who keeps no alcohol in the house is behaving responsibly.

Our conclusion is therefore that there is no fundamental, logical contradiction between the claim to be developing more responsive and responsible government and a vigorous programme of privatizing public assets. There is, however, a series of practical challenges that can, in specific cases, generate tension or divergence between the public interest and privatization (Parker 2000). Governments can sell the assets too cheaply (Waugh 1998), or can fail to put in place effective regulatory machinery, or can simply insist, for doctrinaire reasons, on privatizing activities that a majority of the public strongly wish to retain in public ownership. In these types of cases the principle of privatization is not at fault, but rather the way in which it is executed is.

7.8 Motivate staff and promote cultural change/weaken tenure and downsize

A whole chapter of the NPR booklet *Businesslike Government* was given over to 'Creative license: unleashing the creative power of government employees' (Gore 1997, p. 25). In many countries—particularly those where the civil service was most harshly criticized during the 1980s—the mid-1990s saw attempts to 're-vision' and 're-motivate' public servants. 'The Public Service of Canada requires a transformation in its people, its culture, and its leadership' and 'The Public Service of Canada needs champions and leaders' (Bourgon 1998, pp. 21, 23). 'We must restore faith in the public service ethos, and convey the message that we can only deliver better government if we harness and use the talents of the civil service and other public servants' (Clark—the minister with civil service responsibilities in the new Blair government in the UK—1997, p. 3). And so on. The contradiction here is with the threat to public service jobs, security, and pay posed by expenditure cutbacks, and management reforms. To tell public servants that they are highly valued at the same time that many of them are being 'let go' may strike at least part of the audience as ironic, or worse. Even the most sympathetic official statements often contain a sting in the tail: 'Absolute job security is not something that any employee . . . can expect in the competitive modern world. But we do want to look at ways of reducing insecurity, so as to minimize distractions from policy goals' (Clark 1997, p. 20).

Can this apparent contradiction be resolved? We find it hard to see how it could be. Indeed, there have been obvious instances where the contradiction has been seen only too clearly by the staff concerned (e.g. in New Zealand—Boston et al. 1996, pp. 211–24; in the USA with respect to the NPR's downsizing targets—Kettl 1994, pp. 13–21; or during the public service strikes in France in the mid-1990s). Phrases such as 'expecting the turkeys to vote for Christmas' (UK) and 'from rowing to steering to abandoning ship' (USA) came our way from public servants as we researched this topic.

That said, the contradiction may be lived with—even blunted somewhat. Certain factors promise to assist in this. To begin with, there is the brutal fact that the public servants who matter most will be the ones who survive downsizing. It is possible to envisage a smaller, less bureaucratic, more highly skilled, perhaps even better-remunerated public service within which morale could be restored and a new performance-oriented culture solidly entrenched. Those who lose their jobs frequently also lose their voices—they are now 'outsiders', at best an embarrassment to the survivors. Note, however, that this vision depends on the perception that a new phase of relative stability has been attained. Continuing, repeated downsizing (like those that have taken place in Europe and the USA in industries such as coalmining or shipbuilding) destroys any basis for confidence and commitment. They replace the proposition of 'pain today, jam tomorrow' with the unattractive 'pain today, more tomorrow'. They also destroy institutional memory, reduce the chances of survival for any 'public service ethic', and lead to a 'hollowed-out' and ultimately less competent form of government. Here the basic contradiction is left naked for all to see, and the consequences in terms of morale and trust must be expected swiftly to follow.

7.9 Reduce burden of internal scrutiny and associated paperwork/ sharpen managerial accountability

The evidence seems to indicate that this particular tension is more a question of balance than of outright contradiction—although in practice it is easy for the balance to be lost. The tension between the two arises because to sharpen managerial accountability so often involves operational managers having to make new returns to the top of the organization, to provide data for new PI systems, quality improvement schemes, or performance audit scrutinies. Although what is being asked of operational managers is (in principle at least) a different *kind* of information—output- and outcome-oriented rather than input data—it can still become an onerous burden, perhaps even exceeding in volume and complexity what was required under the *status quo ante*.

Radin (1998) shows how easy it is for a series of individually well-intentioned reform measures to produce a heavy weight of requirements upon public managers. In the USA the Paperwork Reduction Act of 1995 was aimed at eliminating unnecessary paperwork and reducing the burden of form-filling for citizens and firms. Introducing the bill, President Clinton spoke of the need to 'conquer the mountain of paperwork'. This in itself appeared an unexceptional objective, although, as Radin points out, it also placed limits on the collection of the kind of performance data that would be required to fulfil the aspirations of the 1993 GPRA. Meanwhile, however, federal managers groaned under a series of new measures, including:

- The Federal Managers' Financial Integrity Act, 1982—which requires annual assurance of the adequacy of controls.
- The Chief Financial Officers' Act, 1990—which requires annual accountability reports.
- The Government Management Reform Act, 1994—which requires annual financial statements to the Office of Management and Budget.
- The Information Technology Management Reform Act, 1996—which also requires annual reports, this time showing how information technology is being used to help programmes achieve their objectives.
- The Federal Financial Management Improvement Act, 1996—which requires reports on financial systems compliance by agency heads, inspectors-general, and the head of OMB.
- REGO 111 of the NPR, 1996—which requires annual reports from agencies on how they are responding to the principles of the NPR.

The above is by no means a complete listing of all the *new* information demands, let alone the ongoing ones.

This is not just a tale of some particularly American exuberance or excess. Parallels can be found in a number of other countries where reform has been given a high profile. After documenting an 'audit explosion' closely linked to new styles of management, Power (1997, p. 142) comments: [I]t is clear that in the UK and elsewhere during the 1980s and the early 1990s auditing acquired an institutional momentum which insulated it from systemic enquiry.' New processes of audit or quasi-audit were devised and applied in almost every main branch of the UK public sector (Hood et al. 1999). In universities ongoing squabbles took place over the validity and reliability of new 'audits of teaching quality', which imposed huge documentation requirements upon each and every institution, and spawned a substantial cohort of new internal committees, working to prepare their departments or universities to put the best possible face towards its next external review. In schools head teachers complained regularly of the weight of inspections by the new regulatory body, Ofsted (Pollitt 2003a, chapter 2). In the NHS elaborate systems of PI and quality assurance were devised and put in place. In fieldwork during the mid-1990s one of us found the director of quality at a medium-sized hospital frustrated by the fact that the hospital was required to respond to four or five different types of quality reviews simultaneously, each with its own forms and processes (Pollitt et al. 1998, p. 91).

We said at the beginning of this section that we considered the tension between reduced paperwork and increased performance-monitoring to be a question of balance rather than of inherent contradiction. The above examples indicate that balance is not automatically guaranteed—it has to be constructed and then actively maintained. The paperwork burden on middle management *can* be reduced, if the performance-monitoring regime is carefully designed, focused, and regularly reviewed so as to prune 'excess growth'. This is the optimistic view. A slightly less sanguine perspective would be to see the whole process as a cyclic one in which monitoring and auditing systems possessed inbuilt tendencies to 'put on weight', but these were, from time to time, corrected by bursts of 'dieting' (reforms). This would perhaps explain why, in several countries, clear-outs of regulations and paperwork requirements seem to be hardy perennials rather than 'one-off' reforms. It would also allow for the fact that there is some evidence of PI systems cycling between a smaller number of key indicators and a larger number of detailed indicators (Pollitt 1990). What one is seeing here is therefore a trade-off rather than a contradiction: the trade is between, on the one hand, simple, light monitoring controls which permit subtleties and complexities and 'gaming' to squeeze round or through them and, on the other, detailed, heavy systems which capture more of the complexities and ploys, but that are burdensome and expensive to operate (Bruijn 2002). Over time the grass on the other side of the trade-off often looks greener, hence the cycle.

7.10 Create more single-purpose agencies/improve horizontal coordination

The difficulty with this pair of proposals is that, *ceteris paribus*, specialization (into single-purpose agencies) *increases* the difficulty of coordination (Bouckaert et al. 2000). As

Rhodes (1997, p. 53) puts it of the Next Steps reforms in Whitehall, 'the most obvious result of the new system is institutional fragmentation'. There is some evidence that 'agentification' has exacerbated coordination problems in at least New Zealand (Boston et al. 1996, p. 88), the UK (Office of Public Services Reform 2002), and the Netherlands (Roberts 1997, pp. 106–11). In Sweden, where a system of strong, independent agencies has been in existence for a long time, there has also been a recurring concern that ministries lack the capacity and expertise effectively to manage 'their' agencies (see, e.g. OECD 1998, p. 4 of executive summary; Molander et al. 2002). In fieldwork research that one of us undertook in the mid-1990s, it appeared that for hospitals, schools and providers of social housing, greater autonomy for individual service delivery organizations had indeed lessened coordination, at least at the level of individual cities or regions (Pollitt et al. 1998).

None of this is to say that agencification/autonomization does not also carry benefits. There is evidence, in several countries and many different sectors, of greater autonomy leading to improvements in economy, productivity, or user-responsiveness. Such benefits are, of course, not automatic: there is always the danger that poor management will fail to grasp the opportunities that are presented to them. But the existence of benefits is not the point here: the point is that there is a tension between the taking of these benefits and the simultaneous arrival of certain penalties in the form of loss of coordination at a higher level. (To be even-handed between both sides of the equation, it must also be acknowledged that the *potential* for coordination that existed under more centralized systems was by no means always taken advantage of.) Advocates of NPM-type reforms tend to deny or minimize the existence of loss of coordination, and, because 'coordination' is such a difficult concept to operationalize, it is extremely hard to prove them wrong. According to this view, a framework that provides clear performance targets and lines of accountability should obviate fragmentation, and allow the central authorities to continue to 'steer' flotillas of agencies in some strategically sensible direction. To which we would respond that actual frameworks are often much less integrated than that (Talbot 1996), and that, in a number of countries, perceptions of fragmentation among practitioners seem to be quite widespread. What we suspect, therefore, is that there probably *is* a trade-off (not a contradiction) here, and that in practice significantly increased levels of institutional autonomy (and the benefits that brings) are usually purchased by some loss of policy or programme coordination. It is for politicians and public to say whether any given trade-off is acceptable, but so long as the rhetoricians of reform insist that nothing is lost the trade-off issue cannot be properly investigated, weighed, and debated.

7.11 Decentralize management authority/improve programme coordination

The potential problems here are similar to those discussed in the previous section. Pushing authority down and out tends to increase coordination difficulties.

Agencification is just one case of the larger category of decentralization. The popularity of decentralization in many jurisdictions during the 1980s and 1990s eventually led to a growth of concern for 'joined-up government' and 'cross-cutting issues' (OECD 2001; Peters and Bouckaert 2003; Pollitt 2003*b*). A good example here is probably the EU's structural funds programmes: the management of these is highly decentralized—and highly variable. The EU Commission gives out the money, but its attempts to evaluate and steer what is going on cannot be considered to be very impressive (Barbier and Simonin 1997; Toulemonde 1997).

Our conclusion is therefore the same as that for agencification—that is, in many cases there will be a trade-off, but probably not such a steep-sided choice as to justify the title of a 'contradiction'. Sensitive implementation may minimize and even succeed in concealing the trade-off, but on the bottom line shifting authority to the periphery means just that, and carries the implication that the coordinating authority of the centre is diminished. Of course, this consequence can be avoided in cases (not unknown) of pseudo-decentralization—those instances where the central authority claims to have 'empowered the front line' but in fact retains a full battery of controls which are reimposed the moment anything not to its liking occurs.

7.12 Increase effectiveness/sharpen management accountability

It may not be immediately apparent why there should be any tension between these two objectives. Are they not both perfectly sensible and compatible? If we consider the observations of the Canadian Auditor General, reporting on performance management reforms, we can see that this is not necessarily so:

Outputs are results that managers can control, while the outcomes managers are trying to accomplish are influenced by factors outside their programs. (Auditor General of Canada 1997, pp. 5–8)

A glance back at Figure 5.1 will show that effectiveness is a question of securing the hoped-for *outcomes*, while efficiency is a matter of optimizing the *input/output* ratio. A good deal of evidence, spread over many years and from a number of countries, indicates two alternating difficulties:

1. When managers are enjoined to concentrate on concrete outputs (licences issued, grants given, training courses completed), they tend to lose sight of outcomes and, therefore, to stress efficiency rather than effectiveness (East 1997).

2. When managers are asked to concentrate on outcomes and effectiveness, it is hard to hold them responsible and accountable, for several reasons. This is because the attribution of outcomes to the actions of individual units or organizations is frequently obscure or doubtful, and also because, for many public programmes, measurable outcomes manifest themselves over such extended time periods that they cannot provide a sensible basis for annual accountability exercises anyway (Pollitt 1995; Pollitt and Bouckaert 2003).

There appears to be a dilemma, or at least a trade-off, here. Go for outputs and you are likely to lose sight of effectiveness; go for effectiveness and you lose the chance of clear accountability for individual managers and their units. The easy answer is to say 'go for both simultaneously' (Bruijn 2002, p. 17). Unfortunately, that is more easily said than done. Accountability systems are likely to slide towards outputs, as more quickly measurable, more easily attributable, and much less costly to monitor. At a 1997 conference for senior New Zealand public managers, the then minister for the civil service made 'output fixation' and the neglect of outcomes one of his chief themes (East 1997). This theme was also echoed in parts of the UK government's 1999 white paper *Modernising Government* (Prime Minister and Minister for the Cabinet Office 1999).

There is an even more controversial aspect to the effectiveness/accountability relationship. This is pungently expressed by Wright (1997, p. 11):

A great deal of public policy is about rationing, about the distribution of scarce resources, about zero-sum games and opportunity costs. For rationing to work over any length of time it must either be ignored, obfuscated or it must be legitimised. It is an intrinsically difficult exercise to undertake by a democratic society in peacetime and in periods of stagnation or depression...

However, some of the current reforms, driven by good intentions, seem designed to undermine those three essential props: ignorance is being replaced by defined rights and obfuscation by transparency. Even more significant is the *delegitimation* of the process: decisions about rationing are being removed from politicians and self-regulating professions like teachers and doctors and they are being transferred to *managers* and to entrepreneurs, who quite simply lack the essential legitimacy to spread the essential misery.

In the light of these considerations, what can be said about the relationship between the drive for greater effectiveness and the drive for sharper management accountability? First, we are definitely *not* arguing that this is a sharp contradiction, with a steep-sided collapse of an effectiveness-orientation the moment the authorities begin to try to build management accountability, or vice versa. Second, there does, however, seem to be a tension between a focus on outputs and a focus on outcomes, with most of the cards (measurability, timeliness, attributability, cost) being stacked in favour of outputs. This is not so much a trade-off as a balance, which is difficult to hold against the slide towards 'output fixation'. Third, Wright opens up a deeper and more obviously political dilemma: that, for services that are rationed, the process of clarifying accountability and shifting it more to managers and away from public service professionals may result in a loss of legitimacy and an increase in litigation and dispute.

7.13 Improve quality/cut costs

Quality Is Free was the title of a widely referenced book by one of the private sector quality gurus of the 1980s (Crosby 1979). The happy claim was that improving quality was effectively free—that ultimately it always paid for itself. Whether or not this may have been true for commercial organizations operating in competitive markets, it certainly does not hold as an invariable proposition in the public sector. There are many public services where spending on quality improvements is unlikely to increase either the volume of customers, or the budget appropriation, or the income (if any) received from charges. The incentives for quality improvement are accordingly diminished. One of the reasons for the recent epidemic of standard-setting and guideline formulation is a recognition within the public sector that normal commercial reasons for improving service often do not apply, and that additional controls are therefore necessary. Imposing standards, a cynic might say, is cheaper than increasing the budget, and, in the anglophone world, 'standard' has a reassuring professional ring.

The cost/quality equation is an echo—at the level of specific services—of the systemic issue of the relationship between saving money and improving performance (Section 7.6) (Bouckaert and Peters 2002). It partakes of the same difference of emphasis between microeconomic thought and management theory. It also suggests two rather contrasting bases for the legitimation of management actions—one rationale founded on competitiveness and the other on organizational improvement and transformation. Clarke and Newman (1997, p. 67) describe this in the following terms:

The competitive order is characterised by its primary orientation to the market, its modelling of organisations as businesses and by the dominance of discourses of entrepreneurialism and competitive success. The transformational order is characterised by the modelling of organisation as dynamic, progressive and customer-oriented, and by the pre-eminence of the discourses of culture, HRM, quality and values.

Both orders are substantially different from traditional public administration, whether in its 'pure' bureaucratic form (as in a central ministry) or in its bureau-professional form (as in health care and education services). In many situations the two new orders may point in the same direction, at least as far as the choice of a practical line of action is concerned. In some situations, however, divisions can appear. Quality improvement schemes may be held back or underresourced, because they are not seen as contributing directly enough or substantially enough to competitive success. Hitting this year's financial targets to the letter may be regarded as more important to a manager's reputation than achieving quality improvement or cultural change. These tensions are far from being purely theoretical: as one NHS hospital chief executive put it in the mid-1990s: 'In the real world we only get judged on narrow and short-term criteria . . . there is clearly a tension between competition and planning' (Pollitt et al. 1998, p. 101).

Overall, one may hazard that the nature of the cost/quality relationship at a microlevel does indeed resemble the savings/better performance relationship at meso- and macro-levels. That is to say, the issue of trade-offs and contradictions depends on specific features of the particular context. Where an organization goes into a savings programme with plenty of 'fat' or spare capacity, then quality improvement and cost-cutting can coexist. Where managers in a particular context can call upon technological advances (including new ways of organizing the staff) to boost productivity and enhance communications with service users, then, again, quality can be increased at the same time as costs are reduced. However, where no technological breakthrough is available, where the reorganization of staff practices is severely circumscribed by professional and 'tribal' rules and conventions, *and* where previous cost-cutting has already removed most of the fat, the relationship between quality improvement and further savings becomes a trade-off, or even a contradiction. Such circumstances had, for example, become visible in some parts of the UK NHS by the mid-1990s—where tribalism remained extensive and many hospitals had already undergone a decade or so of 'cost improvements' (annual cost-cutting exercises). Some circumstantial evidence of a tension between costs and quality comes from a comparative study of the implementation of a range of TQM projects in NHS settings and in two commercial companies. Joss and Kogan (1995, p. 140) commented: 'It is also clear that the funding of TQM at the NHS sites, while not inconsiderable, was more than an order of magnitude lower than in the two commercial companies.'

7.14 Reflections: balances, limits, dilemmas, and paradoxes

Looking across the various 'candidate contradictions' reviewed above, one can allow that not all are insurmountable. Some can be avoided—they are implementation dangers rather than fundamental logical contradictions. Others are more apparent than real (paradoxes), and in other cases still, there may be a deep-lying tension but the edge can be taken off it by skilled leadership and implementation. A considerable residue, how-ever, remains. The various components of what has become (at least in the core NPM countries) the vision of a modernized public sector do not add up to an integrated and harmonious whole:

Tensions such as the conflict between 'career service' and 'spot hiring' approaches to organising top public servants, legalist and managerial visions of organisational process, competition-centred and oversight-centred approaches to control over public services are not likely to disappear through some ultimate 'modern' resolution. (Hood 1998, p. 221)

The scope of our investigation has in some ways been narrower than Hood's—he seems to be attempting to establish a set of timeless and universal trade-offs, pictured in a group/grid matrix of administrative cultures in which both his four 'pure' administrative philosophies and attempts at hybrid combinations are fundamentally unstable. We have focused more specifically upon selected elements from the NPM 'package'. We are more interested in the extent to which these elements can be reconciled in logic and also confirmed as mutually compatible by empirical observations. Our focus is therefore less on an exploration of the explanatory value of any one overarching taxonomy. Thus, while we entirely concur with Hood's proposition that certain tensions cannot be 'disappeared' by contemporary models of management reform, we also want to discriminate between the more- and the less-'do-able'. In the preceding sections we have therefore reached towards a set of conclusions concerning our ten 'candidate contradictions'. We conclude the chapter by briefly recapitulating these tentative 'findings'.

7.15 **The candidate contradictions revisited**

1. *Increase political control of the bureaucracy/free managers to manage/empower service consumers*: in a perfect world these could just about be compatible. In the real world there is frequently a trade-off between one or more of the three corners of this triangle. In some contexts the trade-off becomes so sharp as to merit the title of a contradiction.

2. *Promote flexibility and innovation/increase citizen trust and therefore governmental legitimacy*: there is no fundamental contradiction here. However, there are specific contexts in which politicians and/or managers are obliged to trade off between, on the one hand, innovation and, on the other, values such as stability, predictability, continuity, and trust. Not infrequently management innovations can relatively disadvantage certain sections of the community.

3. *Give priority to making savings/improving the performance of the public sector*: there is no general contradiction; much depends on the specific circumstances, especially whether the organization(s) in question has/have spare capacity, and/or whether technological advances offer the possibility of productivity gains.

4. *'Responsibilize' government/reduce the range of tasks government is involved with*: again, there is no necessary or general contradiction here. On the other hand, the actual implementation of privatization projects is replete with possibilities for governments to depart from the public interest. But these are implementation risks, not inevitable degradations of responsibility.

5. *Motivate staff and promote cultural change/weaken tenure and downsize*: this appears to be the most obvious and inescapable contradiction. Of course, it can be rhetorically papered over, but it is not clear that many public service staff are persuaded. There is a price to pay for the contradiction in terms of loss of morale, loyalty, the attractiveness of a public service career, and possibly, therefore, effectiveness.

6. *Reduce burden of internal scrutiny and associated paperwork/sharpen managerial accountability*: this seems to be principally a question of balance. However, while it may not be a contradiction, intelligent and determined implemention is required if the balance is to be first constructed and then, subsequently, maintained.

7. *Create more single-purpose agencies/improve policy and programme coordination*: we suggest that there is an underlying trade-off here. It may be sharp or gentle, depending on context. The evidence for this tension is persuasive but not yet conclusive.

8. *Decentralize management authority/improve programme coordination*: a more general formulation of the seventh candidate contradiction. Again, we argue that there is some evidence of a trade-off between these two desiderata.

9. *Increase effectiveness/sharpen managerial accountability*: whilst this does not appear to be a contradiction, there does seem to be some tension between these two objectives, and there is evidence that the balance is hard to hold. There may also be an underlying dilemma—for rationed services—between transparency and legitimacy.

10. *Improve quality/cut costs*: as with the third candidate contradiction this is a relationship that depends heavily on the context and, in particular, whether cost cuts can be achieved through the exploitation of spare capacity and/or technological advances. Where neither of these is possible, then cost-cutting exercises may well trade off directly against quality improvement. Quality is 'free' only under certain circumstances, not always.

8

Reflections: management and governance

> The art of government is in procrastination and in silence and delay;
>   blazing bonfires left to burn will soon consume themselves away.
> Of evils choose the least: great foes will tumble down in time, or wither, one by one.
> He that rules must hear and see what's openly or darkly done.
> All that is not enough: there comes a moment when to rule is to be swift and bold;
>   know at last the time to strike—it may be when the iron is cold!
>
> (Sir Robert Cecil to Queen Elizabeth I from Benjamin Britten's opera *Gloriana*.
> Libretto by William Plomer)

8.1 Introduction

This final chapter expresses some general views on the nature of public management reform. As we move through these reflections, the reader may care to speculate on how far the concept of governance attributed to Sir Robert Cecil should also be applied to public management. In some countries, it seems the iron has never been cold for the past twenty years: the UK and the USA, for example, appear to be locked into cycles of unending, sometimes repetitive, reform. In others, reform has been a much more occasional and selective experience, proceeding not swiftly and boldly (a rather English trajectory, one might think) but in a more measured, negotiated, and drawn-out manner. It may not be a coincidence that it was a Swedish public servant, Hans Blix, who opened our first chapter with the more consensual thought:

> The noble art of losing face
> Will one day save the human race

The chapter is organized in four main sections—two pairs of contrasting perspectives. The first pair concern the overall nature of public management reform—or, at least, the quarter-century slice of it upon which this book has been focused. Here the contrast is between a perspective on reform as a distinct *strategy* and one of reform as a much more hit-and-miss process of muddling through particular crises and pressures as they arise (*incrementalism*). Within the view of reform as a strategy we also deal with the distinction between the NPM and what we have earlier termed the Neo-Weberian State or NWS. The second pair of perspectives also concern the nature of reform, but in a different sense. In this pair we ask about the extent to which useful knowledge of reform is being systematized, accumulated, and applied. This time the contrast is between a first perspective that sees the reform process as a possible basis for developing a 'science' or 'craft' of public management, and another that is considerably more sceptical as to 'what has been learned' and, indeed, what is likely to be learned in the foreseeable future. One might call the first 'reform as science' and the second 'reactive reform'.

We take no final position ourselves with regard to either pair of perspectives. Indeed, for us, part of the experience of writing this book has been an oscillation, manic-depressive style, between more 'optimistic' (reform as a strategy and, potentially, a science) and more 'pessimistic' views of our subject matter (reform as muddling through, and usually a matter of rhetoric, doctrine, and hit-and-miss experiment). Within these contrasts or oscillations readers can find their own points of equilibrium, comfortable or otherwise.

8.2 Public management reform as strategic decision-making

Let us assume a simple world in which three systems interact—political, law and administration, market economy. Each of the three is set within the larger context of civil society, and the citizens of that society both participate in, and form judgements about, the legitimacy of each of these systems (Figure 8.1).

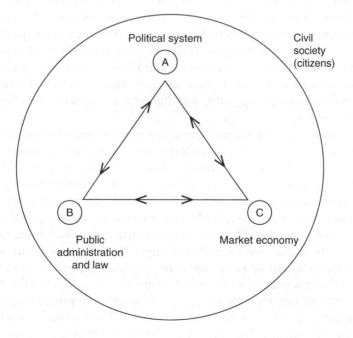

Figure 8.1 Three interactive systems.

Of course, such a model is too simple for some purposes. For example, in the real world executive politicians (ministers) are enmeshed in the administrative systems (typically as heads of departments of state), and some top public servants—such as the President of the European Commission—may have heavily 'political' roles (as described in chapters 3 and 6). However, we are using the model for a particular pedagogic purpose—to explore possible alternative settings for different systems of relationships within society, where each set of relationships (politics, administration, market economy) is characterized by a significantly different set of motivations, incentives, and penalties. For our purpose, therefore, it is not essential that each and every individual can be confidently assigned to one system and one system only, and simply that these broad sets of relationships run on the basis of significantly different norms, values, and procedures.

Thus the three systems are distinguished from each other by a whole range of norms, rules, and cultural assumptions—they are 'high group' in terms of group/grid cultural theory (Douglas 1982; Dunleavy and Hood 1994; Hood 1998). For example, the market runs on the basis of competition and contracts and choice, but the law does not—it is concerned with justice, and the impartial application of a special class of rules to all citizens, irrespective of their personal wealth or preferences.

Let us further assume that the political system faces two particularly large and pressing problems. The first is a *fiscal* problem. It is widely believed (widely enough for it to count, whether or not the belief is in some empirical sense 'true') that the political system has to moderate the amount of resources consumed by the administrative and legal system, which otherwise has a tendency to grow faster than the economy as a whole. Without this restraint, it is said, the economic system will suffer, and the electorate will become more and more discontented. The second problem is a problem of the *legitimacy* of the political system in the eyes of the citizenry. Evidence accumulates that the 'legitimacy rating' of the political system is falling (see Chapter 6). This causes various difficulties: the authority of politicians is eroded; the electoral loyalty and stability of voters is steadily reduced; public trust in political processes as efficacious ways of solving social problems declines; and defiance and evasion of the law may begin to increase. (Here we refer not simply to criminal and public order laws but also to tax laws, social security laws, planning laws, and so on.)

These two problems call for a strategic response from the leaders of the political system. Somehow they need to begin to restrain expenditure (or give the impression that they are doing so) and simultaneously to increase their own legitimacy. How can this be done? In strategic terms there are various possibilities. They can change their own behaviour, rebuilding trust through moderate, consistent, and transparent policy-making. At the same time they can act explicitly and directly to restrain public expenditure. Alternatively, they can search for some way of enhancing economic performance that is 'internal' to the market economy—for example, through some technological break-through. Or they can pursue closer and more mutually supportive links between the political and the economic systems (which some would say is what the EU is mainly about). Or they can take a course that, as we have seen, has proved popular in several countries at different periods—distance themselves as politicians from the system of administration and law and then blame that system for either the expenditure problem and/or the legitimacy problem. These are only three of a larger set of possible strategies, and to some extent they can be and have been pursued in combination rather than in isolation.

Let us dwell, for a moment, on the last strategy. The NPM is, as many commentators have noted, a bundle of disparate elements, but one of those elements has certainly been a process of distancing and blaming by political leaders. Government is the problem, said President Reagan, as though it were some alien entity with which he had only a distant and basically hostile relationship. Other politicians, less rhetorically antigovernment than Reagan, have also linked management reform with increased legitimacy: 'How can people trust government to do big things if we can't do little things like answer the telephone promptly and politely?' (Gore, in National Performance Review 1997a, p. ix). This sentence seems to imply that trust in the nation's political leaders will only return if the telephones are fixed first. If this is what it means, then Vice-President Gore, or his text-writers, attribute astonishingly low powers of discrimination to the American citizenry. Such a proposition flies in the face of evidence that citizens are perfectly capable of holding one attitude towards the 'big things' and a different one towards the specifics of particular services (Chapter 6). Be this as it may, the legitimacy question has been given repeated prominence in North American discussions of management reform.

The strategy of *distancing and blaming* is represented in Figure 8.2. It has, as we have remarked earlier in the book, been used far more in some regimes than others—more in Australasia, North America, and the UK than in Germany, France, or the Nordic states. Even in such ideological settings—sympathetically attuned to suspicions of governmental competence and motivation—the blaming strategy has certain obvious limitations.

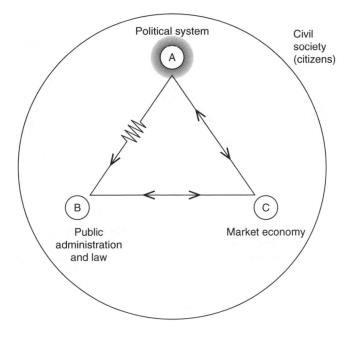

Figure 8.2 Distancing and blaming.

First, politicians will not necessarily be believed. They may say that the problem is 'over there' in the bureaucracy, and that proper managers should be brought in, given greater flexibility, and made more publicly accountable. However, the public may not believe that the problem *is* 'over there'. They may be quite able to distinguish between the political system and the administrative system, and believe that more problems lie with the former than the latter. Some, though not all, of the survey evidence referred to in Chapter 6 appeared to point in this direction. Even if the public *do* focus considerable discontent on the administrative system—the 'bureaucracy'—it may nevertheless continue to hold ministers, not managers, responsible for even quite detailed occurrences and events. Politicians therefore have to be very careful when they attack the state machine, especially if they are trying to portray doctors, nurses, firefighters, and teachers as parts of 'the problem'. Second, even if politicians are believed, they will not be believed for ever. After a few years of 'bureaucrat bashing' the public will begin to enquire when things are actually going to change: when will services improve and begin to live up to the 'visions' held out in citizen's charters, political speeches, and statements of service standards? In other words, distancing and blaming at best only buys a little time.

All of which brings us to the further, more profound issue raised by the distancing-and-blaming strategy. It is the question of what to do next—once political leaders have taken up their Olympian positions, pointing down at the failings of the bureaucratic state, what can they do to reform it? Here there appears to be a number of options. Political leaders can:

Tighten up traditional controls, restrict expenditures, freeze new hiring, run campaigns against waste and corruption, and generally 'squeeze' the system of administration and law (see Figure 8.3). We may call this strategy MAINTAIN.

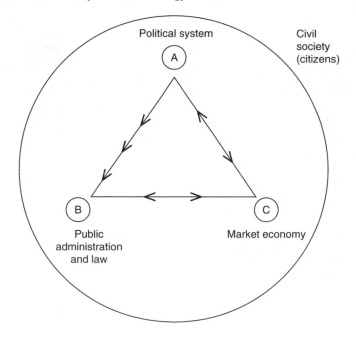

Figure 8.3 Tightening traditional controls.

Modernize the administrative system, bringing in faster, more flexible ways of budgeting, managing, accounting, and delivering services to their users. Some of these new ways of doing things are likely to be borrowed from the market sector (hence the C > B arrow in Figure 8.4). However, such changes are also likely to require some corresponding adjustments to the political system (hence the B > A arrow in Figure 8.4). We call this approach MODERNIZE. It is predicated on the distinctiveness of *public* provision, and the need to strengthen rather than dilute the state. This encompasses the approach we have termed the NWS. As was discussed in Section 4.9, it comes in at least two subvarieties. While not opposed to each other, each of these possesses a different 'spirit'. The first emphasizes the need for professional, performance-oriented management on the assumption that public servants are often full of initiative and will improve their own operations once they are freed from heavy bureaucratic regulation from further up the traditional hierarchies. The second, by contrast, stresses that the best route to modernization is to engage citizens and service users in a variety of participatory processes. It puts its faith in more 'bottom-up' influence from civil society, whereas the first variant is more concerned to reduce the amount of 'top-down' regulation.

Marketize the system, by instituting as many MTMs as possible within the system of administration and law. Public sector organizations are made to compete with each other, in order to increase efficiency and user-responsiveness. This represents a penetration of the administrative system by the culture and values and practices of the market sector—a lowering of 'group' in this respect (see Figure 8.5). MARKETIZE is the label we give to this approach, and it is the dominant influence within the NPM movement. As

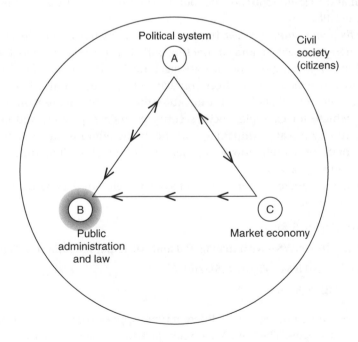

Figure 8.4 Modernize the administrative system.

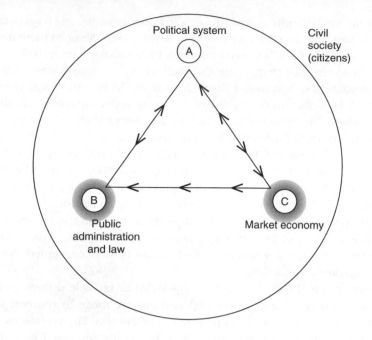

Figure 8.5 Marketize the administrative system.

Christensen and Lægreid (2001, p. 306) put it, 'The supermarket state model is a central feature of the NPM'.

Minimize the administrative system, handing over as many tasks as possible to the market sector (through privatization and contracting-out). This is the case of what some writers have called the 'hollowing-out' of the state machine. It carries a number of implications, including an intensification of direct contacts between the political system and the market economy, unmediated by bureaucratic structures (see Figure 8.6). It represents a scenario in which, for example, social security payments, prisons, and even security services are run by private companies, and the public administrative system dwindles to a shadow of its former self, now acting mainly as a kind of small holding company. We term this vision MINIMIZE.

In this analysis, therefore, there are four basic strategies for dealing with the pressures on the state apparatus:

1. MAINTAIN (Figure 8.3);

2. MODERNIZE (the NWS—with managerial and participatory variants—Figure 8.4);

3. MARKETIZE (the NPM—Figure 8.5); and

4. MINIMIZE (Figure 8.6).

As we have seen, different regimes at different times appear to have leaned towards one or other of these strategies. The 'four Ms' do not have to be taken in a particular order, but neither can they all be convincingly pursued simultaneously. Some countries have gone

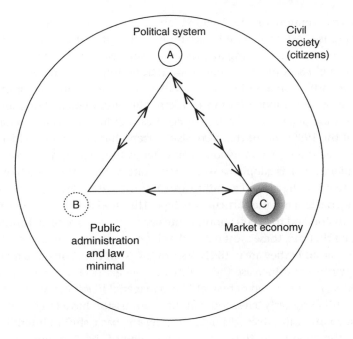

Figure 8.6 Minimize the administrative system.

through the phase of distancing and blaming (Figure 8.2) first, but many have not. The Nordic countries tended to bypass that and aim for modernizing, with some modest marketizing (Figure 8.4 with a flavour of Figure 8.5). They also tended to try to mix the managerial and participatory elements of the MODERNIZE approach (e.g. in Finland, where during the 1980s and early 1990s there was much emphasis on results-oriented management, and on reducing and simplifying regulations, and then, in the late 1990s the stress was placed on more participation—*High Quality Services, Good Governance, and a Responsible Civic Society* 1998*a*, 1998*b*). These are, therefore, in the main examples of an NWS approach. The Germans have also largely avoided the blaming strategy and have moved directly to a mixture of maintaining and modernizing (Figures 8.3 and 8.4). The British, under Thatcher, certainly blamed (Figure 8.2). In the early years (1979–82) this was combined with a mixture of tightening traditional controls (MAINTAIN) and, increasingly, MODERNIZE-style efficiency drives. Later, from the mid-1980s, the Conservative government moved much further towards a mixture of MARKETIZE and MINIMIZE (Figures 8.5 and 8.6)—together with New Zealand in the 1984–93 period and Australia under John Howard, this was the fullest flowering of the NPM. In the UK, Blair later moved back towards MODERNIZE, indeed, this term became one of the mantras of his administration, and suffused the 1999 white paper *Modernising Government* (Prime Minister and the Minister for the Cabinet Office 1999). France has gone mainly for MODERNIZE, though there has clearly been a tension within this strategy as between more participatory and more top-down, managerial versions of reform. The Dutch, too, have preferred to MODERNIZE. Neither the Dutch nor the Nordics nor the Belgians have indulged in much of the exaggerated political rhetoric about public management that has been common in the Anglo-Saxon countries. Their preference for a more modest, consensus-oriented style of debate is well captured by the words of a senior Dutch public servant, responding to questions from a New Zealand public management expert: 'You Anglo-Saxons, you should learn that pulling grass up doesn't make it grow any faster' (reported conversation, 1998). Italy has pursued a mixture of modernization (decentralization and modernization of the public employment laws) and marketization (privatization or part-privatization of significant industries), but the chaotic political upheavals of the 1990s meant that a consistent trend has been hard to identify.

Finally, we see the EU Commission as an organization which, for most of the period under consideration, has adopted a MAINTAIN strategy. Since the launch of SEM 2000 in 1995, there seems to have been a shift to a MODERNIZE strategy, though very much one of the managerial and not the participatory type. This modernization intensified with the Prodi Commission and the 2000 reform white paper. As we have seen, however, despite a decentralizing rhetoric, these most recent developments have a distinct centralizing edge (Levy 2003). Certainly they are in the NWS, not the NPM tradition—the main thrust is to strengthen control and increase the quality of strategic decision-making, not to introduce elements of competition or market-like managerial freedoms. We must also remember that it is still fairly early days, and that the Commission has a large capacity to absorb and exhaust change initiatives without achieving any basic shift in internal structures or cultures. On the other hand, the current enlargement of the Community seems likely to force further reform.

Turning away from Europe, after 1996 the Australian government under Howard opted for a combination of MARKETIZE and MINIMIZE (Figures 8.5 and 8.6), though with a fair amount of blaming (Figure 8.2) thrown in for good measure. 'Put another civil servant on the barbie, mate', was one jokey characterization of their general attitude. The emphasis on privatization (MINIMIZE) and the introduction of competitive pressures into the public sector (MARKETIZE) came earlier in New Zealand which, by the late 1990s, appeared to be entering a period of consolidation and relative calm, after a decade of hectic reform. It is worth reiterating that the concept of a 'strategy' can probably be applied more convincingly to New Zealand than to any other country in our set. For New Zealand there is evidence that strategic principles were adopted, thought through, and applied in a more systematic way than elsewhere (Boston 1995). As for the North American countries, in the USA under Reagan there was much sounding-off of the MINIMIZE rhetoric, but this was never more than very selectively followed through, at least at the federal level. Instead, in practice, most of the measures actually implemented seem to fall within the MARKETIZE and MODERNIZE categories. In Canada the federal level was perhaps more securely embedded (despite a growing challenge from the provincial authorities), so, with the exception of some early Mulroney rhetoric, most of the specific measures seem to be concerned with modernization, occasionally spiced with some marketization (Figure 8.4 flavoured with Figure 8.5).

The important thing to note in all these examples is that *each strategy has implications not only for the administrative corner of the triangle, but for the other two corners as well*. Partly because of this, each strategy also has somewhat different impacts on the original problems of expenditure restraint and government legitimacy. If we take them one by one, MAINTAIN is the strategy that least 'rocks the boat'. Its weakness is that, as some countries have discovered, it may not yield sufficient change materially to affect either the fiscal problem or the legitimacy problem. MODERNIZE (Figure 8.4) represents a more fundamental shift, and appears to have enjoyed considerable success in, for example, Finland, the Netherlands, and Sweden. Both Finland and Sweden have managed to make considerable reductions in public spending. Whether the legitimacy problem has been eased is hard to say, but the issue of 'starting lines' is again relevant here—these were both countries where the legitimacy of government had in any case held up better than in, say, the USA. Belgium and Italy started their reforms later, well into the 1990s, and both were wrestling with particularly acute crises of citizen confidence in 'normal politics'. The Belgian reforms definitely fall within the MODERNIZE NWS camp, and so do some elements of the Italian changes, though others are more market-oriented. It is too soon to say whether, in either country, the legitimacy of government has been much restored. Within a modernization strategy, therefore, leaders can still appeal to traditional public service values, such as career service, probity, equity, equality, and so on. In value terms the basic thrust of this approach is that something valuable and worthwhile is being updated and improved—whereas MARKETIZE and, even more, MINIMIZE entail the substitution of a substantially different set of values and, by implication, a blaming and discarding of the older set (Hacque 2001; Hood 1991; Kernaghan 1997).

MARKETIZE (Figure 8.5) thus has somewhat different implications for the fiscal and legitimacy problems. On the one hand, it may be a powerful strategy for addressing fiscal difficulties—sharp MTMs can oblige public sector agencies and departments to cut costs and search intensively for efficiencies. On the other hand, the legitimacy of some parts of the public service may actually fall further, if the public begin to perceive that fiscal priorities predominate over a service ethic, or that public agencies are more concerned with beating off 'competition' or improving their quasi-market image than with the 'bread and butter' of stable and predictable service for the average client. Something of this may be seen in the UK university sector, where huge efforts have gone into public relations, institutional PIs, and quality control proceduralism, while the actual class contact and individual attention that most students can expect to receive have in many instances fallen considerably. These dangers are especially present where the service concerned is nonstandardized, 'intangible', and generates outcomes that are hard to define and identify, and where generalized values such as equity or fairness are pitted against a harder, more measurable concern for costs/profits (Pollitt 2003a, chapters 6 and 7). Strong resentments can also arise as a result of increasing differentiation within the public service—for example, if rank-and-file staff see their own pay being held back while their chief executive earns a private sector-comparable salary, with substantial performance bonuses.

The MARKETIZE strategy also tends to lead to the creation of flotillas of new, 'hybrid' organizations and PPPs—to a blurring of the line between the market sector and the system of public administration. Whilst these innovations may yield new flexibilities and efficiencies, they also pose new problems for accountability and legitimacy. The literature addressing these issues is only now beginning to emerge (see Osborne 2000; Peterson 2000; Rosenau 2000).

Finally, the MINIMIZE strategy (Figure 8.6) results in a residual public sector, which should certainly equate to lower direct consumption of goods and service by the state.

Whether this solves the fiscal problem remains to be seen, since strong minimization or marketization strategies tend to go hand in hand with efforts at tax reduction; so a balance still has to be struck, even if at a considerably lower level. More fundamentally, the marketized services (health, education, etc.) still have to be paid for; so unless the political system can tolerate extensive exclusion of certain citizens because of their inadequate incomes, state subsidies will be necessary in one form or another. The legitimacy problem is transformed—and possibly clarified—because now the public's expectations are focused directly on the political leadership itself. 'Bureaucracy' and 'big government' are no longer available as whipping boys or scapegoats. Public discontent about the adequacy or quality of the (former) public services is directed towards the market economy, since that is what now provides these necessities, and towards the political leadership who remain responsible (in the public's eyes) for regulating market excesses and externalities. One can perhaps see a mild preview of what this might be like in countries that have already carried through major privatization programmes, such as New Zealand or the UK. In the UK, for example, public discontent at what are perceived as the high prices, high salaries, and poor services of some of the privatized water companies was considerable. Then there were a series of accidents, and consequent upheavals in the privatized railway network, which quickly triggered the public response that the *government* must do something to bring the private companies to order. It would be hard to claim that the legitimacy of these particular parts of the market economy was very impressive.

Both marketization and minimization strategies tend to reduce the distinctiveness of the public sector. As Pierre (1998, p. 3) puts it:

The overall pattern [of public service reform, internationally] suggests that in several important respects the public service has lost much of its organisational and normative specificity; political institutions are developing new points of contact with the surrounding society and encouraging new channels for citizen input on political and administrative matters.

This discussion has necessarily been a very simplified one, and in one respect the simplification has been so great that we must now acknowledge and correct it. Our oversimplification, thus far, has been to write as though management reform is always initiated, shaped, and led by politicians. However, as has been clear from the very first chapter of this book, in the real world this is by no means always the case. Senior public servants are almost always heavily involved in reform attempts, and sometimes provide more of the dynamism than do the politicians. In Finland, France, the Netherlands, and Sweden, for example, public servants have themselves played leading roles in establishing reform agendas and proposing specific types of solutions: '[M]uch of what has emerged in Sweden so far...has been driven by a small number of civil servants and, frequently, without explicit, senior political support' (Pierre 1998, p. 6). Such 'mandarins' are powerful figures in their own right, aware of the pressures emanating from the external environment and willing, in some instances, to take pre-emptive action to preserve or enhance the role of the system of administration and law (or, at least, of their own part of that system).

This additional source of dynamism therefore requires a reconsideration of Figures 8.2–8.6. The system of administration and law is not simply passive, being acted upon by forces from the political and market systems. It can also be proactive, in the sense that its leadership may seek the support of leading politicians and/or business elites for particular modes of reform. Strategies may emerge *from* the bureaucracy rather than being imposed upon it. This has long been recognized by a number of theorists from a range of theoretical traditions. Working within a rational choice frame, Dunleavy (1991), for example, has developed a theory of 'bureau-shaping' in which senior public servants use the reform process to distance themselves from routine management tasks and from responsibility for substantive programmes that can so easily go wrong or appear to fail. Instead they carve out for themselves roles as strategists and policy advisers, redesigning, evaluating, and monitoring the 'operational' organizations 'below' them, but neatly avoiding the 'firing line' themselves. The popularity—in a number of countries—of creating corporatized bodies or executive agencies and of market-testing and contracting-out can readily be fitted into this theoretical framework (Pollitt and Talbot 2004). The testimony of seasoned practitioners also supports such an interpretation: consider Allen Schick's essay on the changing role of central budget offices:

In the typical case the budget office has divested most (or all) *ex ante* control of running costs and now leads the effort for management improvement. It has a major role in devising new institutional arrangements, integrating budgeting and other management processes, prodding departments and other public entities to measure performance and evaluate results, developing new guidelines and methods for holding managers accountable, and installing new information and reporting systems. (OECD 1997*b*, p. 4)

Theorists of quite different persuasions from rational choice recognize many of the same phenomena. Power (1997, p. 11) describes the explosion of audit and audit-like processes in contemporary societies, and comments: 'As the state has become increasingly and explicitly committed to an indirect supervisory role, audit and accounting practices have assumed a decisive function. The state cannot play this indirect role without assuming the efficacy of these practices . . . ' Similarly, Clarke and Newman (1997, p. 82) observe that recent changes have 'installed management as a new command system which features business managers, chief executives, quality coordinators and internal audit staff. They have also installed *managerialism* in the sense of new regimes of power structured through the domination of decision making, agenda setting and normative power.'

Each of these perspectives, although differing profoundly one from another in a variety of ways, holds up a picture of a dynamic strategy which is being pursued by the top tiers of the public service hierarchy. This involves taking control of the *process* of management reform and carving a new role out of the activity of orchestrating continuous change. Restructuring organizations, making strategic plans, launching quality improvement initiatives, measuring, auditing, and evaluating the performance of others—these are the components of a kind of 'metamanagement', the practitioners of which are themselves able to avoid the hurly-burly of 'operations'. They set the targets, others have to achieve them. They redesign the organizations, others then have to manage them. This is a strategy that can be carried out in response to the demands of politicians for lower costs and higher legitimacy, or it can be launched independently by the new mandarinate, requiring nothing more from the political leadership than sympathetic acquiescence.

The substantive content of the strategy is likely to be either modernization (Figure 8.4) or marketization (Figure 8.5) or some mixture of the two. Distancing (Figure 8.2) is not an easy tactic for leading public servants themselves (though they may nonetheless draw sharp contrasts between the 'bad old bureaucratic ways' and the bright new managerialism—Clarke and Newman 1997, p. 65). Tightening up traditional controls (MAINTAIN—Figure 8.3) is widely regarded as insufficient. MINIMIZE (Figure 8.6) is unattractive because it radically diminishes the 'empire' over which the new managerial leaders can exercise their suzerainty. The new mandarinate, therefore, is most likely to go for the 'middle ways' of MODERNIZE and MARKETIZE—the NWS or NPM.

8.3 Management reforms as 'muddling through'

The foregoing perspective, which locates management reforms as part of a process of strategic decision-making by political leaders and/or top public servants, can be criticized as too neat and formulaic. Choosing between the 'four Ms' may make a good lecture or textbook, or even a piece of high-level consultancy, but are these the terms in which many of the participants actually experience reform? It is possible to explain much of what has been described in our book more in terms of 'muddling through' (Lindblom 1959, 1979) than as an exercise in conscious strategy. On this view, the twin problems of fiscal restraint and legitimacy are real enough, but governmental responses to them have usually been ad hoc and partial rather than strategic.

Lindblom's original article (1959) on incrementalism was tremendously influential. In it he described a decision-making process in which policies typically emerged from a process of mutual adjustment between organized interests, with limited analysis of alternatives and frequent mixing of means and ends. The articulation of clear and well-ordered goals was the exception rather than the rule (Harrison et al. 1990, pp. 8–10). Lindblom was concerned to offer what he saw as a more realistic model of most public policy-making than contemporary 'rational–comprehensive' theorists. His focus was mainly on decision-making itself rather than outputs or outcomes (this has sometimes been misunderstood by commentators). At any event, twenty years later the debate between the various schools of thought was still running so strongly that Lindblom was prevailed upon to write an update on his first article. In this he distinguished between three elements:

1. *incremental politics*: the process of changing outputs and outcomes cautiously, in small steps;

2. *incremental analysis*: the process of analysing policy problems one at a time, in an ad hoc manner, rather than attempting grandiose, synoptic, or comprehensive reviews; and

3. *partisan mutual adjustment* (PMA): a process of political decision-making that is fragmented and/or decentralized, and the resultant 'policies' are the amalgam of attempts at mutual persuasion by the main stakeholders, rather than the decision of a single, unitary body.

The strength of the incrementalist model can be felt the closer one approaches most of the specific reforms described in this book. In particular, incremental analysis and the PMA seem to have been very frequent features of public management reform, even if more-than-incremental changes in output were frequently hoped for. For example, it is easy to exaggerate both the comprehensiveness and the strategic forethought that went into the UK reform programme of the Thatcher years. It is now documented that the eventual scale of the privatization programme was simply not envisaged when the Conservatives came to power; that the Next Steps report (which led to the creation of many executive agencies) was the subject of fierce controversy and mutual adjustment within Whitehall (Thain and Wright 1995); and that it was in any case largely a reaction to the perceived failures of the previous reform effort, the Financial Management Initiative (Zifcak 1994). Even the radical MTMs introduced to the NHS through the enormously controversial 1989 white paper, *Working for Patients*, were constantly being adjusted and trimmed by successive Conservative secretaries of state for health, until the incoming Labour government declared that it was 'abolishing the destructive, bureaucratic competition of the internal market' altogether (Chancellor of the Exchequer 1998, p. 46).

These examples could easily be multiplied—similar tales of how radical-sounding reforms, when viewed close-up, begin to appear less startling and more 'bargained', can be told for many countries. The boldness and clarity of vision that marked the New Zealand experiment remains the exception rather than the rule (though even there a good deal of ad hoc compromising took place—see Boston et al. 1996, pp. 81–2). Furthermore, the incrementalist will note that New Zealand was a small country, with an unusually compact elite and an equally unusual absence of checks and balances to force a reforming cabinet into the paths of the PMA. This elite grabbed at what may have been a unique 'window of opportunity' created by the extreme economic circumstances of the mid-1980s (Aberbach and Christensen 2001). All in all, this was not an example that could easily be copied by other jurisdictions. Contrast this case with that of the NPR and GPRA in the USA, where tremendous 'hype' undoubtedly led to particular improvements, and to energetic participation in some of the 'reinvention labs', but, at the same time, a highly pluralistic system of government led to several major departures from the original vision (General Accounting Office 1998; Kettl 1994; Radin 1998; Thompson 2000).

From an incrementalist perspective, therefore, the nature of public management reform is normally 'bitty', ad hoc, and specific, not strategic, comprehensive, and driven by generic models. Models may sometimes still play a headline role, but from this perspective, they are being used as a 'selling angle' for something much more modest, or as a *post hoc* rationalization for the same. Their use, in short, is more as a rhetorical device than as a practical template for action. Our original scheme of reform (Figure 2.1), combined with the analysis of regime differences contained in Chapter 3, explains why this should (usually) be so. To launch, sustain, and implement a comprehensive strategy for reform requires certain conditions, and these are seldom all satisfied in the real world of public management reform. It requires, first, either a single authority or a set of key players who can establish a high degree of consensus over what needs to be done, and who can sustain this consensus over the kind of five-year-plus timescales necessary to put in place fundamental, broad-scope reform. Second, it requires informed leadership, both from executive politicians and from a sufficient proportion of top public servants (mandarins). If either of these elite groups is opposed or uninterested, then opportunities for delay, dilution, and diversion will multiply and will be taken advantage of by the forces of resistance and recalcitrance which are almost bound to exist in the context of reform. Sustaining a strategy also requires a considerable organizational capacity to plan and carry out the operational detail of the reforms, to respond to the unforeseen, and to ensure that suitable new knowledge and skills are brought into the public sector workforce. A degree of public acceptance, or at least acquiescence, is a further sine qua non, at least for reforms that affect the frontline.

Taken together, this is a formidable list of requirements. Occasionally, it may be more or less met—in New Zealand between 1984 and 1990, for example, or for the 1994 Program Review exercise in Canada (Aucoin and Savoie 1998) or in the gradual introduction of results-oriented budgeting—over a period of nearly a decade—in consensualist Finland (Pollitt et al. 1997). Often, however, one or more important requirements cannot be satisfied. It was argued in Chapter 3 that the probability of a stable platform for a well-focused reform strategy varies with regime type. Yet even in the most favourable circumstances (unified, centralized state, strong executive, long period in power), conditions may change. Eventually an election intervenes and a new party comes to power. Or political leadership loses interest as other issues press for attention (e.g. Pollitt 1984, pp. 96–106; Savoie 1994 on Prime Minister Mulroney). Or the implementation capacity is insufficient, and well-meant reforms get bogged down. Thus, talk of 'strategy' can be seen, from this second perspective, as an idealization or *post hoc* rationalization of a set of processes that tend to be partial, reactive, and of unstable priority.

8.4 Management reform as a science?

It is part of the job of an academic enquiry to ask what scientific knowledge may be extracted from the many experiences of public management reform. Is there the actuality—or possibility—of cumulative knowledge, so that future reformers in country X will be able to build on the sure foundations established by the reforms implemented in country Y? There have been quite a few academic and practitioner attempts to 'take stock' and 'draw lessons' (e.g. Aucoin and Savoie 1998; Christensen and Lægreid 2001; Department of Finance and Administration 1998*b*; Development Team 1998; Gore 1997; OECD 1996, 1997*a*, 2002*a*; Olsen and Peters 1996; Peters 1998*a*). What have they yielded?

Peters (1998*a*) reviews some of the main 'principles' of public sector management reform and arrives at the conclusion that these should not be applied sweepingly, as though they were universals, but need rather to be tailored to specific organizational contexts. However, he is not optimistic about the availability of the necessary theory of contexts:

The problem with a highly differentiated approach to organisational reform is that organisation theory in the public sector is not yet sufficiently advanced to provide adequate guidance for would-be reformers . . . Our classification of government organisations tends to be on the basis of what they do—health, defence and so on—rather than on structural or managerial grounds that would provide more of a basis for reform recommendations. While we can think of a number of potentially important criteria, such as size, professionalisation, client involvement, there is not yet sufficient evidence to make good predictive statements to aid reformers. (Peters 1998*a*, p. 96)

Although a few researchers have gone a little further than this in specifying the criteria that are important in particular contexts (Pollitt 2003*a*; Wilson 1989), few would disagree with Peters's final point about insufficient evidence. Social scientists have long written about the need to come up with a robust theory of contexts, but are yet to offer a satisfactory answer to their own call. Group/grid cultural theory, as borrowed from anthropologists by public administrationists, does provide a map of sorts but has a number of limitations, especially from a practitioner's point of view, as Hood (1998, chapter 10) explicitly acknowledges. It is, as its title suggests, a *cultural* theory—it is very broad and does not say much about factors such as the specific service characteristics or dominant technologies, which others have found influential in determining appropriate organizational structures and procedures. Furthermore, the finding '[b]ecause . . . each way of [administrative] life has its built-in blind spots and weaknesses, along with its corresponding strengths . . . surprise and disappointment is inevitable and perpetual' (Hood 1998, p. 191) is not a conclusion likely to be found to be particularly inspiring by reform practitioners. One might say that the present authors are quite prepared to be disappointed, but this is neither 'perpetually' nor on the vast scale seemingly required! Nor is it clear how this theory helps us to understand the many undeniable, tangible improvements that sometimes take place as a result of deliberate reform. Forms become easier to fill in. Services speed up their response times (without any significant increase in error). Staff are trained to deal with users in a more friendly and efficient manner. Hitherto separate services are made available through 'one window'. The costs of a public sector organization are reduced through a more professional procurement procedure. And so on—we would regard these as thoroughly useful reforms that seem to take place 'below the radar' as far as group/grid cultural theory is concerned.

In Chapters 2 and 3 we developed a model of influences on public management reform that stressed constitutional, political, and 'administrative system' factors. Such a model takes one a certain way in understanding why certain reforms 'fit' in one country but would be very difficult to implement in another, yet it is still pitched at a fairly high level of generalization, and may therefore be of limited use to those who are confronting specific reform needs in specific institutions. Perhaps a slightly more detailed theory of contexts can be found in the work of 'realist' evaluators of public policy, who at least provide some detailed methodologies for ascertaining 'what might work for whom in what circumstances' (Pawson and Tilley 1997). However, this has yet to be taken up by the main schools of academic thought on public management reform, and certainly cannot yet be crystallized into the kind of recommendatory checklist beloved of practitioners.

The absence of an adequate theory of contexts leaves many academic writers (including ourselves) very wary of coming out with specific recommendations. True, there are a few well-worn general admonitions, such as: find a 'champion', ensure attention by linking management reforms to processes of resource allocation, go for some inspiring 'early wins' as well as longer-term changes, stay in power long enough to complete what you start, and so on. Unfortunately, taken together, these could hardly be regarded as amounting to a 'science of improvement'. Most academic commentators from the public administration community simply avoid the issue. Peters and Savoie (1998, pp. 6–7) speak for many of their colleagues when they write:

We soon realized that when we take stock of administrative reforms we are invariably confronted with a confusing and contradictory picture of change. On the one hand, we discover that a large number of changes have been adopted and implemented, and appear to have produced some benefits for people inside and outside government . . . On the other hand, we also discover that few, if any, of these reforms have been able to live up to the claims of their advocates.

Of course, not all academic disciplines are so reticent. Economists, in particular, have been much more ready to offer prescriptions. This may be part of the explanation of why microeconomic ideas have been so influential in public sector reforms in several countries. Principal and agent theory and the new 'institutional economics' have left their mark, and some, at least, of their advocates would claim that they were definitely 'scientific'. Certainly they offer politicians and senior public servants a clearer and more specific set of guidelines for reform than most of the analyses provided by academics with backgrounds in public administration and public management.

Practitioner manuals are very different from the corpus of academic work. Generally speaking, such manuals just set out what is supposed to be done, with limited or no attention to context. Some—especially those associated with high-profile political programmes such as the US NPR or the UK *Citizen's Charter*—exude an air of confidence which admits little or no anxiety over the paucity of any scientific basis for the 'knowledge' that they are (implicitly or explicitly) claiming to convey (e.g. European Foundation for Quality Management 1996; Gore 1997). Others are more sober in rhetorical terms, but may still be prone to 'one-best-way-ism' and to inadequate acknowledgement of the variety of contexts that most public sectors display. 'Most what-to-do arguments in public management rely on circumstantial evidence and rhetorical power' (Hood 1998, p. 13). Despite these common limitations, there does seem to be a good deal of practical knowledge about how to do certain things and what problems to watch for—for example, in designing PI sets (Likierman 1995), or introducing performance management (Department of Finance and Administration 1998*a*), or integrating results-based performance management and budgeting (Mayne 1996), or evaluating EU expenditure programmes (European Commission 1997*a*), or making progress with e-government (National Audit Office 1999). This is mainly 'craft knowledge' rather than being scientifically based— though it may be none the worse for that. Craft knowledge can be tremendously useful, always assuming it is applied by craftspersons—those who already have an experienced 'feel' for what allowances to make for local taste and context, the strength or otherwise of the materials being worked with, and so on. It is, perhaps, routinely underestimated and understudied by academics. However, craft knowledge is more likely to come unstuck when applied by newcomers or experts who are just 'passing through' on a limited term or limited focus assignment. It also has obvious limitations when applied to problems or in contexts that are genuinely novel.

We are therefore left with a rich, but only half-cooked mixture of two or three kinds of ingredient. There are academic theories that point in a general way to certain key issues or variables, but seldom develop these into specific recommendations or practical 'tips'. There are—especially in the anglophone countries—'upbeat' proclamations of what should be done to modernize the public service, but these frequently float in a rhetorical stratosphere, lacking any critical or analytical edge. Finally there is the 'grey literature' of guides and manuals, produced by public servants for public servants. These are sometimes mines of useful craft-based experience, but tend to be weak on allowance for contextual factors and—unsurprisingly—to lack theoretical or systematic empirical underpinnings (and therefore scientific authority). In the final section we offer a contrasting perspective on the state of the art of public management reform. Instead of looking at what we know it places more emphasis on how we *talk* and *write* about reform.

8.5 More rhetoric than rigour? Concluding impressions of public management reform

Reform-watching in public management can be a sobering pastime. The gaps between words and deeds, and between the view from the top and the experience at the grassroots are frequently so wide as to provoke scepticism or—according to taste—cynicism. The pace of underlying, embedded achievement tends to be so much slower than the helter-skelter cascade of new announcements and initiatives, each with its own, ephemerally fashionable, abbreviation (to name but a few, PPBS, RCB, PAR, ZBO, TQM, BPR, NPR, PS 2000, SEM 2000, RIA, JUG). The apparent ability of leaders to forget the lessons and limitations of previous administrative reforms is impressive—perhaps *administrative* history, at least, really is dead. One becomes accustomed to hearing large claims touted and to discovering, subsequently, that these are founded on precious little in the way of systematic, relevant, and attributable evidence. It is not unusual for the researcher to read in an official document that accruals-accounting or efficiency-planning or some other new process has started on a particular date, and then, when visiting the organizations concerned, to find that nothing much has happened beyond the circulation of a few policy papers, or that many people in the organization have not even heard of the innovation in question (Pollitt 2002). One's spirits fall when visionary futures are unfurled in terms that are carefully chosen to sound good whilst carrying no specific and testable content. It is hard to avoid a hardening of the heart against a certain kind of hyperbole:

The Government will deliver a world class education service, offering opportunity for all to reach their full potential . . . (Chancellor of the Exchequer 1998, p. 42)

(Four years later the UK education service was widely seen as being in crisis with, *inter alia*, the education minister resigning following the mismanagement of a set of national examinations; loss of confidence in some test scores; an ongoing crisis in the recruitment of teachers; and the admittance by the government that the university sector was chronically underfunded.)

Or

that was the challenge that President Clinton handed down four years ago when he asked me to reinvent the federal government—to put the wheels back on. We agreed right then that we needed to bring a revolution to the federal government. We call it reinventing government. (Gore 1997, p. 1)

(Four years later Vice-President Gore failed, following a lacklustre campaign, to be elected president. His incoming opponent, George W. Bush, swiftly scrapped the remaining reinvention teams, and instituted a quite different reform agenda.)

How, one wonders, did these leaders intend to rebuild trust in government—one of their avowed intentions—when they resorted to such implausibly exaggerated and over-sure language? Who did they think would believe such claims?

It is comparatively easy to identify the rhetorical excesses of some reform leaders. There is, however, another and much more subtle gap between rhetoric and practice. As we have noted, one difference between the current wave of public management reform and earlier phases is that this one has taken on an explicitly international dimension. An international vocabulary (an English one) has developed, actively fostered by organizations such as PUMA, SIGMA, the World Bank, and the IMF, as well as through national governments and academic and professional associations. Terms such as 'privatization', 'agentification', 'contractualization', 'continuous quality improvement', 'efficiency gains', 'activity-costing', 'regulatory impact assessment', and 'performance management' are part of this international lexicon. Their repeated use seems to confirm that everyone is involved in basically the same enterprise, a global shift in the direction of modern management. Yet this is by no means necessarily the case. This special vocabulary may serve to conceal and constrain the nature of beneficial change as well as aid it. The problems are at least threefold.

First, use of these terms often generates an exaggerated impression of the uniformity of what is going on. This is because the same term may be used to refer to very different sorts of change in different places, changes that carry different meanings in different contexts (Pollitt et al. 2001; Sahlin-Andersson 2001). Every consultant or academic who has worked outside his or her mother country or mother tongue has experienced something of this—or, at least, everyone we have spoken to. Anecdotes concerning the phenomenon are commonplace. One of the authors of this book once spent an entire day discussing the meaning of 'efficiency' in a Franco/German/Italian/English expert team, each member of which, at the outset, had mistakenly thought that he or she was perfectly clear as to its conceptual content, and that the day would be spent sorting out the practical details of the consultancy upon which we were supposed to be working. On another occasion, a comparative researcher looking at management reforms in the Netherlands and the UK was obliged to go back and revise his report when he realized that the terms 'privatization' and 'agency' were being used to denote quite different processes/institutions by the civil servants he spoke to in the two countries. These potential confusions are not helped by the fact that many of the most influential and active propagators of the debate are the members of central policy or management units, nationally or internationally, such as the UK Cabinet Office, the Swedish *Statskontoret*, the French *grands corps*, or PUMA itself. By and large these are individuals who, whatever their many other talents may be, will not have had much experience of 'normal' operational management. Rather they tend to be high-flyers, policy advisers, intellectual synthesizers, and academic entrepreneurs. So their own ability to relate the terms and ideas they use to the realities of day-to-day administration and management is limited. Thus the danger that the language of reform can take on a life of its own is further reinforced.

Second, the international vocabulary of management reform carries a definite normative 'charge'. Within the relevant community of discourse, whether it be the NPM or NWS, the assumption has grown that particular things—performance management, TQM, PPPs, and so on—*are* progress. To be progressive one has to be seen doing things to which these particular labels can be stuck. They constitute the *menu du jour*. Yet this is also a limiting process, in so far as items *not* on the current list are seldom discussed, and are easily rejected if and when they do appear. Suggesting, for example, that an existing or new activity would be better placed within an enlarged central ministry or as a direct, state-provided service, becomes an uphill struggle—it is 'beyond the pale', not the done thing. In the NPM countries: 'To borrow a phrase, going public is out. Going private is in' (Rockman 1998, p. 20). Likewise the proposition that working in partnership with a range of private and 'third sector' bodies to deliver a service may be simply time-consuming, wasteful, and a threat to clear public accountability: uttering such a sacrilegious thought can be instantly to brand oneself as a 'reactionary'. Within this managerialist thought-world there is only limited consciousness of the flimsiness of many of the current 'principles' of good public management. A more historically informed awareness would show how such 'principles' or 'proverbs' come and go over time, and are often arranged in opposing and mutually contradictory pairs (Hood 1998; Hood and Jackson 1991; Peters 1998*a*; Simon 1946).

Third—and we address this remark especially to our only-English-speaking readers—the anglophone literature has, perhaps unsurprisingly, been dominated with anglophone ideas, so that it has been easy to assume that (*a*) these are the *only* reform ideas around and/or (*b*) these are clearly the *best* ideas around. These impressions may have been amplified by a cultural factor, namely the Anglo-American keenness to publicize their systems and innovations as being of global relevance. British and American governments have seized on the NPM and reinvention as new logos with which to 'badge' their management 'products' and increase foreign 'sales'. 'All around the world', boasted a British minister in 1993, 'governments are recognizing the opportunity to improve the quality and effectiveness of the public sector. Privatization, market testing and private finance are being used in almost every developed country, and it's not difficult to see why' (Dorrell 1993). As we have seen, this view—linking virtually all reform to a marketizing strategy—was a considerable distortion and oversimplification of what was, and is, happening in the world. The NWS model, by contrast, has suffered from (*a*) not being invented in anglophone countries and (*b*) not being evolved by governments that were culturally ambitious enough to proclaim to the rest of the world that they had invented a winning brand.

And yet there is another side to public management reform, which has a more solid and sensible persona. The pressure, the rhetoric, the loosening of the old ways—under both the NPM and NWS—all these have combined to give many public servants the opportunity to make changes that make local sense to *them*. Such 'improvements' may occasionally be self-serving, but often they are substantially other-directed, and result in gains in productivity, service quality, transparency, fairness, or some other important value. If close-up scrutiny of many 'great operations' tends to reveal incremental rather than strategic decision processes (Section 8.3), it also reveals endless examples of beneficial opportunism and pragmatic reform by public servants at all levels. Some of these innovations may win awards, chartermarks, and the like (Borins 1995; Löffler 1995), but many do not. To end this book on an appropriate note of self-criticism, one of the major limitations of our approach—and the approaches of many others who have concentrated on big reforms and big ideas—is that we capture very little of this micro-improvement. As some of the most successful reform leaders have recognized, a crucial ingredient of a successful reform strategy is that it should create and sustain conditions in which 'small improvements'—many of them unforeseen and unforeseeable—can flourish.

The socio-economic context

A.1 The scope and purpose of Appendices A and B

Chapter 2 introduced the model of public management reform which we have referred to throughout the rest of the book (see Figure 2.1). In that model socio-economic forces (box A in Figure 2.1) are given an important, though not finally determinative, role in setting the climate for management reform. In Appendix A we offer a brief descriptive summary of what that climate has been like during the past twenty-five years. Then, in Appendix B we move on to the specifics of reform in each country.

The two appendices together provide some basic facts about the twelve countries covered in the main text. Unlike many other multicountry studies, this book is *not* organized into single-country chapters. It is deliberately and, we hope, advantageously organized by model and theme—thus permitting a more integrated, less sequential form of intercountry comparison. However, one price that is paid for this type of integration is that the reader is not offered neat little summaries of each country's recent history and arrangements. Left thus, readers who were not already familiar with the relevant aspects of a particular country's constitution, policies, and so on would be at a considerable disadvantage. To offset this possible handicap, Appendices A and B have been prepared so as to offer this type of information in a conveniently packaged form. The contents of the package are closely patterned on the model of public management reform introduced in Chapter 2 (see especially Figure 2.1). The sequence is therefore as follows:

- some information on major economic indicators for each country (i.e. data which help to 'fill in' the larger box A in Figure 2.1)
- some information on key sociodemographic indicators for each country (i.e. data which help fill in box C in Figure 2.1)

- a set of 'country files' which give snapshots of each country, organized in exactly the same categories as Chapter 2 and including, *inter alia*, details of the major management reforms since 1980
- a chronological table listing the key reforms by country, date, and type

A.2 Major economic indicators

Table A.1 lists some key economic indicators for each of the twelve countries. It may help to go through the measures one by one, and to indicate their possible significance for the factors that influence public management reform. Two major limitations to these data should, however, be acknowledged at the outset. First, it is seldom, if ever, possible to read off conclusions about a country's economic health from a single indicator. Second, many of these indicators are 'snapshots'—indicators of the state of a variable at a particular point in time or, at best, over a three- or five-year average. These two limitations indicate that caution is necessary in interpretation. If we take the variable 'general government expenditure', for example, the table tells us what share of GDP this represented in each country in 2001, but nothing about whether the trend over time was up or down within any given country (some information of that kind *is* given in Table A.2 and also in Table 5.2).

Nevertheless, despite these important qualifications, the variables listed in Table A.1 do carry significance—if often indirect—for the structure and management of the public sector in each country. They constitute some important elements of the *context* in which public management reforms unfurled. Some brief remarks to indicate the nature of the linkages are offered in the following paragraphs.

First, there is size—not a factor that usually changes overnight. By and large big populations

Table A.1 Selected key economic variables (2001)

Variable	Australia	Belgium	Canada	Finland	France	Germany	Italy	Netherlands	New Zealand	Sweden	UK	USA
Population (millions)[a]	19.4	10.3	31.0	5.2	59.2	82.3	57.4	16.2	3.9	8.9	59.8	285.0
Per capita GDP (current exchange rates)	18.876	22.291	22.430	23.250	22.125	22.431	18.969	23.463	12.872	23.573	23.814	36.831
Per capita GDP (current PPP)	26.333	26.932	28.911	26.097	25.255	26.542	26.074	27.847	20.250	25.617	24.455	35.619
Average annual gross fixed[b] capital growth over 5 years	0.5	0.6	2.6	1.8	2.1	−0.8	2.0	0.9	−0.9	1.6	2.1	4.3
General government expenditure on goods and services as % of GDP[c]	18.7	21.2	19.6	20.6	23.3	19.0	18.2	22.7	14.7	26.2	18.8	15.2
Average annual consumer price increase, previous 5 years	3.1	2.2	0.7	1.6	1.4	1.7	2.4	4.4	1.8	2.7	0.7	1.6
Export of goods as % of GDP	16.5	82.4	37.4	35.2	22.5	30.9	22.0	57.0	26.1	36.0	20.1	8.0
Average annual % export increase, previous 5 years	1.0	1.5	5.1	1.1	0.5	1.7	−0.8	1.5	−0.9	−1.3	0.9	3.1
Import of goods as % of GDP	17.4	77.4	31.9	26.4	22.3	26.3	21.2	51.4	27.5	29.9	23.8	12.8
Average annual % import increase, previous 5 years	−0.2	1.8	5.4	0.8	1.4	1.2	2.4	1.3	−0.2	−1.3	2.8	7.5

Notes: [a] Figures are for 2001, except for Sweden, UK, and USA that are for 2000.
[b] Figures are for 2001, except for Australia, New Zealand, and USA that are for 2000.
[c] Figures are for 2000, except for Canada (1998), and New Zealand and USA (1997).

Source: OECD, 2002, *Main Economic Indicators*, pp. 272–5, August, Paris, OECD.

Table A.2 Social expenditure (% of GDP), 1980–98

	1980	1985	1990	1995	1998
Australia	11.32	13.50	14.36	17.79	17.81
Belgium	24.18	26.99	24.60	25.07	24.54
Canada	13.26	16.97	18.25	19.23	18.03
Finland	18.51	22.92	24.78	31.24	26.54
France	21.14	26.62	26.45	28.98	28.82
Germany	20.28	20.98	20.29	26.70	27.29
Italy	18.42	21.27	23.87	23.75	25.07
Netherlands	27.26	27.43	27.92	25.92	23.90
New Zealand	19.15	19.43	22.53	19.32	20.97
Sweden	29.00	30.18	31.02	33.03	30.98
UK	18.19	21.27	21.62	25.84	24.70
USA	13.13	12.87	13.36	15.41	14.59

Source: OECD, 2001, *Twenty Years of Social Expenditure: 1980–98*, Paris, OECD.

tend to be more diverse, with a greater variety of social cleavages which are likely to be reflected in a greater complexity of political arrangements. One might argue that the huge and diverse population of the USA—or even the ethnically, regionally, and socially quite diverse sixty million people living in the UK—are inherently less straightforward to govern than the relatively homogenous five million Finns or nine million Swedes.

Second, there is the per capita wealth of a country. By global standards all twelve countries studied in this volume are rich. However, there are considerable differences within this rich countries' club. All other things being equal (which is a big assumption), a super-rich country such as the USA or Germany will have more room for manoeuvre, in both public and private spheres, than a significantly less rich country such as New Zealand or the UK. Obviously size is not everything: Belgium is quite small (population ten million), but the deep tensions between the Wallonian and Flemish communities have certainly made it a difficult country—at the federal level—to govern.

Third, Table A.1 shows diversity in terms of trends in capital growth.

Fourth, the figures for general government expenditure confirm the broad comparative picture developed earlier in the book. There are relatively generous Nordic countries (Finland, 20.6%; Sweden, 26.2%) and relatively parsimoni-

ous Anglo-Saxon countries (Australia, 18.7%; New Zealand, 14.7%; UK, 18.8%; USA, 15.2%). Somewhere in between come Belgium (21.2%) and Germany (19.0%). However, there are also some mild surprises—Italy quite low (18.2%) and the Netherlands (22.7%) second only to Sweden.

Fifth, the figures for wage increases and price increases over five years also show considerable variation. The highest consumer price increases were experienced by the Australians, Dutch, Italians, and Swedes. The Canadians and British enjoyed the lowest price increases. Ultimately, the balance between wage and price increases affects the international competitiveness of an economy as well as the purchasing power of its citizens. These factors, in turn, strongly influence the pressures on governments to spend and/or save. To take just one obvious example, falling international competitiveness (perhaps due to higher-than-average price increases) will lead to increasing unemployment and therefore to higher expenditure on unemployment benefits. Equally, virtuously small price increases (aided by low wage increases) will increase employment, increase the government's tax revenues, and reduce spending on unemployment benefits.

The size of exports and imports as a proportion of the total GDP provides a very rough indicator of the 'openness' of an economy to changes in global trade patterns. Here we may note that exports *and* imports are a higher proportion of the Belgian, Canadian, Finnish, Dutch, and Swedish economies than of the Australian or American economies. Germany, New Zealand, and the UK come somewhere in between these two groups. This pattern illustrates the complexity of factors affecting public management reform. In the abstract one might have hypothesized that countries with large import/export sectors would have been more open to the influences of economic 'globalization'—in particular increasing intensity of competition—and therefore would have been obliged to act most vigorously with respect to public management reform. In practice, however, any such hypothesis is falsified by the data in Table A.1. The 'high reformers' are New Zealand and the UK (in the 'middling' category for import/ export shares), while cautious modernizers such as the Belgians, the Dutch, and the Canadians fall in the 'high' category for import/export shares. This supports the point developed in Chapter 5, that reforms cannot be 'read off' from macroeconomic indicators—the influence of the latter may be profound, but it is often indirect, lagged, and diffuse.

A.3 Key sociodemographic indicators

The need to constrain public expenditure (and thereby hold down rates of taxation) has been a prominent theme throughout the book. Most of the largest elements of expenditure within the twelve public sectors under examination are strongly influenced by sociodemographic factors. Typically, pensions, health care, and education are the largest spending programmes. Unemployment benefits tend to be smaller in volume, but have attracted a great deal of public attention, especially as the nature of both employment and unemployment has been changing during the 1980s and 1990s as compared with the 1950s and 1960s. Part-time employment has grown almost everywhere (although at different rates in different countries) and there has been a shift in employment away from younger people and from older men (OECD 1996, pp. 28–9).

Among our twelve countries welfare states vary hugely, not simply in terms of the shares of expenditure they absorb but also in terms of their basic structures and procedures. However, all, to a significant degree, have both fiscal and social problems to face. Expert studies sometimes classify welfare states into a Scandinavian model, an American model, and a Continental European model. The Scandinavian model is relatively generous, and places emphasis on the provision of social services as well as on cash payments. The American model is relatively parsimonious, leaving a wider range of service provision to the private sector than is the case in its Scandinavian counterpart. There is also a political willingness to tolerate more extreme inequalities in income distribution and therefore, in both the US and the UK cases, the continuing existence of substantial pockets of deep poverty. The Continental model is more 'generous' than the American, but less service-oriented (and therefore less employment-intensive) than the Scandinavian model. The emphasis is on cash transfers. Table A.2 gives an aggregate picture of social expenditure in our twelve countries. Notice that, in the majority of countries, it has grown in importance.

The different models are also financed in different ways. All use some combination of general taxes, payroll taxes, and mandatory insurance, the exact balance between these different forms varying a good deal. As a basis for welfare expenditure, payroll taxes are particularly vulnerable in a globalized economy because they add directly to the cost of labour and, when employment falls, revenue shrinks more rapidly than it would from, say, a tax on consumption or even a general tax on incomes. Summing up an expert analysis of these differences, one recent commentator suggested that

[t]he implication seems clear enough: in order to increase their sustainability, each of these three types of welfare state must primarily attend to its specific problems. The Scandinavian model must reduce its dependence on very high levels of taxation; the American model must find ways of alleviating the distress of the working poor; and the continental model must find ways to increase levels of employment without running into the problems of the other two models. (OECD 1997c, p. 218)

Returning to the sociodemographic particulars, pensions are obviously affected by the age structure of the population. *Ceteris paribus*, the higher the proportion of the population that is retired, the higher will have to be public pension expenditure, and the smaller will be the proportion of the population that is in work and therefore capable of making some contribution to this expenditure through current taxation. In practice, matters are rather more complicated than this, for a variety of reasons. For example, in different countries differ-

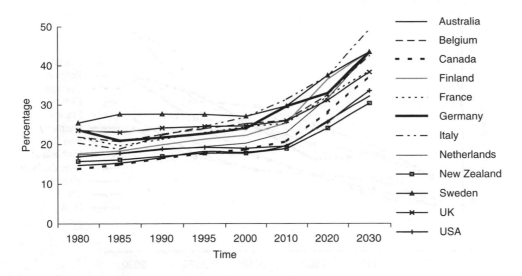

Figure A.1 Population aged 65 and over as a percentage of the population aged 15–64.

Source: OECD, 2000, *Labour Force Statistics*, Paris, and United Nations, 1999, *World Population Prospects: The 1998 Revision*, New York, Paris, OCED.

ent proportions of the retired population are covered by private pension schemes, and the adequacy of these schemes also varies. Also, many older people may still be active participants in the labour market, and variations in the extent to which this takes place can also influence the 'need' for state pensions. Further, it is the case that pensionable age varies from country to country (and since the mid-1980s there has been a trend towards shifting the age of entitlement *upwards*, so as to moderate demands on public expenditure). All these variations are important, but underneath them net changes in the elderly population remain a significant 'driver'. Within the EU the age/dependence ratio has been calculated to increase by 50 per cent within the coming twenty years (OECD 1997c, p. 70). In all twelve countries the percentage of elderly persons in the population as a whole has been increasing, but at different rates and over slightly different time periods. Figure A.1 gives some information about this.

From Figure A.1 it can be seen, for example, that in 1990 Sweden and the UK had the highest percentages of over-65s. In both countries the increase had been considerable since 1960. For all twelve countries, further increases are yet to come. However, looking forward to 2030, the coming increases in, say, Germany and the Netherlands are likely to be significantly greater than the in-creases in Sweden or the UK. In terms of pressures on expenditure one might say that, for Sweden and the UK, 'the worst is past', whereas for Germany and the Netherlands 'the biggest shocks are yet to come'.

The relative size of the elderly population is also very important for health care spending. For example, in the UK it was calculated that, in 1990, the average gross per capita expenditure for hospital and community health services for 16–44-year-olds was £115. The equivalent annual expenditure per 85-plus capita was £1,875. Between 1971 and 1990 the population of people aged 85 and over had risen from 485,000 to 866,000 (Harrison and Pollitt 1994, pp. 19–21). Figure A.2 gives some comparative figures for the growth of this most elderly group. As with Figure A.1, one can see growth everywhere, but from different starting points and at different rates. Thus Sweden has an unusually large population of the very old throughout the period 1980–2010, whereas, in this respect at least, New Zealand appears to be a considerably 'younger' society.

Of course, there is no assumption that each country is equally generous in its social expenditures, or that there is some uniform balance between expenditures on different social groups. Some countries seem to emphasize the needs of the elderly, others the needs of, say, the young, or the unemployed (OECD 1997c, pp. 63–80).

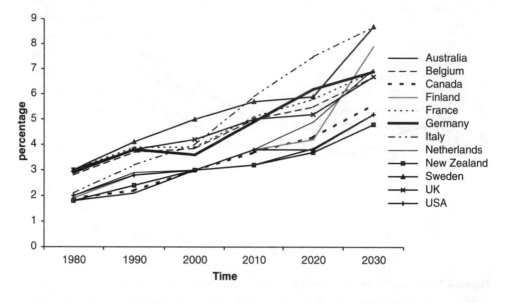

Figure A.2 Percentage of people aged 80 and over in the whole population.

Source: OECD, 2000, *Reforms for an Aging Society*, pp. 134–217, Paris, OECD.

Figures A.1 and A.2 and Table A.1 are focused mainly on the elderly. There is a range of other social developments that can affect social expenditure, apart from changes in the proportion of over-65s or over-85s. For example, studies in several countries have indicated that the creation of single-parent households tends to lead to problems such as increased rates of poverty, poor health, and social exclusion. Both increased rates of marital breakup and a growth in the proportion of children born outside marriage have contributed to this trend. The struggling 'lone mother', burdened with debts and unending childcare responsibilities, has become a focus for concern, especially in the USA and the UK, but also elsewhere. 'In all countries lone-mother families tend to be poorer than two-parent families' (OECD 1997c, p. 84). Table A.3 shows how this type of household has become a significant proportion of all households in most countries, but more so in some (USA, UK, Canada) than in others (the Netherlands, Sweden). New public programmes to address these issues (e.g. through subsidizing childcare facilities) can be expensive. Yet the changing structures of society—and the wider public and social costs of the *consequences* of allowing single-parent households to sink into poverty—provide strong arguments in favour of governments adopting measures to ameliorate the problems associated with this particular trend. As the introduction to a recent OECD report puts it: 'Maintaining lone parents and the long-term unemployed on benefits is seen as a problem rather than a solution' (OECD 1997c, p. 13).

Finally, we live in a period of considerable international migration, for economic, political, and other reasons (one of the authors of this book is currently an immigrant). This movement of persons brings a range of individual and collective benefits, but can also lead to political, economic, and cultural tensions. The presence of a substantial body of immigrants in a country faces the government of that state with various challenges—first of all, what citizen rights should be extended to them? Table A.4 shows that some of our twelve countries (Australia, Canada, New Zealand, USA) contain large percentages of foreign-born residents, while others have only proportionately small groups (Finland, Italy).

Table A.3 Composition of households by type of household in 1995 (%)

	One-person households	Couples without children	Couples with children	Lone-parent families	Other households
Australia[a]	24.2	30.5	27.9	7.6	9.8
Canada[b]	24.2	20.7	32.7	10.5	11.8
Belgium	10.0	20.0	58.0	7.0	4.0
Finland	15.0	21.0	50.0	9.0	5.0
France	12.0	20.0	56.0	7.0	5.0
Germany	14.0	25.0	50.0	5.0	5.0
Italy	8.0	16.0	66.0	7.0	3.0
Netherlands	13.0	25.0	56.0	5.0	1.0
New Zealand	20.1	27.8	23.6	8.9	19.7
Sweden	24.0	31.0	31.0	3.0	11.0
UK	11.0	22.0	52.0	10.0	6.0
USA[c]	25.7	28.3	24.6	9.3	12.1

Notes: [a] Data refer to 1999; [b] data refer to 1996; [c] data refer to 1998.
Notes about composition of households/families
  Australia: Couples without or with children are defined as couple family without or with one or more dependants.
  Canada: For families of married couples there is a distinction between children at home and no children at home without indication on age of children.
  New Zealand: Couples without or with children include couples without or with only dependent children.
  USA: Couples without or with children include couples without or with children under eighteen.
Notes about lone-parent families
  European countries: It is not possible to exactly know what the lone-parent families include: do they include only one parent with one or more dependent children? Or do they include other types of households with a male/female householder?
  Australia: They include only male/female householder with at least one dependant.
  Canada: They are defined as lone-parent male/female living with at least one never-married child.
  New Zealand: They include male/female householder with only dependent children.
  USA: They include male/female householder with children under eighteen.

Source: OECD, 2001, *Society at a Glance: OECD Social Indicators*, Paris, Annex G7.

Table A.4 Foreign and foreign-born population as a percentage of total population

Australia[a]	23.6
Belgium[b]	8.4
Canada[a]	17.4
Finland[b]	1.8
France[b]	5.6
Germany[b]	8.9
Italy[b]	2.4
Netherlands	4.2
New Zealand[a]	19.5
Sweden[b]	5.4
UK[a]	4.0
US[b]	10.4

Notes: [a] Defined as foreign-born population; [b] defined as foreign population.

Source: OECD, 2002, *Trends in international migration*, p. 40, Paris, OECD.

■ APPENDIX B

Country Files

AUSTRALIA

A. Socio-economic forces: general

Australia is a very large country, with a relatively modest population of 19.4 million in 2001. For key economic and sociodemographic data see Sections A.2 and A.3, including Tables A.1–A.3, and Figures A.1 and A.2.

B. Global economic forces

See Section A.2, especially Table A.1. Like New Zealand, Australia has relinquished most of its protectionist policies of the 1950–75 period as no longer viable. In consequence, it has recently laid great stress on competitiveness.

C. Sociodemographic change

See Section A.3. Two features of the 1970s and 1980s that tended to dilute the previous assumptions of Australia as an overwhelmingly white, postcolonial society were, first, an influx of Asian immigrants and, second, an increasingly strong demand for political (including territorial) rights by the aboriginal peoples. By the early twenty-first century, immigration was a major political issue, with the Howard government attempting to make political capital out of its tough stance with respect to asylum seekers and refugees. However, the pressures of an ageing society were somewhat less than those experienced by most western European states (Figure A.2).

D. National socio-economic policies

Australia and New Zealand were both obliged, during the 1980s, to move away from previous protectionist policies which had involved a high degree of state regulation and intervention in the economy. 'Increasingly both countries turned to the private sector and the use of market principles within the public sector, which have been linked to broader programmes of economic reform' (Halligan 1997, p. 17). Also like New Zealand, one component in the shift of economic strategy was a recognition that a higher proportion of both imports and exports was now coming from Asia, rather than from Europe (Castles et al. 1996, pp. 24–6).

From 1983 to 1985 the Australian economy recovered somewhat from its previous crisis. The Hawke Labor government increased public spending as a percentage of GDP. However, the terms of trade deteriorated sharply in 1985/86, and the second half of the 1980s witnessed an intensified effort at expenditure reduction. This, in turn, focused efforts to increase public sector efficiency and streamline government. By the mid-1990s the Australian economy was performing better, and, at the time of writing, has an above-OECD average record over recent years.

In general it might be said that the transition to new macroeconomic and microeconomic policies was both sharper and more painful in New Zealand than in Australia. During the 1985–92 period Australia enjoyed much better economic and employment growth than New Zealand (Castles et al. 1996). Microeconomic reforms were mediated through corporatist negotiations with the Australian trade unions, whereas the New Zealand reforms had a more 'imposed' quality.

E. The political system

Australia is a federal state, in which the state level is strong and, indeed, served as a 'laboratory' for some of the public management reforms which were subsequently introduced at the federal (Commonwealth) level (Halligan and Power 1992).

At the Commonwealth (central) level Australia has a bicameral legislature, with the Upper House being directly elected, with control by nongovernment parties, and quite well endowed with legislative powers. It has a strong committee system and capacity (often mediated through minority party senators) to block legislation. The electoral system is majoritarian, being based on an alternative vote procedure where voters are asked to indicate their first, second, third (etc.) preferences among candidates, and the preferences of those who voted for the candidate with the lowest number of first preferences are redistributed until one candidate emerges with an absolute majority of first preferences. Governments are usually dominated by a single party, either the Australian Labor Party (ALP), as between 1983 and 1992, or Liberal–National coalitions (as for the whole of the period from 1950 to 1972). The dominant style of politics is adversarial. (Australia is mildly famous for the boisterousness of its political exchanges.)

F. New management ideas

Australia was exposed to the same tide of 'Ricardian' or rational choice microeconomic thinking as other Western states, but does not seem to have been as directly and powerfully influenced by this as was New Zealand (Castles et al. 1996)—or, at least, not until the Howard-led National government of the late 1990s. Australia was also within the global reach of the parallel wave of generic managerialist ideas such as TQM, benchmarking, re-engineering. In this case the concept of a distinctive *public* service seems to have been strong enough to dilute the impact of such genericist concepts and their associated techniques somewhat more than in either New Zealand or the UK. Nevertheless, both rational choice and generic managerialism certainly exerted an influence during the late 1970s and 1980s—as in the UK and the USA, right-wing think tanks began to play prominent roles in debates about government and public affairs (Zifcak 1994, p. 19). However, their ultimate impacts on the central government machine were less than sweeping (Halligan and Power 1992, chapter 5). By the late 1990s, however, the Howard government was strongly advocating a familiar mix of downsizing and outsourcing in order to concentrate on 'core activities', more flexible and decentralized labour relations within the public service, stronger and more entrepreneurial public service leadership,

and continuous benchmarking for performance improvement.

G. Pressure from citizens

As with most other countries, there is no evidence of popular opinion demanding some specific and particular programme of management reform. Like elsewhere, however, some effect was probably felt from the public's unwillingness to continue putting up with poor service or bureaucratic obstructions. The Howard government (1996–) sometimes played on negative images of the public service to support its neoconservative policies.

H. Party political ideas

By the time Labor came to power in 1983, there was a growing consensus that the public service elite had become too much of a 'law unto themselves', and there was an appetite for a reassertion of political direction. This generalized sense that the public service required reform was clearly illustrated in the incoming government's white paper on the public service (Commonwealth 1983) and the 1984 Public Service Reform Act.

When, after a narrow victory in 1993, Labor's run of office came to an end in 1996, their National Party successors brought with them an at least equal suspicion of self-interested behaviour by the public service, combined with a stronger enthusiasm for privatization and the institution of MTMs within the public sector. As a departmental secretary in the Howard administration put it in 1997: 'It is important that the APS takes what practices and experiences it usefully can from the private sector. We have often lagged behind private sector efficiencies, largely because we have lacked the edge of competition and the reality of meaningful performance targets'.

I. Chance events

None of great significance for public management reform.

J. Elite decision-making

From 1983 onwards there was a consistent desire by the Labor governments (1983–96) and their National successors to assert full political control over the APS (Halligan 2002). During the 1980s '[m]anagerialism offered both a new approach for directing the public service and a rationalisation for exerting greater political control' (Halligan 1996b, p. 77). On the other hand, while the Labor politicians knew the direction in which they wanted to travel, they were not devotees of one particular model of reform: 'Australia has followed a more pragmatic mixture of principles and practice in contrast to the theory-driven reform in New Zealand' (Halligan 1996b, p. 79). The long period in office after 1983 meant that Labor politicians were able to build up confidence and knowledge in their reform efforts. Thus, for example, important new reforms were launched in 1987, after ministers had had some opportunity to observe what worked and what did not in Canberra.

The Howard government, from 1996, was perhaps more 'pure' in its doctrines, and vigorously espoused the neoconservative ideas of downsizing, contracting-out, and privatizing. However, it stuck to the principle of an apolitical public service, albeit one with much less of a monopoly of policy advice than formerly (Halligan 2002).

K. The administrative system

At the beginning of our period (1980), the APS remained in the classic 'Westminster' mode—separate political and mandarin careers, a strictly party-politically neutral, permanent career service, a near-monopoly of policy advice to ministers, strongly hierarchical, high levels of unionization. This 'Westminster model' has been extensively changed during the two following decades. Tenure is now less secure; the presence of partisan advisers within the system is much more extensive; levels of unionization—and the role of the unions—have been reduced; user-charging, actual or quasi-contracts and outsourcing have extensively replaced administrative hierarchies.

L. Contents of the reform package

In 1983 the first priority of the new Labor government was 'to re-establish ministerial control and greater responsiveness to government policies and priorities' (Halligan 1997, p. 31). This meant reform of the APS so as to shift the balance of power between bureaucrats and politicians more in favour of the latter. Actions included a number of components which were designed to reduce the

permanency of public servants, diversify sources of policy advice to ministers, and increase both managerial competence and the responsiveness of public servants to the government's political priorities. A central vehicle for this was the creation of a Senior Executive Service as part of the 1984 Public Service Reform Act. The effects of this were not particularly radical to begin with, but when combined with the 1987 restructuring, led to much more mobility and diversity in the upper reaches of the service.

Other key developments during the long Labor term of office from 1983 to 1996 included the following:

• 1983: launch of the Financial Management Improvement Program (FMIP), including strong elements of corporate management and programme-budgeting, plus mandatory evaluation to 'close the loop' for a new system of results-oriented management (see Zifcak 1994).

• 1984: Public Service Reform Act—creation of a Senior Executive Service. One aim was to make recruitment to senior public service appointments more open and competitive.

• 1987: major restructuring of central departments. Twenty-eight portfolio ministries were merged to produce sixteen large departments. In particular, 'mega' departments emerged with responsibility for Foreign Affairs and Trade, Education, Employment and Training, and Transport and Communications. These changes forced a considerable reshuffling of senior posts. A Department of Administrative Services (DAS) was formed, which subsequently became associated with a strong drive to increase competition. Greater emphasis was also placed on creating a tighter regime for the Government Business Enterprises (GBEs)—the growing number of public sector units and activities that had been 'corporatized'. (Subsequently many of these were privatized.)

• Late 1980s: beginnings of a sequence of significant sales of public sector assets, for example, Defence Service Homes Corporation (1988–90), Qantas Airline (1992–5), and Commonwealth Bank (1994) (see Halligan 1996b, p. 34 for more detail).

• 1993: publication of the Hilmer Report, *National Competition Policy*, recommendations from which were subsequently embodied in an intergovernmental agreement to seek competitive neutrality (a 'level playing field') as between public and private sectors.

- 1999: Public Service Act, significantly 'de-privileging' the senior public service.

The National Liberal Party came to power under John Howard in 1996, and remained in power at the time of writing (early 2004). Extensive reforms deprivileging the public service were pushed through, with the 1999 Public Service Act as a milestone. The Howard government also carried through further contracting-out, a shift to accruals-accounting, and an intensification of the existing performance measurement regime (McGuire 2004). There was also a major drive to restrain government regulation—a 'meta-regulatory regime'—carried out under the Competition Principles Agreement (1996—see Morgan 1999).

M. The implementation process

Compared with countries such as the Netherlands or even the USA, the implementation of public management reforms in Australia looks to have been a fairly centralized process. Prime ministers and the DAS have generally been able to get their way—although all such observations need to be taken in a context where the focus is principally on the Commonwealth government and not on the (independent) state level. Sometimes the style of implementation has been gradual and incremental (as with much of FMIP), sometimes rapid and sweeping (as with the 1987 restructuring of departments). Most recently (since the advent of the Howard/National government in 1996), the implementation process has sometimes appeared sudden and harsh. This, in turn, has generated unusually virulent opposition.

N. Reforms actually achieved

As indicated above, Australian governments not only carried through a series of significant public management reforms, they also committed themselves to a more extensive application of evaluation than did most of the other countries covered in this book. Thus, for example, the FMIP was subject to a series of evaluations, both internal and independent (Halligan 1996b; Zifcak 1994, pp. 96–9), and in 1992 the whole sweep of reforms was reviewed in an expensive and large-scale study (Task Force on Management Improvement 1992).

The picture revealed by these and other studies is a mixed one. Real change has undoubtedly been achieved: the 'culture' of the public service has shifted; substantial state assets have been privatized; certain techniques such as user-charging, outsourcing, and benchmarking have been widely applied; cost-consciousness and financial management skills have been considerably sharpened. The total size of the public service fell from 180,893 in 1986 (the peak year) to 143,305 in 1996 (Halligan 1997, p. 39).

On the other hand, implementation has often been significantly slower than had been envisaged, and the costs of change have been high. For example, central finance divisions within departments were often reluctant to permit the degree of internal delegation of financial authority implied by the spirit of the FMIP. Or 'corporate planning floundered as a technique designed to enhance political and departmental strategy' (Zifcak 1994, p. 110). The big 1992 evaluation by the Task Force on Management Improvement found that enthusiasm for many aspects of the reforms was much more pronounced at senior levels in the hierarchy than lower down, where considerable scepticism appears to have existed. By the late 1990s the downsizing and perceived antipublic service attitudes of the Howard government seemed to be generating disruption and severe morale problems. However, by 2001 this drive was somewhat moderated, partly because it was realized that imposition from the top could be counterproductive (e.g. problems with ICT outsourcing).

Country file events: Australia

	General	Organization	Personnel	Finance
1981–5	– Fraser: PM (Lib.) (1980) – Hawke: PM (Lab.) (1983) – 'Reforming the Australian Public Service' (APS) (1983) – Amendment of Public Service Act (1983)		– Access and Equity Programme (1985) – Merit Protection and Review Agency (MPRA) (1985)	– 'Budget Reform' (1984) – Financial Management Improvement Programme (FMIP) (1984)
1986–90	– 'APS 2000' (1989) – Hawke: PM (Lab.) (1990)	– From 28 to 18 departments (1987) – Efficiency Scrutiny Unit (1987) – Government Business Enterprises: reform (1987) – Management Advisory Board (MAB) (1987) – Management Improvement Advisory Committee (MIAC) (1989)	– Public Service Commission (PSC) replaces Public Service Board (1987) – Devolve to departments (1987) – Guidelines on Official Conduct of Commonwealth Public Servants (1987) – Wage agreement based on Structural Efficiency Principle (1988) – Equal Employment Opportunity: Further Steps Forward Strategy (1989) – Access and Equity Strategy (1989) – Performance Appraisal Programme for Senior Executive Service (1989) – Joint APS Training Council (1990) – Guidelines for appraisal of performance of SEO (1990)	– 2nd Review FMIP (1988) – Programme Management and Budgeting (1988) – Regulations on Purchasing: revised (1989) – 3rd Review FMIP (1990) – Purchasing Development Centre (1990)
1991–5	– Keating: PM (Lab.) (1991) – MAB/MIAC publications series (1991) – Code for handling conflict of interests (1991) – Unions–Government Framework Agreement: (1992) – Keating: PM (Lab.) (1993) 'Ongoing Reform in the APS' (1994)	– MAB: launch of 'Evaluation of Management Improvement' (1992) – Industry Commission: Benchmarking of Performance (1992) – PSC and MPRA merge into PSMPC (1994) – Privatization of Qantas and Aerospace Technologies (1995) – Reshuffling of departments (1995)	– Middle Management Development Programme (1991) – Framework for HRM (1992) – Strategic Plan for Equal Employment Opportunities (PSC) (1992) – Improving Productivity, Jobs, and Pay in the APS 1992–4 (agency workplace bargaining) (1992)	– Announcement of accruals-accounting (1992) – Revised requirements for departmental annual reporting (1993) – Develop generic performance measures (1993) – Audit Act (1994): – Financial Management and Accountability Bill – Commonwealth Authorities and Companies Bill

Period				
	– Principles and Guidelines for National Standard Setting and Regulatory Action (Council of Australian Governments) (1994) – National Competition Agreement (1994) – 'Review of the Public Service Act Report' (1995)	– Central Redeployment Unit (1993) – Guidelines on Official Conduct of Commonwealth Public Servants (1993) – Public Service Act: amended (choice: tenure or fixed-term appointment) (1994)	– Auditor-General Bill – New Fraud Control Arrangements (1994) – Efficiency dividend arrangements (1%) after signing Property Resource Agreement (1994)	
1996–2000	– Howard: PM (Lib.) (1996) – Several MAB/MIAC projects on costs, risk, ethics, benchmarking (1996) – Public Service Reform legislation introduced into Parliament (1997) – Single Australian Public Service Award (1998) – Government Online Strategy (1999) – Electronic Transactions Act (1999) – APCC (the Australian Procurement and Construction Council) (1999) – Framework for national cooperation on electronic commerce in government procurement (1999)	– Small Business Deregulation Task Force (1996) – Policy Parameters for Agreement-Making in the APS (1997) – Commonwealth Competitive Neutrality Policy through corporatization, commercialization, and cost-reflecting pricing (1999) – Competitive tendering and contracting reaffirmed by the government (1999)	– Workplace Relations Act (1996) – Public Service Bill (1997): apolitical public service; new legal employment framework; rights and obligations – Job Network replacing the Commonwealth Employment Service (1998) – Implementation of Performance Improvement Cycles and Competitive Tendering and Contracting (1998) – Public Service Act (1999), framework for the public sector, replaces old Public Service Act – Independent office for 'Merit Protection Commissioner' (1999) – Government boards and committees, guidelines for agencies and board directors (2000)	– Charter of Budget Honesty (1997) – Financial Management and Accountability Act (FMA) (1997–8) – The Commonwealth Authorities and Companies Act (CAC) (1997–8) – Auditor-General Act (1997–8) – Accruals Budgeting Project (1997–2000): – from cash to accrual; extension of performance measurement system – Charter Budget Honesty Act (1999) – Introduction of Accrual Information Management System (1999) – Government and general government sector (GGS) reporting of actual results (1999) – Accrual-based Outcomes and Outputs Budgeting and Reporting Framework (1999–2000)
2001–2	– Commonwealth Electronic Procurement Implementation Strategy (2000) – Howard re-elected: PM (Lib.) (2001)	– Review of Agreement-Making in the APS: Final Report and Case Studies (2001)	– Release of the Human Resource Capability Model (2001) – Performance management: a strategic framework for the integration of organizational, group, and individual performance (2002)	– Commonwealth procurement guidelines (2002)

BELGIUM

A. Socio-economic forces: general

Belgium is a rather small country (32,500 km^2), with a relatively modest population (10.3 million in 2002). For key economic and sociodemographic data, refer to Sections A.2 and A.3, including Tables A.1–A.4.

B. Global economic forces

Belgium is a particularly open economy with imports and exports representing an unusually high percentage of GDP (see Table A.1). Facing the convergence criteria for accessing the European Monetary Union (EMU) in 1992, Belgium was confronted with the problem of its consolidated gross public debt which rose to 132.1 per cent in 1990. Due to the restriction policy pursued by the government, public debt has been reduced to 102 per cent in 2002 (see Table A.1).

C. Sociodemographic change

Belgium is situated at the junction of the Latin and Germanic languages (Dutch, French, and German) and cultures. For many years these different cultures have been trying to find a fragile balance, leading to the creation of a federal state at the end of the 1980s and the beginning of the 1990s (a process that is still continuing and is explained more broadly in Section E).

Since the late 1970s and the early 1980s, the classical welfare state together with the social security system have been subject to great pressure from the economic climate (increasing unemployment) and the ageing society (increment of pensions and more expenditure on health care). The social welfare system is advanced, though not as elaborate as that in Sweden.

D. National socio-economic policies

Faced with the problems of public debt and the increasing public sector expenditures, central government launched a strong programme of budgetary reform and restraint under the Dehaene government (1992). Thanks to this policy, Belgium was able to fulfil the Maastricht 'convergence criteria' for the EMU (only partially). The

focus was one of downsizing the public sector and coping with the economic crisis by working more efficiently and effectively. The governments of the late 1990s have enjoyed an easier position on public spending than their predecessors.

E. The political system

Belgium is a federal state. In recent years the country has evolved rapidly, via four stages of constitutional reforms (in 1970, 1980, 1988–9, and 1993). The decision-making power in Belgium is no longer exclusively in the hands of the federal government and the federal parliament, but falls to communities on the one hand and regions on the other, which exercise their competences independently in different fields.

The redistribution followed two broad lines. The first concerns linguistics and, more broadly, everything relating to culture. It gave rise to the communities. Belgium has three communities, based on language: the Flemish, the French, and the German. The second main line of the state reform is historically inspired by economic concerns, expressed by regions that wanted to have more autonomous power. This gave rise to the founding of three regions: the Flemish, the Brussels Capital, and the Walloon. To some extent Belgian regions are similar to the American states or the German *Länder*, except that legislation decreed by regions and communities is at the same level as federal legislation.

All these communities and regions have separate governments and parliaments. The federal state retains important areas of competence including foreign affairs, defence, justice, finances, social security, important sectors of public health and domestic affairs. The country is further divided into ten provinces and 589 communes.

On the federal level, as well as on community and the regional level, there is a multiparty political system, and governments are composed by coalitions. The cabinets act collegially, with the prime ministers taking the role of *primus inter pares*.

Between the parliaments there are some differences. On the federal level the legislature is bicameral (tending to a unicameral system in the future), with, on the one hand, the House of Representatives and, on the other hand, the Senate, which are elected every four years. On the community and regional level, legislatures are unicameral and elected every five years.

For a long time the government was composed by Christian Democrats and Liberals or the Socialist Party. In the 1999 federal election, the composition changed and the Christian Democrats lost their place in government. The Liberals made up a coalition (the 'purple–green coalition' of Verhofstadt) together with the Socialist Party and the Green Party.

F. New management ideas

The position at the junction of two main cultures (see Section C) has also an impact on the introduction of new management ideas. Since federalization, especially at the end of the 1980s and at the beginning of the 1990s, different rhetoric on public management was displayed. The Flemish Ministry (ministry for the Flemish Community and Region) was influenced by the NPM principles from the Anglo-Saxon world and organized and modernized itself according to these thoughts (Bouckaert and Auwers 1999). The ministries of the French Community and the Walloon Region, as in France, were more reluctant and applied their own strategy. Recently they both launched modernization plans. Although the aim of making public service more efficient, effective, and responsive is similar, the trajectory in the separate parts in Belgium is different in approach, scope, and speed (Vancoppenolle and Legrain 2002).

Recently the evolution on the national level has followed the same trajectory as the modernization of the Flemish Ministry. A lot of ideas used earlier in the Flemish Ministry are projected on the national level.

G. Party political ideas

Like in the Netherlands, it is clear that the ideas of one single party in the consensual, multiparty governments in Belgium are likely to be less significant and powerful than in countries with one-party government and majoritarian systems (e.g. New Zealand, UK). Belgium has a proportional system and compulsory voting.

In the 1980s and the early 1990s, party political ideas (Christian Democrats and the Socialist Party or Christian Democrats and the Liberal Party) were merely focused on the reduction of the public debt and rebalancing the budget deficit aiming to cope with the Maastricht convergence criteria. Because of this policy the public sector was subject to a downsizing operation. The question in Belgium was not one of the role of the state, and the privatization debate was never as prominent as it was in the Netherlands.

After the elections of 1991 (and also in 1995) and the rise of the extreme right party, government policy was focused on the relation with the citizens, and the amount of (dis)trust in politics and the public sector. Therefore policies aimed at closing these gaps and making the public sector more responsive to the needs of citizens/users (e.g. charter of the user of public services, 1992).

In recent years the purple–green government (1999) has launched a large, in terms of scope and objectives, reform initiative for the federal public service (the Copernicus initiative). This reform programme was initiated by the federal (national) minister of public services, Van den Bossche, based on his experiences in the 1990s in the Flemish administration.

H. Pressure from citizens

It is indeed hard to find out if there was any pressure from citizens, what this pressure was, and whether pressure from citizens instigated the government to launch reform initiatives. In the beginning of the 1990s, with the elections of 1991, trust in the national government was very low at 31 per cent (*la Libre Belgique*, December 1991). The government launched initiatives to reduce this gap.

In 2000, with the proclamation of the Copernicus initiative, a questionnaire was distributed on a large scale. On the one hand, this questionnaire was meant to be an information and communication strategy, but on the other hand, a low response to this questionnaire was seen as a failure of the initiative (Bouckaert et al. 2001).

I. Elite perceptions of what management reforms were desirable and feasible

Most elite attention was focused on the federal process and budgetary problems during the 1980s and 1990s (see Section D). Management reforms therefore emphasized the economy—and input side of the public service.

Next to the budgetary focus, the gap between the government and the citizens was seen as a reason for the launch of initiatives to make the public service more accountable and responsive, following the elections of 1991.

When the budgetary restraints were fewer at the end of the 1990s, the government found an opportunity to launch a major reform initiative (see Section L).

J. Chance events

In the 1991 national elections, the rise of an extreme right party was marked. Politicians and social scientists saw this as a sign of the low legitimacy of the political culture and the widening of the gap between citizens and politicians (Maesschalck et al. 2002).

In 1996 Belgium was startled by a paedophilia scandal (the Dutroux affaire). Due to this scandal the judicial system and the function of the police forces were intensely criticized. The authorities were shaken by 'The White March'—250,000–300,000 demonstrating people in Brussels. Again this showed a decline in trust in the institutions and politics in general.

In 1999 the dioxin food crisis had an impact on the elections and pushed the reform agenda and the creation of the Federal Food Agency.

K. The administrative system

The original administrative structure of the Belgian state as established by the 1831 constitution was quite simple. It was made up of three government levels: the central level and two subnational levels, provinces and municipalities. This structure remained intact until 1970. Four revisions of the constitution made Belgium a federal state in 1993 (see Section E). The federal civil service has been severely reduced as a result of the different state reforms (see Table B.1). In terms of public employment the national level now represents only 33 per cent of the personnel in the public sector. In fact 7 per cent of civil servants are actually employed in the federal ministries. In addition, many functions have been transferred to autonomous public institutions (Brans and Hondeghem 1999, pp. 122–4).

The Belgian civil service is facing two main challenges. The first is associated with the legitimacy crisis of political institutions as a whole (see Sections I and J). The second is related to the budgetary pressures and the ascendancy of the new managerial paradigm in the public sector. Civil service reform has arrived on the agenda, albeit somewhat behind many other nations. There are, however, strong internal constraints

Table B.1 Public employment at the different levels of Belgian government

	1953	1964	1970	1980	1989	1995	2001
Ministries							
National					77.232	62.535	62.188
Regional					7.848	26.804	26.809
Total	83.797	99.198	108.074	88.062	85.080	89.339	88.997
Public institutions							
National					166.098	149.575	131.224
Regional					13.634	47.888	56.673
Total	131.341	126.292	115.969	198.402	179.732	197.463	187.897
Particular bodies	85.830	199.806	272.684	392.336	352.965	358.780	357.311
Local government	97.200	98.010	120.299	184.643	188.556	244.729	285.843
Legislature		1.000	969	1.232	1.773	2.282	2.860
TOTAL	398.168	524.306	617.995	864.675	808.106	892.593	922.908

Source: Brans, M. and Hondeghem, A. (1999), *The Senior Civil Service in Belgium*, p. 123. Federaal Ministerie van Ambtenarenzaken, Dienst Algemeen Bestuur, (2001), *Personeelsgegevens*.

on which reforms are likely to be implemented. These constraints are linked to the strong position of the civil service unions and the preoccupation of political actors with maintaining a balance of party political power within the administrative system (Brans and Hondeghem 1999, p. 121).

The federal civil service is a modest administration, playing only a marginal role in the policy making process. With the loss of important functions and powers to the new state levels, the federal level is now a laggard. Nevertheless major initiatives are launched in the shape of Copernicus reforms to restructure and reform the civil service (see Section L).

L. Contents of the reform package

Since the 1980s, several different initiatives have taken place to reform the federal civil service. Most of these initiatives in the 1980s occurred against the background of stringent cutbacks on public expenditure and the diminution of the general public debt (see Sections D and G). In the first half of the 1980s, under the fifth and sixth Cabinets of Prime Minister Martens, the modernization of the civil service and the vision on the personnel were inspired by these cutbacks. For this reason the modernization of the civil service was a part of the crisis management of that time (Bouckaert and François 1999, p. 12). Although the federal government was forced to cope with the financial restrictions, due to its openness to global economic influences and the pressure of Europe, the modernization of the civil service never led to a rethinking of the role and the scale of the state. In many other OECD countries the privatization debate was more present than it was in Belgium at that time.

Between 1981 and 1989 several initiatives were launched to modernize the civil service:

- 1985: appointment of a state secretary for modernizing the public service, attached to the prime minister
- 1987: creation of modernization cells in the different ministries
- 1987: creation of a secretariat of modernization
- 1989: creation of the College of Secretaries-General (the highest civil servants of the ministries), and the enlargement of the power of this college in 1993

After 1991 the focus of the modernization process shifted. Macroeconomic policy was still a priority. Instead of integrating the personnel management in this macroeconomic policy, the focus moved to the rewarding and motivation of civil servants. Reforms at the ministry of the Flemish Community triggered initiatives at the central level:

- 1991: first edition of the General Principles Royal Decree (KBAP) that stated the overall principles for the civil servants (and replaced the old statute Camu that went back to 1937); the KBAP was finally approved in 1994
- 1993: creation of the office for modernization and organization (ABC)
- 1995: creation of a ministry of the civil service

The modernization of the civil service was more than just an attempt to improve efficiency and effectiveness. It was also used to try to bridge the gap between the citizens and the government (see Sections G and II). After 1991 many initiatives were started to improve legitimacy (Bouckaert and François 1999, p. 30):

- 1991: law on the motivation on administrative actions
- 1993: public services users' charter
- 1994: law on access to information
- 1995: appointment of the federal ombudsmen

Most of the initiatives were launched on an ad hoc basis and lacked an overall strategy. Therefore there was little coherence between the different initiatives. However, with the establishment of the Cabinet in 1999, a major reform initiative was launched. The Copernicus reform, initiated and sponsored by the minister of reform, is a modernization plan covering many fields of the federal civil service. The initiative is built on four main trajectories:

- a modern HRM: In each new ministry HR experts are appointed and HR cells are created. The top managers are selected by an assessment centre and they get a mandate for six years. For all civil servants the evaluation system changed and the remuneration- and career-planning systems are to be reformed. Education and training are a priority.
- a restructuring of the ministries: The former ministries are restructured and reformed. There are ten vertical, four horizontal, and several

programmatic ministries (working on social themes crossing the entire policy field). The new internal structure of the ministries aims to equip them to fulfil an important role in policy design, implementation, and evaluation.

• a new budget and control system: The new ministries have a large degree of autonomy in developing a policy strategy and in spending the budget. For this reason each ministry has its own internal audit, which monitors its economy and efficiency.

• improved communication: On the one hand, there is the internal communication with the civil servants and on the other hand, externally, with citizens.

M. The implementation process

As stated in Section L, in the past, initiatives were not always coherent, and lacked an overall strategy. In 1989 a minister of the civil service was appointed; until then a secretary of state was attached to the prime minister. For a long time reform initiatives were a matter for the prime minister. In 1995 a separate ministry of civil service was created and many reforms have been launched and sponsored by this ministry.

In the past initiatives were ad hoc and fragmented. Many separate ministries launched their own programmes and took individual initiatives. The modernization pressure came from the lower levels of government (communities and regions), especially the Flemish Community. The reforms started in 1999, under the leadership of Minister Luc Van den Bossche, were often perceived as fundamental and drastic. These reforms are coherent and inspired by an overall strategy, but initiated in a stringent top-down way, which evoked some resistance. Since 2003 the new Minister Arena has redefined the reform process.

N. Reforms actually achieved

In Belgium policy and programme evaluation are not widespread. It is only in recent years (since 1998) that the role of the national court of audit (Rekenhof) has changed and moved to performance-auditing as well as traditional financial and compliance audits.

A broad-scope evaluation of management reforms as such is not an internal matter for the civil service, but rather an academic matter. Management reforms were introduced on an ad hoc basis and many individual initiatives have taken place in the separate ministries. Overall initiatives launched in the early and mid-1990s are still effective tools (access to information law, motivation law). Other initiatives have slowly faded out (e.g. users' charter).

The most import assignment for the Copernicus reform is to install a different culture within the civil service. Since 1999 many initiatives have taken place; the restructuring of the ministries, the appointment of the new top managers and leading officials, implementation of BPRs, development of an HRM policy. Although many initiatives have been realized, many others remain to be put in place. At this time it is too early to make a global evaluation of the reforms or an assessment of their sustainability. The new government has emphasized certain new elements (e.g. personnel assessment) while deemphasizing others (e.g. pay for top civil servants.)

Country file events: Belgium

	General	Organization	Personnel	Finance
1981–5	– Martens: PM (Christian Democrats) (1981) – 2nd Reform of the State (1980–2) – Economic recovery actions (1982) – Establishment of the information system BISTEL (1982) – Martens: PM (Christian Democrats) (1985)	– Territorial Reform: creation of communities and regions (1980) – Transfers of national services and ministries to the regions and communities (1982)	– More autonomy for communities and regions (1980) – Transfers of two personnel services (the Direction of General Affairs and the General Direction for Selection and Formation) to the Ministry of Home Affairs (1982)	– Restructuring of departmental budgets (1981) – Programme-budgeting (1985)
1986–90	– Martens: PM (Christian Democrats) (1987) – Martens: PM (Christian Democrats) (1988) – 3rd Reform of the State (1988–9) – Creation of the Crossroads Bank for Social Security (1990)	– State Secretary for modernization and information added to the PM (1985–8) – Report on the modernization of the civil service (1986) – Creation of the modernization secretariat (1986) – Creation of modernizing cells in the federal administration (1987) – Territorial Reform: extension of competences (1988–9) and creation of the Brussels Region (1988) – Appointment of a minister of the civil service (1989) – Creation of the College of Secretaries-General as advisory council for the government (1989) – Privatization of the task of extension of the Brussels Airport by the creation of the Brussels Airport Terminal Company (1989)	– Creation of a School for Finance and Tax Law within the Ministry of Finance (1987) – Policy for equality for men and women (1990) – Creation of the Corps of Civil Service advisers (1990)	– Finance Law (1989) – Zero-based budgeting (1990–5) – Introduction of financial memoranda (annual evaluation of all costs of selected services within a ministry) (1990–4)
1990–5	– Martens: PM (Christian Democrats) (1991) – Law on the motivation for administrative actions (1991)	– Merging of the Ministry of Public Works with the Ministry of Post and Communication in the Ministry of Communication and Infrastructure (1990)	– Reform of the Office for Selection and Recruitment (1991)	– Law on state accountability (1991)

continues

continued

	General	Organization	Personnel	Finance
	– Creation of the Advisory Board for Informatics (1991) – Dehaene: PM (Christian Democrats) (1992) – Restrictions on public spending (1992) – Reducing public debt (1992) – 4th Reform of the State: Belgium becomes a federal state (1992–3) – Charter of the Customer of Public Services (1993) – Law on the access to information (1994) – Appointment of information officers and creation of the Federal Information Service (1995) – Dehaene: PM (Christian Democrats) (1995) – Appointment of the federal ombudsmen (1995) – Introduction of the balanced scorecard in the social security agencies	– Law on the reform of state companies (1991) – Law on the reform of the Public Credit Institutions: creation of two semi-public holdings (1991) – Radioscopy, audit of the federal departments (1991–3) – Creation of autonomous government companies (1991) – 1st wave of asset sale of State Companies and Credit Holdings (1992) – Reform of the College of Secretaries-General (1993) – Merging of the Ministry of Agriculture with the Ministry of Middle Classes (1994) – 2nd wave of asset sale of Credit Institutions (1994–6) – Several autonomous state enterprises (like Belgacom of the Belgian Railways) become public limited companies (1994–5) – Creation of the Federal Participation Society as intermediary step to the privatization of the Credit Institutions (1995)	– Radioscopy, restructuring of wages, career opportunities, and number of personnel (1993) – Creation of the Outplacement Service (1993) – 'Tobback plan': recruitment stop, stimulating mobility – Royal Decree on the general principles of the civil service (1994) – Creation of the Ministry of Civil Service (1995) – Creation of the Office for Organization and Management (ABC) (1995)	– Maastricht convergence criteria (1992)
1996–2000	– Creation of Agency for Administrative Simplification (1998) – Satisfaction barometer (1998) – Establishment of a new intranet: Fedenet (1998)	– Creation of the Ministry for Social Affairs, Public Health, and Environment (1996) – Royal Decree on the autonomy and the accountability of the social security agencies (1997)	– Reform of the Institute for Education and Training of the Federal Civil Service (OFO) (1996)	– Law on the social security system and the pension system (1996) – Commission on the normalization of accountability (1998) – Charging role of inspectors of finance (1998)

- Creation of the Office of Public Debt (1998)
- Introduction of a new budgeting and control cycle (2000)
- Creation of financial cells in the federal ministries (2000)

- Creation of the Office of Budgeting and Control separate from the Ministry of Finance (2000)
- Creation of an internal audit service at each ministry (2000)

- Royal Decree on the regulation and reform of the budget, accounting, and audit system of the social security agencies (2001)

- 'Flahaut plan': instructions on recruitment, evaluation, mobility, vacation, and education (1997)
- Introduction of evaluation system (1997–8)
- Royal Decree on the general principles of the civil service (2000): more liberties for the regions and communities

- Reform of the recruitment and selection office (Selor) (2000)
- Separation of the selection and recruitment process and the enlargement of competences for the ministries (2000)
- Introduction of a mandate system for top managers (2000)

- Creation of the Ministry of Personnel and Organization and of HRM cells in the federal ministries (2001)
- Appointment of HRM officers for the federal ministries (2000–1)
- Public Management Programme: education programme for young high potentials (2000–2)
- Assessment for top managers (2000–3)
- Introduction of the Copernicus reform into the social security agencies (2002)

- Creation of the Federal Agency for the Protection of the Food Chain (2000)

- Introduction of the Copernicus reform plan of Minister Van den Bossche (2000)

- Creation of a virtual matrix as general structure with horizontal, vertical, and planning ministries (2001)
- Reduction and abolishment of ministerial cabinets (2001–3)
- Creation of new structures in ministries: management board and direction board (2001)
- Operational autonomy and new personnel status for 10 social security agencies (2002)
- Business Process Re-engineering in all new ministries (2001–3)
- Bankruptcy of Sabena (2002)

- Verhofstadt: PM (Cons./Soc./Green) (1999)
- Appointment of a minister of administrative reform (1999)
- Action plan for administrative simplification and the appointment of a government commissioner (1999)

2001–2

- Introducing the Common Assessment Framework in the public service (2000–1)
- Organization of a quality conference for all public services in Belgium (2001)
- Creation of a Ministry of Information and Communication Technology (FEDICT), new e-government policy and creation of ICT cells in the federal ministries (2001–2)
- Establishment of the Federal Metropolitan Area Network: all the federal ministries and agencies are connected to each other (2002)
- Creation of the Portal Website for the whole civil service in Belgium (2002)
- Verhofstadt PM (Cons/Soc) from 2003

CANADA

A. Socio-economic forces: general

See Section A.2 and Table A.1.

B. Global economic forces

Again, see references to Canada in Section A.2 and Table A.1.

C. Sociodemographic issues

For general picture, see Section A.3, Figures A.1 and A.2, and Tables A.2 and A.3. Canada is rapidly becoming multi-ethnic and multicultural—partly through immigration (see Table A.4). By 1991 the number of Canadians whose first language was neither French nor English reached 4.1 million (out of the then population of 29.2 million); 626,000 defined themselves as belonging to one of the three recognized aboriginal groups. Canada, like other advanced industrial economies, is also getting older. Between 1961 and 1991 the number of citizens aged sixty-five and over increased by 128 per cent to 3.2 million (see Figure A.1). Canada also has a relatively high divorce rate (2.8/1,000 population in 1992) and 60 per cent of female-headed single-parent families fell below the official low income cut-off (Statistics Canada 1995).

D. National socio-economic policies

Relative to OECD averages, Canada suffered a disappointing economic performance during the 1980s. Control of public spending was a particular weakness. During the Mulroney administration (1984–93), public spending targets were repeatedly set and missed. Between 1984 and 1993 the net public debt increased from Can.$168 bn. to Can.$508 bn. (Harder and Lindquist 1997, pp. 80–1). However, the Chrétien administration (1993–2003) largely met its expenditure reduction targets, and in 1997/98 achieved the first balanced budget in thirty years.

E. The political system

Canada, like Australia, is a federal state with a 'Westminster' system (i.e. a first-past-the-post electoral system, disciplined parties, and strong, majoritarian governments). However, a simple picture of single-minded centralism would be quite inaccurate:

> In a country consisting of two 'founding' linguistic groups, four or five distinct regions, and the usual cleavages between classes and other divisions characteristic of all modern societies, a governing party must try to accommodate a representation of as many interests as possible. Aboriginals, historically marginalised in the political process, are also becoming contenders in the system ... (Mallory 1997, p. 16)

During the nineteenth and early twentieth century central government appeared to dominate most of the significant governmental functions, but the growth of the welfare state shifted the balance in favour of provincial and local governments. Agreements between federal and provincial governments became more and more essential for policy progress on many items, but during the 1980s the political conditions for stable multilevel agreements of this kind became less readily available.

Although in many ways a more 'state-centred' and even 'state-trusting' society than its US neighbour, Ottawa's political elite also suffers popular suspicion. The underpinnings of federal authority have been eroded from several directions:

> [T]he whole system of government in Canada is beset by a number of forces which tend to undermine it. These include a pervasive anti-elitism and populism which undermines the authority of government and thus its will to deal with issues, a pervasive and exaggerated fear of mounting public debt and public bankruptcy, and a threat to the survival of the system by the danger of Quebec separation accompanied by serious regional discontent which could of itself lead to the dissolution of the union. All these threats to survival have occurred in the past, and have been successfully surmounted. This time they seem to have all come together. But one should not underestimate the enormous inertia of the system, as well as its flexibility, which may well ensure its survival and its capacity to adjust (Mallory 1997, p. 23).

F. New management ideas

It is clear that Canadian ministers and senior officials were well aware of the currents of new management thinking, which were flowing through the anglophone world from the late 1970s onwards. Mulroney's administration (1984–93) made extensive use of business people and also 'borrowed'—at least in part—a number of public management reform ideas from the USA and the UK. Mulroney's own rhetoric mirrored the antibureaucratic, pro-private-sector tone of Thatcher and Reagan (Savoie 1994).

Just two examples will suffice. First, the Nielsen task force set up in 1984 took about half its members from the business community, and Nielsen himself was conscious of borrowing from Raynerism (UK) and the Grace Commission (USA) (Savoie 1994, pp. 127–30). Second, the creation of politically sympathetic chiefs of staff in each department drew something from the US 'spoils system', and more specifically from President Reagan's expansion of that system during the early 1980s. The basic idea was to give ministers greater assistance in the task of getting the permanent bureaucracy to do their bidding.

Under the Liberal administration from 1993 the public service regained some of its self-confidence, and by 1998 the Clerk of the Privy Council (the most senior civil servant) felt able to proclaim a 'Canadian model' of public management reform. This included a rejection of the proposal that minimizing government was always a good thing and an embracing of experiment and diversity in organizational forms (Bourgon 1998).

G. Pressure from citizens

As elsewhere, citizens in Canada did not rush forward with specific proposals for management reform. However, a perceived dissatisfaction with government, and alleged citizen demands for greater accountability, were certainly a factor mentioned by executive politicians and senior officials as one reason for public management reform (e.g. President of the Treasury Board 1997, Foreword).

It is important to disentangle the various strands and dimensions of citizen opinion, for example, by distinguishing the satisfaction levels of service users with a particular service from more general citizen views of the competence or trustworthiness of government at large (Canadian Centre for Management Development 1998a). Much of the expressed distrust of government appears to have been focused on politicians and government in general, with public servants being regarded with greater confidence. Furthermore,

when due allowance for differences was made, user satisfaction levels with many public services were not systematically worse than with private sector services (Canadian Centre for Management Development 1998b).

H. Party political ideas

The decisive shift towards public management reform came (as in the UK and the USA) when a right-wing government was elected in place of a somewhat 'worn-out' centre-left government (in the Canadian case, Trudeau's Liberal government). Mulroney's Progressive Conservative administration was imbued with antibureaucratic rhetoric, and carried with it a general suspicion of the established bureaucracy and its seemingly close previous relationships with long-standing Liberal governments. However, although the incoming administration had plenty of generalized prejudices against bureaucracy and in favour of private sector dynamism, there is no evidence that it had any well-worked-out scheme for public management reform, or any coherent set of operationalized ideas on which to base such a plan.

The popularity of private sector management concepts faded somewhat during the long life of the Mulroney government, and was certainly less to the fore during the succeeding, more 'state-friendly' Liberal government. It is not clear that Chrétien's regime had any distinct plan of conception for management reform per se, but it was determined to bring expenditure under control and try to link that to a more positive agenda of modernization and developing alternative modes of public service delivery. Most of the specific ideas, however, seem to have come from the senior bureaucrats themselves.

I. Chance events

Several chance events appear to have had some influence over the trajectory of management reform. One was the dropping of Nielsen from the Mulroney Cabinet in mid-1986—for reasons unconnected with his leadership of the programme review task force. This cannot have helped the implementation of the still-new report, which afterwards largely faded away. A second coincidence, of rather larger impact, was the Mexican currency crisis of late 1994, which by all accounts helped significantly to strengthen the determination of the Chrétien Cabinet to push ahead with the downsizing and programme adjustments of the Program Review exercise, in case Canada became the next state to suffer currency 'meltdown' (Aucoin and Savoie 1998).

J. Elite decision-making

See Section G. The Mulroney administration developed a series of specific initiatives on the basis of some generalized attitudes and prejudices, but there does not seem to have been any coherent overall plan. Even the specific initiatives that were launched frequently encountered implementation difficulties (see Sections L and M).

After the fall of the Progressive Conservative administration in 1993, there was a shift in ministerial preferences. More emphasis was now placed on finding creative forms of 'alternative service delivery', on partnership operations with the provinces, on shrewd use of advanced information technology, and on more transparent accounting to Parliament for results (Aucoin and Savoie 1998; President of the Treasury Board 1997).

Throughout, Canadian ministers and officials had to temper their enthusiasm for particular directions of reform with a recognition of the complex, multilevel, sectoralized nature of the political and administrative systems. They did not enjoy the powers of New Zealand, for example, or UK prime ministers to drive through major reforms even against significant opposition. The picture of the 'Canadian model' drawn by the Secretary to the Privy Council (Bourgon 1998) is essentially incremental and antidoctrinal. It speaks of reform being carried out 'calmly, competently, without much fanfare' (Bourgon 1998, p. 1). Considerable stress is laid on sharing and cooperation with the provinces.

K. The administrative system

In February 1997 there were twenty-four departments, thirty-seven crown corporations, and at least forty-eight other service organizations responsible to federal ministers. Total employment was 370,000 full-time equivalents (FTEs). A strong form of ministerial responsibility prevails (ministers responsible for all the actions of their portfolios, crown corporations, service agencies, tribunals, etc., but no 'accounting officers' along the UK lines).

Within this ensemble the central agencies have remained relatively large and influential. The main ones are the Privy Council Office (approximately 300 staff), the Treasury Board Secretariat (800), the Department of Finance (700), the Prime Minister's Office (80), and the Public Service Commission (2,000) (Savoie 1997). Management reforms tend to be led by the Privy Council Office and the Treasury Board Secretariat.

The public service itself is nonpartisan, and deputy ministers (the chief officials in the departments) usually remain in place when the government changes. Nearly all deputy ministers are career civil servants. There is quite a strong 'mandarin culture', with considerable horizontal communication between senior civil servants in different departments (Bourgault and Carroll 1997, p. 97).

L. Contents of the reform package

From a bird's-eye view much of the recent history of management reforms in the Canadian federal administration appears as a bewildering series of overlapping and only loosely coordinated initiatives, many of which seem to fade away or lose momentum after a relatively short time. Several commentators confirm that—certainly under the Mulroney administration of 1984–93—the political leadership lacked any 'grand design' and gave management issues only intermittent attention (documented in Savoie 1994).

Mulroney came to power following a campaign that had been sharply critical of 'big government' in Ottawa, and that had promised greater 'frugality' and radical changes in the the bureaucracy. He was re-elected in 1988 and finally lost office in 1993. During his period in power he launched a number of initiatives, including:

- A 1984 review, under Deputy Prime Minister Erik Nielsen, of existing government programmes to make them 'simple, more understandable, and more accessible to their clientele', as well as to decentralize them and cut out programmes for which there was not a demonstrable need.

- The creation, in each ministry, of a politically appointed chief-of-staff position at assistant deputy minister level (i.e. the second highest civil service grade).

- A target of a 15,000 downsizing of the civil service within six years.

- The 1985 Increased Ministerial Authority and Accountability initiative (IMAA), designed to give individual ministers and departmental managers

greater flexibility in allocating and reallocating resources within their departments (partly by reducing the detailed control of central agencies). One
part of this was the creation of Treasury Board
Memoranda of Understanding (MOUs) which
were supposed to provide greater freedom to departments that negotiated with the Treasury Board.

• From 1986, a 'make-or-buy' policy to encourage competitive tendering for public services.

• Also from 1986, the establishment of a privatization office.

• The 1988 establishment of the Canadian
Centre for Management Development (CCMD)
to strengthen management training for the Canadian public service.

• It was decided that deputy ministers (the most
senior civil servants) could henceforth be called
before parliamentary committees for questioning
(Bourgault and Carroll 1997, p. 3).

• The effective scrapping of the previous PEMS
and its replacement, from 1989, with a new system
of cabinet committees, centred upon an Expenditure Review Committee (ERC).

• A high-profile, broad-scope exercise entitled
Public Service 2000 (PS 2000) to empower civil
servants, cut red tape, and improve service to the
public. PS 2000 was announced in December
1989. In 1990 a white paper *The Renewal of the
Public Service in Canada* was published.

• The creation of a new type of decentralized
agency, the Special Operating Agency (SOA), to
enjoy greater managerial flexibility, whilst
remaining within the framework of ministerial
departments. The first five SOAs were announced
in December 1989.

• Shared Management Agendas (SMAs), which
evolved alongside PS 2000, were agreements
between the Treasury Board and deputy ministers
in departments to identify the top management
priorities for the forthcoming twelve months.

Further reforms followed the fall of the Mulroney
administration in March 1993. Some of the more
significant were:

• 1993: Service Standards Initiative, to encourage departments and agencies to develop and publish service standards. By 1995 two-thirds of
departments were said to be well advanced in
this exercise.

• June 1993: a radical restructuring of the machinery of central government by Mulroney's Progressive Conservative successor, Kim Campbell.
The size of the Cabinet was reduced from thirty-
five to twenty-three and a number of departments
were merged or eliminated.

• Campbell's government was short-lived. In
October 1993 the Liberals, under Chrétien,
returned to power.

• February 1994: a process of Program Review
was launched. Unlike some previous expenditure
reduction exercises, this one was able to mobilize
considerable collective support within Cabinet,
and was carried through to implementation in
the 1995 and subsequent budgets. It went beyond
simple cost-cutting and entailed a broad reconsideration and prioritization of the role of the federal
government in Canadian society (Aucoin and
Savoie 1998).

• February 1995: a new Expenditure Management System (EMS) was introduced, which
considerably tightened the previous approach
to the use of budgetary reserves. Under EMS
it is assumed that all new programmes and
programme increases will have to be financed
by reallocations within departments' budgetary
envelopes. The government also committed
itself to the introduction of full accruals-
accounting.

• June 1995: a Quality Services Initiative approved by the Cabinet, aimed at increasing measured client satisfaction.

• 1996: introduction of Improved Reporting to
Parliament Project (IRPP) with the aim of enhancing the accountability of ministers and departments to Parliament.

• 1996: Secretary to the Privy Council launched
an initiative named *La Relève*, designed to tackle
what was said to be a 'quiet crisis' in the Canadian
public service. 'This was the result of years of
downsizing and pay freezes, criticism, insufficient
recruitment, and the premature departure of experienced public servants' (Bourgon 1998, p. 18).
Initiatives were invited from departments to revit-
alize the public service.

• 1997: publication of *Accounting for Results*
(President of the Treasury Board 1997), which for
the first time brought together results statements
for all departments.

M. The implementation process

The implementation process in Canada appears to have been a somewhat uncertain one, at least in the sense that a number of the initiatives petered out after a relatively short period, leaving only traces rather than the significant achievements that had been predicted at the time of their initiations. Even the Canadian government's own account, as published in an OECD text, conceded that 'use of performance measures has been uneven, with departments and agencies having considerable discretion over their development and use' (OECD 1997a, p. 39). Examples of such disappointment include:

• 'Notwithstanding its early support, the Mulroney government did not follow through on the great majority of the Nielsen recommendations...Indeed, the great majority of programs reviewed are still in place and virtually intact' (Savoie 1994, p. 130).

• The 'make-or-buy' policy of 1986 did not make much progress beyond the pilot project phase, and was abandoned in 1990.

• Despite the early development of a privatization plan, substantive progress on this policy had dwindled to rather little by 1987. The Department of Finance insisted that revenues from privatization sales should go into the Consolidated Revenue Fund, and departmental ministers became increasingly resistant to 'losing' 'their' crown corporations or subsidiaries.

• The success of IMAA was limited. Six years after its introduction only about one-third of departments had agreed to sign an MOU with the Treasury Board, and those that did sometimes complained of a mass of paperwork for only limited real autonomy.

• 'Even its most ardent supporter admits that PS 2000 is not living up to expectations' (Savoie 1994, p. 241). The expectation that central agencies would be cut back was not fulfilled. There was a widespread perception that PS 2000 remained a top-down exercise that produced more reports than action.

• Mulroney's programme for downsizing the civil service produced a reduction of only 15,000, and about half these positions were actually transferred to provincial governments or other parts of the public sector (Savoie 1994, pp. 266–7).

• 'Although the experiences with SOAs have been positive, it is not clear whether they are sufficiently different from traditional departments to support flexible and innovative service delivery' (OECD 1997a, p. 44).

• During the 1980s 'governments became increasingly preoccupied with the deficit and the debt, but were unable to come to grips with it. The period was characterized by unachievable deficit reduction targets and regular across-the-board cuts, primarily targeted at operations' (Harder and Lindquist 1997, p. 80). Net public debt increased from Can.$168 bn. in 1984 to Can.$508 bn. in 1993.

After 1994 conditions for implementation eased. The Canadian economy began to improve, and Chrétien, a very experienced prime minister, was able to establish a relatively disciplined Cabinet. The 1994 Program Review and the 1995 budget were generally regarded as successful exercises. However, there remains a doubt about the connections between the higher levels of the federal government—especially the central agencies—and 'middle management' in the operational agencies and the departments. Reforms may achieve agreement at the top, but to what extent is implementation 'owned' by those outside Ottawa?

N. Reforms actually achieved

There has been no systematic evaluation of public management reform in Canada during this period, although there have been a number of specific reviews or assessments of particular initiatives. Notable among these have been the sometimes sharply critical reports of the Auditor-General (e.g. Auditor-General of Canada 1993, 1997).

As indicated in Section M, it appears that Canada suffers (or, at least, suffered) from a significant 'implementation gap', with many initiatives failing to meet anything like their full expectations. The 1994 Program Review exercise, thanks to a favourable set of political circumstances surrounding its launch, appears to be an important exception to this, but it would be optimistic to expect such circumstances to continue indefinitely (Aucoin and Savoie 1998).

Country file events: Canada

	General	Organization	Personnel	Finance
1981–5	- Trudeau: PM (Lib.) (1980) - Turner: PM (Lib.) 1984 - Mulroney: PM (Progr. Cons.) (1984) - Focus on reducing public expenditure (1984) - Increased Ministerial Authority and Accountability (IMAA) (1988)	- Office of Privatization and Regulatory Affairs (OPRA) (1986)	- Creation of a 'Management Category' (1981)	- Policy and Expenditure Management System (PEMS): Multi-Year Revenue Expenditure Plan, Multi-Year Operational Plan (MYOP) (programmes with activities) (1981)
1986–90	- 'Public Service 2000' initiative (1989) - 'Enterprising Management' (on IMAA) (1989) - Public Service 2000 white paper (1990) - Service standards and client surveys (1990)	- Canadian Centre for Management Development (CCMD) (1988) - Treasury Board Senior Advisory Committee: re-established (1989) - Special Operating Agencies (SOA) (1989)	- Personnel Management Manual: streamlined (1989) - Administrative Policy Manual: consolidated (1989) - Human Resources Development Council (HRDC) (1990) - Management Trainee Programme (1990)	- Memoranda of Understanding (MOUs) (3-year: performance indicators, targets, expectations, accountability) (1988)
1991–5	- Budgetary measures (1991) - Government's Economic Statement: cuts and freezes (1992) - Public Service 2000: progress report (1992) - Co-location of related federal government services (1992) - Review of regulatory regimes (1992) - Campbell: PM (Progr. Cons.) (1993) - Chrétien: PM (Lib.) (1993) - Budget cuts (1994) - 2nd Annual Report on the Public Service (1994) - Efficiency of the Federation Initiative (1994) - Declaration of Service Quality (1994) - Deputy Ministers Task Forces (1995):	- OPRA functions to DoF and Treasury Board Secretariat (TBS) (1991) - Departments: from 32 to 24 (1993) (1993); - Cabinet members: from 35 to 23 (1993); - Cabinet Committees from 11 to 4 (1993) - Blueprint for Renewing Government Services Using Information Technology (1994) - Intergovernmental and interdepartmental cooperation: Canada Business Service Centres (1994) - Alternative Service Delivery (ASD) (1995)	- Public Service Reform Act: amended (1992): Public Service Employment Act; Public Service Staff Relations Act	- Shared Management Agenda (SMA) (deputy ministers, TBS, comptroller-general) (1991) - 12 operating budgets (1991) - Public Service Reform Act: amended (1992): Financial Administration Act; Surplus Crown Assets Act - Expenditure Management System (EMS) (1995) - Improved Reporting to Parliament Project (IRPP): Performance Reports and Reports on Plans and Priorities; Business Plans replace MYOP; Government Wide Performance Reporting - Reviews (1994): Program Review: Agency Review; Review of Major Sectors and Horizontal Activities; Internal Audits

continues

continued

	General	Organization	Personnel	Finance
	– Future of the Public Service; – Service Delivery Models; – Federal Presence; – Overhead Services; – Value and Ethics; – Policy Planning and Horizontal Issues – 3rd Report (1995) – Quality Service Initiative (1995)			– Annual Strategic Planning Cycle (1994) – Service standards for major business lines required (1995)
1996–2000	– Policy Research Committee established: interdepartmental Group of Assistant Deputy Ministers (1996) – 'Getting Government Right' (1996–7) – Policy Research Secretariat established (1997): to coordinate interdepartmental research networks – First balanced budget since 1969 (1997–8) – 5th Annual Report to the PM on the Public Service of Canada (1998) – The Government of Canada Regulatory updated (1999) – Treasury Board Secretariat published Strategic Direction for Information Management and Information Technology: Enabling 21st Century Service to Canadians (the government's priorities for IM/IT) (1999)	– Canadian Food Inspection Agency (1997) – Creation of the Policy Research Secretariat (1997) – Citizen-Centred Service Network (1998) – Creation of Service Canada Access Centres (1998) – Parks Canada Agency (1999) – A new secretariat in Privy Council Office to support the Special Committee of Council (SCC), Cabinet Committee that approves regulations (1999) – Creation of three Deputy Minister Committees to analyse the issues of recruitment, retention, and learning development in the public service (1999) – The Department of National Revenue became the Canada Customs and Revenue Agency (CCRA) (2000) – Treasury Board creates the Office of Value and a Government of Online Project Management Office (2000)	– 'La Relève: A Commitment to Action' (1997) – Replace 'La Relève Task Force' by 'The Leadership Network' (1998) – The first public service employee survey (1999) – Framework for Good Human Resources Management in the Public Service for measuring the quality of their personnel management in five key areas: leadership, values, productivity, enabling environment, and sustainability (1999) – Employment Equity Positive Measures Program (EEPMP) – Employment Equity Act – The Task Force on the Participation of Visible Minorities—Action Plans: Embracing Change in the Federal Public Service (2000)	– Continuation of EMS (1996) – President of Treasury Board's 2nd Annual Report on Review (1996) – All federal departments and agencies: Performance Reports (1997) – President of Treasury Board's 3rd Annual Report: Accounting for Results (1997) – Financial Information Strategy (FIS): accruals-accounting, upgrading financial management (1997) – Planning Reporting Accountability Structure (PRAS): departments with business lines (1997) – 80 federal departments and agencies: Reports on Plans and Priorities (1998) – Modernization of the Controllership in the Government of Canada (1998) – Balance between investing in service improvement, maintaining the integrity of existing programmes, reducing taxes, and retiring public debt – Continues EMS (1999)

- Managing for Results (1999)
- Update for HR Professionals on Business Planning and Reporting in the Government of Canada (1999)
- Sustaining Growth, Human Development, and Social Cohesion (1999)
- Chrétien: PM (Lib.) (2000)
- 7th Annual Report on the Public Service of Canada (2000)
- Result for Canadians—A Management Framework for the Government of Canada: Citizen Focus, Values; Result-Based Management; Responsible Spending; Citizen-Centred Service Delivery, Government of Canada Online; Modern Controllership; Improved Reporting to Parliament; Program Integrity; Development of Exemplary Workplace (2000)

- Comprehensive Program Integrity Assessments (1999)
- Financial Information Strategy Learning Framework (1999)

2001–2

- The establishment of the Partnership for International Cooperation (2001)
- Service Improvement Initiative (2001–5)

- Continues La Relève Reform: the Leadership Network: website (www.leadership.gc.ca) to connect and support leaders at all levels of the public service (2001)

- Financial Information Strategy (2001)
- Results for Canadians—A Management Framework for the Government of Canada (2001)

EUROPEAN COMMISSION

Introduction

The European Commission is an 'odd one out' in this book, in the sense that it is *not* a national government, and, indeed, to think of it as though it were would be highly misleading. The Commission is one important component—the main 'executive' component—in the unique and tremendously complex formation of institutions that make up the EU (see Peterson and Shackleton 2002 for a clear treatment). A recent Commission reform document describes the Commission's original role as follows:

It was established to act impartially in the interests of the European Community as a whole and to act as guardian of the founding Treaties, notably by exercising its right of legislative initiative; controlling Member States' respect of community law; negotiating commercial agreements on behalf of the Community, implementing the common policies and ensuring that competition in the Community was not distorted. (European Commission 2000, p. 1)

Over the years, however, the Commission took on a wide range of new tasks. Not only did it help to devise new policies and legislative initiatives (as originally intended), and carry out evermore extensive regulatory functions (e.g. in relation to competition within the Single European Market), it also acquired a substantial burden of administrative tasks. By 2000 almost half the Commission's officials were engaged in the management of programmes and projects of various kinds. Thus, it performs a significant set of *management* tasks, and forms a fit subject for treatment in this book.

A. Socio-economic forces: general

For details of the socio-economic forces affecting some of the member states, see the country files for Belgium, Finland, France, Germany, Italy, Sweden, and the UK.

The 'gross value added' for the fifteen member states' economies fell slightly in 1994, but then rose strongly until 2000. The second half of the 1990s—unlike the early 1990s and the early 1980s—was thus a period in which the EU as a whole was generally free from acute economic pressures (Eurostat 2002, pp. 158–61). However, growth slowed significantly from 2001.

B. Global economic forces

Again, details are given in Appendix A and in the country files for EU member states. EU current transactions (both exports and imports) with non-EU countries rose substantially from 1994 to 2000 (Eurostat 2002, p. 350). In 1999 the EU was the world's largest single trading block in services, and was only slightly behind the USA in its share of total world transactions in goods.

C. Sociodemographic change

The total population of the fifteen member states rose steadily from 365 million to 376 million from 1980 to 2000, (Eurostat 2002, pp. 14–15). Within this total, the proportions aged over sixty-five and over eighty rose. In the twenty years from 1980 onwards the number of divorces per 1000 people rose slightly and the number of marriages declined by a rather substantial amount. Life expectancy continued to rise (71.1 years for men and 77.6 for women in 1980–4; 74.4 and 80.8 respectively in 1995–9).

Net migration has been the largest component of total population change in the EU since 1989. In the second half of the 1990s most or all EU countries experienced positive net migration (i.e. immigration exceeded emigration—see Eurostat 2002, pp. 73–84).

D. Socio-economic policies

It is only a slight exaggeration to say that, during the past two decades, the Commission has presided over a revolution in EU economic policy. After a period of stagnation in the late 1970s and early 1980s, the pace of policy development picked up. A landmark was the Commission's 1985 white paper on the Single European Market. This was followed, in the subsequent year, by the Single European Act, which committed member states to completing a single market by 1993. This programme brought with it an enhanced role for the Commission, not only 'internally' as the regulator of the market, but also externally, as the central actor managing the interface between the single market and the wider world trade system. In 1988 the Council asked the Commission to develop a plan for achieving economic and monetary union (EMU). The eventual upshot of this was the launch, on 1 January 2002, of a single currency (the euro), watched over by a single, independent European Central Bank (ECB).

The Commission's presence in the social policy field is not nearly as soundly based in the European treaties as is its economic activity. Most of its resources are directed elsewhere. Nevertheless, by a variety of stratagems, the Commission has edged into social policy, especially in the areas of employment law, equal opportunities, and health and safety issues. Increasingly, also, the largest EU budget line—the Common Agricultural Policy (CAP)—is being converted into a vehicle for a kind of social policy for rural regeneration and diversification.

E. The political system

The political system within which the Commission operates has evolved quite rapidly over the past twenty years. In institutional terms the system comprises the Commission itself (headed by the College of Commissioners—political appointments agreed by the member states), the Council of Ministers (ministers from the member states), and the European Parliament (members directly elected from the member states).

During this period the EU enlarged its membership three times and, at the time of writing, was on the brink of a fourth, and even more dramatic enlargement. In 1981 Greece joined; in 1986 Portugal and Spain; in 1995 Austria, Finland, and Sweden. The 'candidate countries' for membership in the near future are Poland, Romania, the Czech Republic, Hungary, Bulgaria, Slovakia, Lithuania, Latvia, Estonia, Cyprus, and Malta—a much less economically developed group than the existing membership, and one which includes many states that have only emerged from Communist rule/membership of the Soviet Block since 1990. Clearly, each successive enlargement increases the size and complexity of the Council of Ministers. This, in turn, has generated an ongoing evolution of voting procedures, with more and more issues being assigned to qualified majority voting (where the number of votes allocated

to each state is proportionate to its size) so as to avoid the potential deadlock of a requirement of unanimity.

The political system has also changed in other ways. The European Parliament has developed its role considerably (Peterson and Shackleton 2002, chapter 5). The first direct election to this body took place in 1979. In 1980 the *Isoglucose* judgment of the European Court of Justice made it clear that the Council of Ministers could not adopt community legislation without consulting the Parliament. In 1987 the Parliament gained further influence through a new cooperation procedure, which meant that, for certain categories of legislation, the Council of Ministers could only overrule the Parliament if it acted unanimously. The Maastricht Treaty of 1992 further extended the Parliament's role. Finally, the dramatic 1999 resignation of the entire College of Commissioners—the fall of the Santerre Commission—was triggered to a significant extent by fear of an imminent vote of censure in the Parliament. This provided an indelible mark of the growing significance of the Parliament for the work of the Commission. Subsequently, the Parliament carved itself a role in holding hearings and approving the candidates selected for the College of Commissioners.

Despite these numerous and significant changes, one original feature of the Commission's political position remains. As Christiansen (2001, p. 100) puts it, 'there is an inherent contradiction in the Commission providing both political leadership and an impartial civil service to the EU system'.

F. New management ideas

In general it could be said that the Commission has not been particularly receptive to management ideas coming from outside—or, at least, not as far as the reform of its own structures and procedures have been concerned. It is self-consciously 'different'—unique—and has never been as open to private sector management ideas as, say, the governments of the USA or the UK. The reforms since the mid-1990s (details follow) have been very much 'home-grown' and not directly modelled on those of any guru or school of thought such as NPM, even if they have shared some of the rhetoric ('decentralization', 'performance').

That having been said, the Commission has acted to facilitate the spread of certain management ideas among the member states. It has helped to promote TQM, and has supported the development of a simplified version of the EFQM model of excellence, known as the Common Assessment Framework (CAF). For the main part, however, these activities have constituted the promotion of certain techniques *for use elsewhere* (in member states or in EU programmes which are administered on a decentralized basis) rather than within the core of the Commission itself.

G. Pressure from citizens

It is hard for citizens to exert any direct pressure on the Commission. On the whole it has few direct contacts with citizens—most EU programmes are administered by member states, with the Commission acting from a distance to formulate the objectives and rules to supply some or all of the finance, and to regulate or monitor the activities 'on the ground'. So the Commission does not itself provide extensive public services, as do national and local authorities.

Nevertheless, in a more general way, the Commission—together with the Council and the Parliament—is certainly concerned about the general problem of falling trust in EU institutions and declining voter turn-out at European elections (Peterson and Shackleton 2002, pp. 8–9). This concern may well have been one motive behind the theme of 'transparency' which was embraced in the 2000 white paper, *Reforming the Commission* (European Commission 2000).

H. Party political ideas

The reform of the Commission does not seem to have been much affected by party political ideas. The Commission is not 'run' by one or two parties, like most national governments. There is no direct channel by which the ideas of a particular political party could come to dominate the reform discussion within the Commission.

I. Chance events

One may debate whether it was 'chance' or 'an accident waiting to happen', but the series of scandals and inefficiencies that gradually engulfed the Santerre Commission (1995–9) certainly left their mark on the ongoing process of reform. The eventual resignation of that Commission made a fresh reform effort virtually inevitable. Arguably, however, it also biased attention towards an agenda of control (tightening procedures and audit) and away from the agenda of efficiency and performance (see, e.g. Committee of Independent Experts 1999). The ensuing reforms embraced both themes, but circumstantial evidence suggests that the former, rather than the latter, has been more vigorously implemented.

J. Elite decision-making

Whilst there is certainly an 'elite' within the Commission, it is quite a diverse one. As far as reform is concerned the key actors are probably the commissioners themselves plus the directors-general (heads of the main vertical divisions within the Commission). These two groups come from all the member states, and therefore from a wide range of political and administrative cultures. Even when they can agree that a particular reform may be desirable, they face a number of powerful constraints. In practice, major reforms would have to be acceptable to the Council of Ministers, and 'saleable' to the European Parliament. Last but by no means least, the Commission is home to strong trade unions ('syndicates'), which have long practice in defending their members' strong tenure and not inconsiderable privileges.

The elite is advised by personal *cabinets* of officials (often quite young) and by ad hoc teams and task forces. The selection of members of these influential teams and *cabinets* is commonly quite personalized—this is not a transparent process based on qualifications and merit, but rather a commissioner picking (from those who are willing and available) individuals she or he thinks will be effective and loyal helpers in the process of forming and negotiating a set of feasible reform proposals.

K. The administrative system

A popular image in the British mass media is that of a 'bloated Brussels bureaucracy'. In reality, while the Commission certainly possesses many of the classic characteristics of a bureaucracy (strict hierarchy, lots of 'red tape'), it is not at all large, relative to the long list of responsibilities attributed to it. The total number of Commission staff in 2001 was between 21,000 and 31,000 (depending upon exactly how one does the calculation—see Peterson and Shackleton 2002, pp. 148–50). This number included several thousand translators and interpreters (to handle the need to translate the many documents and speeches into all the community languages). The number of A-grade staff (the policy and management group) was just over 6000.

At the top sits the College of Commissioners itself. These twenty-one members (at the time of writing—though this number will change with enlargement) are mainly ex-politicians, and are supposed to work on a collegial basis, not as individual ministers, each with his or her own unique sphere of authority (Christiansen 2001).

The work is divided into more than twenty DGs and a number of other services (most importantly, the Legal Service and the Secretariat General). The DGs (whose exact number varies over time, with mergers and new creations) are functionally defined (e.g. Agriculture, Budget, Energy, and Transport, etc.—see Peterson and Shackleton 2002, p. 145). Most are sectoral ('vertical'—e.g. Energy) but a few are horizontal, cutting across the sectors (e.g. Budget). Traditionally, DGs are fairly hierarchical, and the divisions between them are quite deep. In other words, the directors-general are powerfully placed at the top of strong vertical ladders of authority, and horizontal coordination between these twenty-plus 'commands' is weak. For long the administrative culture of the Commission represented a blend of the hierarchical and legalistically oriented French and German traditions. Current reforms aim to improve strategic coordination but it is not yet clear whether this objective will be achieved.

The most senior official in the Commission is the Secretary-General. All permanent staff enjoy high security of tenure. The nationalities of the A grades in any particular part of the organization are deliberately mixed up so as to try to prevent the formation of 'national groups' which could influence a given programme or project (i.e. if you are an A-grade German, you are unlikely to have another German as your boss). There is an unofficial national quota system for the top three grades (A1–A3). (Details of how all this works are given in Page 1997, but it should be noted that the Kinnock reforms since 2000 have had as one of their aims the reduction of the 'flags on posts', or quota system for top positions.)

The directors-general report to the commissioner responsible for their particular function. The precise definition of functions and the exact portfolios of individual Commissioners change constantly over time, in roughly the same way as frequent reallocations or definitions of function take place in many national governments. Commissioners are supposed to assume full political responsibility for the Commission's actions, with directors-general being responsible for sound implementation. In practice, the line between policy and implementation in the EU is probably even harder to draw than in national governments.

L. Contents of the reform package

Between 1980 and the mid-1990s there were few attempts to reform the management of the Commission. During this period its tasks and size grew considerably, and in particular it took on more executive functions—running projects and programmes. The famous French President of the Commission between 1984 and 1994, Jacques Delors, was keen to expand the range of Commission activities, but seems to have been little interested in issues of efficiency or performance management. Expert observers refer to 'the inefficiencies and *immobilisme* that plagued the services' (Peterson and Shackleton 2002, p. 156).

In 1995 the Santerre Commission launched a programme entitled *Sound and Effective Management 2000* (SEM 2000), quickly followed, in 1997, by a further development called *Modernization of Administration and Personnel Policy* (MAP 2000). SEM 2000 was aimed at updating financial management practices and creating a system whereby EU programmes would be subject to regular, independent evaluation (European Commission 1997a, 1998). MAP 2000 was aimed at decentralizing and simplifying the Byzantine system of personnel and administrative procedures (European Commission 1997b). The Santerre Commission also launched an exercise called DECODE (1997–9), which aimed at inventorizing staff and their functions. It was perhaps significant that such an elaborate and time-consuming exercise was needed simply so that the Commission could accurately see what its own staff were spending their time doing.

SEM 2000, MAP 2000, and DECODE each got quite a long way before the end of the Santerre Commission (1999), although none were entirely complete. A brief assessment of them is given in Section N.

The incoming Prodi Commission built upon these previous attempts at reform, and gave its own effort a high profile. It quickly published a white paper *Reforming the Commission*, followed by a more general paper on *European Governance* (European Commission 2000, 2001*a*). The first white paper announced major changes in:

- Strategic priority setting and resource allocation (particularly a system of Activity-based Management, or ABM plus a policy of 'externalizing' operational tasks and activities so as to be able to refocus on policy priorities—see European Commission 2000, 2001*b*)

- Human resource management (decentralizing responsibility for staff management, and simplifying and clarifying procedures; introducing better training and career planning)

- Financial management (setting up a proper internal audit service and better 'fraud-proofing' of legislation; decentralizing financial controls to individual DGs)

M. Implementation process

Implementation of the SEM 2000 and MAP 2000 reforms conspicuously lacked a central focus and leadership, and they were eventually overtaken by the collapse of the Santerre Commission.

The Kinnock white paper had a clearer action plan (European Commission 2000, Part 2), with many of the important actions falling to the Secretary-General, a man who had previously been chief adviser (*chef de cabinet*) to Prodi, the new president. Nevertheless, a quick perusal of this document should suffice to convince the reader of the complexity of the implementation process for a reform of this type. It was also noticeable how, during implementation, the HRM elements came to take up a larger and larger share of effort (Kinnock himself felt obliged to attend many dozens of meetings with the syndicates) and the performance-oriented elements of the reforms seemed to take second place. Furthermore, the rhetorical flourishes concerning decentralization seem to have lost out to a strong bureaucratic logic of further centralization in the name of tighter control (Levy 2003).

N. Results achieved

It is difficult to assess the results achieved, not least because many elements within the recent reforms have been expressed in very general terms and/or are hard to measure. In any case, it is still too soon to be able to confidently assess the results of the reform package announced by Vice-President Kinnock in March 2000 (European Commission 2000, 2001*a*). There have certainly been important changes in procedure, such as the introduction of ABM and the creation of a proper internal audit service. Financial procedures have changed—though whether they have become more efficient or effective in some fundamental sense can be debated. The new emphasis on the individual responsibility of directors-general, coupled with new promotion and grading procedures and annual activity plans *could* begin to shift the management culture, but at the time of writing this is little more than a hope and a prayer. A Progress Report at the beginning of 2003 claimed that eighty-four out of ninety-three reform actions had been completed or were in the process of being implemented. Certainly, the effort to track implementation was more visible and systematic than had been the case for SEM 2000/MAP 2000. Whether there has been any basic shift in the bureaucratic and hierarchical culture of the Commission remains doubtful. There is a sense in which the reforms have themselves been bureaucratized during implementation, so that the original rhetorical emphasis on a more performance-oriented approach has somewhat evaporated under the welter of new rules on financial procedure, internal audit, and personnel management.

There was a formal evaluation of the earlier (1995–9) SEM 2000 reform programme. The evaluators found that some significant progress had been made in setting up financial units within each DG and in embedding evaluation as a regular practice. However, they were of the opinion that '[T]he effectiveness of the implementation of SEM 2000 is being undermined by some basic problems which inhibit effective change...' (Evaluation Partnership 1999, p. 4). These problems included a lack of ownership and leadership, and a certain incoherence to the reform programme itself. It might also be said that in their original conception SEM 2000 and MAP 2000 were quite cautious and modest, if measured against the standards of major public management reforms in, say, New Zealand and the UK, or even France, Sweden, or the USA. This may not, however, be a fair yardstick. As this case file makes clear, the Commission is in several crucial respects quite *unlike* a national government.

It remains the case that the Commission is an exceptionally complex organization, and one in which it is extraordinarily difficult to formulate and execute fundamental reform. It does not provide many services directly to citizens, being mainly concerned with transferring funds to other bodies, and with regulation and legislative initiatives. Much of its work is carried on within tight legislative frameworks, which permit little discretion to individual managers. The basic rules for setting six-year budget totals through the Council of Ministers (the 'Financial Perspective')

create a situation in which incentives for 'savings' and 'efficiency' have much less force than in some national systems (the European Parliament has frequently criticized the Commission for failing to spend up to the hilt). Its multiculturalism and collegiate principles further militate against implementation of the kind of fast, single-track reforms which have been possible in some of the NPM countries.

Country file events: European Commission

	General	Organization	Personnel	Finance
1981–5	– Thorn Commission (1981–4) – The accession of Greece (1981) – Delors Commission (1984–94)			
1986–90	– The accession of Portugal and Spain (1986)	– Commission grows as, under Delors, it acquires many new programmes and functions		
1990–5	– Treaty of Maastricht (1992) – The Council and the Commission reach agreement on code of conduct governing public access to official documents (1993) – Santerre Commission (1994–9) – The accession of Austria, Finland, and Sweden (1995)			– Sound and Effective Management 2000 programme (SEM 2000) (1995)
1996–2000	– Resignation of entire Santerre Commission following alleged mismanagement and fraud, investigated by a Committee of Independent Experts (1999) – The Court of Auditors publishes the special report concerning the management by the Commission of the implementation of measures to promote equal opportunities for men and women, together with the Commission's replies (1998) – Prodi Commission (1999)	– Kinnock white paper: Reforming the Commission and the Action Plan (2000) – Policy of externalizing operational tasks and activities (2000)	– Modernization of Administration Policy (MAP 2000) (1997) – DECODE: inventorying staff and their functions (1997) – The European Commission publishes the codes of conduct for Commission staff and the relations between commissioners and Commission departments (1999) – Decentralizing responsibility for staff, simplifying procedures (2000) – Introducing better training and career-planning (2000)	– First Commission guide to evaluation of EU programmes (1997) – Strategic Priority Setting and Resource Allocation (system of Activity-Based Management) (2000) – Internal audit service (2000) – Decentralizing financial controls to individual DGs
2001–2	– White paper on *European Governance* (2001)			

FINLAND

A. Socio-economic forces: general

See Table A.1 and discussion in Appendix A.

B. Global economic forces

See Table A.1 and discussion in Appendix A.

C. Sociodemographic issues

See Tables A.2 and A.3 and Figures A.1 and A.2. Finland shares most of the problems of an ageing population that are present in the rest of Western Europe. Generally speaking, Finnish society is relatively homogenous and peaceful. There is a different ethnic group (the *Saami* people) in the far north (Lapland) but their numbers are small, and their significance for a study of the reform of central government limited.

D. National socio-economic policies

Finland enjoyed a good growth rate and relatively low unemployment through most of the 1980s. From 1991, however, the sudden collapse of trade with its neighbour, the Soviet Union, together with the more general recession in the West, sparked a severe economic crisis. Trade fell, banks got into great difficulties, unemployment soared to unprecedented heights (18.4% in 1994). Between 1990 and 1993, GDP volume fell by 12 per cent. Faced with these problems, central government launched a strong programme of budgetary reform and restraint. By 1997 growth had returned, budgetary discipline was maintained, and Finland was fully able to satisfy the Maastricht 'convergence criteria' for EMU. By the late 1990s economic growth was once again healthy, although there was some concern about the high reliance of the economy on one firm—the mobile phone giant, Nokia.

E. The political system

Finland is a unitary state, though with a strong tradition of relatively autonomous municipal government, protected by the constitution (like Sweden). The basic pieces of legislation are the Constitution Act (1919) and the Parliament Act (1928). There is a multiparty political system and governments are usually quite stable coalitions. The Cabinet acts collegially, with the prime minister having less personal prominence than in the 'Westminster' systems of the UK and New Zealand. Formally the power of execution lies with a Council of State, consisting of government ministers and the Chancellor of Justice. There is a president, who is elected every six years, retains some responsibility for foreign policy, and is commander-in-chief of the armed forces. In general it might be said that the Finnish president, while considerably more active and politically powerful than his or her German counterpart, is also not as dominant as the French president. During the last decade it is the Prime Minister's Office that has tended to gain new responsibilities and powers, while the President's Office has not (see Bouckaert et al. 2000).

The legislature (*Eduskunta*) is unicameral, with 200 seats. Eighty per cent of MPs tend also to be municipal politicians—so the interests of the municipalities are strongly represented at the centre. The three big parties in recent years have been the Social Democrats, the National Coalition (Conservatives), and the Centre Party (originally an agrarian party). The reforming coalitions since the late 1980s have been led by the National Coalition (Holkeri 1987–91), the Centre Party (Aho 1991–5), and the Social Democrats (Lipponen's 'Rainbow Coalition' 1995–2003). The Communist Party was a significant political force during the 1960s and 1970s, but has since lost most of its strength.

F. New management ideas

Finland has been an active member of many international organizations, both governmental and academic (e.g. PUMA, European Group for Public Administration). In that sense it has been open to, and acquainted with, the full range of contemporary management concepts and techniques as applied to the public sector. However, it has not slavishly followed fashions but rather carefully selected and piloted those ideas considered suitable for Finnish needs. To take two examples, TQM and ISO 9000 approaches to service quality improvement were widely adopted in Finnish local government (Association of Finnish Local Authorities 1995a, 1995b) and, in central government, accruals-accounting practices in other countries were closely studied but then only partly adopted. Finnish central government has not made intensive use of management consultants to implement reform (in the way that occurred in, say, the UK). Consultants have been used to gather information, and a number of foreign academics have been used as advisers, but actual implementation has remained, for the most part, firmly in the hands of career civil servants.

G. Pressure from citizens

We are not aware of any evidence pointing to sustained pressure for specific reforms from the Finnish public—or, indeed, for reversal of any of the changes that have been implemented. During the 1980s and 1990s public attitudes towards the state appear to have been mixed. On the one hand, 'Finns are a people very loyal to the state, who see change as a governmental process rather than a grass root level reform of the society' (Centre for Finnish Business and Policy Studies 1996, p. 2). The radically antistate attitudes that are common in the USA are rare in the Nordic countries. On the other hand, there have been a limited number of instances where popular discontent has been manifested over specific aspects of the changes—for example, over the closure of some small rural post offices and the substitution of postal counters in local shops. Senior officials are aware of the dangers of loss of legitimacy (Holkeri and Nurmi 2002) and some of them believe that administrative modernization, including improvements in the quality of services, openness to greater citizen participation, and visible efficiency will help contribute to sustaining political stability and trust (see, e.g. *High Quality Services, Good Governance, and a Responsible Civic Society* 1998a, 1998b).

H. Party political ideas

Party political ideas per se have not had a big influence on public management reform in Finland. On the contrary, reforms have been mainly the work of a fairly small elite of senior civil servants and a few politicians. Media interest in the reforms has not been particularly strong either (Ministry of Finance 1997, pp. 73 and 81). Finland did not experience strongly ideological governments with strong views about changing the role of the state in the way that the USA did under President Reagan or the UK under Prime Minister Thatcher.

I. Chance events

One might argue that the collapse of the Soviet Union at the beginning of the 1990s had a significant, if indirect, influence on public management reform. By triggering economic crisis it strengthened the hand of reformers, particularly with respect to budgetary reform (e.g. the rapid implementation of frame-budgeting was seen as a vital part of regaining control of public spending). But most of the reforms (e.g. results-oriented budgeting) were already firmly on the agenda, before the economic downturn.

J. Elite decision-making

The process by which Finnish reforms came into being was quite long-drawn-out and cautious. It was not a matter of a few individuals passionately advocating specific 'solutions' (which would be unusual anyway within the Finnish politico-administrative culture), but rather the gradual, consensual formation of a set of proposals for streamlining the state apparatus and, after 1991, for restraining expenditures in response to the sudden economic downturn. Within this process some central themes were the lightening of the bureaucratic 'weight' of central government (especially by reforming the national-level agencies); a shift from input budgeting to a stronger focus on results; a parallel shift to frame(block)-budgeting for central transfers to municipalities; a commitment to service quality improvement; and some measure of decentralization. Thus, for example, 'the goal is to create a single-level central government; in the central administration only the ministries will in general exercise administrative authority vis-à-vis lower levels' *Principle on Reforms in Central and Regional Government* (1993).

From the late 1990s there was some thinking by senior civil servants about the possibility of a second wave of reform. This would involve a fairly comprehensive restructuring of central government into different relational categories (e.g. organizations where the government was principally exercising the interests of an owner, organizations where the government's interest was as a direct service provider). This then became coupled with a wider agenda, embracing improved steering by ministries, e-governance, and strengthened citizen participation. Under the second Lipponen administration (1999–2003), ministers again became more directly and actively interested in management reform, especially the strengthening of the Prime Minister's Office and the improvement of horizontal coordination between ministries.

K. The administrative system

For many years Finland, like Sweden, had an administrative system consisting of ministries, national-level boards (agencies) with considerable powers of rule-making and detailed intervention, and a municipal level. However, in the mid-1990s the agency level was subject to fairly fundamental reform, shrinking its size and numbers and reorienting its role away from detailed regulation (Ministry of Finance 1995, pp. 1–2—see also Section L). It should be noted that, although this account is focused principally on the central state, local (municipal) government employs roughly three-quarters of the public sector workforce.

The population of central ministries has been fairly stable over the past two decades. In the 1990s there were twelve ministries and the Prime Minister's Office, which itself has the status of a ministry (Prime Minister's Office and Ministries 1995). The Ministries of Finance and the Interior are the two with the most important responsibilities for administrative reform.

Traditionally, each ministry has independent responsibility for implementation and control of laws and policies within their own sphere so, although the Ministry of Finance may be, in some general sense, the most 'powerful' ministry, it usually cannot impose its own programmes on other ministries to the degree that has occasionally been possible in more centralized systems such as that in France, New Zealand, or the UK. However, by the beginning of the new century, concern about this relative lack of coordination was growing, and a major report drew attention to the need for better integration across government (Bouckaert et al. 2000). A strengthening of the Prime Minister's Office, especially but not exclusively with respect to EU coordination, was one consequence of this debate.

There is a career civil service, and political and 'mandarin' careers are usually separate. However, some of the top three levels of civil service appointment go to known sympathizers with particular political parties, according to a kind of informal 'quota' system (Tiihonen 1996, p. 40). In the past, senior Finnish civil servants were mainly lawyers, but this balance has shifted over the past generation, with more people with a training in economics or the social sciences being recruited to senior posts. Public management reform has been mainly an 'insider' process, with senior civil servants playing a crucial role. External consultants, although used for certain purposes, have not been as influential as in, say, the UK or the USA (Ministry of Finance 1997, p. 74).

L. Contents of the reform package

There was much internal discussion of reform during the early and mid-1980s, but the first major initiatives came with the arrival in office of the Holkeri government in 1987. The subsequent decade was then a busy one, with several main lines of reform unfolding simultaneously or in sequence. The three changes of government (1991, 1995, and 1999) did not appear to make any dramatic difference to the general thrust of the reforms, although possibly it could be said that the level of political interest in management reform (never overwhelmingly high among the majority of politicians) declined somewhat after 1994, but then revived from the beginning of the second Lipponen administration in 1999.

The key points of the first wave of reform were as follows (see the pamphlet *Government Decision in Principle on Reforms in Central and Regional Government* 1993):

- Results-oriented budgeting was piloted from 1987 and rolled out to the whole government from 1994. This required a number of potentially important changes including the definition of results indicators for agencies (to enable their performance to be assessed more explicitly by their 'parent' ministries) and the creation of unified running cost budgets for ministries and agencies. The pilot projects appeared to show that significant running cost savings could be achieved, but that some ministries were slow to take up the challenge of using indicators as an active form of performance management (Summa 1995).

- An Administrative Development Agency (ADA) (later retitled the Finnish Institute of Public Management) was set up in 1987 to provide training and consultancy to support reform. The Agency/Institute has been obliged to operate along increasingly commercial/self-financing lines. An attempt to sell it off during the late 1990s/early 2000s failed, and, at the time of writing, its future shape is uncertain.

• The transformation of a number of agencies with commercial functions into, first, State Enterprises (twelve were created 1989–97) and then, subsequently and in some cases, State-Owned Companies. The law enabling the creation of State Enterprises was passed in 1988. The further transformation to state-owned joint stock companies included Post and Telecommunications and Railways.

• The introduction from 1993 of a framework-budgeting system to control central government aid to municipalities. This was partly a decentralization measure, aimed at reducing the amount of detailed central intervention in municipal decision-making, but it was also a way of gaining firm control of the *totals* of municipal spending at a time of great budgetary pressure, and of delegating painful decisions about spending priorities down to municipal leaders. The total aid going to a given municipality was henceforth calculated as a lump sum based on the values taken by certain indicators, such as the number and age structure of the population. Later, framework management was developed into 'a central procedure steering the preparation of the State budget by the government' (*High Quality Services, Good Governance, and a Responsible Civic Society* 1998a, p. 10).

• A restructuring of the central agencies. This was also a decentralization measure. The agencies with commercial functions were turned into State Enterprises. Others were merged or downsized, and their role was changed from that of regulation to one of providing research and development and evaluation to the ministries. Their internal governance structures were also changed—usually away from collegial forms towards more managerial and/or monocratic arrangements.

• Government data collection streamlined and barriers to data transfer between different parts of the state reduced.

• Regional state administration unified and lightened. The offices of different ministries at regional level combined.

• Human Resource Management Reforms, including provision for performance-related pay and more decentralized management of staff.

The main decisions and announcements here were made during the Aho administration (1991–5) but subsequent implementation has been quite slow.

• In 1998 it was announced that '[T]he quality as well as the citizen- and customer-orientation of the services will be developed by means of a new type of Service Charters to be given to the customers' [sic] (*High Quality Services, Good Governance, and a Responsible Civic Society* 1998a p. 15).

Thus the balance of the reforms leant towards decentralization, simplification, and tighter control of spending (Ministry of Finance 1993; Puoskari 1996). There was no great enthusiasm for widespread privatization, although the Finnish governments were quite prepared to privatize selectively, when it seemed to make sense on its own terms (e.g. the government printing company).

In the late 1990s a second wave of reform began. Considerable emphasis was placed on improving the quality of public services and on encouraging citizen participation (Holkeri and Nurmi 2002). To support this and other goals, a sophisticated national electronic portal on the public sector was developed and opened in 2002 (Romakkaniemi 2001). There was also an attempt to tidy up some of the 'unfinished business' from the first wave of reforms, particularly the slowness of ministries to engage in active, performance-oriented steering of their agencies (Joustie 2001).

M. The implementation process

Overall, the implementation process has been gradual and deliberate, with pilot projects and extensive training programmes to ensure the smoothest possible implementation. One does not get the sense of the hectic pace and urgency that prevailed during, say, 1986–92 in New Zealand or 1987–92 in the UK.

At the highest level the coordination of the reform programme was ensured by the creation of a ministerial committee on which all the main political parties in government were represented (Ministry of Finance 1997, p. 69). Stability was also enhanced by the long-term participation of a small number of senior civil servants from the Ministry of Finance and the Ministry of the Interior. One Finnish commentator went so far as to term the Finnish approach 'technocratic' (Puoskari 1996, p. 105).

N. Reforms actually achieved

The reforms mentioned in Section L were all 'achieved', in the sense that relevant legislation was passed and new procedures were put in place. What is harder to determine is how vigorously the originally announced aims of the reforms were pursued, and how far they were eventually realized. In some cases (e.g. corporatization of former agencies into enterprises and then state-owned companies) change has been undeniable and quite rapid. In others (e.g. the introduction of a new personnel regime into the public service) legislation has been passed, but the implementation seems to have been fairly slow. For example, a new system of job classification and payment by results was first introduced in the mid-1980s, but by 1997 covered only about 5 per cent of state employees (Ministry of Finance 1997, p. 78). It is also clear that persuading ministries to adopt the spirit as well as the letter of results-oriented steering has been a fairly long-drawn-out business, still unfinished at the time of writing.

The number of personnel financed directly through the state budget fell by about 40 per cent (from 213,000 to 130,000) between 1989 and 1995 (thanks partly to the creation of off-budget state enterprises and companies, which accounted for about 54,000 of the reductions).

The Finnish government has supported a programme of evaluations of its reforms (Holkeri and Summa 1996). It is not clear that these evaluations (see, e.g. Ministry of Finance 1997; Pollitt et al. 1997) have had any clear and direct effect on subsequent decisions, but the evaluation function has now been firmly established in Finland as an ongoing component of modern public management.

Finally, an interesting reflection on the reforms of the 1987–97 period appeared in the 1998 Government Resolution, *High Quality Services, Good Governance, and a Responsible Civic Society* (1998a, p. 8):

[E]arlier administrative reforms have been experienced to have increased the bureaucracy of administration. The Government wants to ensure the democratic development of the policy of governance... On all administrative levels, the real possibilities of the citizen to influence matters as well as openness and transparency of administration will be increased.

In subsequent years this theme was intensified, and became one of the main dimensions of reform (Holkeri and Nurmi 2002; Romakkaniemi 2001).

Country file events: Finland

	General	Organization	Personnel	Finance
1981–5	– Koivisto (Soc., Centre) (1979) – Sorsa (Soc., Centre) (1983)			
1986–90	– Holkeri (Cons., Soc.) (1987) – First programme for reforms (1988) – Service Declaration: general principles (1988) – Government guidelines on decentralized decision-making (1988) – Decree on use of information technology (1988) – Second programme for reforms (1989) – MoF: measurement of productivity project (1989) – Ministry of Communication: national information and services network (1989) – White paper on information management in central government and role of IT in administrative reform (1989) – Government decision: leaving 10% of open positions unfilled (1990)	– Permanent Ministerial Committee for Public Management Reform (1987) – Administrative Development Agency (ADA) (1987) – General legislation on public enterprises (1988) – New types of public enterprises (1989) – Proposal to re-organize national boards (1989) – Free Municipal Experiment in 56 municipalities (1989) – Simplify procedures for permits and licences (1989) – Railways and Post and Telecom: new types of public enterprise (1990) – Act requiring agencies to renew ordinances and regulations (1990)	– Proposals for productivity-based bonus system, individualized pay system, decentralized classification of posts (1989) – Personnel Committee: proposals to reform personnel policy (1990)	– MoF: new instructions to reform state budget implementation procedure (1989) – Frame-budgeting (1990) – Three pilot agencies: results-oriented budget (1990)
1991–5	– Aho (Centre, Cons.) (1991) – 'Rationalisation' project launched (1991) – Legislation proposed to reform state aid to municipalities (1991) – Public Sector management reform decision: MTM, financial management, personnel management (1992) – Budget cuts (1992) – Comprehensive citizen's guide (1992) – Project: general strategy for information management (1992) – Regional Development Act: transfer of competencies to Joint Municipal Boards (1994)	– All agencies: keep a register of regulations (1991) – 'Rationalisation' project report: focus on decentralization and reorganization (1992) – Proposals to reform regional administration (1992) – Joint Stock Companies for four bodies (1992): computing, printing, restaurants, the Mint – Broaden ownership of six industrial companies (1994)	– Task force: develop a uniform employment category and collective bargaining system (1991) – Pension committee: harmonize with private sector (1991) – Special Top Management Training Programme (1991) – Leaving 15% of open positions unfilled in 1992–5 (1991) – New State Civil Servants Act (1994) – Budgetary ceilings and personnel numbers and costs (1993)	– 12 agencies: results-oriented budget (1991) – Management by results (1993): performance contracts, annual reports, audit by Audit Office, performance measurement systems set up, receive lump sum for operational expenses – Statutory annual reports for all ministries and agencies (1993) – Reform of the state grant system (1993) – Generalize performance-budgeting: all agencies (1995)

	– Comprehensive reform of Municipalities Act (1994) – Lipponen (Soc., Cons.) (1995) – Regional Administration 2000 project (1995) – Ministerial Working Group on Public Management Reform (1995) – Evaluation Programme of Public Management Reforms (1995) – Programme for improving regulatory management (1995) – Membership of the EU (1995)	– Public enterprise: Forest Administration (1994) – Joint Stock Company: Post and Telecom, Map Centre (1994) – Separation of immigration and naturalization service from Ministry of Interior (1995) – Joint Stock Company (1995): Railway, Purchasing Centre, Uniforms Factory, public building service, part of State Granary – Status (1995): 12 public enterprises, 15 public companies – Administrative Development Agency replaced by Finnish Institute of Public Management (1995)		– Budget reform principles (1996): bring budget structure in line with accruals-accounting reforms – MoF (1996): project to improve system of monitoring performance and the quality and coverage of information – Reform of state grant system (1997) – Implement accruals-accounting (1998) – Statutory Annual Reports for Ministries (1998) – Introduction of accruals-accounting for agencies (1998)
1996–2000	– Governance Project (1997) – Evaluation Report (FINREF) (1997): Implementation of Finnish Management reforms – Portfolio for Government Wide Planning (1998) – Reform provincial administration: from 11 to 5 provinces – Quality strategy for public services; Service Charters (1998) – Government resolution on electronic transactions, development services, and reduction of data-gathering (1998) – The Government Resolution *High Quality Services, Good Governance, and a Responsible Civic Society* (1998)	– 110 one-stop shops (1996) – Establishment of Regional Employment and Business Development Centres (1997) – Joint Stock Company (1996–8): car inspection services, state occupational health services, Technical Inspection Centre – Privatize: Map Centre, Finnish Telecom (into Sonera Ltd.) – Revised act on openness of government activities (1999) – Government decision-in-principle on information security in government (1999)	– Government decision on the principles in recruiting senior civil servants; accountability (1997) – Performance-related pay-schemes in some ministries and agencies (1997) – Evaluation of the state personnel policy (1998) – Management development programme for senior civil servants (2000) – Personnel policy barometer and an annual reporting system on human resources (2000)	

continues

continued

	General	Organization	Personnel	Finance
	– Lipponen: PM (Social Democrats) (1999) – Reforming central government (2000): better integration of budgetary and policy decision-making, better policy coordination, strategic planning, ministries' steering role in performance management – Halonen: President (Social Democrats) (2000) – New Constitution (2000) – Survey on the use of quality models (2000) – Evaluation strategy for public services (2000) – National Quality Conference (2000)	– Balanced Scorecard Forum (1999) – Act on electronic service in the administration (2000) – National Quality Initiative (2000–1): increase use of EFQM and charters		– Reforming central government: integration of policy and budgetary decision-making (2000)
2001–2	– Recommendation by the ministers in charge of state reform, based on work of 13 projects (2001) – 'Towards a shared evaluation of public services' (2001) – Second National Quality Conference (2002) – Creation of a satisfaction index by Ministry of Finance (2002)	– National Quality Initiative (2001) – Pilot project on benchmarking (2001)		

FRANCE

A. Socio-economic forces: general

For general background, see Appendix A and Table A.1. France is a large country (population 59.2 million in 2001) in a central position in the most economically advanced part of Europe.

B. Global economic forces

Again, see Appendix A for background.

Economic globalization brought increasing pressure upon the previous system of state-directed 'sectoral corporatism' (Jobert and Muller 1987). In consequence, there has been 'a more general loss of centrality of the state in social mediation and public policy' (Clark 1998, p. 101). Successive governments have been seen to have little success in solving the problem of high unemployment (well over 10% for most of the 1990s).

C. Sociodemographic change

See Appendix A.

D. National socio-economic policies

Traditionally, France has sought a somewhat greater degree of state control over its economy than either Germany or the UK. This stance has come under increasing strain as the forces of economic globalization appear to have favoured more open, competitive economies (see Jobert and Mueller 1987).

E. The political system

The French political system is distinctive, belonging fully neither to the 'majoritarian' camp with the UK and Australasia nor to the consensual systems which prevail in the Netherlands and the Nordic countries (see Chapter 3). Elections are according to plurality and the cabinets are usually one-party or a minimal coalition, but these majoritarian features are offset by the existence of a multiparty system and a strong, directly elected presidency.

Since 1980 there has been a fairly frequent alternation of the parties in office, with these sometimes matching the party identification of the

president but sometimes not (the periods of *cohabitation*, as with the Chirac government under President Mitterand, 1986–8, the Baladur government, also under Mitterand, 1993–5, and the Jospin government under President Chirac, 1997–2002). Obviously, all things being equal, a president is stronger when his own party also forms the government (e.g. Prime Minister Raffarin under President Chirac 2002–).

F. New management ideas

France is usually regarded as a country that has been quite resistant to the NPM ideas which have emerged from the UK and Australasia since the early 1980s. France has continued its own, distinctive thinking and rhetoric about administrative reform, centred on the themes of modernization and decentralization. However, during the 1980s there was a shift towards neoliberal ideas within the elite at the Ministry of Finance, albeit in the form of favouring the modernization of the public sector through private sector methods, rather than maximum privatization or the 'hollowing out' of the state (Clark 1998, p. 103). The contractualization of public services, stressed as a key component of Prime Minister Juppé's 1995 circular, *Réforme de l'Etat et des services publiques*, was a reflection of this tendency.

In 2001 a new institute was established, the Institut de la Gestion Publique et du Développement Economique (Public Management and Economic Development Institute), under the guidance of the Ministry of Economic Affairs, Finance, and Industry. Its purpose is to organize training, research, and general interaction on the issue of public sector modernization.

G. Pressure from citizens

Most political scientists have regarded France as traditionally a state-centred system, where the intensity and variety of pressure group activity has tended to be moderate in comparison with, say, the USA or the UK. The system has tended to sectoral corporatism rather than active pluralism, that is, governments have made deals with a smaller number of peak associations (big employers, big unions) rather than being particularly permeable to a wider range of interest or issue groups. Such deals have been facilitated by the frequency with which members of the *grands corps* move between government and business positions. Certainly, in respect of public management reform, the pressures from the citizenry in general appear to have been limited. Nevertheless, there has been a general decline in public confidence in the French system, and some popular critiques of the rigidity of some public services, and of the corruption and remoteness of some of the state elite.

Societal tensions on, for example, safety, urban development, and migration resulted in a significant protest vote for a far-right candidate during the first round of the presidential elections in 2002.

H. Party political ideas

In France neoliberalism has been embraced by the right (especially when Chirac was prime minister, 1986–8) but has been interpreted in a managerial rather than a doctrinaire, antistate fashion (in our terms, more NWS than NPM). This has meant that the 'modernization' theme was also acceptable (with some changes in the 'filling') by governments of the left. The public service 'renewal' programme of 1989–93 was negotiated with, and broadly supported by, the public service unions. However, left and right parted company over the desirability of reforms to social security and central personnel regulation, where the right's attempts to push through changes sparked major public service strikes during 1995 (Howard 1998). Also education reform was high on the agenda, causing major strikes in 2002.

I. Chance events

From one angle, the emergence of various cases of corruption could be viewed as chance events that have contributed to a crisis of confidence in 'an elite that had discredited itself' (Howard 1998, p. 201). From another perspective, however, these cases are not so much one-off, chance events as 'business as usual' within a system in which certain forms of corruption and 'cronyism' had become endemic.

J. Elite decision-making

This general loss of perceived legitimacy has been a factor in encouraging the elite to launch such initiatives as the public service charter (Ministère

de la Fonction Publique et des Réformes Administratives 1992) and the *L'année de l'accueil dans les services publiques* (Ministère de la Fonction Publique 1994*a*). During the French presidency of the EU (2000) there was an explicit focus on 'the public service: the social dialogue as a contribution to improvement'.

The limited move towards neoliberal ideas as a basis for modernization has already been mentioned. There has been a widely shared desire to rehabilitate the reputation of the state apparatus but there have been differences as to how this might best be done. One line of tension is between the central politico-administrative elite (*Inspections des Finances, Cour des Comptes, Conseil d'Etat*) and the growing autonomy of the field services of ministries and the regional and local authorities. The division of opinion here is perhaps between those who still believe that technocratic reforms, imposed by the centre, can ultimately succeed, and those who argue for a new and more inclusive form of political action. One view is that

[t]he strikes of 1995 made clear what should have been evident: France cannot be reformed by decree. Technocratic solutions, however well conceived, are not possible in modern, individualist democracies. (Howard 1998, p. 216)

K. The administrative system

France has possessed a strong administrative tradition since at least Napoleonic times. Five main features of the system as it existed in the late 1970s may be noted (Clark 1998, pp. 98–100):

• A tradition of state direction of the economy and society (*dirigisme*).

• Centralized direction of the state apparatus by two sets of *grands corps*. The first set are administrative and comprise the *Inspection des Finances* (a kind of financial inspectorate), the *Conseil d'Etat* (the Council of State—a supreme administrative court), and the *Cour des Comptes* (the national audit office). This group recruit their members (*Enarques*) from the prestigious *Ecole Nationale d'Administration* (ENA). The second set are technical (e.g. *Ponts et Chaussées*) and recruit from the *Ecole Polytechnique* via various *Grands Ecoles*. Members of the *Grands Corps* enjoy highly mobile careers and frequently take up top executive positions in the private sector or, indeed, in politics.

For example, up to 1993, 8 of the previous 11 Prime Ministers had been civil servants.

• A strong central presence subnationally through the presence of a *préfet* (prefect) and many local units of central ministries (deconcentrated state services) in each *département* and region. The prefect co-ordinates the deconcentrated state services and also has, since 1982, a steering authority. He/she is the representative of central government and used to hold a direct supervisory authority (*tutelle*) on the budgets of the local authorities. In 1982, prefects lost the direct supervisory authority over local administrative decisions.

• Division of the civil service into a large number of *corps* (1,800 at the end of the 1980s) each with its own educational entry requirements and its own set of hierarchically arranged posts, defined by a general civil service law. This feature of the French administrative system has proved a source of considerable rigidity and resistance in the context of management reform.

• The importance of a special body of administrative law in regulating administrative procedures and appointments. The French system 'is a "legal model" in the sense that it is regulated by legal rules which conceive the state administration as inhabiting an autonomous domain apart from civil society'.

Each of these five features has come under strain during the last twenty years, but the modernization process thus far has probably made greater impact on the first and third than on the other three.

L. Contents of the reform package

There was no one single package that lasted for very long, but rather a series of separate initiatives by different governments which could, at best, be said to be grouped around certain broad themes. The two most prominent were, first, decentralization and deconcentration and, second, modernization. The strategic shift towards decentralization came in the mid-1980s, when the socialist government under President Mitterand removed the prefects' *tutelle* and created local collectivities as autonomous authorities. Direct elections were established for regional councils, and legislation during 1982 gave local collectivities significant new taxing and budget-making powers. The ripples spreading out from this deep

change have continued through to the present (Montricher 1996), and have been amplified by the effects of EU regional policies. The 'deconcentration charter' of 1992 marked a further step in shifting authority from the centre to the periphery. In the French context:

[D]ecentralisation means transfer of authority from the central state to regional and local governments. Deconcentration means devolution of competence and managerial authority to the local administrative units of central government . . . as well as the agencies. (OECD 1997*d*, p. 67)

Autonomy in personnel management, in budget management, and for administrative decisions has been transferred to the deconcentrated state services and the prefects. The main purpose was the promotion of a better policy coordination at the deconcentrated level (Albertini 1998, pp. 145–56). Initiatives have been taken and new policy instruments have been introduced for a better *interministérialité*: extension of the coordination's mission of the prefects (1999), creation of a college of the *chefs de service* (directors of a deconcentrated state service), creation of discussion platforms between deconcentrated state services (*pôles de compétences*), introduction of a strategic approach at the regional level (1999), and so on. In 1997 management autonomy was given to several national management support services by the creation of a new kind of internal agency: the Services of National Scope.

The second theme—modernization—came to prominence under Prime Minister Rocard in 1989, although earlier discussions and initiatives had occurred throughout the 1980s. In February 1989 Rocard issued an important circular entitled *Renouveau du service publique*, which contained a series of initiatives: the creation of responsibility centres (*centres de responsabilité*, CDRs) within ministries, personnel reforms, greater emphasis on decentralized management of field services and responsiveness to public service users, and the institutionalization of policy evaluation across many sectors of government. Renewal—or modernization—continued under the succeeding Cresson and Bérégovoy governments. In 1995 Prime Minister Juppé issued a circular, *Réforme de l'Etat et des services publiques*, which proposed the reorganization of certain field services and an experiment in contractualizing the relationship between central ministries and their field services. The Jospin government set up several objectives on the second step of the *Réforme de l'Etat* (1997–2002): permanent evaluation of public policy, modernization of the deconcentrated level, modernization of the prefect's tasks, introduction of the strategic management, better transparency in public administration, better responsiveness to citizens' wishes and demands, and e-government. Thus 'the successive phases of "administrative modernization" have been characterised by a broad continuity of policy, rather than by partisan differences between governments of the Left and the Right' (Clark 1998, pp. 106–7).

A third theme—one characterized by much greater divergence between the parties which held power—was that of privatization. During the period of the socialist government of 1981–6, extensive nationalizations were carried through (exactly the opposite of the trend that was beginning to develop in the UK). However, the neoliberal government of Chirac (1986–8) reversed this, listing 65 companies that were to be sold off. During a relatively short period in office, nearly 300,000 industrial workers and 100,000 bank staff were 'privatised' (Wright 1989, p. 105). This flurry came to an end with the return of left governments in 1988, but when the right regained power in 1993, significant privatization resumed (e.g. steel in 1995). Despite the left-wing label, the Jospin government sold assets of public companies (e.g. *Crédit Lyonnais* and *France Telecom*) to the private sector. However, the critics inside the Socialist Party after the presidential election in 2002 showed that a majority of the left political world remains opposed to further privatizations. Overall, the period since 1980 has seen a significant fall in the public sector's share of the French labour force.

M. The implementation process

The French reforms have been implemented in a fairly piecemeal way, with different initiatives coming from different ministries at different times, and a good deal of successive 'repackaging' of some basically similar ideas (e.g. about being more responsive to citizen-users). For example, CDRs have been pushed much further in some ministries than in others (Trosa 1995). However, the *grands corps* appear to have remained in control of most of the changes, and their central roles have not been seriously undermined (Rouban 1997, pp. 154–5).

Prime ministers have often played a leading role in reforms, especially Chirac, Rocard, Juppé, and Jospin. The procedural device of the circular has been much resorted to. The ministries most heavily involved have been the Ministry of Public Service (which has undergone several slight changes of name), the Ministry of Finance, and the Ministry of the Interior (patron ministry for the prefects, and heavily involved in decentralization and deconcentration reforms). Naturally, the *grands corps* have been major players. The main decisions have been taken in specific interministerial committees. An officially stated feature of implementation has been that it should be a judicious mixture of 'top-down' and 'bottom-up':

Performance management programmes are initiated from the central level through legal instruments but they are usually not very prescriptive. The actual content of the reforms is therefore to a large extent determined at the level of local agencies and services. (OECD 1997*a*, p. 68)

In practice it seems that reform implementation has moved more smoothly and quickly in technical ministries and field services than elsewhere.

N. Reforms actually achieved

Despite the construction, from 1989, of an elaborate network of evaluation institutions (Duran et al. 1995), there seems to have been no across-the-board systematic evaluation of French management reforms. There have, however, been some assessments of particular aspects, for example, the 1996 *Cour des Comptes* report on CDRs, the 2002 Ministry of Public Service report on the Public Establishments (external agencies), and the 2002 Interministerial Delegation on the Reform of the State report on contractualization.

Less formal assessments have been made by some academics (e.g. Clark 1998; Montricher 1996; Flynn and Strehl 1996; Rouban 1997) and some officials (Trosa 1995, 1996). In general it might be said that outcome data is hard to come by, but that, thematically, French governments have held more closely to the values of a strong administrative state committed to some form of strategic planning than did Australia, New Zealand, or the UK. Significant modernization has taken place, and the decentralization reforms of 1982 seem to have been a genuine political and managerial watershed. However, much of the machinery of a centralized civil service remains fundamentally unaltered. In particular, centralized control of personnel still survives, and reforms aimed at bringing budgeting, accounting, and performance measurement within a single, compatible framework have only recently been given much momentum (Trosa 2002). Partly because of these constraints, the experiments with organizational diversity and user-responsiveness, though certainly substantial, have been somewhat less pervasive than in Australasia or the UK.

Country file events: France

	General	Organization	Personnel	Finance
1981–5	– Mitterand: President (Soc.) (1981) – Mauroy: PM (Soc.) (1981) – Decentralization Acts (1982) – Fabius: PM (Soc.) (1984) – Plan '10 objectives for the modernization' (1985)	– Nationalization of 7 industrial groups, 39 banks, and 2 financial groups (1981–2)	– Economic restructuring: salary constraints and staff reduction (1982) – Creation of 82,000 new jobs into the public service (1981–3) – Reform of the personnel's status (1983)	
1986–90	– First elections of regional councils (1986) – Chirac: PM (Cons.) (1986) – Mitterand: President (Soc.) (1988) – Rocard: PM (Soc.) (1988) – Reform of Administrative Courts (1988) – 'Renewal of the Public Service': PM (1989) – Economic and Social Council: report on modernization (1989) – Committee on government effectiveness: preparation of Tenth Plan (1989) – First government seminar led by PM (1989) – Second government seminar (1990) – Diagnosis of deconcentrated central administration (by each prefect) (1990) – Interministerial Committee on Evaluation (1990) – Decree on the evaluation of public policies (1990)	– First privatization wave (1986–7) – Each ministry: modernization plan including IT Master Plan (1989) – 200 service projects (redefine responsibilities) (1990) – 60 centres of responsibility (1990) – Innovation Network by DG for Administration and the Public Service (1990) – 101 decentralization and regulatory simplification measures identified (1990) – Reform of Post and Telecom starts (1990)	– Elimination of 12,000 jobs between 1984 and 1986 – Pay agreements with five of seven public servant trade unions (1988) – Two Decrees on broader promotion opportunities (1988) – Elimination of 33,000 jobs between 1986 and 1988 – New personnel's policy based on three themes: innovation and quality, HRM, and participation (1987–8) – Circular on the modernization of the HRM (1988) – Framework Agreement with five unions: continuing training (1989) – Agreement on the lifetime formation (1989) – Protocol of Agreement with five public servant trade unions (qualifications and salary scales) (1990) – 29 regional colloquia on renewal (1990)	– Circular on government working methods, introducing the concept of cost-effectiveness (1988) – Experiments in budgetary autonomy for the centres of responsibility (1990)
1990–5	– Cresson: PM (Soc.) (1991) – Third government seminar (1991) – Committee for Renewal of Public Service chaired by Minister of Public Service (unions, administration, experts) (1991) – Interministerial Committee on Evaluation: five policy areas for evaluation (1991) – Interministerial Committee for Territorial Administration (CIATER) (1991): relocate 5% of employees outside Ile-de-France within 3 years	– Opening of the public companies' capital to private investors (1990–3) and second privatization wave under Juppé (1993) – 470 service projects – 85 centres of responsibility (1991) – PTT transformed into two independent public establishments linked to the state by a planning contract (1991)	– Salary Agreement with four public servant trade unions (1991) – Deconcentration of interministerial training appropriations to regional prefects (1991) – Law: opening public employment to EC citizens (1991) – Renewal of Framework Agreement on continuing training with six unions (1992)	– Simplify budgetary and accounting procedures (consolidation of operating appropriation) (1991) – Circular on the control of financial management (1994)

- Bérégovoy: PM (Soc.) (1992)
- New Act on regional administration (1992): redefine roles and forms of cooperation
- Decree (containing the Deconcentration Charter (1992)
- Circular on reform of state structures (implementation of subsidiarity principle) (1992)
- Balladur: PM (Cons.) (1993)
- Report (by Picq) on measures to improve the efficiency of the state (1993)
- Joint declaration: central government, local authorities, public establishments, welfare agencies: quality of customer services (1994)
- 11 interregional platforms on quality (1994)
- Adjustment to judicial boundaries (1994)
- Chirac: President (Cons.) (1995)
- Juppé: PM (Cons.) (1995)
- National Synthesis Forum chaired by PM on customer services
- Government seminar on State Reform (1995)
- Circular: PM on customer service improvements (1995)
- Circular: PM on implementation of the reform (1995)

- Implementation of deconcentration measures for regulatory procedures (1991)
- Deconcentration Charter (1992)
- Implementation of policy for cities with development of local partnerships (1992)
- 127 centres of responsibility (contract on objectives and resources with parent department) (1992)
- 315 deconcentration measures: CIATER (1993)
- New Committee for the Reorganization and Deconcentration of the State Administration (1993)
- 4-year ministerial plan for reorganization and deconcentration (1993)
- Interministerial Committee for Rural Planning and Development (CIDAR) (1994): special centres to ensure equal access to high-quality services
- Creation of the Collège des Chefs de Service at the departmental level (1992) and diffusion of the instrument Pôles de Compétences at the regional level (from 1994)
- New Interministerial Committee for State Reform and State Reform Commission (1995)
- Committee for the Simplification of Administrative Formalities (COSIFORM) (1995)

- Ethics Committee to supervise the departure of civil servants (1993)
- Act: conditions for appointments of civil servants and supervising departures (1994)
- Act on the organization of work time, recruitment, transfers: makes it possible for motivated public servants to be posted to urban areas suffering from severe social problems and high social insecurity (1994)
- Circular: management of state employees to deconcentrated services (1994)
- All decisions concerning reorganization or abolition must be preceded by an impact study on the opportunities of distance working (1995)

- Pilot experiment: deconcentration of financial control of deconcentrated spending (1995)

continues

continued

	General	Organization	Personnel	Finance
1996–2000	– *Cour des Comptes*: report on responsibility centres (1996) – Jospin: PM (Soc.) (1997) – Circular: PM on government's way of working (1997) – Report (by Santel) on the deconcentration process (1998) – Establishment of the Interministerial Committee for the Information Society (1998) – Policy of public sector modernization (1999) – Opened up the whole of its telecom markets to competition (1999) – E-government becomes one of the objectives of the State Reform's programme (2000): establishment of a central intranet, the AdEr (2000), establishment of information systems at the deconcentrated level, the Territorial Information Systems (2000), New Government Internet Portal: (www.service-public.fr) (2000)	– All prefectures become responsibility centres (1996) – Balladur launches TQM (1997) – Deconcentration of some administrative competencies of ministries to prefectures (1997) – Creation of the Services of National Scope (1997) – Establishment of new general rules for the organization of central ministries and Services of National Scope (1997) – Replacement of the State Reform Commission by the General Direction of the Administration and Civil Service (1998) – Introduction of a strategic approach within the ministerial departments with the Multiannual Programme of Modernization (1998) – Third privatization wave under Jospin: first part (1998) – Interministerial Delegation for State Reform (DIRE) replaces the State Reform Commission and the Sub-Directorate for modernization of the General Directorate for Administration and Public Service (DGAFP) (1999) – Standing Commission for the Modernization of Public Service was renewed (1999)	– Third 3-Year Framework Agreement on continuing training (1996) – Report (by Roché) on working hours in the public sector (1999) – Limited introduction of the 35-hour working week into the public sector (2000) – The creation of a public employment 'observatory', responsible for modernizing and developing tools for information collection and forward-looking management of staff (2000) – Improvement of the professionalism of managers, by continuing training (2000) – Creation of specialist networks around specific management and modernization subjects (College of Modernization and Deconcentration's Top Managers, Evaluations Club, Human Resources Managements Club, etc.) (1999–2000)	– Circular on the reform of the budgetary process (1996) – Extension of the reform of financial control of deconcentrated spending (1996)

- Introduction of a strategic approach at the deconcentrated level for the regions with the Territorial Project of the State and for the prefectures with the Multiannual Actions Plan (1999)
- Acceleration of the deconcentration process (1999)
- Extension of the coordination mission of the prefects (1999)
- Third privatization wave under Jospin: second part (1999)
- Introduction of a modern system of public management based on optimal allocation of resources, staff motivation to foresee and adapt to new developments in the society (2000)

- Integration of IIAP, the International Institute for Public Administration in the ENA (2001)

- The Introduction of a Business Start-Up Loan (Prêt à la Création d'Entreprise or PCE)
- The New Economic Regulations Law: provide more effective protection against abuses in commercial practices, improve the operation of the markets (2001)
- Creation of the Agence France Trésor (2001)

2001–2
- Report by Carcenac on e-government (2001)
- The electricity market opened to competition: access to Electricity Transmission Network is regulated by the Electricity Regulatory Commission (2000)
- Reform of the Public Procurement Code (simplification of procedures, and clarification and simplification of the law on public procurement) (2001)
- Report (by Mauroy) on the decentralization process (2001)
- Chirac: President (Cons.) (2002)
- Raffarin: PM (2002)

GERMANY

A. Socio-economic forces: general

See Section A.2 and Table A.1. Germany is by far the biggest and most populous, as well as one of the richest, of the eight European states in this book.

B. Global economic forces

Again, see Appendix A.

C. Sociodemographic forces

Although there were some pressures (e.g. the integration with the former German Democratic Republic) that affected all three levels of German administration, there are other social problems faced mainly by local authorities.

These include high rates of unemployment with more people depending on social welfare benefits, which are provided by local authorities. Local authorities, not state or federal administrative bodies, have to deal directly with the problems of citizens. Citizens have also become more demanding and more self-confident in their relationship with public services, many of which are provided by local authorities. Local government is therefore under much greater pressure to introduce improved services for citizens. Furthermore, due to increasing competition for production facilities, local authorities are involved in policies of regional economic development, and have to provide new services for business communities (Röber 1996, p. 175).

One problem for government at all levels has been the high rate of immigration and asylum-seeking which Germany has experienced. This has led to racial tensions, especially in some parts of the east.

D. National socio-economic policies

Compared to the EU norm Germany still has a large manufacturing sector. This results in significant competition with the USA and the former Asian 'tigers'. Prior to the introduction of the euro in 2001, German currency, the DM, had been one of the strongest in the world. Monetary policy had been directed by the *Bundesbank*, which developed its policy independently from the political executive, and which served as a model for the new ECB. Germany is a country with a strong corporatist tradition, in which firms and banks and trade unions have tended to work closely together. However, Germany's poor economic performance since 2000 has brought these arrangements into question.

E. The political system

The German system is a chancellor model (*Kanzlerdemokratie*), which means that the chancellor is above other ministers and is more than the *primus inter pares*. The president has a primarily symbolic function, unlike the French or even (to a lesser extent) the Finnish president.

At the federal level there are two major parties, the Christian Democratic Union of Germany (CDU)/Christian Social Union (CSU), of the former Chancellor Helmut Kohl and the Social Democratic Party (SPD), which won the 1998 and 2002 elections and at the time of writing is led by Gerhard Schröder. Except for the big coalition between CDU/CSU and the SPD from 1966 to 1969, federal politics was dominated by coalitions of CDU/CSU with the small Free Democratic Party (FDP) (Liberal Party) from 1946 to 1966 and again from 1982 to 1998. There was also a coalition of the SPD with the FDP from 1969 to 1982. At the *Länder* level the SPD and the Greens have formed coalition governments. The smaller parties are:

• The FDP, which never went beyond 10 per cent of the national vote but has always been important as a coalition partner for either the CDU or the SPD. After the unification of Germany, its relative share of votes decreased because of a lack of programme and leadership.

• The Greens started as a movement and turned into a political party. As a consequence they still have two major tendencies, 'fundamentalists' and 'realists'. The more it becomes feasible to join governments, the more influence the *realos* seem to have. The Greens are part of some *Länder* and of the post-1998 federal governments.

• The former communists—the Party of Democratic Socialism (PDS, former SED)—have gained momentum, especially in former East Germany.

To get into the federal Parliament (*Bundestag*) political parties have to have a minimum of 5 per cent of the votes. This eliminates the smaller parties and sometimes posed problems for the FDP and the Greens. The voting system is mixed. The first vote (*Erststimme*) is majoritarian, and the second vote (*Zweitstimme*) is proportional.

F. New management ideas

The German changes could be characterized more by administrative tightening-up and modernization (see MAINTAIN and MODERNIZE in Chapter 8) than by marketization or minimization (Derlien 1998). The German trajectory has also been marked more by incrementalism ('permanent flexibility of institutional frameworks') than by fundamental change (Benz and Götz 1996, p. 5), and more by improvement of the existing system rather than an import of other systems (König 1997).

At the local level, where most management reforms have taken place, new management ideas were promoted by the Local Management Co-op or the Joint Local Government Agency for the Simplification of Administrative Procedures (*Kommunale Gemeinschaftstelle für Verwaltungsvereinfachung*, KGSt). The KGSt is an independent consultancy agency organized by a voluntary membership of municipalities, counties, and local authorities with more than 10,000 inhabitants.

Following the Tilburg model from the Netherlands, the KGSt propagated a modern system of local government, which was labelled the 'New Steering Model' (*Das Neues Steuerungsmodell*). Main characteristics of this model are 'clear-cut responsibilities between politics and administration, a system of contract management, integrated departmental structures and an emphasis on output control' (Röber 1996, p. 176; see also Klages and Löffler 1996, p. 135). Elements of this New Steering Model have been applied in a growing number of big cities and counties, and during the 1990s a variety of participatory innovations were also made at local levels, especially the use of local referenda (Wollmann 2001).

Modernization has also been a major focus of the Bertelsmann Foundation through its research initiatives and publications, its international network for better local government (since 1995), and, since 1993, its Carl Bertelsmann Prize 'Democracy and Efficiency in Local Government'.

On the whole, therefore, changes in Germany have been informed by ideas developed within the public sector, rather than by private sector managers or 'gurus'. One partial exception to this is the field of quality improvement, where TQM ideas have exerted a significant influence.

G. Pressure from citizens

The focus on democracy and citizen participation was always very present in Germany and was labelled as *Ausserparlamentarische Opposition* (APO), which is citizen opposition outside parliament. The fact that the CDU/CSU was in power for almost twenty years encouraged leftist intellectuals to organize themselves to fight government policies and to protect democracy outside the legislature. Since the SPD joined government, first as part of the Big Coalition, then as the ruling party in the 1970s, APO was weakened. In the 1970s the pressure from citizens resulted in Citizen Initiatives (*Bürgerinitiativen*), where citizens gathered and tried (unlike the APO, which opposed those in power) to approach positively political parties, administrations, and institutions. Thousands of initiatives were taken in the fields of public infrastructures, environmental matters, housing, transport, or education. In the 1970s there was also the concept of 'democratic, participatory public administration'. In the 1990s there was the important new development of local referenda, which became widely used (Wollmann 2001).

H. Party political ideas

There is no radical challenge to the *Rechtsstaat* and the basic functioning of the system. The concept of modernization does not really include extreme downsizing and is the product of agreements made between management and the trade unions (Röber and Löffler 1999). The talk of a 'slim state', which was popular at the end of the Kohl chancellorship, did not in fact result in any major changes at the federal level.

In 1992 the then candidate Chancellor Engholm (SPD) released a managerialist public sector reform paper. In 1993 there was a similar party paper by the ruling Christian Democrats. In general, specifically party political 'lines' on administration seem to be absent. Party political ideas are not developed at the federal level but basically at the state and local levels since the electoral process is focused at these levels. This results in sometimes diverging visions and practices according to specific situations, which are then not translated in a common federal party line. *Landtage* became interested in the New Steering Model, especially in 'global budgets', which are more flexible.

I. Chance events

At the end of the 1970s the Baader–Meinhof Group (Red Army Faction, RAF) developed terrorist activities against representatives of the political, industrial, and administrative establishment. This resulted in a discussion on the presence and the removal of 'extremists' in the public service (*Berufsverbot*). This was in line with a concern to neutralize civil servants who had been Nazis, then communists, as well as sympathizers with the terrorist RAF.

German unification caused serious pressure at all levels and aspects of society (though whether this can really be deemed a 'chance event' is debatable). Financially, there was the political decision to equal an eastern to a western *Deutsche Mark*. Economically, the *Treuhandanstalt* organized the privatization of most of the East Germany economy and the resulting unemployment had to be absorbed by the social security system. The former *Deutsche Demokratische Republik* (DDR, German Democratic Republic) administrative system was reformed according to the *Bundesrepublik Deutschland* (BRD, Federal Republic of Germany) system, and even the location of the capital changed from Bonn to Berlin. The transformation of local government in East Germany was 'between imposed and innovative institutionalization' (Wollmann 1997).

J. Elite decision-making

At present, the perspective of the state as a provider of services remains predominant in Germany. However, the federal plan for the elderly of 1993 was a first indication that the German state will increasingly act as facilitator rather than as a direct provider, and there have been a number of further moves in this direction. Nevertheless, the idea of local authorities as multifunctional providers has probably remained more closely intact than in most other western European countries—certainly more than, for example, in the UK or the Netherlands.

The legal status of the civil service has always been a political issue of administrative reforms. The constitutionally guaranteed status of civil servants remains untouched and is unlikely to change fundamentally (partly because so many German MPs are themselves civil servants).

Finally, '[t]he question whether to impose a national administrative reform program from above or whether to leave freedom for local and actoral initiatives is only a theoretical one in the Federal Republic of Germany where federal structure and tradition by nature forbid a centralized approach to administrative reforms' (Klages and Löffler 1996, p. 143).

K. The administrative system

The 'legal state' or *Rechtsstaat* is a key element in the German system.

While the *Rechtsstaat* and federal principles constitute the essential formal parameters for policy making and public-sector change, the market economy and the welfare state establish substantial norms which delineate functions and responsibilities of the state ... These complex arrangements between state and market economy, based on neo-corporatist linkages and intermediary organizations, allow the co-existence of market ideals such as free enterprise, individualism and subsidiarity, with a positive evaluation of the welfare state. (Benz and Götz 1996, p. 17)

Within this setting, the Federal Republic of Germany has sixteen *Länder*, of which three are city states (Berlin, Bremen, and Hamburg), and local governments. The size of the *Länder* varies from 17.7 million inhabitants (N. Rhine-Westphalia) to 700,000 (Bremen), or from 70,000 km^2 (Bavaria) to 400 km^2 (Bremen). Local government consists of 329 counties (*Kreise*), 115 noncounty municipalities (*Kreisefreie Städte*), and 14,915 municipalities (*Gemeinde*), which are governed according to different models.

The administrative structure in the Federal Republic of Germany is moulded by three principles. First is the principle of 'separation of powers', which distributes legislative, executive, and judicial powers among separate institutions. The second principle is 'federalism', which defines *Länder* as 'members of the Federation yet retaining a sovereign state power of their own' (Röber 1996, p. 170). 'Local government' is the third founding principle. Local government in Germany mainly operates on two levels, that of the local authorities and that of the counties (Röber 1996, p. 170). Local self-government has a long tradition in Germany. The Basic Law and all *Land* constitutions guarantee the right of every community to govern local affairs under its own responsibility (OECD 1992 p. 126; OECD 1997*d*).

The development of public management in Germany has not been uniform because German administration is extremely varied and complex. Central government only plays a modest part in the direct administration of public services. Many public duties (e.g. education, police) are administered by the states (*Länder*) that have considerable political and administrative power, whilst other public duties (e.g. social services) are administered by local authorities. As a consequence the impact of public management and public managers varies throughout Germany and at different levels of public administration (Röber 1996, pp. 169–70; Wollmann 2001).

The role of federal administration is mainly limited to law-making and is not concerned with service delivery as such, which therefore reduces the need for administrative reform at that level. The concept of *Rechtsstaat* and the principle of legality are embedded in a negotiating and contracting state (Sommerman 1998). The German system of public administration is characterized by the classical bureaucratic model with strong emphasis on legality and proper fulfilment of regulatory functions (*Ordnungsaufgaben*). This model is based on the Weberian ideal type of bureaucracy with a tall hierarchy of positions, functional specialization, strict rules, impersonal relationships, and a high degree of formalization

(Röber 1996, p. 170). However, the upper levels of the federal civil service are extensively politicized. It is common for many such senior officials to change jobs or take study leave when the political colour of the government changes (Götz 1997).

L. Contents of the reform package

The modernization of public administration in Germany has to be understood in 'terms of a "bottom-up" revolution: there are few reform initiatives at the federal level, at least some German *Länder* show up as modernization pioneers, but the truly new entrepreneurs in the field of modernization are the local governments' (Klages and Löffler 1996, p. 134).

The elements of the New Steering Model that local governments and some *Länder* have put into practice are the following:

- results-oriented budgeting;
- cost calculation of administrative products;
- introduction of commercial bookkeeping;
- decentralized resource accountability;
- definition of indicators for quality standards;
- customer orientation;
- outsourcing, contracting-out, and privatization; and
- openness to 'competition'.

Klages and Löffler (1996, pp. 137–41) assert that there was an east–west division in the modernization approach of local government, due to the specific problems facing public administration in East Germany. The restructuring of the East

Table B.2 Stages of German administrative reform

Stage	Decade	Reform or reform objective	Main content
1	1950s	Deregulation	New legal system and de-Nazification
2	1950s and 1960s	Territorial reform	*Länder* and municipal gerrymandering
3	1960s	Reform of functions	Recentralization and decentralization
4	1970s and 1980s	Citizen-oriented administrative simplification	Debureaucratization, increased transparency, improved participation
5	1990s	Modernize administration: *Neues Steuerungsmodell*	Administration as performance-oriented service delivery to citizens

Source: Naschold et al., 1994.

German public sector was so dramatic that it is accurate to refer to it as a transformation. The transformation encompassed changes in governmental competencies (from holistic planning authority to a balancing function, typical for a market economy), civil service (from political cadre administration to a civil service based on professional qualifications), organization (from unity of powers to horizontal and vertical separation of powers), and procedures (from the guidance principle of the party to legalistic administrative behaviour). Territorial restructuring of local authorities was necessary in the face of the enormous financial problems the local authorities faced. As to the characteristics of the local public sector in the eastern part of Germany, the Weberian model was put in place, while, by contrast, in the western part there were local experiments with the NPM (e.g. in the city of Passau and in the city state of Berlin). A summary of the broad stages of German administrative reforms is given in Table B2.

M. The implementation process

The initiation and implementation of changes in Germany is through pilot projects rather than by a comprehensive approach (Klages 1998). This creates problems of dual structures and can jeopardize islands of reforms. Lower levels of governments are the experimenters. This is well summarized in the title of a research project of Naschold and colleagues (1994), 'The country needs new cities'. The modernization pressure comes from the lower levels of government and is pushing through the *Länder* to the federal level. However, the merger with East Germany and the related modernization was definitely a top-down process.

N. Reforms actually achieved

There is no evaluation of the outcomes of reform at the various levels of government. There are surveys of the German Association of Cities (and the KGSt) on the degree of implementation of the New Steering Model (see also Grömig and Gruner 1998; Grömig and Thielen 1996). Reform processes and initiatives have been described by Hill and Klages (1993, 1995, 1996a, 1996b) referring to the general implementation of the New Steering Model in local governments (Duisburg, Bad Oldesloe, Saarbrücken, Rheine, Pforzheim, Soest, Heidelberg, München, and Nürnberg), or to more specific dimensions of the modernization such as controlling (Offenbach, Ludwigshafen, Heidelberg, Leipzig, Soest, and Detmold), team-building (Aachen), cost reduction (Kronach), decentralized service centres (Ludwigsburg), performance-related organizing (Main-Kinzig, Meissen), holding structure (Oberhavel), benchmarking (Osnabrück), contracting-out (Pinneberg), and budgeting (Waldshut).

The 'Cities for Tomorrow' initiative of the Bertelsmann Foundation includes the HRM case of the City of Duisburg. Systematic evidence at the level of *Länder* and definitely at the federal level is not available, although there are some academic assessments (e.g. Konig and Siedentopf 2001; Wollmann 2001).

Country file events: Germany

	General	Organization	Personnel	Finance
1981–5	– Schmidt: Chancellor (Soc.) (1980) – Kohl: Chancellor (CD) (1982) – Government resolution to promote debureaucratization (1983) – Independent Federal Commission to Simplify Law and Administration (Interiors) (1983) – Major cutback budgets and curbing legal rights of citizens to receive benefits (1983) – Study Act to Repeal Unnecessary Regulations and Consolidate Existing Law (1983)	– Comprehensive attempt to reform ministerial bureaucracy in Baden-Württemberg (1985) – Cooperation with private industry (1985) – Debureaucratization reforms in all *Länder*, and sunset for administrative regulations (1980–9)		– Amendment to Federal Budget Code: uniform accounting system in three steps involving organizational simplification and better use of IT (1986)
1986–90	– Bertelsmann Foundation sponsors research on public management (1987) – Kohl: Chancellor (1987) – First stage of Trade Union ÖTV Programme (Public Service, Transport, and Traffic: 'Future of Public Services' (ZÖD) (1988) – Federal: guidelines for the use of IT (1988) – Federal: strategy for improving federal legislation (1989) – German Unification Treaty (1990) – Construction of *Länder* governments in East Germany (1990) – Major local government constitution reform in East Germany (1990) – Debate about necessity of regional authorities in new *Länder* (1990)	– Ministry of Environmental Affairs (1986) – First steps to privatize federal mail and telecom (1987) – Start of privatization in East Germany (1990)	– Law amending provisions for working conditions (part time, unpaid leave, etc.) (1989) – Speyer Federal Academy of PA: in-service training programme for *Länder* (1990)	– New controlling systems in various cities (1987) – Transfer of budget law to East Germany (1990)

continues

continued

	General	Organization	Personnel	Finance
1991–5	– Kohl: Chancellor (CD) (1991) – Move capital from Bonn to Berlin (1991) – Major cutback budgets (1992) – Basic Law: *Länder* more power to influence decision-making on matters of the EU (1992) – Ad hoc group on 'simplification of the administration and reduction of government tasks' (Conference of Federal and *Länder* Ministers of Interiors) (1993) – Joint working group on privatization (Federal MoF and Economics, *Länder*, local authorities) (1993) – Reform of revenue redistribution system between *Länder* and federal government (1993) – Kohl: Chancellor (1994) – Interministerial working group on 'increasing efficiency/critical review of tasks' (Interiors) to report to Committee for Organizational Matters (1994) – Federal Ministry of Interiors: Lean State Advisory Council (1995)	– Local Management Co-op (KGSt) launches the New Steering Model (1991) – Ongoing implementation of the New Steering Model in *Länder* and local government; Adjust Household Laws (1991–5) – All federal ministries: divisions to examine European legislation issues, coordination, and implementation requirements (1992) – Working group 'on expediting, planning, and licensing procedures' (Economics): reduce unnecessary functions, charge third parties with tasks, simplify procedures, streamline organization of administration (1993) – Privatization of federal rail (1993) – Number of junior ministers reduced to 27 (1993)	– Large secondments of civil servants to new *Länder* (1991) – Public Service Reform Act (1994)	– Working group on 'possibility of promoting efficiency through an improvement of accounting in the government sector of public administration' (Conference of Federal and *Länder* Ministers of Interiors) (1993) – Working group on 'methods of business accounting in government' (1993) – Test pilot schemes of flexible budget instruments (carry over unspent resources) (1995) – Cost-accounting in specific areas (1995)
1996–2000	– Amendment Administrative Procedure Act (permitting flexibility) (1996) – Second stage of Trade Union ÖTV Programme (Public Service, Transport, and Traffic): Future of Public Services (ZÖD) (1996) – Final Report of Lean State Advisory Committee (1997)	– *Länder* and cities continue to implement the so-called New Steering Model (1996) – Federal: improving organizational structure: reduction of number of federal authorities (1996) – Change of the Federal Framework Household Law (1997)	– Amendment of the Federal Civil Servant Law (1996) – Act to Reform the Law on the Civil Service: performance, mobility, management (1997)	– Cabinet commissions Federal MoF to develop Cost and Results Accounting (CRA) (1997) – Standardized Cost-Result Accounting System (MAS) (1997) – CRA introduced in more than 20 authorities or ministries (1998)

– Schröder: Chancellor (Soc.) (1998) – 'Modern state–Modern Administration' programme (emphasis on efficiency) (1999)	– Steering Committee on Administrative Organization (1997) – Reform of the Joint Procedural Act that introduces strategic approach, agreements, and controls for the agencies, and a limitation of the direct control of the responsible ministerial department on its agencies (2000)	– Reduction of staff caused by unification (from 381,000 in 1992 to 315,000 in 1998); reduction of staff in ministries (from 21,300 in 1991 to 18,500 in 1998) – Pensions Reform Act (1998) – Federal government on gender mainstreaming (2000) – 'Equality Act for the Federal Administration and the Courts of the Federation' (2000)	– Act on the Further Development of Budgetary Law (more flexibility) (1998) – Pilot project on product-oriented budgeting (2000)
2001–2			
– Launch of the 'BundOnline 2005' Campaign: all Internet-capable public service shall be online by 2005 – Guideline for processing and administrating documents (2001) – Act to reform civil procedure (2001) – Federal Data Protection Act (2001) – Framework guideline for modern creativity and innovation management (2002) – Schröder: Chancellor (Soc.) (2002)	– Reorganization of the federal interior administration (2001) – Structural developments in the federal finance administration (2001) – Restructuring of the federal armed forces administration (2001)	– 'Act to modernize the pay structure', no limited recruitment to a specific pay scale, allowance for temporary performance of superior functions, transferring regulatory competence for maximum achievable grades to the *Länder* (2001) – Introduction of staff development goals in federal ministries by the State Secretary Committee (2001) – Elimination of 18,000 jobs in the federal administration between 1998–2002	– Introduction of cost and activity accounting, budgeting, and controlling in federal ministries (2001) – New pilots on product-oriented budgeting (2002)

ITALY

A. Socio-economic forces: general

With a population of fifty-seven million, Italy is, together with Germany, France, and the UK, one of the big states of Western Europe. See Appendix A.

B. Global economic forces

See Appendix A. Italy has a lower level of imports and exports as a percentage of GDP than Belgium, Germany, or the Netherlands, but a higher level than Australia or the USA.

C. Sociodemographic issues

Italy is experiencing the same growth in the elderly population as other EU and North American countries and despite the stereotypical Italian image of the strong, extended family, this is putting significant strains on the social and health care services (see Figure A.1). Italy has also been subject to sudden upsurges in the number of asylum seekers, in a country that has hitherto had quite a low percentage of foreign-born residents (Table A.4).

D. National socio-economic policies

There is a tradition of extensive state direction over the economy, including state ownership of banking and insurance, as well as industrial companies. Furthermore, industrial policy was traditionally oriented towards the support of the big Italian private firms. Globalization and the opening of national markets within the EU have put strong pressure on this situation. There has been widespread privatization of state firms.

During the 1990s the EU's 'convergence criteria' obliged governments to address the very high level of national debt, and propelled 'savings' to the top of the political agenda. This, in turn, impacted upon welfare state policies.

An important feature of the Italian economic and political situation is the long-standing contrast between the rich, industrialized, and urbanized north and the much poorer, more rural south.

E. The political system

Until the political crisis of 1993–4, there were two main parties, the Christian Democrats (with vote shares of 33–40% during the 1980s) and the Communist Party (with around 30%). There was also a Socialist Party, and various other smaller parties of the right and left. Governments changed frequently and were often of the grand-coalition type. In the early and mid-1990s, however, a political and economic crisis (political bribery and other illegal activities, the need for large public expenditure cuts) led to changes in both the electoral system (from proportional towards more majoritarian arrangements) and the pattern of parties (the effective collapse of both the Christian Democrats and the Communists).

Since 1994 the Italian political system looks more majoritarian, but displays fragmented coalitions, antisystem parties (e.g. the Northern League, the refounded, smaller Communist Party), and parties identified principally with charismatic leaders (e.g. Prime Minister Berlusconi's *Forza Italia*, Di Pietro's Italy of Values Party). During these upheavals the position of the President of the Republic (previously a largely symbolic role) became somewhat more influential.

There was also a period where many senior civil servants began to be appointed to political positions, indeed, there were two 'technical' governments—the Ciampi administration of 1993 and the Dini administration of 1995—which were headed by former central bank executives.

There has also been a move away from centralization and towards federalism, with major constitutional reforms in 2001. At the local level the influence of party machines has declined and there has been a trend towards elected mayors and provincial presidents.

F. New management ideas

In the 1980s there was a fashion for promoting a corporate, managerial culture in bodies such as regional and local authorities and hospitals and health care units. During the 1990s there was a strange *mélange* of traditional, French-derived administrative doctrines and NPM ideas.

The EU also had a distinct influence, particularly because of the reform of the structural funds from the late 1980s, which helped introduce new ideas about financial management, planning, and evaluation (mandatory evaluations became a feature of the reformed structural funds system). The Treasury was an important channel for these influences. As Italy moved into the twenty-first century, the intensification of international networking at regional and local levels facilitated the introduction of new ideas from the 'bottom-up'.

G. Pressures from citizens

Trust in government generally is not high in Italy (see Table 5.14). However, attitudes to public services have tended to be more favourable than attitudes towards politicians per se. Trust in the civil service appeared to increase between 1990 and 2000 (see Table 5.13). In general, it might be said that there has been strong, if diffuse, public pressure for reform—a growing awareness (fuelled by the greater international traffic in ideas) that inefficiency and even corruption are not just 'part of the way things are', but are problems that can be tackled.

H. Party political ideas

The fragmentation and volatility of the party system during the recent period makes it hard to identify consistently 'leading' ideas. Rather there have been certain groups of (sometimes contradictory) themes like:

- privatization
- downsizing and contracting-out
- some 'governance' ideas, including enhanced emphasis on public participation and third-sector partnership in service provision
- emphasis on the primacy of political control (often entailing a tightening of traditional, hierarchical) controls

I. Chance events

Bribery is not a chance event, but its discovery, perhaps, may be so regarded! The 'clean hands' inquiry, which began in the winter of 1992, was something of a watershed. It discredited a large part of the political and business elite, and pro- vided a catalyst for deep changes in the party system and the whole political class.

The monetary crisis in the summer of 1992 also made a major impact. It led to a new approach to the national deficit and to tremendous pressure on public organizations to find savings.

J. Elite decision-making

The crisis of 1992–4 made it politically very important to be seen as a 'reformer', and provided a background to many of the more specific proposals and ideas. Proposals to distance administrative responsibility from the political leadership (while leaving them with steering instruments) were understandably popular, and offered nodes for consensus. Privatization was one example of this, and one that also helped provide cash during a period of budgetary restraint. Decentralization was another rallying cry, expressed with particular vigour by the Northern League. The relative public popularity of the EU made it less difficult for politicians to carry through policies of privatization and downsizing, since these could be represented as being essential responses to EU convergence criteria.

K. The administrative system

The Italian administrative system is related to its French cousin, and has sometimes been described as 'Napoleonic'. Significant elements include:

- state direction of the economy and society;
- an elite state cadre, including the *Consiglio di Stato* (Council of State), the *Corte dei Conti* (NAO), and the *Ispettorato Generale* (a financial inspectorate);
- central state at regional level, personified in the *prefetto* (prefect);
- a special body of administrative law, based on the concept that the state occupies an autonomous domain (see discussion of the *Rechtsstaat* in Chapter 3). A public service culture that is hence strongly juridical;
- a four-tier system—state, region, province, municipality, with large central ministries that until recently managed many functions. Until the 1990s the provinces had only limited functions; and
- strong regional and cultural differences, despite the detailed framework of national rules and regulations.

L. Contents of the reform package

There was no single, defining 'package'. During the 1980s there was a good deal of innovation at local levels and in the health service, much of which was aimed at strengthening management and modernizing budgeting and planning procedures. However, it was not until the 1990s that major national reforms got underway. At the beginning of that decade local authorities were given greater autonomy to organize their services in different ways, and an important law on transparency in public administration was introduced.

Then, during the crisis of 1992–4 various reform packages took shape:

• Privatization and liberalization of banking and insurance; the dismantling of the state industrial conglomerate Istituto per la Ricostruzione Industriale (IRI) the partial liberalization of the mobile phone sector.

• Changes to the basis of public employment, in an attempt to introduce more decentralized collective bargaining and more private-sector-like disciplines.

• Clearer lines being drawn between the roles of elected officials and public managers, particularly at the local level. In practice this demarcation between setting priorities (political) and managing resources (managerial) proved very hard to implement.

• Financial management reforms: more recourse to block-budgeting (giving lower-tier authorities greater discretion to suballocate) but simultaneously a tightening of cash management.

• Introduction of a citizen's charter (Schiavo 2000) and of 'offices for relations with the public'.

• Reform of the NAO, reducing its administrative power and partly reorienting it from *ex post* controls towards *ex post* controls and performance audit.

A second wave of reform took place in 1997–9:

• Major decentralization. Invoking the principle of 'subsiduarity', many functions were transferred to the regional and local levels. This was reinforced by a new constitutional law in 2001.

• Further employment reform, strengthening private sector disciplines and introducing performance-related pay.

• A broad package of administrative simplification, including the widespread introduction of 'one-stop shops'.

• Restructuring of central government, including mergers of ministries and the creation of executive agencies that were supposed to operate through performance contracts.

• Reform of the general system of controls, distinguishing between administrative controls, management controls, and strategic controls.

• Accounting reform, aggregating expenditures into larger 'units'.

• Increased autonomy given to schools, universities, and chambers of commerce.

M. The implementation process

Those reforms that were directly driven by the financial pressure of the economic crisis in the early 1990s tended to be implemented relatively quickly. The intensity of implementation of other reforms was very varied, with long delays and 'dilutions' being quite common.

There has been a considerable debate within Italy as to whether the reforms of the 1990s were mainly 'top-down' or 'bottom-up'. The answer seems to be 'both'. Some reforms were clearly driven by national laws. But, on the other hand, the autonomization and decentralization processes released many innovatory experiments in municipalities and local hospitals. The spread of 'city managers' was also a largely bottom-up phenomenon.

N. Results achieved

No general evaluation is available. It is clear that considerable structural change has taken place, and it seems likely that, in many instances, the client orientation has also increased. In the mid-1990s considerable reductions in public spending were achieved, although it may be debated how far this was due to any managerial skill. Some particular evaluations have been made of specific reforms, for example, Pessina and Cantu (2000—for health care) or Valotti (2000—for local government).

Country file events: Italy

	General	Organization	Personnel	Finance
1981–5		– Reform of health care (1978–80) – Reform of local government (increased autonomy in organizational schemes 1980–1)		
1985–90	– Structural Funds Agenda for the period 1989–94 – Sixth and seventh Andreotti governments – Monorchio becomes director-general of the General Accounting Department (1989) – Reform of local government: redefinition of politico-administrative relations and of service delivery options (1990) – New rules on administrative transparency (1990)	– Reform of the presidency of the Council of Ministers (1988) – Higher education reform: autonomy of universities (1989–91) – Increased autonomy of INPS (pensions) and INAIL (safety at work) (1988–9)	– Constraints on turnover (1985–6)	– Financial constraints (1985–6)
1991–5	– Delegation law to the government concerning reform of ministries and other important topics (1992): 'economic public bodies' are transformed into companies – 'Clean hands' inquiry (1992) – Amato government (1992) – Monetary crisis (1992) – Ciampi government (1993) – Berlusconi first government (1994) – Reform of structural funds agenda (1994) – Dini government (1995) – Reform of pension system (1995)	– Organization of Treasury Ministry in departments—Draghi is appointed director-general of Treasury Department (1991) – Reform of Finance Ministry (1991) – Reform of health care (regionalization and competition mechanisms—1992 and 1993) – Decree on the organization of the public service (1993) – Merger of Balance and Economic Programming Ministry and Treasury Ministry; emerging departmental model in Treasury Ministry – Big privatization plan is started (1993) – Credito Italiano e Comit (among the major Italian banks) are privatized (1993 and 1994)	– Reform of public employment and public manager responsibility (1993)	– Law on public finance corrective measures (1993) – Systematic cutbacks (1993) – Increased use of block grants (in different sector of the public system) – Increased cash constraints (1993) – Reform of the Court of the Accounts (1994) – Law on measure to rationalize government finances (1994) – Accounting reform law (local authorities) (1995)

continues

continued

	General	Organization	Personnel	Finance
		– Liberalization of the telecommunication sector – Reform in health care (regionalization and competition mechanisms) (1992–3) – Delegation law to the government to reform ministries and establish new authorities in utilities and industrial sectors (1994) – Introduction of the charters of services (1994) and of the offices for the relationships with the public (1993) – A relevant share of INA (a large insurance group) and IMI (investment bank) is sold (1994)		
1996–2000	– Prodi government (1996) – The third Bicameral Commission for reforming the constitution is established (1996–7) – Italy joins the European single currency (1998) – D'Alema first government (1998) – Parliamentary debate on the reform of utilities (local level) – D'Alema second government (1999) – Amato second government (2000) – Action plan for e-government (2000)	– A first tranche of ENI (oil and gas industry) is sold – Other four tranches of ENI are sold (1996–8); the Treasury keeps the control – Establishment of regulatory and other authorities (notably telecommunications, energy): decentralization law (1997); law on administrative simplification (1997) – Other sectoral reforms (1997–9) – Telecom Italia (the former public monopoly) is sold (1997) – One-stop shops for undertakings at the local level start (1998) – Development of the negotiated planning and the pacts for economic development (1997–8)	– Second reform law of public employment (1997) – Increased mobility of central government civil servants (2000) – National collective work contracts introduce relevant innovations in the different sectors (particularly health care and regional and local governments) (1998–2000)	– State budget reform (1997) – Various financial manoeuvres for controlling cash and restructuring the public debt (1996–8) – Reform law on the development of performance measures in the public sector (1997) – Redefinition of the system of controls: administrative controls are clearly separated from management and strategic control (the last one introduced by this law) and from the evaluation of public managers (1999) – Reform of regional accounting and financial system (2000) – Reform of regional accounting and financial system (2000)

	– Education: increased autonomy—directors of schools become public managers (1998, to be started in 2000); proposed reform of the school system (currently not implemented) – Reform law on the reduction in the number of ministries, establishing in particular the merger of Treasury and Finance Ministry, to be started in 2001 (1999) – Establishment of 12 new executive agencies, ruled by a performance contract (1999) – Reform of prefect's offices (1999) – Reform of the presidency of the Council of Ministers (1999) – Liberalization of the electricity sector, a first share of ENEL is sold (2000) – Relevant organizational changes in local and regional authorities (second half of 1990s)	– The Inland Revenue Agency is the first one to start (2001) – Reform of university system (1999–2001) – Reform of public procurement – Establishment of the Ministry for Technological Innovation (2001) – Reduction of ministries (2001) – Merger of state local offices into single interministerial units (2001)	– Spoil system mechanisms strengthened (2001)
2001–2	– Berlusconi second government (2001) – Establishment of the Ministry of Technological Innovation (2001) – Siniscalco appointed director-general of Treasury Department (2001) – Federal reform of the constitution, subsequently confirmed by a referendum (2001)		

NETHERLANDS

A. Socio-economic forces: general

See Appendix A.

Population ageing will reduce economic growth and increase resource transfers to the elderly. This will put pressure on the retirement income–health care insurance systems. The Netherlands is better placed than most OECD countries to meet these pressures because it has a large, funded occupational pension system. Even so, the government budget balance is projected to deteriorate when the baby boom generation passes into retirement. (OECD 2002c, p. 3)

B. Global economic forces

Again, see Appendix A.

C. Sociodemographic issues

See Appendix A, Figure A.1, and Tables A.2 and A.3. Since the 1980s and even at the beginning of the 1990s, the Netherlands was second only to Sweden (among the twelve countries reviewed), in respect of the high proportion of GDP devoted to social expenditure. During the 1990s and especially in the late 1990s the proportion stabilized and even decreased, as is shown in Table A.2. At the end of the 1990s immigration became a major political issue (the Netherlands is a small, densely populated country with large immigrant communities in most cities).

D. National socio-economic policies

Until the recession of the 1970s the post-war history of the Dutch public sector had been one of more or less continuous expansion. Then, between 1974 and 1982, the budget situation deteriorated from surplus to a large deficit. Unsurprisingly, the 1980s were a period of sharp cutbacks in the public sector, combined with a series of measures to develop tighter control over state expenditures. These measures caused a cutback of the central government debt by 11 per cent between 1990 and 2000 (Table 5.4). Since 1989 the Dutch economy has performed better, although it shared in the international slowdown of the early 1990s. Employment growth since 1994 has been ahead of many other EU member states. Although the governments of the mid and late 1990s have enjoyed a less threatening position on public spending than their 1980s predecessors, the economic circumstances are changing:

These are undoubtedly testing times for the Netherlands, with the economy moving away from sustained non-inflationary growth, which had been the hallmark of the Dutch model for nearly two decades. (OECD 2002c, p. 1)

E. The political system

The Netherlands is a unitary, but decentralized state: 'traditionally, the Dutch state . . . has always resisted centralisation of state authority' (Kickert and In't Veld 1995, p. 45). The political system is consociational, consensual, multiparty, and corporatist (Lijphart 1984). Elections take place according to a system of proportional representation. In the recent period the main parties have been Christian Democratic (a 1980s merger of previously separate Christian parties), Liberal (Conservative), Progressive Liberal, and Social Democratic. The Christian parties were continuously in government from the First World War until 1994, allied to varying grouping of other parties. Through the 1970s the governing coalitions were centre–left, and in the 1980s centre–right. Unusually, in 1994 and 1998, a 'purple' (left–right) coalition was formed *without* Christian Democratic participation. However, from the late 1990s, the party system became volatile, with the rapid emergence, and then equally rapid decline, of Pim Fortuyn's anti-establishment LPF party. After the elections of May 2002 and January 2003, the Christian Democrats returned to government.

In the Netherlands almost every sector of government policy consists of a myriad of consultative and advisory councils, which are deeply intertwined with government and form an 'iron ring' around the ministerial departments . . . Deliberation, consultation, and pursuit of compromise and consensus form the deeply rooted basic traits of Dutch political culture. (Kickert and In't Veld 1995, p. 53)

F. New management ideas

The system of consultative and advisory councils (see Section E) affords many channels for both business-based and academic ideas to enter public administration:

[T]he Dutch ministries are relatively open organisations. They are not only populated by career civil servants, but also by many external consultants and scientists who contribute enthusiastically to policy making in general. (Kickert and In't Veld 1995, p. 56)

In this respect, therefore, the Netherlands is dissimilar to more closed, *Rechtsstaat*-type regimes such as Germany or France. Following the Second World War there was a noticeable 'dejuridification' of public administration. During the 1980s specific reform ideas came from a number of other countries, especially Sweden, the UK, and the USA (Roberts 1997, p. 101).

As in many other countries, during the 1980s, notions of comprehensive planning were in rapid retreat, and business-origin management ideas increasingly penetrated the public sector. However, in the Netherlands, the drive for efficiency and savings did not carry the same antigovernment ideological edge as it did, for example, in the UK under Thatcher or in the USA under Reagan.

It should also be noted that the Netherlands, relative to its size, has one of the largest communities of public administration academics in Western Europe. Many professors played some part in advising government on administrative reform. During the 1980s open systems approaches and network theories provided alternative perspectives to business management approaches and, during the 1990s, the Dutch academic community played an important part in developing the 'new steering model' of governance (Kickert and In't Veld 1995, pp. 59–60).

G. Pressure from citizens

Whilst there is a popular suspicion that 'the bureaucracy' is inefficient, and while public service seems to have become a less attractive career for young people, Dutch public opinion does not seem to support the strongly antigovernment attitudes, which have been quite popular in the USA and, to a lesser extent, in Australia, New Zealand, and the UK. Also in regard to other European countries, the public opinion in the Netherlands has a positive attitude towards the government (Table 5.13). The Dutch public opinion too gives high ratings to institutions such as Parliament, social security, health care, and education.

One might further mention that the Dutch have a certain cultural aversion to public figures 'showing off', which suggests that the potential popular appeal of politicians with bold, doctrinaire

programmes (such as Thatcher, Reagan, Howard, Lange, or Mulroney) is less in the Netherlands than in some other countries. However, since 1999, the rise of Pim Fortuyn has somewhat dented this image of Dutch 'steadiness'.

In general: 'The Dutch seem to like representative government by general local, regional or national governments. The underlying idea is that intersectoral judgements can best be made in this type of democratic body' (Kickert and In't Veld 1995, p. 58).

H. Party political ideas

Whilst political parties undoubtedly developed broad notions about how Dutch government should be reformed, it is necessary to remember that the significance of the ideas of any one party for practical action is likely to be less in a consensual, multiparty system than in the kind of one-party dominance that has usually characterized government in New Zealand and the UK. That having been said, one may note a number of party political themes that gained some salience.

First, it is clear that the first Lubbers government, which came to power as a centre–right coalition in 1982, was influenced by the right-wing Anglo-American neoliberal governments of the time. It adopted a rhetoric that was pro-privatization and in favour of slimming the central state. Over time, this emphasis became somewhat diluted, especially when the third Lubbers administration (1989–94) included the Social Democrats as major partners (instead of the Liberals, as in the first and second Lubbers governments). Simultaneously, however, the Social Democrats muted their previous ideological resistance to various forms of business-like practices being (selectively) introduced to the public sector. Additionally, the pressures to cut back public spending receded during the 1990s, so that the context for debate was less acute.

Later, during the 1990s, there was a certain disenchantment with some of the reforms. Following some critical analyses (e.g. Algemene Rekenkamer 1995) of the many ZBOs (autonomous administrative bodies) created during the 1980s, the new 'purple coalition' government of the mid-1990s declared its intention of restoring the 'primacy of politics', meaning a greater measure of public accountability and transparency for nonministerial public bodies (Thiel 2001).

I. Chance events

Confidence in the administrative and political system has been under pressure. There was a fireworks factory that exploded in Enschede with many people killed and injured, resulting in questions on procedures related to permits and inspections. There was the 2002 murder of Pim Fortuyn that also caused a parliamentary commission to look hard at the responsibilities and levels of accountability of different administrative and political actors involved. There was a public works fraud that emphasized the importance of ethical standards in public sector reform. All these incidents combined to raise the question of whether 'cosy consensualism' had gone too far.

J. Elite decision-making

Much elite attention was focused on budgetary problems. The development of performance indicators (PIs), contractualization, and output budgeting were all seen as desirable. During the 1980s and early 1990s, the political elite was most interested in strategies for achieving cutbacks. Top officials, however, were more enthusiastic about the possibilities of management reforms per se. During the election campaign in May 2002, the populist candidate Fortuyn emphasized the malfunctioning of administrations and certain public policies. (For a detailed account of elite thinking, see Kickert 2000.)

K. The administrative system

'*Ministerial responsibility* is the cornerstone of our system' (Kickert and In't Veld 1995, p. 46). Ministers are responsible politically, in criminal and in civil law. Collective decision-making takes place in the weekly council of ministers. The prime minister is not as strong a coordinating and centralizing force as in the UK system—indeed, various attempts during the 1980s and 1990s to strengthen the Prime Minister's Office have been rejected or dropped. She or he remains *primus inter pares*.

In the mid-1990s there were fourteen ministries (the number has varied over time, e.g. in 1982 the new government abolished the Ministry of Public Health and Environment and transferred its functions to two new ministries). Because of the absence of a strong central power each has considerable autonomy—more so than would be the case in either New Zealand or the UK. The highest civil servant in each ministry is the Secretary-General, and ministries are generally divided into DGs. In 1995 the ABD (Algemene Bestuursdienst) was created (a Senior Executive Service), which numbered, at the end of 2000, 628 civil servants.

The civil service is not partisan, and civil service and political careers are separate. Ministries are fairly open organizations, at least in the sense that they frequently bring outside experts into the processes of policy deliberation.

The provincial and municipal levels are highly significant in terms of services, expenditure, and personnel. There are twelve provinces and 625 municipalities. These subnational tiers are responsible for most of the expensive, labour-intensive welfare state services (municipalities account for roughly one-third of public expenditure, though much of this is financed by central government). Many of the cutbacks of the 1980s were directed at these levels.

L. Contents of the reform package

The content of the reform package developed over time, with shifts in the coalition government, and with changes in the fortunes of the Dutch economy. In general terms it might be said that the package appeared most radical in the early part of our period, especially under the 'Lubbers 1' centre–right coalition of 1982–6. Privatization was a prominent theme, but the scope for returning state bodies to private ownership was less than in the UK or New Zealand because the extent of pre-existing state ownership was more modest. Nevertheless, the Postbank (10,500 staff), Posts and Telecommunications (95,000 staff), the Royal Mint, and the Fishery Port Authority—the four main state companies—were either corporatized or wholly or partly sold off.

Alongside privatization, the Lubbers 1 administration announced a series of 'great operations'. These comprised measures to trim central government spending, decentralize activities to lower levels of government, and simplify legal and bureaucratic procedures.

The 1980s was also a period in which many new ZBOs were created. A survey showed that, by 1992, 18 per cent of total state expenditure passed through these semi-autonomous bodies. Some were long-established (e.g. the state universities) but more than 40 per cent dated from after 1980 (Algemene Rekenkamer 1995).

In the 1990s the departmental agency, rather than the ZBO, became the fashionable format for decentralizing administrative authority. Between 1991 and 2002 the number of agencies went up to twenty-three and the number of ZBOs was 340 (Ministerie van Financiën 2002). These included agencies for Meteorology, Immigration and Naturalization, Defence Telematics, and the Government Buildings Service.

In HRM/personnel management there was a gradual shift towards the 'normalization' of the terms of public services, that is, bringing them more in line with private sector labour conditions. The Netherlands, along with most other countries in this study, experienced a tension between the desire to use HRM to build a more skilled and highly motivated workforce and the desire to shed jobs and economize (Korsten and van der Krogt 1995).

Throughout the period there was a trend to develop and refine PIs for a widening range of public services. Mol (1995) provides an interesting case study of the strengths and weaknesses of this process in the National Logistic Command.

During the 1980s extensive financial management reforms were instituted in both central and local government:

A key element of this initiative consisted in the introduction of encumbrance accounting in central government, to be applied in conjunction to the cash concept of accounting already in use. Accounting for obligations may be considered a key factor in controlling central government spending, as cash disbursements will inevitably result from previously established operations. (Boorsma and Mol 1995, p. 229)

As the government finances were again under control in the early 1990s, results-oriented budgeting and management regained attention. There was also an increasing trend to integrate performance measures in the budget documents. Finally, in 2001, performance-budgeting (VBTB) was legally implemented: the format of the budget bill became outcome-oriented and policy objectives and performance measures were integrated in the explanatory memorandum. In 2001 the Ministry of Finance also started planning to extend the accruals-budgeting system from the agencies to the departments.

M. The implementation process

In many, perhaps most, countries the rhetoric of public management reform outdistances the actual changes in practice. This has certainly been true for the Netherlands during the 1980–97 period. The implementation of decentralization is a good example:

[T]he decentralisation process in the 1980s and 1990s became largely a power struggle. Spending departments often held out resolutely (and with success) against the transfer of power to provinces and municipalities. Decentralisation only began to assume any importance when spending cuts and decentralisation were brought together in a single context: municipalities were permitted to take over certain tasks if they were prepared to accept 90% funding; the 10% contraction was (without much evidence) justified as 'efficiency gains'. (Derksen and Korsten 1995, p. 83)

More generally, implementation has been an incremental and selective process—much less of a series of dramatic 'waves' as in the UK or New Zealand. This is perhaps only to be expected of a politico-administrative system that prides itself on its consensual character.

N. Reforms actually achieved

The Netherlands is a country where programme and policy evaluation has been fairly widely practised (a 1991 survey recorded 300 evaluations being undertaken across fourteen ministries) but relatively little of this effort seems to be been focused upon management reforms per se. For example, many ZBOs were created during the 1980s, but, writing in the mid-1990s, one Dutch expert considered that their performance was a blind spot (Leeuw 1995). Certainly, there does not seem to have been any overall evaluation of the reforms or even of their significant sections, such as the 'great operations' of the Lubbers 1 and 2 administrations. There have, however, been a few academic assessments (e.g. Kam and De Haan 1991).

Some questioning of the reforms has come from the National Court of Audit (Algemene Rekenkamer 1995). In particular, they published a 1995 report that was highly critical of the lack of public accountability of some ZBOs. For example, the report indicated that only 22 per cent of the ZBOs surveyed produced PI data for their parent ministries. Financial control procedures were often weak and in some cases the legal basis for certain tasks was not clear (Algemene Rekenkamer 1995).

More recently, the Ministry of Finance has sponsored an assessment of the programme (1991–8) of creating agencies (Ministerie van Financiën 1998).

Country file events: The Netherlands

	General	Organization	Personnel	Finance
1981–5	– Van Agt: PM (CD, Soc.) (1981) – 'Major Operations': deregulation, privatization, reconsideration (1981) – Lubbers: PM (CD, Lib.) (1982)	– Reorganization including decentralization (1982) – Transfer competencies to lower-level line managers (1984)	– Bonus payments for special efforts (1984) – Central Steering Committee on Personnel Policy (1984)	
1986–90	– Lubbers: PM (CD, Lib.) (1986) – Targets for job reduction (1988) – Lubbers: PM (CD, Soc.) (1989) – Management Development Advice Centre (Interiors) (1989) – Ministerial Committee for 'Great Efficiency Operation' (reducing tasks, improving organization, cost reduction) (1990)		– Ministry of Interiors asks universities to set up management training (1988) – System of pay differentials (1989) – School of Public Administration (1989) – 'Small-Scale Efficiency Operation': increases labour productivity (1990)	– Performance indicators (PIs) in budget (estimates, efficiency, effectiveness): first stage: (input) estimates (1990)
1991–5	– 'Core Business' operation: central tasks; reduces personnel (1991) – Minister of Justice presents report to Parliament on shortcomings in legislation (1991) – 'Towards More Results-Oriented Management' report of government (1992) – 'Great Efficiency Operation' (Interiors): privatization and staff reduction (1992) – Committee on Constitutional Renewal (Parliament) (1992) – 'Tailor-Made Advice': revision of advisory bodies (1993) – 'Towards Core Ministries': small administration centres (1993) – 'Organization and Working Methods of the Civil Service': core tasks (1993) – Kok: PM (Soc., Lib.) (1994) – 'Choices for the Future' (1994)	– Civil service centres: experiment (1991) – Agreement between central and local government to transfer tasks (1992) – Start agencies: 4 (1994) – Agencies: 7 – Government position: semi-privatized bodies (1995) – Government position: autonomous administrative authorities (AAAs) vs. ministerial responsibility (1995) – Start screening 253 AAAs (1995)	– Significant steps to 'normalize' status of government employees (1991) – Evaluation of performance-related pay schemes (1991) – Agreement between government and trade unions to privatize the General Pension Fund for public employees by 1996 (1992) – Increase mobility by 'temporary assignments' (1992) – People and Management in the Civil Service: 1st annual report on personnel management (1994) – Senior Public Service (SPS) (PM and Interiors): intertop database, mobility (1995)	– Closing of 'Financial Accountability Operation' (1986–91) – MoF: quantitative and qualitative improvement of measurement: estimates, planning, and controlling systems, allocation of resources (1991) – Completion of 'Financial Accountability Operation': each ministry responsible for accounting system, independent agencies, streamline budget process, reassess rules on financial and personnel management (1992) – Ministries obliged to report on policy evaluation programmes in annual budget explanation (1992) – Strengthen Accounting Law 1976: more PIs (1992) – Application of broader rules of budgetary discipline (end-of-year margin: 0.25%) (1993)

	– Ministerial Committee for Political Reform (Interiors) (1994) – Ministerial (PM) Committee for Market Improvement, Deregulation, and Legislative Quality (1994) – Government policy document: 'Back to the Future': ICT and use of information (1995)		– Policy: charges cover costs (1993) – Set-up of Policy Evaluation Programme: budget looks at current, planned, completec evaluations (1993) – Project: indicators for the cost of implementing regulations (1993) – Control of the integrated operating budget (personnel and equipment) (1994) – MoF: manual PI (1994) – 'Reconsideration' Procedure replaced by 'Interdepartmental Policy Audit' (1994) – Agencies: five double bookkeeping (1995) – End-of-year margin: 1% (1995) – Review prccedure topic: financial reform (1995) – Adjust Accounting Law (1995)
1996–2000	– Framework Act on Advisory System (1996) – Financial Relations Act (1996): redistribution of finances among municipalities – Evaluation of agencies (1997) – Cohen report: market and government (1997) – Further reduction of number of municipalities to about 550 (1998) – Kok: PM (Soc., Lib.) (1998) – Further reduction of municipalities to about 538 (1999) – Growing problems in health care (2000)	– 19 agencies (1998) – Policy intention to restructure parts of the implementation of social security in autonomous administrative authorities (1998) – Reform of the employment guidance system (AOB) (2000)	– 36-hour week introduced in most sectors of public service (1997) – Extension of the SPS to all management positions (more than 1,500 public servants) (1998) – Review of Senior Public Service (2000) – Study to find out whether the salary scales of agency executives were in proper proportion to the scales in policy departments. A number of adjustments were recommended to put salaries into a similar position (2000)	– More stringent rules for contract and equipment management (1996) – Parliament: Commission of Finance Audits PIs (1996) – PIs in budget: second stage: outputs (1997) – PIs in budget: third stage: link cost/ expenses–outputs (efficiency) (1998) – 'Interdepartmental Management Audit' (1998) – VBTB: departmental budget and annual accounts structured along policy goals (1999) – Introduction of Government Governance (2000) – Regulation and reform of the budget and accounting system of the ZBO (2000)

continues

continued

	General	Organization	Personnel	Finance
2001–2	– Second research on quality management instruments in the public sector (2001) – Regulation on Performance Management and Policy Evaluation (2002) – Balkenende: PM (CDA/Fortuyn) (2002) – Nationwide conference on best practice (2002)	– Creation of new agencies (6 between 1999 and 2001). The number of agencies has now moved up to 23 (2001) and the number of ZBOs, to 340 (2002) – Generalization of the establishment rules for agencies to the establishment of new ZBOs (2001) – Some ZBOs have lost their status of ZBO and have been drawn back under ministerial responsibility. They received a status of temporary agency to meet, within the 3 years, the requirements of the results-oriented management system of the agencies (2001) – Reorganization of public employment services, including marketization (from RBA to CWIs) (2002) – Proposal for a Framework Law on ZBOs (2002)	– Further rise of public employment by 1.3% p.a. – Growing share of the agencies in the total civil service (30% in 2001, expectation for 2004 is 80%)	– First policy-oriented departmental budgets authorized (2001) – Modern budgeting: intention to move to accruals-budgeting in 2006 (2001) – Regulation on Performance Information and Policy Evaluation (2002) – Regulation on Management Reporting in the Budget (2002) – Public Finance Act 2001 (2002) – Report on new financial instruments for public–private partnership (PPP) (2002)

NEW ZEALAND

A. Socio-economic forces: general

New Zealand is a small country (population 3.9 million) in a peripheral geographical location (2,000 km from Australia). GNP per capita fell from ninety in 1985 to seventy-six in 1992 (where OECD average = 100). There were close economic and cultural ties to the UK, but these began to dwindle after the UK joined the European Community in 1973, and it was obvious that the favoured arrangements for New Zealand agricultural exports to the UK market could not survive indefinitely. There are two main population groups—whites and Maoris. The latter (12% of the population) have been increasingly politically active in insisting on their rights and pointing to inequalities—a process sometimes described as 'internal decolonization' (Castles et al. 1996, chapter 7).

See Appendix A, and especially Table A.1 for details of New Zealand's comparative position.

B. Global economic forces

The system of protectionism that had been in place since the Second World War was close to the point of collapse by the early 1980s. In 1952, 65 per cent of exports had gone to the UK and only 1.7 per cent to Asia. By 1982 the first figure had fallen to 14.7 per cent and the second had risen to 31.8 per cent (Castles et al. 1996, p. 25).

When the new Labour government led by David Lange came to power in July 1984, the economy was stagnant and the national debt was large. The New Zealand Reserve Bank suspended trading in the New Zealand dollar and a 20 per cent devaluation quickly followed. The government's first priorities were tax reform, financial deregulation, and privatization. The comprehensive public management reforms of 1984–90 flowed directly from this financial and economic crisis. There continues to be controversy about the extent to which the exchange rate crisis was also the symptom of a deeper economic crisis—critics say the new government exploited the situation to push through its radical agenda.

Restructuring the economy was undertaken at high speed, but the beneficial impacts took more than five years to show through. The interim period was very tough. In 1985 inflation reached 13 per cent. Overseas firms were prominent beneficiaries of the privatization programme, being mainly responsible for the purchase of the railways, the telephone system, and (thanks to financial deregulation) most of the major banks. Between 1985 and 1992 the economy actually shrank by 1 per cent. As Table A.1 makes clear, both per capita GDP and fixed capital growth have recently been lower in New Zealand than most of the other countries covered by this book.

C. Sociodemographic change

Prior to 1984 unemployment had usually been low (less than 5%) in New Zealand. It rose rapidly between 1985 and the early 1990s, reaching more than 10 per cent in 1992/93. The social effects of this were widespread and harsh. This was partly because many social benefits were linked to employment status but also because from 1990 the National Government initiated the rapid dismantling of much of the previous welfare state system. Speaking of the 1980s Castles and colleagues (1996, p. 101) observe that

a very substantial decline in real wages over the latter half of the period was accompanied by distributional effects...These included an increased incidence of low pay for men, a decline in the share of real gross income of wage and salary earners accruing to each of the bottom three quintiles and a marked increase in the share of the top quintile.

One might add that, as might be expected, women and ethnic minorities were particularly hard hit by the simultaneous worsening of employment conditions and slimming down of welfare provision.

D. National socio-economic policies

A very clear commitment to a comprehensive economic restructuring: tax reform (to lower the tax burdens on business); financial deregulation (to attract foreign capital); privatization (to promote efficiency and relieve pressure on public spending). The generous New Zealand welfare state was left largely intact at first, but major reforms aimed at reducing welfare and social security expenditure were instituted by the incoming National Party government of 1990. An Employment

Equity Act introduced by the Labour Government in 1990 was soon repealed by its national successor. The Employment Contracts Act significantly deregulated the labour market.

E. The political system

The political executive is drawn exclusively from a small legislature, organized on Westminster principles. There is no upper house. There is no single written constitutional document nor any other major constraint on the government in power.

Until 1996 the electoral system was based on a single-constituency member, 'first-past-the-post' system, which usually delivered a single party to power. Once in power '[p]ublic servants and their managers have long operated in a context in which the Prime Minister and cabinet could, if they wished, ride roughshod over any opposition' (Boston et al. 1996, p. 68). However, following a constitutional referendum in 1993 the electoral system was changed (1996) to one based on mixed member proportional (MMP) representation. Subsequently, coalition governments have become the norm, and there has been considerable rearrangement of the political parties.

Unlike other small countries in our set (Finland, the Netherlands), New Zealand has traditionally been fairly centralized. There has been '[a] preference for retaining key governmental powers and responsibilities at the central government level, with only limited devolution to sub-national government, despite considerable rhetoric about devolution in the 1980s' (Boston et al. 1996, p. 5).

F. New management ideas

The public management reforms in New Zealand were unusual both in their comprehensiveness and in the relatively high degree to which they were based on explicitly theoretical ideas about management. The then Central Financial Controller to the Treasury wrote: 'A number of literatures contributed...The sources included public choice theory, managerialism, transaction cost economics, public policy, public sector financial management and accounting' (Ball 1993, p. 5).

There was a shared intellectual background within the quite small group of key ministers, senior civil servants, and businessmen who drove

through the reforms: '[T]here were a series of quite close relationships set up, from about 1982 on, by a group that encompassed the corporate business sector, the senior Labour parliamentary group' (Canadian Broadcasting Corporation 1994, p. 3). The highly theoretical character of much of this thinking was novel:

> Like their British counterparts, senior New Zealand public servants had not been known in the past for their interest in theory. The emphasis on using theory to guide policy was, therefore, a novelty. It seems to have been due, at least in part, to the growing influence of economists and the particular kind of higher education which many of these economists, especially those in the Treasury, received. (Boston 1995, p. 168)

The content of this thinking, in institutional terms, may be expressed as follows (borrowing from Boston et al. 1996, pp. 81–2):

1. prefer private sector over state sector organizations wherever possible, especially for commercial functions;

2. prefer nondepartmental organizations over ministerial departments, especially for policy implementation;

3. prefer small to large organizations;

4. prefer single-purpose to multi-purpose organizations;

5. allow pluriform administrative structures rather than seeking uniformity ('horses for courses');

6. separate policy from operations;

7. separate funding from purchasing and purchasing from providing;

8. separate operations from regulation;

9. separate provision from review and audit;

10. prefer multi-source to single-source supply;

11. place like with like (primarily on the basis of the purpose or the type of activity);

12. aim for short ('flat') rather than long hierarchies;

13. aim for 'straight-line' accountability/avoid 'multiple principals'; and

14. decentralize wherever possible.

G. Pressure from citizens

The rush of reforms from 1984 to 1994 could not be described as a response to direct pressure from citizens; in fact at first they were controversial and widely unpopular. They were a package pushed through quickly by an elite that took the 'window of' opportunity for radical reform (Aberbach and Christensen 2001). Since the 1996 shift to a system of proportional representation, such untrammelled elite actions have been rather more difficult, and the pace and scope of reform has been reduced.

H. Party political ideas

Until the advent of proportional representation in 1996, the main electoral competition had taken place between the Labour Party (broadly Social Democratic) and the National Party (broadly Conservative). It is noticeable that the New Zealand Labour and Australian Labor governments were the only Labour/Social Democrat executives in the OECD to respond to the global economic pressures of the 1980s by actively embracing market-oriented reforms (Castles et al. 1996, p. 2). Labour had been in power from 1935 until 1949, and during that time had established what was arguably the world's first comprehensive welfare state. After this, however, Labour enjoyed only brief periods in power (1957–60 and 1972–5) before its coming to office in 1984.

Specifically, *party* political ideas do not appear to have had much influence on the New Zealand reforms of 1984–90. The policies that were put in place were developed rapidly and without much external consultation by the governing elite (Castles et al. 1996). Unlike the Australian Labor Party, the New Zealand Party did not have particularly close links with the trade union movement, and its relatively unrestrained constitutional position allowed it to choose its policies with few major constraints.

I. Chance events

It is not obvious that any chance events had a major and direct influence on the course and content of the public management reforms. However, it might be said that, towards the end of our period, the Cave Creek disaster (in which, in 1993, fourteen young people died when an observation platform collapsed in a Department of Conservation nature reserve) provided a focus for much public unease about the changes that had been implemented over the previous decade. One theme in the media treatment of the Cave Creek tragedy was the lack of individual responsibility in the decentralized public service (Gregory 1998).

J. Elite decision-making

The small, elite group of Labour Party ministers and civil servants who drove the New Zealand reforms from 1984 to 1990 were, in the main, enthusiasts for the new management ideas spelled out in Section F. When the National Party returned to power in 1990, there was no great change to this 'menu' other than, perhaps, a willingness to apply these concepts even more vigorously than before to the social protection system. Nevertheless, it would be erroneous to see the New Zealand example as the pure and undiluted application of a set of tightly knit theoretical ideas. To begin with, the ideas do not all fit together perfectly— sometimes different principles or guidelines seem to point in different directions. Furthermore, many detailed, practical compromises had to be made (Boston et al. 1996, pp. 82–6). For example,

[d]espite the substantial privatisation programme during the late 1980s, a number of important commercial organisations remain in public ownership, and there has been little public or political support for privatisation in areas like education, health care, and scientific research. (Boston et al. 1996, p. 82)

By the turn of the century the mood had shifted somewhat and, without favouring any fundamental reversal of the great changes of 1984–94, governments became more concerned with issues of better institutional coordination, restoring morale and leadership within the public service and more community involvement in policy-making and service design and delivery (State Services Commission 2001, 2002).

K. The administrative system

At the outset of the reforms the New Zealand public service was a unified, non-party-political, career service. Senior public servants 'tended to take a broad service-wide perspective at least as much as a narrow departmental focus' (Boston et al. 1996, p. 56). It was heavily rule-bound (especially in matters of personnel and industrial relations), and by the early 1980s was widely regarded as inefficient.

Much of this was changed by the 1988 State Sector Act and other reforms. Personnel powers were decentralized and senior civil servants were henceforth employed on performance-related contracts. Large departmental structures were broken up into a larger number of smaller agencies, each with a more closely defined set of objectives and targets. The turnover of chief executives was quite rapid—over 80 per cent of those initially appointed had gone by 1995. Nevertheless, the State Services Commission has retained effective control of senior appointments—the system has not become as politicized as in Australia (Halligan 2002). Furthermore, although more fragmented than formerly, it remains a highly centralized system in comparison with countries such as Finland, Germany, Sweden, or the USA (see Table 3.2).

L. Contents of the reform package

The key management changes were embodied in four pieces of legislation:

- *The State-Owned Enterprises Act, 1986*—provided the basis for converting the old trading departments and corporations into businesses along private sector lines.

- *The State Sector Act, 1988*—chief executives became fully accountable for managing their departments efficiently and effectively. The role of the State Services Commissioner shifted from that of employer and manager of the public service to that of employer of the chief executives and adviser to the government on general management and personnel issues. Chief executives became the managers of their own departmental staff.

- *The Public Finance Act, 1989*—introduced accruals-accounting and insisted on a focus on outputs and outcomes rather than inputs and activities.

- *The Fiscal Responsibility Act, 1994*—obliged the government to set out its fiscal objectives and explain how these were related to stated principles of responsible fiscal management.

After 1994 the pace of reform slowed. There were (understandably) signs of 'reform fatigue', and there were modest retreats and readjustments where the purity of the original doctrines seemed to have led to obviously negative consequences. Significantly, a major report in 2001 (the *Review of the Centre*, see State Services Commission 2001, 2002) emphasized the following problems:

- The need for better coordination in what had become a fragmented system of state sector organizations

- The need to concentrate more on the formulation and pursuit of desired outcomes, rather than simply mechanically pursuing outputs

- The need to involve citizens and communities more with policy making, service design, and service delivery

- The need to strengthen the public service culture and invest in public service leadership

M. The implementation process

The implementation process was vigorous—at times harsh—and fairly continuous for the eight years following the 1984 election. The key civil servants at the Treasury and the State Services Commission played central roles. Much use was also made of management consultants and other experts brought in from outside. The human relations climate was often poor—formally a fairly humanist model of HRM was adopted during the 1980s, but in practice there were many job losses, large restructurings, great pressures, and many upheavals (Boston et al. 1996, p. 213).

By the early twenty-first century it seemed that one of the longer-term results of the reforms—especially the budget and financial management reforms—had been a serious running down of the capability of government departments (Newberry 2002). Resource starvation and short-termism appear to have been built-in (intentionally or otherwise) to the procedures through which the Fiscal Responsibility Act and the Public Finance Act have been implemented.

N. Reforms actually achieved

The New Zealand government achieved what was probably the most comprehensive and radical set of public management reforms of any OECD country. For example, between 1988 and 1994, employment in the public service declined from 88,000 to 37,000 (though this includes civil servants who were transferred 'off books' to Crown Entities or State-Owned Enterprises).

Unlike many other countries, New Zealand governments have commissioned at least two broad-scope evaluations of the reforms (Schick 1996; Steering Group 1991). Both came to positive conclusions, while identifying some areas of continuing concern. The Steering Group believed that '[i]n the view of most people we spoke to or heard from, the framework is sound and substantial benefits are being realized' (Steering Group 1991, p. 11). Allen Schick, the American expert, concluded that 'the reforms have lived up to most of the lofty expectations held for them' (Schick 1996, executive summary). Major productivity and quality improvements have been won in the state trading sector. The range of policy advice to ministers seems to have broadened. There is much greater flexibility of employment, and operational managers wield genuinely decentralized powers. There is much more performance information in the public domain (Boston et al. 1996, pp. 359–61).

Less positive results include:

- The costs of reform have not been closely estimated but seem very likely to be high. These include extensive disruption, loss of continuity, and 'institutional memory'.

- A greater focus on outputs has been achieved, but sometimes at the expense of some loss of attention to *outcomes* (see State Services Commission 2001, 2002).

- The accountability and monitoring arrangements for the somewhat diverse Crown Entity category of institutions are unclear.

- It seems that there has been a gradual erosion of both the financial and the human resources of government departments (Newberry 2002).

Country file events: New Zealand

	General	Organization	Personnel	Finance
1981–5	– Muldoon: PM (NP) (1975) – Lange: PM (Lib.) (1984) – Start departmental restructuring (1985)	– Establishment of new population-based ministries (Women's Affairs, Youth Affairs, Pacific Island Affairs) (1985)	– Start equal employment initiatives (1985)	– User-pays principle introduced for many state services (1985)
1986–90	– State-Owned Enterprises (SOEs) Act (1986) – Intention to reform local government system (1987) – State Sector Act (SSA) (1988) – SSA: autonomy, accountability, service to community, integrity, state as good employer (1988) – Palmer: PM (Lib.) (1989) – Amend SSA: include education, other state services, restructured SSC (1989) – Moore: PM (Lib.) (1990) – Bolger: PM (NP) (1990)	– SOE: separating trading activities from administrative and regulatory ones (1986) – Corporatization of trading activities in SOEs (1987) – Restructuring government departments: separate policy advice—operational functions (agriculture, labour, justice, social welfare) (1987) – Separate policy advice from regulatory, review, and monitoring (education, transport) (1987) – Privatization: government assets, trading activities (1988) – Local government: from 600 (more than 700: Boston) to 94; abolition of most special purpose authorities (1989) – Corporatization of Local Authority Trading Enterprises (LATEs) (1989) – PM's Office and Cabinet Office: new structure to improve coordination and quality of advice (1989)	– SSA: devolve personnel management to chief executive (1988) – Establishment of Senior Executive Service (SES) (1988) – Annual performance agreements between CEs and ministers (1988) – SSA: major changes in industrial relations and wage-fixing (1988) – State Services Commission (SSC): restructured to focus more ministers (1989) – SSC: 'Public Service Code of Conduct': minimum standards of integrity and conduct (1990)	– SSA: devolve financial management to chief executive (1988) – Announce new budget cycle, performance agreements (1988) – Public Finance Act (PFA) (1989) – PFA: output/outcome; owner/purchaser; modes of appropriation (accrual vs. revolving funds) (1989) – Comprehensive Bill: reform resource management and allocate responsibility for implementation (1989) – All core public sector bodies move to new financial management system: outputs specified and agreed, operating full accruals-accounting, cash arrangement system, new financial reporting (1990)
1991–5	– Logan Review of State Sector Reforms (1991): accountability and collective interest; departmental performance, cost/benefit of reporting and audit requirements, quality of senior management	– PM and Cabinet: adjust for policy coordination and PP task forces (1991) – Establishment of 10 Crown Research Institutes (1991) – Sale of shares in airports, port companies, and local utilities (1991)	– Employment Contracts Act (ECA) (1991) – ECA: new legal and institutional arrangements for private and public sector industrial relations; SSC for core state sector; delegation of bargaining authority (1991)	– Introduce capital charges to reflect cost of capital used by departments in price of outputs (1991) – Part (user) charges in health (1992) – Legislation identifies uniform accountability and financial reporting structure (1992)

– IT in tax and social welfare (1991) – Various ministerial task forces to develop more competitive mechanisms for service delivery (1992) – Referendum to move to proportional system (1993) – 'The Next Three Years' (1994) – Reinforcing the 'collective interests': government's Strategic Results Areas (SRAs) (1994) – SRA reflected in departments: Key Results Areas (KRAs) (1994) – Guidance issued on public service principles, conventions, practices (1995) – 'Investing in Our Future' (1995)	– Crown Research Institutes, Crown Health Enterprises, Regional Health Authorities, new (commercial) organizational forms used in social services (hospitals, housing, and transport, etc.) (1992) – Establishment of 23 Crown Health Enterprises (1993) – Privatizations: Government Computing Services Ltd, Prime Rate Housing Corporation (1994) – New Fishery Department (separate policy from management, research in Crown entity) (1995) – Restructuring of Department of Justice separating policy from implementation, clarity of organizational purpose (1995)	– Review government pension scheme (1991) – More individual contracts than collective arrangements (1991) – Union bargaining rights contestable (1991) – SSC collaborates with chief executives to develop guidelines and codes of ethics (1992) – Public Sector Training Organization (detect needs and provide or coordinate training) (1995)	– Financial statements include Crown-owned and core bodies (1993) – Separate purchase from performance agreements (1993) – Fiscal Responsibility Act (FRA) (1994): responsible fiscal management and strengthening reporting requirements of the Crown – Estimates vs. DFRs (Departmental Forecast Reports) (1994) – DFR: reflect producer/capital user orientation; forward-looking versions of annual reports; 'Vote Minister's' purchase expectations vs. 'Responsible Minister's' ownership interest (1994)
1996–2000 – 'The Spirit of Reform' (Schick Review) (1996) – Major review of management framework: structure, organizational capacity, managing public money, accounting for results (1996) – First election under proportional electoral system (1996) – Standing orders for operation of House of Representatives (1996) – Local Government Act (1996) (transparency and accountability) – Shipley: PM (NP) (1997) – Improving the quality of policy advice (1999) – Clark: PM (Lab.) (1999) – The State Services Commission's role as ownership adviser to the government is formalized (1999)	– Merger of four Regional Health Authorities (RHAs) into one Health Funding Authority (1996) – The Ministry of Culture and Heritage was formed (1999) – Reform of the Accident Compensation Corporation (1999) – Strategic Results Area Networks for better policy coordination and political accountability (1999) – Crown Entities Bill (2000)	– Management Development Centre: cater to needs of public sector managers (1996) – Equal Employment Opportunities Policy (1997) – Employment Relations Acts (2000) that determines the status ('employee of the state sector') of the Crown Entities Employees	– House: changes in annual financial cycle (1996) – Compliance Cost Assessment Framework: Compliance Cost Statement; Compliance Cost Assessment Report (1996) – Strategic Results Area Networks for better performance and budget integration (1999) – Departments develop Strategic Business Plans (2000)

continues

continued

	General	Organization	Personnel	Finance
	– Capability, accountability, and performance (CAP) pilots (1999) – New SRAs (1997–2000) – Cabinet approved an e-government vision statement and massive investments in e-government policy and initiatives (2000) – Reform of the strategic system (SRA/KRA) by the introduction of Strategic Results Area Networks, the replacement of the SRA by Strategic Priorities and Overarching Goals (1999), and the Pathfinder project (2000)			– Public Audit Act (2001) – Statement of intent: new accountability system (2001) – Managing for Outcomes: integrating outcome information in the output-oriented management information systems (2002)
2001–2	– The New Government, and in particular the Minister of State Services and the PM, have pledged to reinvigorate the state sector (2001) – Statement of intent (2001) – Three important developments in the roles of central agencies: focus on the State Services Commission, an enhanced role for the Ministry of Maori Development, and Crown Entity Reform (2001) – Agreement in principle to changes in the accountability and reporting systems (2001)	– The Department of Work and Income was created (2001) – The Ministry of Social Development was formed from the policy arms of the former Department of Social Welfare and the Ministry of Housing (2001) – The Department of Child, Youth, and Family Services was reformed (2001) – Establishment of an e-government unit within the State Services Commission (2001) – State Services Commission Review at Centre (2001)	– Training programme for senior public servants (2001) – Senior leadership and development initiative (2002)	

SWEDEN

A. Socio-economic forces: general

See Appendix A.

B. Global economic forces

Sweden is a small country with a fairly open economy. For economic details, see Appendix A, especially Table A.1.

C. Sociodemographic issues

According to political scientists Lane and Ersson (1991, chapter 2), who surveyed data on a number of social cleavages, Sweden was among the most homogenous, least socially and/or ethnically divided countries in Western Europe. Nevertheless, it has experienced the same difficulties of an ageing population and increasing rates of family breakup as most other Western European and North American states. In the late 1980s and early 1990s, the growth in the elderly population was particularly fast (see Figure A.2 and Section A.3 generally). Also, rapid immigration for the last decade or more is beginning to lessen the homogeneity.

D. National socio-economic policies

Throughout the period under study Sweden maintained the largest (as a proportion of GDP) public sector in the western world. It built and has maintained one of the world's most generous and egalitarian welfare states (Esping-Andersen 1990). This was already giving rise to fiscal problems in

the late 1970s, and the budget deficit peaked at 13 per cent of GDP in 1982. Although the budget moved briefly into surplus in 1987, Sweden subsequently experienced a further—and spectacular—deterioration in its budget balance. Some expert commentators began to see this as a virtually insoluble problem within the existing political and administrative system (Lane 1995). Certainly, the late 1980s and early 1990s were a particularly difficult time (see Table B.3).

A Conservative government came to power in 1991, and the early and mid-1990s were dominated by the acute necessity of making cuts and efficiency savings. However, by the late 1990s, budget balance had been restored (OECD 1998). Nevertheless, Sweden continues to experience a difficult economic situation, as a small but open economy, sustaining the largest public sector in Western Europe.

E. The political system

Sweden is a unitary, but highly decentralized state. It has had a constitutional monarch since 1866, but the monarch's role is almost exclusively ceremonial. Executive power rests with the Prime Minister and the Cabinet (*Regering*). Most important decisions are made collectively, not by individual ministers. The legislature (*Riksdag*) is a unicameral body with 349 seats. Part of its work goes on in a relatively nonpartisan spirit unlike, say, the UK House of Commons or the Australian Parliament. Nevertheless, the significance of party is pervasive. The process of forming a government is initiated by the Speaker of the *Riksdag* (who

Table B.3 Swedish economic growth, 1970–93(%)

	1970–7	1978–86	1987–93
Sweden	1.7	2.1	0.1
OECD Europe	2.5	2.0	2.3
All OECD	3.8	2.5	2.3

Source: Adapted from Lane, 1995, p. 580, based on OECD data.

plays a nonpartisan role). She or he nominates a candidate for prime minister, but if more than 50 per cent of the members vote against, then another name must be put forward.

Elections to the *Riksdag* and to local governments take place every four years under a system of proportional representation. However, since the 1970s:

Not only has power been transferred from the *Riksdag* to the Cabinet, but public power appears to have become more diffused among several groups of actors, among which may be mentioned various bureaucracies that have grown from the exceptional expansion of the Swedish public sector, different organised interests, regional and local groups of actors. (Lane and Ersson 1991, p. 262)

Since the 1920s, the Social Democratic Party has become the 'establishment' party in Sweden. It was continuously in government (often in coalition with smaller parties) from 1932 to 1976. Lane and Ersson (1991, p. 262) write:

The strong position of the Social Democratic Party in state and society opened the way for the participation of organised interests in policy-making, exercising influence at various stages of the policy process. The major interest organisations include: the LO (*Landsorganisationen*), the TCO (white collar workers), the SACO-SR (academics), the SAF (employers' association) and the LRF (farmers' association).

F. New management ideas

The new management ideas that were circulating so vigorously in the Anglo-Saxon world during the 1980s and 1990s also reached Sweden. The Swedish system is a very 'open' one, in the sense that Swedish officials and academics play an active role in many international fora (probably disproportionately so for a country of Sweden's modest population), and most educated Swedes can speak English. However, the Swedish governing elite did not embrace fashionable management ideas as enthusiastically as did their counterparts in some other countries. 'Marketization' ideas, although briefly in official favour from 1991 to 1994, never achieved the penetration that they enjoyed in New Zealand and the UK during the 1980s. Other new management concepts were more readily assimilated—for example, TQM was quite widely adopted in various forms. Performance management and Management by Objectives (MbO), based on a shift from an orientation to input and procedural controls to a system based on the achievement of measured results, became a central philosophy of the public management reforms from the late 1980s onwards.

G. Pressure from citizens

According to Premfors (1998), Swedish public attitudes towards their governments have been quite fickle. For example, the public sector, together with the Social Democrat leadership, fell rapidly from favour in the late 1980s and early 1990s, but as soon as in 1992 there were signs that confidence in public sector institutions was increasing, and that the electorate feared any radical dismantling of the generous Swedish welfare state. In general it might be said that, during the period under consideration, most Swedes were impatient of the more bureaucratic aspects of the large government machine, but were protective of most of their welfare provisions, and were certainly not enamoured of the kind of 'new right', pro-market doctrines that were fashionable in the UK and the USA during the 1980s.

H. Party political ideas

Premfors (1991) explains the internal political debate during the first half of the 1980s as a struggle between three camps—the decentralists, the traditionalists, and the economizers. The 1985 programme favoured decentralist ideas (which were also a means of off-loading fiscal responsibilities) but, quite quickly thereafter, the minister most concerned was heavily criticized on the grounds that he was more talk than action. In any case, by the late 1980s, with a fiscal crisis fully in process, decentralization and participation tended to seem less pressing than cutting expenditures. The economizers took over as the dominant group. Management by results became one of the most salient themes in administrative reform.

At the 1991 elections Sweden acquired its first Conservative Prime Minister since 1930. Neoliberal ideas such as privatization and market-testing, extensively borrowed from New Zealand and the UK, were now in favour among the political elite (Premfors 1998, pp. 151–2). However, this was a relatively brief phase, and when the Social Democrats were voted back into power in September 1994 the 'reform talk' soon lost its high emphasis on the power of markets to solve problems. The stress on economy and efficiency continues, as budget problems are too deep to be solved overnight.

I. Chance events

None of particular prominence.

J. Elite decision-making

One Swedish expert has suggested that, during the period covered by this study, there were three main schools of thought and opinion as to how the Swedish government should respond to its problems (Premfors 1991—see Section H). Decentralizers wanted to relax the detailed grip of the central state, and push out both operational management decisions and some increasingly uncomfortable resource allocation decisions to other levels of government, and even down to individual institutions, such as schools and hospitals. Economizers were mainly concerned with the looming deficit, and the inbuilt tendencies for welfare expenditure to expand. They sought to weaken the 'distributional coalitions' in Swedish policy-making. Traditionalists concentrated on preserving as much as they could of both the substance and the process of the Swedish state, as it had existed during its 'golden age' in the 1960s and early 1970s. From the late 1980s the economizers appeared to gain the upper hand, but Premfors (1998) suggests that, by the late 1990s, the decentralizers were once more gaining ground.

Issues of feasibility are usually determined partly by the strongly entrenched *process* by which government decisions are arrived at in Sweden. Typically, agencies plan with the aid of boards on which trade unions, employers' associations, and other interest groups are strongly represented. Thus, feasibility questions are soon aired with those who will have to 'live' with any proposed reform, unlike the policy-making systems in, for example, the UK and New Zealand, where some reforms were conceived and promulgated by quite small groups of politicians and senior officials. The consensualist and corporatist ways of doing things remain strong in Sweden.

K. The administrative system

As of 1994 only 17.3 per cent of public servants worked for central government (compared to 48.7% in France and 47.7% in the UK—see Table 3.2). This reflects the importance of the county and municipal levels in the Swedish administrative system. There are twenty-three counties and 289 municipalities. The counties are responsible for most health care and are entitled to raise an income tax. Municipalities are responsible for housing, education, and social welfare.

Central government is also fairly decentralized by international standards, and has long been so. Swedish central government agencies have their operational autonomy protected by the constitution, and are responsible to the Cabinet collectively, not to individual ministers. There are over 200 of them, and at the end of the 1990s they employed over 200,000 staff (compared to the ministries, which employed fewer than 4,000). Thus, the ministries themselves tend to be small and largely devoted to policy advice and the preparation of legislation. Doubts have frequently been expressed concerning their capacity to guide or control the agencies (Molander et al. 2002; OECD 1997a, p. 94, 1998; Wilks 1996).

The Swedish civil service is nonpartisan, and minister/mandarin career paths are normally separate (see Table 3.1). The culture has been one of meritocracy and neutral competence. However, the top three officials in ministries—the undersecretary of state, the permanent secretary, and the under-secretary of legal affairs—are appointed by the minister. It is also said that senior appointments to the powerful agencies (which are responsible for most implementation activities) have tended to become more party-political in recent years (Molander et al. 2002).

Policy-making is typically an open process, with extensive participation by experts and interested groups. Commissions play an important role in preparing new policies. Freedom of information legislation gives the public access to almost all official papers, including most of the prime minister's correspondence.

L. Contents of the reform package

Following its 1976 ousting from government, the Social Democratic Party rethought its policies. One factor in their defeat appeared to be the way in which many people associated it, as the 'establishment' party, with bureaucratic inertia. When the Social Democrats returned to power in 1982, they were therefore determined to change their image in this respect, and to make the state machine more responsive and accessible to the ordinary citizen. They created a Ministry of Public Administration as a symbol of their reforming intent. In 1985 a Government Modernization Programme laid considerable stress on decentralization from the centre to counties and municipalities.

Increased choice and user-responsiveness were also emphasized. Deregulation and debureaucratization were further themes. Personnel authority was decentralized, so that agencies could now hire their own staff and set their own salary ranges, within national frameworks. At that stage privatization was not favoured. As one senior civil servant put it in 1987:

The Swedish government in principle rejects privatisation as a means of solving the problems of the [public] sector. The main objection is that this would lead to distributive injustices. (Gustaffson 1987, p. 180)

In the late 1980s a second phase of reform began, overshadowed by the growing fiscal crisis. The need to make efficiency gains and savings was paramount. In 1990 an Administration Programme was announced which aimed to generate a 10 per cent reduction in the size of the public sector. This was supposed to be achieved through a combination of measures: abolishing or merging agencies, increased delegation, and various productivity improvement initiatives. The focus on economy intensified with the arrival of a conservative (Bildt) government in 1991. At this point there was considerable rhetoric in favour of privatization, but in practice the government soon had to compromise on its original and quite extensive privatization schemes. In any case, the Social Democrats returned to power in 1994, though by that time they had abandoned their opposition in principle to privatization and were prepared to accept it on a selective and pragmatic basis. Between 1990 and 1996, thirteen agencies did become public companies (the Swedes, like the Finns, tended to prefer a combination of the corporate format with state ownership rather than outright privatization like New Zealand and the UK). During the 1990s there was a good deal of thinking about what principles should govern each of the main types of organizations in the Swedish public sector—legal and regulatory agencies, agencies providing public services, state enterprises, state companies, and so on.

From 1988 to 1993 a series of strong financial management reforms were implemented, including results-oriented budgeting, frame appropriations, and accruals-accounting. Results-oriented management was officially adopted for all state organizations from 1988. The rise of this form of output- and outcome-oriented approach was accompanied by a parallel decline in the previously

formidable machinery of Swedish planning (Wilks 1996). Since 1993 each agency has been required to publish an annual report which includes performance data, an income statement, a balance sheet, an appropriation account, and a financial analysis (OECD 1997a, p. 90). In 1996 the budget process itself was reformed, with a better-defined first stage to the process in which firm ceilings to overall expenditure were fixed (OECD 1998). On into the twenty-first century, further budget modernization remained a central plank of Swedish reform efforts. Proposals emerging from the VESTA workgroup aimed at putting central government and the national accounts on the same performance-oriented, accruals-accounted basis as the agencies (Gustafsson 2000). A new management philosophy, which is being gradually phased in as a replacement to management by results, is management focused on activities or *verksamhetsstyrning*. The new model draws on a huge number of PIs and could thus be seen as a path-dependent continuation of previous management reforms.

Limiting public expenditure was never off the agenda. In 1993 a new system of central government grants to the municipalities strengthened the latter's autonomy (fewer detailed regulations from the centre) but also permitted central government to fix tight frame budgets and leave the local authorities to sort out how they would allocate their circumscribed allocations.

Over the whole period from the mid-1980s, a variety of service quality improvement schemes were adopted, often based on TQM or ISO 9000 principles. These were implemented at all levels of government but there was no central plan or framework equivalent to, say, the UK *Citizen's Charter* (OECD 1997a, p. 91). There was, however, a Swedish Institute for Quality (SIQ) model which has been quite widely adopted in the public sector, and the EFQM model has also been used.

M. The implementation process

Sweden has tended to avoid the sometimes strident or harsh styles of implementation favoured by Thatcher's administration in the UK, Lange's in New Zealand, or Howard's in Australia. The traditional Swedish processes of intensive, corporatist discussions between the main interested parties prior to action have, with a few exceptions, persisted. However, the employers' association, SAF, walked out of the agency boards in the early 1990s, which has meant a significant blow to the corporatist arrangements. Informal discussions are important, not only in the evolution of new policies, but also in the continuous steering of agencies (Pierre 2003). As in Finland, extensive use has been made of pilot projects to test out key innovations (e.g. results-oriented budgeting) before they were 'rolled out' to the government more generally. An example would be the 1984 'Free municipalities' experiment, in which nine municipalities and three county councils piloted a system of greater freedom from central state regulation. Strenuous efforts were also made to minimize compulsory redundancies among public servants.

N. Reforms actually achieved

There is no doubt that substantial decentralization of powers to counties and municipalities was achieved during the 1980s and 1990s. It is also clear that budgeting systems have been extensively modernized, and that a much more output-oriented set of arrangements has been firmly put in place since the late 1980s. Productivity studies, after showing a large overall deterioration in public sector productivity during the 1970s, and a smaller one even during the 1980s,

indicated a productivity gain for the early 1990s (see discussion in Chapter 5).

Sweden has developed a strong interest in evaluation and a variety of evaluation bodies. The NAO (RRV) has an extensive role in evaluation and performance-auditing, and has taken an interest in a number of public management reforms (Pollitt et al. 1999). There is also an Expert Group on Public Finance, which has conducted large-scale studies of public productivity, and a Swedish Agency for Administrative Development. Despite the existence of these units, no overall evaluation of the main reforms appears to have been undertaken.

Against these substantial achievements must be set the continuing concern that the central ministries lack the capability to set a really well-informed yet demanding set of performance targets for the agencies (Molander et al. 2002; OECD 1997a, 1998). Furthermore, it is by no means clear that the members of the *Riksdag* are overwhelmingly interested in making use of the increased flow of performance data that is now available. Finally, and most importantly, it is too soon to be confident that the underlying problem of chronic budget deficit has been definitively solved.

Country file events: Sweden

	General	Organization	Personnel	Finance
1981–5	– Fälldin: PM (Agrar., Lib.) (1979) – MoF: Independent Expert Group on Public Finance (ESO) (1981) – Palme: PM (Soc.) (1982) – Palme: PM (Soc.) (1985)			– Experiment: 3-year budget frames (administrative expenditures) (1985)
1986–90	– Carlsson: PM (Soc.) (1986) – Parliamentary Decision on Public Management (1987) – Government Agency Ordinance: guidelines for administrative reform (1987) – Carlsson: PM (Soc.) (1988) – Free Municipal Experiment: increasing autonomy, restructuring central, regional, municipal relations (1988) – Administration: slim down by 10%: decentralization, deregulation, internationalization (1990) – Expanded survey of regulatory impact (1990) – Number of laws and ordinances in force: lowest level: result of regulatory review and computerization (1990) – New Local Government Act: clearer powers, financial management reforms, more importance for accounting and auditing, freer committee structure (1990)	– New instructions for 200 agencies: decentralization, results, long-term objectives, increased autonomy, discretionary authority for managers (1988) – Ministry of Public Administration: reorganization, re-enforcement, leader of renewal process (1988)	– Act delegating employment responsibilities to agency directors (1988) – More flexibility: recruitment, mobility of senior executives (1988) – Study on pay scales, remuneration (1988) – Public Employment Act modernized (1988)	– Supplementary Budget Bill: 3-year budget frames (1988) – Results-based management: measurement, accounting, budget cycles (request and *regleringsbrev*) (1988) – In-depth budget requests: analyses of resources, environment, results (minus 2 years) (1988) – Methodology for determining costs of regulations refined (1988) – Government Budget Ordinance (goals and results) (1988) – Supplementary Budget Bill: guidelines for public sector renewal (1988) – Ongoing reorganization of budget process: specify results (1990)
1991–5	– Bildt: PM (Cons.) (1991) – Management by results: emphasis on analysis and evaluation (1991) – Budget Bill Annex: report on progress with rule simplification (1991) – Deregulation efforts speeded up: over 1,000 agency regulations abolished (1991) – Local Authority Act: free to structure activities, promote deregulation, privatization, market orientation (1991) – Economic Policy Statement: budget deficit reduction (1992)	– MoF: responsible for central matters of public administration (1991) – Ministry of Public Administration: regional and local authorities; rest is transferred to MoF, Agency for Administrative Development, National Audit Bureau, National Agency for Government Employers (1991) – Cabinet Office: Political Coordination Chancery (1991) – Privatization of certain state-owned enterprises (1991)	– Comprehensive Job Security System (1991) – Job Security Foundation (1991) – Pension system similar to private sector (1991) – New classification system for civil service wage and salary statistics (1991) – Each agency responsible for training and development (1992) – State and Employee Organization report: unions should pay for help received in negotiations (1992)	– Review of budget process (1992) – National Audit Bureau Commission: rating system to evaluate the capacity of agencies (1992) – Flexible budget frame periods introduced (1992) – Agencies deliver 1st annual financial report directly to government (audited by National Audit Bureau): balance sheet, income statement, appropriation report, changes in financial position, performance report (1992) – Agencies pay interests on drawings on the state budget (1993)

Period				
	– Criteria to determine when State Company is suitable for privatization, transformation, closure (1992) – Decrease structural deficit (1993) – Criteria for corporatization of state activities (1993) – Management by results proceeds (1993) – Carlsson: PM (Soc.) (1994) – Commission on Administrative Policy (1995)	– Ordinances for all agencies: clearer goals and results control (1992) – Reorganize Government Chancery, framework budget (1992) – Dissolve National Institute for Civil Service Training and Development (SIPU) (1992) – Abolish Postal Giro's monopoly of state payments (1993) – Selling 49% of shares of forest industry (1994). They were bought back in 2001.	– Programme of training in financial management (1992) – New Organization for State Employers controlled and financed by government agencies (1994)	– Agencies: borrow money for investments, risk analysis (1993) – Changes in financial control of agencies: new accruals-accounting model, technique of frame appropriation, interest accounts, loan model for investments in fixed assets (1993) – Ordinance on Internal Audit of Government Agencies (1994) – Booster project: 10 ministries and 10 agencies (1995)
1996–2000	– Persson: PM (Soc. Dem.) (1996) – *Riksdag* resolution on implementing expenditure ceiling (1995) – VESTA: integrated, consolidated system for central government forecasting, budgeting, consolidated accounting, performance monitoring, and payment information by 2000 (1997) – Central Government Administration in the Citizen's Service: Government Bill (1997–8) – Improvement of administration emphasis on concentration, quality and skill development, performance, effective provision of information and services (2000) – Government adopted action plan and set guidelines and general directions of public management reforms (2000) – Parliament resolution on Government Bill: An Information Society for All (2000) – Government e-link project for a better information exchange between administrations and between the administration and the public service users (2000)	– Further corporatization of various state activities (1996–) – Establishment of the National Financial Management Authority (1998) – Establishment of the National Council for Quality and Development (1999) – A special unit within the Ministry of Industry, Employment, and Communication was established to monitor the new system for impact of analysis of the effects of rules for small businesses (1999) – A special committee for the promotion of democracy has been established (2000) – A commission concerning information and the principle of public access to official records to stimulate openness and transparency (2000)		– Budget year coincides with calendar year (1997) – 260 agencies: performance follow-up reports (1998) – Establishment of the National Financial Management Authority (1998) – Performance-Budgeting Project (VESTA): from accruals-accounting to accruals-budgeting within an activity-based structure: Present the central government budget in terms of revenues and costs, incoming and outgoing payments, assets and liabilities (2000) Propose the costs of central government activities (2000) Management of individual agencies and their specialized activities shall be adapted to each activity (2000)
2001–2	– Citizens are entitled to central government administration as a high quality (2001) – Sweden's chairmanship of the EU Council of Ministers (2001) – Persson: PM (Soc. Dem.) (2002)	– The Top Leader's Forum (Toppledar Forum) has been removed and replaced by the Statens e-Forum (2001)		– High skills on the part of the public servants. Impose new requirements on public servants in terms of both technology and new work procedures (2001)

UNITED KINGDOM

A. Socio-economic forces: general

See Appendix A.2.

B. Global economic forces

See Appendix A.2.

C. Sociodemographic issues

See Appendix A.3.

D. National socio-economic policies

The advent of Thatcher's Conservative government in 1979 marked the final abandonment of Keynesian policies of macroeconomic management and the beginning of an era of vigorous monetarism. The general view was that the Public Sector Borrowing Requirement (PSBR) was a key variable that a responsible government should seek to minimize. This, in turn, implied a tight fiscal policy. So did the government's continuing determination to control inflation (which had reached frighteningly high levels during the 1970s and which was still running faster than that of most of the UK's main economic competitors). Thus the Conservative governments were committed to reducing the proportion of GDP that was represented by public spending. In practice, however, they were not tremendously successful at first (see Thain and Wright 1995 for the details). Public sector borrowing fluctuated widely during the period of Conservative rule. In the beginning it had been 5 per cent of GDP. In 1987/88 it had fallen to −0.5 per cent (i.e. there was a surplus), but by 1993/94 it was up to 7.3 per cent.

The incoming 1997 Labour government inherited a fairly healthy economic situation, but committed itself to maintaining the previous government's tough spending plans for at least two years. However, it introduced important new principles and procedures for public expenditure planning and control, including periodic 'comprehensive spending reviews' (the first of these came in 1998, the second in 2000—see Chancellor of the Exchequer 1998). The 2000 review resulted in substantial increases in spending on health care and education.

E. The political system

The UK is a unitary and highly centralized state. The political system is majoritarian and adversarial, with a first-past-the-post electoral basis. There are two major parties (Conservative, Labour) and a number of minor parties, the most important of which is the Liberal Democrat party. All governments since the Second World War have been Labour or Conservative. The Cabinet is mainly concerned with enforcing collective responsibility among ministers and endorsing new policies. Most policies, however, are developed outside the Cabinet, in departments or cabinet committees. The executive is powerful, reinforced by tight party discipline in the Lower House of the legislature (the Commons). In normal times it can almost always get its legislation through. The Upper House, a mixture of a heridtary aristocracy and appointed 'life peers', is, at the time of writing, undergoing major reform to remove the hereditary element. Despite five years of debate there is both confusion and disagreement about what the relative proportions of elected and appointed members should be. In any case the Upper House basically only has the power to delay, not to reject, government legislation.

Another important constitutional change has been the creation of separate parliaments/assemblies for Scotland and Wales. The significance of these for public administration is still unfolding but there is certainly some effect—for example, the national forestry agency being broken up into separate English, Scottish, and Welsh bodies.

F. New management ideas

The UK has been very much part of the anglophone, US-dominated world of managerialism, management consultants, and management gurus (Pollitt 1993, chapters 1 and 2). The Conservative governments of 1979–97 were particularly open to generic management thinking, and to ideas injected into government by the private sector. Thatcher's first efficiency adviser, Derek Rayner, was a businessman, and many other managers were subsequently brought into government in various advisory capacities (Metcalfe and Richards 1990). The succeeding Labour administration has continued to use high-profile business people for important public roles (e.g. reviewing the *Citizen's Charter* initiative).

G. Pressure from citizens

There was no single, citizen-inspired movement for reform. Management changes came from political, business, and administrative elites. Nevertheless, public opinion played a part. The popularity of early measures of privatization (selling public housing to the tenants, issuing shares for British Telecom) helped convince the government that this was a policy that could be pursued much further. The public was also receptive to the government's message that the quality of public services should be raised although, ironically, the 1991 *Citizen's Charter* was launched very much as a top-down exercise, with little consultation of public opinion (Prime Minister 1991). The general 'decline of deference' was also a significant background influence on a number of user-oriented reforms.

During the New Labour administrations after 1997, public opinion tended to focus on the performance of the major welfare state services, health care, and education. The government made these its top domestic priorities, and substantially increased expenditure in both sectors. Results, however, were slow in coming and, at the time of writing, it was far from clear whether the government would achieve most of its performance targets in these sectors and, even to the extent that they did so, whether the public would believe that services really were improved.

H. Party political ideas

The decisive shift towards managerialism came in 1979, when a neoconservative government was elected in place of a centre–left administration (see also Canada and the USA—but note that managerialist reforms in Australia and New Zealand were launched principally by centre–left parties, see Castles et al. 1996). However, that is not to say that at the beginning Conservative politicians necessarily had very precise ideas about management reform. Rather it was a case of certain broad beliefs and doctrines that inclined the government in a particular direction. Among these were beliefs that the private sector was inherently more efficient than the public sector, that the civil service was too privileged and complacent, and that the state was too big and too interventionist

(Pollitt 1993). However, ideas evolved during the long period of office.

The New Labour government that took over from 1997 contained many traditional supporters of public services. Party policy stressed 'partnerships', 'modernization', and (later) 'joined-up government' rather than private sector solutions. The internal market mechanisms in the NHS were much disliked, and were partly dismantled, as was the compulsoriness of contracting-out local services. Nevertheless, behind these surface shifts away from marketization, many elements of NPM thinking continued—not least performance measurement, which was further intensified. More generally, the Blair government's early identification with a 'third way' in politics translated into a 'third way' in public administration also— more public–private partnerships, extension of the Private Finance Initiative, more benchmarking, and so on.

I. Chance events

There are none which stand out as having an immediate, large, and direct effect of management reform (unless one counts the Falklands War as a chance, with its tonic effect on the Conservative government's electoral ratings and subsequent success in the 1983 general election—though even this would have to be seen as an indirect influence).

On the other hand there have been particular events in particular organizations or sectors which have had significant local influences. Examples would include a series of tragic failures in child protection (which obliged governments to address the reform of social services departments) and the behaviour of certain left-wing local councils, which provided central government (under Thatcher) with one of its pretexts for abolishing certain large, urban councils and instituting various additional controls on the remainder (Cochrane 1993). Under New Labour a series of fatal train accidents led directly to a reconsideration of the organizational arrangements for the privatized railway system and some strengthening of the public presence on the regulating body. The NHS continued under Labour, as under the Conservatives, to supply the media with a steady trickle of tragic and unfortunate episodes which were inevitably used as political ammunition in the ongoing struggle to reform that huge and complex set of organizations.

J. Elite decision-making

The boldness of Thatcher's Conservative government grew as its political confidence was boosted by the election victories of 1983 and 1987. By the late 1980s some members of the Cabinet, probably including Thatcher herself, perceived the possibility of a mixture of marketizing and minimizing, that is, the return of many hitherto public functions and activities to the private sector combined with the introduction of MTMs to much of the remaining, 'rump' public sector. This general orientation continued into the Major administration (1990–7), as evidenced by the further privatizations of the railways and British Coal, the selling-off of some Next Steps executive agencies and the expansion of the Private Finance Initiative. The aspirations of the incoming Labour government of 1997 were different, but not enormously so. The urge to privatize disappeared, but there was no countervailing desire to take organizations or functions back into public ownership. The Private Finance Initiative was retained and expanded. Even if the tone was more sympathetic to public sector staff, the general belief in the scope for improving public management and providing more efficient and high quality services persisted.

The unusual dominance of a single party form of executive within the British system gives governments an equally unusual ability to realize their reform desires, even when these are controversial in Parliament or unpopular in the country (e.g. the 1989 reform of the NHS was hugely unpopular, both among NHS staff and the wider public, but the 'provider market' was forced through all the same; see Pollitt et al. 1998). It is clear that, since 1979, governments of both major parties have regarded continuing and deep administrative change as perfectly feasible. In the UK the barriers to (and political costs of) this kind of reform are considerably lower than in many other countries. However, while reforms can be forced through again and again, the consequences for those who run public services can easily become negative. By the time New Labour won its second election in 2001, there were signs of 'reform fatigue' and 'measurement fatigue' in several major public services.

K. The administrative system

The permanent civil service is still the main source of advice and support for ministers, though it is almost certainly less dominant in this role than it was thirty years ago, and the use of substantial numbers of partisan political advisers is now firmly entrenched. The civil service is neutral in party political terms, right up to the most senior level (permanent secretary). The culture of the upper civil service is generalist (and nonlegalist). The single most important constitutional doctrine for senior civil servants remains that of 'ministerial responsibility', which means that ministers must answer to the House of Commons for all the doings of their ministries, and that civil servants normally remain anonymous but have a prime duty to support and protect 'their' minister. Therefore, civil servants are *not* held to have any higher duty towards 'the State' (a concept not much in use), the legislature, or the citizenry.

Central government is organized into departments, most of which are headed by a Cabinet minister. The majority of civil servants now work in semi-autonomous executive agencies, which are still, constitutionally, part of their 'parent' departments (O'Toole and Jordan 1995; Pollitt and Talbot 2003).

Local government is less protected from central government interventions than in most other European states. The period of Conservative government from 1979 to 1997 was one of considerable tension between the centre and local authorities. Central government passed many new pieces of legislation restricting the discretion of local authorities (especially in relation to finance) and gave many functions to local quangos and other non-elected bodies (Cochrane 1993; Painter et al. 1996; Stoker 1988). Relations between central and local government were easier after the New Labour government came to power in 1997, but the habit of close central regulation and supervision of local authorities has continued.

L. Contents of the reform package

With the advantage of hindsight, the period of Conservative government could be said to have three broad phases of development in respect to management reform. From 1979 until 1982/83 there was a fierce drive for economies and the elimination of waste. Civil service numbers were cut, first by 14 per cent and then, subsequently, by a further 6 per cent. Rayner scrutinies (see Metcalfe and Richards 1990) sought to find more efficient ways of undertaking tasks, and usually concluded that staffing reductions were possible.

In the early 1980s, however, the emphasis shifted to improving financial and general management, and increasing efficiency. The Financial Management Initiative was launched in 1982 and embraced the whole of central government with its philosophy of more decentralized management, more decentralized budgets, more targets, and more professionalism (Zifcak 1994). The NAO and Audit Commission were brought into being (the relevant legislation being passed in 1983 and 1982 respectively), and each was given a mandate that stressed the 'three Es'—economy, efficiency, and effectiveness. In the NHS, central government insisted on the introduction of general managers to every health authority (Harrison et al. 1992). PI systems began to sprout for most public services, central and local (Pollitt 1986).

During the mid-1980s the privatization programme gathered momentum, with the sales of British Telecom (1984), British Gas (1986), the British Airports Authority (1987), and water supply and sewerage (1989). Between 1979 and 1990 about 800,000 employees were transferred from the public sector to the private.

The third phase of Conservative reform was the most radical. Following their convincing victory in the 1987 election, Thatcher's administration launched a series of fundamental restructurings. MTMs were introduced on a large scale—in health care, community care, and education. The 'purchaser/provider split' was imposed by central government as a basic model for most locally provided services (Pollitt et al. 1998). Performance measurement systems were sharpened, and the annual publication of national league tables for schools and hospitals became significant media events. Privatization continued (electricity, 1990–3; railways 1994). In central government the Next Steps report of 1988 led to the creation, within ten years, of more than 140 executive agencies, which employed in excess of 70 per cent of the nonindustrial civil service (Chancellor of the Duchy of Lancaster 1997; O'Toole and Jordan 1995). During the mid-1990s a number of central ministries were significantly downsized, following a programme of management reviews (e.g. HM Treasury 1994). In 1991 both the *Citizen's Charter* (Prime Minister 1991) and ambitious programmes of contracting-out and market-testing were launched (*Competing for quality*—HM Treasury 1991). These two well represented the main tendencies of the 1990s: a huge emphasis on 'customer service' (Clarke and Newman 1997) and an equally intense concern to keep up the pace of contracting-out and marketization.

The new Labour government of 1997 reversed very little of what had gone before. Although ideologically more sympathetic to the public sector, they did not reverse the privatizations or the purchaser/provider splits even though they took some steps to ameliorate the least popular consequences of the latter. If anything, they intensified the 'league table' system still further, and 'rebranded' the *Citizen's Charter* programme as the 'Service First' initiative. Many of their proposals shared the underlying assumptions about the transformatory capacity of better, more professional public management which had been characteristic of their Conservative predecessors (e.g. the idea of a benchmarked Procurement Excellence model or the 'Best value' initiative in local government—see Chancellor of the Exchequer 1998). In 1999 the Prime Minister issued a white paper, *Modernizing government*, which offered a slightly curious mixture of old themes (e.g. greater responsiveness and quality) with faintly millenarial visions of the government's role in the 'Information Age' (Prime Minister and the Minister for the Cabinet Office 1999). Subsequently, the increases in public spending, particularly in health care and education, were accompanied by further intensification of central target-setting and performance measurement, continuing the trend towards 're-regulation' of the public sector which had begun under the Conservatives (Hood et al. 1999). As Blair famously said, his second term of office came to be about 'delivery, delivery, delivery'.

M. The implementation process

In the UK reform has been continual, often intense, and sometimes harsh. Public sector employees have become accustomed to constant restructurings, downsizing, and new 'initiatives'. Much of the change has been strongly driven from the top. The Treasury and the Cabinet Office have been the main actors, though most departments have been heavily involved, especially Health (for the NHS), Environment (for local government), Education (the reform of schools, colleges, and universities), and Social Security. Under New Labour, No. 10 Downing Street itself became a significant reform 'player', housing the Prime Minister's Delivery Unit and Office of Public Services Reform.

N. Reforms actually achieved

As noted above, British central government is relatively unfettered in its ability to make administrative changes. So when it determines to carry something through, it usually can. As Section L made clear, many large-scale reforms have been put in place. That is not to say that all have achieved the results forecast or claimed for them. Sometimes one can 'take a horse to water but not make him drink' (see Pollitt et al. 1998 for an assessment of this factor in health care, education, and housing reforms).

The Conservative governments of 1979–97 were not enthusiastic about mounting large-scale evaluations of their management reforms. Ministers tended to take the line that reform was essential and self-evidently desirable, and that formal, public evaluation might prove a delay and distraction. Internal management reviews were more common. The Labour government since 1997 has been more committed to formal evaluation, but it is too soon to say how far the results will be fully taken on board, especially if evaluation findings indicate that high-profile reforms are not working well.

There have, however, been a number of specific evaluations of particular initiatives, and some of these were made available within the public domain. For example, there was a useful series of assessments of the Next Steps programme that were basically positive in tone (e.g. Trosa 1994) although acknowledging the danger of fragmentation and loss of departmental control (Office of Public Services Reform 2002).

Some academic evaluations have begun to appear. One of the most thorough of these suggests that there have probably been substantial though not spectacular efficiency gains, increased responsiveness to service users, but significant loss of equity (Boyne et al. 2003).

Country file events: United Kingdom

	General	Organization	Personnel	Finance
1981–5	– Thatcher: PM (Cons.) (1979) – Thatcher: PM (Cons.) (1983) – First set of national PI for the NHS (1983) – White paper: *Lifting the Burden*: on deregulation (1985)	– Management and Personnel Office (MPO) created in Cabinet Office (1981) – Privatization B Aerospace (1981) – Central Unit on Purchasing created: report annually on progress in VFM targets (1984) – Privatization B Telecom (1984)	– Civil Service Department disbanded (1981)	– Rayner scrutinies (efficiency studies) launched (1979) – Financial Management Initiative (FMI): delegate financial and personnel matters to line managers (1982)
1986–90	– White paper: *Building Business... Not Barriers* (1986) – Thatcher: PM (Cons.) (1987) – White paper: *Releasing Enterprise* on deregulation (1988) – NHS white paper *Working for Patients*: Introduction for MTM in the health sector (1989) – Major: PM (Cons.) (1990) – Central government takes power to cap local authority budgets, to set tax rate on local business (1990)	– Privatization B Gas (1986) – Privatization BAA (1987) – Next Steps initiative: executive agencies: CE accountable to ministers who set performance targets (1988) – Privatization Water (1989) – 34 agencies (80,000 staff) established (1990) – 29 candidates (200,000) identified (1990) – Privatization: 1990–3: Electricity Generation (1990) – Trading Fund Act: extend range of government business able to benefit from trading fund status (the Royal Mint, Central Office of Information, Fire Service College) (1990)	– Office of the Minister of Civil Service (OMCS): reconstituted MPO (1987) – Treasury: 21 flexibilities for department and agencies on personnel management, pay, allowances (1989) – New career arrangements for IT and Purchasing and Supply Staff: more professionalism (1989) – Flexible pay, recruitment, management development, training (1989) – Equal opportunity initiatives; revision of Code of Practice for employing the disabled (1990) – 600 secondments between civil service and industry/commerce (1990)	– Progress report on budgeting reforms (1988)
1991–5	– 'Making the most of Next Steps': relation of departments and agencies (1991) – Major: PM (Cons.) (1992) – White paper: *Citizen's Charter* (1991) – Booklet: *Cutting Red Tape for Business*: on deregulation (1991) – White paper: *Competing for Quality* (1991)	– Privatization: 900,000 jobs transferred; state-owned sector reduced by two-thirds since 1979 (1991) – Office of Public Service and Science (OPSS) in Cabinet Office: merger of OMCS, Next Steps Team, *Citizen's Charter*, Efficiency Unit, Market-Testing Unit (1992)	– Treasury: 40 flexibilities for departments and agencies on personnel managements pay, allowances (1991) – Programme of Action for Women in Civil Service (1992) – 13 agencies: group bonus schemes linked to quality of service targets and funded from efficiency savings (1992)	– Audit Commission: 77 indicators for local governments to report on performance (1992) – Private Finance Initiative (PFI) launched (1994) – Green paper: resource accounting by 1998, resource budgeting by 2000 (1994)

continues

continued

	General	Organization	Personnel	Finance
	- First *Citizen's Charter* Report and 28 follow-up charters published (1992) - Plans to market test £1.5 bn. of public service (1992) - Conservative election victory (small majority) (1992) - Programme of Fundamental Reviews of Ministries launched (1993) - White paper: *Continuity and Change* (1994) - Next Steps: civil service reform 'Moving on' (1994) - White paper: *Competitiveness* (1994) - *Citizen's Charter Second Report*; 98 chartermarks; 53 reviews of Complaints Task Force; 16 Charter Quality Networks (1994) - Code of Practice on Access to Government Information (1994) - Deregulation and Contracting-Out Act (1994)	- Scheme to increase interchange with local authorities launched (1992) - Government Office for the region (one window for Transport, Trade and Industry, Employment, Environment) (1994) - Beginning of a series of 'fundamental reviews' of major ministerial departments, leading to average downsizing of more than 20% (1994) - OPSS loses Sciences and becomes OPS (1995) - Central Information Technology Unit in OPS (1995) - Remaining Treasury responsibilities for Civil Service Management transferred to OPS (1995) - Privatization B Coal (1995)	- Civil Service (Management Functions) Act: facilitate delegation of central management responsibilities (1992) - Efficiency Unit Report: Career Management and Succession Planning (1993) - Introduction of central funding scheme: help departments meet costs of early departures (1994) - All departments: forward 'Investors in People' plans (1994) - White paper: *Taking Forward Continuity and Change* (1995)	- Fundamental Review of Expenditure: leads to 25% downsizing of HM Treasury (1994) - Departments: prepare efficiency plans each year (1995) - White paper: *Resource Accounting and Budgeting in Government*: from cash management to management of resources against achievement of objectives' (1995) - 'Burdens of Bureaucracy': efficiency scrutinies (1995) - Efficiency Scrutiny of Management Information Systems published (1995)
1996–2000	- Evaluation of first 3 years of 'Competing for Quality' (1996) - Benchmarking initiative for executive agencies (1996–8) - Blair: PM (Lab.) (1997) (large majority) - White paper: *Better Government* (1997) - 'Service First' (*Citizen's Charter* relaunch) (1998) - *Modernizing Government* white paper (1999) - E-Government Strategy paper (1999) - *Our Healthier Nation* white paper (1999) - Freedom of Information Act (1999)	- 127 agencies (387,000 civil servants: 72%); 37 candidates (1996) - Privatization B Railways (1996) - Extended service hours for the National Health Service via NHS Direct and NHS Direct online (1999) - Prime Minister's Delivery Unit and Office of Public Service Reform (1999) - Introduction of Beacon Council Scheme (2000) - Social Care Quality Programme (SCQP) (2000) - Modernizing Dentistry (2000) - Primary Health Care Trusts	- Civil Service Code into effect (1996) - New Senior Civil Service created (1996) - Senior Management Reviews completed (1996) - White paper: *Development and Training for Civil Servants* (1996) - Centre for Management and Policy Studies established (1999) - Adoption of EFQM model (1999) - Public Service Agreement 1999–2002 - European Benchmarking (2000) - New performance management system for senior civil servants (2000)	- Efficiency Plans of Agencies (1997) - Adaptation of Private Finance Initiative and extension to local government (1997–8) - Comprehensive Spending Review (1998): Public Expenditure Plans 1999–2000, - Public Service Agreements, Service Delivery Agreements and Output, and Performance Analysis - E-Business: forms to file VAT returns online (2000) - 2000 Spending Review (2000)

– Code of Practice on written consultation (2000)
– Performance Targets Review (2000)
– Sharing of performance information online (2000)
– Housing green paper (*Quality and Choice: A Decent Home for All*) (2000)

– Merger of Performance Innovation Unit with Prime Minister's Office's Forward Strategy Unit to form the new Strategy Unit (2000)

– TNT modernizing government partnership award (2001)

– Introduction of Resource Accounting and Budgeting (2001)
– Modernizing government's use of loans (2002)

2001–2
– Evaluation of e-government
– Energy Review (2002)
– E-Government Strategy (2002)

– E-Government Health Initiative
– Medicdirect (2001)
– Health and Social Care Act 2001, transfer of funds from PSS SSA to NHS (2001)
– Partial privatization of Air Traffic Control (2001)

UNITED STATES OF AMERICA

A. Socio-economic forces: general

The USA is unique among the twelve countries in this study in its status as a military and economic 'superpower'. It is rich and powerful (see Table A.1). Thus it is probably in a better position than other states to influence the course of global trends. Nevertheless, there are limits to its power, and it, too, is subject to the challenges of an ageing society, changing social values and norms, and mass immigration.

B. Global economic forces

Imports and exports form a considerably smaller proportion of the US economy than for any of the other eleven countries reviewed in this book. Yet, as with social trends, the USA is far from immune to international economic trends. See Appendix A for key statistics.

C. Sociodemographic issues

Although rich on the basis of average per capita incomes (Table A.1), the USA spends a surprisingly small amount of government money on social expenditure (Table A.2). By comparison with most European countries it has only a 'thin' welfare state.

D. National socio-economic policies

The 1980s was a period during which political and popular awareness of the federal deficit grew—alongside the growth of the deficit itself. Very high levels of defence spending under the Reagan administration, together with its failure to cut back on social programmes as sharply as had originally been intended, contributed to this problem (Stockman 1986). These increases dwarfed the savings and cuts that flowed from managerial efficiency improvements (see Section M). Under Clinton, from 1992, however, more effective measures were taken to control the deficit, and at the same time the economy entered a long boom. In 1997 President Clinton and the Republican-dominated Congress agreed a five-year plan to balance the budget, and by the time President Clinton made his 1999 State of the Union address, a political debate was building up on the question of what to do with the anticipated budget surpluses. George W. Bush inherited a rapidly changing economic situation, and after the September 11, 2001 terrorist attacks, it became abundantly clear that the US economy was slowing down. By background and conviction, the new President was fiscally conservative, pro–big business and pro-market, but (like Reagan) his increased military and security spending soon threatened the federal fiscal balance.

E. The political system

The USA possesses a unique political system, with no close parallel within our set of ten countries. It is a federal state, with a constitutionally entrenched division of powers between the executive, legislature and judiciary. From its foundations, the American political elite has been much concerned with maintaining a system of 'checks and balances' to ensure that no one of the three main branches of government can become dominant. (Maidment and McGrew 1986)

There is a two-party system (Republican and Democrat) but the parties are each 'broad churches', and, by European standards, there is little party discipline within the legislature, each Congressperson or Senator being free to vote and act according to his or her own dictates. Individual committees within the legislature also enjoy high independence, and the chairs of the senior committees are major political figures in their own right. Specific constituency interests have a strong influence on voting patterns. There is no equivalent to the Social Democrat or Socialist Parties which are such a familiar presence in Western European politics. The president is directly elected every four years and cannot serve more than two successive terms.

The legislature is bicameral and, relative to the executive, unusually powerful by European standards. The president and the executive cannot rely on getting their way—certainly not in matters of administrative reform (Savoie 1994, p. 213). The agencies of the executive may be partly or wholly 'captured' by interest groups represented within the legislature. Many expert commentators have remarked on the legislature's predilection for 'micromanaging' the federal bureaucracy (e.g. Kettl 1994).

Washington politics is also characterized by a 'spoils system', in which an incoming administration hands out large numbers of senior administrative posts to political sympathizers. These (often short-term) political appointees then work alongside career civil servants (Heclo 1977). During the 1980s the spoils system grew in size under Presidents Reagan and Bush.

Finally, it must not be forgotten that, although the main focus of this book is on national level governments, the USA has an extensively decentralized and democratized system of governance (see Table 3.2—there are more than 80,000 'governments' within the USA).

F. New management ideas

The USA is characterized by a 'business-oriented', 'free enterprise' culture. Its system of government is also very open and fragmented. These factors have meant that it has been very easy for private sector management concepts to enter the public sector. At various times the federal administration has expressed enthusiasm towards most of the contemporary management techniques and approaches, including MbOs, downsizing, TQM, benchmarking, and re-engineering.

A historical perspective indicates that there is nothing particularly new in this openness to business techniques. For example, in the 1960s the federal government famously adopted PPBS, and in the 1970s other techniques with private sector conceptual origins, such as ZBB and organizational development, were also enthusiastically embraced.

G. Pressure from citizens

Since the 1970s US public opinion has tended to become increasingly critical of both the motives and the competence of federal government (Bok 1997; Kaufman 1981). Most Americans believe that the federal bureaucracy wastes huge sums of money. However, the accuracy of popular perceptions of its federal government can be questioned: for example, as mentioned earlier, a majority believe that the administrative overheads eat up more than 50 per cent of the social security programme, whereas the true figure is less than 2 per cent (Bok 1997, p. 56). Nevertheless, US presidents and their colleagues have to operate against a

background in which the proportion of Americans who believe that public officials don't care what people think has grown from 36 per cent in 1964 to 66 per cent in 1996, and the proportion who think that quite a few people in government are crooked has risen (over the same period) from 29 per cent to 51 per cent. This set of attitudes does not so much point towards specific management reforms as it does handicap all reformers, in so far as their efforts and motives are likely to be regarded with widespread scepticism by the public.

At the same time, however, citizen approval of particular services coexists with their generalized mistrust of 'the feds'. Major institutions such as the Social Security Administration, the Internal Revenue Service, and the Postal Service regularly score highly on customer satisfaction, and at least equal private sector satisfaction scores.

H. Party political ideas

These, too, were influenced by the general 'free enterprise' culture and by the absence of a Social Democratic or Socialist Party of any size or salience. Thus, a majority of both Republicans and Democrats have been willing to sign up to notions of more 'businesslike' government. Since the late 1970s, however, a substantial group of right-wing Republicans have taken a more radical stance. Deeply sceptical of the efficacy of federal actions, they have argued for fundamental downsizing of the civil service and a general reduction in 'government interference'. At the time of writing, the Republicans are in control of Congress, and the antifederal-bureaucracy theme is being propounded as vigorously as ever.

I. Chance events

Some events had an impact on specific aspects or sectors of the federal administration. Two examples are the 1986 *Challenger* space shuttle explosion (which had a huge impact on the National Aeronautics and Space Administration, NASA, one of the largest federal agencies) and the 1994 Oklahoma City bombing, which starkly illustrated the depths of hatred for the federal authorities felt by some groups on the radical right of the American political spectrum.

However, the clearest example of event-driven policy-making is the range of measures adopted following the Al Quaeda terrorist attacks of

September 11, 2001. These led directly to a major federal reorganization, with the creation of the Department of Homeland Security as its centrepiece.

J. Elite decision-making

It is less appropriate to speak of a (singular) elite perception in the USA than in some more centralized and homogenous European countries. Traditionally, in the USA, executive perceptions of what was needed tended to be somewhat at variance with the perceptions of leading groups within the legislature. Whilst it may have been relatively easy to secure consensus on the proposition that the federal government needs to be more flexible, efficient, customer-friendly, and coordinated, it has been much more difficult to build a broad coalition of support for a package of specific and concrete measures to achieve this. As Bush's *Management Agenda* document puts it, 'All too often, Congress is part of the government's managerial problems' (Office of Management and Budget 2002, p. 6).

As indicated above, reformers had to contend with a general loss of trust in the federal machine, a tendency which was frequently encouraged by presidents themselves. In the US system reform feasibility frequently depends heavily on the mood of Congress and the current standing of the incumbent President. It is noticeable that large-scale structural reforms (e.g. merging agencies, consolidating or splitting up major departments), though prominent in the earlier reform attempts of the 1930s and 1950s, have been tried rather less frequently by the Presidents of the 1980s and 1990s (and with disappointing results—Reagan's 1986 Civil Service Simplification Act and Clinton's Personnel System Reinvention and Omnibus Civil Service Reform Acts failed). Evidently, changes in technique—budgetary and accounting systems, customer service systems, performance management—have been regarded as more feasible/less politically controversial than wholesale redesign of the government machine.

By the end of the 1980s there were signs of a real collapse of morale within the federal service (Volcker 1989). This was hardly in anyone's interest, and provided the incoming Clinton administration with a base on which to build support for a new attempt at reform. This took the form of the NPR and the GPRA (see Section N).

The Bush presidency, from 2000, seemed mainly oriented to a marketizing treatment of the federal machine, making 'actively promoting . . . innovation through competition' one of its three main principles (the other two being to be 'citizen-centred' and 'results-oriented'—Office of Management and Budget 2002, p. 4).

K. The administrative system

The US administrative system is quite fragmented and highly permeable to influences from outside the executive itself. Unlike many European countries, the USA never developed a unified and powerful central state apparatus. It democratized before it industrialized, and industrialized before the main era of state-building (Amenta and Skocpol 1989). During the twentieth century a patchwork of departments and agencies grew up, which successive attempts at reform (especially the Brownlow Committee of 1936 and the Hoover Commissions of 1949 and 1955) only partly succeeded in rationalizing (Savoie 1994).

By the mid-1990s the federal machine consisted of a wide variety of organizational forms (Peters 1995). These included fourteen Cabinet departments, a large number of independent executive organizations (e.g. the NASA), independent regulatory commissions (e.g. the Federal Trade Commission), and public corporations (e.g. the Tenessee Valley Authority, the Federal Deposit Insurance Corporation). There are also organizations within the sphere of the legislature that are important players in financial and management issues—especially the Congressional Budget Office (CBO) and the General Accounting Office (GAO).

While a modest employer in terms of its proportion of the total labour force (2.4%) or of the total public labour force (only 15%), the federal government is still a big employer in absolute terms. It employed three million or so staff prior to the downsizing of the mid and late 1990s (Peters 1995, p. 22) and still 1.8 million in 2001 (the lowest level since 1950).

L. Contents of the reform package

Of the twelve countries in this study the USA is probably the one which has been home to the strongest antigovernment rhetoric and the lowest public trust of government (it is not clear which is the cart and which is the horse). Each of the last five Presidents (Carter in 1976, Reagan in 1980,

Clinton and George Bush, sen. in 1992, George Bush, jun. in 2000) felt it politically advantageous to include criticism of the federal bureaucracy as a significant element in their electoral campaigns. In practice, however, their actions have varied from attempts at sympathetic modernization of the federal departments and agencies (Carter and Clinton) to attacks on alleged bureaucratic 'waste' and duplication, combined with the introduction of more and more political appointees (Reagan, Bush).

One reform that took place just before the period covered by this book, but which needs to be mentioned, was President Carter's 1978 Civil Service Reform Act (CSRA—see Ban and Ingraham 1984). This created an SES of about 8,000 and introduced performance appraisal and merit pay. The SES provision had been designed partly to cater for growing public/private pay differentials (in favour of the latter) but Congress soon cut the share of SES positions that were eligible for bonuses from 50 per cent to 20 per cent. One rueful contemporary comment on the implementation of the CSRA was that Congressional support for it was 'a mile wide but an inch deep'. President Reagan was subsequently able to make good use of the 1978 Act to dominate personnel administration to a greater extent than his predecessors had been able to. A quarter of a century later Bush was promising to 'establish a meaningful system to measure performance. Create awards for employees who surpass expectations', as though this were a new idea (Office of Management and Budget 2002, p. 11).

The Reagan administration introduced a welter of reforms, many of them designed to bring 'business disciplines' to the federal civil service. It was also systematic in exploiting the Presidency's huge power of patronage to appoint Conservatives to key positions throughout Washington (Savoie 1994). Some of the principal initiatives were:

- Appointing Donald Devine, an arch-Conservative and virulent critic of the federal bureaucracy, to be head of the Office of Personnel Management (OPM). 'Career officials were shocked and demoralized by Devine's hostility to them' (Savoie 1994, p. 222).
- The President's Council on Integrity and Efficiency (founded 1981). 'It questioned many practices, identified billions of savings as a result of audits, launched civil and criminal actions, and introduced many sanctions against

government agencies or employees' (Savoie 1994, p. 189).

- Reform 88 (launched in 1982). This was a broad-scope programme, somewhat lacking in focus. Actions under its umbrella included upgrading computer systems and improving financial management and accountability.
- The Council on Management and Administration (1982).
- The President's Private Sector Survey on Cost Control (PPSSCC, better known as the 'Grace Commission' 1982).
- The Council on Management Improvement (1984). This was a council of Assistant Secretaries from across federal departments and agencies, tasked to develop long-range management improvement plans and reinforce the implementation of Reform 88.
- The President's Productivity Program (from 1985). This was aimed at increasing the productivity of government agencies by 20 per cent by 1992. Measures included the widespread adoption of TQM.
- 'Although not nearly as successful as he would have liked, Reagan promoted privatisation, contracting out, and user fees at every opportunity' (Savoie 1994, p. 215).

The Grace Commission was one of the most publicized of these initiatives, and in some ways typified the Reagan administration's approach. It involved bringing in large numbers of business people (2,000 supported by 859 companies) with a brief to identify bureaucratic 'waste'. Over a two-year period it generated forty-seven reports containing 2,478 recommendations. It claimed potential savings of $298 bn., though a GAO analysis suggested that the true figure was more like $98 bn. Some of its recommendations were partly or wholly implemented, but many were not (Pollitt 1993, pp. 91–5). In proportion to the size of the effort (and of the fanfare—see Grace 1984) it left only a small trace. The much less widely publicized Council on Integrity and Efficiency probably had a considerably greater impact.

President Bush (1988–92) was less overtly anti-bureaucrat than Reagan—possibly because he had a lifetime of public service behind him. He presided over a growing crisis in the morale of the federal service, but was seemingly unable to take any particularly strong action to counter it. In 1989 a task force identified serious weaknesses in the public service (including pay, performance appraisal, and career development systems and morale—Volcker 1989). In 1990 a GAO study came to broadly similar conclusions (General Accounting Office 1990). Yet no major reforms were undertaken. As one observer wrote at the time: 'America's flame of managerial reform seems to have died down to a glowing ember' (Hede 1991, pp. 507–8). President Bush's main interests seem to have lain with high policy issues rather than management reform.

By contrast, the incoming Clinton administration of 1992 was keen to restore status to the federal machine, and to do so by pursuing a high-profile reform which would lead to a government that 'works better and costs less'. The centrepiece of their programme, entrusted to Vice-President Gore, was the NPR (see Gore 1996, 1997; National Performance Review 1997 *a* and *b*; and countless other publications). This package included proposals for savings (promises of $108 bn. worth) and downsizing (by 252,000 subsequently raised by Congress to 272,900), as well as for 'empowerment' and 'reinvention'. Different stakeholders have stressed different aspects, and from the start it was clear that there were tensions between, for example, the 'savings and downsizing' theme and the 'empowerment and reinvention' theme. 'In practice NPR has been a messy and sometimes disorganised multi-front war against the government's performance problems' (Kettl 1994, p. 5).

A second major management reform proceeded alongside the NPR. The 1993 GPRA mandated the development of strategic planning and performance measurement throughout the federal government (National Academy of Public Administration 1994). Its origins went back to draft Congressional legislation from the Bush era (Radin 1998, p. 308). Three years of pilot projects were planned before the reporting requirements were 'rolled out' to the rest of the federal government in 1997.

After 2000, the approach of Bush in some ways echoed that of Reagan. He placed great emphasis on competitive outsourcing and the advantages of competition. He 'reinvented' the idea of performance-budgeting, and made results orientation one of his central themes. Like almost every other western government, he lauded the potential of e-government. Without referring to the Clinton–Gore NPR (which, in rhetorical terms at least, quickly disappeared from view), he discovered that federal managers lacked discretion,

and headlined 'freedom to manage' as a goal (Office of Management and Budget 2002, p. 5). However, in the aftermath of 9/11 he also set up a Department of Homeland Security, and used this as a vehicle for achieving greater managerial flexibility and freedom from Congressional control.

M. The implementation process

Implementing management reform has always been difficult for US presidents. As noted above, the powers of Congress to intervene in organizational restructurings are as extensive as its powers to reshape budgets. Neither are the agencies themselves under such clear and unequivocal hierarchical authority as would be usual in the case of, say, a British or French agency. Many exist as one corner in an 'iron triangle', with Congress as a second corner and one or more major interest groups as a third (e.g. farmers, or the oil companies, or the defence industries). These links can give agencies the capacity to resist unwelcome changes through political channels.

Furthermore, implementation of some important reforms has been entrusted mainly to political appointees (rather than career civil servants). For example, the 'reinvention' teams established under the NPR were usually led by Clinton appointees. Sometimes this helps give impetus, but at other times it produces oscillations and discontinuities, as political appointees find their attentions are drawn away to other issues of current political salience, or, indeed, they themselves leave their posts (the turnover among political appointees can be brisk).

Unsurprisingly, therefore, the record of implementation of reforms has been patchy. Organizationally, the key player in management changes would normally be the Office of Management and Budget (OMB). In practice, however, this has not always been a substantial force for management reform. Within the OMB the emphasis on management has varied, and for considerable periods the bulk of their effort has been directed to short-term budgetary issues, with management improvement taking a poor second place (see Savoie 1994 for an account of the changing role of the OMB under Reagan). Under Clinton, the OMB took a lead role in implementing the GPRA but, by contrast, made only limited inputs to the NPR reinvention activities. Even with the GPRA, however, the nature of the US governmental system led to implementation difficulties:

Although the aims of GPRA suggest that the information produced under the Act will support more rational decision-making, both the structure of the US government and current developments in other areas make this extremely difficult. The structure creates a disconnect between budget functions, agency organisation, and the jurisdictions of appropriations committees. The fragmented nature of decision-making, including budget decision-making, limits the ability of any institution of government in either the executive or the legislative branch to look at crosscutting issues and the government as a whole (Radin 1998, p. 311).

N. Reforms actually achieved

Despite the existence of a flourishing evaluation culture in the US public sector, it is extremely difficult to come to any sure assessment of the impact of the reforms since 1980. At a microlevel there have clearly been many examples and cases of efficiency gains, modernization of systems, and increased attention to customer-responsiveness. Some of the NPR publications are spattered with upbeat examples of such performance improvements (e.g. Gore 1997). However, broad-scope evaluations seem thin on the ground. An academic review of NPR reinvention laboratories identifies some successes (especially where there has been 'stubborn' leadership) but also some failures and continuing problems (Ingraham et al. 1998). Certainly, most of the reforms of the Reagan administration were not subject to scientific evaluation—the mood of the times was somewhat against evaluation, as being itself a further symptom of bureaucratic empire-building and obfuscation. Assessments of GPRA by the GAO indicate a mixed picture with some performance plans following well short of what the act seems to require (e.g. General Accounting Office 1998; 2001). As for the NPR, one authoritative academic assessment is mixed—in the main, federal agencies technically complied with NPR, but effectively dampened much of its intended force. Cultural change has been patchy (Thompson 2000). Subsequently, in his incoming management agenda, Bush laid great stress on the fact that 'What matters in the end is completion. Performance. Results.' (Office of Management and Budget 2002, p. 1). However, although setting targets for most of its initiatives, the President's agenda was largely silent about arrangements for evaluation and accountability. Perhaps this is 'business as usual', since, as the Agenda itself notes:

Congress, the Executive Branch, and the media have all shown far greater interest in the launch of new initiatives than in following up to see if anything useful ever occurred. (Office of Management and Budget 2002, p. 3)

Country file events: United States of America

	General	Organization	Personnel	Finance
1981–5	– Reagan: President (Rep.) (1980) – Reagan: President (Rep.) (1984) – Simplification efforts include cutting 30,000 pages from Federal Acquisition Regulation (1984)			– Replacement of central budget system by single government-wide financial system (1981)
1985–90	– Extensive effort to improve quality (1986) – Bush: President (Rep.) (1988) – Increase number of contracts subject to competition from 41% (1981) to 58% (1988) – President's Management Improvement Program: Reform 88 (1988) – Overview of broad issues for programme emphasis into the next century (1989) – Review of development and use of IT (1989) – MBO system to allow President and senior officials to monitor and evaluate some 50 programmes/policies (1989) – Programme evaluation: accelerates (1990) – Office of Management and Budget (OMB): monitor 100 high-risk areas (1989)	– President's Council on Competitiveness (1989) – Review of adequacy of management controls in 65 departments (1989)	– Reduce number of personnel payroll systems from 132 (1983) to 53 (1988) – Studies to hire and retain skilled personnel (1989) – Federal Employees Pay Comparability Act (1990)	– Increase in number of agencies having inspectors general: audit and investigate wasteful and inefficient practices (1988) – Improvement of lending programmes – Reduce number of financial systems from 379 (1984) to 253 (1988) – Establish a formal integrated structure for financial management (goal-setting, preparation of annual statements, chief financial officer in 23 agencies) (1990) – Federal Accounting Standards Advisory Board established (1990) – Presidential Legislation on Financial Management (1990) – New Budget Deficit Reduction Law – Budget Enforcement Act (1990) – Federal Credit Reform Act (1990)
1991–5	– Clinton: President (Dem.) (1992) – Voucher programmes in childcare and housing extended (1992) – President: moratorium on new regulations (1992) – Senate: Government Performance and Results Act (GPRA) (1992) – Vice-President Gore: National Performance Review (NPR) (1993)	– CFOA: establishment of Office of Federal Financial Management in the OMB (1991) – National Economic Council (White House): domestic issues (1993) – Abolish President's Council on Competitiveness (1993) – President's Management Council: all chief operating officers of departments and agencies (1993)	– Postal Services: 5% employee reduction (1992) – Cut 100,000 positions, cut White House staff by 25% (1993) – National Partnership Council (NPC): federal management and employees: collaboration, customer service, cutting costs (1993) – Federal Workforce Restructuring Act (FWRA) (1994): cut 272,000 FTE by 1999, buyout authority – Elimination of the 10,000-page Federal Personnel Manual (1994)	– Chief Financial Officers Act (CFOA) (1991): publication of guidelines and standards for financial reporting/accounting – Initial set of annual audited financial statements (several agencies and 27 corporations) (1991) – Pilot regulatory budget (covered by CAA) (1991) – Increased emphasis on measurement of programme performance (1991) – OMB asks agencies to provide cost/benefit data for all significant regulations (1991)

	– NPR: 'From Red Tape to Results: Creating a Government that Works Better and Costs Less' (1993) – Presidential EO: Regulatory Planning Review (cut obsolete regulations, reward result, get out of Washington, negotiate, grassroots partnerships) (1993) – Presidential EO: 'Setting Customer Service Standards' (1993) – GPRA (Congress) (1993) – Federal Acquisition Streamlining Act (FASA) (1994): reform procurement – Government-wide electronic contracting system (1995) – Reauthorize Paperwork Reduction Act (1995)	– 200 Reinvention Labs (1993) – Federal interagency–state partnerships with Oregon and Connecticut (1994) – First Performance-Based Organization (PBO): Patent and Trademark Office (1995)		– MBO discontinued (1991) – GPRA: all federal agencies: 5-year strategic plan, annual performance plans, report on performance (1993) – Expand Government Management Reform Act (GMRA) (1994): audit of financial statements for entire operations to all 24 CFO agencies – Pilot projects in all 14 Cabinet departments and 13 agencies: annual plans, performance goals, and reports on actual and planned performance (also in military combat and R&D) (1994) – No mandates for state, local, and tribal governments without money (1995) – Unfunded Mandates Reform Act (1995)
1996–2000	– Clinton: President (Dem.) (1996) – Budget: (1997): consolidation, devolution, privatization, termination (from 271 programmes to 27 'Performance Partnerships' (1996) – Federal Acquisition Reform Act (FARA) (1996) – National Performance Review becomes National Partnership for Reinventing Government (1998) – President articulates a vision for e-government (1999) – Bush: President (Rep.) (2000) – Government that is citizen-centred, result-oriented, market-based (2000)	– Information Technology Management Reform Act (ITMRA): chief information officer in each agency, new schemes for management and acquisition (1996) – Education Department's Student Financial Aid Office: first congressionally created performance-based organization (PBO) (1998) – First government-wide survey for customer satisfaction index (ASCI) (2000)	– Establishment of the Office of Personnel Management (OPM) (2000)	– Line Item Veto Act (LIVA) President may cancel discretionary spending, new entitlement authorization, and tax provisions (1996) – All agencies submit strategic plans under GPRA (1997) – First balanced budget in 30 years (1998) – Federal government issued its first audited government-wide financial statement (1999) – Executive Office of the President, OMB CFOs integrate financial management agencies, produce annual audited financial statements (2000)

continues

continued

	General	Organization	Personnel	Finance
2001–2	– President Bush established his Management Agenda, containing five government-wide goals for improving federal management: strategic HRM, competitive sourcing, e-government, better financial management and budget, and performance integration (2001) – Management Scorecards to follow up the President's Management Agenda (2001) – 9/11 terrorist attacks on World Trade Center (New York) and Pentagon (Washington, DC)	– Integration of IT capital planning with agency budget, acquisition, financial management with strategic planning process (2000) – Office of Government Ethics (OGE): provides overall direction of executive branch policies in preventing conflicts of interest (2000) – Competitive Sourcing: setting up private and public competition (2001) – Development of Executive Scorecards: measure strategic competencies, leadership, performance culture, learning, or knowledge management (2001) – Department of Homeland Security (2002)	– President's Management Agenda: Strategic Human Resources Management (2001)	– Establishment of Debt Collection Improvement Act (DCIA) (2001) – President's Management Agenda: budget and performance integration (2001) – Program Assessment Rating Tool for 20% programmes FY04 budget (2002) – Development of Common Performance Measures (2002)

BIBLIOGRAPHY

Aberbach, J. and Christensen, T. (2001) 'Radical Reform in New Zealand: Crisis, Windows of Opportunity, and Rational Actors', *Public Administration*, 79:2, pp. 403–22.

Ahonen, P. and Salminen, A. (1997) *Metamorphosis of the Administrative State*. Frankfurt am Main: Peter Lang.

Albertini, J.-B. (1998) *Contribution à une théorie de l'Etat déconcentré*. Bruxelles: Bruylant.

Algemene Rekenkamer (1995) *Tweede Kamer*, 1994/95, 24120, no. 3.

—— (2002) *Verantwoording en toezicht bij rechtspersonen met een wettelijke taak deel 3*. 's-Gravenhage: Sdu Uitgevers.

Amenta, E. and Skocpol, T. (1989) 'Taking Exception: Explaining the Distinctiveness of American Public Policies in the Last Century', pp. 292–333, in F. Castles (ed) *The Comparative History of Public Policy*. Oxford: Polity.

Aristotle (1963) *Aristotle's Politics* (translated by B. Jowett). Oxford: Clarendon Press.

Ascher, K. (1987) *The Politics of Privatisation: Contracting out Public Services*. Basingstoke: Macmillan.

Association of Finnish Local Authorities (1995*a*) *Total Quality Management in Municipal Service Provision*. Helsinki: Association of Finnish Local Authorities.

—— (1995*b*) *Quality in the Procurement of Municipal Services*. Helsinki: Association of Finnish Local Authorities.

Aucoin, P. (1998) *Accountability in Public Management: Making Performance Count*. Paper presented to the authors' roundtable, Revitalising the Public Service. Ottawa: Canadian Centre for Management Development. 12–14 November.

—— and Savoie, D. (1998) *Program Review: Lessons for Strategic Change in Governance*. Ottawa: Canadian Centre for Management Development.

Auditor-General of Canada (1993) 'Canada's Public Service Reform, and Lessons Learned from Selective Jurisdictions', *Report, 1993*, chapter 6. Ottawa: Auditor-General of Canada.

—— (1997) *Annual Report*. Ottawa: Auditor-General of Canada.

Balk, W. (1996) *Managerial Reform and Professional Empowerment in the Public Service*. Westport: Quorum Books.

Ball, I. (1993) *New Zealand Public Sector Management*. Paper presented to the 1993 National Accountants in Government Convention, Hobart. 26–28 May.

Ban, C. and Ingraham, P. (1984) *Legislating Bureaucratic Change: the Civil Service Reform Act of 1978*. New York: SUNY Press.

Barberis, P. (1998) 'The New Public Management and a New Accountability', *Public Administration*, 76:3, pp. 451–70, Autumn.

Barbier, J.-C. and Simonin, B. (1997) 'European Social Programmes: Can Evaluation of Implementation Increase the Appropriateness of Findings?', *Evaluation*, 3:4, pp. 391–407, October.

Beale, V. and Pollitt, C. (1994) 'Charters at the Grass roots: A First Report', *Local Government Studies*, 20:2, pp. 202–25, Summer.

Behn, R. (2001) *Re-thinking Democratic Accountability*. Washington, DC: Brookings Institution.

Bellamy, C. and Taylor, J. (1998) *Governing in the Information Age*. Buckingham: Open University Press.

Benz, A. and Götz, K. (1996) 'The German Public Sector: National Priorities and the International Reform Agenda', pp. 1–26, in A. Benz and K. Götz (eds) *A New German Public Sector? Reform, Adaptation and Stability*. Aldershot: Dartmouth.

Boje, D., Gephart, R., and Thatchenkey, T. (eds) (1996) *Postmodern Management and Organization Theory*. London: Sage.

Bok, D. (1997) 'Measuring the Performance of Government', pp. 55–76, in J. Nye, P. Zelikow, and D. King (eds) *Why People Don't Trust*

Government. Cambridge, Mass.: Harvard University Press.

Boorsma, P. and Mol, N. (1995) 'The Dutch Public Financial Revolution', pp. 219–32, in W. Kickert and F. van Vught (eds) *Public Policy and Administration Sciences in the Netherlands*. London: Prentice-Hall/Harvester Wheatsheaf.

Borins, S. (1995) 'Public Sector Innovation: The Implications of New Forms of Organisation and Work', pp. 260–87, in G. Peters and D. Savoie (eds) *Governance in a Changing Environment*. Montreal and Kingston: Canadian Centre for Management Development and McGill-Queen's University Press.

Boston, J. (1995) 'Lessons from the Antipodes', pp. 161–77, in B. O'Toole and G. Jordan (eds) *Next Steps: Improving Management in Government?* Aldershot: Dartmouth.

—— Martin, J., Pallot, J., and Walsh, P. (1996) *Public Management: The New Zealand Model*. Auckland: Oxford University Press.

Bouckaert, G. (1994) 'The History of the Productivity Movement', pp. 361–97, in M. Holzer and A. Halachmi (eds) *Competent Government: Theory and Practice: The Best of Public Productivity and Management Review, 1985–1993*. Burke: Chatelaine Press.

—— (1995a) 'Charters as Frameworks for Awarding Quality: The Belgian, British and French Experience', pp. 185–200, in H. Hill and H. Klages (eds) *Trends in Public Sector Renewal, Recent Developments and Concepts of Awarding Excellence*. Europäischer Verlag der Wissenschaften, Beiträge zur Politikwissenschaft, Band 58, Frankfurt am Main: Peter Lang.

—— (1995b) 'Improving Performance Measurement', pp. 379–412, in A. Halachmi and G. Bouckaert (eds) *The Enduring Challenges of Public Management: Surviving and Excelling in a Changing World*. San Francisco: Jossey-Bass.

—— (1996a) 'Informing the Clients: The Role of Public Service Standards Statements', pp. 109–16, in OECD, *Responsive Government, Service Quality Initiatives*. Paris: OECD, PUMA.

—— (1996b) 'Measurement of Public Sector Performance: Some European Perspectives', pp. 223–37, in A. Halachmi and G. Bouckaert (eds) *Organisational Performance and Measurement in the Public Sector*. London: Quorum Books.

—— (2000a) 'Techniques de modernisation et modernisation des techniques: Evaluer la modernisation de la gestion publique', pp. 107–28, in L. Rouban (réd) *Le Service Public en Devenir*. Paris: L'Harmattan.

—— (2000b) 'Trajectories of Modernisation and Reform in Financial Management in the Public Sector', pp. 123–36, in F. Theron, A. Van Rooyen, and J. Van Baalen (eds) *Good Governance for People: Policy and Management*. South Africa: School of Public Management and Planning, University of Stellenbosch.

—— (2001) 'Pride and Performance in Public Service: Some Patterns of Analysis', in *International Review of Administrative Sciences*, 67, pp. 9–20.

—— (2002a) 'Modernising the Rechtsstaat: Paradoxes of the Management Agenda', pp. 71–83, in K.-P. Sommermann and J. Ziekow (eds) *Perspectiven der Verwaltungsforschung*. Berlin: Duncker & Humblot.

—— (2002b) 'Administrative Convergence in the EU: Some Conclusions for CEEC's', pp. 59–68, in F. Van den Berg, G. Jenei, and L.T. LeLoup (eds) *East-West Co-Operation in Public Sector Reform: Cases and Results in Central and Eastern Europe*. Amsterdam: International Institute of Administrative Sciences Monographs (Vol 18), IOS Press.

—— (2002c) 'Reform of Budgetary Systems in the Public Sector', pp. 17–42, in M. Högye (ed) *Local Government Budgeting*. Budapest: OSI/LGI, Open Society Institute (Local Government and Public Service Reform Initiative).

—— and Auwers, T. (1999) *Modernisering van de Vlaamse overheid*, Brugge: Die Keure.

—— (2003a) 'Renewing Public Leadership: The Context for Public Service Delivery Reform' in Finlay Jane, Debicki Marek (eds) *Delivering Public Services in CEE Countries: Trends and Developments*. NISPAcee, Bratislava, pp. 15–26.

—— (2003b) 'La Réforme de la Gestion Publique change-t'elle les Systémes Administratifs?' *Revue Française d'Administration Publique*, No 105/106, pp. 39–54.

—— and François, A. (1999) *Modernisation de l'administration: les questions de recherche*. Bruxelles: SSTC.

—— Kampen, J., Maddens, B., and van de Walle, S. (2001) *Klantentevredenheidsmetingen bij de Overheid: cerste rapport "Burgergericht Besturen: Kwaliteit en Vertrouwen in de Overheid"*, Leuven: Instituut voor de Overheid.

——and Ulens, W. (1998) *Mesure de la performance dans le service public: exemples étrangers pour les pouvoirs publics Belges*. Bruxelles: Service Fédereaux des Affaires Scientifiques, Techniques et Culturelles.

——and Van Reeth, W. (1998) 'Budget Modelling for Efficiency and Effectiveness: The Case of the Flemish Government', pp. 43–53, in G. de Graan and F. Volmer (eds) *Performance Budgeting: A Perspective on Modelling and Strategic Planning*. Delft: Eburon.

——and Verhoest, K. (1999) 'A Comparative Perspective on Decentralisation as a Context for Contracting in the Public Sector, Practice and Theory', pp. 199–239, in Y. Fortin (ed) *La Contractualisation dans le Secteur Public dans des Pays Industrialisés depuis 1980*. Paris: L'Harmattan.

Bouckaert, G. Ormond, D., and Peters, G. (2000) *A Potential Governance Agenda for Finland*, Research Report No.8. Helsinki: Ministry of Finance.

——and Peters, B. G. (2002) 'Performance Measurement and Management: The Achilles' Heel in Administrative Modernization', in *Public Performance & Management Review*. London: Sage, 25:4, pp. 359–62.

——van Dooren W. (2003) 'Performance Measurement and Management in Public Sector Organizations', in Bovaird Tony & Löffler Elke (eds) *Public Management and Governance*, Routledge, London, pp. 127–136.

——Van Dooren, W., Verschuere, B., Voets, J., and Wayenberg, E. (2002) 'Trajectories for Modernizing Local Governance, Revisiting the Flanders Case', in *Public Management Review, an international journal of research and theory*. Routledge, 4:3, pp. 309–42.

——and Thijs, N. (2003) *Kwaliteit in de publieke sector. Een handboek voor kwaliteitsmanagement in de publieke sector o.b.v. een internationaal comparatieve studie*. Gent: Academia Press.

Bourgault, J. and Carroll, B. (1997) 'The Canadian Senior Public Service: The Last Vestiges of the Whitehall Model?', pp. 91–100, in J. Bougault, M. Demers, and C. Williams (eds) *Public Administration and Public Management in Canada*. Quebec: Les Publications du Quebec.

——and Savoie, D. (1998) *Managing at the Top*. Paper for the authors' roundtable, Revitalising the Public Service. Ottawa: Canadian Centre for Management Development. 12–14 November.

——Dion, S. and Lemay, M. (1993) 'Creating Corporate Culture: Lessons from the Canadian Federal Government', *Public Administration Review*, 53:1, pp. 73–80.

Bourgon, J. (1998) *Fifth Annual Report to the Prime Minister on the Public Service of Canada*. Ottawa: Privy Council Office.

Bovens, M. (1998) *The Quest for Responsibility: Accountability and Citizenship in Complex Organizations*. Cambridge: Cambridge University Press.

——and Zouridis, S. (2002) 'From Street-level to System-level Bureaucracies: How Information and Communication Technology is Transforming Administrative Discretion and Constitutional Control', *Public Administration Review*, 62:2, pp. 174–84.

Boyne, G. (1998) 'Bureaucratic Theory Meets Reality: Public Choice and Service Contracting in US Local Government', *Public Administration Review*, 58:6, pp. 474–84 November/December.

——Farrell, C., Law, J., Powell, M., and Walker, R. (2003) *Evaluating Public Management Reforms*. Buckingham: Open University Press.

Brans, M. and Hondeghem, A. (1999) 'The Senior Civil Service in Belgium', pp. 121–46, in E. C. Page and V. Wright (eds), *Bureaucratic Élites in Western European States*. London: Oxford University Press.

Bruijn, H. de (2002) *Managing Performance in the Public Sector*. London: Routledge.

Brunsson, N. (1989) *The Organisation of Hypocrisy: Talk, Decisions and Actions in Organisations*. Chichester, UK: John Wiley.

——and Olsen, J. (1993) *The Reforming Organization*. London and New York: Routledge.

Bureau of Transport and Communications Economics (1995) *Evaluation of the Black Spot Program*. Canberra: Australia Government Publishing Service.

Burrell, G. (1997) *Pandemonium: Towards a Retro-organization Theory*. London: Sage.

Caiden, N. (1988) 'Shaping Things to Come', pp. 43–58, in I. Rubin (ed) *New Directions in Budget Theory*. Albany: SUNY Press.

Camp, R. (1989) *Benchmarking: The Search for Industry Best Practices That Lead to a Superior Performance*. Milwaukee: Quality Press.

Canadian Broadcasting Corporation (1994) *The Remaking of New Zealand*. Toronto: CBC Radio Works.

Canadian Centre for Management Development (1998a) *Citizen/client Surveys: Dispelling Myths and Redrawing Maps*. Ottawa: CCMD.

——(1998b) *Government at Your Service: A Progress Report from the Citizen-Centred Service Network*. Ottawa: CCMD.

Carter, N. (1998) 'On the Performance of Performance Indicators', pp. 177–94, in M.-C. Kesler, P. Lascoumbes, M. Setbon, and J.-C. Thoenig (eds) *Évaluation des politiques publiques*. Paris: L'Harmattan.

——Klein, R. and Day, P. (1992) *How Organisations Measure Success: The Use of Performance Indicators in Government*. London: Routledge.

Castles, F., Gerritsen, R., and Vowles, J. (eds) (1996) *The Great Experiment: Labour Parties and Public Policy Transformation in Australia and New Zealand*. St Leonards, NSW: Allen & Unwin.

Centre for Finnish Business and Policy Studies (1996) *Not Revolution but Re-evaluation: A Report of Political Decision-making in Finland*. Helsinki (translated by the Public Management Department, Ministry of Finance). April.

Chancellor of the Duchy of Lancaster (1997) *Next Steps: Agencies in Government: Review, 1996*, Cm3579. London: The Stationery Office.

Chancellor of the Exchequer (1998) *Modern Public Services for Britain: Investing in Reform*, Cm4011. London: The Stationery Office.

Chapman, R. (1998) 'Problems of Ethics in Public Sector Management', *Public Money and Management*, 18:1, pp. 9–13, January/March.

Christiansen, T. (2001) 'The European Commission: Administration in Turbulent Times', pp. 95–114, in J. Richardson (ed) *European Union: Power and Policymaking*, 2nd edn. London: Routledge.

Christensen, T. and Lægreid, P. (eds) (2001) *New Public Management: The Transformation of Ideas and Practice*. Aldershot: Ashgate.

Clark, D. (1997) *The Civil Service and New Government*, speech by the Rt. Hon. Dr David Clark, MP, Chancellor of the Duchy of Lancaster, QEII Centre, London, 17 June.

——(1998) 'The Modernization of the French Civil Service: Crisis, Change and Continuity', *Public Administration*, 76:1, pp. 97–115, Spring.

Clarke, J. and Newman, J. (1997) *The Managerial State*. London: Sage.

Cochrane, A. (1993) *Whatever Happened to Local Government?* Buckingham: Open University Press.

Comité pour la réorganisation et la déconcentration de l'administration (1995) *33 propositions pour rendre plus efficace l'administrat territoriale de l'État*. Rapport du Comité, Paris, April.

Committee of Independent Experts (1999) *First Report on Allegations Regarding Fraud, Mismangement and Nepotism in the European Commission*. Brussels, 15 March.

Commonwealth (1983) *RAPS/Reforming the Australian Public Service: A Statement of the Government's Intentions*. Canberra: AGPS.

Commonwealth Secretariat (1993) *Administrative and Managerial Reform: A Commonwealth Portfolio of Current Good Practice*. London: Management Development Programme, Commonwealth Secretariat.

Cowper, J. and Samuels, M. (1997), 'Performance Benchmarking in the Public Sector: The United Kingdom Experience', pp. 11–31, in OECD, *Benchmarking, Evaluation and Strategic Management in the Public Sector*. Paris: PUMA/OECD.

Crosby, P. (1979) *Quality is Free*. New York: McGraw-Hill.

Czarniawska, B. and Sevón, G. (eds) (1996) *Translating Organizational change*. New York: de Gruyter.

Denham, A. and Garnett, M. (1998) *British Think Tanks and the Climate of Opinion*. London: UCL Press.

Department of Finance (1996) *Measuring Up: A Primer for Benchmarking in the Australian Public Service*. Discussion Paper No. 4. Canberra: Resource Management Improvement Branch.

Department of Finance and Administration (1998a) *The Performance Improvement Cycle: Guidance for Managers*. Canberra: Department of Finance and Administration.

——(1998b) *Lessons Learned from Others: International Experience on the Identification and Monitoring of Outputs and Outcomes*. Discussion Paper 2. Canberra: Department of Administration and Finance.

Derksen, W. and Kortsen, A. (1995) 'Local Government: A Survey', pp. 63–86, in W. Kickert and F. van Vught (eds) *Public Policy and*

Administration Sciences in the Netherlands. London: Prentice-Hall/Harvester Wheatsheaf.

Derlien, H.-U. (1998) *From Administrative Reform to Administrative Modernization.* Bamberg: Verwaltungswissenschaftliche Beitrage 33.

Development Team (1998) *International Experience on the Identification and Monitoring of Outputs and Outcomes.* Canberra: Department of Finance and Administration, March.

Dorrell, S. (1993) *Public Sector Change is a World-wide Movement.* Speech by the Financial Secretary to the Treasury, Stephen Dorrell, to the Chartered Institute of Public Finance and Accountancy, London, 23 September.

Douglas, M. (1982) *In the Active Voice.* London: Routledge.

Driscoll, A. and Morris, J. (2001) 'Stepping Out: Rhetorical Devices and Culture Change in Management in the UK Civil Service', *Public Administration*, 79:4, pp. 803–24.

Dryzek, J. (1996) 'The Informal Logic of Institutional Design', pp. 103–25, in R. Goodin (ed) *The Theory of Institutional Design*, Cambridge: Cambridge University Press.

Du Gay, P. (2000) *In Praise of Bureaucracy.* London: Sage.

Duhamel, R. (1996) *Evaluation Report: Improved Reporting to Parliament Project on Performance Indicators.* A report of the Parliamentary Working Group. Ottawa, December.

Dunleavy, P. (1991) *Democracy, Bureaucracy and Public Choice: Economic Explanations in Political Science.* Hemel Hempstead: Harvester Wheatsheaf.

—— (1994) 'The Globalisation of Public Service Production: Can Government be the "Best in the World"?', *Public Policy and Administration*, 9:2, pp. 36–65, Summer.

—— and Hood, C. (1994) 'From Old Public Administration to New Public Management', *Public Money and Management*, 14:3, pp. 9–16, July/September.

Dunn, W. (1993) 'Policy Reforms as Arguments', pp. 254–90, in F. Fischer and J. Forester (eds) *The Argumentative Turn in Policy Analysis and Planning.* London: UCL Press.

Dunsire, A. (1973) *Administration: The Word and the Science.* London: Martin Robertson.

—— (1993) 'Modes of Governance', pp. 21–34, in J. Kooiman (ed) *Modern Governance:*

New Government–Society Interactions. London: Sage.

Duran, P., Monnier, E., and Smith, A. (1995) 'Evaluation *à la française*', *Evaluation*, 1:1, pp. 45–63, July.

East, P. (1997) *Opening address to Public Service Senior Management Conference.* Wellington: New Zealand. 9 October.

Efficiency Unit (1988) *Improving Management in Government: The Next Steps.* London: HMSO.

Employment Service (1994) *Employment Service: An Evaluation of the Effects of Agency Status, 1990–1993.* London: Employment Department Group.

Esping-Andersen, G. (1990) *The Three Worlds of Welfare Capitalism.* Cambridge: Polity.

—— (1997*a*) *Evaluating EU Expenditure Programmes: A Guide.* Brussels: DGXIX/02, European Commission.

—— (1997*b*) *MAP 2000: Modernisation of Administration and Personnel Policy for the Year 2000* (draft memorandum from Mr Liikanen in agreement with the President: doc.IX/486/97). Brussels: DGIX.

—— (1998) *SEM 2000: Implementation by the Services: Information Note from the President, Mrs Gradin and Mr Liikanen.* SEC(98)760 final. Brussels: Secretariat General. 14 May.

—— (2000) *Reforming the Commission: A White Paper* (Parts 1 and 2). Communication from Mr Kinnock, in agreement with the President and Mrs Schreyer. Brussels: European Commission. 1 March.

—— (2001*a*) *European Governance: A White Paper.* COM2001/408. Brussels: European Commission.

—— (2001*b*) *Implementing Activity Based Management in the Commission.* Communication from the President in agreement with Mr Kinnock and Mrs Schreyer to the Commission. SEC92001) 1197/6&7. Brussels: European Commission.

European Foundation for Quality Management (1996) *Self-assessment, 1997: Guidelines for the Public Sector.* Brussels: EFQM.

Eurostat (2002) *Eurostat Yearbook 2002: The Statistical Guide to Europe.* Luxembourg: Eurostat/ European Commission.

Evaluation Partnership (1999) *Evaluation of the Implementation and Results of SEM2000 and Its*

Contribution to the Overall Management Reform of the Commission. Brussels: European Commission.

Evers, A., Haverinen, R., Leichsenring, K., and Wistow, G. (1997) *Developing Quality in Personal Social Services: Concepts, Cases and Comments*. Aldershot: Ashgate.

Executive Office of the President of the United States (1995) *Budget of the United States Government, Fiscal Year 1995*. Washington, DC.

Farnham, D., Horton, S., Barlow, J., and Hondeghem, A. (eds) (1996) *New Public Managers in Europe: Public Servants in Transition*. Basingstoke: Macmillan.

Fischer, F. and Forester, J. (eds) (1993) *The Argumentative Turn in Policy Analysis and Planning*. London: UCL Press.

Flösser, G. and Otto, H.-U. (1998) *Towards More Democracy in Social Services: Models of Culture and Welfare*. Berlin: de Gruyter.

Flynn, N. and Strehl, F. (eds) (1996) *Public Sector Management in Europe*. London: Prentice Hall/ Harvester Wheatsheaf.

Foster, C. (1992) *Privatization, Public Ownership and the Regulation of Natural Monopolies*. Oxford: Blackwell.

—— and Plowden, F. (1996) *The State Under Stress*. Buckingham: Open University Press.

Gaertner, K. and Gaertner, G. (1985) 'Performance-contingent Pay for Federal Managers', *Administration and Society*, 17:1, pp. 7–20.

Geertz, C. (1973) *The Interpretation of Culture*. London: Hutchinson.

General Accounting Office (1990) *Why and How the GAO is Reviewing Federal College Recruiting*. Washington, DC: US House of Representatives.

—— (1994) *Deficit Reduction: Experiences of Other Nations*. Washington, DC: GAO/AIMD-95-30. December.

—— (1995) *Managing for Results: Experiences Abroad Suggest Insights for Federal Management Reforms*. Washington, DC: GAO/GGD-95-120.

—— (1997) *Performance Budgeting: Past Initiatives Offer Insight for GPRA Implementation*. Washington, DC: GAO/AIMD-97-46. March.

—— (1998) *The Results Act: Observations on the Department of State's Fiscal Year 1999 Annual Performance Plan*. Washington, DC: GAO/NSIAD-98-210R. June.

—— (2001) *Managing for Results: Federal Managers' Views on Key Management Issues Vary Widely Across Agencies*. Washington, DC: GAO-01-592.

Giddens, A. (1990) *The Consequences of Modernity*. Cambridge: Polity Press.

Gillibrand, A. and Hilton, B. (1998) 'Resource Accounting and Budgeting: Principles, Concepts and Practice', *Public Money and Management*, 18:2, pp. 21–8, April/June.

Götz, K. (1997) 'Acquiring Political Craft: Training Grounds for Top Officials in the German Core Executive', *Public Administration*, 75:4, pp. 753–75, Winter.

Goodin, R. (1996) *The Theory of Institutional Design*. Cambridge: Cambridge University Press.

Gore, A. (1995) *Common sense government: works betters, costs less*. Washington DC: US Government Printing Office.

—— (1996) *The Best-kept Secrets in Government: A Report to President Bill Clinton*. Washington, DC: National Performance Review.

—— (1997) *Businesslike Government: Lessons Learned from America's Best Companies*. Washington, DC: National Performance Review.

Government Decision in Principle on Reforms in Central and Regional Government (1993) Helsinki: Council of State.

Grace, P. (1984) *Burning Money: The Waste of Your Tax Dollars*. New York: Macmillan.

Gregory, R. (1998) 'Political Responsibility for Bureaucratic Incompetence: Tragedy at Cave Creek', *Public Administration*, 76:3, pp. 519–38, Autumn.

Greve, C., Flinders, M., and van Thiel, S. (1999) 'Quangos—What's in a Name: Defining Quangos from a Comparative Perspective', *Governance*, 12:1 pp. 129–46.

Grömig, E. and Gruner, K. (1998) 'Reform in den Rathäusern. Neueste umfrage des Deutschen Städtetages zum them Verwaltungsmodernisierung', *Der Städtetag*, 8, pp. 581–7.

—— and Thielen, H. (1996) 'Städte auf dem reformweg: zum stand der Verwaltungs modernisierung', *Der Städtetag*, 9, pp. 596–600.

Gunn, L. (1987) 'Perspectives on Public Management', pp. 33–46, in J. Kooiman and K. Eliassen (eds), *Managing Public Organizations:*

Lessons from European Experience. London: Sage.

Gustafsson, A. (2000) *Performance Budgeting in Sweden: Outline of a Reform programme.* Paper presented to an International Symposium on Accruals Accounting and Budgeting, Paris, 13/14 November. Stockholm: Ministry of Finance

Gustafsson, L. (1987) 'Renewal of the Public Sector in Sweden', *Public Administration*, 65:2, pp. 179–92.

Guyomarch, A. (1999) '"Public Service", "Public Management" and the Modernization of French Public Administration', *Public Administration*, 77:1, pp. 171–93.

Habermas, J. (1976) *Legitimation Crisis*. London: Heinemann.

Hacque, S. (2001) 'The Diminishing Publicness of Public Service Under the Current Mode of Governance', *Public Administration Review*, 61:1, pp. 65–82, January/February.

Halachmi, A. and Bouckaert, G. (1995) *The Enduring Challenges of Public Management*. San Francisco: Jossey-Bass.

Halligan, J. (1996a) 'The Diffusion of Civil Service Reform', pp. 288–317, in H. Bekke, J. Perry, and T. Toonen (eds) *Civil Service Systems in Comparative Perspective*. Bloomington, IND: Indiana University Press.

—— (1996b) 'Australia: Balancing Principles and Pragmatism', pp. 71–112, in J. Olsen and B. Peters (eds) *Lessons from Experience: Experiential Learning in Administrative Reforms in Eight Democracies*. Oslo: Scandinavian University Press.

—— (1997) 'New Public Sector Models: Reform in Australia and New Zealand', pp. 17–46, in J.-E. Lane (ed) *Public Sector Reform: Rationale, Trends and Problems*. London: Sage.

—— (2002) 'Politicians, Bureaucrats and Public Sector Reform in Australia and New Zealand', pp. 157–68, in G. Peters and J. Pierre (eds) *Politicians, Bureaucrats and Administrative Reform*. London: Routledge.

—— and Power, J. (1992) *Political Management in the 1990s*. Melbourne: Oxford University Press.

Hammer, M. and Champy, J. (1995) *Re-engineering the Corporation: A Manifesto for a Business Revolution* (rev. edn). London: Nicholas Brealey.

Hammond, K. (1996) *Human Judgement and Social Policy: Irreducible Uncertainty, Inevitable Error,*

Unavoidable Injustice. New York: Oxford University Press.

Handy, C. (1993) *Understanding Organisations*. Harmondsworth: Penguin.

Harden, I. (1992) *The Contracting State*. Buckingham: Open University Press.

Harder, P. and Lindquist, E. (1997) 'Expenditure Management and Reporting in the Government of Canada: Recent Development and Backgrounds', pp. 71–89, in J. Bougault, M. Demers, and C. Williams (eds) *Public Administration and Public Management: Experiences in Canada*. Québec: Les Publications de Québec.

Harrison, S. and Pollitt, C. (1994) *Controlling Health Professionals: The Future of Work and Organisation in the NHS*. Buckingham: Open University Press.

—— Hunter, D. J., and Pollitt, C. (1990) *The Dynamics of British Health Policy*. London: Unwin Hyman.

—— Marnoch, G., and Pollitt, C. (1992) *Just Managing: Power and Culture in the National Health Service*. Basingstoke: Macmillan.

Hartley, J. (1983) 'Ideology and Organizational Behaviour', *International Studies of Management and Organization*, 13:3, pp. 26–7.

Heclo, H. (1977) *A Government of Strangers*. Washington, DC: Brookings Institution.

Hede, A. (1991) 'Trends in the Civil Services of Anglo-American Systems', *Governance*, 4:4, pp. 489–510, October.

Held, D. (1987) *Models of Democracy*. Cambridge: Polity.

——, McGrew, A., Goldblatt, D., and Perraton, J. (1999) *Global Transformation*. Cambridge: Polity Press.

Heintzman, R. (1997) 'Canada and Public Administration', pp. 1–12, in J. Bourgault, M. Demers, and C. Williams (eds) *Public Administration and Public Management: Experiences in Canada*. Québec: Les Publications du Québec.

Hencke, D. (1998) 'Jobcentres Fiddled the Figures', *Guardian*, p. 2, 8 January.

Heseltine, M. (1980) 'Ministers and Management in Whitehall', *Management Services in Government*, 35.

High Quality Services, Good Governance, and a Responsible Civic Society (1998a) The

Government Resolution. Helsinki: Oy Edita Ab.

—— (1998*b*) Background Material. Helsinki: Oy Edita Ab.

Hill, H. and Klages, H. (1995) 'Verbindung mit dem Deutschen Landkreistag', in H. Hill and H. Klages (eds) *Kreisverwaltung der zukunft. Vergleichende untersuchung aktueller modernisierungsansätze in ausgewählten Kreisverwaltungen.* Düsseldorf: Raabe Fachverlag.

——(eds) (1993) *Qualitäts- und erfolgsorientiertes verwaltungsmanagement. Aktuelle tendenzen und entwurfe.* Berlin: Duncker and Humblot.

——(eds) (1996*a*) *Wege in die neue Steurung.* Düsseldorf: Raabe Fachverlag.

——(eds) (1996*b*) *Controlling im neuen Steurungsmodell. Werkstattberichte zur Einführung von Controlling.* Düsseldorf: Raabe Fachverlag.

Hill, M. and Hupe, P. (2002) *Implementing Public Policy.* London: Sage.

HM Treasury (1991) *Competing for Quality,* Cm1730. London: HMSO. November.

—— (1994) *Fundamental Review of HM Treasury's Running Costs* (The 'Southgate Report'). London: HM Treasury.

—— (1998) *Whole of Government Accounts.* London: HM Treasury. July.

Hofstede, G. (2001) *Culture's Consequences: Comparing Values, Behaviors, Institutions and Organizations Across Nations.* Thousand Oaks: CA, Sage.

Hojnacki, W. (1996) 'Politicization as a Civil Service Dilemma', pp. 137–64, in H. Bekke, J. Perry, and T. Toonen (eds) *Civil Service Systems in Comparative Perspective.* Bloomington and Indiana polis?: Indiana University Press.

Holkeri, K. and Summa, H. (1996) *Contemporary Developments in Performance Management: Evaluation of Public Management Reforms in Finland: from ad hoc Studies to a Programmatic Approach.* Paper presented to PUMA/OECD, Paris. 4–5 November.

—— and Nurmi, J. (2002) *Quality, Satisfaction and Trust in Government: The Finnish Case.* Paper presented to the Conference of the European Group of Public Administration, Potsdam. 4–7 September.

Holmes, M. and Shand, D. (1995) 'Management Reform: Some Practitioner Perspectives on the Past Ten Years', *Governance,* 8:4, pp. 551–78, October.

Hondeghem, A. (2000) 'The National Civil Service in Belgium', pp. 120–8, in H. J. G. M. Bekke and F. Van der Meer (eds), *Civil Service Systems in Western Europe,* Cheltenham: Edward Elgar.

—— and Vandermeulen, F. (2000) 'Competency Management in the Flemish and Dutch Civil Service', *The International Journal of Public Sector Management,* 13:4, pp. 342–53.

—— and Nelen, S.(2002) *L'égalité des sexes et la politique du personnel dans le secteur public,* Paris: L'Harmattan.

Hood, C. (1976) *The Limits of Administration.* Chichester: John Wiley.

—— (1991) 'A Public Management for all Seasons', *Public Administration,* 69:1, pp. 3–19, Spring.

—— (1995) 'Contemporary Public Management: A New Global Paradigm?', *Public Policy and Administration,* 10:2, pp. 104–17, Summer.

—— (1996) 'Exploring Variations in Public Management Reform of the 1980s', pp. 268–317, in H. Bekke, J. Perry, and T. Toonen (eds) *Civil Service Systems in Comparative Perspective.* Bloomington, IND: Indiana University Press.

—— (1998) *The Art of the State: Culture, Rhetoric and Public Management.* Oxford: Oxford University Press.

—— (2002) 'Control, Bargains, and Cheating: The Politics of Public-service Reform', *Journal of Public Administration Research and Theory (J-Part),* 12:3, pp. 309–32.

—— and Jackson, M. (1991) *Administrative Argument.* Aldershot: Dartmouth.

—— Scott, C., James, O., Jones, G., and Travers, A. (1999) *Regulation Inside Government: Waste Watchers, Quality Police, and Sleaze-busters.* Oxford: Oxford University Press.

Horton, S., Hondeghem, A., and Farnham, D. (eds) (2002) *Competency Management in the Public Sector.* Amsterdam/Brussels: IOS Press, International Institute of Administrative Sciences.

Howard, D. (1998) 'The French Strikes of 1995 and Their Political Aftermath', *Government and Opposition,* 33:2, pp. 199–220, Spring.

Hudson, J. (1999) *Informatization and the Delivery of Government Services: A Political Science Perspective*, Ph.D. thesis. Department of Government: Brunel University.

Hughes O. (1998) *Public Management and Administration: An Introduction* (2nd edn). Basingstoke: Macmillan.

ICM (1993) *Citizen's Charter Customer Survey* (conducted for the Citizen's Charter Unit). London: ICM Research.

Ingraham, P. (1997) 'Play it Again Sam; It's Still not Right: Searching for the Right Notes in Administrative Reform', *Public Administration Review*, 57:4, pp. 325–31, July/August.

——Thompson, J., and Sanders, P. (eds) (1998) *Transforming Government: Lessons from the Reinvention Laboratories*. San Francisco: Jossey-Bass.

Innovative Public Services Group (2002) *Survey Regarding Quality Activities in the Public Administrations of the European Union Member States*. Madrid: Subdireccion General de Gestion de Calidad (unpublished).

Jackson, P. (2001) 'Public Sector Value-added: Can the Public Sector Deliver?', *Public Administration*, 79:1, pp. 5–28.

Jobert, B. and Muller, P. (1987) *L'État en action*. Paris: Presses Universitaires de France.

Joss, R. and Kogan, M. (1995) *Advancing Quality: Total Quality Management in the National Health Service*. Buckingham: Open University Press.

Joustie, H. (2001) 'Performance Management in Finnish State Administration', pp. 18–19, in *Public Management in Finland*. Helsinki: Ministry of Finance.

Kam, C. and de Haan, J. (eds) (1991) *Terugtredende overheid: een evaluatie van de Grote Operaties*, Schoonhoven, Academic Services.

Kaufman, H. (1981) 'Fear of Bureaucracy: A Raging Pandemic', *Public Administration Review*, 41:1, pp. 1–9, January/February.

Kaufmann, F., Majone, G., and Ostrom, V. (eds) (1997) *Guidance, Control and Evaluation in the Public Sector*. Berlin: de Gruyter.

Keeling, D. (1972) *Management in Government*. London: Allen & Unwin.

Keohane, R. and Nye, J. (eds) (2000) *Governance in a Globalization World*. Washington, DC: Brookings Institution.

Kernaghan, K. (1997) 'Values, Ethics and Public Service', pp. 101–11, in J. Bourgault, M. Demers, and C. Williams (eds) *Public Administration and Public Management: Experiences in Canada*. Québec: Les Publications du Québec.

Kettl, D. (1994) *Reinventing Government? Appraising the National Performance Review*. Washington, DC: The Brookings Institution.

——(2000) *The Global Public Management Revolution: A Report on the Transformation of Governance*, Washington, DC: The Brookings Institution.

——Ingraham, P., Sanders, R., and Horner, C. (1996) *Civil Service Reform: Building a Government That Works*. Washington, DC: The Brookings Institution.

Kickert, W. (ed) (1997) *Public Management and Administrative Reform in Western Europe*. Cheltenham: Edward Elgar.

——(2000) *Public Management Reforms in the Netherlands: Social Reconstruction of Reform Ideas and Underlying Frames of Reference*. Delft: Eburon.

——and In't Veld, R. (1995) 'National Government, Governance and Administration', pp. 45–62, in W. Kickert and F. van Vught (eds) *Public Policy and Administration Sciences in the Netherlands*. London: Prentice-Hall/Harvester Wheatsheaf.

——Klijn, E.-H. and Koppenjan, J. (eds) (1997) *Managing Complex Networks: Strategies for the Public Sector*. London: Sage.

King, G., Keohane, R., and Verber, S. (1994) *Designing Social Enquiry: Scientific Inference in Qualitative Research*. New Jersey: Princeton University Press.

Klages, H. and Löffler, E. (1996) 'Public Sector Modernisation in Germany: Recent Trends and Emerging Strategies', pp. 132–45, in N. Flynn and F. Strehl (eds) *Public Sector Management in Europe*. London: Prentice-Hall/Harvester Wheatsheaf.

——(1998) 'New Public Management in Germany: The Implementation Process of the New Steering Model', *International Review of Administrative Sciences*, 64, pp. 41–54.

König, K. (1996) *On the Critique of New Public Management*. Speyer, 155: Speyerer Forschungsberichte.

——(1997) 'Entrepreneurial Management or Executive Administration: The Perspective of Classical Administration', pp. 217–36, in

W. Kickert (ed) *Public Management and Administrative Reform in Western Europe*. Cheltenham: Edward Elgar.

——and Siedentopf, H. (eds) (2001) *Public Administration in Germany*. Baden-Baden: Nomos.

Korsten, A. and van der Krogt, T. (1995) 'Human Resources Management', pp. 233–48, in W. Kickert and F. van Vught (eds) *Public Policy and Administration Sciences in the Netherlands*. London: Prentice-Hall/Harvester Wheatsheaf.

Lalenis, K., de Jong, M., and Mamadouh, V. (2002) '*Families of Nations and Institutional Transplantation*', pp. 33–52, in M. de Jong, K. Lalenis, and V. Mamadouh (eds) *The Theory and Practice of Institutional Transplantation: Experiences with the Transfer of Policy Institutions*. Dordrecht: Kluwer.

Lane, J. E. (1991) *Politics and Society in Western Europe*. (2nd edition). London: Sage.

——(1995) 'The Decline of the Swedish Model', *Governance*, 8:4, pp. 579–90.

——(ed) (1997) *Public Sector Reform: Rationale, Trends and Problems*. London: Sage.

——(2000) *New Public Management*. London: Routledge.

——and Emson, S. (2002) *Culture and Politics: A Comparative Approach*. Aldershot: Ashgate.

Laurance, J. (1997) 'New National Checks after Breast Cancer Screening "Disgrace"', *The Independent*, 4 November, p. 5.

Leeuw, F. (1995) *The Dutch Perspective: Trends in Performance Measurement*. Paper presented at the International Evaluation Conference, Vancouver, 1–5 November.

Leftwich, A. (ed) (1984) *What is Politics? The Activity and its Study*. Oxford: Blackwell.

Le Grand, J. and Bartlett, W. (1993) *Quasi Markets and Social Policy*. Basingstoke: Macmillan.

Le Loup, L. (1988) 'From micro-budgeting to macro-budgeting', pp. 19–42, in I. Rubin (ed) *New Directions in Budget Theory*. Albany: SUNY Press.

Levy, R. (2003) 'Confused Expectations: Decentralizing the Management of EU Programmes', *Public Money and Management*, 23:2, pp. 83–92.

Lewis, D. (1987) *Hidden Agendas: Politics, Law and Disorder* London: Hamish Hamilton.

Lijphart, A. (1984) *Democracies: Patterns of Majoritarian and Consensus Government in Twenty-one Countries*. London: Yale University Press.

——(1999) *Patterns of Democracy: Governance Forms and Performance in 36 Countries*. New Haven: Yale University Press.

Likierman, A. (1995) 'Performance Indicators: Twenty Lessons from Early Managerial Use', pp. 57–66, in P. Jackson (ed) *Measures for Success in the Public Sector*. London: Public Finance Foundation/Chartered Institute of Public Finance and Accountancy.

——(1998*a*) 'Resource Accounting and Budgeting: Where Are We Now?', *Public Money and Management*, 18:2, pp. 17–20, April/June.

——(1998*b*) 'Report: Recent Developments in Resource Accounting and Budgeting (RAB)', *Public Money and Management*, 18:4, pp. 62–4, October/December.

Lindblom, C. (1959) 'The Science of Muddling Through', *Public Administration Review*, 19:3, pp. 79–88.

——(1979) 'Still Muddling, Not Yet Through', *Public Administration Review*, 39:6, pp. 517–26.

Listhaug, O. and Wiberg, M. (1995) 'Confidence in Public and Private Institutions', pp. 298–322, in H.-D. Klingemann and D. Fuchs (eds) *Citizens and the State: Beliefs in Government*, vol.1. Oxford: Oxford University Press.

Löffler, E. (1995) *The Modernisation of the Public Sector in an International Perspective: Concepts and Methods of Awarding and Assessing Quality in the Public Sector in OECD Countries*. Speyer Forschungsberichte 151, Speyer: Forschungsinstitut für Öffentliche Verwaltung.

Lomas, K. (1991) *Contemporary Finnish Poetry*. Newcastle-upon-Tyne: Bloodaxe Books.

Lowndes, V. (1996) 'Varieties of New Institutionalism: A Critical Appraisal', *Public Administration*, 74:2, pp. 181–97, Summer.

——and Skelcher, C. (1998) 'The Dynamics of Multi-organisational Partnerships: an Analysis of Changing Modes of Governance', *Public Administration*, 76:2, pp. 313–33, Summer.

Lynn, L., Heinrich, C., and Hill, C. (2001) *Improving Governance: A New Logic for Empirical Research*. Washington, DC: Georgetown University Press.

Maas, G. and van Nispen, F. (1999) 'The Quest for a Leaner, not a Meaner Government', *Research in Public Administration*, 5, pp. 63–86.

Maeschalk, J., Hondeghem, A., and Pelgrims, C. (2002) 'Die evolutie naar een "Nieuwe Politieke Cultuur" in België: een beleidswetenschappelijke analyse' in *Beleidswetenschap*, 16, 4, pp. 295–317.

Maidment, R. and McGrew, A. (1986) *The American Political Process*. London: Sage.

Mallory, J. (1997) 'Particularities and Systems of Government', pp. 15–23, in J. Bourgault, M. Demers, and C. Williams (eds) *Public Administration and Public Management: Experiences in Canada*. Québec: Les Publications du Québec.

—— (1993*b*) *Building a Better Public Service*, Canberra, MAB/MIAC No.12, June.

—— (1994) *On-going Reform in the Australian Public Service: An Occasional Paper to the Prime Minister*, Canberra, MAB/MIAC No. 15, October.

Manning, N. (2001) 'The Legacy of the New Public Management in Developing Countries', *International Review of Administrative Sciences*, 76:2, pp. 297–312.

—— and Parison, N. (2004) *International public administration reform: implications for the Russian Federation*, Washington, DC: World Bank.

March, J. and Olsen, J. (1995) *Democratic Governance*. New York: Free Press.

Margetts, H. (1998) *Information Technology in Government: Britain and America*. London: Routledge.

Marmor, T., Mashaw, J., and Harvey, P. (1990) *America's Misunderstood Welfare State*. New York: Basic Books.

Matheson, A., Scanlan, G., and Tanner, R. (1997) 'Strategic Management in Government: Extending the Reform Model in New Zealand', pp. 81–99, in OECD, *Benchmarking, Evaluation and Strategic Management in the Public Sector*. Paris: PUMA/OECD.

Mayne, J. (1996) *Implementing Results-based Management and Performance-based Budgeting: Lessons from the Literature*, Discussion Paper No. 73. Ottawa: Office of the Auditor General of Canada.

Mazel, V. (1998) 'Supporting Managerial Growth of Top Dutch Civil Servants', *Public Management Forum*, IV:6, pp. 4–5, November/December.

McGuire, L. (2004) 'Contractualisation and performance measurement in Australia', pp. 113–39, in C. Pollitt and C. Talbot (eds)

Unbundled government, London and New York: Taylor and Francis.

Metcalfe, L. (1993) 'Public Management: From Imitation to Innovation', pp. 173–89, in J. Kooiman (ed) *Modern Governance: New Government–Society Interactions*. London: Sage.

—— and Richards, S. (1987) 'Evolving Public Management Cultures', pp. 65–86, in J. Kooiman and K. Eliassen (eds) *Managing Public Organizations*. London: Sage.

—— —— (1990) *Improving Public Management* (enlarged edition). London: Sage/European Institute of Public Administration.

Meyer, J. and Gupta, V. (1994) 'The Performance Paradox', *Research in Organizational Behavior*, 16, pp. 309–69.

—— and Rowan, B. (1991) 'Institutionalised Organisations: Formal Structure as Myth and Ceremony', in W. Powell and P. DiMaggio (eds) *The New Institutionalism in Organisational Analysis*. Chicago: University of Chicago Press.

Micheletti, M. (2000) 'The End of Big Government: is it Happening in the Nordic Countries?', *Governance*, 13:2, pp. 265–78.

Middlemass, K. (1995) *Orchestrating Europe: The Informal Politics of European Union, 1973–1995*. London: Fontana.

Mihm, C. J. (2001) 'Implementing GPRA: Progress and Challenges', pp. 101–12, in D. W. Forsythe (ed) *Quicker, Better, Cheaper? Managing Performance in American Government*. New York: The Rockefeller Institute Press.

Ministère de la Fonction Publique et des Réformes Administratives (1992) *La charte des services publiques*. Paris: Ministère de la Fonction Publique.

—— (1994*a*) *L'année de l'accueil dans les services publiques*. Paris: Ministère de la Fonction Publique.

—— (1994*b*) *Circulaire sur la création de points publiques en milieu rural*. Paris: Ministère de l'Intérieur et de l'Aménagement du Territoire, 8 August.

Ministerie van Financiën (1998) *Verder met resultaat: het agentschapsmodel 1991–1997*. Den Haag: Dutch Ministry of Finance.

Ministry of Finance (1993) *Government Decision in Principle on Reforms in Central and Regional Government*. Helsinki: Ministry of Finance.

—— (1995) *The Public Sector in Finland*. Helsinki (document prepared for a meeting of EU Directors-General).

—— (1997) *Public Management Reforms: Five Country Studies*. Helsinki: Ministry of Finance.

Mol, N. (1995) 'Quality improvement in the Dutch Department of Defence', pp. 103–28, in C. Pollitt and G. Bouckaert (eds) *Quality Improvement in European Public Services: Concepts, Cases and Commentary*. London: Sage.

Molander, P., Nilsson, J-E., and Schick, A. (2002) *Does Anyone Govern? The Relationship Between the Government Office and the Agencies in Sweden*. Report from the SNS Constitutional Project. Stockholm: SNS.

Montricher, N. de (1996) 'France: In Search of Relevant Changes', pp. 243–71, in J. Olsen and B. Peters (eds) *Lessons from Experience: Experiential Learning in Administrative Reforms in Eight Democracies*. Oslo: Scandinavian University Press.

Morgan, B. (1999) 'Regulating the Regulators: Meta-regulation as a Strategy for Re-inventing Government in Australia', *Public Management*, 1:1, pp. 49–65.

Murray, R. (1998) *Productivity as a Tool for Evaluation of Public Management Reform*. Paper presented to the European Evaluation Society Conference, Rome, 29–31 October.

Naschold, F., Oppen, M., Tondorf, K., and Wegener, A. (1994) *Neue Städte braucht das Land*. Berlin: Wissenschaftszentrum Berlin für Sozialforschung.

National Academy of Public Administration (1994) *Towards Useful Performance Measurement: Lessons Learned from Initial Pilot Performance Plans Prepared Under the Government Performance and Results Act*. Washington, DC: National Academy of Public Administration. November.

National Audit Office (1995) *The Meteorological Office: Evaluation of Performance*, HC693. London: HMSO. 25 August.

—— (1996) *State Audit in the European Union*. London: National Audit Office.

—— (1997) *Annual Report, 1997*. London: National Audit Office.

—— (1999) *Government on the Web*, HC87. London: The Stationary Office.

National Performance Review (1997*a*) *Blair House Papers*. Washington, DC: National Performance Review (see also NPR website, http://www.npr.gov). January.

—— (1997*b*) *Serving the American Publics: Best Practices in Customer-driven Strategic Planning*, Federal Benchmarking Consortium Study Report. Washington, DC: National Performance Review.

Newberry, S. (2002) 'New Zealand's Public Sector Financial Management System: Resource Erosion in Government Departments', Ph.D. thesis. University of Canterbury, New Zealand.

Next Steps Team (1998) *Towards Best Practice: An Evaluation of the First Two Years of the Public Sector Benchmarking Project, 1996–98*. London: Efficiency and Effectiveness Group, Cabinet Office.

Nivette, N. (1996) *The Decline of Deference*. Peterborough: Broadview Press.

Nye, J. Jr., Zelikow, P., and King, D. (eds) (1997) *Why People Don't Trust Government*. Cambridge, Mass.: Harvard University Press.

OECD (1987) *Administration as Service: The public as client*. Paris: PUMA/OECD.

—— (1992) *OECD Country Profiles*. Paris: OECD.

—— (1993*a*) *Managing with Market-type Mechanisms*. Paris: PUMA/OECD.

—— (1993*b*) *Private Pay for Public Work: Performance-related Pay for Public Service Managers*. Paris: PUMA/OECD.

—— (1994) *Public Management Developments: Survey 1993*. Paris: PUMA/OECD.

—— (1995) *Governance in Transition: Public Management Reforms in OECD Countries*. Paris: PUMA/OECD.

—— (1996) *Responsive Government: Service Quality Initiatives*. Paris: PUMA/OECD.

—— (1997*a*) *In Search of Results: Performance Management Practices*. Paris: PUMA/OECD.

—— (1997*b*) *The Changing Role of the Central Budget Office*. OCDE/GD(97)109. Paris: PUMA/OECD.

—— (1997*c*) *Family, Market and Community: Equity and Efficiency in Social Policy*. Social Policy Studies No. 21. Paris: OECD.

—— (1997*d*) *OECD Country Profiles*. Paris: OECD.

—— (1998) *Budgeting in Sweden*. Paris: PUMA/OECD.

—— (2000) Reforms for an Aging Society, Paris: OECD.

—— (2001) *Managing cross-cutting issues*. Paris: PUMA/OECD (www.oecd.org/puma/strat/managing.htm).

—— (2002*a*) *Public Sector Modernisation: A New Agenda*, CCNM/GF/GOV/PUBG(2002)1. Paper presented at the OECD Global Forum on Governance Seminar at the London School of Economics, 2–3 December. Paris: OECD.

—— (2002*b*) *Governing for Results*, CCNM/GF/GOV/PUBG (2002)3. Paper presented at the OECD Global Forum on Governance Seminar at the London School of Economics, 2–3 December. Paris: OECD.

—— (2002*c*) *Economic Survey of the Netherlands*. Paris: OECD.

—— (2003) *Managing senior management: senior civil service reform in OECD member countries*, GOV/PUMA (2003) 17, Paris: OECD, 30 October.

Office of Management and Budget (2002) *The President's Management Agenda*. Washington, DC: Government Printing Office (http://www.whitehouse.gov/omb/).

Office of Public Services Reform (2002) *Better Government Services: Executive Agencies in the 21st Century*. London: Cabinet Office (www.civilservice.gov.uk/agencies).

Olsen, J. and Peters, B. (eds) (1996) *Lessons from Experience: Experiential Learning in Administrative Reforms in Eight Democracies*. Oslo: Scandinavian University Press.

Osborne, D. and Gaebler, T. (1992) *Reinventing Government: How the Entrepreneurial Spirit is Transforming the Public Sector*. Reading, Mass.: Adison Wesley.

Osborne, S. (ed) (2000) *Public–Private partnerships: Theory and Practice in International Perspective*. London: Routledge.

O'Toole, B. and Jordan, G. (eds) (1995) *Next Steps: Improving Management in Government*. Dartmouth: Aldershot.

Packwood, T., Pollitt, C., and Roberts, S. (1998) 'Good Medicine? A Case Study of Business Re-engineering in a Hospital', *Policy and Politics*, 26:4, pp. 401–15.

Page, E. (1997) *People Who Run Europe*. Oxford: Clarendon Press.

Painter, C., Rouse, J., Isaac-Henry, K., and Munk, L. (1996) *Changing Local Governance: Local Authorities and Non-elected Agencies*. Luton: Local Government Management Board.

Parker, D. (1999) 'Regulating Public Utilities: What Other Countries Can Learn from the UK Experience', *Public Management*, 1:1, pp. 93–120.

Parker, D. (ed) (2000) *Privatisation and Corporate Performance*. Cheltenham: Elgar.

Pawson, R. and Tilley, N. (1997) *Realistic Evaluation*. London: Sage.

Pederson, T. (2002) 'Consumer Power Will Transform the Public Sector', *2Q Conference* (newspaper of the 2nd Quality Conference for Public Administrations in the EU, Copenhagen, October), pp. 2–3.

Perrow, C. (1972) *Complex Organisations*. Glenview: Scott Foreman.

Perry, J. and Kraemer, K. (eds) (1983) *Public Management: Public and Private Perspectives*. California: Mayfield.

——and Pearce, J. (1985) 'Civil Service Reform and the Politics of Performance Appraisal', pp. 140–60, in D. Rosenbloom (ed) *Public Personnel Policy: The Politics of Civil Service*. London: Associated Faculty Press.

Peters, G. (1995) 'Bureaucracy in a Divided Regime: The United States', pp. 18–38, in J. Pierre (ed) *Bureaucracy in the Modern State: An Introduction to Comparative Public Administration*. Aldershot: Edward Elgar.

—— (1996*a*) 'Theory and Methodology', pp. 13–41, in H. Bekke, J. Perry, and T. Toonen (eds) *Civil Service Systems in Comparative Perspective*. Bloomington, IND: Indiana University Press.

—— (1996*b*) *The Future of Governing: Four Emerging Models*. Kansas: University Press of Kansas.

—— (1998*a*) 'What Works? The Antiphons of Administrative Reform', pp. 78–107, in B. G. Peters and D. Savoie (eds) *Taking Stock: Assessing Public Sector Reforms*. Montreal and Kingston: Canadian Centre for Management Development and McGill-Queen's University Press.

—— (1998*b*) 'Managing Horizontal Government: The Politics of Co-ordination', *Public Administration*, 76:2, pp. 295–311, Summer.

——and Savoie, D. (1998) 'Introduction', pp. 3–19, in B. G. Peters and D. Savoie (eds) *Taking Stock: Assessing Public Sector Reforms*, Montreal and Kingston: Canadian Centre for Management Development and McGill-Queen's University Press.

—— and Pierre, J. (eds) (2001) *Politicians, Bureaucrats and Administrative Reform*. London: Routledge.

—— and Bouckaert, G. (2004) 'What is Available and What is Missing in the Study of Quangos?', in C. Pollitt and C. Talbot (eds) *Unbundled Government*. London: Routledge pp. 22–49.

Peters, T. (1987) *Thriving on Chaos: Handbook for a Management Revolution*. London: Pan.

Peterson, J. and Shackleton, M. (2002) *The Institutions of the European Union*. Oxford: Oxford University Press.

Peterson, M. (2000) 'The Fate of "Big Government" in the United States: Not Over, but Undermined', *Governance*, 13:2, pp. 251–64.

Pew Research Centre (1998) *Deconstructing Distrust: How Americans View Government*. (hhtp://www.people-press.org/trustrpt.htm).

Pierre, J. (1998) *Externalities and Relationships: Rethinking the Boundaries of the Public Service*. Paper for the authors' roundtable, Revitalising the Public Service. Ottawa: Canadian Centre for Management Development. 12–14 November.

—— (ed) (1995) *Bureaucracy in the Modern State: An Introduction to Comparative Public Administration*. Aldershot: Edward Elgar.

—— (2004) 'Central Agencies in Sweden: A Report from Utopia', in C. Pollitt and C. Talbot (eds) *Unbundled Government*, pp. 203–14. London: Taylor and Francis.

—— and Peters, G. (2000) *Governance, Politics and the State*. Basingstoke: Macmillan.

Pierson, P. (2000) 'Increasing Returns, Path Dependence and the Study of Politics', *American Political Science Review*, 94:2, pp. 251–67.

Pollitt, C. (1984) *Manipulating the Machine: Changing the Pattern of Ministerial Departments, 1960–83*. London: Allen & Unwin.

—— (1986) 'Beyond the Managerial Model: The Case for Broadening Performance Assessment in Government and the Public Services', *Financial Accountability and Management*, 2:3, pp. 155–70, Autumn.

—— (1990) 'Performance Indicators: Root and Branch', pp. 167–78, in M. Cave, M. Kogan, and R. Smith (eds) *Output and Performance Measurement in Government: The State of the Art*. London: Jessica Kingsley.

—— (1993) *Managerialism and the Public Services* (2nd edn). Oxford: Blackwell.

—— (1995) 'Justification by Works or by Faith? Evaluating the New Public Management', *Evaluation*, 1:2, pp. 133–54, October.

—— (1996a) 'Anti-statist Reforms and New Administrative Directions: Public Administration in the United Kingdom', *Public Administration Review*, 56:1, pp. 81–7, January/ February.

—— (1996b) 'Public Administration', pp. 699–701, in A. Kuper and J. Kuper (eds) *The Social Science Encyclopaedia* (2nd edn). London: Routledge.

—— (2000) 'Institutional Amnesia: A Paradox of the "Information Age"?', *Prometheus*, 18:1, pp. 5–16.

—— (2001) 'Integrating Financial and Performance Management', *OECD Journal on Budgeting*, 1:2, pp. 7–37.

—— (2002) 'Clarifying Convergence: Striking Similarities and Durable Differences in Public Management Reform', *Public Management Review*, 4:1, pp. 471–92.

—— (2003a) *The Essential Public Manager*. Buckingham: Open University Press/ McGraw-Hill.

—— (2003b) 'Joined-up Government: A Survey', *Political Studies Review*, 1:1, pp. 34–49.

—— (2005) 'Decentralisation: a central concept in contemporary public management', in E. Ferlie, L. Lynn Jr. and C. Pollitt (eds) *The Oxford handbook of public management*, Oxford: Oxford University Press (forthcoming).

——, Bathgate, K., Caulfield, J., Smullen, A., and Talbot, C. (2001) 'Agency Fever? Analysis of an International Fashion', *Journal of Comparative Policy Analysis: Research and Practice*, 3, pp. 271–90.

——, Birchall, J. and Putman, K. (1998) *Decentralising Public Service Management: the British Experience*. Basingstoke: Macmillan.

—— and Bouckaert, G. (eds) (1995) *Quality Improvement in European Public Services: Concepts, Cases and Commentary*. London: Sage.

—— —— (2003) 'Evaluating Public Management Reforms: An International Perspective', in H.Wollman (ed) *Evaluating Public Sector Reforms, an International Perspective*, pp. 12–35, Chettenham: Edward Elgar.

——Cave, M. and Joss, R. (1994) 'International Benchmarking as a Tool to Improve Public Sector Performance: A Critical Overview', pp. 7–22, in PUMA Public Management Occasional Papers 1994, No. 4, *Performance Measurement in Government: Issues and Illustrations*. Paris: OECD.

——, Girre, X., Lonsdale, J., Mul, R., Summa, H., and Waerness, M. (1999) *Performance or Compliance? Performance Audit and Public Management in Five Countries*. Oxford: Clarendon Press.

——, Hanney, S., Packwood, T., Rothwell, S., and Roberts, S. (1997) *Trajectories and Options: An International Perspective on the Implementation of Finnish Public Management Reforms*. Helsinki: Ministry of Finance.

——and Summa, H. (1997) 'Reflexive Watchdogs? How Supreme Audit Institutions Account for Themselves', *Public Administration*, 75:2, pp. 313–36, Summer.

——and Talbot, C. (eds) (2004) *Unbundled government: a critical analysis of the global trend to agencies, quangos and contractualisation*, London and New York: Routledge/Taylor and Francis.

Power, M. (1997) *The Audit Society: Rituals of Verification*. Oxford: Oxford University Press.

Premfors, R. (1991) 'The "Swedish Model" and Public Sector Reform', *Western European Politics*, 14:3, 83–95 July.

——(1998) 'Reshaping the Democratic State: Swedish Experiences in a Comparative Perspective', *Public Administration*, 76:1, pp. 141–59, Spring.

President of the Treasury Board (1997) *Accounting for Results, 1997*. Ottawa: Treasury Board Secretariat.

Pressman, J. and Wildavsky, A. (1973) *Implementation*. Berkeley: University of California Press.

Prime Minister (1988) *Civil Service Management Reform: The Next Steps*, Cm.542. London: HMSO.

——(1991) *The Citizen's Charter: Raising the Standard*, Cm.1599. London: HMSO.

——Chancellor of the Exchequer, and Chancellor of the Duchy of Lancaster (1994) *The Civil Service: Continuity and Change*, Cm.2627. London: HMSO.

Prime Minister and the Minister for the Cabinet Office (1999) *Modernising Government*, Cm.413. London: The Stationery Office.

Prime Minister's Office and Ministries (1995) Helsinki: Prime Minister's Office (a short description and organization chart).

Puoskari, P. (1996) *Transformation of the Public Sector*. Helsinki: Ministry of Finance.

Radin, B. (1998) 'The Government Performance and Results Act (GPRA): Hydra-headed Monster or Flexible Management Tool?', *Public Administration Review*, 58:4, pp. 307–16, July/August.

——(2000) 'The Government Performance and Results Act and the Tradition of Federal Management Reform: Square Pegs in Round Holes', *Journal of Public Administration and Research Theory*, 10:1, pp. 111–35.

Rainey, H. and Steinbauer, P. (1999) 'Galloping Elephants: Developing Elements of a Theory of Effective Government Organizations', *Journal of Public Administration Research and Theory (J-Part)*, 9:1, pp. 1–32.

Rhodes, R. (1997) 'Re-inventing Whitehall, 1979–1995', pp. 43–60, in W. Kickert (ed) *Public Management and Administrative Reform in Western Europe*. Cheltenham: Edward Elgar.

Röber, M. (1996) 'Germany', pp. 169–94, in D. Farnham, S. Horton, J. Barlow, and A. Hondeghem, *New Public Managers in Europe*. Basingstoke: Macmillan.

——and Löffler, E. (1999) 'Flexibilities in the German Civil Service', in S. Horton and D. Farnham (eds) *Human Resource Flexibilities in the Public Services: International Comparisons*. Basingstoke: Macmillan.

Roberts, S. (1997) 'The implementation of Dutch Public Management Reforms 1980–1996', pp. 91–130, in *Public Management Reforms: Five Country Studies*. Helsinki: Ministry of Finance.

Rockman, B. (1998) 'The Changing Role of the State', pp. 20–44, in B. G. Peters and D. Savoie (eds) *Taking Stock: Assessing Public Sector Reforms*. Montreal and Kingston: Canadian Centre for Management Development and McGill-Queen's University Press.

Romakkaniemi, P. (2001) 'Access to Finnish Public Sector Information and Its Services', pp. 4–7, in *Public Management in Finland*. Helsinki: Ministry of Finance.

Rosenau, P. (ed) (2000) *Public–Private Policy Partnerships*. Westwood, Mass.: Massachusetts Institute of Technology.

Rouban, L. (1995) 'The Civil Service Culture and Administrative Reform', pp. 23–54, in B. G. Peters and D. Savoie (eds) *Governance in a Changing Environment*. Montreal and Kingston: Canadian Centre for Management Development and McGill-Queen's University Press.

—— (1997) 'The Administrative Modernisation Policy in France', pp. 143–58, in W. Kickert (ed) *Public Management and Administrative Reform in Western Europe*. Cheltenham: Edward Elgar.

Rubin, I. (1992) 'Budgeting: Theory, Concepts, Methods and Issues', pp. 3–22, in J. Rabin (ed) *Handbook of Public Budgeting*. New York: Marcel Dekker.

Sahlin-Andersson, K. (2001) 'National, International and Transnational Constructions of New Public Management', pp. 43–72, in T. Christensen and P. Lægreid (eds) *New Public Management: The Transformation of Ideas and Practice*. Aldershot: Ashgate.

Saint-Martin, D. (2000) *Building the new managerialist state: consultants and the politics of public sector reform in comparative perspective*, Oxford: Oxford University Press.

Savoie, D. (1994) *Thatcher, Reagan, Mulroney: In Search of a New Bureaucracy*. Toronto: University of Toronto Press.

—— (1997) 'Central Agencies: A Government of Canada Perspective', pp. 59–69, in J. Bourgault, M. Demers, and C. Williams (eds) *Public Administration and Public Management: Experiences in Canada*. Quebec: Les Publications du Québec.

Schick, A. (1996) *The Spirit of Reform: Managing the New Zealand State Sector in a Time of Change*. Wellington: State Services Commission.

—— (2001) 'Getting Performance Measures to Measure Up', pp. 39–60, in D.W. Forsythe, *Quicker, Better, Cheaper? Managing Performance in American Government*. New York: The Rockefeller Institute Press.

Schiavo, L. (2000) 'Quality Standards in the Public Sector: Differences Between Italy and the UK in the Citizen's Charter Initiative', *Public Administration*, 78:3, pp. 679–98.

Scholte, J. (2000) *Globalization: A Critical Introduction*. Basingstoke: Macmillan.

Schröter, E. and Wollmann, H. (1997) 'Public Sector Reforms in Germany: Whence and Where? A Case of Ambivalence', *Administrative Studies/Hallinnon Tutkimus*, 3, pp. 184–200.

Shergold, P. (1997) 'A New Public Service Act: The End of the Westminster Tradition?', edited text of an address, *Canberra Bulletin of Public Administration*, no. 85, pp. 32–7, August.

Simon, H. (1946) 'The Proverbs of Administration', *Public Administration Review*, 6, pp. 53–67.

Smithers, R. (2002) 'Schools Cheat to Boost Exam Results', *Guardian*, p. 1, 5 June.

Smullen, A. (2004) 'Lost in Translation? Shifting Interpretations of the Concept of "Agency": The Dutch Case' pp. 184–202, in C. Pollitt and C. Talbot (eds) *Unbundled Government*. London: Taylor & Francis.

Sorber, B. (1996) 'Experiences with Performance Measurement in the Central Government: The Case of the Netherlands', pp. 309–18, in A. Halachmi and G. Bouckaert (eds) *Organisational Performance and Measurement in the Public Sector: Towards Service, Effort and Accomplishment Reporting*. Westport, Conn.: Quorum Books.

Spierenberg, D. (1979) *Proposals for Reform of the Commission of the European Communities and Its Services*. Brussels: Commission of the European Communities.

State Services Commission (2001) *Review of the Centre*. Wellington (NZ) (http://www.ssc.govt.nz/roc).

State Services Commission (2002) *Current Problems in Public Management*. Wellington (NZ) (http://www.ssc.govt. nz/current-problems-public-management).

Statistics Canada (1995) *Canada: A Portrait*. Ottawa: Minister of Industry.

Steering Group (1991) *Review of State Sector Reforms*. Auckland: State Service Commission.

Steunenberg, B. and Mol, N. (1997) 'Fiscal and Financial Decentralization: A Comparative Analysis of Six West European Countries', pp. 235–56, in J.-E. Lane (ed) *Public Sector Reform: Rationale, Trends and Problems*. London: Sage.

Stevens, A. and Stevens, H. (2001) *Brussels Bureaucracts? The Administration of the European Union*. Basingstoke: Palgrave Macmillan.

Stewart, J. (1992) *Managing Difference: The Analysis of Service Characteristics*. Birmingham: Institute of Local Government Studies.

——(1994) 'The Rebuilding of Public Accountability', pp. 75–9, in N. Flynn (ed) *Reader: Change in the Civil Service*. London: Public Finance Foundations.

Stockman, D. (1986) *The Triumph of Politics*. London: Bodley Head.

Stoker, G. (1988) *The Politics of Local Government*. Basingstoke: Macmillan.

Stone, B. (1995) 'Administrative Accountability in the "Westminster" Democracies: Towards a New Conceptual Framework', *Governance*, 8:4, pp. 505–26.

Stone, D. (1996) *Capturing the Political Imagination: Think Tanks and the Policy Process*. London: Frank Cass.

Straw, J. (1998) 'Resource Accounting and NHS Trusts', *Public Money and Management*, 18:2, pp. 35–8, April/June.

Summa, H. (1995) 'Old and New Techniques for Productivity Promotion: From Cheese-Slicing to a Quest for Quality', pp. 155–65, in A. Halachmi and G. Bouckaert (eds) *Public Productivity Through Quality and Strategic Management*. Amsterdam: IOS Press.

Swedish Ministry of Finance (1997) *Public Sector Productivity in Sweden*. Stockholm: Budget Department/Swedish Ministry of Finance.

Talbot, C. (1994) *Re-inventing Public Management: A Survey of Public Sector Managers' Reactions to Change*. Northants: Institute of Management.

——(1996) *Ministers and Agencies: Control, Performance and Accountability*. London: CIPFA.

——(1997) *Public Performance: Towards a Public Service Excellence Model*, Discussion Paper No. 1. Monmouthshire: Public Futures.

Task Force on Management Improvement (1992) *The Australian Public Service Reformed: An Evaluation of a Decade of Management Reform*. Canberra: Management Advisory Board, AGPS.

Thain, C. and Wright, M. (1995) *The Treasury and Whitehall: The Planning and Control of Public Expenditure, 1976–1993*. Oxford: Clarendon Press.

Thiel, S. van (2001) *Quangos: Trends, Causes and Consequences*. Aldershot: Ashgate.

Thompson, G., Frances, J., Levacic, R., and Mitchell, J. (eds) (1991) *Markets, Hierarchies and Networks: The co-ordination of Social life*. London: Sage.

Thompson, J. (2000) 'Reinvention as Reform: Assessing the National Performance Review', *Public Administration Review*, 60:6, pp. 508–21, November/December.

Tiihonen, S. (1996) *The Administration of the Summit in Finland* (unpublished conference paper).

Toulemonde, J. (1997) 'Europe and the Member States: Cooperating and Competing on Evaluation Grounds', pp. 117–32, in O. Rieper and J. Toulemonde (eds) *Politics and Practices of Intergovernmental Evaluation*. London: Transaction.

Treasury Board of Canada (1996) *Getting Government Right: Improving Results Measurement and Accountability*. Ottawa: Ministry of Public Works and Government Services.

Trosa, S. (1994) *Moving on: Next Steps*. London: Efficiency Unit, Cabinet Office.

——(1995) *Moderniser l'administration: comment font les autres?*, Paris: Les Éditions d'Organisation.

——(1996) 'Quality Strategies in Three Countries: France, the United Kingdom and Australia', pp. 265–97, in OECD, *Responsive Government: Service Quality Initiatives*. Paris: PUMA/OECD.

——(1997) 'Chairman's Summary', pp. 5–9, in OECD, *Benchmarking, Evaluation and Strategic Management in the Public Sector*. Paris: PUMA/OECD.

——(2002) *Le guide de la gestion par programmes: vers une culture du résultat*. Paris: Éditions d'Organisation.

United Nations (2001) *World Public Sector Report: Globalization and the State*. New York: Department of Economic and Social Affairs, UN.

Vallemont, S. (1998) 'France Moves From a Rating System to a Performance Appraisal System', *Public Management Forum*, IV:6, pp. 8, 16, November/December.

Vancoppenolle, D. and Legrain, A. (2003) 'Le New Public Management en Belgique: Comparaison des réformes en Flandres et en Wallonie', *Administration Publique* (in press).

Van de Walle, S. and Bouckaert, G. (2003) 'Public service performance and trust in government: The problem of causality', *International Journal of Public Administration*, Vol 26 Nrs. 8–9: 891–913.

Volcker, P. (1989) *Leadership for America: Rebuilding the Public Service*. Task force report to the National Commission on the Public Service. Washington, DC: National Commission on the Public Service.

Vowles, J., Aimer, P., Catt, H., Lamarre, J., and Miller, R. (1995) *Towards Consensus: The 1993 Election in New Zealand and the Transition to Proportional Representation*. Auckland: Auckland University Press.

Waugh, P. (1998) 'State Sell-off Errors "Cost UK Billions"', *Independent*, p. 4, 3 September.

Weber, M. (1947) *The Theory of Social and Economic Organisation* (translated by A. M. Henderson and Talcott Parsons). Glencoe, IL: The Free Press.

Weiss, C. (1992) *Organisations for policy analysis: helping government think*. London: Sage.

Wilks, S. (1996) 'Sweden', pp. 23–49, in N. Flynn and F. Strehl (eds) *Public Sector Management in Europe*. London: Prentice-Hall/Harvester Wheatsheaf.

Williams, D. (2000) 'Reinventing the proverbs of government', *Public Administration Review*, 60:6, pp. 522–34, November/December.

Williamson, O. (1975) *Markets and Hierarchies: Analysis and Anti-trust Implications*. New York: Free Press.

Wilson, J. Q. (1989) *Bureaucracy*. New York: Basic Books

Wise, C. (1990) 'Public Service Configurations and Public Organizations: Public Organizational Design in the Post-privatization Era', *Public Administration Review*, 50:2, pp. 141–55.

Wollmann, H. (1997) 'Modernization of the Public Sector and Public Administration in the Federal Republic of Germany: (Mostly) a Story of Fragmented Incrementalism', pp. 79–103, in M. Muramatsu and F. Naschold (eds) *State and Administration in Japan and Germany: A Comparative Perspective on Continuity and Change*. Berlin: de Gruyter.

Wollmann, H. (2001) 'Germany's Trajectory of Public Sector Modernization: Continuities and Discontinuities', *Policy and Politics*, 29:2, pp. 151–69.

Wright, V. (1989) *The Government and Politics of France* (3rd edn). London: Unwin Hyman.

——(1997) 'The Paradoxes of Administrative Reform', pp. 7–13, in W. Kickert (ed) *Public Management and Administrative Reform in Western Europe*. Cheltenham: Edward Elgar.

Yin, R. (1994) *Case Study Research: Design and Methods* (2nd edn). London: Sage.

Younge, G. (2003) 'Shades of Grey' (an interview with Hans Blix), *Guardian G2*, pp. 2–3, 28 March.

Zifcak, S. (1994) *New Managerialism: Administrative Reform in Whitehall and Canberra*. Buckingham: Open University Press.

■ WEBSITES—OVERVIEW

General

http://www.oecd.org Organization for Economic Cooperation and Development
http://www.gksoft.com/govt/en/world.html Worldwide governments on the Internet
http://www.europa.eu.int European Union
http://www.eipa.nl European Institute for Public Administration
http://www.3qconference.org/ (Third Quality Conference for Public Administration in the EU)
http://www.worldbank.org World Bank
http://www.imf.org International Monetary Fund
http://www.iiasiisa.be/ International Institute of Administrative Sciences

By country

Australia

http://www.fed.gov.au/KSP/ Australian Commonwealth Government Entry Point
http://www.gg.gov.au/ Governor General of Australia
http://www.aph.gov.au/ Parliament of the Commonwealth of Australia
http://www.dpmc.gov.au/ Department of the Prime Minister and Cabinet
http://www.apsc.gov.au/ Public Service and Merit Protection Commission (PSMPC)
http://www.dofa.gov.au/ Department of Finance and Administration (DoFA)
http://www.ogo.gov.au/ Office for Government Online (OGO)
http://www.anao.gov.au/ Australian National Audit Office (ANAO)
http://www.nolg.gov.au/ National Office of Local Government (NOLG)
http://www.treasury.gov.au/ Department of the Treasury
http://www.ncc.gov.au/ National Competition Council (NCC)
http://www.rba.gov.au/ Reserve Bank of Australia (RBA)
http://www.ramint.gov.au/ Royal Australian Mint

Belgium

http://www.copernic-us.be Federal Government Reforms
http://www.vlaanderen.be Flemish Government and Civil Service
http://www.fed-parl.be Federal Parliament
http://www.belgium.fgov.be Federal Government—General Overview
http://www.statbel.fgov.be Statistical Information on Belgium
http://www.bnb.be/sg/index.htm National Bank
http://www.ccrek.be Court of Accounts
http://www.pcf.be/ Parliament of the French Community of Belgium
http://www.cfwb.be/default2.asp Government of the French Community of Belgium

http://parlement.wallonie.be/ Walloon Parliament
http://www.wallonie.be/ Walloon Government
http://mrw.wallonie.be/mrw/ Ministry of the Walloon Region
http://www.dgov.be/start.html Government of the German-speaking Community
http://www.publicquality.be Website on the Belgian Quality Conferences

Canada
http://www.gg.ca/ Governor General of Canada
http://www.parl.gc.ca Parliament
http://www.gc.ca/ Government of Canada
http://www.pm.gc.ca/ Prime Minister's Office
http://www.myschool-monecole.gc.ca/main_e.html/ Canada School of Public Service
http://www.pssrb-crtfp.gc.ca/ Public Service Staff Relations Board (PSSRB)
http://www.fin.gc.ca/ Department of Finance
http://www.bank-banque-canada.ca/ Bank of Canada
http://www.statcan.gc.ca/ Statistics Canada
http://mc.ic.gc.ca/ Measurement Canada
http://www.scc.ca/ Standards Council of Canada
http://www.nrc.ca/ National Research Council of Canada (NRC)
http://www.cac.gc.ca/ Department of Public Works and Government Services (PWGSC)
http://www.infocan.gc.ca/ Canada Information Office (CIO)
http://www.cac.gc.ca/ Consulting and Audit Canada (CAC)
http://www.infocan.gc.ca/ Canadian General Standards Board (CGSB)
http://www.tbs-sct.gc.ca/ Treasury Board of Canada
http://www.pco-bcp.gc.ca/ Privy Council Office (PCO)
http://www.psc-cfp.gc.ca/ Public Service Commission of Canada (PSC)
http://www.oag-bvg.gc.ca/ Office of the Auditor-General
http://www.policyresearch.gc.ca Policy Research Initiative
http://www.leadership.gc.ca The Leadership Network
http://www.ipaciacp.ca Public Management Institute

Finland
http://virtual.finland.fi/ Finland General Overview
http://www.tpk.fi/netcomm/ President of the Republic
http://www.eduskunta.fi/ Finnish Parliament
http://www.vn.fi/ Council of State
http://www.valtioneuvosto.fi Prime Minister's Office
http://www.vm.fi/ Ministry of Finance
http://www.vero.fi/ Tax Administration
http://www.tilastokeskus.fi/ Centre for Statistics
http://www.vatt.fi/ State Economic Research Centre
http://www.bof.fi/ Bank of Finland

France

http://www.service-public.fr/ Public Service

http://www.elysee.fr/ Presidency of the French Republic

http://www.assemblee-nat.fr/ National Assembly

http://www.senat.fr/ Senate

http://www.premier-ministre.gouv.fr/ Prime Minister and Government

http://www.fonction-publique.gouv.fr/ Ministry of Public Service and Reform of the State

http://www.plan.gouv.fr/ General Commissariat of Planning

http://www.finances.gouv.fr/ Ministry of Economy, Finance and Industry

http://www.insee.fr/ National Institute of Statistics and Economic Studies

http://www.interieur.gouv.fr/ Ministry of the Interior

http://www.cnrs.fr/ National Centre of Scientific Research

http://www.banque-france.fr/ Bank of France

http://www.ccomptes.fr/ Court of Accounts

http://www.innovations-services-publics.gouv.fr Administrative Reforms

Germany

http://www.bund.de General Overview

http://www.staat-modern.de Modernization Programme

http://eng.bundespraesident.de Federal President

http://www.bundestag.de/ Federal Diet

http://www.bundesrat.de/ Federal Council

http://www.bundesregierung.de/ Federal Government

http://www.bundeskanzler.de/ Federal Chancellor

http://www.zivildienst.de/ Federal Office for the Civil Service

http://www.bundesfinanzministerium.de/ Federal Ministry of Finance

http://www.bsv.de/ Federal Debt Administration

http://www.bff-online.de/ Federal Office for Finance

http://www.bmi.bund.de/ Federal Ministry of the Interior

http://www.destatis.de/ Federal Statistical Office

http://www.bundesverwaltungsamt.de/ Federal Administration Office

http://www.bundesbank.de/ German Federal Bank

http://www2.din.de/ German Institute for Standardization

Italy

http://www.quirinale.it/ Presidency of the Republic

http://www.parlamento.it/ Italian Parliament

http://www.camera.it/ Chamber of Deputies

http://www.senato.it/senato.htm Senate of the Republic

http://www.palazzochigi.it/ Presidency of the Council of Ministers

http://www.funzionepubblica.it Department of Public Service

http://www.istat.it/ National Institute of Statistics

http://www.mininterno.it/ Ministry of the Interior

http://pers.mininterno.it/ General Directorate for General Administration and for Personnel Affairs

http://**cedweb.mininterno.it**/ General Directorate of Civil Administration
http://**www.tesoro.it**/ Ministry of Treasury, Budget and Economic Planning
http://**www.dgt.tesoro.it**/ Department of Treasury
http://**www.bancaditalia.it**/ Bank of Italy
http://**www.corteconti.it**/ Court of Accounts
http://**www.unicei.it**/ Italian National Agency for Standardization

Netherlands

http://**www.overheid.nl**/ The Netherlands General Overview
http://**www.koninklijkhuis.nl**/ Royal House
http://**www.parlement.nl**/ Parliament
http://**www.eerstekamer.nl**/ First Chamber
http://**www.minez.nl** Ministry of Economic Affairs
http://**www.cbs.nl**/ Central Office of Statistics
http://**www.cpb.nl**/ Central Planning Office
http://**www.minfin.nl**/ Ministry of Finance
http://**www.dutchstate.nl**/ Dutch State Treasury Agency
http://**www.minaz.nl**/ Ministry of General Affairs
http://**www.wrr.nl**/ Scientific Council for Government Policy
http://**www.ser.nl**/ Social and Economic Council
http://**www.dnb.nl**/ National Bank of the Netherlands
http://**www.ombudsman.nl**/ National Ombudsman
http://**www.rekenkamer.nl**/ General Chamber of Accounts
http://**www.minbzk.nl**/ Ministry of Interior Affairs and Kingdom Relations
http://**www.nni.nl**/ Netherlands Standardization Institute
http://**www.benchmarkinginthepublicsector.nl** Knowledge bank with practical cases

New Zealand

http://**www.govt.nz**/ New Zealand Government Online
http://**www.gov-gen.govt.nz**/ Governor General of New Zealand
http://**www.parliament.govt.nz**/ Parliament
http://**www.executive.govt.nz**/ New Zealand Government
http://**www.dpmc.govt.nz**/ Department of the Prime Minister and Cabinet
http://**www.dia.govt.nz**/ Department of Internal Affairs
http://**www.ministers.govt.nz**/ Ministerial Services Unit
http://**www.treasury.govt.nz**/ New Zealand Treasury
http://**www.nzdmo.govt.nz** New Zealand Debt Management Office (NZDMO)
http://**www.stats.govt.nz**/ Statistics New Zealand
http://**www.ombudsmen.govt.nz**/ Office of the Ombudsmen
http://**www.rbnz.govt.nz**/ Reserve Bank of New Zealand (RBNZ)
http://**www.oag.govt.nz**/ Office of the Controller and Auditor-General
http://**www.ssc.govt.nz**/ State Services Commission

Sweden

http://**www.sverigedirekt.gov.se** General overview

WEBSITES—OVERVIEW **331**

http://www.virtualsweden.net VirtualSweden—the Official Gateway to Sweden
http://www.royalcourt.se Royal Court
http://www.riksdagen.se/ Parliament
http://www.regeringen.se/ Government
http://statsradsberedningen.regeringen.se/ Prime Minister's Office
http://finans.regeringen.se/ Ministry of Finance
http://www.rsv.se/ National Tax Administration
http://www.esv.se/ Financial Management Administration
http://www.rrv.se/ National Audit Administration
http://www.lst.se/ Counties Agency
http://www.rgk.se/ National Debt Office
http://www.konj.se Economic Research Institute
http://www.fi.se/ Finance Inspectorate
http://www.scb.se/ Central Bureau of Statistics
http://www.statskontoret.se/ Office of Public Management
http://fa.regeringen.se/ Department of Administration
http://www.riksbank.se National Bank of Sweden
http://www.sis.se Swedish Standards Institute (SIS)
http://www.kkr.se/ National Council for Quality and Development

UK
http://www.open.gov.uk/ Government Information Service
http://www.official-documents.co.uk/ Official Documents
http://www.royal.gov.uk/ British Monarchy
http://www.parliament.uk/ Parliament
http://www.pm.gov.uk/ Prime Minister's Office
http://www.cabinet-office.gov.uk/ Cabinet Office
http://www.servicefirst.gov.uk/ Service First Unit
http://www.gics.gov.uk/default.htm Government Information and Communication Service (GICS)
http://www.e-envoy.gov.uk/ Office of the e-Envoy
http://www.hmso.gov.uk/ Her Majesty's Stationery Office (HMSO)
http://www.public-standards.gov.uk/ Committee on Standards in Public Life
http://www.publictrust.gov.uk/ Public Trust Office
http://www.hm-treasury.gov.uk/ Her Majesty's Treasury (HMT)
http://www.inlandrevenue.gov.uk/ Inland Revenue
http://www.royalmint.com/ British Royal Mint
http://www.statistics.gov.uk/ Office for National Statistics (ONS)
http://www.dmo.gov.uk/ Debt Management Office (DMO)
http://www.privy-council.org.uk/ Privy Council Office
http://www.civilservicecommissioners.gov.uk/ Office of the Civil Service Commissioners (OCSC)
http://www.bankofengland.co.uk/ Bank of England
http://www.nao.gov.uk/ National Audit Office (NAO)
http://www.lga.gov.uk/ Local Government Association (LGA)

http://www.bsi-global.com British Standards Institution (BSI)
http://www.benchmarking.gov.uk Public Service Benchmarking Service
http://www.chartermark.gov.uk Chartermark Initiative

USA

http://www.firstgov.gov/ General Overview
http://www.whitehouse.gov/ Office of the President
http://www.whitehouse.gov/omb/ Office of Management and Budget (OMB)
http://www.house.gov/ House of Representatives
http://www.senate.gov/index.htm Senate
http://www.esa.doc.gov/ Economics and Statistics Administration (ESA)
http://www.bea.doc.gov/ Bureau of Economic Analysis (BEA)
http://www.stat-usa.gov/ Statistics USA
http://www.treas.gov/ Department of Treasury
http://www.fms.treas.gov/ Financial Management Service (FMS)
http://www.publicdebt.treas.gov/ Bureau of Public Debt (BPD)
http://www.usmint.gov/ US Mint (USM)
http://www.gao.gov/ General Accounting Office (GAO)
http://www.usoge.gov/ Office of Government Ethics (OGE)
http://www.gsa.gov/ General Services Administration (GSA)
http://www.fts.gsa.gov/ Federal Technology Service (FTS)
http://www.policyworks.gov/ Office of Governmentwide Policy (OGP)
http://www.federalreserve.gov/ Federal Reserve System

■ INDEX

A

aboriginal peoples:
  Australia 210
  Canada 224
  New Zealand 277
academic literature: on public
      management reform 1–2,
      20
academic subject: public
      management as 9
academics:
  ideal models 135
  loss of legitimacy 152
  Netherlands 271
  public management
      reform 19–20, 196–9
    assessment of results 104,
      138
acceptance, public: for reform 196
accountability 6, 101, 128, 157
  Canada 227
  civil servants 163
  management 146–7, 173–4,
      176–7
  Netherlands 273
accounting: importance of 193
accounting systems:
  accruals 72
    Canada 227
  double-entry
      bookkeeping 71–2
  modernization of 70–2
  pure cash 71, 72
activities:
  definition of political 144
  public sector 114–15
Activity-Based Management
      (ABM) 236
administration:
  replacement of term by
      management 12
  see also public administration
administrative systems:
  Australia 212
  Belgium 218–19
  Canada 226
  change in 39–40
  European Commission 234–5
  Finland 240–1
  France 247–9

Germany 257–9
  in interactive model 183–94
  Italy 265
  Netherlands 276
  New Zealand 279–80
  in public management reform
      model 25, 27, 34–7
  Sweden 287
  UK 294
  USA 302
  see also culture, administrative
advice, policy:
  from business 57–8
    USA 20, 32
  for European Union 60
  for political leadership 123
  sources of 57–8
  UK 293
  see also consultants; think tanks
age: pensionable 207
  see also elderly
agencies:
  creation of 1, 83, 174–5
  Finland 241
  ideal 89
  Netherlands 273
  UK 295
ancien régime 40, 61–3
announcements, reform 35–6,
      151
Asian immigrants: Australia 210
asylum seekers:
  Germany 256
  Italy 264
attitudes, public see citizens,
      attitudes
audit offices: perspective on
      results 138–9
audits and auditing:
  explosion of 174, 193
  external and internal 74
  performance 73–4, 92, 104
  with performance issues 73
  reforms 72–4
  traditional financial and
      compliance 72–3
Ausserparlamentarische Opposition
      (APO) 257
Australia:
  accounting systems 70, 72
  administrative culture 56, 148
  administrative system 212

auditing 73
  benchmarking 119–20
  boundaries between politics
      and management 147
  budget reform 69
  citizen pressure for reforms 211
  civil service 44, 78, 79
    reform 74, 75, 76
  client orientation 125
  country files 210–13
  cultural change 130
  economic indicators 204
  elite decision-making 211–12
  foreign and foreign-born
      population 209
  global economic forces 210
  household composition 209
  as marketizer 98
  new management ideas 211
  organizational reform 81, 86
  party political ideas 211
  performance measurement 91
  political system 210–11
  politico-administrative
      regime 42
  privatization 171
  public management
      reform 161, 189, 190
    content 212–13;
      implementation 213;
      results 111–12, 118, 213
  social expenditure 205
  sociodemographic change 210
  socio-economic forces 210
  socio-economic policies 210
  strategic management 127
  table of events 214–15
  think tanks 211
autonomy 175

B

balances 163
Belgium:
  accounting systems 70
  administrative culture 56, 55–7
  administrative system 218–19
  auditing 73, 74
  boundaries between politics
      and management 147,
      149–50
  chance events 147, 218

Belgium: (*cont.*)
  citizen pressure for reforms 217
  citizens' charter 152
  civil service 44, 80
    reform 74, 77
  country files 216–20
  decentralization 88
  deregulated government
    model 136–7
  economic indicators 204
  foreign and foreign-born
    population 209
  global economic forces 216
  idealism 135
  household composition 209
  new management ideas 217
  organizational reform 81
  party political ideas 217
  performance measures 86
  political system 216–17
  politico-administrative
    regime 42, 63, 134
  public management reform 2,
    97, 161, 189–90, 191
    contents 219–20; elite
      perceptions of 217–18;
      implementation 220;
      results 220; role of
      politicians after 150, 151
  social expenditure 205
  sociodemographic change 216
  socio-economic forces 216
  table of events 220–3
  trust
    in government 133; in
      institutions 131, 132, 150
  see also Copernicus reforms
benchmarking 92, 118–20
blaming 184–6, 188–9
bookkeeping: double-entry
  71–2
budgets and budgeting:
  inputs and savings 107–13
  link with performance
    measurement 126
  reform
    Belgium 216; Finland 239,
      240; interpretation of 69;
      Netherlands 272–3;
      trajectories 67–74
  results-oriented
    Finland 69, 152, 241;
      Sweden 69
  state structure and 43–4
bureau-professionalism 62
bureau-shaping, theory of 19, 193

bureaucracy, traditional 40, 61–3
business: advice from *see* advice

C

Canada:
  administrative culture 55, 56
  administrative system 226
  auditing 73
  budget reform 69–70
  chance events 225
  citizen pressure for reforms 225
  civil service 44, 52, 77, 80, 172
    reform 74
  country files 224–9
  economic indicators 204
  elite decision-making 226
  foreign and foreign-born
    population 209
  household composition 209
  new management ideas 224–5
  organizational reform 81, 82,
    84, 85, 86
  party political ideas 225
  performance management 176
  political system 224–5
  politico-administrative
    regime 42
  public and private sector
    services 153
  public management
    reform 36–7, 98, 161, 190,
    196
    contents 226–8;
      implementation 102, 228;
      results 138–9, 141, 228–9
  quality assessment 121, 122
  social expenditure 205
  sociodemographic issues 224
  socio-economic policies 224
  sources of policy advice 58
  table of events 229–31
capacity:
  of institutions 105, 129
  organizational 196
  for reform 102
capital growth 204, 205
centralization 81, 89
  see also decentralization
centralized states 43–5
  nature of executive
    governments and 47–50
chance events:
  Belgium 218
  Canada 226
  crisis management 101, 147

European Commission 234
Finland 240
France 248
Germany 258
Italy 265
Netherlands 272
New Zealand 279
in public management reform
  model 25, 32–3
UK 293
USA 301–2
citizens:
  attitudes to politicians and civil
    servants 150, 154–5
  attitudes to reform 146, 152–6
  Belgium 217–18
  client orientation 125–6
  empowerment 136, 149
  Germany 256
  impact of reform 22
  involvement in reform 19
  pressure from 25, 31
    Australia 211; Belgium 217;
      Canada 224–5; European
      Commission 234;
      Finland 239–40;
      France 247–8;
      Germany 257; Italy 265;
      Netherlands 271; New
      Zealand 279; Sweden 286;
      UK 293; USA 301
  quality assessment 120–2
  see also legitimacy; trust
citizens' charters 1, 19
  Belgium 152
  Italy 152, 266
  UK 103–4, 125, 152, 198, 293, 295
civil servants:
  accountability 163
  cultural change 130
  de-privilegisation 79–80
  empowerment in Canada 227
  improvements by 201–2
  motivation 171–2
  performance-related pay 78–9,
    80, 126–7, 242
  promotion 78–9
  public attitudes to 154–5
  in public interest model 53
  public management reform 19
    influence on 16
    ownership of 48, 57
  relationship with
    politicians 144, 156
  state structure and 44, 45
  tenure 77–8, 171–2

civil servants, senior 12
  Australia 211
  as battletroops and
      trustees 40–1, 48, 60
  European Commission 60–1
  Finland 240–1
  institutional memories 159–60
  Italy 264
  New Zealand 280
  political activities of 144
  public management reform 19,
      192–4, 196
  in public management reform
      model 26–7
  relationship with
      ministers 40–1, 50–2
    in European Union 59–60
  role of 146
  UK 294–5
  see also elite
civil service:
  Australia 211
  Belgium 218–19, 219–20
  boundaries with politics
      144–5
  Canada 226, 228
  Finland 241
  France 248
  Germany 258
  Netherlands 272
  political control of 86, 165–7
  public management
      reform 34–5
  reductions in 112–13, 171–2
  Sweden 287
  trust in 131, 132, 150
  UK 293–4
  as unified service 79–80
  USA 301–2
  see also human resource
      management
civil society 11–12
  see also citizens
client orientation 125–6
cohabitation 247
collectivism: as cultural
      element 55
College of Commissioners 235
Common Agricultural Policy
      (CAP) 233
Common Assessment Framework
      (CAF) 119, 234
Commonwealth Institute 20
communities: Belgium 216
companies *see* state-owned
comprehensiveness in reform 26

UK 195
compulsory competitive
      tendering (CCT) 83
consensual government 46–50
  European Commission as 59
consensus: in reform 195–6
constraints:
  administrative 159
  for public management
      reform 160–81
consultants, management 19–20,
      30
  Finland 240–1
  influence of 16
  New Zealand 280
  perspective on results 138
consumers: empowerment
      of 146–7, 165–7
consumption:
      government 110–11
contents of reform 25, 35–6
contexts, theory of 196–8
continuity 51–2
  tension with innovation 167–9
contracting-out 114, 117, 188
contracts: organizational
      reform 84
contradictions 161, 163
  candidate 164–81
convergence criteria, EU 29,
      107–8, 216
  Belgium 216
  Finland 239
  Italy 265
cooperation: voluntary 83
coordination:
  connection with
      specialization 84–5
  Finland 241
  horizontal
    European Commission 59,
      235;
    improvement of 174–5;
    state 41, 45
  improvement of
      programme 175–6
  in organizations 81, 83–6
Copernicus reforms: Belgium 74,
      102, 135, 136–7, 217,
      219–20
corruption:
  France 248
  Italy 265
cost cutting: tension with quality
      improvement 177–9
costs of change 33–4, 139

Australia 213
county government: Sweden
      287
craft:
  knowledge 198
  public management reform
      as 183
crisis management 101, 147
criteria, reform 140
critical modernism 22–3
cultural factors:
  change in 129–30
  political systems 30
  politico-administrative
      systems 40–1
cultures, administrative 3, 41
  change in 148
  elements of 54–7
  European Commission 60, 61
  models of 52–4
  process improvements
      and 123–4

D

data, reform 21
  collection, in Finland 241
  on results 139–40
  use by legislatures 139, 157
  validation 115
debt, government 112
decentralization:
  civil service 79–80
  competitive and
      noncompetitive 87, 88
  France 249
  internal and external 87, 88–9
  Italy 265–66
  management authority 175–6
  Netherlands 273
  organizational reform 81
  performance measures 87–9
  political and administrative 87,
      88, 149
  Sweden 287, 288
  tensions with accountability
      and consumer power
      146–7
decentralized states 43–5
  nature of executive
      governments and 47–50
decisions, reform 139, 141
  strategic *see* strategy
  see also elite, decision-making
DECODE 235
deference: decline in 152, 155

delegation: to provincial or
     regional
     government 146–7
Denmark: public management
     reform 35
Department of Administrative
     Services (DAS) 212, 213
departments, government:
     merging 86
desirability of reform 25, 26
devolution 89
     New Zealand 278
     UK 293
dilemmas 7, 160, 161
     definition 162–3
discourse, community of 18, 20
distancing 184–6, 188–9, 194
downsizing 87, 89
     civil service 112–13, 171–2
     from national to subnational
          government 146–7
dynamism, reform 50
     senior civil servants as source
          of 192–4

E

economic:
     crises
          Finland 238, 240; New
               Zealand 276
     indicators 203–6
     reforms: Netherlands 271
     see also socio-economic
economic and monetary union
     (EMU) 233
economists: public management
     reform 198
economy:
     in input/output model 73,
          106
     results and 110
education 206
     UK 199
     see also schools; universities
effective government: theory
     of 118
effectiveness 6
     concept of 106
     increasing 176–7
     performance measurement 73,
          92
efficiency 6, 176–7
     concept of 106
     European Commission 237
     Netherlands 271

performance measurement 73,
     92
egalitarianism: tension with
     innovation 168
elderly population:
     aged 80 and over 208
     Canada 224
     Finland 239
     Germany 256
     Italy 264
     Netherlands 270
     pensionable 207
     percentage of 207
     Sweden 285
elite:
     Belgium 217–18
     decision-making 25, 26–7,
          184–6 Australia 211–12;
          Canada 226; European
          Commission 234;
          Finland 240; France 248;
          Germany 258;
          implementation of
          reform 37; Italy 265;
          Netherlands 271; New
          Zealand 279;
          Sweden 287; UK 294;
          USA 302
     moral standards 154
     New Zealand 195
     see also civil servants, senior;
          ministers
employment 206
     Netherlands 270
     see also unemployment
empowerment:
     citizens 136, 149
     civil servants: Canada 227
     consumers 146–7, 165–7
enterprises: state-owned *see* state-
          owned
ethnic minorities: New
     Zealand 277
European Commission 1
     accounting systems 70, 71
     administrative system 234–5
     budget reform 70
     candidate countries 233
     chance events 234
     citizen pressure for reforms
          234
     civil service 80
          reform 75, 77
     country files 232–7
     elite decision-making 234
     global economic forces 232

     membership 233
     new management ideas 233–4
     organizational reform 81, 90
     party political ideas 234
     performance measures 86, 126
     political system 233
     politico-administrative
          regime 58–61
     programme coordination 176
     public management reform 2,
          19, 97, 162, 190
          contents 235–6;
          implementation 102, 236;
          results 139, 236–7; role of
          politicians after 151
     quality assessment 119
     role of 232
     sociodemographic change 232
     socio-economic forces 232
     socio-economic policies 232–3
     table of events 237–8
European Court of Auditors 73–4
European Foundation for Quality
     Management
     (EFQM) 118–19
European Group for Public
     Administration (EGPA) 20
European Parliament: role of 233
European Union (EU):
     convergence criteria 29, 107–8,
          216, 239, 265
     harmonization 89
     influence on Italy 264
     trust in governments 133
evaluation:
     in auditing 73
     Australia 213
     Canada 228–9
     Finland 243
     France 249–50
     Netherlands 273
     New Zealand 280–81
     Sweden 291
     UK 296
     USA 305
executives, political *see* elite;
     ministers
expectations:
     citizens 153
     client orientation 125
Expenditure Management System
     (EMS) 70, 227
expenditure, public 204, 205
     Canada 224
     centralization and 89
     ratio to GDP 109–10

reduction of 67, 101
Sweden 288
see also savings; social
  expenditure
exports 204, 205–6
  European Commission 232
  Italy 264
  New Zealand 277
  USA 300

F

feasibility, reform 25, 26
  European Commission 60
  Sweden 287
federal states 41–3
  European Commission as 58–9
femininity: as cultural element 55
finance *see* budgets; expenditure;
    savings; social expenditure
Financial Management
    Improvement Program
    (FMIP) 212, 213
Finland:
  accounting systems 70, 72
  administrative culture 54, 55,
    56
  administrative system 241–2
  auditing 73
  boundaries between politics
    and management 147,
    148–9
  chance events 240
  citizen pressure for reforms 239
  civil service 34, 44, 51, 54, 77,
    78–9, 80
    reform 75
  country file 238–42
  decentralization 87–8, 89
  economic indicators 204
  elite decision-making 240
  foreign and foreign-born
    population 209
  frame-budgeting 68, 240, 241
  household composition 209
  idealism 135
  new management ideas 239
  organizational reform 81, 85,
    90
  party political ideas 240
  political system 30, 239–40
  politico-administrative regime
    42, 48–9, 64, 129, 136
  post offices 167–8, 240
  privatization 171
  productivity 116

public management reform 97,
    161, 189–90, 191, 192, 196
  contents 241–2;
    implementation 94–5,
    242; public knowledge
    of 152; results 109, 113,
    243; role of politicians
    after 151
results-oriented budgeting 69,
    152, 241
social expenditure 205
sociodemographic issues 239
socio-economic policies 239
sources of policy advice 58
state structure 43, 44, 45
strategic management 127
table of events 243–5
trust
    in government 131, 133; in
      institutions 132, 150
flexibility: promotion of 167–9
focus: of public management
    reforms 43–4
foreign and foreign-born
    population *see* migration;
    specific countries
fragmentation 175
frame-budgeting 68–9, 146–7
  Finland 68, 240, 241
France:
  administrative culture 55–7
  administrative system 248–9
  auditing 73
  boundaries between politics
    and management 149
  budget reform 70
  chance events 248
  citizen pressure for
    reforms 247–8
  civil service 41, 44, 76, 77, 80,
    172
    reform 75
  country file 247–51
  cultural change 130
  decentralization 87–8
  economic indicators 204
  elite decision-making 248
  foreign and foreign-born
    population 209
  global economic forces 247
  household composition 209
  new management ideas 247
  organizational reform 81, 82,
    85
  ownership of reforms 51
  party political ideas 248

political system 247
politico-administrative
    regime 42, 48, 63, 129
privatization 171
public management reform 97,
    100, 161, 189, 192
  contents 249–50;
    implementation 102, 250;
    results 112, 250–1
Rural Service Outlets 85
social expenditure 205
socio-economic forces 247
socio-economic policies 247
sources of policy advice 57
state structure 44, 45
table of events 252–55
trust
    in government 133; in
      institutions 131, 132, 150
frontier: between politics and
    management 143–58
functional elements: politico-
    administrative
    systems 40–1

G

Germany:
  accounting systems 70
  administrative culture 53, 55,
    56
  administrative system 258–9
  auditing 73
  boundaries between politics
    and management 147, 149
  budget reform 70
  chance events 258
  citizen pressure for reforms 257
  civil service 41, 44, 49, 51, 77,
    80
    reform 75
  country file 256–260
  decentralization 88
  economic indicators 204
  elite decision-making 258
  foreign and foreign-born
    population 209
  household composition 209
  idealism 135
  Länder 43, 49, 85, 257, 258–9
  local government 83
  new management ideas 257
  organizational reform 81, 82,
    85
  party political ideas 257–58
  performance measures 86

Germany: (*cont.*)
    political system 29, 30, 256–7
    politico-administrative
        regime 42, 49, 63, 134
    public management reform 97,
        161, 189
        contents 259–60;
          implementation 95, 260;
          results 112, 114, 115, 141,
          259
    social expenditure 205
    sociodemographic forces
        255
    socio-economic forces 255
    socio-economic policies 255
    sources of policy advice 57
    state structure 43, 45
    table of events 261–63
    think tanks 20
    trust
        in government 133; in
          institutions 131, 132,
          150
global economic forces 206
    Australia 210
    Belgium 216
    European Commission 232
    France 247
    Italy 264
    New Zealand 277
    in public management reform
        model 25, 27–8, 33
    USA 300
goals: high-priority 127
governance:
    culture of 52–7
    definitions 10–11
    European Commission 59
government:
    delegation to provincial or
        regional 146–7
    joined-up 31–2, 82, 85–6, 101,
        176
    more responsible 170–1
    perspective on results 138–9
    theory of effective 118
    typology of 46–50
    see also legitimacy; local;
        municipal; trust
Government Business Enterprises
    (GBEs) 212
Government Performance and
    Results Act (GPRA):
    USA 127–8, 130, 195, 302,
        304, 305
Grace Commission 58, 303

grand corps: France 248–50
group/grid theory 197

H

health services 28–9, 206
    expenditure on 207
    performance measurement 91,
        93
    service quality indicators 120–2
    see also National Health Service
hierarchies: coordination in 83–4,
    86
history: lessons of 159–60, 199
Hofstede, G. 60
    Culture's Consequences 54–7
horizontal coordination *see*
    coordination
households:
    composition of 209
    single-person 28, 208, 209
        Canada 224
human resource management
    (HRM):
    Belgium 219
    Finland 241
    Netherlands 273
    New Zealand 280
    performance orientation 126–7
    trajectories in 74–80

I

ideal state: movement toward 105
idealism 135
ideology 16
    managerialism as 12–13
immigration *see* migration
impacts: in input/output
    model 106, 107, 117–22
implementation, reform 22, 164
    Australia 213
    Belgium 220
    Canada 228, 229
    difficulties 101–2
    European Commission 236
    Finland 242
    France 249
    Germany 260
    habitats 39
    Italy 266
    modes of 93–6
    Netherlands 273
    New Zealand 280
    in public management reform
        model 25, 36–7

Sweden 289
    top-down and bottom-up 94–5
    UK 296
    USA 304
imports 204, 205–6
    European Commission 232
    Italy 264
    USA 300
Increased Ministerial Authority
    and Accountability
    initiative (IMAA) 227, 228
incremental analysis 194, 195
incrementalism 182, 194–5
    Germany 257
individualism: as cultural
    element 55
inflation: UK 292
information and communication
    technology (ICT) 3, 161
    in flexible government 136
    performance and 91, 170
information kiosks,
    electronic 168
innovation: promotion of 167–9
input linkage: public management
    as 12
input/output model 106–7
inputs 107–13
    boundaries between politics
        and management 147
institutionalism 23
institutions: trust in 131, 132
    see also specific institutions e.g.
        civil service
intensity: reform 94
intentionality 26–7, 134
international factors: public
    management reform
    implementation 36
International Institute for
    Administrative Sciences
    (IIAS) 20
International Monetary Fund 20
internationalization:
    management ideas 31
Italy:
    accounting systems 70, 72
    administrative culture 55, 56
    administrative system 265–6
    auditing 73
    boundaries between politics
        and management 149–50
    chance events 265
    citizen pressure for reforms 265
    citizens' charter 152, 266
    civil service 44, 79–80

reform 75, 77
country file 264–6
decentralization 68, 88
economic indicators 204
elite decision-making 265
foreign and foreign-born
    population 209
household composition 209
new management ideas 264–5
organizational reform 82, 86
party political ideas 265
performance measures 86
political system 264
politico-administrative
    regime 42, 48, 63–4, 129
public management reform 2,
    97, 162, 190, 191
    contents 266;
        implementation 266;
        results 266
social expenditure 205
sociodemographic issues 264
socio-economic policies 264
table of events 267–9
trust
    in government 131; in
        institutions 132

K
Key Results Areas (KRAs) 85, 127
Kinnock reforms 80, 127, 235, 236
knowledge:
    citizens 152–3, 155
    craft 198
    of reform 182–3
Kommunale Gemeinschaftstelle
    für
        Verwaltungsvereinfachung
        (KGSt) 257

L
laboratories:
    federal states as natural 43
    reinvention 96, 152, 195
Länder: Germany 43, 49, 85, 258,
    259
language: of reform 18, 22–3,
    200–1
    see also rhetoric
law:
    administrative 3
    impact on public management
        reform 29
    in interactive model 183–94

in Rechstaadt model 52–3
leaders *see* civil servants, senior;
    elite; ministers
leadership: as dynamic agency 50
league tables 149
    UK 89, 93, 120, 149, 295
learning process: public
    management reform as 18
legislatures:
    perspective on results 138–9
    use of performance data 139,
        157
legitimacy:
    Belgium 218, 219
    complexity of concept 155
    Finland 240
    France 248
    loss of 145, 152, 153
    of public management
        reform 6, 18
    problem of 184, 192
    promotion of 101, 167–9, 185
leverage, degree of 48
limits 159, 160–1
    definition 162
local government:
    Finland 240
    Germany 255, 257, 258–9
    organizational reform 82–3, 85
    UK 82–3, 294
long-term orientation: as cultural
    element 55

M
macro process: public
    management as 10, 11
MAINTAIN strategy of public
    management reform
    186–7, 188–9, 190–1, 194
majoritarian governments 46–50
    European Commission as 59
management:
    administration replaced by 12
    decentralization of
        authority 175–6
    generic 9
        incorporation of 98;
        influence of 20;
        relationship with public
            management 14
    potential of 159–60
    see also public management;
        public management
        reform
management ideas, new:

Australia 211
Belgium 217
Canada 225
European Commission 233–4
Finland 240
France 247
Germany 257
Italy 264–5
Netherlands 270–1
New Zealand 278
in public management reform
    model 25, 30, 33
Sweden 286
UK 292–3
USA 301
managerialism 12–13, 193
    Australia 211
managers:
    accountability 173–4
    freedom to manage 165–7
mandarins *see* civil servants,
    senior
manuals, practitioner 198, 199
Maoris 277
market economy: in interactive
    model 183–94
market-type mechanisms
    (MTMs) 187, 191
    coordination and 83–4, 85
    UK 82–3, 101, 195, 294, 295
MARKETIZE strategy of public
    management
    reform 187–8, 188–9, 191,
    194, 201
marketizers 97–8
masculinity: as cultural
    element 55
media:
    Finland 240
    influence of 32
    performance measurement 93
    scepticism of 146
memories, institutional 159–60,
    199
metamanagement 193
micro process: public
    management as 10, 11, 14
microeconomic theory 30–1, 169,
    198
migration 208, 209
    Australia 210
    Canada 224
    European Commission 232
    Germany 256
    Netherlands 270
    Sweden 285

minimal states 98
MINIMIZE strategy of public
  management
  reform 188–9, 191–2, 194
ministers:
  attitudes to 154–5
  boundaries between politics
    and management 144–5,
    147
  Canada 227
  difficulty of role of 146
  European Commission 60–1
  moral standards 154
  Netherlands 271
  policy advice 57–8
  public management reform 19,
    196
    implications of 150–1;
      perspective on
      results 138–9; role
      after 156–7
  in public management reform
    model 26–7
  relationship with senior civil
    servants 40–1, 50–2
    European
      Commission 59–60
  strategic decision-
    making 184–6
  see also elite
ministries:
  Australia 212
  Belgium 219–20
  France 249–50
  Netherlands 272
  reform of 81–90
  Sweden 287
modernism, critical 22–3
modernization:
  France 249–50
  Germany 257
  managerial and
    participatory 97
MODERNIZE strategy of public
  management reform 187,
    188–9, 191, 194
modernizers 97, 98–9, 102
Modernizing Administrative and
  Personnel Policy (MAP)
  2000 61, 80, 102, 139, 235,
    236
monetarism: UK 292
monetary crisis: Italy 265
moral standards: political
  leaders 154
movements, popular 32

MPs see politicians
muddling through: public
  management
  reforms as 194–6
multiculturalism:
  Canada 224
  European Commission 237
municipal government:
  Netherlands 272
  Sweden 287

N

National Audit Offices (NAOs) 73,
    74, 92, 115, 148
National Health Service: UK 179,
    195
  quality assurance 174
National Performance Review
    (NPR): US 135, 195, 198,
    302
  assessment of 124, 130, 131,
    151–2, 303–5
  disappearance of 52
  launch of 34
  status report on 123
Neo-Weberian State (NWS) 3, 187,
    189, 190, 201
  described 99–102
Netherlands:
  accounting systems 70, 72
  administrative culture 54, 55,
    56
  administrative system 272
  agencies 175
  auditing 73
  boundaries between politics
    and management 147,
    148–9
  budget reform 70
  chance events 31, 32–3, 147,
    272
  citizen pressure for reforms
    271
  civil service 44, 80
    reform 75, 76–7
  country file 270–73
  decentralization 88–9
  economic indicators 204
  elite decision-making 272
  foreign and foreign-born
    population 209
  household composition 209
  idealism 135
  new management ideas
    270–1

organizational reform 81, 82,
    85
party political ideas 271
performance measurement 91
policy shifts 114
political system 270
politico-administrative
    regime 42, 64
privatization 171
public management reform 97,
    161, 189–90, 191, 192
  contents 272–3;
    implementation 102, 273;
    results 109, 113, 115, 137,
    273; role of politicians
    after 150, 151
social expenditure 205
sociodemographic issues 270
socio-economic forces 270
socio-economic policies 270
sources of policy advice 58
state structure 45
table of events 274–6
trust
  in government 131, 133; in
    institutions 132, 150
networking 167
networks: cooperation in 83
New Public Management (NPM)
  group, core 99, 100, 102
  countries in 98
New Steering Model:
  Germany 257, 259,
    260
New Zealand:
  accounting systems 70, 72
  administrative culture 56,
    55–7, 148
  administrative system 279–80
  agencies 175
  auditing 73
  boundaries between politics
    and management 147
  budget reform 69
  chance events 32, 279
  citizen pressure for reforms
    279
  civil service 44, 52, 77, 79, 172
    reform 75
  country file 277–80
  economic indicators 204
  elite decision-making 279
  foreign and foreign-born
    population 209
  global economic forces 277
  high-priority goals 127

household composition 209
management 165
market model 136
as marketizer 98
new management ideas 278
organizational reform 81, 82,
    84, 85, 86, 90
outcomes 92, 117–18, 280
outputs 92, 177, 280
party political ideas 279
performance management 37,
    91, 92
political system 278
politico-administrative
    system 42, 129, 134
privatization 170
protectionist policies 210
public management reform 7,
    26, 161, 189, 190, 192, 195,
    196
  contents 280;
    implementation 280;
    results 109, 111–12,
    117–18, 141, 280–81
social expenditure 205
sociodemographic change
    277
socio-economic forces 277
socio-economic policies
    277–8
state structure 44, 45
table of events 282–4
visions 135
Next Steps agencies 82, 119,
    129, 174–5, 195, 294,
    295
Nielsen task force 225, 227
Norway:
  administrative culture 148
  finance 67

O

objectives: in input/output
    model 106; reform 101
obstacles: to public management
    reform 26
old see elderly
opinion, popular see citizens,
    attitudes
optimism, reform 159–62
organizational capacity: for public
    management reform 196
organizations:
  creation of new 94, 191
  implementation of reform 36

trajectories 81–90
outcomes 69, 113, 140, 176
  described 117–22
  in input/output model 107
  links with process
    improvements 123–4
  New Zealand 92, 117–18, 280
output linkages 16
  public management as 11–12
outputs 69, 176
  boundaries between politics
    and management 147
  described 113–15
  input/output model 107
  New Zealand 92, 177, 280
ownership of reforms 48, 51, 57

P

paperwork: reduction 173–4
paradoxes: definition 163
parliaments see legislatures
participation, citizen 155, 187
  Finland 242
parties, political:
  ideas 25
    Australia 211; Belgium 217;
    Canada 225; European
    Commission 234;
    Finland 239–40;
    France 248;
    Germany 257–8; Italy 265;
    Netherlands 271; New
    Zealand 278; in public
    management reform
    model 25, 31–2;
    Sweden 286; UK 293;
    USA 301
  influence on civil service
    jobs 50, 51–2
partisan mutual adjustment
    (PMA) 194, 195
partnerships:
  popularity of 167
  public-private 191
past: relevance of 159–60, 199
path dependency 33, 39
pay: performance-related 78,
    126–7
  Finland 78–9, 241
  Sweden 78–9, 80
pensions 168, 206–7
performance:
  audits 73–4, 92, 104
  budgeting
    Netherlands 273; USA 303

data: use by legislatures 139, 157
  improvement 18, 67
    savings and 68; tension with
    public expenditure
    savings 169–70
  orientation 126–8
  trajectories 69–70
performance indicator (PI)
    systems 89
performance measurement 86,
    90–3
  Canada 228
  extent of 91–2
  external use of 93
  intensive use of 92–3
  Netherlands 273
  Sweden 288–9
  UK 295
  USA 303
personnel management see
    human resource
    management
planning, strategic 85–6
policies, government: changes in
    key 7
Policy and Expenditure
    Management System
    (PEMS): Canada 70
political systems 2, 25, 40, 101
  Australia 210–11
  Belgium 216–17
  Canada 224–5
  change in 39–40
  European Commission 233
  Finland 239
  France 247
  Germany 256–7
  in interactive model 183–94
  Italy 264
  Netherlands 270
  New Zealand 278
  in public management reform
    model 27, 29–32
  Sweden 285–6
  UK 292
  USA 300–1
politicians:
  control over bureaucracy 86,
    165–7
  elite see ministers
  implications of reforms for 6,
    148, 151–2
  influence on reforms 16–17
  need for induction and
    training 157–8
  public attitudes to 150, 154–5

politicians (*cont.*)
  relationship with civil
      servants 144, 156
  role after reforms 151–2
  use of public
      management 13–14
  visions 135
politico-administrative regimes:
  boundaries between politics
      and management 147
  change in 129–34
  key features 40–1
  types of 39–64
politics: boundaries with public
      management 143–58
population, size of 203–5
post offices 167
  Finland 167–8, 239–40
  UK 167
poverty 208
power distance: as cultural
      element 54, 60
préfets: France 249
price increases, consumer 204,
      205
priorities 127
private sector services: compared
      to public services 153–4
privatization 19, 82, 97, 188
  Canada 228
  Finland 242
  France 250
  impact of 31
  Italy 265, 266
  in market model 135
  Netherlands 272
  New Zealand 278
  productivity ratios 117
  as savings 108
  Sweden 288
  tension with more responsible
      government 170–1
  UK 170, 171, 195, 293,
      295
processes:
  boundaries between politics
      and management 147
  change 8
  improvement 105, 170
    client orientation 125–6;
    performance
      orientation 126–8;
    results as 122–8
  in input/output model 107
  political 144
  public management 10

Prodi Commission 89, 127, 190,
      235–6
productivity:
  ratios 115–17
  Sweden 289
protectionist policies:
  Australia 210
provincial government:
  Netherlands 272
pseudo-decentralization 176
public *see* citizens
public administration:
  distinctiveness of 13
  use of term 9–10, 13
public interest model 52–4
  civil service 76
  European Commission as 60
public management:
  boundaries with
      politics 143–58
  definitions 8–15
  relationship with generic
      management 14
  scope of 14–15
  use of term 13–14
public management reform:
  academic literature on 1–2,
      20
  contents of 25, 35–6
  contraints for 160–81
  definitions of 8, 16–17
  international spread of 1
  model of 2, 21–2, 25–38, 197,
      203
  as muddling through 194–6
  nature of 6–23
  objectives 6–8
  optimism for 159–60
  options 182–202
  people involved in 18–20
  potential and limitations 2
  quantity of 24
  as science 196–9
  timescale of 7–8
  see also implementation;
      management ideas, new;
      results; trajectories;
      specific countries
public sector 22
  activities 114–15
  distinctiveness of 192
  values 9
public servants *see* civil servants
Public Service 2000 227, 228
public services:
  better-performing 101

compared to private sector
      services 153–4
  delivery 19
  France 248
  improvements to 6
public-private partnerships
      (PPPs) 114, 191
PUMA 1, 30, 31
  public management reform 20

Q

quality control 92, 118–22, 170,
      174
  Canada 227
  Finland 239–40, 243
  Germany 257
  Sweden 288
  techniques 125
  tension with cost cutting 177–9
quasi nongovernmental
      organizations
      (quangos) 83
  Netherlands 148
quasi-audits 174
quasi-contracts 84
quota system:
  European Commission 235
  Finland 241

R

racial tensions: Germany 256
rationing resources 177
reactive reform 183
Rechstaat model 52–4
  civil service 76
  European Commission as 60,
      61
  traditional bureaucracy 62
reform: definitions of 15–16
  see also public management
      reform
regions: Belgium 216
reinvention laboratories 96, 152,
      195
resistance: to reform 33
results, reform 2, 25, 103–42, 197
  Canada 228–9
  concept of 103–4
  data for 139–40
  European Commission 236–7
  Finland 243
  France 250–1
  Germany 260
  in input/output model 107

Italy 266
key concepts 106–7
necessity for 140–1
Netherlands 273
New Zealand 280–1
operational 104–5, 107–22
perspectives on 137–9
by politico-administrative
regime 141–2
as process improvements 105,
122–8
in public management reform
model 26–7, 37
as realization of visions 134–7
Sweden 289
as system improvement 105,
128–34
UK 296
USA 305
see also performance
rhetoric 22, 137, 139, 141
gap with practice 199–200
of reform announcements
35–6
of systems
improvements 133–4
Rural Service Outlets 85

S

Santerre Commission 74, 233,
235
savings, public expenditure 6, 67,
68–9, 184
European Commission 237
Italy 264
Netherlands 270
as operational result 107–13
tension with performance
improvement 169–70
scale:
of decentralization 89–90
of organizational reform 81
scenarios: definition of 66
schools: audits 174
science: public management
reform as 183, 196–9
selection bias 124–5
SEM 2000 61, 102, 139, 190, 235,
236
Senior Executive Service (SES) 77,
78, 212
service delivery:
one-stop 85, 105
state structure and 43
service quality see quality control

shared management agendas
(SMAs) 227
short-term orientation: as cultural
element 55
size: countries 203–5
small-N analysis 21
social expenditure 205, 206
Netherlands 270
social policies: European
Commission 233
social security 29
Belgium 216
consumer empowerment
166
implications of reform 34–5
process improvement 170
sociodemographic issues 203,
206–9
Australia 210
Belgium 216
Canada 224
European Commission 232
Finland 238
Germany 256
Italy 264
Netherlands 270
New Zealand 277
in public management reform
model 25, 28–9
Sweden 285
USA 300
socio-economic forces 101
Australia 210
Belgium 216
description of 203–9
European Commission 232
Germany 256
Italy 264
Netherlands 270
New Zealand 277
in public management reform
model 25, 27–8, 33
USA 300
socio-economic policies:
Australia 210
Belgium 216
Canada 224
European Commission 232–3
Finland 238
France 247
Germany 256
Italy 264
Netherlands 270
New Zealand 277–8
in public management reform
model 25

Sweden 286
UK 292
USA 301
Soviet Union, collapse of: effect on
Finland 240
Special Operating Agencies
(SOA) 82, 84, 227, 228
specialization:
connection with
coordination 84–5
of organizations 81–3
spending see expenditure; social
expenditure
spoils system: USA 51–2, 225, 301
stability 48, 51–2
structural change and 129
tension with innovation 167–9
state:
sphere of 11–12, 13
structure 40, 41–5
centralized and
decentralized 43–5;
European
Commission 58–9;
federal 41–3;
horizontal 41, 45; nature
of executive government
and 47–50; unitary 41,
43–5; vertical 41–5
temporary 136
state-owned enterprises 82, 97
Finland 242
New Zealand 280
strategic management: increasing
performance
orientation 127–8
strategic planning 85–6
Strategic Results Areas (SRAs) 85,
127
strategy: reform as 182, 183–94
structural factors:
political systems 30
politico-administrative
systems 40–1
in public management
reform 8, 27
in systems 129
subsidies, state 192
super budgeting 67
Supreme Audit Institutions
(SAI) 73, 74
Sweden:
accounting systems 70, 72
administrative culture 54, 55,
56, 148
administrative system 287

Sweden (*cont.*)
   agencies 175
   auditing 73
   boundaries between politics
      and management 147,
      148–9
   budget reform 69
   citizen pressure for reforms 286
   civil service 34, 44, 54, 77,
      78–9, 80
   country file 285–9
   decentralization 87–8, 89
   economic indicators 204
   elite decision-making 287
   foreign and foreign-born
      population 209
   household composition 209
   new management ideas 287
   organizational reform 81
   party political ideas 286
   political system 30, 285–6
   politico-administrative
      regime 42, 64
   productivity 116
   public management reform 97,
      161, 189–90, 191, 192
      contents 287–88;
         implementation 288–9;
         public knowledge of 152;
         results 110–11, 113, 114,
         137, 289; role of politicians
         after 151
   public services 154
   social expenditure 205
   sources of policy advice 58
   state structure 43, 44
   table of events 290–1
   trust
      in government 133; in
         institutions 132, 150
systems 11
   cultural change in 129–30
   improvement
      concept of 128; results
         as 128–34
   structural change in 129

T

talk, reform *see* rhetoric
technological advances:
      performance improvement
         and 170, 178–9, 184
      see also information and
         communication
         technology

terrorism: Germany 258
theoretical thinking 3
   New Zealand 278
think tanks 19–20, 57
   Australia 211
   Germany 20
   UK 20
   USA 20
timescale of reform 7–8, 195–6
timing of reform 28
trade-offs 7, 159, 160, 161, 163
   definition 162
trajectories, reform 65–102
   components of 66–7
   definition of 65–6
   in financial
      management 67–74
   Germany 257
   in human resource
      management 74–80
   organizations 81–90
   results 141–2
transparency 157, 177
   Italy 266
tribalism 179
trust:
   Belgium 217–18
   in civil service 132, 150
   complexity of 152–5
   in governments 131–4, 147,
      152, 153
   in institutions 132
   Italy 264
   promotion of 167–9
   USA 303

U

UK:
   accounting systems 70, 72
   administrative culture 53, 55–7
   administrative system 294
   agencies 174–5
   audits 73, 174
   boundaries between politics
      and management 147
   budget reform 69
   bureau-professionalism 62
   chance events 33, 293
   citizen pressure for reforms 293
   citizens' charter 103–4, 125,
      152, 198, 293, 295
   civil service 34, 44, 52, 53, 76,
      78, 79, 145, 172
      reform 20, 75
   cost cutting 179

   costs of change 33
   country file 292–6
   cultural change 130
   decentralization 87–8
   economic indicators 204
   education 199
   electronic information
      kiosks 168
   elite decision-making 294
   foreign and foreign-born
      population 209
   household composition
      209
   league tables 89, 93, 120, 149,
      295
   local government 82–3, 294
   as marketizer 98
   new management ideas 292–3
   organizational reform 81–2, 84,
      85–6, 90
   party political ideas 293
   performance measurement 89,
      91, 93
   political system 29, 30, 292
   politico-administrative
      system 42, 129, 134
   post offices 167
   privatization 170, 171, 195,
      293, 295
   process improvement 170
   public and private sector
      services 154
   public management reform 32,
      50, 101, 161, 182, 191, 192,
      195, 201
      contents 294–5;
         implementation 95–6,
         102, 295; public
         knowledge of 153;
         results 109, 111–12, 113,
         114, 115, 137, 296; role of
         politicians after 150–2
   quality assessment 119
   social expenditure 205
   socio-economic policies 292
   sources of policy advice 57
   state structure 43, 44, 45
   strategic management 127
   table of events 297–9
   think tanks 20
   trust
      in government 131, 133; in
         institutions 131, 132, 150
   visions 135
uncertainty avoidance: as cultural
      element 54, 60

unemployment 27–8, 205
   France 247
   Germany 256, 258
   New Zealand 277
unemployment benefits 206
unification, German 258
uniformity: of public
         management
         reform 200–1
unitary states 41, 43–5
   European Commission as 58–9
universities:
   audits 174
   market economy 191
   performance measurement 92
   public management as subject
         in 9
   public management reform 20
   see also academics
USA:
   accounting systems 70
   administrative culture 55, 56
   administrative system 302
   auditing 73
   boundaries between politics
         and management 147
   budget reform 70
   business advisers 20, 32
   chance events 33, 301–02
   citizen pressure for reforms 300
   civil service 34, 41, 44, 77–8,
         80, 172
      reform 75
   contracting-out 117
   country file 300–05
   cultural change 130
   economic indicators 204
   elite decision-making 302
   foreign and foreign-born
         population 209
   global economic forces 300
   household composition 209
   legitimacy 185
   new management ideas 301

organizational reform 81,
      89–90
paperwork 173
party political ideas 301
performance measurement 91
political system 300–01
politico-administrative
      regime 42, 49–50
process improvement 123
public and private sector
      services 154
public management reform 35,
      98, 101, 145, 161, 182, 190,
      201
   contents 301–3;
      implementation 96, 102,
      303; public knowledge of
      reforms 152; results 113,
      137, 141, 305; role of
      politicians after 151–2
reinvention laboratories 96,
      152, 195
social expenditure 205
social security programmes 153
sociodemographic issues 300
socio-economic forces 300
sources of policy advice 57–8
spoils system 51–2, 225, 301
state structure 45
strategic management 127–8
table of events 306–8
think tanks 20
trust in government 131–3
visions 135
see also National Performance
      Review
utopia 66

V

validation:
   auditing 73
   results 115

value:
   in input/output model 107
   lambda 10
   public sector 9
   sigma-type 10
   theta-type 10, 62
visions 96–7, 141–2, 199
   deregulated government
         model 136
   flexible government model 136
   market model 135
   participatory state model 136
   results as realization of
         134–7
volatility: increase in 145

W

Weber, Max: ideal-type
         bureaucracy 62, 259
   see also Neo-Weberian State
welfare state 146, 154, 157,
         206
   American model 206
   Belgium 216
   consumer empowerment 166
   Continental model 206
   cuts 169
   financing of 206
   New Zealand 277, 279
   Scandinavian model 206
   Sweden 285, 286
   USA 301
will, political 50
World Bank 1, 20, 30

Z

ZBOs: Netherlands 148, 271, 272,
         273